MODERN
NATIONALISM
and
RELIGION

MODERN
NATIONALISM
and
RELIGION

SALO WITTMAYER BARON

MERIDIAN BOOKS, INC. *New York*

THE JEWISH PUBLICATION SOCIETY OF AMERICA *Philadelphia*

SALO WITTMAYER BARON

*Salo Wittmayer Baron was born in Tarnow, Austria, in 1895. He received
higher degrees in history, law, and political science from the University of
Vienna and a rabbinical degree from the Jewish Theological Seminary
in Vienna. From 1926 to 1930 he served as Professor of History and Librarian
at the Jewish Institute of Religion in New York. Since then he has
occupied the chair of Jewish History, Literature, and Institutions on the
Miller Foundation at Columbia University. Among his many works are*
THE JEWISH COMMUNITY: ITS HISTORY AND STRUCTURE TO THE AMERICAN
REVOLUTION *and* A SOCIAL AND RELIGIOUS HISTORY OF THE JEWS.

M

Published by Meridian Books, Inc., and The Jewish Publication Society of
America, November 1960
First printing October 1960

CONTENTS

FOREWORD

NATIONALISM has been in the focus of human attention for several generations. It is in considerable disrepute today. Many people, especially in the Anglo-Saxon countries, blame it for all the world's ills. There are, on the other hand, millions of professed nationalists who view nations, and particularly their own nation, as the chief instrument of historic progression. In approval or disapproval they all discuss nationalism, often with more heat than discernment.

Curiously, a discussion of religious issues generates far less heat today. Once the basic source of fanaticism and intolerance, the various denominations have established a certain *modus vivendi* with one another as well as with the outside world. Even atheism has become less militant. The very citadel of "godless" agitation, the Soviet Union, has made its peace with the majority church and toned down its perennial attacks on this "opiate" of the people. Although such absence of opposition does not necessarily accrue to the advantage of religion, to which indifference or lukewarm approval are often more dangerous than outright persecution, many unbiased observers have detected signs of an incipient religious revival. They believe that religion is once again destined to play a major role in all human affairs.

In view of the overwhelming importance of both nationalism and organized religion in the modern world, it is doubly astonishing to find that no comprehensive study of their interrelations has yet appeared in any language. Entire libraries could be assembled dealing with one or another aspect of modern religion or nationalism. Among these myriads of books and articles there are quite a few which deserve serious scholarly consideration. There is, for example, a fine three-volume treatment of the religion of such a prominent nationalist as Jean Jacques Rousseau. Quite a few worthy dissertations have been written on the theological views of a nationalist like Fichte, or the nationalist teachings of a theologian like Schleiermacher. A selection of these and other writings will be found in the notes to this volume which, even if somewhat disproportionate in size, intend to offer only documentation of specific points mentioned in the text. On the whole, however, the attitudes of the varying churches to the modern national trends all over the world have never been subjected to precise monographic treatment. It may be hoped, therefore, that the present analysis of the fundamental interrelations between the western religions and modern nationalism will stimulate sustained endeavors to fill this significant lacuna in our knowledge.

At the same time this is not merely a major scholarly problem, but also a basic public issue, the clarification of which ought to prove helpful to believers and unbelievers, to nationalists and internationalists alike. In addressing myself, therefore, to the intelligent general reader, as well as to the scholar and publicist, I have omitted many technical elaborations and relegated others to the notes. I have also accepted the editor's advice to be inconsistent rather than abstruse in spelling such widely accepted Russian names as Dostoevski and Trotsky.

My thanks are due, in the first place, to the Rauschenbusch Foundation of Colgate-Rochester Divinity School for having given the initial stimulus to this undertaking. The original four Rauschenbusch lectures delivered in April, 1944, have since been expanded by the inclusion of additional chapters, the investigation of many ramifications of problems then discussed and fuller documentation. But it was undoubtedly the cordial hospitality of the members of the Rauschenbusch Committee, headed by Professor Earle B. Cross, and their associates among faculty, alumni and students of the Divinity School, which served as permanent encouragement to delving into the ever-expanding area of this study, the scope of which doubtless transcends the intellectual resources of any individual.

I should also like to express thanks to my wife, Jeannette M. Baron, who, from the earliest stages of preparation of these lectures to the final proofreading, has been of immeasurable assistance to me. My secretary, Mrs. Miriam A. Brownstone, has relieved me of much of the responsibility for the vast technical details involved in the writing and rewriting of this volume.

S. W. B.

Canaan, Connecticut
May 31, 1947

Foreword to the Second Edition

Much has happened since the appearance of this book to affect profoundly both nationalism and religion as well as the interrelations between them. Some 700,000,000 persons, or a quarter of all mankind, have interveningly achieved national independence and thus entered a new phase of their national evolution.

Unfortunately the prevailing brand of Afro-Asian nationalism is but part of the process of Westernization of these new countries. It has been imported from the West at a time when it was degenerating there. We find, therefore, in it few traces of that "heroic" nationalism which characterized the ideologies of the "nationalist fathers" from Rousseau to Mazzini as discussed in the present volume. One feels here little of the impact of Jefferson's "manifest destiny," Fichte's *Menschheitsnation*, or Mazzini's messianic nationalism, which viewed the destinies of their nations largely in terms of the great mission they were to fulfill in behalf of humanity at large. Nor is the primary emphasis laid now on the profound cultural regeneration of the people, but rather on its power politics and its ambitions for territorial expansion and material self-aggrandizement. While lacking some of fascism's glorification of the state and its totalitarian control over all national life, the nationalist brand of a Nasser and his confreres bears far greater resemblance to that of the nationalist "epigoni" than to that of the founders. True, some of the new nations, great and small, like India and the African states, begin to realize the dangers of this extreme political nationalism. But whether they will succeed in escaping the pitfalls of this unlimited thirst for power, remains to be seen.

Religion, too, has undergone some important transformations. On the one hand, there has been the much-debated reawakening of religious feeling in most Western lands. While some observers have minimized the depth and duration of this "return to religion," I have long felt that we are confronted here, indeed, with a long-range manifestation of the "Impact of Wars on Religion" (about which I wrote at length in the *Political Science Quarterly* of December, 1952). On the other hand, the technological advances of the Soviet Union and the unprecedentedly speedy program of Red China have established a powerful bloc of communist nations preaching, with a truly missionary zeal, their brand of anti-religion. The rise of the other Afro-Asian nations, combined with the world-wide population "explosion," has likewise placed the traditional religions on the defensive. Certainly, the Judeo-Christian civilization, even if combined with Islam, no longer enjoys that preponderance in numbers and influence and that confident drive to new heights of achievement which it possessed but a few decades ago. Together they are but minority religions under attack from both the anti-religious forces and those of other religious traditions. More, under the impact of the Western type of nationalism, the countries of Islam are now going through the process of secularization which is undermining their traditional outlook on life and the mores of their peoples. With the rise of the State of Israel, Zionism, too, has entered a new phase of its evolution with as yet unforeseeable consequences for the future of the Jewish people and its religion.

Nevertheless, the lessons of the past as marshalled in the present volume may hopefully assist the reader in thinking through some of these perplexing problems so deeply affecting the future of all humanity. In rereading the text, I have found that no substantial corrections were required with respect to the broader range of the historic interplay of national and religious factors from the vantage point of our newer situation and our increased knowledge. Even the optimistic overtones of the concluding forward-looking chapter still may, in my opinion, serve as useful antidotes to the prevailing sense of gloom and widespread despondency over the latest crisis in world affairs.

S. W. B.

Canaan, Connecticut
June 3, 1960

MODERN
NATIONALISM
and
RELIGION

Chapter I

VARIETIES OF NATIONALIST EXPERIENCE

NATIONALISM and class struggle have been determinant factors in the evolution of the modern world. Nearly four decades ago Walter Rauschenbusch, writing his classical work on *Christianity and the Social Crisis*, rightly emphasized that "Western civilization is passing through a social revolution unparalleled in history for its scope and power." [1] This social revolution, often dividing nations against themselves and transcending national boundaries, was vastly complicated by the simultaneous nationalist revolution, equally unprecedented in scope and intensity. While the social revolution was growing ever more international in outlook and its most activist forces were marshaled under the flag of the socialist "International," the nationalist revolution was gaining some of its most substantial victories. In the name of the national principle Italy and Germany, long hopelessly divided, found a new unity and the map of Europe was constantly and forcibly redrawn. A new legitimacy was thereby secured for the most subversive and insurrectional movements in old and venerable empires embracing more than one nationality. Curiously, just when nationalism seemed to reach the apogee of its achievements, when during the First World War it succeeded in breaking up Austria-Hungary, Turkey, and Czarist Russia and in securing ever-wider recognition of the principle of "national self-determination," the socialist International achieved its first major victory in the Communist Revolution.

The high-strung, almost messianic hopes then animating mankind failed to materialize. The expectation of millions, no less genuine and profound because of subsequent derision, that that war would "end all wars" and remove all legitimate national grievances was quickly frustrated in the din of postwar controversies. The nationalist revolution now entered an unholy alliance with its greatest enemy, the social revolution. In fascism the two strains seemed to blend into the new totality of a national-socialist revolution.

Their unity was apparent, however, rather than real. Unreconciled they lay side by side undermining each other and destroying whatever residuum of harmony and peace there still remained in the world. To achieve formal national unity the class struggle had to be eliminated at all costs and the restless under-

1

privileged masses held down by the overweening power of the state. To become bearable, such enslavement had to be sugar-coated by some real or imaginary economic benefits and by a newly won nationalist glory. These aims stimulated the mutually exclusive trends toward self-sufficiency at home and an expansionist search of markets and sources of raw materials abroad. Sooner or later the resulting impasse had to be resolved by military conquest which alone could guarantee the supply of cheap raw materials and even cheaper foreign labor, enabling the nazi workers to become a new kind of aristocracy of labor. Carried to their logical conclusion these expansionist trends thus generated a new violent brand of imperialism transcending national boundaries and hence betraying the very nationalist principles from which they had started. Even those who were ready to condone Italy's conquest of Ethiopia, the Italo-German intervention in Spain, and the absorption of German-speaking Austria and the Sudeten lands by Germany awoke with a start when, in March, 1939, the Nazis marched into Prague and took over the control of an ethnically alien and culturally advanced nation. It then became clear to all but the most indifferent or prejudiced that sooner or later these inner contradictions of fascism would lead to the catastrophe of the Second World War.

The heritage of both revolutions is still with us today. Never in history was the term "revolution" as popular as it is now. Never before have so many leaders of governments owed their power to a revolution nor did so many other, more regularly constituted authorities claim to be the "true" promoters of a worldwide revolutionary transformation. The popular mind, too, although far more sober and skeptical today than after the First World War, again cherishes the irresistible hope that a new world may now emerge which will obliterate the staggering conflicts of the past generations. Historic experience, however, does not warrant any such expectation. The democratic alliance was still intact when Winston Churchill, one of its indomitable leaders, made the ominous declaration that the war had progressively become less and less "ideological." This simple statement of fact was the more serious as it confirmed and was mutually confirmed by historic experience. In the two previous world-shaking ideological conflagrations, the Thirty Years' and French Revolutionary wars, the conflicting national and social interests likewise progressively reasserted themselves behind the clashes in religious or political creeds.

Nor can we place all the blame for this transformation on the scheming of greedy or power-hungry individuals. Karl Marx, indubitably the most influential revolutionary thinker of the modern era, once rightly called the revolution a "locomotive of history." He meant to say that revolutionary movements, however dramatic, do not create new social forces but merely bring to a speedy climax those which had slowly been gathering strength before. Wars, too, might legitimately be called such locomotives of history. Through the tragedy of bloodshed, through the extreme concentration of the national will on a single objective they, too, have often succeeded in resolving summarily political, economic and cultural conflicts, long simmering under the surface. Even today in the midst of a world revolution of unprecedented scope and after a global war of unrivaled magnitude we may expect only the fruition, however speedy and complete, of those basic trends which had been with us for decades and generations. If, indeed, the deepest yearning of suffering humanity today is for some new regime of social and national justice, of the Four Freedoms and the Atlantic Charter, which would bring to rest the tragic convulsions of the social and nationalist revolutions, it is doubly imperative for us to reach a proper understanding of the true nature of both. Only if we realize the magnitude and complexity of the forces inherent in them can we hope to carry out this magnificent experiment.

The great world religions with their deep-rooted ethical ideals and their supranational dogmas and rituals may be called upon to play a decisive role in this achievement. They must be cognizant, however, of their own turbulent historic experience before their leadership can successfully cope with the endless complexities of the emerging new order. The following analysis of the interrelations between the Western religions and the modern national evolution is intended as a small contribution toward such clarification.

1. Confusing Nomenclature

Nationalism has been in ill-repute in recent years. Witnessing the excesses of nationalist strife and especially the extravagant claims of fascism many peace-loving people have begun denouncing nationalism as the source of all evil. In their righteous anger they are often prone to forget that they themselves are nationalistic in so far as they are loyal, patriotic citizens of their country and deeply cherish their cultural and linguistic heritage. When confronted by this contradiction they immediately try to draw a line between what they consider the legitimate and the illegitimate aspects of nationalism. Martin Buber, himself a nationalist, once beautifully described the difference between the related terms, people, nationality and nationalism. He said,

> Being a people is simply like having eyes in one's head which are capable of seeing; being a nationality is like having learned to perceive their function and to understand their purpose; nationalism is like having diseased eyes and hence being constantly preoccupied with the fact of having eyes. A people is a phenomenon of life, nationality (which cannot exist without national feeling) is one of consciousness, nationalism one of superconsciousness.[2]

But even if we accept this factually tenuous distinction between "national feeling" as a legitimate form of nationalism and "nationalism" as its illegitimate offshoot, what are we going to do about it? Certainly if one's eyes *are* diseased, it will not do to declaim against one's preoccupation with them, but we must try to cure the disease. Much of the existing confusion may indeed be explained by the baffling variety of uses to which the term "nationalism" has been put. It has come to cover an astounding multitude of both sins and virtues.

To say that there is a profound dichotomy between cultural and political nationalism is almost like repeating a truism. Cultural nationalism springs from the deep-rooted attachment of most men to the language, literature and mores of their forefathers. Such loyalty to one's cultural heritage is an extremely personal affair and varies with individuals and groups. In many respects cultural nationalism is really an extension of the feeling for one's family, although it is not necessarily based upon community of descent. Fichte, one of the greatest expounders of nationalism, remarked: "How can a totally changed posterity derive its unifying bond from the battle of Arminius the Teuton? That spirit is dead and who can tell *where* the descendants of those fighters now are." [3]

It has long been recognized that there are no objective criteria which in the ultimate sense determine cultural allegiance. In many cases, but not all, it is the common language that creates the feeling of sharing the same national values. But the common use of English has not made Americans and Britons members of one nationality and even the most radical exponents of Spanish-American solidarity never claimed to belong to a single Spanish nation. Nor has the use of German by many Alsatians prevented their cultural allegiance to the French nationality or that of three diverse languages stopped the Swiss from counting themselves members of a single cultural entity. An inscription on a Lugano monument reading "Free and Swiss or Death" still reminds the visitor of the fateful decision taken by Ticino's Italian-speaking population to resist inclusion in the Italian Cisalpine Republic founded by Napoleon. Living on the same soil also has often created the feeling of national allegiance. But transplantation even to distant lands has not always obliterated that feeling. It is generally agreed, therefore, that lacking clean-cut objective attributes, cultural nationalities are best defined vaguely as "communities of destiny and culture." In dubious cases personal allegiance ultimately depends on individual conscience or private preference, often dictated by external reasons. Those nationalists, however, who have elevated any such objective elements as blood or soil into sole criteria of nationality have necessarily expounded some form of integral nationalism or racism which, as we shall presently see, profoundly negates any purely cultural allegiance.

In contrast thereto political nationalism is, on its first level, but a form of patriotism. Politically nations (not nationalities) are identical with states, whatever may be their ethnic or cultural composition. In this sense political nationalism, basically an extension of the human attachment to one's home, is as old as civilization. Its modern manifestations have merely been sharpened by the doctrine of unrestricted sovereignty of each nation and the complementary doctrine of noninterference in the inner affairs of one's neighbors. The latter doctrine, designed to stave off quarrels, was often honored in its breach by the major powers, but was readily enforced in regard to the lesser states. As a means of shirking moral responsibilities, however, it has proved a greater obstacle to effective international collaboration than perhaps any other doctrine of international law.

It is the combination of political and cultural nationalism and such subsidiary manifestations as economic and religious nationalism which explains the richness and intensity of modern nationalist experience. Cultural nationalism has often tended to turn into political nationalism by demanding political independence for each cultural and ethnic group. The doctrine of national self-determination implies that every ethnic-cultural group constituting the majority in a particular area has the right of creating a national state of its own. The very term "national state" thus indicates the subordination of the state to nationality, although it also involves the right of the state to demand patriotic allegiance from its national minorities. On the other hand, self-determination also implies that cultural minorities, too small or too dispersed to claim states of their own, are nevertheless entitled to safeguards for their cultural nationalism. This constant intermingling of political and cultural nationalism and the ensuing endless controversies between majorities and minorities have become, as we have learned to our deep chagrin, a major source of disturbance in the modern world.

Economic nationalism is a specific variety of political nationalism. In fact, even more than the latter it depends on national boundaries. In fostering the economic well-being of their population few states have hesitated to use their political and economic power in a way accruing to the disadvantage of other nationals. In the game of power politics the weakening of one's neighbor often appeared as an end in itself.[4] Such nationalism has frequently been combined with political and economic imperialism. Its connection with cultural nationalism has always been rather remote. A certain latitude of terminological usage is required to apply the term "economic nationalism" to such demands of ethnic-cultural minorities as equality of opportunity in civil service and private employment. Not that economic nationalism has been a recent invention of evil men. Even its theory and methods were fairly well developed in the mercantilist era and it admirably served the political schemes of a Cromwell or a Colbert. However, its ravages would have been greater in our far more interdependent world even if they had not been aggravated by the simultaneous excesses of political nationalism and imperialism. Economic thinking, too, has dominated the minds of men in recent generations much more than in any previous historical period. Rapid technological changes and sudden depressions have created, as Thorstein Veblen has pointed out, a semireligious fear of the Unknown in the operation of business cycles of which man became a victim without warning or personal guilt and which he could not mollify by personal expiation. Economic conflicts became invested with the fury of religious hatreds and the irrationality of fear. Under these circumstances economic nationalism deepened the ills it had set out to cure, disastrously exacerbated the rivalries generated by political nationalism and added to them a great many of its own making.

Religious nationalism, on the other hand, is more akin to cultural than to political nationalism. To be sure, in the original tribal and national religions there existed a most intimate connection between the state and its religion. Almost every ancient religion was a state religion, its gods expanding and disappearing together with the state. Even after the establishment of the great world religions, denominationalism long remained a major factor in the rise and decline of nations and in their relations with one another. Basically, however, religious nationalism has shared the fate of cultural nationalism of which, through the longest periods of human history, it was the main manifestation. Even today it is the ultimate source of the cultural nationalists' underlying conviction of the superiority of moral values over political convenience, as well as of much of their intrinsic intolerance and heresy hunting.

Racism, finally, while in many ways the culmination of cultural, political and economic nationalism, is in some respects a denial of them all. By emphasizing racial superiority, it injects the idea of "chosenness" into culture and statehood and elevates them both to a supreme position by mooring them in an unalterable natural law. At the same time, however, it undermines the voluntaristic, personal principle of cultural nationalism or what Renan had in mind when he said that "the existence of a nationality is a plebiscite repeated daily." [5] It controverts the great historic reality of statehood as a man-made institution in its historic dynamism and ability to change. It profoundly denies the legitimacy of those purely economic motivations which ultimately determine the rise and disappearance of economic nationalism. It compromises with religious nationalism only in so far as it is able to develop a religion of its own. In short, by making man but a creature of his soil and blood, it preaches a racial determinism which controverts the basic principle of all nationalism, namely the capacity to shape destiny by the historic workings of the national will.

Certainly the word "nationalism" may mean a variety of things to a variety of men, or even to the same men at different times. Nor would a new nomenclature designating each particular aspect of nationalism, however desirable on other grounds, offer a permanent remedy. For all these facets are so deeply interlocked that their differentiation is frequently more germane to scholarly analysis than to the world of action. Nevertheless, a fuller understanding of these diversities of nationalist experience may help us find some line of demarcation between "good" and "bad" nationalism, which is of so deep a concern to our generation. It may prove doubly helpful to us in discerning the role religion is to play in fostering the former and counteracting the latter.

2. EMERGENCE OF NATIONAL FEELING

Modern nationalism has displaced religion as the chief factor in human group relationships. Throughout human history, however, there has been a constant interplay between religious denominationalism and those basic elements of state and territory, ethnic descent and language which have always constituted the major ingredients of national feeling. Positively or negatively, religions served as the most powerful vehicle of both nationalization and denationalization, while receiving in turn enormous stimuli from the patriotic, ethnic and cultural loyalties of their adherents. True of the millennia before the French Revolution, this profound relationship continued to operate in recent generations, when the nationalist factors emerged from their relative obscurity into the full light of history. Religion, now displaced from its position of primacy, continued to influence profoundly national life both through the various state-controlled, state-subsidized or even state-separated churches and through their supranational, nonpolitical ethical teachings.

A few brief illustrations must suffice here. In the early tribal religions the whole social structure was suffused with religious beliefs and rituals. They formed a single entity, arising, flourishing and decaying together in an organic wholeness. Robbed of its gods or, what was the same, persuaded that its gods had been defeated by those of its enemy, the tribe quickly disintegrated and was easily absorbed by the conqueror. Even in antiquity, however, religion often transcended tribal boundaries. As a rule operating through the instrumentality of a state, but sometimes in opposition to it, it succeeded in cementing super-tribal entities bearing all the earmarks of nationality. We may disagree with the extreme views of a contemporary historian that

> the nationalisms of the ancient Near East were on the whole sharper, more violent and more irreducible than modern nationalisms. For the counterweight of international and supranational factors was far weaker in the ancient Near East than in the modern period. There was absent, particularly, that unity of civilization which the Western world has inherited from the Roman Empire. The civilizations of the ancient Near East were national civilizations in a much higher degree than all the subsequent civilizations.[6]

We may, especially, point to the existence of several successive supranational empires, to the more or less permanent diffusion of Babylonian culture throughout the Near East and to the widespread absence of national consciousness as differentiated from state allegiance. But we shall have to admit that, even when unconscious, political and cultural nationalism, deeply interwoven with religion, profoundly influenced the rise and decline of these venerable ancient civilizations.

More significantly, there arose in antiquity a new type of ethnic-religious nationalism which, transcending political boundaries, served as a new unifying force. For reasons both numerous and complex, the main pioneering was done by the same two creative nations, Israel and Hellas, which were destined to influence deeply all subsequent civilizations. As far back as the days of the Israelitic "judges" the twelve tribes, united by a common creed and ritual, had their common center in the sanctuary at Shiloh and seem to have formed a regular religious "amphictyony." [7] In periods of stress their ethnic-religious unity made them forget their tribal differences, which in normal times they were likely to exaggerate. United resistance to the conquering Philistines ultimately led to the establishment of the Israelitic monarchy. Later, too, their common Yahwism, however diluted from the pure Mosaic tradition, overcame the centuries-long separation between Northern Israel and Judah and maintained their national unity above the local divergences in speech and mores, conflicting economic interests, and frequent political struggles.

> The common geographic designation, "from Dan to Beersheba," still marked the essential ethnic boundaries, whereas at no time can the political borderline between Israel and Judah be traced without difficulty. . . . Neither the Judean Yahwist nor the Israelite Elohist seems to pay the slightest attention to the political separation.[8]

This religious-national unity survived even the greatest political catastrophe, the loss of national independence. Out of its religious fervor and messianic hope the exilic nation succeeded in re-establishing its shattered political life. In another period of great religious conflict, during the Maccabean Revolt, it even regained for a time complete political sovereignty.

Less conspicuous, but no less profound, was the unifying role of the ancient Greek religion. Divided into many wholly "sovereign" city-states and dispersed over a wide colonial area, the Greeks retained their common nationality and distinctiveness from the "barbarian" world by adhering to their common religious traditions and rituals. According to Herodotus, the Athenians once invoked the "kinship of all Greeks in blood and speech and the shrines of gods and the sacrifices we have in common, and the likeness of our way of life." [9] In amphictyonic festivals and semireligious Olympian games this national unity outlasted the Persian conquest of Greek Asia Minor and the destructive wars between Athens and Sparta. True, the idea of a Greek national state never advanced beyond the "sophistries" of Gorgias or Isocrates, and a genuinely Panhellenic political action occurred only during the Trojan War. Later on, even regional unity was attained only by the superior force of one state (in the "hegemonies" of Sparta, Athens and Thebes) or by the conquest of Philip II of Macedonia. But the very use of force was usually backed by an ideological appeal to the religious-cultural unity of all Greeks. There also existed a Panhellenic public opinion, almost as strong as that of all Israel. One had "in Hellas no peer" or was a "curse of Hellas," just as one had "wrought folly in Israel." [10] This ethnic-religious unity continued for centuries under Roman domination, but was totally lost as soon as the Greeks abandoned their national religion and embraced Christianity. As if to document this forfeiture of national consciousness the Byzantine Greeks gave up their venerable name of "Hellenes," which became synonymous with pagans, and adopted that of their former enemies. As "Romans" they were the chief bearers of the new church-state of medieval Byzantium.

The story of the Baal worship as the main cohesive force tying together the Phoenician cities with their far-flung colonies in Africa and Spain is yet to be told in full and illuminating detail. But certainly when the Phoenician subjects of Persia were willing to go "all out" in their war against the Greeks, but roundly refused to participate in any campaign against Carthage, they were animated by a feeling of religious and ethnic kinship which long outlived the broken political and economic ties between that African colony and the mother country. And Hannibal, Rome's greatest opponent, testified by his very name to the national impact of Baalism on the western Mediterranean.

The conquering empires, too, were perfectly aware of these nationality-forming and nationality-preserving features of religion. For the most part the conquered populations were persuaded that their gods, too, had been defeated and that the conquering deities had proved to be both more powerful and more true. Assyria practiced large-scale deportation of peoples or their leaders. Living in a distant land these were prone to forget their former local deities and shrines and, together with them, to abandon their national aspirations. Imperial Persia, on the other hand, which embraced a vaster and ethnically more heterogeneous area than the later Roman Empire, converted the subjected religions themselves into instruments of imperial policy. By establishing self-governing local theocracies the Persian "kings of kings" satisfied their subjects' craving for religious and cultural autonomy while developing strong vested interests in support of the existing order. The Persian example was, on the whole, followed by the equally "tolerant" Hellenistic and Roman empires. Without serving directly as a means of ethnic denationalization such religious toleration at least prevented the translation of ethnic and religious solidarity into political irredentas.

Of course, there existed no greater community of destiny and culture than that of living for many generations under the same imperial regime. Joint defense against foreign enemies, common economic interests, the leveling power of imperial bureaucracy, mutual imitation of mores and fashions, and constant exchange of ideas converted each such imperial entity into a regular "melting pot." When its duration was sufficiently long, its dominant culture sufficiently strong, and its assimilatory pressures so moderate as not to provoke violent nationalist reactions, it tended to develop a new homogeneity and ultimately to create a new national consciousness. Even the Roman Empire's conglomeration of races, cultures and religions was gradually becoming such a new nationality. The two centuries from Augustus, a convinced Italic na-tionalist, to Caracalla, himself apparently of Carthaginian descent, witnessed a radical transformation of the imperial structure. Where formerly a haughty minority of Romans dictated to an overwhelming majority of "barbarian" provincials, nearly all imperial subjects were now called "Romans" and enjoyed equal rights of citizenship. Correspondingly there was an unparalleled growth of religious syncretism which, reflecting this nascent national homogeneity, became the major support of the new egalitarian regime. Both processes culminated in the Christian empire. Christianity, that greatest fusion of Jewish, Oriental and Graeco-Roman beliefs, ceremonies and ecclesiastical forms, though starting as a new divisive force, ultimately became the main leveling factor in the formation of the new all-embracing Roman Catholic civilization.

The diverse nationalities were not completely submerged, however, for the empire had not lasted long enough. With a constantly weakening socioeco-nomic and cultural structure, slight technological advances and continued slow-ness of communications it could not overcome completely the old ethnic and religious loyalties of the provincial populations. Peasants living at a distance from the emporia of trade and culture and traditionally conservative, long stanchly adhered to their local mores and deities. *Paganus* (peasant) now came to be identified with the heathen inordinately resistant to the Christian mis-sion. Even when he ultimately surrendered and adopted Christianity he often succeeded in smuggling into the new religion his local gods as "saints" and in mixing the new ritual with his ancient worship. More, to preserve his own national identity, he often sought refuge in sectarianism. Monophysitism, for instance, served as a convenient cloak for Egyptian as well as Armenian na-tionalism, which refused to be submerged in the sea of Romanism.[11]

3. HIDDEN CLASHES

Sectarianism served as a major disguise for nationalism in medieval Europe as well. Of course, many "heretical" movements were due to genuine religious dissent or the worldly ambitions of individual heresiarchs. Social and economic conflicts often resulted in social upheavals which, in that enthusiastically re-ligious age, were usually invested with heterodox meaning. Much also depended on chance and a fortuitous concatenation of circumstances. But there is little doubt that overt or latent nationalism lurked behind many sectarian trends, lending them powerful support from groups not otherwise affected, adding to the effectiveness of their emotional appeal and maintaining their organiza-tional structure long after the original incentive had ceased to operate. The Arianism of the Gothic conquerors of Spain long differentiated them from the conquered "Roman" population as well as from the Catholic Franks across the border. Based on the Bible translation of Ulfilas, it had many decidedly nationalist features.[12] But when the Goths lost their national identity and became absorbed by the superior culture of the natives, they readily surrendered their sectarian beliefs as well. Much hidden or overt nationalism affected also, positively or negatively, the rise of the Albigensian sect or the reformatory work of Wyclif, Huss and Luther. "First and foremost," says a modern historian, "he [Wyclif] was a *nationalist.* . . . His ideal was a national State with a national Church subordinate to it." [13] Despite Huss's public denial of having incited the Czechs against the Germans, Hussitism became the major expression of the Czech struggle for national independence. One need but recall the expressive Czech appeal circularized throughout Bohemia by the Hussite leaders after their victory at Vyšehrad (November 5, 1420).

> Therefore we appeal to you [they wrote] out of love and compassion, that you have mercy on yourselves and your kindred nation and work together with us so that God's law and all the salutary truths which may be proved from Holy Scripture be freed and safeguarded against the oppression planned by the King and his accomplices. He wishes to despoil us of our salvation, foist upon us his heretical creed as proclaimed in Constance and lead us to damnation. Should you, despite it all, wish to take his side, we should be forced to believe that you also favor the extinction of the Bohemian nation and to treat you, with God's help, on a par with the Lord's and our nation's public enemies.

The memory of this struggle has played a great national role even in the resurrected Czechoslovakia of our days.[14]

Opposition to the church, especially the papacy, often was a mainspring of medieval nationalism, even if it did not result in outright sectarianism. The struggle between the medieval state and the church over mutual control underlay not only the memorable conflict between the empire and the papacy but also colored many purely "domestic" issues.[15] Emperor Frederick I's proud declaration of 1157 to the papal legate in Besançon—"Not as a benefice from the pope have We received Our royal and imperial dignity, but through the princes' election from God alone"—also served as a rallying point for Germany's national aspirations. Leading German historians have long seen in the supranational task of maintaining the Holy Roman Empire the most cohesive force of medieval German nationalism. That is also why the first of Germany's neighbors linguistically to recognize its national wholeness, rather than its tribal subdivisions, were the Italians, the pope's immediate compatriots. Until today all Germans are known to Frenchmen under the tribal name of Alemans, to Scandinavians, Finns and Estonians they all appear as Saxons, while many southeastern neighbors speak only of Swabians. The Italians alone have long called them *tedeschi.* This was a variant of that national designation *teutiscus* which, first recorded in Trent in 845, later led to the German designation *deutsch* and to its overhasty historical identification with the ancient Latin *teutonus.*[16]

Repudiation of the combined imperial and papal overlordship, on the other hand, and of the underlying interpretation of history served as a powerful incentive for the national self-assertion of the French and English. Few, if any, Frenchmen were ready to recognize Pope Boniface VIII's sweeping pronunciamento that "the emperor is the ruler over all kings and princes." Even official canon law subscribed to the opposite, more realistic view, voiced by Innocent III a century earlier, that "the [French] king recognized no superior in temporal matters." John of Paris preached the ideal of a French national state, arguing that differences in climate and human character called for a variety of national states. In England John of Salisbury, angered by Frederick Barbarossa's presumptuous tone, asked in 1159: "Who has appointed these Germans as judges over the nations?" Several decades earlier an anonymous York cleric (possibly Archbishop Girved himself) actually postulated the submission of both country and church to the will of the divinely appointed English king. This demand was allowed to sink into oblivion, however, until John Wyclif apparently discovered it in a York manuscript.[17]

Before long the new doctrine of the "divine right of kings," invented by royal theorists for the selfish ends of monarchs, offered both a national counterpart to the international claims of papacy and empire and a national focus to overcome the centrifugal forces of tribalism and feudal regionalism. Since among the feudal lords there were also a great many ecclesiastics, the royal control over the church assumed a twofold national significance. Sometimes national opposition to papal control was fostered within the church itself. Gallicanism, though as orthodox a movement as any in the history of the church, became, through its repudiation of the "ultramontane" interventions in the inner affairs of the church of France, a major factor in the evolution of French nationalism. The "*gravamina* [complaints] of the German nation against the Roman See," too, became in the fifteenth century a permanent feature in the deliberations of the imperial Diet and a major unifying bond in the declining national consciousness of the German people.

Curiously, the church itself unwittingly contributed to the rise of European nationalism. Overtly, to be sure, leading churchmen often condemned it. The master-general of the young but expansive Dominican order (about A.D. 1250) declared that one who loved his native land had not yet overcome nature in favor of grace. Even a ruler, St. Stephen of Hungary (997-1038), enjoined his son, St. Emeric, to emulate the ancient Roman emperors and treat all ethnic groups well, "for a kingdom of a single tongue and identical mores is both inane and fragile." But the eternal rivalry between the Greek Orthodox and Latin churches, itself largely the offshoot of nationalist tensions, often served to reinforce the struggle for national survival. By accepting, for instance, Czar Johannitsa of Bulgaria (1197-1207) as a vassal of the Holy See, the pope indirectly supported Bulgaria's national resistance against the overpowering influence of Byzantium. The very espousal of the cause of religion and church often became a source of national pride. The earliest medieval glorification of the national past, a typical ingredient of all national feeling, is found in the preamble to the Salic Law (about A.D. 500). Its Frankish author climaxed his enumeration of the Franks' manifold virtues by exclaiming:

> This is the people which, valiant and strong, shook off the Romans' heavy yoke in battle. After accepting baptism, the Franks heaped gold and costly jewels in order to adorn the bodies of those holy martyrs whom the Romans had destroyed by fire, mutilated by the sword or thrown to be devoured by savage beasts.

This idea of *gesta Dei per Francos* (God's deeds through the Franks) has sounded the keynote of French national history ever since. Nor can one comprehend fully Spanish nationalism without the centuries of crusading against both a national enemy and a religious infidel, or Polish and Hungarian nationalism without the pride of serving as the "bulwark of Christianity" against the onrushing Turk.[18]

Nationalist dissensions penetrated even such international religious undertakings as the Crusades and the monastic orders. A French bishop asked Innocent III not to allow French and German crusaders to march together since "they are said never to have been of one mind in any solemn partnership." In the universities, largely run by theologians, students were divided into formal national groups. Such division, which had existed in the cosmopolitan fourth century University of Athens as described by St. Gregory Nazianzen, was emulated in medieval Bologna which for a time had thirty-five "nations" until they were combined into two major sections of Citra- and Ultramontanes. Although, on the whole fostering international amity, these groups occasionally indulged in nationalistic feuds and always enhanced the national consciousness of their members. The oath required from the sixteenth century master of St. John's College at Cambridge that he "will not sow hatred or discord, nor bear himself contumeliously to any man by reason of his country or race or other matters of that kind" illustrates both the existence of national prejudices and the attempted impartiality of the administration.[19]

Catholic clerics, being the main intelligentsia in medieval society, were also the main promoters of national literature and recorders of national history. Isidore of Seville often censured the Arian heresies of the earlier Visigothic rulers, but he patriotically extolled their victories over the Catholic Romans and Franks and pointedly contrasted their mild regime with Rome's oppressive rule in Spain. More than any other man he contributed to the formation of an Hispanic national consciousness, the memory of which survived into the days of the *reconquista*. When writing in the vernacular churchmen generally addressed themselves to a wider public and hence favored the broader dialects which they thus helped develop into national languages. This was particularly true of books written for direct religious use, i.e., psalters or other translations from Scripture, prayer books, homilies and martyrologies.[20]

The provincial organization of the church was another contributory factor. In its collections of dues and pious donations from the innumerable feudal units the papal treasury preferred large areas called *Gallia, Germania, Italia* and *Anglia*, long before these countries were organized into national states. Hence next to, often above the royal office that of the ecclesiastical "primate" upheld the memory of erstwhile national unity against centrifugal forces generated by feudalism and the early breakdown of monarchical power.[21]

It is small wonder that the lay masses thought even of their religious problems in nationalist terms. They revered such national saints, as St. Denis in France and St. Patrick in Ireland. They canonized national heroes like Joan of Arc. Subconsciously they still viewed the Christian God himself as their particular national patron. "The Burgundians were down at heart," reads a contemporary report of 1471, "they said that God was French this year, although in times past He has been Burgundian." [22]

Before long the universal Church Councils resembled international political congresses, the individual churchmen acting as spokesmen of their particular nations rather than of the church universal. This system, informally set up at the Council of Lyons in 1274 was fully developed at those of Vienne (1311-12), Pisa (1409) and Constance (1414-18). For the sake of expediency only France and Italy represented at Constance single national units, while the German representation included Hungary and Poland. The English group covered the British Isles and the Scandinavian countries. The last to join, Spain represented the mutually hostile Castilians, Aragonese and Portuguese. But even such regional groups helped stimulate both national animosities and affirmations. The English representation, although numerically weak (it included only one-thirtieth of the membership) was allowed to vote as one of four or five "nations," because, as it argued in reply to numerous objectors, it represented a large population. Nationalist biases were even more pronounced in the following century when, at the height of the Protestant revolt, Francis I of France tried to prevent the convocation of the Council of Trent. Having failed, he instigated the attending French churchmen to do everything they could to thwart its purposes. Recognizing in 1454 the futility of his appeal for a general crusade against the Turkish conquerors of Constantinople, Aeneas Silvius (later Pope Pius II) exclaimed resignedly, "There are so very many different nations, and who could shepherd such a mixed flock?" [23]

The pope's nationality itself became the subject of nationalist controversy, Adrian VI (1522-23) being the last non-Italian to occupy the Holy See. The growingly nationalistic Roman populace and Italian ecclesiastics argued in favor of Italy as the oldest Christian country and the seat of ancient popes and Roman emperors. "We still have the apostleship," exclaimed Aeneas Silvius while campaigning for election, "though we have lost the imperium." [24] On the other hand, the ever-sharpening nationalist conflicts between the major powers, especially the Habsburgs and Bourbons, made the election of a Frenchman, German or Spaniard extremely inexpedient. This preference for their weak and divided nationality, however, did not prevent a Julius II or Pius IX from dreaming of Italian unification under the papal scepter.

4. IN THE OPEN

This brief and rather sketchy survey must suffice here to demonstrate the immemorial ties between religion and nationalism. The universal church, chief heir of the *pax Romana*, insisted upon the universal *corpus christianum* as embracing all mankind, including infidels. It nevertheless emphasized the unity of the Christian as against the Muslim and pagan worlds, and more specifically that of Latin Christianity as opposed to Greek Orthodoxy. While thus nurturing at least the idea of Occidental solidarity, it also greatly contributed, as we have seen, to the formation of national cultures and even to the rise of national states.[25] Generally helping to break down racial differences and as a church universal denying them all religious validity, it nevertheless indirectly contributed to some of the early manifestations of racialism in the treatment of the Iberian *conversos* many generations after their conversion from Judaism or Islam.[26]

Whatever remained of Western unity was exposed to severe shocks during the Protestant Reformation which sprang from the nationalist revolt against "foreign," papal control as much as from the widespread disaffection with the existing state of religion. Often against the will of its founders Protestantism was driven into a direct alliance with the state. Even when it did not form a new national church, as in England, it had to recognize the state's right to regulate ecclesiastical affairs. While adhering to the principles of universal Christianity and demanding the return to the otherworldliness of the apostolic age, it thus accentuated, in practice, national unity as against the superior unity of Western Christendom.

Far beyond this conscious recognition went the indirect effects of the Wars of Religion. They not only tore asunder the body of Latin Christianity but also greatly strengthened the princely control over the militarily defenseless churches. At their height they led to the adoption of the pernicious principle of *cuius regio eius religio*, which gave the princes the right to determine the religious beliefs of their subjects. This principle soon proved untenable and was gradually replaced by religious toleration and liberty of conscience. But the ensuing need of a unifying bond in states embracing members of various denominations demonstrated, from another angle, the supremacy of national loyalties. In the game of international power politics, too, the latter cut across religious party lines. The "most Christian" king of France was permanently allied with the caliph of Istanbul against the Habsburgs, while his chief ministers during the Thirty Years' War, Richelieu and Mazarin, though cardinals of the Church of Rome, joined hands with the Protestant powers in subverting the influence of Catholic Spain and Austria. In this fashion the Wars of Religion paved the way for modern secular nationalism which severed religion's perennial ties with the state and relegated it to the status of a "private affair" of each individual.

It would be erroneous to assume, however, that religion had thus completely vanished as a source of national feeling. In Eastern Europe, particularly, it continued to play a major role in all nationalist controversies. The so-called "national minorities" in the Ottoman Empire were to the very end religious rather than linguistic or ethnic minorities. In the 1920's the exchange of Turkish and Greek populations, under the supervision of the League of Nations, consisted in the removal of some 190,000 Greek Orthodox from Turkey and of some 360,000 Muslims from Greece.[27] It mattered little that many of these Orthodox exiles were of Turkish origin and spoke no Greek. When the Albanian delegate at the League, Msgr. F. S. Noli, protested and demanded expatriation on the basis of language rather than religion, the Greek delegate, Politis, pointedly replied that "at that rate Greece could claim Msgr. Noli, who speaks the same language as myself, and Albania could carry off the President of the Greek Republic, Admiral Condouriotis, who in the intimacy of his own home speaks nothing but Albanian." [28]

The national identity of the Saxon and Hungarian colonists in the Danubian Principalities was likewise successfully maintained only so long as they remained Catholic in contrast to the Orthodox Rumanians. Even in its syncretistic degeneration, when it allowed many local observances to intrude into its ritual and when, on occasions, Lutheran pastors were impressed into its services, Catholicism served as the main bulwark against denationalization, which otherwise proceeded at a rapid pace. A sixteenth century Italian churchman, Bandini, visiting the city of Baia found there only 256 Saxons, a small remnant of an earlier community of some 6,000. In Tecuci all vestiges of the 200 Hungarian families formerly residing there had disappeared and he could not even locate their former Catholic church and cemetery.[29] The essential distinction between Serb and Croat, too, has been religious only. Descended from the same Slavonic group, speaking the same language with minor dialectal deviations, the two peoples have considered themselves separate nationalities only because of an historic accident. The Croats had been converted to Roman Catholicism and hence adopted the Latin alphabet, while the Serbs followed the Church of Constantinople and used the specific Slavonic script going under the name of their Greek apostle, St. Cyril. We have all learned with dismay what tragic effects the overhasty attempts at merging both peoples into a new Yugoslav nationality had for the peace and security of that entire region.

Neither was Western Europe ever devoid of national conflicts originating from or stimulated by religious disparity. The antagonism between the English and the Irish can be traced far back into the medieval period when both peoples professed Catholicism. A Brother Simon of the Friars Minor taught, in defiance of the official church, "that it is no sin to slay an Irishman." [30] Mutual hostility was aggravated by the English landlords' exploitation of their Irish villeins and their excessively cruel suppression of the ensuing revolts. Nevertheless, living for many generations under the same crown, economically interdependent, speaking the same language and reading the same literature (even in the present Irish Free State but relatively few speak Gaelic), the two nationalities would probably have established a modicum of that harmony which now exists between the Scotch or Welsh or even the Scotch-Irish inhabitants of Ulster and their English neighbors. But the continued Roman Catholic allegiance of the Irish majority superimposed upon its nationalist and economic revolts the fanaticism of a religious struggle with effects clearly noticeable to average newspaper readers today.

The story of the Netherlands furnishes another well-known illustration. The successful Dutch War of Independence was as much (or more) a Protestant revolt against Catholic as a national revolt against Spanish overlordship. The southern section, Belgium, by remaining Catholic, speedily developed into a separate nationality. Reunited, after the Napoleonic occupation, in a liberal and prosperous Kingdom of the Netherlands, they drifted apart at the first critical juncture, the Revolution of 1830. The Flemish population of northern Belgium, almost equal in size and importance to the French-speaking Walloons of the south, now threw in its lot with the latter. Despite the persistence of their linguistic frontier for more than a millennium and their far-reaching ethnic affinities with the Dutch, the Flemings preferred, principally on denominational grounds, to share the fate of Catholic Belgium. It was only within Belgium that the Flemish question began to loom large among Europe's national minority problems.[31]

Agnosticism, too, could become a nationalist issue. In 1799 Naples resisted the French revolutionary armies, Cardinal Ruffo forming a peasant "army of faith" to combat the French "infidels." Nine years later the Portuguese priests sounded the effective battle cry, "Death to the Jews and Jacobins," though they knew perfectly well that there were few Jews among the invaders and that Napoleon had long replaced Jacobin anti-Catholicism by a concordat with the pope.

5. Tenacity of Ethnic-Religious Frontiers

Notwithstanding the checkered history of European sectarianism all major Continental nationalities, except the long-divided Germans and Hungarians, overwhelmingly belong to a single denomination. Ever since the decision had been reached in the separation between the Eastern and Western churches and again in the struggle between the Reformation and the Counterreformation, the ethnic-religious boundaries have remained fairly intact. The manifold efforts at denationalizing or converting minorities, though often supported by strong governmental and ecclesiastical pressures, have proved increasingly ineffective in modern times. Even in such a heterogeneous empire as Austria-Hungary the successive censuses between 1880 and 1910 showed but slight changes in the ratios of the various denominations and nationalities. Wherever comparative statistics revealed more significant shifts, closer examination invariably showed them to be the result of mass migrations or differing birth rates rather than of conversion or assimilation. These social factors accounted, for instance, for almost all of the momentous expansion of Catholicism in the United States or for the increase of its adherents in England and Scotland from some 120,000 in 1800 to more than 2,000,000 a century later.

Perhaps the only major exception was the enforced reconversion of the Uniate, or Greek Catholic, Ruthenians upon their annexation by Russia during the partitions of Poland. They were told that, having entered their "Union" with Rome in 1596 under Polish pressure, they should now rejoin the faith of their Russian brethren. Their return was not quite so speedy and universal as the czarist administration desired, but in the long run proved both extensive and enduring. When, in 1906, the first Russian Revolution gave them a modicum of religious freedom, only some 300,000 descendants of former Uniates seem to have relinquished their Orthodox faith. One must bear in mind, however, that few Ruthenians at that time possessed national consciousness, many submitting to the Russian nationalist claim that, regardless of minor dialectal differences, they were but "Little Russians." In refusing a license for the printing of a Ukrainian grammar, a Russian administrator wrote with characteristic candor that "the printing of the grammar of a language which is condemned to nonexistence cannot be permitted." Not until the Revolution of 1917 were these southern Russians officially recognized as a separate Ukrainian nationality.[32]

The quest for religious conformity within each nation was so strong, at least until liberty of conscience became a basic tenet of modern public life, that contemporaries were startled by the suddenness and extremism rather than by the motives of Louis XIV's repudiation of the Edict of Nantes (1685). These motives were neither purely religious nor economic, for the king was no fanatic and was doubtless aware of the heavy losses he would sustain from the emigration of a quarter million of his wealthiest and most industrious subjects. He merely sought to fortify the cultural cohesion of his dominions by eliminating their most important religious minority. Germany's imperial weakness, on the other hand, and its permanent division into hundreds of more or less sovereign principalities militated against its achieving the same kind of religious and national identity. On the whole, the southern states under the leadership of Austria and Bavaria remained Catholic, while the North led by Brandenburg-Prussia remained pre-eminently Protestant. But constant territorial changes, absorption of lesser ecclesiastical and lay principalities by more powerful neighbors and frequent internal migrations kept the imperial population in a state of flux. In some respects these denominational divisions served as a great intellectual challenge. They produced some of the most profound and fruitful, but also the most destructive, nationalist ideologies in the modern world.

No sooner, however, was Germany unified in the new Hohenzollern empire than it underwent a strong nationalist revulsion. Austria had been forcibly shut out, but Bavaria, Württemberg and other Catholic states joined the new empire, not without misgivings about their religious future. Unable to suppress the enormous Catholic minority and reluctant to run counter to the widely heralded principle of liberty of conscience, Bismarck, in his famous *Kulturkampf*, endeavored to eliminate those characteristic forms of Catholic group life which he considered subversive of German national unity. Though he failed and, in order to secure internal peace, had to retrace his steps, the election of a member of the Catholic Center party as president of the imperial Diet caused bitter resentment in nationalist circles. The inauguration of services at the Cologne Cathedral after its completion in 1880 was a strictly Catholic celebration and not the realization of those fervent nationalist hopes which had been voiced at the laying of the cornerstone in 1842.[33] It was clear that Bismarck bequeathed to his nationalist successors the task of suppressing what they were wont to call "political Catholicism." The builders of the Third Reich, however, went far beyond Bismarck. They tried to undermine both Catholicism and Protestantism and to replace them by a new racist creed which would better safeguard the national homogeneity of their people.

This racist upheaval is thrown into bolder relief by the simultaneous evolution across the Alps. Despite its priority in fascist doctrine and practice and its equal glorification of unbridled political nationalism, Italy acquired its racist ideology as a late importation from the stronger Axis partner. Nor did the fascist government ever become quite so hostile to the established church which, because of the country's overpowering Catholic traditions, it had long treated as a peculiar manifestation of the Italian national spirit.

More subtle, but no less decisive, was the permeation of the new European nationalism with the religious fervor of medieval Christianity, as illustrated by the frequent borrowing of religious ideas and terms by leaders of oppressed nationalities. The mystic Andrew Towianski and the great poet Adam Mickiewicz saw in the Polish people a personification of the suffering Messiah and ascribed to it an Israellike mission in the redemption of humanity. Under Mickiewicz's influence, Mazzini, on his part, proclaimed the Italian nation to be the divinely instituted messiah, destined to overcome the dualism between Heaven and Earth, Spirit and Matter, Thought and Action.[34] More significantly, even in its purely secular forms modern nationalism became the inheritor of the exclusiveness of medieval Christendom. Political nationalism always was basically expansive. *Ubique pugnatur pro patria* (everywhere people fight for their country) wrote a medieval monk [35] in the midst of the universalist Catholic civilization. But ancient nationalism was on the whole tolerant of ethnic disparity, so long as it did not affect political loyalties. In many ways it thus merely reflected the basic recognition by polytheistic religions of the legitimacy of manifold creeds. Generally prepared to acknowledge the existence of numerous deities outside their own and, sometimes, to incorporate them into their pantheons, the ancients often approached ethnic problems, too, with considerable latitude. The monotheistic creeds, however, from Judaism to Christianity and Islam, rejected all syncretistic harmonizations. For them there was only the one God, and those who refused to recognize and worship Him necessarily lived in error. This basic religious intolerance was inherited by European nationalism even in its formative stage. The present writer has long been convinced that, for instance, the medieval persecutions and expulsions of Jews were, to a large extent, the effect of that largely subconscious nationalist intolerance.[36] Modern nationalism, in its extreme, has inherited some of the worst attributes of medieval religious fanaticism without any of the latter's redeeming features of mercy and eschatological justice.

6. PRIMACY OF FAITH

A survey of the entire course of human evolution clearly confirms Leopold von Ranke's observation that "in most periods of world history nations were held together by religious ties alone." [37] In antiquity religion, state and nationality were, for the most part, complementary terms covering the same human groups. On occasions there arose multinational structures like Egypt, Babylonia and Assyria, or even such universal empires as Achaemenid Persia and Rome, each covering, at least in the consciousness of its subjects, a worldwide civilization. Each of them was, nonetheless, controlled by a dominant ethnic group professing a particular national creed. Even in tolerant Persia Zoroastrian propaganda tended to reinforce the rule of the Persian minority. Syncretistic identification of the Roman pantheon with the gods of the Greek and other subjected nations helped maintain a semblance of religious unity in imperial Rome. Religious sanctions further buttressed imperial unity by attributing divine character to the emperor (dead or alive) and establishing national-religious festivals uniting the whole population. Imperial worship was readily accepted by polytheistic subjects, although the more exclusive Jews and Christians had to be exempted. During the long reign of the *pax Romana*, that "holiday of world history," [38] all the nationalities of the Mediterranean civilization seemed gradually to be merging into a universal Roman nationality, forming a universal Roman Empire and professing universal Roman Christianity.

If religion here reinforced the supremacy of the state over nationality and even helped fashion new national entities, in ancient Israel, Hellas and, to a lesser extent, in the Phoenician settlements religion proved to be the main factor in securing the supremacy of nationality over the state. The Jewish people, through its religion, actually survived as a nationality without a state. In other words, alliance with either nationality or state or, more frequently, with both was the most characteristic feature of ancient religions.

The rise of the great monotheistic civilizations of Christianity and Islam seemed to terminate this nexus between religion and nationalism. We have seen, however, that sooner or later national disparity reasserted itself behind those unitarian façades. Church and mosque themselves, with their manifold sectarian offshoots, often helped shape the new forms of national consciousness. In the Byzantine emperor, Russian czar or English king, moreover, church and state seemed to blend into a single Janus-faced sovereign entity. Established churches were long the rule rather than the exception also in Catholic Christianity, where the separation of papacy and empire ultimately led to the decline of both and to the emergence of the new national or multinational states. While from the political angle such establishment may have appeared as state control over the church, it was more often tantamount to a church-dominated state. Conversely, Christianity, especially in its early expansive period, urgently required state support. Its greatest and most dramatic advances were made not through the persuasion of individuals, but by the conversion of whole peoples, as a rule, with the backing of state power, if not outright military crusading (by Charlemagne and others). Religion thus used the state and national allegiance as means for achieving its own, primarily otherworldly aims.

Not until the breakdown of religious sanctions and the accompanying abatement of denominationalism in modern times did ethnic-cultural nationalism emerge as the primary force. By setting up the national state and interdenominational liberty of conscience as interrelated ideals, it relegated both religion and statehood into somewhat secondary positions. Secondary, but no less vital.[39] The manifold new combinations entered into by these three major forms of social organization, as yet far from adequately explored, would help explain some of the most crucial phases of modern history.

Of course, any generalization is hazardous, even if it is seemingly derived from a millennial experience. It is doubly so if one is forced to neglect the constant intermingling of such other vital factors as geographic backgrounds, population movements, or changes in productive capacity, with some of which the present writer hopes to deal on future occasions. However, one may venture a general observation that, whenever either religion or the state clearly predominated, the other, as well as the national element, was so consciously pushed into the background as to be but a secondary object of jealousy and friction. An empire embracing many creeds and nationalities usually proved tolerant of religious and ethnic disparity. Under circumstances, as in imperial Persia, it went out of its way to encourage ethnic and religious autonomy. In the Middle Ages, on the other hand, religion was not only tolerant of a diversity of political regimes, but often encouraged the formation of new nationalities by its Bible translations and vernacular liturgies. The medieval political and dynastic wars were fought despite rather than because of religious convictions. Paradoxically, we find a modern parallel in the early attempt of the Soviet regime to instill its supranational ideals in some one hundred eighty different nationalities under its sway. Aiming at the establishment of a new universal civilization, it not only steered clear of the deep-rooted nationalist controversies but consciously fostered the preservation of all minority cultures. In order to bring communist literature to their most backward subjects, the Soviet leaders often had to adapt new alphabets to primitive dialects. By thus creating, as had Christian missionaries before them, first literary products in these languages they laid the foundations for many a new national evolution.

Has nationalism, conversely, in its recent period of pre-eminence been equally tolerant of religious and political disparity? The following analysis of some of its highlights, as represented by the teachings of several nationalist fathers and their nationalist epigoni, may help us obtain a clearer picture of these fundamental relationships.

Chapter II

NATIONALIST FATHERS

WHETHER as an ally or as a rival, religion forced nationalism to take a stand. Even when formally banished from public life by separation of state and church it remained a powerful social factor. The very declaration, so frequent in socialist programs, that religion is but a "private affair" of the individual has been a battlecry rather than a quiet statement of fact. When the German Labor party first inserted this declaration into its program (1875), Marx derided it as a concession to the liberal bourgeoisie. Less sharply, Lenin condemned it as unwise, for it could serve as a subterfuge for religious-minded communists. "We demand," he wrote in 1905, "that religion should be a private affair as far as the state is concerned, but under no circumstances can we regard religion as a private affair as far as our own party is concerned." [1] The religious issue reappeared, under one guise or another, in every major political and social movement. Hence any attempt at analyzing the varying attitudes of nationalists to religion in the course of the last two centuries would in itself be a gargantuan task. It would be sheer foolhardiness to try to do justice to it within the confines of a chapter or two.

We must also take account of another essential difficulty. If we are principally interested in the history of interrelations between nationalist and religious ideas, we may, with some degree of legitimacy, concentrate on the works of their outstanding exponents. We need only bear in mind that, as individuals, these leaders were affected by many accidents of personal experience, heredity, breeding and environment. But to the social historian, interested in the broader intermingling of two powerful social currents, the social background of these ideas and their effects on the socioreligious evolution are of even greater significance. He will try to ascertain the reactions of the mass mind and the reflections of this interplay of ideas in both the popular psychology and the realm of political or social action. He will thus be driven into the obscure domain of public opinion and of action and counteraction in the political, economic, legislative, educational and personal relationships which baffle even the investigator of a small segment of social life and might completely defy generalization in an area of so vast a scope. If, therefore, owing

23

to necessity, our narrative will follow established precedent and merely discuss a few highlights of nationalist thinking as exemplified by five leading nationalists of the early, "heroic" era of modern nationalism, we shall do so with considerable misgivings and the full realization of the fragmentary nature of this treatment. In Jean Jacques Rousseau, Edmund Burke, Thomas Jefferson, Johann Gottlieb Fichte and Giuseppe Mazzini we find representatives of only five nations (Rousseau was not even a full-fledged Frenchman). But these nations have led all others in either the intensity of their nationalist sentiment, the comprehensiveness and depth of their nationalist doctrines, or their general influence on the evolution of the modern world. These five men, moreover, have profoundly influenced not only their own compatriots but nationalists of nearly all shades of opinion all over the world.

1. ROUSSEAU

Many doctrines of the French Revolution and hence also of modern French nationalism stem directly from Rousseau's teachings. Most contemporaries would have agreed with Napoleon's alleged saying that "he [Rousseau] was the cause of the Revolution." [2] The equivocal nature of Rousseau's doctrine, however, is clearly attested by his having inspired also Chateaubriand's *Genius of Christianity*, the ablest exposition of the counterrevolutionary Catholic reaction. A spokesman for the "Society of Friends of Rousseau" assured the French public in 1803 that, were the master alive, he would have acclaimed "the wisdom of the new Concordat." [3] At the same time he was sharply repudiated by such leading twentieth century nationalists as Jules Lemaître and Charles Maurras, and such Catholic thinkers as Jacques Maritain. Rightly or wrongly styled "half-mad" (Carlyle), "charlatan" (Moreau), "egomaniac" (Carrère), "degenerate" (Hudson), and "irresponsible" (Maritain), he has positively or negatively influenced the highest reaches of modern thought as well as the popular mind; indeed, people who had never heard his name. "One studies and discusses Aristotle, Grotius, Hobbes, Spinoza, Locke and Montesquieu, but one either loves or hates Rousseau." [4]

This highly emotional, often self-contradictory attitude to Rousseau's ideas is but a reflection of their own intrinsically emotional and contradictory nature. Rousseau always preached the supremacy of feeling over reason and unabashedly rationalized his frequent inconsistencies, as when he wrote (or rather intended to write) to the elder Mirabeau, that "all the evil I have done in my life, I did on reflection, and what little good I have been able to do, I did by impulse." [5] But this very irrationality best reflected the mainly nonrational springs of both nationalism and religion. To many emotional contemporaries, his paradoxical assurance "that the state of reflection is a state against nature and that a man who meditates is a depraved animal" must have had a welcome ring. Tired of the endless dialectics in proving or disproving the existence of

God and of the brilliant but arid atheistic arguments of Diderot or Holbach, they considered Rousseau's appeal to the "sincerity of one's heart" as an ultimate and conclusive answer. Teulon Jr. of Bordeaux wrote to Rousseau in 1765, that "the *Profession of Faith of the Savoyard Vicar*—that divine book so appropriate in my opinion to make genuine Christians—has dispelled my doubts." [6] Therefore, without taking every one of Rousseau's utterances at its face value,[7] we may try to reconstruct his basic attitude to religion from two major chapters and innumerable briefer utterances scattered throughout his writings.[8]

Emotionally he yearned to return to the Christianity of the Gospels as contrasted with that of the "priests." A descendant of Calvinists who for twenty-odd years lived as a convert to Catholicism and then reverted to his earlier creed, he often professed to be a "sincere Christian." "If it is mean," he once censured a parlor atheist, "to allow one's absent friend to be spoken of badly, it is a crime to allow one to speak badly of one's God who is present; and I, gentlemen, believe in God." Drawing the then popular parallel between Socrates and Jesus, he let his mouthpiece, the Savoyard vicar, exclaim, "If the life and death of Socrates are those of a sage, the life and death of Jesus are those of a God," thereby evoking Voltaire's irate query, "What is the death of a God?" [9] Socially, too, his contempt for advanced civilization and his call to return to nature well harmonized with his ideas of primitive Christianity. His appeal to the untutored common man in many ways resembled those of the contemporary German Pietists or East European Jewish Hasidim, all of them reminiscent of the simple but fervent Galilean peasants some seventeen centuries before. It also corresponded to his antimonarchical, democratic ideals and, being essentially subversive of the established order, had a positively revolutionary ring.[10]

He entertained serious doubts, however, whether return to early Christianity was still feasible: On two different occasions he declared that "if one were entitled to draw from men's actions conclusions concerning their feelings, one would have to state that love of justice is banished from all hearts and that there is not a single Christian in the world today." He also realized that evangelical otherworldly Christianity might run counter to national interests. Like many of his contemporaries (Bayle, Hume and others) he resented especially Christian meekness, the readiness to surrender to state power and the nearly fatalistic acceptance of suffering as willed by God. He warned that this Christian attitude would breed dictatorship and foreign domination, for a population taught to acquiesce in any political change would sooner or later fall prey to an ambitious Catiline or Cromwell domestically, and to a militaristic Sparta in wars among nations.[11]

For these reasons, he believed, Christianity had long been converted into a "religion of the priest," similar to that of the lamas or the Japanese. From the national standpoint Roman Christianity was "a bizarre religion which, by giving people two sets of law, two chiefs, two fatherlands, subjects them to conflicting duties and prevents them from ever becoming simultaneously pious men and [good] citizens." In another connection he said:

> Those who wished to make Christianity a national religion and to introduce it as a constituent part of their legislative system committed two grievous errors to the injury of both religion and state. They tore themselves away from the spirit of Jesus Christ whose kingdom is not of this world. Mixing worldly interests with those of religion they soiled its celestial purity and converted it into a weapon of tyrants and an instrument of persecutors.

Being generally averse to the growing cosmopolitan leveling of European culture, he objected to the very internationality of the church. On more than one occasion he bitterly complained of the progressive disappearance of the national characteristics which had distinguished Frenchmen from Germans, Spaniards or Englishmen, all of whom now increasingly shared the same tastes, the same passions and mores. This unity of mores, letters and commerce, together with religious unity and a uniform international law, was, in his opinion, responsible for that unstable European balance of power which necessarily led to wars. For only one law ultimately governed relations among peoples: the law of the strong.[12]

Under these circumstances Rousseau was led to advocate a kind of national isolationism based on restriction of foreign trade, conscious cultivation of xenophobia along Spartan lines, concentration on national mores, secularization of education and social welfare, and ultimately, the formulation of a new national religion. In his *Profession of Faith of the Savoyard Vicar* he touchingly described the individualistic appeal of Christianity, but in his *Social Contract* he argued for its total inadequacy within the framework of an ideal national state. Saturated with the traditions of ancient Rome and Sparta, which he always admired, he wished to see the modern state built on the firm foundations of a national religion, thereby once again reuniting the "two eagles" of state and church—an old phrase of French Gallicanism and Hobbesian absolutism. Such a religion of the citizen, Rousseau declared, "embracing but a single country gives it its deities, its proper and tutelary patrons. It has its dogmas and rituals, its external cult prescribed by law. Outside the single nation adhering to it the rest of the world is unbelieving, foreign, barbarian." The development of such national rites would also enhance the nation's longevity. That much one may learn from the work of Moses. One may disregard its revealed character—in his letter to the archbishop of Paris, he flippantly asked whether God had to go "look for Moses to speak to Jean Jacques Rousseau?"—but one must admit the effectiveness of its ritualistic legislation.

> Through it alone that extraordinary nation [the Jews] so often subjugated, so often dispersed and outwardly destroyed, but always idolatrous of its Law, has preserved itself unto our days, scattered among the others, but never con-

founded with them. Its mores, laws and rituals persist and will persist to the end of the world, despite the hatred and persecution by the rest of mankind.[13]

By developing national rituals modern nationalities, too, could survive the loss of national independence. This was, indeed, Rousseau's main counsel to the Poles, then being partitioned off among their mighty neighbors. By developing an integrated system of national rituals and holidays, he wrote to his anxious Polish friends, they could so fortify the national loyalties of their people that the country would never be absorbed by its Russian masters.

The dogmatic side of the new religion, however, should be restricted to a few simple beliefs. A true Genevan, Rousseau always believed that "good religion consists far less in what one believes than in what one does." [14] In his ideal state the citizen would have to believe only in the "existence of a powerful, intelligent, beneficent, foreseeing and provident Deity, life in the hereafter, happiness of the just and retribution for the evildoers, the sanctity of the social contract and of the laws." These four positive dogmas thus included one ethical and two purely religious beliefs (the existence of God, the hereafter and reward and punishment) which could easily be shared by all humanity. "If one listened only," Rousseau asserted in another connection, "to what God says to man's heart, there would never have been but one religion on earth." Only each people's particular social contract and laws would remain distinct. That is why Rousseau laid so much stress on the sanctity of the social contract and demanded that any citizen refusing publicly to subscribe to it should automatically forfeit his citizenship and go into exile—not because of his heterodoxy, but because of his unsociability. A citizen who, after accepting it publicly, broke his pledge and conducted himself as an unbeliever, should be executed for "he had committed the greatest of all crimes, he had lied before the laws." [15]

All apologetic explanations to the contrary Rousseau must have realized the totalitarian implications of his program. Even in offering practical advice for Corsica's new constitution he advocated the following oath of fealty from each and every citizen:

> In the name of God Almighty and on the holy Gospels I herewith, by a sacred and irrevocable oath, bind myself with my body, my property, my will and all my might to the Corsican nation to belong to it in complete ownership with all my dependents. I swear to live and die for it, to observe all its laws and to obey all its legitimate chiefs and officials in everything conforming with the laws. . . .

Through one of his characteristic inconsistencies, however, he added to the above four positive dogmas of his new religion a single negative dogma, outlawing intolerance. He evidently believed that, since the social contract would be imposed by the *volonté générale* (the general will) of the people, every citizen would merely obey himself rather than an authority outside himself. Rousseau did not hesitate to sacrifice the minority even in cases involving conscientious scruples, readily brushing aside, for instance, Montesquieu's classical observation on the revocation of the Edict of Nantes, "In religion, as in all matters of thought, there exists no majority, or, if one prefers it, the majority does not have the presumption of truth on its side." [16]

Equally illusory was Rousseau's belief that national religions would help eliminate international and domestic friction. Wars of religion would become meaningless, he stated, when no country would encroach upon its neighbor's faith, while domestic peace would be safeguarded by the re-established harmony between the obligations of the citizen and those of the believer. He readily overlooked the historic lessons of his ancient prototypes, Rome and Sparta, whose national, state-idolizing religions neither stemmed expansionist ambitions abroad nor eliminated factional and class struggles in the interior.

Nor was peace promoted when Rousseau's doctrines stood their first test in the crucible of revolution. True, such a national religion as enunciated by some of his disciples could ultimately become the religion of all humanity. The speech of Marie Joseph Chénier at the revolutionary Convention may have represented the ultimate humanitarian goals of Rousseauist nationalism better than some of the master's own impromptu formulations.

> Wrench the sons of the Republic [Chénier exclaimed] from the yoke of theocracy which now weighs upon them . . . then, free from prejudice and worthy to represent the French nation, you will be able, on the ruin of fallen superstition, to found the one universal religion which has neither secrets nor mysteries, whose one dogma is equality, whose orators are the laws, whose pontiffs are the magistrates, which asks no incense from the great human family to burn, save before the altar of our country, our mother and our deity.[17]

But Robespierre, another ardent disciple, drew equally legitimate deductions from Rousseau's teachings when he violently suppressed all shades of national and religious nonconformity. Ultimately the national Religion of Reason embroiled France in bitter civil strife, and only its speedy downfall accounted for the latter's shorter duration than the quarter century of European wars engendered by the social and national Revolution.

Of course, we must not blame Rousseau for all the revolutionary and Napoleonic excesses, just as we cannot give him all the credit for the Revolution's undeniable achievements. We may neither join the chorus of contemporary ecclesiastics who condemned both the national-religious implications of his "social contract" and the enthusiastic personalized Christianity of his "Savoyard vicar" nor attribute to him more than an incidental share in the powerful religious reaction to French Enlightenment and the triumphant progress of the church militant within a few decades after his death. But seeds for them all were contained in his teachings which, strewn to the winds, fell upon different soils and flowered into plants of fantastically different shape and coloring. Each of these in its own way demonstrated the heroically constructive, as well as dangerously destructive, implications of the new radical nationalist doctrine.

2. BURKE

Among the men who blamed the revolution on Rousseau was Edmund Burke.[18] Although occasionally admitting that "were Rousseau alive, and in one of his lucid intervals, he would be shocked at the practical frenzy of his scholars," the English statesman considered him and Voltaire its intellectual fathers. As a practical politician he was particularly impatient with the theoretical generalizations of thinkers without practical experience. "Who ever dreamt of Voltaire and Rousseau as legislators?" he asked. "The first has the merit of writing agreeably; and nobody has ever united blasphemy and obscenity so happily together. The other was not a little deranged in his intellects to my almost certain knowledge. But he saw things in bold and uncommon lights, and he was very eloquent."[19]

Burke, too, was a nationalist, but his nationalism was of the historical and conservative rather than the romantic and revolutionary type. He objected to both the Enlightenment's reliance on reason and Rousseau's emotionalism. "Politics ought to be adjusted," he sweepingly declared, "not to human reasonings but to human nature; of which the reason is but a part and by no means the greatest part." Nationalism seemed to him to be nurtured from such deeper irrational yearnings. In his famous speech on *Conciliation with America* he, therefore, bitterly denounced the governmental policy of repression and exclaimed, "My hold of the colonies is in the close affection which grows from common names, from kindred blood, from similar privileges and equal protection. These are ties which, though light as air, are as strong as links of iron." [20]

This emphasis on common descent had none of the "racial" overtones of contemporary nationalism, however. For Burke "kindred blood" was merely one of many contributory elements to that "mutual affection and confidence on which the glory and safety of the British empire depend." He believed that historic continuity in political and cultural institutions, those main connecting links between past and future generations, was vital to the health of any nation. He acidly derided the "easy manner" with which "annual constitutions" were enacted by the French revolutionaries and their English followers like Thomas Paine. "A spirit of innovation," he declaimed, "is generally the result of a selfish temper and confined views. People will not look forward to posterity who never look backward to their ancestors." The sepulcher appeared to him, indeed, as one of the major ingredients of national feeling. Consciously forgetful of the storms of the English Revolution under Cromwell which had convinced Voltaire "that the government of that island [England] is more tempestuous than the sea around it," Burke stressed only the far less radical uprising of 1688 and the ensuing Bill of Rights which rather forestalled the Revolution. He considered it a superior trait of English nationalism that "thanks to our sullen resistance to innovation, thanks to the cold sluggishness of our national character, we still bear the stamp of our forefathers." [21]

On the other hand, Burke was also opposed to Rousseau's emotionalism and ridiculed return to nature by comparing it with the rocking of a grown man in the cradle of an infant. The "social contract" struck him as one of the theories advanced by "political theologians and theological politicians" on grounds of metaphysics rather than experience.

> Society is, indeed, a contract [he exclaimed]. Subordinate contracts for objects of mere occasional interest may be dissolved at pleasure; but the state . . . is to be looked on with other reverence; because it is not a partnership in things subservient only to the gross animal existence of a temporary and perishable nature. It is a partnership in all science, a partnership in all art, a partnership in every virtue and in all perfection. As the ends of such a partnership cannot be obtained in many generations, it becomes a partnership not only between those who are living, but between those who are living, those who are dead, and those who are to be born.

John MacCunn correctly stresses this passage as indicative of the gulf separating Burke from both Rousseau and Bentham. "For Contract it, in effect, substitutes Growth: for Greatest Number it reads Social Organism. The categories of law and arithmetic are dethroned, and the conceptions of biology advanced to the supremacy." [22]

In this view of the nations' organic growth Burke decidedly adumbrated the "organic" theories of the nineteenth century nationalists. But he envisaged such growth exclusively in terms of the English Constitution, "whose merits are confirmed by the solid test of long experience." Liberty exercised without wisdom and the restraint of virtue was for him the greatest of all evils. A perfect democracy was "the most shameless thing in the world," since a people at large cannot be punished for abusing its liberty, all punishments being designed only for its own protection. The limited democracy, however, of the English Constitution with its extensive checks and balances appeared to him as the ideal custodian of British liberties. No one knew better than he that, under the existing limitations of franchise, fully 234 of the 558 seats in Parliament were then controlled by individual patrons. He himself once figured out that the interested British "public" (both voters and nonvoters) whose opinion carried weight consisted of only a small minority of some four hundred thousand persons. Nevertheless, he sincerely believed that England's time-tested practice of liberty was far superior to anything yet devised by man. "We fear God," he proudly challenged the revolutionaries across the Channel, "we look up with awe to Kings, with affection to Parliaments, with duty to magistrates, with reverence to priests, and with respect to nobility." [23]

Such constitutional nationalism could very well be reconciled with the British imperial order. "It is the spirit of the English Constitution," Burke declared, "which, infused through the mighty mass, pervades, feeds, unites, invigorates, vivifies every part of the empire, even down to the minutest member." This spirit rather than force had conquered Wales, Ireland and the colonies and its combination of subordination and liberty, of imperial unity and local self-government accounted for the solidity of imperial ties. Even if the original colonists had signed a compact of perpetual servitude, it would have been in England's interest to preserve their liberties. For this reason "conciliation with America" was much more germane to the spirit of the Constitution than the legalistic quibbles about the prerogatives of crown or Parliament. True nationalist that he was—nationalist of the heroic age—Burke felt that here lay the kernel of the British people's mission on earth. A year before his death he spoke to his friend, French Laurence, of his lifelong "defiance of the judgments of those who consider the dominion of this glorious empire, given by an incomprehensible dispensation of the Divine Providence into our hands, as nothing more than an opportunity of gratifying, for the lowest of their purposes, the lowest of their passions. . . ." [24]

Despite his profound admiration for the English national character and institutions, Burke was an internationalist through his deep belief in the unity of Christendom. Itself a fountainhead of the English Constitution, Christian morality transcended national boundaries and underlay the diverse national forms of government. It alone accounted for whatever strength there was in the law of nations, "this great ligament of mankind." Unlike Rousseau he held that "nothing is so strong a tie of amity between nation and nation as correspondence in laws, customs, manners and habits of life. They have more than the force of treaties in themselves. They are obligations written in the heart." The French Revolution, by undermining the Christian heritage and the sanctions of Christian ethics, was bound to disrupt that international amity. It certainly went beyond the usual predatory efforts of a conquering country, being rather "a sect aiming at universal empire, and beginning with the conquest of France." As such it was disruptive of the established order everywhere and had the makings of a civil war cutting across all national boundaries. A general war against it, therefore, that "sole means of justice among nations," was "not only a right but an indispensable duty." [25] In short, while seeing in the American Revolution the realization, however radical, of Christian ethics and British liberties, Burke abhorred the French Revolution as the most peremptory denial of both.

These ideas, espoused with zest and eloquence, appeared inconsistent to Burke's contemporaries.[26] Consistency was, indeed, not his great strength. By nature very impulsive, he often allowed rhetoric to run away with him. His espousal of conflicting causes often earned him the denunciation of Jesuitism, made the more plausible as his bespectacled face bore some resemblance to the popular caricatures of Jesuits. Even his friend, Oliver Goldsmith, retaliated at a club dinner for some humorous epitaphs by emphasizing the contradictory traits in his character and career:

> Though equal to all things, for all things unfit;
> Too nice for a statesman, too proud for a wit;
> For a patriot, too cool; for a drudge, disobedient;
> And too fond of the right to pursue the expedient.

The last criticism must have sounded doubly ironical to the later champion of "circumstances" against the French theorists' stress on principles. Lord Morley, keen analyst of Burke's extreme reaction to the French Revolution, came to the more justifiable conclusion that Burke "had changed his front but never changed his ground." [27]

Burke's attitude to religion and church, though often shockingly contradictory to day-to-day observers, likewise maintained a certain basic line in consonance with his nationalist and humanitarian convictions. First and foremost, he was a stanch believer in the established Church of England. Though realizing the merits of Christian humility and poverty, he insisted that governmental provisions for the clergy made it independent of wealthy members and kept its prestige high among all parishioners. The French Revolution, by disestablishing the Catholic priesthood, exposed it to the whims of the populace which resulted in the churches' becoming but "funeral monuments of departed religion," while nineteen to twenty theaters, maintained at public expense in Paris alone, were crowded every night. More, the new Religion of Reason was to all intents and purposes a newly established godless creed.

> When in the place of that [Christian] religion of social benevolence and of individual self-denial, in mockery of all religion, they institute impious, blasphemous, indecent theatric rites, in honour of their vitiated, perverted reason, and erect altars to the personification of their own corrupted and bloody Republic,—when schools and seminaries are founded at public expense to poison mankind, from generation to generation, with the horrible maxims of this impiety,—when, wearied out with incessant martyrdom, and the cries of a people hungering and thirsting for religion, they permit it only as a tolerated evil,—I call this *Atheism by Establishment*.[28]

Burke could not envisage organized society without organized religion. For him man was just as much a religious as he was a "political animal," religion being the very "basis of civil society and the source of all good and of all comfort." Religious guidance and sanctions were the more urgently needed in self-governing societies, as all free citizens held a certain position of trust and confidence. "All persons possessing any portion of power ought to be strongly and awfully impressed with an idea that they act in trust, and that they are to account for their conduct in that trust to the one great Master, Author and

Founder of society." He could not understand how the state could ever refrain from interfering in matters of religion. "Religion is so far, in my opinion, from being out of the province or the duty of a Christian magistrate," he declared in one of his early speeches, "that it is, and it ought to be, not only his care, but the principal thing in his care, because it is one of the great bonds of human society and its object the supreme good, the ultimate end and object of man himself." Separation of state and church appeared to him unthinkable, for it presupposed that in certain areas of life man could divorce himself from his all-embracing faith. He even objected to the phrase of an alliance between church and state, for "an alliance is between two things that are in their nature distinct and independent such as between two sovereign states. But in a Christian commonwealth the Church and the state are one and the same thing, being different integral parts of the same whole." God has willed that man's nature be perfected by virtue and the "divine tactic" gave it the state as the necessary means of such perfection.[29]

All these theories, advanced on various occasions over a period of two decades, though most sharply formulated during Burke's frenzied attacks on the French Revolution, well fitted together into his general espousal of national religion, viz., the Established Church in England. Of course, he was not a totalitarian. Just as he reconciled his nationalist credo with the self-government of the various parts of the British Empire and the internationalism of Christendom, so he harmonized the existence of an Established Church with toleration of other creeds. "Violently condemning," he exclaimed, "neither the Greek nor the Armenian, nor since heats are subsided, the Roman system of religion, we prefer the Protestant: not because we think it has less of the Christian religion in it, but because in our judgment it has more. We are Protestants, not from indifference but from zeal." Time and again he championed the cause of Catholic emancipation, at least as it was then understood as the relief of Catholics from certain legal disabilities, clearly realizing the nonreligious aspects of the Irish problem. "It is not about popes," he once wrote to his son, "but about potatoes that the minds of this unhappy people are agitated. It is not from the spirit of zeal, but the spirit of whisky, that these wretches act." Equally humane were his sentiments toward Jews. True, there are slightly anti-Jewish allusions in his attack on the French Revolution, although he could not possibly blame the Terror on the tiny and politically inactive Jewish minority in France. Basically, however, his parliamentary speech of 1781, in which he attacked the ill-treatment of "the poor Jews" during the British occupation of the West Indian island of St. Eustatius, more truly reflected his views.[30]

At the same time Burke viewed with alarm the broad toleration of Protestant dissenters in England, though he conceded its need in the colonies. In fact, he found memorable words for the nexus between religious and political freedom in the American Revolution.

All Protestantism, even the most cold and passive, is a sort of dissent. But the religion most prevalent in our northern colonies is a refinement on the principle of resistance; it is the dissidence of dissent, and the Protestantism of the Protestant religion. This religion, under a variety of denominations, agreeing in nothing but in the communion of the spirit of liberty, is predominant in most of the northern provinces; where the Church of England, notwithstanding its legal rights, is in reality no more than a sort of private sect, not composing most probably, the tenth of the people.

In the British Isles, however, he advocated the "Relief of Protestant Dissenters" from enforced adherence to the Thirty-Nine Articles of the Church of England only in so far as they were not Unitarians who still formally belonged to the official church (1772-73). Invoking Locke's analogy with the admission of members by a private society, he believed that the state, too, had the right of admitting religious dissenters on its own terms. "Dissent not satisfied with toleration, is not conscience but ambition." In 1789 he even opposed the formal repeal of the Tests and Corporation Acts barring dissenters from public office, although these acts had long been nullified in practice by the annual renewal of the Acts of Indemnity. He confessed that ten years earlier he would have voted for repeal, but he had come to resent the dissenters' open hostility to the very principle of Establishment and their overt sympathy with the French Revolution.[31]

Put in a nutshell Burke's view was: "Do not promote diversity; when you have it, bear it." Only in regard to atheists he was prone to forget his beautiful sentiments on toleration which he took "to be a part of religion." The infidels, he declared, "are outlaws of the constitution, not of this country, but of the human race. They are never, never to be supported, never to be tolerated." [32]

This obvious discrepancy between Burke's warm advocacy of Catholic emancipation, his equivocal attitude toward dissenters, and his outright intolerance toward freethinkers was often ascribed by contemporaries to personal biases. They knew that Burke's mother and sister had been born and lived as Catholics, that his wife had been a member of that church before their marriage and that he had spent some five years at a Catholic school.[33] But a student of Burke's nationalist philosophy will easily discern in retrospect the deeper reasons. The Irish majority among the Catholics on the British Isles appeared to him less of a menace to the inner consistency and vigor of the national Church of England than the English dissenters or atheists. Toleration of dissent had been sanctioned by the earlier historic evolution, but any further extension of religious disparity, he feared, might well undermine that much-cherished intermingling of nationality and religion which he saw embodied in the Church of England operating as an integral part of the English Constitution.

At this point we may note some crucial similarities as well as divergences between Rousseau and Burke. They were sharply opposed to atheism on both religious and national grounds. Rousseau was ready to deliver to the public executioner any citizen denying the theistic dogmas of his ideal national state, while Burke preached world-wide intolerance toward these "outlaws of the Constitution." Although holding different views on "natural rights," they also agreed that political, like religious, truths were ultimately founded on faith.[34] But Rousseau, a theorist viewing the hopeless political situation in France, appealed from the existing realities to the "general will," i.e., the sovereignty of the people and postulated an ideal future state which was to emerge from the new "social contract." At the same time Burke, a statesman looking back to the marvelous expansion of the British Empire since 1688, glorified England's existing constitution and national church as the historic expressions of the English national will. Rousseau could readily accept Burke's definition that "nation is a moral essence, not a geographical arrangement, or a denomination of the nomenclator." But whereas for Burke the ardent love of the people sprang from "their attachment to their government, from the sense of the deep stake they have in such a glorious institution," for Rousseau the citizens "will obey the laws, and will not seek to elude them because these will suit them, and will have the internal assent of their wills." [35] In short, Burke's constitutional nationalism envisaged the preservation of the peculiar English blend of nationality and religion amidst a heterogeneous empire and much-divided Christendom through the people's conservatory adherence to the existing constitution and church. Rousseau's revolutionary nationalism, on the other hand, postulated the overthrow of all existing unsatisfactory regimes and their replacement by new national entities built upon new "social contracts" and endowed with new national rituals.

3. JEFFERSON

Like Burke, Thomas Jefferson was largely the product of the British Constitution. Compared with the influence of the English constitutional lawyers, especially in his formative years, the much-vaunted impact of French Enlightenment on Jefferson was almost negligible. With fine insight, Burke, arguing for conciliation with America, emphasized that the colonists were "not only devoted to liberty, but to liberty according to English ideas and on English principles." [36] Unlike Burke, however, Jefferson was not a blind admirer of the English Constitution. As a revolutionary leader he somewhat resembled the French constitution makers, who followed basic principles rather than historic continuity. But he radically departed from the accepted British patterns only where such changes were enforced by differing American realities. It was the upsurge of popular will, rather than any conscious a priori determination, that converted Jefferson and his confreres into champions of the rights of man and the separation of state and church.[37]

Like Washington, Franklin, Hamilton and Madison, indeed like nearly two-thirds of all signers of the Declaration of Independence,[38] Jefferson was a member of the Anglican Communion. But he clearly realized, as did Burke, that his denomination embraced only a small minority of his American compatriots and that it was not even in formal control of several colonies. As an Episcopalian he had less to fear than the Congregationalist, John Adams, that, "if Parliament can erect dioceses and appoint bishops, they may introduce the whole hierarchy, establish tithes, forbid marriages and funerals, establish religions, forbid dissenters, make schism heresy, impose penalties extending to life and limb, as well as to liberty and property." But he, too, resented the possibility of Parliament ever exercising such authority. Moreover, if "taxation without representation" became the immediate revolutionary issue and if, as Burke pointed out, the whole history of the struggle for British liberties had centered around the power of taxation, the taxing of dissenters for the benefit of the Established Church became doubly vexing in predominantly non-Anglican areas. The numerous Baptists among Jefferson and Madison's neighbors in Virginia became the earliest protagonists of both independence from England and complete religious freedom and, as such, helped pave the way for the former's memorable *Bill for Religious Freedom* adopted by the Virginia Assembly in 1779. [39] Certainly the aforementioned Burkean formula of the balanced British loyalties toward God, kings, parliaments, magistrates, priests and noblity had little to recommend itself even to these "aristocratic" Americans.

Jefferson had, on the other hand, little of that anti-British animus characteristic of sections of the American public from his days to ours which, as is usual in fratricidal struggles, has been more constant and bitter than the recurrent fits of antagonism toward other peoples. True, he said many a harsh word about the British. Writing to Thomas Paine, another severe critic of his former compatriots, he denounced the average Englishman who "slumbering under a kind of half reformation in politics and religion, is not excited by anything he sees or feels to question the remains of prejudice." He also felt that by removing the "former vassalage in religion and civil government," the American Constitution had marked a tremendous step forward in the history of mankind. Nevertheless, he admitted the great similarity of American and English mores and laws. In his early years he was averse to immigration and in his *Notes on Virginia* he even resorted to specious arithmetic to prove that the American population would increase with equal rapidity without "the importation of foreigners." But he seriously objected only to immigrants from countries of diverse culture and absolutist form of government and not to Englishmen who "differ from us little but in their principles of government, and most of those (merchants excepted) who come here, are sufficiently disposed to adopt ours." Despite recurrent diplomatic tension with Britain, moreover, which in his lifetime led to two wars, Jefferson also realized the importance of the British fleet for the free development of America and looked forward to the time when both nations would live in permanent peace. Perhaps the most mature part of his wisdom was expressed in a letter to John Adams written a few years after the conflict of 1812.

And were they [the English] once under a government which should treat us with justice and equity, I should myself feel with great strength the ties which bind us together, of origin, language, laws and manners; and I am persuaded the two peoples would become in future as it was with the ancient Greeks among whom it was reproachful for Greek to be found fighting against Greek in a foreign army . . . . [and they] will see in us what we really are, their natural friends and brethren and more interested in a fraternal connection with them than with any other nation on earth.[40]

Unlike Burke, however, Jefferson considered every generation entitled to adjust its constitutional life freely and without undue reverence for tradition or precedent. Even in his last years he insisted "that our Creator made the earth for the use of the living and not of the dead . . . that one generation of men cannot foreclose or burden its use to another, which comes to it in its own right and by the same divine beneficence." In this preference for the living Jefferson differed greatly from most other nationalists. "I like the dreams of the future," he admitted to Adams, "better than the history of the past." History to him, as to many optimists of the Enlightenment era, was but the record of past wars and depredations, political intrigues and cruelties in sharp contrast with the dawning era of reason and human happiness. He repudiated the "Gothic idea" of looking backward to the annals of ancestors, rather than to the postulates of reason. It seemed to him "worthy of those bigots in religion and government, by whom it has been recommended, and whose purposes it would answer." Just as he believed that every generation should pay off its public debts and not burden its successors, so he demanded complete overhauling of all laws every two decades, for he had figured out, on the basis of European statistics, that an average generation of adults lasted but nineteen years. It is small wonder that he wrote in 1816 to Samuel Kerchival:

> Some men look at constitutions with sanctimonious reverence, and deem them like the ark of the covenant, too sacred to be touched. They ascribe to the men of the preceding age a wisdom more than human, and suppose what they did to be beyond amendment. I knew that age well; I belonged to it, and labored with it. It deserved well of its country. It was very like the present, but without the experience of the present; and forty years of experience in government is worth a century of book-reading; and this they would say themselves, were they to rise from the dead.[41]

Little did he foresee that the British constitutional heritage would before long elevate the American Constitution to a major article of America's nationalist faith.

At the same time Jefferson himself viewed the new system of American liberties as an essential part of America's distinction in the human family, in fact, as the chief ingredient of its historic mission. His nationalistic ideals, too, were projected into the future. One need not take too literally such temperamental exclamations as that Philadelphia was much more beautiful than either London or Paris, that only vice and modern languages were taught in Europe better than in America, or that "there is not a crowned head in Europe whose talents or merits would entitle him to be elected a vestryman by the people of any parish in America." Even his much-quoted letter to Monroe, like the foregoing written while he was living in Paris, must be taken with a grain of salt. He asked his distinguished disciple and future successor to come to France, which "will make you adore your own country, its soil, its climate, its equality, liberty, laws, people, and manners. . . . I will venture to say, no man now living will ever see an instance of an American removing to settle in Europe, and continuing there." But he was realist enough to know that conversely French émigrés settling in America would have tremendous difficulties of adjustment and might not be happy there for many years.[42]

Certainly Jefferson's nationalism was not of the expansive kind. He knew that every people had its own mores, laws and culture and evinced no desire to change them. He merely believed that they would slowly change of themselves under the influence of the American example. For this reason he ultimately came to favor free immigration, especially of the persecuted in other lands. He had always been a stanch believer in the right of expatriation which he considered an individual's "natural right" to seek happiness wherever he chose. He now recognized that, as its necessary counterpart, one must provide "a sanctuary for those whom the misrule of Europe may compel to seek happiness in other climes. This refuge once known will produce reaction on the happiness even of those who remain there." At the same time he so deeply abhorred the idea of conquest that he feared "entangling alliances" and even decried the rapid growth of America's commerce as ultimately conducive to war. Nor did he know of any greater praise for George Washington than to emphasize the identity of the latter's national and private ethics, for it well paid for nations to be "faithful to their engagements, even in the worst of circumstances." [43]

Curiously, he failed to notice the incongruously imperialistic nature of his expectation that the North American Anglo-Saxon civilization would ultimately unite the whole Western Hemisphere in a single large republic. He looked down upon the Latin Americans and often expressed doubts as to their capacity for self-government. He considered them much too priest-ridden and backward. Hence there was to be a purely pacific expansion of American civilization of the kind represented by his Louisiana Purchase or the Monroe Doctrine which, he knew, had actually been initiated by the British Chancery. To allay apprehensions that such rapid growth might endanger the country's republican structure, as long taught by Montesquieu, he assured a French correspondent that the simultaneous growth of national resources would fortify the republic, "if founded, not on conquest, but in principles of compact and equality." He certainly saw no conflict between such peaceful extension of

America's influence and its setting an example for all peoples desiring freedom and independence. He once even argued that the geographic peculiarities of the Western Hemisphere "may call for a different code of natural law to govern relations with other nations." In 1816 he still saw his country's great destiny in serving as "a barrier against the returns of ignorance and barbarism. Old Europe will have to lean on our shoulders, and to hobble along by our side, under the monkish trammels of priests and kings, as she can. What a Colossus shall we be when the southern continent comes up to our mark!" [44]

In this area of freedom from religious control Jefferson saw America's major departure from historic precedent and, hence, the main criterion of American nationalism. Personally, he seems to have been an agnostic. His assurance that he was a Christian "in the only sense in which he [Jesus] wished any one to be, sincerely attached to his doctrines," carries far less conviction than similar declarations by Rousseau. His world outlook was, in many respects, far closer to the pre-Rousseauan Enlightenment of Locke or Diderot. In his early injunctions to his ward, Peter Carr, he discussed religion in terms of a painfully impartial judge instructing a jury rather than in those of a believer. His personal interpretation of Christianity, moreover, had little in common with that of any established denomination, all of whose dogmatic structures he lightheartedly dismissed as speculations of "crazy theologists" and "metaphysical insanities." In an illuminating letter to Ezra Stiles he frankly admitted, "You say you are a Calvinist. I am not. I am of a sect by myself as far as I know." [45]

Materialism, not of the mechanistic Holbachian but more of the ancient Epicurean or Priestleyan kind, was a major ingredient of Jefferson's faith. "I am a materialist," he told William Short on April 13, 1820. A few months later he wrote to John Adams that "to say that the human soul, angels, God, are immaterial, is to say they are *nothings* or that there is no God, no angels, no soul. I cannot reason otherwise." He regarded Jesus himself as "unquestionably" a materialist looking forward to physical resurrection. Hence his reiterated severe denunciations of Calvin, as in his later letter to Adams, "I can never join Calvin in addressing *his* God. He was indeed an atheist, which I can never be; or rather his religion was daemonism. If ever men worshipped a false God he did. The being described in his five points, is not the God whom you and I acknowledge and adore, the creator and benevolent governor of the world; but a daemon of malignant spirit." Equally bitter was his condemnation of St. Paul. In his letter to Short he insisted on sharply differentiating the genuine utterances of Jesus which contained "many passages of fine imagination, correct morality and of the most lovely benevolence" from other sayings revealing "so much ignorance, so much absurdity, so much untruth, charlatanism and imposture as to pronounce it impossible that such contradictions should have proceeded from the same being." Having been early impressed by Bolingbroke's Bible criticism, he ascribed the wrong sayings to some of Jesus' disciples and biographers who often sinned on the side of both stupidity and roguery. "Of this band of dupes and impostors, Paul was the great Coryphaeus and first corruptor of the doctrines of Jesus." In short, the only real good in early Christianity was its system of ethics which resembled that of Epictetus and other ancient Epicureans.[46]

Even more significant than these doctrinal views were Jefferson's political applications. "The riddles of all the priesthoods," he wrote to the like-minded John Adams, "end in four more [words]: *ubi panis, ibi deus*." If one could only discard the priestly "metaphysical" accretions to Jesus' teachings there would be no room for sectarian divergences and all mankind would profess one religion. Sectarianism, however, became the necessary counterpart of the alliance of state and church which, as in England, "has ever made their judges accomplices to the frauds of the clergy." Jefferson's fulminations especially against the New England "hierocracy" sprang in part from his personal resentment of the latter's undisguised hostility during his electoral campaigns. "From the clergy I expect no mercy," he wrote in 1801, "they crucified their Saviour who preached that their Kingdom was not of this world; and all who practice on that precept must expect the extreme of their wrath." In part, however, it reflected his life-long conviction that America needed complete religious freedom, a conviction reinforced by his close observation of the detrimental effects of the French alliance of church and state.[47]

Here Jefferson's religious agnosticism well supplemented his nationalism. Although officially member of the Church of England and fairly regular churchgoer, he painfully remembered the former intolerant laws in Virginia. Had they been strictly enforced, he knew, he himself would have been a fit subject for many criminal prosecutions. Any one of his anti-Trinitarian harangues would have made him liable to three-year imprisonment. As a freethinker or even Unitarian—by 1822 he could privately state his conviction "that there is not a *young man* now living in the United States who will not die an Unitarian"—he would have been disqualified from serving as guardian of his own children. Even in their neglect these laws were sufficiently rigorous to make him witness the so-called "Period of the Great Persecution" of Baptists in 1768-74. He also knew that during the Revolution the loyalists had derived much support from such Anglican preachers, as Inglis, Seabury and Cooper, while in the mother country the Established Church had almost unanimously opposed conciliation of the kind preached by Burke and the dissenters, Price and Priestley. Even the Quakers did not escape Jefferson's nationalist wrath. On occasion he spoke admiringly of their repudiation of priesthood, but he considered them

a religious sect which, there [in Delaware], in the other states, in England, are a homogeneous mass, acting with one mind, and that directed by the mother society in England. Dispersed, as the Jews, they still form, as those do, one nation, foreign to the land they live in. They are Protestant Jesuits, implicitly devoted to the will of their superior, and forgetting all duties to their country in the execution of the policy of their order. When war is proposed with England, they have religious scruples; but when with France, these are laid by, and they become clamorous for it.[48]

Jefferson conceded, in other words, that in their "metaphysical" aspects religious bodies might differ widely, but demanded that as social organizations they should all conform to the new political patterns of American democracy. Generally a cultural cosmopolitan, Jefferson even as a nationalist did not envisage immediate cultural and, still less, religious uniformity. But in the long run he looked forward to the increasing amalgamation of the various cultural strains into a single American culture, which in its essentials he liked to trace back to early Anglo-Saxon origins. He even dreamed of America's ultimate religious unification, if not in a deistic creed which would hardly satisfy the masses, at least in some sort of enlightened Unitarianism. To all intents and purposes such a faith, if adopted by the vast majority of Americans, would be their new national religion. Although not an essential feature of Jeffersonian nationalism which, primarily conceived in terms of continental solidarity and constitutional liberties, left much room for cultural differences, the ultimate emergence of an American faith based upon the "pursuit of happiness" by all loomed large in the desires of its founder. Being a stanch believer in man's intrinsic goodness (he specifically repudiated the pessimistic views on human nature of a Rochefoucauld and Montaigne) he always believed in the progressive diffusion of light and education as the best means "for ameliorating the condition, promoting the virtue and advancing the happiness of men." [49]

In this hedonistic emphasis Jefferson again revealed his kinship with the individualistic and materialistic trends in pre-Rousseauan Enlightenment. Of course, even he looked for "happiness" far beyond the material well-being and economic prosperity of the individual or the nation. His ideal good life depended on virtuous and socially restrained living as much as on material abundance. It was approximated most closely by the life of American farmers, "the only farmers who can read Homer." Hence his reiterated denunciation of commerce and manufacture which, if engaged in beyond the satisfaction of domestic needs, tended "to increase our dependence on foreign nations and our liability to war."[50] We may look askance at such praise of economic self-sufficiency in the midst of his own strenuous negotiations in behalf of his country's foreign trade. Nor shall we completely dismiss the influence of that fashionable literary enthusiasm for the "noble savage" which, with special reference to American conditions, had inspired Rousseau and other critics of European civilization. Nonetheless, economic self-sufficiency so well fitted into Jefferson's general nationalist doctrine, which, in contrast to many European forms of nationalism, was isolationist rather than expansionist, that we have no reason to doubt his basic sincerity.

Neither shall we dispute Jefferson's genuine interest in popular education. Here his nationalist views combined with his agnostic bias to make him a champion of state-supported secular education which, if not reaching the extremes advocated by Rousseau, exceeded anything envisaged by Burke. Popular education was generally becoming a major nationalist ideal and serving, in turn, as the main vehicle of nationalist propaganda. From its inception it naturally clashed with the existing church-controlled educational systems. Forced, during his stay as ambassador in Paris, to place his daughter, Martha, in a Catholic convent school, Jefferson informed his sister, Mrs. Bolling, with much relief, that many other Protestant children attended that school and "that not a word is ever spoken to them on the subject of religion." Among his early legislative contributions in Virginia was the abolition of the school of theology at William and Mary, a college originally established for the very purpose of propagating Christianity among the Indians. When in later years he founded the University of Virginia, an act which, next to the Bill for Religious Freedom and the Declaration of Independence, he considered his major claim to immortality, he insisted upon its nonsectarian character. He thus laid the foundations for the secularization and, hence, also complete Americanization of education. For, he wrote in his aforementioned letter to Adams, "bigotry is the disease of ignorance, of morbid minds; enthusiasm of the free and buoyant. Education and free discussion are the antidotes of both. We are destined to be a barrier against the returns of ignorance and barbarism." [51]

4. FICHTE

In the midst of the world turmoil generated by the American and French revolutions Fichte, too, became a nationalist. If Rousseau's nationalist consistency suffered from lack of precision and often contradictory emotional reactions, that of Burke from his divergent attitudes to the "constitutional" American and the anticonstitutional French revolutions, and that of Jefferson from the ambivalence of the nascent nationalism in a new country, Fichte was inconsistent chiefly because of his gradual evolution from cosmopolitanism to extreme nationalism. Many an utterance in his earlier works was sharply controverted by his subsequent statements. Being a man of action rather than words, or more correctly a man for whom words constituted action, Fichte reacted to the rapidly changing European and German realities by constantly adjusting his ideology.[52]

At the same time he despised the "realism" of Enlightenment and believed that ideas alone ultimately molded reality. Time and again he ridiculed these contemporaries who made a fetish of experience and echoed Burke's arguments against "metaphysical" generalizations. "Rousseau . . . has treated you, empiricists, much too leniently," Fichte exclaimed, "this was his mistake. You will hear different talk some day." So convinced was he of the superiority of philosophical speculation over practical experience that he coined the paradox "Life is essentially non-philosophizing; philosophizing is essentially non-living." [53]

At first Fichte was carried away by the humanitarian message of the French Revolution. He was ready to become a French citizen and later to teach at the projected German University of Mayence under French auspices. In 1793 he wrote a volume trying to dispel current misconceptions about the Revolution. He even argued courageously against a German reconquest of Alsace-Lorraine.

> Do you really think [he wrote] that the German artist and farmer is so very much interested in whether the artist and farmer of Alsace-Lorraine will in the future find his town or village listed in geography textbooks under the heading of the German Empire? Or that he would throw away his graving tool and farming utensil in order to put it there? [54]

As the revolutionary leadership gradually veered away from its early humanitarianism, however, and became an expansive, imperialistic dictatorship, Fichte became infected with the rising spirit of national resistance. But unlike his compatriot, Ernst Moritz Arndt, he still refused to recognize attachment to the soil and territorial mooring as the main characteristics of nationality. He also repudiated racial descent as a distinguishing mark, pointing out the Germans' historic mixtures with Gauls and Cantabrians abroad and with Slavs in their own country. Rather, with Herder, he insisted upon the intellectual criteria of language and culture, for "men are formed by language far more than language is by men." [55] Despite the widespread usage of the term "Prussian nation" or "Bavarian nation" even in official documents, he consistently championed on these grounds only the idea of an all-German nationality which, he admitted, still was but a nationality in the making. More so, in some respects, than the American nation, for it had no stable boundaries and was rapidly losing whatever nominal unity it had possessed under the Holy Roman Empire. Fichte's resourceful mind made a virtue of this necessity. Out of the German people's political divisiveness he construed his momentous theory of cultural nationalism which, going far beyond that of Rousseau, was destined to play a decisive role in the evolution of political nationalism as well.

Fichtean nationalism had many religious facets. As a fervent Christian preacher, despite lifelong pantheistic leanings and frequent ridicule of the popular ideas of Providence and the fear of God, he never allowed his nationalism completely to displace his early humanitarianism. "Cosmopolitanism," he declared, 'is the dominant will to attain humanity's purpose of existence in humanity itself. Patriotism is the will to attain the same purpose first in that nation, of which we are members, and then to let this success expand from that nation to the whole of humanity." [56] Even in his last, most nationalistic years he always visualized his nation as a *Menschheitsnation,* performing a permanent function for mankind as a whole. He merely might add, with Schiller, another citizen of the world turned nationalist, that "every nation has its day in history, but the day of the Germans is the harvest of all time." Everything serving the purposes of German nationalism, therefore, would, in his opinion, ultimately serve mankind as well.

Semireligious universalism dictated even his retrogressive proposals for the organization of the "commercial state," [57] which were one of the earliest adumbrations of fascism. His truly Rousseauist xenophobia; his advocacy of national autarchy far beyond Jefferson; his insistence that foreign trade, that "anarchy of trade," be restricted to a governmentally controlled indispensable minimum of raw materials; that foreign travel be limited to a few intellectuals in search of knowledge; and that, as a prerequisite to all that, each such "real state" seek to attain its natural boundaries—were all intended to counteract the mercantilistic quest for foreign markets which in his opinion had long been the main incentive to war. While admitting that such a program would entail a lowering of living standards and suppression of many ordinary comforts, he believed that the nation, and indirectly all humanity, would be more than compensated by the ensuing simplicity in customs and a sharper delineation of national characters.

> It is evident that such a self-contained nation, whose members have only intercourse with one another, and very little with foreigners, which through these measures preserves its peculiar way of life, institutions and mores and loves dearly its fatherland and all pertaining to the fatherland, will soon generate a high degree of national honor and a sharply delineated national character. It will become a different, wholly novel nation.

Autarchy, moreover, would enable the government to control "property," which he identified with "the right to work," regulate wages and incomes, prevent indulgence in luxuries before the satisfaction of all legitimate ordinary wants, tax heavily for cultural and educational purposes and expropriate inheritances.

Even in his later years Fichte advocated "national education" for children of both sexes, withdrawn by the state from parental control and living together with their teachers and supervisors. At the same time, he favored strengthening family life as the best method of enhancing the nation's economic and political power. Population growth was for him the first and unpreventable "pacific conquest." Other conquests might readily follow, inasmuch as a generation which had undergone the stringent physical and mental training outlined by him would furnish such a reservoir of military power as to make a standing army altogether superfluous. The new Germany could truly entertain the ambitious desire of every state "either to form a universal Christian monarchy or at least to secure the possibility of striving for one." [58]

That such a regime could not possibly be achieved without the use of force hardly bothered this apostle of "liberty." For him liberty, too, was but an intellectual concept. In his *Theory of State* (1813) he demanded highest authority for the supreme intellect and insisted that so long as there is one man who "understands better any given situation, he be entitled to overrule the majority, by force, if he is strong enough." When he came to weigh the possibilities of Prussia serving as Germany's unifying authority, he spoke of the Prussian king as the *Zwingherr zur Deutschheit* (coercive master for Germanism), a designation later hailed with enthusiasm by Prusso-German chauvinists like Treitschke. Even an offensive war could, therefore, be a holy war if undertaken in the defense of spiritual and ethical values. Just before Prussia's defeat at Jena, Fichte was ready to invoke the shades of Machiavelli and become the champion of outright power politics.[59]

The religious fervor of Fichte's nationalism affected also his concept of Christianity. Just as he had followed Kant in repudiating the utilitarian "pursuit of happiness" as the chief aim of the state, so he rejected the religious teachings of reward and punishment as a vulgar, eudaemonistic distortion of the Christian faith. True patriotism meant to him self-sacrifice in behalf of one's country, and a completely selfless communion with the Deity was the sole legitimate form of religion. That is why he condemned the "social contract," and even its roots in the Old Testament doctrine of the "Covenant," as lowering a given relationship between citizen and state to a contractual give-and-take.

True Christianity was reflected, in his opinion, only in the Gospel of John which taught the belief in God "in whom we all are and may live and attain salvation, and outside of whom there is only death and non-existence." Such Christianity was but the restoration of the ancient religion of Melchizedek, that first genuine religion, anterior to Judaism. In its Pauline form, however, adopted also by the three other Gospels, it made Jesus a descendant of Jews and construed the New Testament to be superimposed upon the Old Covenant which, in itself, had been but an inferior version of Melchizedek's faith. Pauline "Christianity, which in its degeneration had become even more Asiatic and preached quiet humility and blind faith, had appeared as something strange to the Romans." Only after being implanted in the primitive German tribes did it contain the germs of the ultimate Protestant Reformation. In Luther, finally, the original "absolute nature of Christianity" was fully realized, even Catholicism having then been forced to re-examine its fundamentals. This peculiar predisposition of the German national character for the Reformation had its sociopolitical roots in the "German thoroughness of the rulers and the German good-naturedness of the people," i.e., the understanding leadership of the princes and the quiet acceptance of duties by the masses. In the future true religiosity will still depend on the German masses' sense of duty, whereas the princes will play a decidedly secondary role.[60]

Fichte thus took over lock, stock and barrel the old Israelitic idea of the "chosen people." He did not mean to flatter his people's vanity, as his critics accused him of doing.[61] Despite his occasional disparaging remarks on the Old Testament, he often emulated the Israelitic prophets and castigated the "sinfulness" of his compatriots. What is more, like these prophets, he rationalized the national catastrophe of 1806 into a great historic lesson for his people. He proclaimed that its humiliation by Napoleon was a God-sent challenge to complete regeneration, not only in its own behalf, but for all of mankind. In the apogee of his nationalist doctrine (in a much-debated fragment written in the last year of his life) [62] he declared that the unique distinction of the German nation consisted in its having grown until then without a state and "without history." In other words, its political divisions, contrasted with the national unity of most other Western nations, had accounted for its growth without a common national history and for its being an exclusively cultural and linguistic entity. At the same time it possessed an unspoiled "original" language, extraordinary cultural achievements and high ideals. This unique situation offered the Germans also a unique opportunity for developing out of their spiritual values a full-fledged nation transcending the limitations of statehood. Out of their clear recognition of what ought to be, their *Sollen*, they were to reshape the existing realities, their *Sein*. Their ultimate cultural state would serve as a model for all nations and simultaneously remove the obstacles theretofore obstructing the spread of the German brand of Christianity. It is unlikely that Fichte failed to realize the implications of that doctrine for world peace. Discussing the Israelitic feeling of chosenness he himself remarked that, with such a national character, the ancient Jews were better prepared for a career of conquest than any other people, Moses and his successors having failed especially in their "paying too little heed to arming their people." Only through some speculative acrobatics could Fichte harmonize these views with his early dreams, under Kantian inspiration, of a league of nations enforcing permanent peace and universal rights of men.[63]

Deep down in the recesses of his mind Fichte seems to have felt that such a program required a far greater unity between the new "chosen people" and its religion. Living in a period of a Christian reaction to Enlightenment and personally far less rebellious than Rousseau, he did not venture publicly to advocate a national religion. But he allowed himself to dream privately of a German utopia in which nationality and religion would be reunited in a new national creed. In a brief curiosity on *The Republic of Germans at the Beginning of the Twenty-Second Century under its Fifth Imperial Bailiff,* written in 1807 under the impact of Prussia's ignominious defeat but evidently not intended for publication,[64] Fichte gave free rein to his imagination.

In this sketch Fichte described how the German nation, after an initial period of dissolution occasioned by the disloyalty of its princes and writers, ultimately found its desired unity. Being intrinsically more self-contained than other nations, it developed a new constitution as well as a new faith and ritual. The legislators left the three existing Christian denominations in the undisturbed possession of their rights. But they admitted also a fourth denomination which was gradually accepted by "all persons of liberal education." The adherents of the new faith were soon called "general Christians" in contrast to the older "Christianists," because they revered in Jesus Christ the first divulger "of the highest goal of all truth," though no longer an authority to be followed blindly. They assumed the same attitude toward the Bible which they recognized as a matchless part of their national literature. The state as such insisted only on the article of faith that religious disparity does not bar any citizen from ultimate salvation. With an unmistakable dig at Catholic intransigence, Fichte emphasized that public acceptance of this doctrine had been made a prerequisite for admission to citizenship—a clear throwback to Rousseau's civic profession of faith. Ultimately all Protestants and the majority of Catholics joined the new creed; only "a few scattered Catholic communities remained" in the twenty-second century, when they still enjoyed full equality.

This newly found national unity was underscored by the new ritual. Generally much simplified, it laid stress upon civic virtues and military valor. The display of arms in the new churches was a natural part of the ceremonial in a society, where "every German, with minor exceptions, served as a soldier from the age of twenty to his death." If he fell in the defense of his country, his remains (cremation having replaced burial) were preserved in the first, most honored niche in the wall surrounding the church. Another niche, second in distinction, was assigned to those "who had counseled the fatherland with clarity and intelligence."

One must not dismiss these fantastic lucubrations with a shrug. They are too closely akin to Arndt's widely heralded patriotic program for the Wars of Liberation which culminated in "German freedom, a German God, German faith without a scoff." Publicly Fichte always professed a national brand of Christianity which, in so far more humanitarian as ultimately all mankind was to embrace it, was nevertheless equally nationalist and expansive. "Moreover," he declared on one occasion, "every nation will try to spread its peculiar good so far as it is able to do and, if it can, will endeavor to incorporate all humanity in itself. This is the result of a God-given impulse from which have sprung the community of nations, their mutual frictions and their progress." [65]

We thus see that in opposing Jacobin nationalism Fichte developed a theory of German nationalism based upon the unity of the German language and culture, further cemented by the expected progression of Lutheran Christianity. Protestantism, he believed, was in perfect agreement with his own ethical philosophy and did not necessarily preach Christian submissiveness to fate and government—a typical doctrine of tyrants. On the contrary, "we ought to prevent, wherever we can, that the Earth be converted into hell, so as to arouse greater yearnings for Heaven." We ought, indeed, look for happiness and even immortality in this world, for one's nation and fatherland are actually the bearers of such worldly immortality.[66]

In that period of extreme German weakness and despondency Fichte thus pointed the way to the marshaling of all German forces around the nation and its peculiar type of religion which, he believed, would ultimately be accepted by the world at large. It was indeed his basic conception—that of his cosmopolitan youth and of his nationalist years of maturity alike—that science, or more specifically his peculiar Theory of Science, would forge the unity of mankind. In this fashion the traditional dogmatism and eudaemonism in both religion and politics would be replaced by his brand of idealism and moralism. Not without justification, therefore, these Fichtean reasonings, like those of Kant and Hegel, were viewed by posterity as a quest for a new "religion of German idealism," rather than as the upholding of traditional Christianity.

Was this ideology, so eloquent and persuasive for a weak nationality in the making, to prove equally acceptable to a united powerful nation conscious of its strength and apparently no longer in need of shaping realities to conform to its spiritual yearnings? Half a century was to pass before Bismarckian Germany was to furnish the first answer, just as the French Revolution had served as the first testing ground for the problems raised by Rousseau's nationalism. In contrast thereto, Giuseppe Mazzini, leading Italian nationalist, lived to see his ideas tested in the new united Italy—and he died brokenhearted.

5. Mazzini

Mazzini and Gioberti, the spiritual leaders of *Risorgimento*, were in many ways Italian counterparts to the nationalist thinkers of the German Wars of Liberation. Apart from Herder's influence, which was strongly felt on both sides of the Alps, the objective conditions of the two disunited peoples were bound to produce great kinship in their nationalist thought. Like Fichte's *Sollen*, Mazzini's doctrine of duty became the more readily the cornerstone of his nationalist philosophy, as he, too, was deeply dissatisfied with the existing political realities. Not "rights of man" or pursuit of happiness, he contended, but fulfillment of one's duty to nation and mankind was the true aim of national existence.

Right is the faith of the individual; duty is a collective faith. Right can only organize resistance, it can destroy but not lay foundations. Duty builds and creates collaboration. . . . Right undermines sacrifice and eliminates martyrdom from the world. In any theory of individual rights interests alone predominate and martyrdom becomes an absurdity. No interests could survive one's death. Nevertheless, it is martyrdom which frequently serves as the baptism of a new world and the initiation of progress.[67]

With this accent on sacrifice and fulfillment of duty, Mazzini had all the makings of a religious nationalist. In fact, he could not conceive society without religion, society itself being but "a great religious fact." He also extolled the essentially religious idea of mission for both individuals and nations. One of his fullest definitions of nationality (not of nationalism, which term he abhorred) was that it "is the association of all men forming a single group through language, certain geographic conditions or the role assigned to them by history, recognizing the same principle, conducting themselves under the rule of a uniform law and working for the accomplishment of the same aim. . . . Nationality is the role assigned by God to each people in the work of humanity; the mission and task which it ought to fulfill on earth so that the divine purpose may be attained in the world." We note that language is an important national characteristic. So are common laws (confronted with Italy's political divisions, Mazzini preferred laws to statehood). But above all loom each nationality's God-given geographic background and religious mission.[68]

Mazzini was, of course, cognizant of Italy's natural frontiers between the Alps and the sea which were, to cite Napoleon, "defined with as much precision as if she were an island." This geographic emphasis was something of a throwback to Albertus Magnus and the English prelates at the Council of Constance who had argued for basic geographic divisions rather than the innumerable linguistic frontiers or the more or less temporary political organizations. Ernst Moritz Arndt was ready in 1802 to concede to Poland German areas along the Baltic, if only Germany were given access to the North Sea on both sides of the Rhine, i.e., parts of the Netherlands. Arndt believed that "natural frontiers consist first of all in the free access to the sea for every land and in the second place in linguistic divisions." [69] Mazzini not only demanded for Italy, "Europe's best defined fatherland," the entire peninsula to the Alps together with the adjoining islands, but also most of North Africa as falling within the same geographic orbit. Time and again he redrew the whole European map in the name of this national geographic principle. He calmly suggested, for instance, the merger of the three Scandinavian peoples or of Spain and Portugal into a single nationality. He even advocated the annexation by Italy's archenemy, Austria, or after its anticipated early disintegration by one or another of its successor states, of the score of linguistic groups inhabiting the Danubian basin.[70]

This geographic factor had for Mazzini profound religious sanctions, for each nationality reflected "God's design . . . clearly outlined . . . in the course of the large rivers, in the curves of the high mountains and in other geographic conditions." Nations, therefore, should not resist the divine will so clearly stated, but rather serve as the collective instruments of its realization on earth and as real "prophets of the Lord." The Italian nation, particularly, should ultimately emerge as the divine Messiah for the redemption of all mankind. Mazzini's formula for the oath to be taken by each new initiate in the Young Italy Association was a perfect illustration of this strong intermingling of his religious and nationalist faiths. Every newcomer was to swear:

> In the name of God and of Italy—in the name of all the martyrs for the holy Italian cause, fallen under the strokes of tyranny, foreign or domestic— for the duties which bind me to the earth on which God has placed me and to the brethren whom God has given me—for the love, innate in any man, towards the places where my mother was born and where my children will live— for the hatred, innate in any man, towards evil, injustice, usurpation, and arbitrary rule—for the shame which makes me blush in front of citizens of other nations because I have neither the name nor the rights of a citizen, nor the flag of a nation, nor a fatherland—for the quaking of my soul, created for liberty, but unable to exercise it, created for doing good, but unable to achieve it in the silence and isolation of serfdom—for the memory of our ancient power—for the consciousness of our present abject state—for the tears of Italian mothers—for the sons who died by impaling, in prison, or in exile— for the misery of millions,
>
> I, John Doe, believing in the mission entrusted by God to Italy and the duty of every man born an Italian to contribute to its accomplishment—convinced that, where God wished that there be a nation, exist the forces necessary for its creation—that the people is the depositary of these forces—and that in directing them for the people and with the people rests the secret of victory—convinced that virtue consists in action and sacrifice and that power comes from unity and constancy of will—I give my name to *Young Italy*, an association of men believing in the same faith. . . .[71]

Unlike his contemporary Vincenzo Gioberti, however, whose *Moral and Civil Primacy* (1843) postulated Italian unity under papal leadership, Mazzini was decidedly anti-Catholic. "The papacy is a cadaver, as is the monarchy," he exclaimed. Speaking of the Turkish caliphate, he predicted that "like the Catholic papacy, the Mohammedan papacy will expire before the end of the century." He sincerely believed that, whatever its faults, the eighteenth century had already effectively controverted the entire past, including its feudal, aristocratic and monarchical traditions. It had also "negated the Catholic dogma, the dogma of absolute passivity, which had poisoned the springs of liberty and implanted despotism at the top of the social edifice." [72]

Philosophically, too, Mazzini had genuine objections to both the Christian teachings and the Christian theocracy. Apart from rejecting the supernatural beliefs in miracles, a celestial hierarchy, sacraments and other mysteries, he was convinced that true religion should teach the existence of a God immanent in the nation and reject theocracy's dependence on the aid of a transcendental God. Individualistic Christianity, he stated, "ignores collective humanity," whereas true religion must reflect the progressive evolution of national and humanitarian thought. The founders of Christianity had also committed the grievous error of ignoring the love of one's fatherland "which embraces all future generations" and of believing in a single, immediate revelation, whereas in fact "a continuous revelation descends from God to man across all humanity" and through all the ages. That is why Catholicism had for the last six centuries been merely an obstacle to progress. "Not one of the great steps forward accomplished in our century," Mazzini told the church dignitaries assembled at the Vatican Council of 1870, "was initiated or consecrated by your word." The time was indeed ripe for a new religious reformation going far beyond the Protestant Reformation. For, despite its incontestable historical merits, Protestantism, too, had failed because it had likewise denied progress and tried "to accomplish the impossible task of bringing a religion back to its beginnings." It was now breaking asunder into innumerable little sects. In short, "humanity is like a man living indefinitely and always learning. Hence there neither is, nor can be any infallibility of men or of organs; there neither is nor can be a privileged caste of depositaries and interpreters of the Law; there neither is nor can be any need of an intermediary between God and man other than humanity." In an early letter Mazzini frankly admitted that, according to his interpretation of Christianity, he was not a Christian, but that the time was not yet ripe for the propagation of "pure Deism, which is my religion." [73]

At the same time he was perfectly aware of the Catholic loyalties and the conservatism of the Italian masses. Whatever grievances they had against the proverbial mismanagement of the papal bureaucracy in Rome (even friendly Metternich called it a "government which has not the faintest notion how to govern"), they appreciated the social and educational services of the Italian clergy in other provinces. Mazzini himself challenged the contemporary individualists by pointing out that, despite all the clamor about the dying faith, "the multitudes proceed slowly on the road of sacrifice and association." He also knew that the revolution would deeply antagonize the people were it to start by destroying churches. He merely believed that the nation would calmly accept the strict delimitation of the church to its own province, and even such dogmatic departures as the placing of Socrates on a par with Jesus. [74]

Mazzini made no claim to being the founder of a new religion, or even its main apostle. God had not given him, he believed, enough strength for an apostolate. But he was certain that he saw the dim contours of a new faith on the horizon. Warned in 1832 by his friend, Jean Charles Sismondi, against the pretension, or imposture, of founding a new faith Mazzini replied that "everything develops by degrees. Religion, too, which is for me but the most noble and sublime formula of human evolution at a given period, will necessarily follow the progressive stages in the development of humanity." The new religion would still be theistic, for the science "now called Free Thought and Reason" was but an "arid, bloodless, saddest parody of science." But it would cherish a God immanent in the earthly nations and revealing himself through their political and artistic, rather than their sacerdotal leaders. Mazzini's book on *Faith and the Future*, written in 1835 but considered by him even ten years later as his most important work, fairly well summarized his lifelong religious convictions.

Faith requires [he wrote] a purpose embracing all of life, in some fashion concentrating in itself all of life's manifestations. It directs their various forms or suppresses them all for the sake of the activity of a single form. It requires an ardent irrevocable belief that this purpose will be attained; a conviction of one's mission and of the duty to fulfill it; also the consciousness of a supreme power protecting the believers on their path toward this goal. All these are indispensable elements. Where one is lacking, we may have a sect, school, political party, but not a *faith*, nor the constant hourly devotion to the service of a high religious ideal.[75]

In the formulation and propaganda of this new faith lay, in Mazzini's view, the great mission of the Italian people. Using Hegelian antitheses, Mazzini worked out a neat contrast between the great achievements of ancient and medieval Rome and the still greater destinies of the Rome of the future. "As the Rome of the Caesars which had, through action, unified a large part of Europe was replaced by the Rome of the Popes which, through thought, united both Europe and America, so will the Rome of the People replace them both and, through a faith combining thought and action, amalgamate Europe, America and the rest of the world into a single whole." This exalted opportunity was given the Italian people because of its peculiarly difficult situation. "Italy cannot live without living for all men. . . . We cannot have Rome without initiating a new religious epoch!" The Third Rome would thus ultimately unite all nations in an all-embracing "union of the faithful," in which "Hebrews, Mohammedans, Buddhists, all those who in eighteen centuries of effort could not subscribe to a universal religion" would finally feel as brethren. Under the impact of the Revolution of 1848 Mazzini contrasted this free and democratic association of nations with the Holy Alliance of Princes which had stifled every free national movement in Europe. To the old "legitimism" of the monarchs he opposed the new legitimist principle "based not upon the arbitrary privileges of the few, but upon the rights, or rather upon the duties, of all." [76]

Such religiously inspired nations could not possibly uphold separation of state and church, the very idea of which Mazzini condemned as "an immoral concept." Temporarily, he conceded, separation might help reduce the detrimental influence of the Catholic Church and the Jesuits upon Italy's national life. But in the long run he felt that after the successful reconciliation of the new state and the new religion, the latter would "be the soul, the thought of the new state." In general he not only objected to Machiavelli's doctrine of the primacy of politics over morals and religion, but also repudiated any idea of their mutual independence. "To pretend that one can ever completely separate matters pertaining to Earth from those pertaining to Heaven, the temporal from the spiritual, is neither moral, nor logical, nor possible." He insisted that "religion represents the principle; politics the application" of the same interdependent national goals. In other words, a new national religion, remotely derived from Italian Catholicism but easily adaptable to the national creeds of all other peoples, was to furnish the ultimate answer to the quest of ages.[77]

In one respect, however, Mazzini differed essentially from the other Nationalist Fathers. Under the influence of the Saint-Simonians (Salvemini claims that fully four-fifths of his ideas were of Saint-Simonian origin) he realized the meaning of the new conditions created by the Industrial Revolution. The working classes, he declared, had become "the principal new element of history" and, hence, "no revolution is either legitimate or enduring if it fails to combine the social with the political question." From the religious angle, too, he believed that "when the world will have no more Brahmins and Pariahs, masters and serfs, but men alone—we shall adore, with quite different a faith, quite different a love, the great name of God." [78]

Mazzini's socialism was of the evolutionary rather than the revolutionary kind. He who preached bloody insurrection as a legitimate means of national liberation, justified national wars however sanguinary, and intimated the permissibility of regicide, favored none but an absolutely pacific social revolution. Especially after Napoleon III's rise to power by a successful manipulation of popular franchise, Mazzini blamed the new caesarism on the French socialists who, through excessive haste and lack of discretion, had frightened the people into acquiescence with the dictator's coup d'état. "'By virtue of preaching material interests to the worker and farmer, they made him egotistical and violent." From broader theoretical considerations, too, he condemned communism as impossible "without altogether subverting the social order, drying up the process of production, impeding progress, abolishing the freedom of the individual and chaining him to a military and tyrannical order." He was even more sharply opposed to its Marxian brand because of its materialistic philosophy of history, its emphasis on the class struggle and the material well-being of the workers, which he placed on the same level with the liberalistic "pursuit of happiness." He ridiculed this type of progress as "the progress of mankind's kitchen." At times he was even wary of applying to himself the term "socialist," which had come in vogue with the Saint-Simonians in the 1830's. By 1851 he declared in behalf of himself and his associates, "We are

neither communists nor levellers, nor hostile to private ownership, nor socialists in the sense given to this term by the systematical sectarians of a neighboring country [France]." [79]

He resented most the socialists' interference with Italian unification. For the
sake of this ideal he and his fellow triumvirs of 1849 even proclaimed Catholicism as the official creed of the Italian Republic. Later he had to compromise
with the hated monarchical system. He was similarly prepared to adjourn
indefinitely all vital social reforms. His sense of guilt, when reproached by
opponents that his socialist teachings had helped divide the Italian people,
was aggravated by the frequent indiscretions of his own followers. On learning
in 1838 of a secret society in Sardinia propagating antireligious and anti-
property doctrines, he exclaimed, "Senseless and worthless people! If Metternich had furnished them a program of organization he could not have done
better." Moreover, he considered all communist propaganda a dangerous
diversion of the proletariat's energies from its main goal of "creating for itself
a fatherland and a name" [80]—a curious inversion of the well-known Marxist
condemnation of most nationalist movements as a diversion of its energies from
the communist goal.

Socialist leaders in and outside of Italy reacted strongly. Irritated by Mazzini's theological verbiage and messianic mannerisms, Karl Marx dismissed
him curtly as *teopompo* (God-pompous). Proudhon charged that "he wanted
to become pope." At the same time the church and the ruling classes saw in
him a dangerous "fellow traveler." When on April 29, 1849, Pius IX publicly condemned the "horrible and most fatal system of socialism as well as
communism," he included the Mazzinist movement in his anathema. In a
lighter vain Farini in his *Roman State* (1853) claimed that Mazzini was "a
pontifex and a prince, an apostle and a priest. Run away, you clerics; in Rome
he is at home." Even Gioberti, whom Mazzini claimed as an associate in
"Young Italy" (Gioberti later denied it), criticized him severely as an imag-
inative, rather than rational politician, obsessed by a single, the republican idea.
"Since anyone having a single idea cannot vary it (for every permutation
involves at least two concepts), it is small wonder that Mazzini should adhere
to his thought and reveal a constancy in his fancies which simpletons admire,
but which sages call 'obstinacy.'" [81]

Notwithstanding this chorus of accusers, it was neither Mazzini's theology
nor his republicanism or socialism which accounted for his great influence on
his countrymen and his position in the history of the nineteenth century. He
was first and last a champion of Italian unification. Despite his evident sincerity
and eloquence his religious ideas made a greater impression in England than
in Italy, and even in England they were subjects of intellectual playfulness
rather than of deep, emotional concern. Most Italians preferred either to
follow the established Church or to embrace some form of contemporary

agnosticism. He himself abandoned his republicanism and accepted the Sardinian dynasty, making the "greatest possible sacrifice" for the sake of unity and out of deference to the wishes of the majority of the Italian people.[82] Even his socialism, notwithstanding his constantly growing proletarian following, was speedily superseded by the social democratic and communistic influences emanating from Germany, France and Russia. Not until the advent of fascism did Mazzinian socialism become a force in Italian public life, and then chiefly because of its intermingling with nationalist ingredients which lent themselves to easy distortion in support of the new national socialist ideology.

Mazzini, the nationalist, however, was a powerful factor in the Italian, indeed in the European, evolution. No matter how small the official membership of "Young Europe" always was (it was founded in 1834 by eighteen German, Polish and Italian refugees) or how much the "responsible" leaders of Italian unification deprecated his noisy following as a perennial nuisance, his teachings engendered, or at least lent expression to, forces which ultimately shook the most venerable thrones and chanceries of the Continent. What Fichte was to the Germans, Mazzini was to the youthful nationalists of many peoples: the effective idealist preacher. With greater eloquence, because he shunned the jargon of German philosophic idealism, Mazzini spread all over Europe the new credo that "he who wants humanity wants a fatherland." [83]

6. Crucial Epoch

Although more than a century and a half passed from Rousseau's birth in 1712 to Mazzini's death in 1872, the five thinkers here reviewed were almost contemporaries. At Rousseau's death in 1778 Burke was approximately forty-nine years old, Jefferson thirty-five and Fichte sixteen. On the other hand, at Mazzini's birth in 1805 both Jefferson and Fichte were still alive, and many passages quoted above were culled from their writings during Mazzini's childhood or adolescence. The chronological sequence accounts for some differences in their teachings. Events of such magnitude as the American and French revolutions and the rise of the European proletariat would have left a permanent imprint even on less sensitive minds. Basically, however, the differences in their geographic and cultural habitat, historic background and national necessity proved far more decisive. This genuine correspondence between their ideas and their peoples' peculiar historic experiences and social trends lent them their amazingly persistent vitality. Few political writers of that period still attract a reading public like theirs or possess their flair for actuality.[84] If Burke's speeches have lost their popularity as living literature and are largely studied by youngsters under the compulsion of a schoolmasterly tradition, they have at least remained an inexhaustible mine of apt parliamentary quotations.

It is always dangerous to reduce complex systems of thought and emotion to single sloganlike formulas. The present writer is painfully aware that, in trying to analyze briefly the ramified views on nationalism and religion expressed by thinkers over a period of years and under the stimulus of ever-changing circumstances, he had to disregard many significant qualifications and to ride roughshod over numerous side issues however significant. He nevertheless believes that certain fundamental characteristics, peculiar to each of these doctrines,[85] may most graphically, if not most adequately, be summed up in a few pregnant adjectives. He suggests, therefore, with all due reservations, that Rousseau's essentially "voluntaristic" nationalism clearly differed from the "constitutional" nationalism of Burke and the "democratic" nationalism of Jefferson. These in turn were far apart from Fichte's "linguistic-cultural" and Mazzini's "geographic-cultural" nationalism. What is more, these were essentially the dominant features of modern French, English, American, German and Italian national consciousness in general.

Rousseau's exhortation to the Poles sounded the keynote of later French nationalism. He admonished his despairing friends to cherish genuine love for fatherland and freedom, for "so long as that love will burn in your hearts, it may perhaps not safeguard you against temporary subjugation, but sooner or later it will cause an explosion, break the yoke and set you free." [86] The objective criteria of territory, state, language, religion or custom may help us understand national allegiance, but the ultimate decision rests only with the will of the people, which in a sovereign manner determines its "social contract," cultivates its own customs, and creates its own religious and political institutions. Viewed historically, this French will to nationality (Renan's "plebiscite repeated daily") could assume in speedy succession such diverse forms as the championing of "equality, liberty and fraternity" during the Revolution, achieving military "glory" under the imperial dictatorship or propagating a truly Catholic "genius of Christianity" under the Restoration. It could be royalist, republican or caesarist, capitalist or socialist—so long as it was genuinely and professedly French. The ultimate tests came when the French Revolution took Avignon from the papacy and Napoleon III incorporated Savoy and Nice. In both cases it was the incontrovertible will of the people that proved decisive. In a genuine plebiscite of 1860 under Sardinia's supervision the people of Savoy cast 130,533 votes in favor of joining France as against only 225 in the negative. The people's will thus overruled all arguments drawn from its linguistic affinities with Italian and its centuries-old associations with the papacy and the House of Savoy which had now become the royal house of Italy.[87]

As against this voluntaristic, subjective form of national allegiance Fichte and his successors stressed ever more the objective criteria of a common "original" language and historic-cultural heritage. Before long, Johann Christoph

Rühs, Fichte's colleague at the University of Berlin, advocated the liberation of Schleswig-Holstein from the "Danish yoke," without producing a shred of evidence that its German inhabitants desired to be liberated. Half a century later the German-speaking majority of Alsace was "freed," clearly and avowedly against its will. None of the German nationalists dared openly to controvert Merlin de Douai's declaration at the French National Assembly of 1790 that "the Alsatian people has become united with the French people because it has so willed; it was its will alone and not the Treaty of Münster which has legitimized this union." Heinrich von Treitschke, though theoretically admitting, with special reference to the English-speaking Irish, that language was not an absolutely valid criterion, invoked the shades of generations long passed against the will of his Alsatian contemporaries. He rhapsodized on the millennium of Alsace's partnership in German destiny as against the brief two centuries of its participation in French history. Even such a mild-mannered humanitarian as Friedrich Theodor Vischer argued that one did not ask children whether they *wished* to belong to their mother.[88] As late as the early twentieth century there still existed a characteristic cleavage between the Austrian and the German socialists. Karl Renner and Otto Bauer, confronted by the perplexities of the multinational Austro-Hungarian Empire, developed their momentous "personal," i.e., subjective theory of nationality. But the Germans, led by Karl Kautsky, still insisted upon the primacy of the objective, linguistic standards.[89]

Mazzini's nationalist doctrine, which, despite his French residence and general dependence on the Saint-Simonians, was more strongly influenced by German than by French teachings, tended to replace the linguistic by another objective, the geographic factor. Passionately convinced of Italy's superior national unity, he had to find a rationale which would overcome its undeniable regional divergences stemming from great linguistic and dialectal variations, economic and political conflicts, and deep-rooted cultural and historical differences. Even in the twentieth century, writes a modern observer,

> It is Europe that one finds in the valley of the Po, and, to all intents and purposes, Africa in Sicily. For the last seven centuries the history of Italy has been that of Lombardy, Tuscany, Venice and the South. It has been that of France, Germany and Austria rather than that of Italy herself. Italy has a dozen capitals, some of which have had closer connections with foreign countries than with other Italian centers, or so it was up until the opening of the railway system which has been a chief factor in the unification of Italy.[90]

Only in the name of "natural frontiers" could unity be achieved in 1849, in 1871, and in some respects again, under the fascist regime. We have seen that such geographic nationalism could be used even in Mazzini's day to deny national self-determination to many less fortunate peoples. That it also could be abused as an instrument of imperial aggrandizement was to become tragically clear in the days of Italian fascism.

No such theoretical conflict existed between Burke's "constitutional" nationalism and the expansion of the British Empire. Of all the five men here reviewed Burke alone reflected established facts rather than their projection into the future. As early as the fourteenth century Fortescue had already contrasted English freedom with French absolutism. Now English constitutional liberties, safeguarded by the reforms of 1688, could well be reconciled with theories, elsewhere "subversive," of natural law and social contract. Locke himself merely intended to systematize and supply a rationale for the regnant opinion in public and civil law. Rousseau's contemporary, Blackstone, achieved a remarkable conservative synthesis of natural law and the existing English laws. Describing Hutcheson's typical rather than original contributions, a French historian of political theory noted the amazing fact that "these doctrines, which soon were to play in France so formidable a role, were summarized here for students as evident propositions become absolutely innocuous in the course of years." It is small wonder that to Continental readers like the German romanticist Novalis (Friedrich von Hardenberg), Burke's impassioned harangues against the French Revolution seemed unwittingly to convey a revolutionary message.[91] Secure in the possession of these liberties, English nationalism could go on expanding across the seven seas and assuming the "white man's burden" without giving up its traditions of balanced civil and constitutional rights of Englishmen living anywhere in the vast expanse of their empire or commonwealth.

Jefferson's "democratic" nationalism, combining many features of constitutional and voluntaristic nationalism, superimposed upon the traditional British liberties the new humanitarian sweep of the Rights of Man. Voluntary allegiance raised public opinion to a national fetish. Generations of readers have wondered over Jefferson's paradox that having to choose between a government without newspapers and newspapers without a government "I should not hesitate a moment to prefer the latter." Considering the unprincipled journalism of his day, this was indeed a strong dose to swallow. But Jefferson really meant to stress chiefly America's historic achievement in local and national self-government, crowned by a voluntaristic federative system, all based upon the free exchange of ideas. "The eyes of the virtuous all over the earth," he wrote to John Hollins thirty-five years after the Declaration of Independence, "are turned with anxiety on us, as the only depositories of the sacred fires of liberty, and our falling into anarchy would decide forever the destinies of mankind and seal the political heresy that man is incapable of self-government." [92] Based upon the optimistic belief that mistakes made by majority decisions would right themselves in time, this democratic nationalism, like its English constitutional counterpart, respected minority will only in so far as it did not affect fundamentals. When later, at a critical moment, the majority decided to emancipate slaves and incorporate them into the body politic

(Jefferson himself had envisaged only permanent territorial segregation), Lincoln was a true protagonist of Jeffersonian democracy when he denied the minority the voluntaristic choice of secession. Great liberties within the Constitution, but none outside it, have ever since remained the keynote of both English and American nationalism.

Despite the great variety of their nationalist formulations and the sharp divergences of individual temper and upbringing, the five Nationalist Fathers reveal a remarkable kinship in their attitude toward religion. If to attain full inner harmony all nationalism tended toward some sort of national religion, Burke had merely to fall back again on the established Anglican Church. Jefferson, on the contrary, lived in a nation embracing only religious minorities, for whom separation of state and church had become an imperative practical need. Even he, however, could not resist dreaming of Unitarianism ultimately superseding all other creeds as the Western Hemisphere's national religion. In the meantime he could view separation as such as a novel contribution to civilization in both the national and religious sense. In his first Inaugural Address as president of the United States he spoke feelingly of his nation being "enlightened by a benign religion, professed, indeed, and practiced in various forms, yet all of them including honesty, truth, temperance, gratitude and the love of man." [93] Such an all-embracing humanitarian religion (in the singular!) could indeed be conceived as America's characteristic faith and part of its manifest destiny.

France and Italy had to attack these problems differently, on account of both the international character of their church and the small number of their religious dissenters. Rousseau, whose emotional yearnings had brought him back to the Christian fold and unwittingly made him copartner in the great Catholic Restoration, preached as an individual the religion of the Savoyard Priest, i.e., an adumbration of Catholic modernism.[94] But as a nationalist he envisaged only a strictly national religion established by the sovereign people's "general will" as a part of its social contract. In both respects this Genevan influenced the course of French intellectual history, as few Frenchmen did. Mazzini, too, though glorifying the Second Rome of the popes as an intermediary stage in Italy's humanitarian mission, looked forward to the Third Rome with its new religion, new ritual and priesthood, to usher in man's final salvation. This new faith, in some unspecified way reconciling dogmatic beliefs with modern science, was to begin as Italy's national creed and only gradually develop into the universal faith of all men.

For Fichte, finally, Lutheranism was, or at least could become, Germany's national religion. He genuinely believed that a new Superreformation, based on Luther but refined by German idealist philosophy and especially his own Theory of Science, would lend the German people its much-needed spiritual unity to complement its expected political unification. In the deep recesses of his mind, we recall, Fichte went even further and dreamed of some new form of Christianity embracing practically the whole German nation and stressing the citizen's political self-abnegation and military valor.

What did this growing pressure of nationalism on religion imply? Some nationalists thought that, by declaring religion a "private affair," they could eliminate it as an issue of public concern and thus rid their nationalism of a disturbing factor. This formula, however, was in so far self-deceptive as it wished to convey more than the evident effects of liberty of conscience and governmental noninterference with individual beliefs. It covered up rather than solved the real difficulties inherent in the intricate relationships between national and religious loyalties. Such camouflage worked well in years of religious and national harmony, but it speedily broke down in every period of crisis. Certain critical developments in twentieth century nationalism were to furnish, therefore, some startlingly new answers to the perennial problem.

Chapter III

NATIONALIST EPIGONI

IN THE teachings and practices of Charles Maurras, Benito Mussolini and Alfred Rosenberg the nationalist doctrine went to extremes far surpassing the wildest dreams of the Nationalist Fathers. Of course, we deal here with "intellectual rascals," with men who sought and often attained power by irresponsible and reckless propaganda. But no matter how inconsistent and intellectually dishonest they were or how reprehensible the methods they used, one must take account of their enthusiastic, even fanatical following, as well as of their large appendage of pseudo-scholarly "yes men" who, with a vast scientific apparatus, tried to smooth out the wrinkles in their masters' impulsive and opportunist political theories.

We have now witnessed the dramatic decline of these demigods. The septuagenarian Maurras is a broken man, prisoner for life of reborn France. Mussolini, for the past several years but one of Hitler's Gauleiters, has suffered an ignominious death at the hands of his own people. Rosenberg, a native of Czarist Russia, lost the vast eastern empire carved out for him by the German war machine and ended on the gallows. However, even if fascism, nazism and French collaborationism were more thoroughly uprooted, the social, political and cultural factors which gave rise to these tragic aberrations of the human mind would not automatically disappear. Certainly to the student of both nationalism and religion their fuller understanding may serve not only as a warning, but also as a measuring rod for the depth and genuineness of other national and religious formulas and of the various attempts at their reconciliation.

1. MAURRAS

In the century following the Revolution, France had become saturated with nationalism. During the Napoleonic Wars it carried the nationalist slogans into most European countries. It contributed more than any other power to Italian unification, partly against the objections of its own Catholic population. Polish and other insurrectionists always looked to it for assistance. Frequently disappointed, these Francophile rebels ultimately proved right, for it was

61

France and her allies in the First World War that ultimately liberated Poland and other suppressed nationalities. German unity, on the other hand, was achieved only after a protracted struggle with the French.

The great national defeat of 1871, combined with the loss of Alsace-Lorraine, rankled the more deeply. Even Renan, who, disgusted with Napoleon III's caesarist vagaries, had declared that "if God and free will are empty words, patriotism is even more empty" and supposedly was "unable to feel any of the moral indignation with which foreign domination filled patriotic hearts," now became intensely preoccupied with his country's "intellectual and moral reform." [1] French patriots noticed with dismay that in the expansive age of imperialism France constantly receded as a world power and trailed behind both the British Empire and the new Germany. The social question, too, and the ever-sharpening conflict over separation of state and church increasingly divided it into warring camps. Before long Boulangism and the controversy over the accusation of Dreyfus became serious threats to the very survival of the Third Republic.

It was in this overheated atmosphere approximating civil war amidst a Continent rapidly sliding down into the abyss of a world war that French "integral nationalism" was born. Charles Maurras, who, in 1900, was the first to coin that phrase and who, together with his elder contemporary, Maurice Barrès, was its chief intellectual exponent, personified more than anyone else Lord Hugh Cecil's apt characterization of the nationalist who hates all countries but his own. [2] In his positive program Maurras was full of vagaries and inconsistencies and ready to borrow from anybody ideas and phrases even if mutually exclusive. But throughout his life he persevered in most of his pet hatreds.

Curiously, he hated Rousseau, the very father of French nationalism. Blaming both revolution and romanticism on the "false prophet," he declared that Rousseau's various reasonings "never harmonize except in the cadence of his lamentation." On another occasion he compared Rousseau to the Old Testament prophets, "the energumens vomited out by the desert," and exclaimed, "Folly, savagery, ignorance, singularity, solitude, pride and revolt, this is what the adventurer, nurtured on biblical marrow, has erected upon the altar under the name of virtue." [3] He was more friendly to the German, Fichte. Though calling him a pure-blooded barbarian and, on aesthetic grounds, objecting to his stylistic peculiarities, he wished to see Fichte's *Addresses to the German Nation* distributed in millions of copies throughout France. [4]

At the same time he objected to Protestantism, "the worst enemy of the species," not on Catholic grounds, but because of its revival of biblical Christianity, i.e., of that kind of "Semitic leprosy" which had invaded ancient Rome. For him the Reformation was but another barbarian invasion which had menaced the survival of Western civilization as much as had the barbarian

migrations eleven centuries before. One of his main objections to Enlightenment was that Montesquieu and Voltaire had brought back from their visits
to England the seeds of that fever and anarchy which Jewish and German
thought had implanted in that country. "In France Reform is always anarchical. Protestantism here protests eternally." The Protestant minority, which,
owing to its wealth and ensuing birth control, was fortunately decreasing in
number, had thoroughly departed from the established mores and even
language of the French majority and been infected with many foreign idio-
syncrasies. It had thus become a dangerous element of denationalization.
Maurras's anti-Protestant bias went so far as to prevent his advocacy of a
national church.

> The idea of a national church [he declared], similar to the Russian, Prussian,
> Anglican churches, once cherished by certain nationalists, is henceforth con-
> sidered a calamity. One need but realize that as soon as the Roman See goes
> into discard, the absence of the traditions and interpretations of the Church
> will cause the Hebraic letter of the Scriptures, the commentaries of the rabbis
> and their exegesis, in one word, the Jewish spirit, to gain everything that is
> lost by the spirit of Catholicism.

Even "integral Gallicanism" made him apprehensive lest France be "inun-
dated with Bibles in the vernacular." [5]

Essentially Maurras was an atheist subscribing to Comte's positivist doctrine
of humanity as the Great Being. He also acknowledged his indebtedness to
men of such diverse attitudes to life as Renan, Taine and Proudhon. Explaining his failure to produce a program for a new relationship between state and
church, he declared that the latter ought to be arranged between the hierarchy
of believers and the sovereign. "I do not consider myself the sovereign, and
I am not a believer." On historical grounds, however, he admired Roman
Catholicism as the long dominant factor in the French cultural evolution.
One must not forget, he contended, that "if the Capetians made France, the
bishops and clerics were their first collaborators." Even its internationalism
was preferable to a national church, which would "tend to denationalize us."
The Roman attachment, so often criticized, is exactly "that which conserves
for Catholicism in France its double character, ordered and French." A Catholic critic was perfectly right in saying that "Maurras loves and sings the praises
of the Catholic Church, because he believes to see in it the only successful
agent in the dechristianization of the world, the authentic pagan form of
our era." [6]

This curious "cerebral Catholicism" [7] was purely intellectual and historical
and had little to do with Catholic ritual or dogma. Its derivation from opportunistic political considerations was too obvious to carry conviction. Maurras himself admitted that he saw in the Catholic hierarchy his chief ally in
the struggle against the Third Republic. He also vigorously applauded the

Catholic clergy's attitude during the Dreyfus affair, which was admittedly the fountainhead of his own *Action française*. This attitude, he declared, had brought back the much-needed alliance between church and army, religious orders and officers' corps, which was fully reminiscent of the good old monarchical regime. Behind it all, however, lurked the true dogma of the new school: the heathen worship of the soil and of the ancestors long dead. Following Barrès, Maurras declaimed:

> Our manner of thinking, determined in the first instance by our fathers and mothers, retains hold of all that our ancestors have been; they are dead only in appearance. They maintain in our nature the character which has been marked in them in other days. . . . The living expression of French nationalism is the result of the vigor of the good and pure blood which we have received from our fathers and mothers.[8]

Unlike Fichte and Mazzini, who in order to cement their peoples' unity had to preach national solidarity transcending regional and tribal disparities, the French integral nationalists viewed with alarm the growing centralization of France and the controlling influence exercised by Paris on all national life. In his *Déracinés* (The Uprooted) Barrès graphically described the ravages wrought in the minds of provincials who came to Paris to make their careers. Here Barrès not only abandoned his early flirtations with decadentism and anarchism and became an ardent nationalist—Max Nordau commented on this "antisocial Saul transformed into a Paul of the *raison d'état*" [9]—but also began to preach French federalism. Maurras followed him therein, too, and demanded complete regional autonomy which, in his opinion, would engender true attachment to the country at large in lieu of the "administrative patriotism" animating the present centralized nation.

Before long Maurras became the chief French theorist of a nationalism based on blood and soil—the French counterpart to Houston Stewart Chamberlain and other German forerunners of nazism. It matters little that, ardently disliking this company, he heatedly protested that, with all doctoring of the texts, "no one can make of us racists and gobinists." As a native of the Provence and expounder of Provençal regionalism, he well realized that few European areas had a greater historic succession of racial mixtures. He even admitted to being himself a descendant of Provençal Moors, as was indicated in his name, but contended that these Moors had been of African rather than Semitic origin. Often derided on this score and called by an antiroyalist Sidi Maurras ben Ma'aras, he nevertheless glorified the French "race" with increasing vehemence.[10]

As elsewhere, the Jew, real or imaginary, served as a welcome counterfoil. Not only during the fervid Dreyfus Affair, but ever after Maurras and the *Action française* harped on the theme of Jewish "foreignness." As strangers to the soil of France and of foreign ancestry, they contended, Jews could never absorb the physical and mental make-up of bygone generations of Frenchmen. Therefore, they should never have become naturalized, but permanently kept apart in the status of ancient *metics* (second-class citizens). Instead, misled by the Revolution's democratic doctrines—which, explained Paul Bourget, Maurras's collaborator, might work in America with its traditions of lawlessness, but would never do in authoritarian and law-abiding France [11]—the French people allowed the Jewish immigrants to seize control over its economic and political life. In view of their solidarity and extraordinary aptitude for finance the Jews were well on the way to achieving world domination, their rise to power having become relatively easy once they had destroyed the world's religious unity through the Reformation and its political unity through the Revolution. Only two other powers were still disputing their universal dominion. "There exists a great maritime power: it is Anglo-Saxon and Protestant, and hence twice barbarian. There exists a great military power: it is German, Protestant, twice barbarian. There exists a great financial power: it is cosmopolite and Jewish, that is both barbarian and anarchist." Catholic France, therefore, could only be saved by reverting to its own leadership of pre-Revolutionary days.[12]

Maurras saw red when he spoke of the Hebrew-Protestant philosophy of life and international outlook. He cited with great regret Anatole France extolling, in Biblical terms, the future peace among nations. These words, "which could have been spoken by Jaurès," revealed the extent to which the great Voltairian had been taken in tow by a Renan at his worst and generally testified to the meek submission of the leaders of French thought to Jewish ideas and the Jewish style of writing. Together with Protestantism, Judaism was responsible also for the optimistic affirmation of progress, that widespread "theology" of freethinkers which "is but messianism secularized." Without going back all the way to ancient Jewish sources, "it is enough to watch the saint, invoked by Haeckel, namely Spinoza." This dangerous Judeo-Protestant influence was abetted by both Freemasons and metics, or foreigners of all kinds.

> The confederation of these four estates . . . has immensely increased their total power. Jewish gold, consolidating the spontaneous discipline and thought of the Protestants, causes a certain type of intelligence to prevail. Masonic servility assures execution in detail. The buzzing swarm of metics, finally, establishes the necessary relations to and connivance from abroad, an abundant source of reinforcements and subsidies whenever needed.[13]

Xenophobia, that old shibboleth of nationalists, was in Maurras's way of thinking also the best means of solving the increasingly critical social problems. Like Barrès he believed that, to promote the interests of the workers, one merely had to shut down the gates of immigration and erect high tariff walls. Although he did not dare to preach extreme economic isolationism à la Fichte, he early propagated social reconstruction along medieval corporate lines. In 1902 he argued that the state never had any direct dealings with individual citizens other than officials, unless they be criminals, heroes or saints, and that hence it ought always to act only through groups, professional or otherwise. "Through the Dreyfus Affair," he declared, "the Judeo-Protestant confederation has induced us to clarify, by strengthening it, our conception of the state. Through the affair of religious societies, the Judeo-Protestant confederation has caused us to define our conception of society." But at no time did the *Action* elaborate its schemes of corporate reorganization. Generally unconcerned about the operation of purely economic factors, it hoped to ameliorate the status of French workers through a series of prohibitive, essentially negativistic measures. At the same time, unable to stem the rising tide of socialism, it was ready to accept its name, for a "socialism freed of the democratic and cosmopolitan element fits nationalism like a well-made glove on a beautiful hand," provided it would forswear international peace and domestic class struggle.[14]

Maurras often solicited the support of the official church. He regularly publicized whatever commendation he received from churchmen and Catholic journals. He mentioned, for instance, that his article on "Church and Democracy" published in 1906 had brought him a congratulatory note from an "eminent ecclesiastic" stating that "a professional theologian would not have expressed himself with greater precision and orthodoxy." The Jesuit *Etudes* and the *Revue Thomiste* of 1913 had likewise highly praised his views on the rights and liberties of the church as well as on democracy. In his letter to Pope Pius X in 1914 he assured the pontiff that ever since the publication of the encyclical on "Christian Democracy" by Leo XIII in 1902 all the "antidemocrats" of the *Action*, "without regard to their profound differences of opinion, have turned toward Rome." [15]

The Church of Rome resisted these advances. Maurras's conglomeration of hatreds, defined by a colleague (Vaugeois) as "antisemitic, anti-Masonic, anti-Protestant, antiparliamentary and antidemocratic nationalism," appeared to orthodox Catholics as little short of heresy. Particularly so when it was combined with the desired worship of the "goddess of France," and racialist, pagan emphases. Despite its occasional flirtations with the royalist party and the frequent collaboration of militant French Catholics with Maurras and his school on political issues, the papacy never fully recognized that alliance. The French ecclesiastics who had nothing but praise for Maurras's political views nevertheless made the necessary reservations concerning his heterodox doctrinal opinions. Their more or less benevolent neutrality came altogether to an end after the First World War, when the victorious Third Republic emerged as the leading Continental power and resumed its diplomatic relations with the Vatican. In 1925 came the final break. The newspaper, *Action française*, and Maurras's writings were placed on the papal Index. Maurras protested that what really mattered were not sentiments, but results, and recalled that he had always supported the French clerical party in France in its struggle against separation of state and church and in its attempt to control education. In his remarkable letter to Pope Pius XI of October 12, 1926, he described the tenor of all his writings as devoted to "a picturesque critique and violent satire against pantheism, German idealism, Anglo-Saxon atomism and romantic or revolutionary moralism" and to the glorification of the Church "as the mother of France and of civilization." He also showed the Action's effective missionary work on the example of its central committee, which had begun in 1908 with a membership of "six believers, one Protestant and six unbelievers." In the following eighteen years two of the unbelievers died as convinced Catholics, while two others, as well as the Protestant member, gave their children a truly Catholic education. These arguments proved unavailing, however. The pope by his expressive silence and Cardinal Gasparri by his enforced, uncivil reply clearly indicated the displeasure of the Holy See with this recalcitrant and embarrassing ally.[16]

The real crisis was to come a few years later. At a time when Hitler's Germany was adopting Maurras's teachings and when his French following was growing by leaps and bounds, he saw himself placed on the horns of a dilemma. As a French patriot who taught that "a true nationalist places his country above everything" he realized the growing menace to French security. As a champion of the royalist reaction, on the other hand, and lifetime foe of the Third Republic and internationalism he was actually afraid of seeing Germany defeated. As his disciple, Thierry-Maulnier, explained in 1938, after France's diplomatic breakdown at Munich:

> These parties [of the Right] had the impression that in case of war not only would the disaster be immense, not only was defeat and devastation of France possible, but *a German defeat would mean the crumbling of the authoritarian systems, which constitute the main rampart to the communist revolution, and perhaps the immediate bolshevization of Europe.* In other words, a French defeat would really have been a defeat of France, and a French victory would have been less a victory of France than a victory of the principles rightly considered as leading straight to her ruin and to that of civilization itself.[17]

That is why before and after Munich he and his followers developed a streak of isolationist pacifism in foreign affairs combined with extreme belligerency against the forces of democratic France in all matters of domestic concern.

Notwithstanding the sporadic earlier successes of the *Camelots de roi* and the *Croix de feu*, integral nationalism became a dominant doctrine in French politics only after the German occupation. Maurras himself, while fleeing before the invader, gave his blessing to the reorganization of France along regional lines, the new emphasis on family and church and the persecution of Jews and foreigners. In pathetic, but unregenerate "reflections on the disaster" published in 1942 he placed the entire responsibility for the war on the progressive leaders, among whom even "the most innocent had certainly preferred the interests of England or of Jewry to the evident interest of their fatherland." But this crowning victory of his lifelong struggle, coming as it did in the form of Pétain and Laval's collaborationism with the archenemy and followed by an equally sudden defeat, threw into sharp relief the inner weaknesses and irreconcilable contradictions of integral nationalism.[18]

2. MUSSOLINI

This hesitancy of many rightist elements, who could not reconcile their Catholic piety and their opposition to the "impious" democratic regime with the neopagan worship of the nation, came to the fore also in Italy, the very fountainhead of Catholicism. Because of fascism's early seizure of power, however, and the long unsolved "Roman Question," Italy was to offer a far more telling test for the relations between the church and extreme nationalism. Since the "philosophy" of Italian fascism was but a rationalization of Mussolini's ever-changing and often contradictory attitudes and utterances, the checkered story of his ecclesiastical policies well illustrates the successive stages of both conflict and compromise.

The Italian situation was, of course, in many ways different from the French. If Maurras and his associates attacked their country's republican regime in the name of the old monarchy, Italy was ruled by the royal House of Savoy which, rivaling the Bourbons and Habsburgs in antiquity, had had an indubitable major share in the historic achievement of Italian unification. Whatever opposition it engendered came from socialist and liberal internationalists rather than from nationalist groups. While Maurras and Barrès waged unrelenting war against the centralization of French public life and toyed with regionalism as a new backbone of national feeling, in Italy regionalism was an indisputable fact and, as such, a major obstacle to national unity.

Nor were three of the four pet animosities of the *Action française* of any realistic interest across the Alps. To begin with, Protestantism had never been a powerful divisive force in Italy, which had suffered neither from devastating Wars of Religion nor from the strong residuum of bitterness left behind in France by the revocation of the Edict of Nantes. The small Protestant minority exercised little influence on Italian economy and culture. It was only during the heated debates on the Lateran Treaties of 1929 and their effect on religious dissidence that a fascist writer discovered the historic tradition, too terrible for him to behold, that to Protestant churches Italy was a missionary area similar to Papua or Central Africa. But neither fascist leadership nor the Italian people showed any anxiety over these remote dangers. Antisemitism, too, which, as a result of Drumont's agitation and the vicissitudes of the Dreyfus Affair, had become a major factor in French politics in Maurras's youth, was of minor significance in Italy. On the contrary, religious intolerance remained associated in the popular mind with those reactionary forces which had long interfered with national unity. Only when the question was artificially raised in 1938 by the government, which tried to live up to its recent alliance with Hitler, did Jew-baiting become both fashionable and politically profitable. Maurras's so-called metics, finally, so important in the growingly stationary population of France, played no role in Italy, a country of surplus population. Time and again Fascists, led by Mussolini, spoke of the ten million Italians "who have emigrated to all the continents and beyond all the oceans" and whose national loyalties they tried to exploit for their fascist aims. Within four years after the March on Rome there were already 470 *fasci* functioning abroad, allegedly organized merely for the promotion of Italian trade and culture.[19] If, therefore, the foreign influx into France could, however remotely, be construed as a menace to French nationalism, the presence of millions of Italians in foreign lands, that "imperialism of the poor," could well be utilized for the promotion of real fascist imperialism.

Freemasonry alone was attacked by the Italian nationalists with a vehemence rivaling that of their French colleagues. While the Masonic brotherhood of men was an obvious irritant, it must be left to future historians to uncover all the ramifications of the world-wide anti-Masonic propaganda. Neither numerically nor through cohesive organization or interlodge solidarity had Masons ever exercised any real influence on European affairs. The "ballyhoo" of that agitation may perhaps best be explained by the mysterious nature of masonic rites which bred suspicion among the masses and lent plausibility to the hysterical accusations of some dreadful cabals being hatched against nation and religion in these secret conventicles.

Communism, however, had become a truly paramount issue which Mussolini and his confreres had to face. While Marxian socialism had long been a major problem in both France and Italy, it was only after the Russian Revolution that it became a serious threat to the existing order. Italy, greatly suffering from war exhaustion and economic dislocations, became in 1919-20 the scene of disturbances approximating civil war. In France, on the other hand, such sharp clashes came only in the 1930's in the wake of nazism, the Spanish Civil War, and the organization of numerous semimilitary formations. Italy's war record also rankled deeply. Endless nationalist rhetoric on the final "victory" at Vittorio Veneto failed to pacify the people's persistent sense of frustration in view of the army's poor performance, followed by diplomacy's lack of success in extending the country's European frontiers or establishing the vast hoped-for colonial empire. The middle classes, particularly, which during the shift from the Triple Alliance to the Allied side had clamored for intervention, now realized that they had lost the war. To retrieve what they could from the disaster, they welcomed Mussolini and his cohorts who promised to restore order and weaken trade-unionism. The royal dynasty, too, confronted by the strong socialist and antimonarchical tide saw in fascism a prop for its own survival. The story of the March on Rome has never yet been told in full detail. But there seems to be little question that this allegedly antigovernmental move had found strong abettors in royal circles which paralyzed all countermeasures by Premier Facta's indubitably "legitimate," liberal government.

Unlike the other nationalists here reviewed, except Jefferson, Mussolini served as a high governmental official who had to weigh every word for its effects on listeners and readers. However lightly he seemed to take this responsibility and however blunt and outspoken many of his speeches sounded to outsiders, they not only reflected changing momentary circumstances, but were often calculated to conceal his innermost thoughts. In contrast, moreover, to the present availability of Jefferson's numerous letters, mostly written when he was out of office, we are still largely restricted to Mussolini's published addresses and such other materials as were made public with his or his appointees' consent.

These difficulties are further aggravated by fascism's inherent vagaries and Mussolini's emphasis upon action rather than thought. He often spoke of the Mazzinian combination of action *and* thought, but one cannot help feeling that the latter was for him really but an afterthought. "Like all sound political conceptions," ran the curious formula, "fascism is action and it is thought; action in which doctrine is immanent, and doctrine arising from a given system of historical forces in which it is inserted, and working on them from within." Even such an orthodox Fascist as Armando Carlini, who tried to systematize the "philosophy and religion in the thought of Mussolini," had to admit with despair "that in the face of Mussolini's work we feel *disoriented*. We only wish that others, too, should confess to such disorientation." Mussolini himself poignantly, because unwittingly, expressed his contempt for all rationalizations when he wished, as he wrote to Michele Bianchi in 1921, "that during the two months which are still to elapse before our National Assembly meets, the philosophy of fascism could be created." [20] It was also rather dangerous for an Italian to attempt dialectical harmonization unless it stemmed directly from the dictator or other highly posted fascist leaders like Gentile, Rocco or Farinacci. The mere juxtaposition, however, of these three names reveals to the initiated the helpless contradictions in the theory of a movement which embraced exponents of diametrically opposed views so long as they agreed upon common action.

As a long-time orthodox Marxist and admirer of Nietzsche, Mussolini personally was not only a confirmed anticlerical, but basically an anti-Christian.

Even his early book on John Huss was written not out of any predilection for the reformer, whom he largely condemned with faint praise, but as a background for his vivid description of the Catholic atrocities during the Hussite Wars. At the same time he wrote on Machiavelli, a far more permanent influence in his life. He always felt deep kinship to the great Florentine's rationale for those unprincipled warlords of the fifteenth century with whom he was to be constantly compared.[21] Whatever sentimental attachment he had for Catholicism came from romantic recollections of his childhood fondness for certain earthy Catholic rituals.

On achieving power, however, Mussolini (in contrast to his first allies, the futurists led by Marinetti) realized that the Italian peasant masses still stanchly adhered to their ancestral creed. From the imperial angle, too, he viewed Catholicism as an essentially expansionist Italian movement. Consciously misreading Mazzini he emphasized that the Second Rome of the popes was the foundation for the Third Rome of the fascist order. To be sure, he often tried to pacify foreign public opinion by declaring that fascism was not for export. But he did not hesitate to proclaim in his "Message for the Year IX" (1930) that "today" he considered fascism a universal idea. "It is Italian in its particular institutions, but it is universal in the spirit." He foresaw a fascist Europe drawing inspiration from Italian fascism which "solves the threefold problem of relations between state and individual, between state and associations [gruppi], between associations and organized associations." [22]

For these reasons and in order to exploit the open breach between the papacy and the liberal regime ever since 1871, Mussolini early evinced sympathy for Italy's reconciliation with the Vatican. While still struggling for power, he delivered a remarkable speech in the Chamber, designed to enlist the support of Don Louis Sturzo's Popular (Catholic) party and, if possible, to supplant it in the affections of the church. Admitting that there had regrettably occurred "some chastisements" of clerics and popularists by fascist extremists, he denied assassinations and stressed the affinities between his program and that of the Popular party in regard to the liberty of schools, the agrarian problem and administrative decentralization.

> I maintain that the Imperial and Latin tradition of Rome is represented today by Catholicism. . . . I am very disturbed when I see national churches being formed, because I think of the millions and millions of men who will no longer look towards Italy and Rome. For this reason I advance this hypothesis, that if the Vatican should definitely renounce its temporal ambitions—and I think it is already on that road—Italy ought to furnish it with the necessary material help for the schools, churches, hospitals, etc., that a temporal power has at its disposal. Because the increase of Catholicism in the world, the addition of four hundred millions of men who from all quarters of the globe look towards Rome, is a source of pride and of special interest to us Italians.

As prime minister he set in motion a series of conciliatory "incidents," which were duly publicized in the controlled press, and arranged for "accidental" meetings between high fascist officials and leading cardinals. Sturzo's dismissal from the secretaryship of the Popular party was duly reciprocated by the exclusion of two unfrocked priests from the fascist party. "The name of God was perpetually on the lips of the King after years of silence; Mussolini attended religious services with much display of devotion; the Cross once more adorned the Capitol." [23]

Even more significant were Giovanni Gentile's far-reaching educational reforms culminating in the reintroduction of Catholic religious instruction into the public schools. To justify this departure from a long-glorified achievement of Italian progressivism, Gentile argued in terms reminiscent of Mazzini's objections to separation of state and church. "The school must be agnostic," wrote the former liberal philosopher, "neither in religion nor in philosophy, for it dare not be agnostic in morals. Hence neither can it be agnostic in politics. Agnosticism is a suspension of judgment and a consequent refusal to take sides actively with any party. It is the separation of one's personality from life." Gentile's undersecretary, Dario Lupi, ordered that every schoolroom should exhibit a crucifix next to the picture of the king.[24]

By 1926 Mussolini, feeling firm in the saddle, allowed the prominent fascist jurist, Barone, formally to discuss with an unnamed monsignor the possibilities of a compromise solution for the ever-festering Roman question. In February, 1929, finally, he concluded with the papacy a concordat, accompanied by a treaty which proclaimed the pope temporal ruler of the tiny Vatican State and allotted to him a large financial indemnity (750,000,000 lire in cash and 1,000,000,000 lire in bonds, the latter according to Mussolini's own admission worth no more than 800,000,000 lire at current prices). The pope promised to recognize, in return, Italian sovereignty over the rest of the country and to refrain from interfering in its inner affairs.[25]

This agreement, evidently unsatisfactory to either party, was concluded only because the papacy wished the concordat and hence accepted the treaty, while Mussolini wished the treaty and hence accepted the concordat. It was nevertheless heralded all over the world as an epochal decision of the church to withdraw from the temporal field and to concentrate on its purely spiritual functions. The Jesuit *Civiltà Cattolica* spoke of the "hour of the Lord" and "the beginning of a new era of peace and religious restoration." Fascist propagandists, on their part, used the reconciliation to appeal to foreign Catholics in behalf of the common Catholic and fascist emphases on discipline, authority and hierarchy. Conversely, Italy's neighbors became deeply perturbed. The communist *Humanité* stressed the imperialist aspects of the new pacts. The upper-bourgeois *Neue Freie Presse* stated that, the ancient French mantle of church championship having now fallen on the Duce's shoulders, one shall thenceforth speak of the *gesta Dei per Mussolini*. Herriot threatened that the democratic world would always remember the papacy's alliance with a regime which had "suppressed the constitutional liberties of a great nation." After a detailed analysis of the treaties Maurice Pernot came to the conclusion that the Catholic world at large was the main loser. "What the pope gives, he gives in his capacity of head of the church universal. What he receives, he receives in his capacity of bishop of Rome." Even Maurras, though expressing admiration for the "most advantageous" deal in Mussolini's career, professed inability to reconcile it with his high conception of "the papacy's ambitions and pride." [26]

Even in Italy, however, the discussions on the ratification of the treaties soon revealed numerous areas of conflict. Article I, for instance, proclaimed Catholicism as the "sole religion" of the state, but added that "the other existing faiths are tolerated in accordance with the laws." The church interpreted these provisions as well as the privileges extended to clergy and ecclesiastical organizations and the regulation of marriages among Catholics to conform with canon law far more strictly than seemed acceptable to fascist leadership. The underlying historic conceptions also were challenged. The "sacred character" of the city of Rome was interpreted by the church to refer exclusively to Catholic monuments and traditions. In Mussolini's speech of May 13, 1929, however, even greater stress was laid upon imperial Rome with its "legal norms and its venerable and memorable relics" and upon modern Rome with its Tomb of the Unknown Soldier and its Memorial for the Fallen of the Fascist Revolution. In general, Mussolini's interpretation of the role of ancient Rome in transforming Eastern Christianity into Western Catholicism, reminiscent of Maurras, was speedily repudiated by the pope. In his letter to Cardinal Gasparri, Pius XI bluntly characterized some passages in Mussolini's speech to the Senate of May 25 as "a case of modernism of the worst kind and most worthy of condemnation" and as containing "heretical or worse than heretical statements on the very essence of Christianity and Catholicism." [27]

The educational provisions also gave rise to divergent interpretation. The state agreed to consult the church in regard to textbooks and methods of instruction, but according to the official interpretation of Alfredo Rocco, minister of public instruction, it did "not renounce the function, essential to it, of instructing and educating the youth." Catholic leaders, on the other hand, often assumed that they had been given a free hand to realize the program formulated by Professor Giuseppe Monti, namely, that "the supervision and scholastic inspection by the Church should extend also to the teaching of secular subjects insofar as they had any connection with religious and moral instruction. It should pursue the end of preventing the former from paralyzing and destroying the effects of Catholic instruction and education." [28] Education, in their view, was the principal domain of either family or church, both of which—the one as a divine institution and the other as a divinely willed natural organ—were anterior to the state chronologically and ideally.

No true Fascist could admit that. In his speech to the Senate Mussolini stressed the inability of the modern family, preoccupied with the struggle for subsistence, to take care of the children's education, and insisted upon the need of integration, by the state, of religious instruction in the entire educational program. "What kind of education is it, then, which we demand in a totalitarian fashion? The education of the citizen." More broadly he wrote on another occasion:

> It [fascism] sees not only the individual but the nation and the country; individuals and generations bound together by a moral law, with common traditions and a mission which suppressing the instinct for life closed in a brief circle of pleasure, builds up a higher life, founded on duty, a life free from the limitations of time and space, in which the individual by self-sacrifice, the renunciation of self-interest, by death itself, can achieve that purely spiritual existence in which his value as a man consists.

For, as he reaffirmed in 1927 in the Chamber of Deputies what he had once declared at the Scala in Milan, "Everything in the state, nothing against the state, nothing outside the state." Fascism was, in short, a "religious" conception of life "in which man is viewed in his immanent relation to a higher law, endowed with an objective will transcending the individual and raising him to conscious membership of a spiritual society." [29] This was a road which no conscientious Catholic could follow.

In its attempt, particularly, to indoctrinate children in its principles and train them in military valor, fascism condemned Catholic "meekness" as the perennial obstacle. Mussolini invoked the shades of Renan, "who had prefascist intuitions," to prove that the nations which had contributed most to human civilization, Israel, Greece and medieval Italy, had, because of that self-sacrificing contribution, become victims of less civilized aggressors. Twentieth century Italy was not to repeat that mistake. Through intensive training of its youth it was to resurrect its military virtues which, long dormant, had only begun to awaken during the First World War. Fascism, he declared in his most reasoned exposition of its doctrine, "discards pacifism as a cloak for cowardly supine renunciation in contra-distinction to self-sacrifice. War alone keys up all human energies to their maximum tension and sets seal of nobility on those peoples who have the courage to face it." [30]

All this summed up into an extreme worship of the state which Gentile, speaking as a fascist ideologist, had called "the great will of the nation and hence its great intelligence." Even Mussolini's nationalism became ever more statist. He challenged the established nationalist doctrine and the Wilsonian program of self-determination of small nations by claiming that it is the state which creates nationality rather than the "antiquated naturalistic concept" that nationality generates the state.[31] Combining the new statism with Mazzini's geographic nationalism, fascist imperialism could now demand the extension of Italy's power far beyond its linguistic frontiers. "Natural" boundaries expanded, of course, with every new territorial accretion. Nice, Corsica, Tunis, Dalmatia, Corfu and Malta furnished both geographic-historical and linguistic arguments. Distant Ethiopia was a neighbor of the older Italian colonies of Eritrea and Somaliland. Ultimately the whole Mediterranean basin could become Italy's natural frontier, especially since it had once before been ruled and administered from Rome.

The climax of this statist and imperialist interpretation came after Mussolini's fateful agreement with Hitler and the ensuing incursion of racist doctrines. The racist ideology, theretofore alien to the Italian people and even to most Fascists, was suddenly discovered in 1937 by several "authorities." Paolo Orano, who had long denied fascism's indebtedness to any "forerunners," now tried to prove also the originality of Italian racism and anti-semitism.[32] The floodgates were thus opened to the new teachings of an Italian master race destined ultimately to attain world domination. It all sounded highly unrealistic to those familiar with Italy's lack of industrial resources. It filled with dismay foreign sympathizers who realized the dangers of Italy's growing dependence on Germany. But it had an irresistible appeal to the "heroic" youth in the country.

Here an abyss opened between Catholicism and fascism which no amount of reasoning could bridge over. Mussolini was forced increasingly to disregard his earlier warning to Hitler. The whole history of Western civilization, the Duce had written in 1934,

> from Diocletian to Bismarck teaches us that whenever there is a conflict between the state and religion it is always the state that loses the battle. A battle against religion is a battle against the imponderable. It is open warfare against the spirit, at the point where the spirit is deepest and most inward. It is proven to-day that in the course of such a battle even the sharpest weapons at the disposal of the state are ineffectual mortally to wound the Church. The Church, and more especially the Catholic Church, emerges from the bitterest battles unchanged and victorious.

By 1941, however, he is said to have expressed surprise over the Nazis' failure to abolish Christmas. This holiday, Count Ciano reports him as saying, "reminds only of the birth of a Jew who gave the world debilitating and devitalizing theories, and who especially contrived to trick Italy through the disintegrating power of the popes." [33] Fascism, completely overpowered by the German steamroller, increasingly shared the vicissitudes of nazism's nationalist and religious ideologies.

3. Rosenberg

The seeds planted by French and Italian extremists fell in Germany upon fertile soil. Unlike their French and Italian confreres, however, who could view Catholicism as a major unifying force, German nationalists had long striven for a "third denomination" to overcome the existing denominational divisions. Already Fichte's glorification of Lutheranism had all the earmarks of a nationalist reinterpretation of Protestant Christianity. It made of the German idealistic philosophy that "religion of the educated" of which Hegel spoke as chief continuator of Fichte's philosophic and nationalist doctrines. By the end of the century the nationalist fervor, whetted by the country's political unification and imperial expansion, generated antidenominational forces of unprecedented scope and vitality.

Foremost among the anti-Christian crusaders was Friedrich Nietzsche. His "revaluation of all values," doctrine of the "superman" and worship of power played havoc with a generation of young Germans, even more by what they thought he had said than by what he really had said. Certainly such sentences, as they read in *Thus Spake Zarathustra*, "You I advise not to work, but to fight. You I advise not to peace, but to victory"; or "A man shall be raised to be a warrior, a woman for the warrior's recreation—all else is folly"; or "Write with blood and you will learn that spirit is blood," stirred the martial spirit and imagination of the people, drunk with the new glory wrought by their chancellor of "blood and iron." So did Nietzsche's new conception of truth. The generation listened with rapt attention to the doctrine that "falseness of an opinion is not yet a valid argument against the opinion. . . . The question is how much it helps to promote life, to preserve life, to preserve a species, perhaps even to breed a species." It interpreted this to mean that it could, with impunity, replace any of the existing systems of morals and beliefs by any other "life-promoting" and "species-breeding" schemes, regardless of their rational validity. It also believed Nietzsche when he claimed that he had ushered in an unprecedented crisis in human history and that with him had begun the era of truly "great politics." [34]

Germany's sudden emergence as a world power seemed, through the sheer weight of success, to validate these teachings. The fact that Prussian military force and ruthless Bismarckian diplomacy realized in short shrift the ineffectual dreams of statesmen, thinkers and poets for several generations left a permanent imprint on the people's appreciation of political realities. "I have never lived according to principles," the iron chancellor had proudly declared in a letter to General Leopold von Gerlach, not realizing that he had thus removed all dams before the surging tide of the lust for power. No wonder that, in the years of his greatest ascendancy, he heard the voice of an influential Bible scholar, Paul de Lagarde, arguing, on both nationalist and religious grounds, that the new Reich had no vitality and that "there had never yet existed a German state." Lagarde rejected even the *Kulturkampf*, for "Romanism and Catholicism will never be overcome in Germany by an abstract religion, but only by a national German religion," and asserted bluntly:

> Catholicism, Protestantism, Judaism, naturalism must give way to a new conception of life so that they be remembered no more than are the lamps used at night after the sun shines over the mountains. Or else the unity of Germany will become ever more questionable from day to day.[35]

As the world crisis drew closer and closer these ideas were re-echoed, with increasing crudity, by a host of fanatical or self-seeking demagogues. A credulous and avid section of the German public heard Ernst Wachler proclaim from the rostrum of the main anti-Jewish organ, *Der Hammer*, "Woe unto the people which will behave in a Christian fashion in an era when the struggle has begun for the possession of the earth." Another pamphleteer, Heinrich Pudor, complained in the same year 1909 that "from a heroic and master race the Teutons have become a people of dreamers, worshipers and penitents. Wherefore? On account of their Christianity." He exhorted his compatriots, "Get rid of Judaism and Christianity and go back to the sources of Teutonism. . . . Christianity is a Jewish invention. . . . All Christianity is Judeo-Christianity and as such the most stupendous fraud ever committed on races and peoples in world history." [36]

Hysterical denunciations of this kind, heard sporadically before 1914, became a deafening chorus after the downfall of the Hohenzollern Empire. Wartime national unity, combined with front-line religious experiences, reinforced the quest for an all-German "third denomination." This quest was facilitated by the untrammeled antiecclesiastical propaganda under the Weimar Republic's separation of state and church. At the same time defeat and the constant economic and political crisis fostered extreme nationalism. The socialist rulers of the republic soon forfeited their great historic achievement by renouncing the revolution, under the menace of the communist revolt. Successful in Bavaria, the latter threatened indeed to engulf all of Germany and, to quote Karl Radek's address to the German workers in Cologne, establish a united Russo-German front on the Rhine for the final battle against Anglo-Saxon capitalism. After this internecine struggle between the proletarian parties, the republic deteriorated into a weak continuation of Hohenzollern Germany. The revolutionary transformation, still an historic necessity, thus curiously devolved on the "national opposition" which, originally consisting of the conservative parties of Bismarckian Germany, was gradually taken over by the National Socialists.

Hitler himself realized the great power and resilience of religious feeling. Although occasionally betraying his innermost belief, "We will have no other

God than Germany," he generally adhered to the party platform of 1920, which broadly favored the freedom of all denominations provided "they are not a danger to it [the state] and do not militate against the morality and moral sense of the German race." In *Mein Kampf* he even pretended to champion "positive Christianity," a term vague enough to allow for almost any interpretation. In a passage frequently quoted by religious apologists under the Third Reich he contended that "the political leader will always consider inviolable the religious teachings and institutions of his people. Otherwise he ought not to become a politician but a religious reformer, if he has the makings of one." But, as the self-professed inspired mouthpiece of his people's national rebirth, he was, indeed, something of a religious reformer. While advocating his new conception of life (*Weltanschauung*) he often complained of the "infernal intolerance" which Christianity had brought into the world and declared that "force will only be broken by force, terror by counterterror." He denied that national socialism was but a political movement and exclaimed, "Political parties are inclined to compromise; conceptions of life never do. Political parties take into consideration opposing parties; conceptions of life proclaim their infallibility." [37] Hitler feared, however, that a public proclamation of his "infallible" credo as the "third denomination" would provoke that type of religious resistance which might lead to religious martyrdom, an unfailing source of religious regeneration. That is why his methodical persecution of opposing clergy always was carefully cloaked by accusations of political ambition, sexual immorality and illicit traffic in foreign exchange.

Nazism's true face revealed itself far more clearly in its tacit toleration of the propaganda for a German national church and the encouragement given to the various sectarian associations headed by Ludendorff, Count Reventlow and Professor Bergmann. Certain wings in the party were even allowed to assume an overtly anti-Christian position in their early declarations. A resolution adopted, for instance, by the National Socialist Student League in 1935 made it perfectly clear that

> The Führer has declared at the Party Congress (1933) that national-socialism is a conception of life. This conception has been synthesized in Rosenberg's *Myth of the Twentieth Century* for use in the forthcoming . . . struggle for the German soul, viz. in the spirit and with the approval of the Führer. . . . There are now in Germany three basic conceptions of life, the Christian, the Marxist and the national-socialist. One uncompromisingly excludes the other. . . . Both the Christian and the Marxist are essentially liberalistic, because they are individualistic. The national-socialist conception is intended only for the Teutonic race, not like Christianity for all races. . . . It must ultimately come to grips with these denominations, though the struggle will not be violent, for they will die out by themselves. We repudiate not only the hundred different forms of Christianity, but Christianity as such. [38]

The evangelist of the new faith was Alfred Rosenberg, the Baltic German appointed by Hitler in 1934 to supervise the total system of Nazi ideological education. In this capacity he deeply influenced the thinking of millions of party members. His *Myth of the Twentieth Century*, first published in 1930, reached 181 editions totaling 960,000 copies in the first eleven years, despite its bulk, clumsy style and obscure content. A typically nazi decree of the Reich Ministry of Education stating that no one had to purchase the book and that it could be freely criticized was tantamount to declaring the book required reading for conscientious Nazis. But it allowed at least some circumspect discussion which uncovered the author's multifarious deficiencies. Unabashed Rosenberg replied in a widely read pamphlet, *To the Obscurantists of our Time* (1935), intended to remind the reader of the sixteenth century antimonastic satire. Similarly his attack on the Protestant clergy, *Protestant Pilgrims to Rome. A Betrayal of Luther and "The Myth of the Twentieth Century"* (1937), was speedily distributed in ten editions. Supported by a vociferous following, Rosenberg's high-pressure salesmanship easily outshouted the subdued voices of the official Christian leaders.

Rosenberg's nationalism was as heterodox as his religion. Since democracy, he believed, cannot operate beyond a village community and the masses of modern citizenry have no independent judgment on any public issue, nationalism had fallen prey either to dynastic interests or to financiers and other shady manipulators of public opinion. He admitted that, having blossomed in full glory in the German Wars of Liberation (the French Revolution was, of course, not to be mentioned in any laudatory context), it had brought about the unification of Italy and had freed the Balkan and South American peoples. But it had since become a playball of the cabinets of Vienna and Napoleon III or an instrument of international cartels.

> The great Panama scandal in France, certain developments of the *Gründer-era* of Bismarck's Germany, the futile efforts of French Boulangism, unheeded prophetic calls of Nietzsche and Paul de Lagarde—they all reveal that same struggle between the genuine national will and those forces which regarded money as the main stimulus to power and which abused the power of nations for their speculative private interests. Nationalism had thus ceased to be rooted in the people and had become a counterfeit slogan for denationalized litterateurs, citizens of the world and big businessmen.

Even Bismarck's empire, therefore, was not yet the true German Reich of national aspiration. With all its memorable achievements the Hohenzollern dynasty could not divest itself of the last vestiges of the Thirty Years' War and rally the nation behind an integrated national conception of life to supplement the newly won political unity. Germany thus sank into a mire of "mythless" rationalism, of the bourgeois or the Marxist variety. At the outbreak of the War of 1914, to be sure, the highest military values seemed on the way to becoming the supreme values of the nation. "Moltke seemed to vanquish Bleichröder." But the Kaiser missed the great historic opportunity of "hanging on gallows" the entire crew of promoters and pacifists who had infested the Second Reich. Instead "he gave his outstretched hand to the Marxist leaders and thereby unwittingly rehabilitated the traitors, setting the vermin up as masters over the state now struggling for survival." It was, therefore, left to the National Socialist Revolution to establish the first German national state in history.[39]

Nonetheless, Mussolini's statist reinterpretation of nationalism remained, on the whole, alien to nazi ideology. Rosenberg preferred to speak of the "totality of the national socialist movement" rather than of the "total state" which, in his opinion, had merely become identical with the people and hence an inherent "instrumentality of the national socialist conception of life." Of course, only the big nations had the strength, and therewith the right, to forge for themselves such effective instrumentalities. As a professed disciple of Nietzsche, Rosenberg consistently followed Callicles's "wisest gospel" (in Plato's *Gorgias*) that "the law of nature wills it that the superior shall rule over the inferior." But he repudiated, perhaps in conscious opposition to Mussolini, both caesarism and hierarchy. His doctrine of authority was based not on the state, but on the people's "blood and honor"—watchwords soon inscribed on the dagger of every member of the Hitler Youth—and, hence, invested with the implacability of a law of nature. This authority would save civilization, which had hitherto been undermined by the Christian teachings of mercy and compassion, or their "new guise," Masonic humanitarianism. "From the compulsory dogma of limitless love," Rosenberg summarized, "and the equality of everything human before God, on the one hand, and from the doctrine of democratic 'rights of man,' devoid of all racial feeling and all nationally rooted sense of honor, on the other hand, European society has 'developed' into but a guardian of the inferior, the sick, and the crippled, of the criminal and the putrid." He would have liked, therefore, to retrace German history to the days of Charlemagne's "first Thirty Years' War" and their great duke, Widukind, who had fought for the freedom of all Nordic peoples. "There can be no doubt today that we are on the side of those forces which guided him rather than of those which helped Charlemagne to secure victory." Widukind's spirit was still riding through Germany's forests and valleys, calling the nation to rethinking its destiny in terms of blood and soil. "Today, at the turn of a millennium,we may declare that, although in the eighth century Duke Widukind had been defeated, he has proved for ever victorious in the twentieth century in the person of Adolf Hitler." [40]

Rosenberg was forced to admit, however, with something like a sigh, that there was no way of reviving the old Teuton heathenism. "Wotan as a denomination is dead," he declared, "he died not on account of St. Boniface but of his own [weakness]." The Nazis should, therefore, take over from Christianity teachings and rituals of Germanic origin, and repudiate all that stemmed from Judaism or—a new bogy!—was of "Etruscan" provenance. Rosenberg accepted Jesus, because St. Ephrem the Syrian had written about Jesus' Syrian mother and Roman father and, more recently, Houston Stewart Chamberlain, Frederick Delitzsch and E. Jung had "proved" his "Aryan" parentage. European art, too, had almost invariably depicted Christ as a tall, blond Nordic and careful reading of the Gospels convincingly showed the emphasis on his humility and sufferings as a later adulteration of Jewish evangelists. "To us today Jesus appears a self-assertive master, in the best and highest meaning of the term." To the Teuton his life was far more significant than his painful death, "to which he owed his success among the Alpine and Mediterranean peoples." The young generation of Germans, particularly, was determined to understand the Founder out of its own "Teutonic values," not through those "forged accretions which Jewish zealots like Matthew, materialistic rabbis like Paul, African jurists like Tertullian, or unstable half-breeds like Augustine have imposed on us as a most unbearable spiritual ballast." [41]

Rosenberg vented his ire on St. Paul with particular venom. Just as Socrates, whose only extant bust failed to live up to the standards of racial beauty, had been but an "international social democrat," so did Paul attempt to attain "world domination with the aid of the declassed of all states and peoples." With his egalitarian nihilism, which undermined all ancient organic growths, Paul preached a world revolution which lent international significance to the suppressed Jewish national revolt. For this purpose he and other Christian missionaries invented the doctrine of original sin together with the complementary doctrine of grace, both of which would have been utterly incomprehensible to healthy and racially unbroken peoples. "The eternal sense of sinfulness is but the accompaniment of physical bastardization" which alone creates split personalities and a permanent feeling of insecurity. Making use of the racial heterogeneity of the Roman Empire, Paul inflicted these doctrines on the Christian world. But the time had now come for the renascent racial feeling of young Teutons to rebel against them. [42]

The Pauline heritage also gave rise to the Catholic system of "indulgences" which, already repudiated by Luther, was but a typical "commercial doctrine" instituted by the "African" Tertullian. The "horrible doctrine of predestination," on the other hand, was the invention of the "unfree, bastardized, half-African Augustine" in order to convert the believers into "born slaves" of the church. The public burning of witches was an Etruscan heritage, while the Inquisition merely represented the struggle of the Syro-Alpine bastardized, and hence fanatically intolerant, Latin soul against the tolerant, heroic soul of the Nordics. Luther, to be sure, undertook to destroy the alien priesthood and thereby laid the foundations for the Teutonization of Christianity. But he did not go far enough in disposing of the Jewish materialistic heritage. In his doctrine of the Eucharist he still worshiped matter, while "in the materialistic dogma of resurrection comes to the fore the hopeless Judaization of [all] churches." What is more, the Christian doctrine of a transcendent God "controverts the autonomous workings of natural processes. This is a conception of life held by Semites, Jews and Rome." Similarly the Christian doctrine of love has always run counter to the essential Teuton sense of honor and, like its offshoot, the modern humanitarian idea, has proved to be but an "abstract wishful phantom." Under its third and latest guise, nurtured by the Russian ideas of suffering and mercy as exemplified in Dostoevski's characters, it infected the world with the bolshevist contagion. In short, "the myth of God's Roman deputy must be as sharply repudiated as the myth of the 'holy letter' in Protestantism." Or more generally,

> The old Syrian-Jewish, Eastern ecclesiasticism dethrones itself. Starting from a dogmatism which never corresponded to the spiritual structure of the Nordic West, trying to set aside or to subjugate the Nordic race's ideas of honor, freedom, duty which alone can sustain or create culture, this process of poisoning has led many times to most serious breakdowns. We realize today that the central and supreme values of the Roman and Protestant Churches, being but negative Christianity, do not satisfy our soul, that they are an obstacle to the progression of the organic forces of peoples determined by their Nordic race, that they ought to give way to a revaluation in the spirit of Teuton Christianity. This is the meaning of the present religious quest.[43]

This new religion must have only one criterion: the Teutonic race. "The Nordic blood," Rosenberg declared, "represents that mystery which has replaced and overcome the old sacraments," for "soul is race viewed from the inside; and conversely race is the exterior of soul." For this reason racial history is simultaneously natural history and mysticism of the soul. "Conversely the history of the religion of blood is the great world narration of the rise and decline of peoples, their heroes and thinkers, their inventors and artists." Everything of value in human civilization had been created by the four Aryan races of Indians, Persians, Graeco-Romans and Teutons. Even the best elements of the Judeo-Christian tradition were but distorted borrowings from the Persians. Hence given free rein now, the creativity of the Nordic race would attract for its "myth of blood" the most diverse peoples.[44]

Rosenberg had to admit reluctantly that the Teutons, or for that matter all of Europe, had not yet produced a religious genius of the rank of Jesus or Buddha, Zoroaster or Lao-tse. Blaming this distressing shortcoming on the stifling pressures of Christianity, he predicted the speedy emergence of such a new religious founder, himself serving in the more modest role of precursor. The greatest German reformer so far had been not Luther, but the medieval mystic, Magister Eckhart. Building up certain equivocal passages in the mystic writings (long hidden from public view in scarce medieval manuscripts) of that Cologne Dominican, Rosenberg attributed to him the basic elements of the "religion of blood," combined with the "myth of the ever-free soul." A revival of the teachings of the medieval monk, which, he insisted, could appeal only to men "of the same or cognate blood," would finally furnish the foundations for the much-needed new German Church. Preaching the supreme virtues of honor and duty rather than love, the new church would erect in its houses of worship symbols of the hero in lieu of crucifixes.

> Reverence for the soldier fighting for the honor of his people [he declared] is the new, recently developed living sentiment of our time. In the name of the new religion of national honor we may expect the awakening of Nordic-European consciousness. . . . In this matter the German must recall his magnificent mysticism, reacquire and relive the spiritual greatness of Magister Eckhart, so that that man and the hero in the field-gray under his helmet shall become one and the same person. Then the road shall be opened for the German national religion of the future, the truly German Church and the uniform German national culture.[45]

It was with such high-sounding "mystical" rubbish that the minds of German youth were turned from Christian ethics to the worship of an apotheosized "race" and the glorification of war. The new faith, they were told, would be bound "to subordinate unconditionally the ideal of neighborly love to the idea of national honor." These preachments were reinforced by unbridled attacks on all Christian denominations, particularly Catholicism. Rosenberg proclaimed obsolete the Nicean creed, adopted by illiterate monks, and the canons of other "synods of robbers," among which the "dishonorable Vatican Council" had completely dispossessed even the "medicine man," Jesus. He condemned the Jesuits because, with their Moorish antecedents, they had always been the sworn enemies of national cultures. Referring to the more recent past, he bitterly complained of the Protestant alliance with liberalism, the Center party's frequent collaboration with the Socialists, the priests' meddling in politics and their undisguised hostility to the Nazi party. He claimed that many priests had abused the confessional, some enjoining devout women to refuse cohabitation with nazi husbands. He sharply condemned Catholic and Protestant scholarship but, denying the fruitfulness of "a science without premises," demanded substitution for it of nazi scholarship. He also demanded the elimination of all clerical influences in schools and the evolution of a new system of education, which would develop not personalities—an obsolete aim of liberalistic education—but types. Women, especially, would be "emancipated from their emancipation" and completely removed from public life. The new "heroic" conception of life must become the conception of strong men and have as its protagonists, as did all successful movements in history, well-knit societies of men. Nor could dissent be tolerated in any way, for "national socialism arrogates unto itself the totality of man" and, to quote an Indian apothegm from Nordic antiquity, "Right is what Aryan men consider right." In short, "the boundary line," as one of Rosenberg's critics ventured to write even under the Third Reich, "has been drawn not as between good and evil, but between Aryan and non-Aryan." Or, as Rosenberg himself defined it, "religious denominations are not an aim in themselves, but merely varying means in the service of the sentiment of national vitality and the values of the Teuton character." For in all ultimate decisions "the nation comes *first* and *last* and *everything* else must be subordinate to it." This was, indeed, nationalism run amuck.[46]

It mattered little, therefore, that within a few months after Hitler's rise to power (July 20, 1933) Vice-Chancellor von Papen negotiated a concordat with Cardinal Pacelli (the present Pope Pius XII). With even less scruples than Mussolini, the German dictator constantly violated this treaty which, like other international agreements, he despised as but a scrap of paper. The administration of Protestant churches, on the other hand, was increasingly concentrated in the hands of a Reich bishop who, eternally at loggerheads with the established ecclesiastical organs, sought to level down all denominational differences. The small, but articulate, minority of "German Christians" was favored in every possible way, despite its obviously slight popular following (except in Thuringia). The objectives were plainly stated by Reich Minister for Church Affairs Kerrl in 1937. "There has now arisen," he declared, "a new authority as to what Christ and Christianity really is. This new authority is Adolf Hitler. . . . If this had been recognized, there would have been no split between Christianity and national socialism. All could have worked together to carry out the will of God, which is to secure the survival of our people." [47]

These repressive measures, designed to co-ordinate (*gleichschalten*) all organized religion with the new totalitarian society and state, were cleverly camouflaged as secular acts of a government forced to defend itself against the encroachments of a politically minded clergy. Even Rosenberg was but rarely allowed to speak his mind as bluntly as he did in a much-debated speech of 1938, where he said that "the Catholic Church and also the Confessional Church in their present form must disappear from the life of the people is my full conviction, and I believe I am entitled to say that this is also our Führer's viewpoint." The average German, whose opinions were molded by the controlled press, was unaware of the thousands of pastors and devout laymen sent to concentration camps. If he personally knew any such victims he believed that they had been punished for some secular offenses. Church publications trying to inform the public of the real issues were suppressed by the Gestapo. Outside Germany, however, the record of these religious persecutions could not be suppressed by reiterated official denials. To quote Pope Pius XI's Christmas message to the College of Cardinals of 1937:

In Germany there is indeed a real religious persecution. It is said, and it has been said for some time past, that this is not true. We know, on the contrary, that there is a terrible persecution; only a few times previously has there been a persecution so terrible, so fearful, so grievous and so lamentable in its far-reaching consequences.

Foreign protests, however, were unable to stem that persecution, until nearly all of Europe had come under the heel of the "master race." [48]

4. Heritage of Tolerance

In surveying the teachings of both the Nationalist Fathers and the Nationalist Epigoni we have noted that, despite great divergences in time and mental stature, the eight men reveal certain basic similarities in their attitude toward national religion, which can be explained only by the affinity of their nationalist doctrines. Personally they were as different as men can be. Perhaps the only common denominator of the six Continental writers, though not of the two Anglo-Americans, was their extraordinary vanity and the conviction that they were destined to play a great historic role. Modern nationalism had many messianic facets; not the least was that so many of its expounders behaved as if they were divinely ordained saviors.

The first and most popular among them, Rousseau actually came close to being so revered. During the enthusiastic years of the "Religion of Reason," particularly, admirers searched for his relics and made regular pilgrimages to his grave. Fichte, whose great self-assertiveness had often been rebuked by the powers that were, nevertheless was the first German philosopher whose hundredth anniversary was celebrated as a great national festival. So many memorial essays and addresses (including two by Ferdinand Lassalle, founder of the German Socialist party) were published on that occasion (1862) as to call for a special bibliographical survey. Mazzini, too, though most of his life an exile, had an ever-growing following in his country and was lionized in England to an extent hardly justified by his mental stature or the logical consistency of his thought. Even in contemporary Italy his shade has constantly been invoked by political democrats and liberal theologians, radical socialists and fascist reactionaries, the very Catholics having long ago made their peace with the troublesome rebel. Maurras was less fortunate in so far as his teachings were embodied in France's national fabric only under the pressure of a foreign invader. Nevertheless, in his long and stormy life he has had more than his fair share of adulation. Similarly upon Germany's repudiation of the international Nobel prize Rosenberg was chosen as the first recipient of the new annual German prize for citizens of greatest distinction. He was eclipsed there only by the overshadowing figure of Adolf Hitler, whose divinization as the Führer of the new national religion of nazism exceeded anything known in the apotheosis of living men in many generations. Apart from Lenin or Stalin,

Mussolini alone among Hitler's contemporaries approximated such a religious appeal to millions of fanatical worshipers.[49]

Nothing of the kind happened to Burke or Jefferson. True, the sharp, often bitter criticisms leveled against them by political or religious opponents were gradually mollified in the subsequent historic perspective. In their old age they were revered by the majority of their grateful countrymen as unofficial "elder statesmen" to be consulted on all problems of public concern. But they never became the subjects of self-denying adulation by unreasoning multitudes. With remarkable self-irony they themselves were rather inclined to minimize the role they had played in the evolution of their peoples.

This distinction goes far deeper than a mere difference in personal temperaments or the prevailing fashions of speech. The careful reader will have observed that in our analysis the five Nationalist Fathers, representing five important countries, have been contrasted by only three Nationalist Epigoni, from France, Italy and Germany. The present writer was unable to locate in either England or America any truly representative spokesman of the younger, more extremist forms of nationalist thinking. Not that either country was devoid of nazi or fascist sympathizers. But in America the latter clearly belonged to that "lunatic fringe," of which Franklin Roosevelt spoke in one of his campaign addresses of 1944. Not one of the American agitators, not even Huey Long or Father Coughlin, attained truly national stature or enjoyed more than transient popularity. In their slavish imitation of European prototypes, moreover, these would-be dictators utterly failed in developing any truly original, native-American variety of extreme nationalism. The same absence of both originality and national recognition characterized also the noisy, but abortive fascist movement in England. Even before the war, which for a time terminated their careers, Sir Oswald Mosley and his more spectacular than devoted followers could not, by any stretch of imagination, be classified as spokesmen of a large and influential wing of English nationalist thought. The far more serious and penetrating form of extreme nationalism preached by G. K. Chesterton or Hilaire Belloc, on the other hand, was little more than a literary mood affecting a tiny nonactivist intellectual minority. Those of its followers who took it as an earnest call to action found that its combination with Anglo-Catholicism and the medieval universalist conception of life greatly weakened its nationalist fervor. Certainly the program advocated by Belloc (born in France of a French father and an English mother) in his *Crisis of our Civilization*, though written in the heyday of fascism, carried far more of its corporative than of its nationalist implications. Belloc mainly wished "to apply the fruits which the Catholic culture had produced when it was in full vigor, the restriction of monopoly, the curbing of the money power, the establishment of co-operative work, and the wide distribution of private property, the main principle of the Guild and the jealous restriction of usury and competition, which between them have come so near to destroying us." [50]

That is not to say that "*it* cannot happen" in America or in England. Only that if anything of the kind should come to pass, it would no longer be *it*. English or American nationalism would have to reverse its entire course before it could adopt an exact replica of nazism or fascism. We recall Herder's penetrating remark about each nationality's unique standard of perfection. Herder's contemporary, Karl Friedrich von Moser, likewise an acute observer of early nationalist trends, noted that "every nation is motivated by a determining principle: obedience in Germany, freedom in England, trade in Holland, the honor of the king in France." [51] We need not share Moser's metaphysical view of a predetermined "national spirit" permeating every people and subject to change only as a result of major, cataclysmic events. But we shall nonetheless admit that certain national characteristics, often gradually developing from peculiar historic conditions, may be transmitted to subsequent generations, which modify them but slowly and imperceptibly in consonance with their own new historic experiences. [52]

The traditions of both English "constitutional" nationalism and American "democratic" nationalism have surely run counter to any brand of "integral" nationalism. Based on individual liberties, they have always imposed severe limitations on the nation's supremacy over the individual. No matter how "organic" Burke's nationalist theory may often appear (e.g., in his definition of state), he could never preach that total submission of the individual, which characterized the quasi-totalitarian ideologies of Rousseau, Fichte or Mazzini. For Americans individualistic "Jeffersonian democracy" became such a vital ingredient of national feeling that some of the chief opponents of international co-operation have also been most vigorous exponents of "rugged individualism" and governmental noninterference. Americans and English had neither the Germanic traditions of "obedience," nor the Prussian heritage of military glory in the service of national unification, nor the corresponding "objective" ideologies of a linguistic-cultural or racial organism totally dominating the individual will. They also lacked the vagaries of French "voluntaristic" nationalism, which within a century and a half could, without self-betrayal, enter successive alliances with individualistic and liberal as well as with Bonapartist, Proudhonian or Pétainist movements. Nor was "the honor of the king," the revival of which underlay Maurras's "integral" nationalism, of any consequence either under the British constitutional monarchy or in the American republic. Even if the search for national "glory" and honor, moreover, had been more deeply rooted in the Anglo-Saxon peoples, the marvelous expansion of British and American power during the past century and a half would surely have prevented that recurrent feeling of frustration which nurtured so much of French, German or Italian nationalist resentment. Certainly no Englishman or American could feel that bitterness which filled passionately patriotic Italians when they contrasted the universalist power of ancient Rome, the religious supremacy of the medieval papacy and the cultural influence of the Italian Renaissance with their country's recent political and economic backwardness. He did not have to "compensate" for it with an exaggerated, Giobertian chosenness, a Mazzinian geographic-cultural messianism, or a Mussolinian hierarchical totalitarianism.

These differences in outlook were, of course, determined not only by the diversity of nationalist tradition but also by the totality of those economic, political, social and religious forces which, in the ultimate sense, had helped shape and maintain that tradition. It may suffice to state here that the long and arduous, but ultimately successful struggle for religious freedom had injected into the Anglo-Saxon nationalist ideologies certain unparalleled, so far irrevocable safeguards for civil liberties as well. The checkered story of Anglo-Saxon sectarianism, culminating in America where no single sect enjoyed clear numerical preponderance, fundamentally differed from the struggle between Catholicism and freethought in France or Italy or even from the three-cornered conflict between Protestantism, Catholicism and bourgeois or Marxist agnosticism in Germany. In the latter countries, even in Germany with respect to most member states, there existed a single pre-eminent creed which had to resist the onrushing waves of agnosticism rather than the attacks of an opposing dogma and ritual. Under these circumstances the same constitutional safeguards, even if verbatim adopted on the Continent, did not mean quite the same thing in living reality. Similarly separation of state and church, so indispensable under the conditions of American denominationalism, became in France a much-embattled issue. The sudden acceptance of religious freedom under the Weimar Republic merely glossed over temporarily the difficulties arising from a division of a homogeneous nation into two, perhaps three denominations, the small Jewish minority being negligible in numbers, if not in economic and cultural influence.

These difficulties added fuel to the existing revolutionary unrest and stimulated those nationalist forces which sought denominational unity in the new religion of blood and honor. With no deep-rooted respect for *individual* liberty of conscience and for genuine equality among sects there seemed to be no valid reason for the inherited religious disparity to stand in the way of the new Pan-German unity. Nor seemed there to be any plausible ground why here, as well as in denominationally undivided Italy, organized religion, like any other group, should not come under the direct control of the totalitarian state or, what amounted to the same thing, of the totalitarian party in control of the state. Today the victory of the United Nations has saved the existing churches from imminent dangers. Without venturing to foretell precise developments on the European Continent, one may expect not only the suppression of the overt forms of fascism and nazism, but also the adoption in the countries west of the Soviet sphere of influence of the basic patterns of Anglo-American constitutional and religious freedoms. Certainly the words of a Catholic reviewer of Rosenberg's outpourings, courageously published in a Frankfort magazine in 1934, seem to be coming true sooner than the author himself dared expect.

> The Church views this spectacle [he wrote] with sovereign condescension and the calmness of a victor. It has subdued ancient paganism and its false culture, it has mastered the barbarians, it has survived Arianism, which had permeated nearly all of Catholic Christianity, it has conquered giants of great intellectual stature. What is much more: it has overcome the infinitely graver dangers which threatened it because of its own weaknesses of former days. . . . The Church of God shall endure, when no one will ever mention the book by Rosenberg and when a melancholy traveler will sketch the ruins of the University of Leipzig.[53]

But will the church, indeed all churches, overcome their own nationalist weaknesses?

Chapter IV

CATHOLIC INTERTERRITORIALISM

H AVING surveyed the relationships between some of the most vigorous nationalist movements and organized religion, we may now turn to the
analysis of the complementary attitudes of the Christian churches toward nationalism. Here, too, any attempt at generalization within the confines of a few
chapters will necessarily suffer from frequent oversimplification of complex
crosscurrents. As an outsider—and everyone is an outsider in regard to attitudes
of churches other than his own—the analyst will be at the additional disadvantage of, to use a phrase of ancient sages, "teaching in the presence of his
masters" superior to him in both knowledge and living experience. On the
other hand, as Max Nordau once wrote in reviewing newer trends in French
literature a short time after his arrival in France, an outsider has some of the
virtues of "posterity." Where he falls short in regard to direct observation he
makes up in part by detachment and freshness of approach.

In the case of the Catholic Church the difficulties are somewhat mitigated
by the existence of a central authority, the papacy. To be sure, in the vast area
of human relations where nationalism impinges on religion, Catholic attitudes have necessarily varied from country to country and from generation
to generation. One could hardly expect uniformity in a body embracing some
350,000,000 members, whose leading hierarchy alone, according to a computation made some time ago, included 219 archbishops, 882 bishops, 207 vicars
and 82 prefects apostolic. This number has constantly increased and, if the experience of the early 1920's is to be repeated in the present postwar era, we may
witness another period of rapid expansion.[1] The papacy itself has been forced
to consider these local and chronological divergences and often to express its
views on controversial subjects with so much circumspection as to become
rather abstract and noncommittal. Long before British diplomacy that of the
Holy See had learned that outspokenness and unambiguous clarity of definition
are often the mark of political amateurs. Occasionally a pope stating his opinion with concrete decisiveness found that he had run counter to some local
interests and prejudices. Did not Pope Pius XI complain that his famous encyclical *Quadragesimo anno*, demanding equitable treatment for workers,

could not be read publicly in certain churches because of the opposition of employers? [2] More frequently, as that very encyclical illustrates, popes had to modify opinions laid down by their predecessors.

Despite these constant adaptations of theory to ever-changing reality, however, there has undeniably existed a basic continuity in Catholic thinking through the ages. It has been greatly abetted by the singleness of purpose effected by centralized authority and a remarkable tenacity in the face of adversity.

1. STATE AND CHURCH

Although the church unwittingly fathered the rise of medieval national states and frequently lent succor to the modern national aspirations of Poles and Irish, Pope Pius XII was right in emphasizing in his Christmas Allocution of 1945 that it "is supranational by its very nature. . . . She must be now more than ever supranational." It has often aroused thereby the bitter resentment of extreme nationalists. The American Know-Nothing party, for instance, in its national platform of 1855 not only attacked its "aggressive policy and corrupting tendencies," but also advocated the exclusion from public office of any person holding "civil allegiance, directly or indirectly, to any foreign power whether civil or ecclesiastical." Several decades later Bishop Doane of Albany still contended that "it is hard to find any other word [than that of 'alien'] which describes the whole communion of a church which owes its highest allegiance to a single head, who is a foreigner across the sea." [3]

This rationale for withholding religious toleration from Catholics satisfied even genuine humanitarians like Milton or Locke. To weaken its force the revolutionary leaders of the small and dispersed Catholic communities in America petitioned the pope that he sever at least their connection with the vicar apostolic in London and allow them to elect their own superiors under the direct jurisdiction of the Holy See (1783). They were prepared stanchly to adhere to "that which is essential to our religion" and to acknowledge, in particular, "the pope's spiritual supremacy over the whole Christian world." But any other dependence on foreign jurisdiction, they averred, would greatly impair their newly won equality. The need of jurisdictional autonomy had in fact "very frequently been intimated to us in very positive terms by the rulers of this Republic." After prolonged hesitation Rome finally consented to the election of an American bishop subject only to papal confirmation (1789). [4]

Before long it became the church's established policy to grant complete self-government to all substantial Catholic minorities in Protestant lands. The British hierarchy, headed by the Archbishop of Westminster, was removed in 1850 from the jurisdiction of the Sacred Congregation for the Propagation of the Faith which controlled missionary areas, and placed under the pope's direct tutelage. Even where the "Propaganda" retained its control, moreover, a concerted effort was made to develop an indigenous clergy. According to a survey of 1907, the "heathen" lands of Asia, Africa and the Pacific had no less than 135 Catholic seminaries with an enrollment of more than 5,000 native theological students.[5]

In the light of these extensive concessions to native cultures, Aristide Briand was not altogether wrong in objecting to the alleged "foreign" sovereignty of the pope. In his defense, on November 9, 1906, of the bill of separation of state and church he drew an ingenious distinction. The pope was for the French, he said, not a foreign sovereign, but a Catholic and French chief, just as he was for the Germans a Catholic and German chief. As such he was in every country a "domestic sovereign [souverain intérieur]." [6] This formula, strikingly novel in international law, perhaps too readily overlooked the Vatican's temporal interests. But it reflected the fundamental fact that the papacy did not participate in international power politics as a direct partner, but weighed all issues on the scales of its traditional values or, at worst, of its institutional interests. These considerations would have lost little force if, in some miraculous way, the pope could simultaneously have resided in each and every country.

The church's main concern was with political rather than cultural nationalism. From its inception it had to reconcile its members' duties toward the "Kingdom of Heaven" with those toward their respective kingdoms on earth. The "give unto Caesar" of the Gospels was too general to delineate clearly the boundaries between the two areas. In the pre-Constantine period a Christian author could state in all sincerity that "Christians inhabit their own fatherland as aliens. Each foreign country is their fatherland, and each fatherland a foreign country." Such early Church Fathers and teachers, as Origen and Tertullian, opposed military service by Christians, conceding only that they should help their kings by prayers. Although this otherwordliness speedily gave way when Christianity became the dominant religion in the empire, it influenced most medieval scholastics who objected to any mastery of man over man and declared the state to be but the fruit of sin. They only admitted that it was at the same time the divinely instituted remedy for sin. Throughout the Middle Ages the papacy also claimed to be not only the supreme spiritual power of the entire corpus christianum, but also the ultimate source of temporal power. Theoretically the pope could depose the emperor, Christendom's recognized temporal chief. Drawing an equation between sin and rightlessness Aegidius Colonna, a distinguished theologian of the circle of Boniface VIII, concluded that all laymen were but villeins of the church. Another canon jurist stated that "the pope can do what he wants, he can take from one and give it to another, for no one can tell him, Why do you do it." Although never put to a practical test, these extravagant claims were cherished by numerous extremists among the champions of papal supremacy.[7]

In modern times, however, the church had to learn to get along with the ever more self-assertive state power. Few popes now ventured explicitly to re-affirm the supremacy of the religious over civil authority, as Pius IX still did in his encyclical *Quanta cura* of 1864. But none of them ever conceded inferiority. The farthest they, or Catholic apologists elaborating Thomistic theories, were ready to go was to allow the state "co-ordinate authority" with the church and to recognize them both as stemming directly from "natural law," i.e., from God. Unavoidably, political nationalism postulating ever-greater state control came into sharp conflict with this church doctrine. The solution often sought was separation of state and church, which, outwardly leaving the church in un-disputed control of purely spiritual affairs, basically recognized the ultimate sovereignty of the state. It was the state which, subject only to internal pres-sures, was free to define the boundaries of this spiritual area and the extent to which it was ready to concede self-government to its religious bodies. The Catholics, however, "had come to consider Catholicism," as G. K. Chesterton wrote,[8] "as one thing, all the parts of which are in one sense equally assailed and in another sense equally unassailable."

According to canon law the papacy retained its spiritual jurisdiction over the whole of Christendom, including its schismatic and heretical sections. As late as August 7, 1873, Pius IX, in a letter to Emperor William I, vigorously re-stated this claim. But the emperor, in his reply of September 3, just as vigor-ously repudiated it. So did all other Protestant and Greek Orthodox rulers. In practical operation, however, separation often accrued to the benefit of the church in non-Catholic countries. The religiosity of the Catholic community was less infringed upon by strictly political concerns inescapably arising from the state's participation in ecclesiastical affairs, while the worldly advantages of state backing were greatly diminished under a non-Catholic monarch or a non-Catholic popular majority. The church has certainly prospered under the American system of separation. Under the Weimar Republic, too, it speedily overcame the initial shock of revolution and, putting to best advantage the opportunities offered by separation, made unexpected progress, both spiritual and temporal. The removal of some restrictions, carried over from the *Kultur-kampf*, made possible a new "spring of monasticism," an unprecedented ex-pansion of Catholic orders and parochial schools. Politically, too, the Catholic Center party long held the balance of power between the "national opposi-tion" and the socialist-liberal government. Some of its apologists boasted that Centrist influence in the Catholic districts alone had prevented the Marxist parties from securing an absolute majority in the National Assembly and from promulgating a wholly socialist constitution.[9]

It was different in Catholic lands. In his encyclical *Longinqua oceani*, Leo XIII pointed out that, despite the prosperous state of the American church, "it would be very erroneous to draw the conclusion that in America is to be sought the type of the most desirable status of the church, or that it would be universally lawful or expedient for state and church to be, as in America, dissevered and divorced." [10] Indeed, when the French people, which for centuries had been kept in a state of unrest by the incessant friction between political and ecclesiastical authorities, decided twice, in 1795 and 1905, to separate its state from the church, it provoked a storm of Catholic protests. The controversy was seriously aggravated by financial issues, inasmuch as the decree of 1795 had failed to restore to the church its vast estates expropriated by the Revolution, while that of 1905 discontinued all state subsidies.

The strong Catholic opposition induced Napoleon, then first consul, to restore the historic connection with the church by the concordat of 1801. Personally an agnostic and downright opportunist, he believed that "society cannot exist without inequalities of fortune, and the inequality of fortune cannot be maintained without religion," namely, the belief in God's inscrutable will and retributive justice in the hereafter. In the concordat he saw a means not only of restoring internal peace, but also of buttressing his dictatorial regime. Article 6 of the pact provided for an oath of loyalty to be taken by all priests which pledged them to inform the government of anything prejudicial to its interests which might come to their attention. Cardinal Maury stated that "with a good police and a good clergy, the emperor would always be assured of public order, for an archbishop is also a prefect of the police." Before long a catechism was distributed among the churches enjoining all pious Christians to remember that they owed their emperor "love, respect, obedience, fidelity, military service, and taxes . . . [also] fervent prayers for his salvation and for the spiritual and temporal prosperity of the state." For "to honor and serve the emperor is to honor and serve God himself." [11]

The real victor, however, was the church. Under the restoration it gained an ascendancy unparalleled in the prerevolutionary era. The main Gallican declaration of 1682, which proclaimed royal independence in temporal matters, the supremacy of universal councils over popes and papal noninterference with the rules of the Gallican church, though never formally abrogated, was no longer taught as a part of the official credo at theological seminaries. Despite the well-known tenacity of religious rituals, the Roman liturgy gradually replaced the Gallican rites in all French dioceses between 1839 and 1875. The church's intellectual spokesmen, de Bonald, Chateaubriand, Lamennais and de Maistre, found not only new eloquent words to glorify its ideals and a new enthusiasm to fill it with missionary zeal, but also new formulas to reconcile it with the rising spirit of nationalism. Far beyond the boundaries of France their writings gained new converts, including such distinguished German writers as Friedrich von Schlegel and Adam Müller. They created the spiritual background for the new international system of the Holy Alliance. Crossing the Channel, this "Catholic Renaissance" (so styled by Thureau-Dangin) led to the much-debated conversions of Cardinals Newman and Manning, the latter objecting, in particular, to the "appellate jurisdiction of the crown in matters spiritual." Even the new French liberal regime of Louis Philippe did not dare to infringe upon any church prerogatives. In his crude way the king warned that "one must never stick one's finger into the affairs of the church, for one can never withdraw it," reiterating the fears expressed in the popular adage, *qui mange du pape en meurt.*[12]

The Third Republic was far less circumspect, however. Its nationalist, democratic regime increasingly emphasized secular education. In the Fleury decrees of 1879 it challenged the all-powerful parochial school. In 1880 it dissolved the Jesuit order. In 1886 it insisted on exclusively lay instruction. Leo XIII's efforts in the 1890's to come to terms with the republican regime whose growing stability and probable longevity he clearly perceived (the so-called *ralliement*), were greatly hindered by the French clerical party which supported all reactionary movements from Boulangism to Bonapartism, royalism and even, as we have seen, integral nationalism. The break came in 1905 with the law of separation which, far from securing the promised reconciliation, for a time exacerbated the mutual recriminations. Pius X did not exaggerate when he wrote (in his encyclical *Vehementer nos*):

> We cannot, therefore, without the keenest sorrow, observe that the French government has just done a deed which inflames, on religious grounds, passions already too dangerously excited, and which, therefore, seems to be calculated to plunge the whole country into disorder.[13]

After the First World War, however, the papacy made its peace with the French Republic. Along with such other neutrals as Switzerland and Holland, the Vatican had become the diplomatic storm center of a belligerent world. France badly needed absolute national unity in her crucial struggle for survival, while internationally she sought the church's aid in establishing a system of security which would protect her against future aggression. The papacy, too, found that it was in its best interests to secure the friendly co-operation of the now leading Continental power whose republican form of government rested apparently on unshakable foundations. In 1918 a leftist senator, de Monzie, began publicly to advocate that France resume diplomatic relations with the Vatican, which, in his opinion, she could negotiate without going to Canossa. Arguing for resumption at the Chamber of Deputies several governmental spokesmen emphasized the numerous nationality problems awaiting decision and their intimate tie-up with denominational divisions and ecclesiastical institutions. In May, 1921, finally, an agreement was reached. France established a regular embassy at the Vatican and recognized a papal nuncio in Paris.[14] Four years later, we recall, Pius XI condemned the *Action française.*

This brief summary of the historic relationship between the modern French state and church may serve as an illustration of the importance ascribed by the church, both regional and universal, to this aspect of political nationalism.

Wherever Catholics lived in substantial numbers, their ecclesiastical autonomy often involved them in controversies over governmental policy which evoked the ire of the church's political opponents. It became fashionable for such Protestant statesmen as Bismarck, even long before the *Kulturkampf*, to fulminate against the *ecclesia militans*.[15] Others spoke with increasing venom of "political Catholicism." Even discounting the usual partisan exaggerations, there remained an undeniable residuum of "politics" not only in the efforts of devout Catholics to mold all political and social realities to conform to their Thomistic views, but also in their attempts to safeguard the full autonomy of their ecclesiastical organs and the latter's jurisdiction over education and family life. The complexity of these problems often called for the Vatican's direct intervention and the conclusion of formal international treaties. Pius XI alone, during the seventeen years of his reign (1922-39), signed concordats with Poland, Lithuania, Latvia and Rumania, with Bavaria, Prussia, Baden and the Reich, with Italy, Austria and Yugoslavia. He also secured less formal working agreements with Czechoslovakia and Portugal.

2. CULTURAL NATIONALISM

In comparison with these major political issues the problems of cultural nationalism or even the political struggles of national minorities received scant consideration. On the fringe of the Greek Orthodox world Catholic missionaries had long been accustomed to making concessions to popular folk-ways and native languages. The Uniates of southeastern Poland were generally allowed to use Ruthenian in their liturgy and to employ married priests. In the Danubian Principalities the hard-pressed Catholic leaders tried to stem the tide of assimilation by conceding to their immigrant flocks the use of the old Julian calendar, the nonobservance of certain Catholic holidays, and the wide employment of Rumanian sermons. Only in so far as cultural nationalism stressed the purely secular aspects of national unity, as against the divisive influences of denominationalism, and tried to indoctrinate the youth with its standard of values, it was condemned by the church as the mainspring of "secularism" and "materialism." In his famous encyclical *Ad beatissimi* of November 1, 1914, Benedict XV enumerated among the basic causes of the First World War the influence of "godless schools" and an "unscrupulous press" which had "succeeded in propagating the deadly error that man ought not to look for a happy eternity; that is only here that happiness is to be found in the riches, the honors, the pleasures of this life." [16]

Not that the record of Europe's Catholic education had been particularly impressive. Discussing the difficulties of Italian unification in 1866 a modern historian observed that "the real Quadrilateral that has stopped us is our seventeen million illiterates and five million *dilettanti*." Statistics had shown, indeed, an average ratio of 78 per cent of illiterates throughout Italy and of fully 90 per cent in priest-dominated Naples. Even in 1900, after several decades of concerted liberal and nationalist efforts, Italy's incidence of illiteracy was the second highest in Western Europe, second only to Portugal, where the church had likewise long dominated popular education. Only where the Catholic school faced stiff secular competition, as in France or the United States, it often rose to considerable heights of educational achievement and popular effectiveness. Arguing that the parochial school was a divisive factor forcing French youth to grow up under two different approaches to education, the French Chamber extended, in 1901, the laws of 1879-86 which had restricted teaching to lay personnel. Now "congregational" schools were completely outlawed. The Catholic schools persisted, however, under a different guise and a decade later still showed an enrollment of nearly a million pupils.[17]

In the United States, too, there was much opposition to the parochial school on nationalist grounds. The "Oregon Statute" of 1922, adopted by popular vote, required public school attendance up to the eighth grade by nearly all children aged eight to sixteen. Brought before the United States Supreme Court, the statute was defended by Oregon's attorney general with the plausible argument that the state must make its citizens "fitted both in body and in mind" for the performance of their civic duties. The separation of school children along religious lines, he argued, was likely to produce permanent mutual suspicion to the injury of the whole community. Nevertheless, the statute was declared unconstitutional by the Supreme Court, which in its memorable decision of June 1, 1925, broadly affirmed that

> the fundamental theory of liberty upon which all governments in this Union repose excludes any general power of the state to standardize its children by forcing them to accept instruction from public teachers only. The child is not the mere creature of the state; those who nurture him and direct his destiny have the right, coupled with the high duty, to recognize and prepare him for additional obligations.

Unlike the languishing parochial schools of other denominations, the American Catholic schools had in 1939 an attendance of more than two and a half million pupils. But Catholic leadership is far from satisfied. The fact that some 56 per cent of Catholic children fail to attend parochial schools shows how far from realization still is the original program of the Third Plenary Council of Baltimore (1884), which had demanded means of education for "every Catholic child." But the progress already made has demonstrated the persuasiveness to Catholic masses of the principle enunciated by that council that "to shut religion out of the school, and keep it for home and the church is . . . to train up a generation that will consider religion good for home and the church, but not for the practical business of life." [18]

In his encyclical *Rappresentanti in terra* of December 31, 1929, Pope Pius XI saw in the American Supreme Court's recognition of the educational rights of each family an example of what a nation must properly do if it is "anxious to respect the natural law." The church often invoked the family's natural rights even more directly in the realm of family laws as such and valiantly fought for state acceptance of the canon law regulations governing the marriage and divorce of Catholics. The German Center party, in its electoral proclamation of 1912, asserted that "only true religiosity offers a permanent guarantee of national strength and national health." The church's consistent opposition to birth control, because of its favorable effects upon population growth, was indeed considered by many nationalists as a major asset, though they, as a rule, resented as a divisive force Catholic objections to intermarriage, except on terms favoring the Catholic faith. Clearly the church was bound to repudiate the nazi sterilization laws. Even before the establishment of the nazi regime Pius XI in his encyclical *Casti connubii* of December 31, 1930, sharply denied the right of civil authorities to inflict bodily mutilations. The Nazis added, therefore, insult to injury, when they issued, in 1935, orders regulating the procedure in the sterilization of members of religious orders, notwithstanding their vows of chastity.[19]

The church evinced greater interest in cultural nationalism only where a Catholic national minority fought for the preservation of its culture, religious as well as secular, but even then its political conservatism long counseled moderation and abstention from violence. Not that the church had always been opposed to insurrection. In the endless conflicts between papacy and empire or the recurrent struggles against oppressive monarchs, as well as in the doctrines of such teachers as Suarez, rebellion against the state had long been accepted as a frequent necessity. Thomas Aquinas himself had taught that sometimes it was the tyrant whose acts were seditious. Stanch resistance was certainly deemed a duty, whenever the state infringed upon the religious conscience of its subjects. But the church was hesitant in extending the same privilege to subjects disturbed in their nationalist or social conscience. In fact, under the impact of the revolutionary upheavals, its regnant political theory tended to move away, slowly but unmistakably, from the Suarezian doctrine. That is why Cardinal Rampolla, Leo XIII's chief collaborator, so sharply denounced the seditious implications of the nationality principle. "The so-called nationality right [*diritto di nazionalità*]," he wrote in his circular instructions to the papal nuncios of June 22, 1887, "is not only entirely disregarded by positive law which regulates the reciprocal relations between civilized nations, but, if an attempt were made to apply it to existing states, it would become the source of universal disturbance. Society would revert again to the era of barbarian invasions accomplished under the exclusive reign of material force." Leo XIII himself ordered the bishops of Bohemia and Moravia to advise the Catholic clergy not to become involved in the heated nationalist controversies between Czechs and Germans. "They will easily," he wrote in 1901, "unless they abstain from all appearance of contention, become hateful and offensive to both parties, and nothing is more detrimental to the exercise of their sacred office than this." [20] Of course, both the Bohemian Germans and Czechs were Catholics; the latter not wholly above suspicion of cherishing memories of their Hussite national church.

The papacy also long hesitated to permit the Catholic Croats the use of ancient Slavonic in their ritual for fear of offending the Austrian regime which regarded it as an entering wedge to their national unity with the Serbs. Similarly, so long as the Flemish national movement seemed to run counter to the interests of the established Belgian church, Cardinal Mercier enjoined his priests to desist from pro-Flemish agitation. The Catholic party, often in control of the whole state, was especially powerful in Flanders. It nevertheless came to espouse the Flemish cause very late and with evident lack of enthusiasm.[21]

The situation of the Canadian, Irish and Polish Catholics living in Protestant or Greek Orthodox countries was altogether different. In Quebec the problem was largely linguistic and educational. In his letters to the Canadian bishops of 1916-18, Benedict XV could recommend "that all the priests should seek to acquire the habit of speaking competently each of the two languages, English and French and, casting all prejudices aside, should use now one, now the other to meet the needs of the faithful." Only in recent years conflicting attitudes in international affairs and the emergence of strong semifascist and antisemitic trends have created among the French Canadians new seminationalist movements, with which the church will undoubtedly have to cope in the future. The Irish and Polish problems, however, combined, from the outset, a struggle for cultural and religious autonomy with a more overtly "seditious" political irredenta. Leo XIII, at that time (1888) seeking better relations with the British government, counseled the Irish to abstain from revolutionary acts, "because nothing is more fatal to a cause, no matter how just it may be, than that it be defended by violence and injustice." He also told the Poles in 1894:

> As for those who are under the dependence of authority, they are bound to observe respect and fidelity towards princes as exercising towards God His authority through the intermediation of men; they must obey them, not only from fear of chastisement, but also from conscience, pray for them and give thanks in their behalf, religiously respect the order of the state, abstain from the plots of men of disorder and from adhesion to secret societies; they must commit no seditious act, but must assist with all their efforts in maintaining peace in justice.

His successor, Pius X, had even more reason to advise the Poles to "stand on the side of peace and order" during the Russian Revolution of 1905, which was led by Marxian Socialists.[22]

This doctrine of unflinching obedience gave way during the First World War, when national rebellions attained unexpected legitimacy. First the Germans and then the Allies began to play on the disaffection of national minorities in enemy lands. National self-determination was soon hailed as a major war objective. The resurrection of an independent Poland and Irish Free State, in particular, appeared highly desirable also from the religious viewpoint. In 1918, at the height of the revolutionary agitation, Benedict XV found warm words of appreciation for the Irish in their tenacious struggle for "religious and civil rights" which, the pope asserted, had also safeguarded the rights of their British coreligionists. These sentiments were re-echoed by Cardinal Bourne, archbishop of Westminster. The pope also pointed out that, among his predecessors, Clement XIV had tried, however unsuccessfully, to forestall the partitions of Poland, while Gregory XVI and Pius IX had "lifted their voices in vigorous protest in behalf of the oppressed" inhabitants of that country. Papal enthusiasm was not lessened by the fact that the Poles, by now regaining their independence, were withdrawn from communist control. These considerations may well have prompted the pope to formulate (in the same letter to Archbishop Kakowski, October 15, 1918) his general views on the national aspirations of minorities. For the first time he expressed his "fond hope" that Russia's other subject nationalities "may be allowed to decide their own lot and develop and prosper according to their native genius and their own individual resources." [23]

No sooner was Poland reconstituted, however, than, defying the Vatican's calmer counsels, she embarked upon a policy of denationalizing the Ruthenian, White Russian and Lithuanian minorities inhabiting her less densely populated eastern areas. The papacy wished to reconstitute, especially, the venerable Uniate bishoprics of Chelm and Polock as religious centers for the millions of Ukrainians inside and outside of Poland. It was ready to reaffirm its old concessions to their language and folkways and generally to strengthen their Ukrainian, and hence anti-Russian, national consciousness. Under Polish pressure, however, the Holy See was forced in the concordat of 1925 to deliver them to the jurisdiction of bishops of the Latin rite, Eastern Galicia alone retaining its Uniate hierarchy inherited from the Austrian regime. Nor were the interests of the church advanced in any way by the raging nationalist controversy over Silesia which was claimed by both Poland and Germany. Since a part of the Breslau diocese was involved in the Upper Silesian plebiscite, every move by Archbishop Bertram was suspected of aiding the Germans to secure a majority. Polish bishops, on the other hand, were accused of unlawfully sending numerous Polish agitators in priestly garb into the region. The papal nuncio in Warsaw, Msgr. Achille Ratti, who within two years was to become Pope Pius XI, served as papal commissioner and naturally earned the gratitude of neither party. He was sharply denounced in the German, especially Protestant, press as a Polish agent. At the same time, forgetful of his great services during Poland's crucial war with the Soviet Union, the Polish government now secured his unostentatious revocation.[24]

Other difficulties arose in the new Czechoslovakian republic. Apart from having to find adequate replacements for the German Magyar ecclesiastical chiefs, the church had to deal with powerful reformatory trends along national lines. The demand that new bishops be elected by clergy and laymen alike was overshadowed by the insistence on the abrogation of celibacy and patronage. Some demanded a Czech prayer book, others that the Czech church be headed by a native patriarch who would visit the pope but once in three years. More than two-thirds of the Catholic clergy itself (1,788 of a total of 2,620) voted for these and other reforms. "When Vienna falls, Rome must fall, too!" became a watchword of national liberation. Even more serious was the agitation for the "rehabilitation" of John Huss and the proclamation of the anniversary of his martyr's death as a national day of mourning. The implied condemnation of the church was underscored by recurrent riots on the holiday commemorating St. John Nepomuk who, as Huss's chief opponent, was now called the "saint of darkness." After several years this nationalist frenzy calmed down in the face of the Vatican's stubborn resistance supported by Czechoslovak bodies in foreign lands, especially the United States. The unsuccessful attempt to secure ordination of new national bishops by the Serbian Orthodox Church likewise undermined the new hierarchy by raising the specter of a serious breach in the apostolic succession. The government, too, lent but relatively scant support to the Reformist groups. Committed to the policy of essential separation of church and state, President Thomas Masaryk in his New Year's message for 1925 declared that "the churches should strengthen the spiritual life and progress from their own resources, just as the state should rely upon its own strength and inner worth." But whatever comfort the church may have derived from this weakening of the opposition was outweighed by the realization that ever more Czechs were severing all ties with organized religion.[25]

It is small wonder that the papacy long tried to steer clear of the more complex and emotionally overburdened nationalist controversies. During the Second World War, however, their undeniable import for world peace forced Pius XII vigorously to espouse the legitimate rights of national minorities. In his encyclical *Summi pontificatus* of October 20, 1939, and his Christmas Allocutions of 1939 and 1941 the pope analyzed the requisites of a just and honorable peace and stressed that "every nation has its own genius, its own qualities, springing from the hidden roots of its being." The church, aiming at unity rather than uniformity, he declared, was ready to befriend with its prayers the cultivation of such national characteristics, "so long as all is done without prejudice to those duties which the common origin and the common destiny of the whole human race impose upon us." The message of 1941 no less clearly stated:

> Within the limits of a new order founded on moral principles there is no place for open or secret oppression of the cultural and linguistic characteristics of national minorities, for the hindrance or restriction of their economic resources, for the limitation or abolition of their natural fertility. The more conscientiously the government of a state respects the rights of minorities, the more confidently and the more effectively can it demand from its subjects a loyal fulfillment of those civil obligations which are common to all citizens.[26]

3. INTERNATIONALISM AND ROMAN SOVEREIGNTY

In such statements as these has come to the fore, as in all periods of great crisis, the intrinsic supranationalism of the church. Its well-knit hierarchical organization always was necessarily interterritorial. Whether or not the pope directly appointed archbishops and bishops, he controlled through them that vast "corporate body of clergy," whose interterritorial social compact had been characterized by Rousseau as a "masterpiece" of political organization. While the provincial setup of monastic orders fostered their autonomy and frequently opened the gates to the influx of nationalist ideologies, the centralization of authority in the hands of "generals" (this title is quite properly reminiscent of the orders' quasi-military discipline) made them a foremost centripetal force. Enemies, like Gambetta, could style them "that multicolored militia, without a fatherland," or rather one "whose fatherland is based only on the last of the seven hills of Rome." The effective jurisdiction exercised over the far-flung Catholic missions by the papal Congregation for the Propagation of the Faith added still another cohesive force to the hierarchical structure.[27]

Of course, nationalism was too powerful a force in modern times not to penetrate deeply even the sacred asylums of churches and monasteries. Cardinal Richelieu's alliance with German Protestant princes against their Catholic emperor commanded the unstinted support of the Sorbonne theologians. His successor, Cardinal Mazarin, brought the Thirty Years' War to a successful conclusion from the standpoint of French rather than Catholic interests, though he never relinquished his Italian name (Mazarini) and his obvious aspirations to the papal tiara. If, at the end of the nineteenth century, France supported some 70 per cent of all Catholic missions, she never lost sight of their contribution to the spread of French influence in the Orient. The divergent policies pursued by provinces of the Society of Jesus largely reflected differences in national aspirations and interests. After 1918 the pope leaned ever more heavily upon Anglo-Catholic churchmen in the Near East which had come under British control, defying the French and Italian hierarchy which had viewed the Levant's Latin populations as their traditional preserve. This resentment was dramatized by the Franciscan bishop, Msgr. Briante who left Alexandria without previous consultation with the Vatican in protest against the appointment of the English Dominican father, Coutourier, as apostolic delegate to Egypt.[28]

These instances could easily be multiplied. Where Catholic loyalties, however, coincided with national interest, religious allegiance often deeply colored political attitudes. American revolutionary leadership, for instance, succeeded in enlisting almost unanimous support of Catholics in an overt rebellion against established authority only because the Revolution held out the promise of greater religious freedom and the removal of Catholic disabilities. Patriotic fervor rose to an even higher pitch when the Catholic powers of France and Spain rallied behind it. Nor were the Congressional leaders slow in realizing the opportunity thus given for the inclusion of Catholic Canada in the anti-British insurrection. Despite strong anti-Catholic sentiments in its own midst and its vocal protests against the "Quebec Act" which had granted full religious autonomy to the French Canadians, Congress dispatched to Canada a diplomatic mission which, headed by Benjamin Franklin, included the two Catholic brothers Charles and John Carroll (1776). This mission was instructed to reassure the Canadians with respect to the free and undisturbed exercise of their religion and to promise "to the clergy the full, perfect and peaceable possession and enjoyment of all their estates; that the government relating to their religion and clergy shall be left entirely in the hands of the good people of that province and such legislation as they shall constitute." More recently, too, the attitude of many, though not all, American Catholics to the Anglo-Irish conflict, the Mexican and Spanish revolutions and other matters of international concern was greatly colored by their Catholic biases. Domestically, the existence of a "Catholic vote" in national and local elections, along with a "Jewish vote," a "Negro vote," a "labor vote," though far from unanimous, need not be denied even by those who disagree with the hostile interpretation placed upon it by opponents. Similarly the frequent support extended by the German Center party between 1871 and 1914 to Poles and Alsatians had many earmarks of Catholic solidarity cutting across national lines.[29]

Such intermingling of religious and nationalist biases continued to exist, notwithstanding the frequent denials by Catholics living in an atmosphere of fervent nationalism and confronted by recurrent denunciations of "political Catholicism." Bishop Ketteler of Mayence hotly disputed in 1873 Bismarck's aspersions and asserted that, apart from the usual quinquennial reports on ecclesiastical affairs, he had been in no communication whatsoever with the Holy See. "My entire activity has absolutely nothing to do with 'papal policy.' Rome has never made any such demands on me." Ketteler could not deny, however, that only two and a half years earlier, at the constitution of the German Empire, he had formally appealed in behalf of the Center party for "the restoration of the temporal rule of the Roman See as one of the first acts of the emperor's wisdom and sense of justice." The papal Department of State, on its part, did not always refrain from interfering with the policies of the Center party. In his confidential note of January 3, 1887, Cardinal Jacobini instructed the nuncio to induce the Centrist leaders to vote in favor of a military bill then pending at the Reichstag. Such a vote would cause "the government to be ever more friendly to Catholics as well as to the Holy See" and facilitate the passage of favorable ecclesiastical laws at the Prussian Diet. Even the generally tractable Centrist leaders resented such bluntness and reciprocated by replying to the nuncio that they had never pledged obedience to the Vatican except in matters of purely spiritual concern. Prompted, in part, by fear of such excessive Roman dictates some leading German churchmen (e.g., Döllinger) balked at the doctrine of papal infallibility. Other theologians, too, largely trained at state universities rather than church-controlled seminaries, even if personally not outright "modernists," grew up in the climate of historical-critical scholarship and were deeply impressed by the nationalist orientation of German historiography. Father Schell actually expected the Teuton spirit to regenerate the whole church and to lend it a degree of inwardness unachieved by Latin nations.[30]

Latin Catholics, and especially Italians, on the other hand, often considered Catholicism as the true expression of Latin culture. The constant succession of Italian popes, the predominance of Italians in the College of Cardinals, and the papal residence on Italian soil seemed to bear out this claim. Leo XIII himself vented his grievance against newly united Italy by pointing out in 1882:

> The truth is that Italy owes it to the Roman pontiffs that her glory has gone abroad to distant peoples, that she has sustained the repeated attacks of barbarians, that she has repulsed the dreaded Turk, that she has so long preserved in so many things her just and lawful liberties, and enriched her cities with so many immortal works of art. And it is not the least of the services of the popes that the various provinces of Italy, differing as they do in character and in customs, have been kept united by a common faith and a common religion, and free from the most fatal of all sources of discord.[31]

Only the catastrophic outcome of the Second World War, which definitely relegated Italy to the position of a lesser power, has forced the papacy to broaden the College of Cardinals so as to embrace a non-Italian majority. Pius XII's assurance (in his Christmas Allocution of 1945) that Italy would not "suffer any loss of prestige; rather will she be resplendent in the eyes of all people as sharing in this greatness and this universality" offered little comfort to confirmed Italian nationalists.

These Italian attachments, however, and problems of papal sovereignty involved the church in political conflicts little germane to its religious calling or ecclesiastical organization. Throughout modern history the popes acted both as spiritual leaders of a world-wide church and as sovereigns of a small state, a dichotomy which they were not always able to reconcile. In the crucial Thirty Years' War, which ultimately checked all further progress of the Counterreformation, Urban VIII extended but lukewarm support to the main Catholic powers of Spain and Austria, for he feared the Habsburg aspirations in Italy and their possible domination over the whole church. Only when the war was reaching a stalemate did the Jesuits vigorously agitate against the unavoidable negotiated peace and subsequently pope after pope protested in vain against the tolerant provisions of the Treaty of Westphalia. Pius VII's far-reaching and dangerous concessions to Napoleon I can likewise be explained only by his desire to regain his possessions at almost any cost. Napoleon reminisced later on St. Helena, "I never gave up hope, sooner or later by one or another means, to gain control over the pope. And after that what influence! What lever of opinion for the rest of the world!" [32] We know that ultimately the pope proved the real victor. But in 1801 no one could foresee this outcome, made possible only by Moscow and Waterloo.

A few years later, during the final settlements at the Congress of Vienna, papal policy was again torn between these conflicting loyalties. The pope extended but equivocal support to Johann Wessenberg's all-German reform movement or even to his own secretary of state, Cardinal Consalvi, who worked for a concordat with a strong Germanic Confederation. The papal administration preferred its envoy to concentrate on his main job, "the recovery of the dominions of the Holy See," leaving the ultimate arrangements in Germany to subsequent negotiations with individual states. It agreed with Consalvi's method of procedure, however, graphically described in one of his earlier dispatches: "One takes what one can get, and protests about the rest." [33]

In the following decades the agitation for Italy's unification brought to a head the simmering conflict between Italian nationalism and the papacy. Having given up the ancient dream of unifying the peninsula under their own leadership, the popes were now forced into the unenviable position of obstructing the realization of its legitimate national aspirations. During the critical period of 1849-71 the Catholic hierarchy rallied around its chief. Never before had so many pilgrims, including church dignitaries, gathered at the See of St. Peter to lend it their moral and financial support. Two hundred bishops assembled for the definition of the dogma of Immaculate Conception in 1854. Eight years later two hundred seventy-five bishops appeared at the canonization of the Japanese martyrs. In 1867 the celebration of the eighteen hundredth anniversary of the martyrdom of Peter and Paul attracted to Rome 500 bishops, 20,000 other priests, and 120,000 Catholic laymen. Cardinal Antonelli's call in 1859 for volunteers to defend the Papal States led to the formation of an international pontifical brigade, 15,000 strong. The French government, unmindful of the national interests of both France and Italy, pledged its honor in 1867 that Rome would "never" be occupied by the Italian king. When this declaration was read in the French Chamber two hundred deputies chanted in unison, "Never, never!" [34] Three years later Garibaldi marched into Rome and proclaimed it the capital of the unified kingdom.

Curiously, the Italian clergy put up no resistance to unification; certainly none comparable with that of their French compeers. The papacy as such, however, long rejected all offers at amicable settlement and repudiated the Law of Papal Guarantees wherewith the new Italy had hoped to safeguard its interests. Acrimony rose to such a high pitch that on Pius IX's death in 1878 the cardinals seriously debated the holding of their conclave in another Catholic country. The new pope, Leo XIII, even entertained the idea of temporary expatriation paralleling the medieval exile to Avignon. In numerous letters to the Austrian emperor, Francis Joseph, long hidden away in secret archives, he asked, with ever-increasing urgency, for Austrian hospitality. He paid little heed to the likely complications for the imperial government, at a time when liberal parties were in control of Parliament and the recently concluded Triple Alliance with Germany and Italy had become a cornerstone of Austria's foreign policy. Although the emperor succeeded in evading the issue, he failed to repay a visit of his Italian ally because he could not come to Rome without hurting papal sensitivities. When, to undermine the Triple Alliance, President Loubet of France visited the Italian king in 1904, his visit called forth a papal protest followed by a storm of clerical opposition in the Chamber and the rightist press. Such "unpatriotic" disparagement of a shrewd diplomatic move was one of the final incentives to separation. This curious anomaly, more embarrassing to foreign monarchs than to the king of Italy, was swept away by the storms of the First World War and the subsequent social revolution, with which the Vatican could not possibly make common cause. In his encyclical *Pacem Dei munus pulcherrimum* of May 23, 1920, Benedict XV gave up his objections to the visits of crowned Catholics. He merely made the reservation that "this concession, which seems counseled or rather demanded by the grave circumstances in which today society is placed, must not be interpreted as a tacit renunciation of its sacrosanct rights by the Apostolic See." Similarly the prohibition forbidding Catholic voters to participate in national elections, often repeated and but slightly relaxed in 1904 and 1909, was repealed in 1919, after many Catholic leaders had in vain objected to their country's alliance with "godless" France and schismatic Russia.[35]

The Italian crown retaliated by shutting the Vatican out of all international gatherings. When in 1899 Czar Nicholas II initiated the Peace Conference at The Hague, he envisaged full participation by the Holy See. But the Dutch government, acting as host, could not issue the invitation because of Italian opposition. Similarly, on joining the Allies in 1915, Italy exacted the definite pledge that "France, Great Britain and Russia shall support such opposition as Italy may make to any proposal in the direction of introducing a representative of the Holy See in any peace negotiations for the settlement of questions raised by the present war." Some papal representatives ultimately entered the Paris peace negotiations through the back door, in connection with issues affecting Catholic missions, but they could not directly influence any major decision. Repeated efforts of English, Brazilian and other Catholic groups to the contrary, Italy succeeded also in blocking formal papal collaboration with the League of Nations which had looked very promising during President Wilson's dramatic visit to the Vatican in 1919. This enforced absence may, in the long run, have spared the papacy its share of responsibility for the League's downfall. But in the early years it merely emphasized the contrast between its temporal weakness and its great international mission. Even when in the Lateran Treaties of 1929 Pius XI finally renounced all temporal claims to territory outside of Vatican City, he was induced by "our noble sovereign and his incomparable minister" (the pope himself so styled the king and Mussolini in his Christmas Allocution of 1938) to sign the pledge that the Holy See

> wishes to remain and will remain extraneous to all temporal disputes between nations and to international congresses convoked for the settlement of such disputes, unless the contending parties make a concordant appeal to its mission of peace; nevertheless it reserves the right in every case to exercise its moral and spiritual power.[36]

There is no record of any such concordant appeal since Italy embarked upon her policy of retaliation, which sharply contrasts with the papacy's frequent earlier successes in arbitrating international disputes. In 1885, for example, it had effectively helped settle the acrid controversy between Germany and Spain over the possession of the Caroline Islands.

If the ramifications of the "Roman Question" thus seriously interfered with the papacy's active co-operation with international political bodies, its dogmatic intransigence prevented it from participating in international undertakings under religious auspices. Such collaboration would have implied some recognition of the relative merits of other denominations. To be sure, Napoleon's minister of cults, Portalis, in his peroration before the French legislative body in 1802 could cite many authorities in support of his contention that "Catholic priests could not preach intolerance without offending reason, violating the principles of universal charity, rebelling against the laws of the Republic, and placing their conduct in opposition to the laws of Providence." But a few decades later Lamennais and others were traditionally on safer ground, when they glorified the Inquisition, then re-established in Spain by French troops, and contended that "toleration was a violation of the law divine." Cardinal Manning, too, voiced majority sentiment when, among the twenty-one canons to be adopted by the Vatican Council, he included also an anathema on all persons believing "that men can be saved by the profession of any faith." Although anathemas had lost much of their pristine vigor, this threat reflected the church's unflinching condemnation of all other creeds as fundamentally erroneous. Under these circumstances it could collaborate with a heathen state much more readily than with an "heretical" Christian Church.[37]

That is why, in 1878, when William Gladstone thought of organizing a world church, he anticipated and received greater response from the Russian, than from the Roman Church. The same negative attitude was maintained in regard to such mixed assemblies as the Parliament of Religion, attendance at which was forbidden to Catholics by Leo XIII, despite the implied censure of Cardinal Gibbons, who had addressed the Chicago session of 1893.[38] It persisted after the First World War when, under the leadership of Robert Hallowell Gardiner, a group of Protestant churchmen attempted to convoke a "world conference on faith and order." To establish the preliminary contacts three delegates visited, in 1919, many European capitals including Rome, which they considered a logical meeting place for the conference. The pope was to serve as chairman. But though courteously received by the pontiff, the delegates were handed a clean-cut refusal, buttressed by references to similar negativistic decisions dating from the years 1864-96. The Swedish pastor delegated in 1925 by Archbishop Nathan Söderblom of Upsala to invite Pius XI to the forthcoming Stockholm "World Conference on Life and Work" was bluntly informed by the pope that, while the cónference was to be a congress of seekers, the church had long found the truth. Pius XI thus summed up not only the long-accepted church doctrine, but also his own eloquent restatement thereof in the encyclical *Ubi arcano Dei* of December 23, 1922. Even more clearly he defined this negative attitude in the encyclical *Mortalium animos*, issued on January 6, 1928. "The Unity of Christians," he declared, "cannot be otherwise obtained than by securing the return of the separated to the one true Church of Christ from which they once unhappily withdrew." Even when the Second World War had already begun to cast its shadows upon the Continent and the Oxford and Edinburgh conferences of 1937 tried to forestall it by the united forces of organized religion, the Catholic Church persevered in its policy of splendid isolation. It paid no heed whatsoever to such fervent appeals as were made from the House of Lords by Archbishop Temple of Canterbury. "There are some things more sacred than peace," the archbishop had said, "and these must be defended. If his Holiness would give the lead, I can promise that all the leaders of the Anglican, Orthodox and Protestant Churches would give their support." The papacy refused to lead.[39]

4. Fascism and Communism

The Roman Church was by no means blind to the menace of totalitarian nationalism. The very Lateran Treaties inspired little confidence in view of the fascist regime's long record of broken promises and general fascist political ethics. To allay widespread fears the pope could only emphasize his reliance on the legitimacy of his claims, the conscience of the Italian people, and the foreign demonstrations of sympathy "so solemn, so grandiose that they replaced and immeasurably surpassed all guarantees which we might have desired." No one was surprised, therefore, when within two years a sharp conflict broke out about the interpretation of the treaties and the rights of laymen organized for "Catholic action." The church felt once again the truth of Lord Acton's observation about the perennial enmity to the church of modern absolutist regimes. "In France, Spain and Germany, by Gallicanism, Josephinism and the Inquisition, she came to be reduced to a state of dependence, the more fatal and deplorable that the clergy were often instrumental in maintaining it." Certainly none of these early absolutist regimes approximated fascism's totalitarian claims and practices. The doctrine of *sacro egoismo*, moreover, ran counter to the very fundamentals of Christian ethics. Long before her adoption of nazi racialism in 1938 fascist Italy's exaggerated patriotism evoked Pius XI's memorable encyclical *Ubi arcano Dei* (1922).

> Patriotism [the pope wrote]—the stimulus of so many virtues and of so many noble acts of heroism when kept within the bounds of the law of Christ—becomes merely an occasion, an added incentive to grave injustice when true love of country is debased to the condition of an extreme nationalism, when we forget that all men are our brothers and members of the same great human family, that other nations have an equal right with us both to life and to prosperity, that it is never lawful nor even wise, to dissociate morality from the affairs of practical life, that, in the last analysis, it is *justice which exalteth a nation: but sin maketh nations miserable* [Proverbs 14: 34].[40]

If the papacy and the Catholic Church in general were not even more vocal in their condemnation of this frightful new threat to the doctrine of brotherhood of man, indeed to the entire Christian civilization, this was largely due to their overpowering fear of communism. Throughout the nineteenth century even those Christian-socialist groups which wanted to secure the reign of social justice on the basis of Christian, or more specifically, Catholic teachings, repudiated Marxism and, especially, Marxist materialism. Only under the Weimar Republic did social democracy's great advance induce a few Catholic leaders (e.g., the circle around the *Rhein-Mainzer Volkszeitung*) to look for harmonization. They cherished the hope that, by joining the movement, they might infuse it with Catholic spirituality. Organized German Catholicism, however, represented by the Center party, collaborated with the Socialists only in political and economic fields, but drew a sharp line of demarcation in areas affecting the general conception of life or education. In most other countries no restraints were necessary. Invoking Pius IX's sharp condemnation of communism in 1846, the subsequent popes continued to denounce the "untenableness of socialism and similar errors." At the same time they searched for new solutions to mitigate the ever-sharpening class struggle. The encyclicals of Leo XIII, *Rerum novarum* (1891), and Pius XI, *Quadragesimo anno* (1931), are memorable documents of stirred-up public conscience during the last half century. But, unable to remedy that "great scandal of the nineteenth century that the church lost the working class" which Pius XI regretfully conceded, they merely aggravated an already deep-rooted conflict.[41]

The Communist Revolution in Russia brought the conflict to a head. The effect of its antireligious policies on the Catholic minority was summarized by a Catholic observer in 1931:

> Within the territorial limits now controlled by the Soviet power, there were, in 1917, the year of the Bolshevik Revolution, 614 Catholic churches in operation; today 182 remain. In addition, there were 581 chapels; today not one remains. There were 896 priests; today 110 are at liberty while 200 languish in bolshevik prisons. The remainder have perished from privation and starvation or have been exiled and executed.

Mutual hostility was further aggravated by the hereditary antagonism between Rome and the Eastern schism. The ancient Polish-Russian controversy now precipitated the Russo-Polish War of 1920. Notwithstanding its keen disappointment with Poland's excessive appetites, the papacy was forced actively to support the Polish cause. Similarly, Lithuania's self-designation as the "northern defense guard of Catholicism" was accepted by Pius XII with the exhortation that she make herself worthy of that task "even if sacrifice should become the necessary price for the affirmation and realization of such an ideal." [42]

The threat of world revolution, moreover, and the spread of communist propaganda to Italy endangered the very citadel of the Roman Church. Personal experiences of the two great pontiffs, whose policies determined the church's attitude since 1922, underscored this undisguised hostility. As papal nuncio, Msgr. Achille Ratti was the only foreign diplomat to remain in Warsaw in 1920, ready to face the approaching Red Army. Though spared this painful experience, he lived too long in the terror-stricken atmosphere of the Polish capital not to carry with him that deep emotional dread of communism which, quite apart from all rational considerations, was to color his policies as Pope Pius XI. Monsignor Eugenio Pacelli, on the other hand, served as nuncio in Munich under Kurt Eisner and witnessed the new regime's antireligious fervor. His friends from the Bavarian People's party filled his ears with fearsome tales of persecution which to a world as yet unhardened by nazi atrocities must have appeared as stark tragedies. These impressions left an indelible imprint upon the mind of the subsequently influential papal secretary of state and present Pope Pius XII. Nor could all members of the pope's entourage, including cardinals permanently residing in Rome, entirely escape the impact of the constant anticommunist exhortations of fascist propagandists.

The result was that, casting aside their customary diplomatic restraints, pope after pope sharply denounced communism as the source of "dreadful horrors" (Benedict XV) and as "the first, the greatest and most widespread menace" (Pius XI). World Catholicism, under papal leadership, collaborated with the fascist dictators in the Spanish Civil War. Even after the nazi occupation of Czechoslovakia, Pius XII broadcast a message to "heroic Spain" in which he extolled it as the nation which "chosen by God as the principal instrument for the evangelization of the new world, and as the impregnable bulwark of the Catholic faith, has given the loftiest proof to the champions of the materialistic atheism of our age, that above everything stand the eternal values of religion and the spirit." [43]

In the subsequent months the Vatican's efforts to secure an amicable settlement of the Danzig controversy and a general rapprochement between the Axis and Britain, France and Poland lost all efficacy because of the underlying anticommunist bias. Unwittingly they thickened that atmosphere of mutual suspicion which led to Stalin's nonaggression treaty with Hitler and thus to the immediate outbreak of the war. It was perhaps the greatest tragedy of our era that the two major genuinely international movements, Catholicism and communism (or what the Nazis chose to call the Black and Red Internationals), through their mutual hostility largely neutralized each other's efforts in combating excessive nationalism.

It stands to reason that, were it not for this overpowering fear of communism, the Catholic Church would have more effectively counteracted the spread of the new paganism. True, before 1933 German bishops frequently warned their flock against nazi preachments. The Mayence administration, especially, ordered in 1930 that no member of the National Socialist party be admitted to the usual sacraments. A nazi Gauleiter was refused church burial. Somewhat later (February 10, 1931) the Bavarian bishops formally declared that "what national socialism calls Christianity is no longer the Christianity of Christ." Even after Hitler's rise to power Cardinal Schulte of Cologne ventured to teach publicly that "it is heathenism and apostasy from Christ and Christianity" to view blood and race as essential elements of religion. He also dared to publish this statement in the official bulletin of his archdiocese (March 1, 1934). Cardinal Faulhaber of Munich publicly defied the nazi interpretation of the Old Testament and the Teuton antiquities. An organization of Catholic Nazis (*Arbeitsgemeinschaft katholischer Christen*), organized by von Papen as a counterpart to the Protestant "German Christians," died of inanition and was officially dissolved in the fall of 1934.[44]

In other countries, too, after the initial period of hesitation, Catholic leaders found memorable words of condemnation for the new doctrine. Pius XI's encyclical of 1937, *Mit brennender Sorge*, particularly gave classical expression to the deep apprehensions of men of all faiths. The unusual circumstances of its publication emphasized the feeling of urgency that permeates its text. Written in German, it was smuggled into Germany and speedily distributed in hundreds of parishes before the first copies were seized by the Gestapo. On Palm Sunday millions of German Catholics simultaneously listened to the moving injunctions read from the pulpits.

He who takes the race [the pope declared] or the people, or the state or the form of government, the bearers of the power of the state or other fundamental elements of human society—which in the temporal order of things have an essential and honorable place—out of the system of their earthly valuation, and makes them the ultimate norm of all, even of religious values, and deifies them with an idolatrous worship, perverts and falsifies the order of things created and commanded by God. Such a one is far from true belief in God and a conception of life corresponding to true belief. . . . Only superficial minds can lapse into the heresy of speaking of a national God, of a national religion; only such can make the mad attempt of trying to confine within the boundaries of a single people, within the narrow blood stream of a single race, God, the Creator of the World, the King and Lawgiver of all peoples before Whose greatness all peoples are as small as a drop in a bucket.

These sentiments were speedily echoed in other lands, as when the American hierarchy meeting in Washington in November, 1937, voiced the universal sense of outrage "by the Satanic resourcefulness of these leaders of modern paganism and by the incredible excesses committed by them in their attempt to exterminate religion and to blot out from the minds of the German people all true knowledge and love of God." [45]

Not until after the nazi invasion of the Soviet Union, however, did it dawn upon influential circles at the Vatican that nazism might indeed be the greater menace.

Atheist bolshevism [observed at that time an unnamed high prelate to a correspondent of the New York Times] is less preoccupying for the reason that, although it has forcibly eliminated God, man cannot live without believing in a superior being. On the other hand, nazism has replaced God with a pagan theory which, though it does not meet his spiritual needs, yet gives him something to look up to.[46]

But there is no evidence that this had become the prevailing opinion even then.

Earlier the pope and his German advisers tried to appease the nazi regime by snubbing Cardinal Faulhaber and reinstating a clergyman suspended for preaching a pronazi sermon. The papacy itself concluded with Hitler a concordat, for the first time covering the whole Reich rather than its member states. This compact, allegedly intended to supplement the existing treaties with Prussia, Bavaria and Baden, was ruthlessly infringed upon by the Nazis even before its final ratification. Throughout the six prewar years pious German Catholics, though slightly more resistant to nazi inroads than their Protestant compatriots, bent their heads before the onrushing wave. An occasion to suffer religious martyrdom, unparalleled for generations, was allowed to pass without producing any significant number of genuine witnesses to the superiority of the spirit over the flesh. Some Catholic priests and laymen were put into concentration camps, but the controlled press, in part nominally Catholic, had no difficulty in persuading the Catholic public that these prosecutions had been instituted on other than religious grounds. Certainly during the war, despite the regime's unrelenting persecutions, the majority of German Catholics rallied behind Hitler, totally forgetful that in such cases rebellion would have been their sacred duty.[47]

Most astonishingly, nazi propaganda gained Catholic adherents abroad, despite the availability of unbiased information concerning the nazi onslaught on their faith. Even in the United States Coughlinism was not recognized for what it truly was, a profound betrayal of Catholicism. Collaborationist priests like Father Forestier, chaplain of the French Scouts, argued that "to obey is to submit to the reason and to the will of the legitimate chief with the conviction that he is nearer to the truth than oneself." In Franco Spain and Argentina nazi and fascist doctrines were harmonized with the Spanish Catholic tradition. Harking back to the Spanish Inquisition, such Argentinian writers as Cesar E. Pico (leading representative of the *Cursos de Cultura Catolica*) have spoken of "the Kingdom that has been promised to the violent." Violent suppression of democratic liberties had, in their opinion, the "penitential" quality of punishment for the sins of unchristian democracy. The same government, which on December 31, 1943, had restored Catholic religious instruction in public schools and whose apologists had preached the state's submission to religious authority even in temporal matters, also directed schoolteachers in June, 1944, to hold special classes devoted to the discussion of such nationalist propositions as:

> The Fatherland is always right.
> Argentina has a liberating and teaching mission: it has an
> inalienable right to exercise a directing function in Latin America.
> Whoever denies this is an enemy of the Fatherland.
> To be worthy of our traditional leadership we must live arrogantly.

Coughlinites and Argentinian nationalists uncritically swallowed also the nazi antisemitic arguments, notwithstanding the Holy Office's condemnation of antisemitism in 1928 and Pius XI's solemn warning ten years later against "a movement in which we Christians can have no part whatsoever. . . . Spiritually we are Semites." [48]

5. THOMISTIC IDEALS

Notwithstanding these serious lapses into nationalist frenzy, the church as such has constantly adhered to its international outlook. Romantically exaggerating the beauties of the past, popes and Catholic teachers have frequently glorified the medieval system as the pinnacle of human achievement. Contrasting Christendom's medieval unity with the breakup of modern civilization into hostile sovereign nations, they implicitly appealed for the restoration of that unity.

> No merely human institution of today [wrote Pius XI in 1922] can be as successful in devising a set of international laws which will be in harmony with world conditions as the Middle Ages were in the possession of that true League of Nations, Christianity. It cannot be denied that in the Middle Ages this law was often violated; still it always existed as an ideal, according to which one might judge the acts of nations, and a beacon light calling those who had lost their way back to the safe road. . . .
> It is therefore to be hoped [he added half a year later in a special encyclical on St. Thomas] that the doctrines of Aquinas concerning the ruling of peoples and the laws which establish their relations with one another may be better known, since they contain the true foundations of that which is termed the "League of Nations."

Thomistic philosophy has been considered by Catholic apologists as the only fountainhead of truthful thinking, as the "perennial" philosophy in contrast to the transitory modern philosophic systems. After the conclusion of the Lateran Treaties, Jesuit teachers tried to replace instruction in Kantian and Hegelian philosophy at Italian colleges by indoctrination in the philosophy of the "Angelic doctor." Here and here alone, in their opinion, "philosophy and religion, though distinct, are marvelously co-ordinated and, far from combating each other, coëxist on the basis of most perfect harmony." [49]

Feeling itself the proud possessor of the truth eternal, whose fundamentals were rooted in divine revelations and whose important ramifications had long since been authoritatively stated by a great galaxy of "infallible" popes, ecumenic councils and inspired teachers, the Roman Church faced the perplexities of the modern world with comparative calm. It had undoubtedly traveled a long way from the days of the Wars of Religion, when it protested any concession to heretics and when, in the opinion of zealotic advisers of Maximilian I of Bavaria, it could without much ado abrogate any pledges of toleration given them under the stress of circumstances.[50] It had also greatly toned down its opposition to freedom of speech which, as late as 1791, Pius VI condemned as "a monstrous law, contrary to the law of the Creator." But it could not help persisting in its objections to the modern implications of "liberty of conscience." In his comments on the Lateran Treaties Pius XI made it perfectly clear that absolute freedom of conscience would never be accepted by the church. "This would be tantamount to saying that the creature is not subject to the Creator; it would be tantamount to legitimizing every form, or rather deforming, of conscience, however criminal and socially disastrous." In a Catholic state, therefore, the pope concluded, "liberty of conscience, and of discussion ought to be understood and practiced in accordance with the Catholic doctrine and law." In this sense Hilaire Belloc voiced regnant Catholic opinion, lay as well as ecclesiastical, when he climaxed his diatribe on the "crisis of our civilization" by exclaiming, "Therefore does it remain true that we shall only recover a moral society . . . if we also recover the general spirit of Catholicism. In other words, you will not remedy the world until you have converted the world." [51]

Though excluded from international political bodies at Italy's insistence and from international church bodies by its own intransigence, the Roman Church has exerted great international influence. In 1834 Ranke, a keen student of papal history, claimed that the papacy had reached the end of its great historic career. But he failed to take into account its extraordinary adaptability to changing conditions. Some seventy years later William Barry, a Catholic professor of theology, surveying the great strides made by the church under the vigorous leadership of Leo XIII, asserted with greater justification that "when all is said, the nineteenth century leaves the church visibly stronger than she was a hundred years ago." Helped by its own unique constitutional structure, it succeeded, though mostly after a period of hesitation and theoretical adjustment, to make its peace with any existing form of government. In the fifteenth century John Gerson observed that the church had successfully combined the three major governmental forms known from Aristotle's classical division. In the pope it possessed a monarchical head, in the College of Cardinals an electoral and administrative aristocracy, while in its councils it had the nucleus of democratic representation. One might add that the basic equality of opportunity within the clergy and the possibility for a poor farmer's boy to ascend the throne of St. Peter had long opened the gate to reconciliation with a democratic world. In this sense Leo XIII's designation of the church as a "Christian democracy," often repeated by the American hierarchy, was more than sheer rhetoric. Its meaning was fully elaborated in the 1944 Christmas Allocution of Pius XII, with obvious reference to the defeat of the Axis and the growing world trend toward democracy.[52]

In recent years, to be sure, the church had not yet seen its way clear to a complete and sincere agreement with the ever-growing socialist movements. The latter's professed "godlessness" and the apparent instability of Russia's communist regime before the war, surrounded as it was by a world of enemies and but a few uncertain friends, largely accounted for this delay in finding some real *modus vivendi*. The halfhearted attempts of the papal Chancery to secure some agreement with the Soviets during the Genoa Conference of 1922 merely underscored its subsequent deviations when it supported almost any form of anticommunist crusade, even if propagated by out-and-out Fascists and Falangists. Not until the antireligious nazi persecutions did church leadership get an inkling of the dangers to its own survival arising from such alliance with reactionary forces. Judging from past experience, however, one may expect that, in the face of the Soviet regime's proved stability and diminishing godlessness, some new efforts will soon be made by the papacy to reach an understanding with both the Soviets and whatever new order will emerge from the debris of war-torn Europe. The great Catholic parties in France and Italy have already adopted strongly socialist programs. Such understanding will be further facilitated if the Vatican will utilize wisely—and there is no reason to doubt its doing so—its moral prestige in a generation suffering from the sharp dichotomy between idealistic aspiration and imperialistic practice. One already hears G. A. Borgese, himself anything but a partisan of "political Catholicism," decry the whittling down of the great promises of the Atlantic Charter and contrast it with the Holy See's championship of the cause of the vanquished and the neutrals. "Hence the political prestige wielded today by the Roman curia, unequaled perhaps since its medieval culmination, with the paradox of the Lilliputian and thoroughly unmechanized Vatican state growing to be the one power with which the victors may have to come to terms." [53]

In wielding this unquestionable moral influence the church is greatly aided by its unflinching adherence to what it considers the mainsprings of the law of nations.

> There exists [wrote Pius XI in 1922] an institution able to safeguard the sanctity of the law of nations. This institution is a part of every nation; at the same time it is above all nations. She enjoys, too, the highest authority, the fullness of the teaching power of the Apostles. Such an institution is the Church of Christ.

We may disagree with this narrower concept in lieu of the broader foundations of international law as rooted in the general Judeo-Christian-Muslim tradition, which was conceded by Pius XI himself in his famous declaration that "spiritually we are Semites." Many of us may also cherish a different conception of history. We may believe that, for instance, the foremost Thomistic principle in international relations based on the respect due by all nations to "natural law" is outworn today. But we shall certainly not consider outworn the much older principle of justice, not even in Leo XIII's homiletical interpretation that "justice derives life from faith, *iustus ex fide vivit.*" Especially so, if justice be mitigated by the other ancient principle of charity. There is no question that, by holding fast to the combination of both, the church may yet furnish powerful antidotes to the excesses of modern nationalism and contribute to the establishment of a true and lasting peace which, to quote again Pius XI citing Aquinas, "is more a matter of love than of justice." [54]

Chapter V

PROTESTANT INDIVIDUALISM

UNLIKE the Catholic Church, the Protestant denominations have no all-embracing ecclesiastical authority. Some Protestants object to the very term "Protestantism" as the only common designation of their numerous sects, for it seems to imply negativism and divisiveness.[1] Even the international church gatherings between the two World Wars merely underscored the national divisions, for they did not consider the setting up of international organs endowed with compulsory authority over the constituent national groups. Leading German churchmen viewed them as mere traps intended to captivate the German people for the ideology of the League of Nations, which they, largely belonging to the "national opposition," considered but a cloak for Western imperialism.

Absence of international organization often placed the Protestant churches before the alternative of either total otherworldliness or compromise with nationalism. On the one hand, there was concentration on Christian mysticism and complete separation between state and church, not only organizationally but as the counterpart to widespread sectarianism. Separation was also germane to the very idea of religious individualism which underlay the Protestant revolt against the authoritarian medieval church. Even Luther started from the premise of strict delimitation of state versus ecclesiastical power, recognizing state as supreme in its own domain and thereby giving up the medieval church's postulate of Christianizing it. On the other hand, by more than a coincidence, the Reformation came at a time when medieval nationalism celebrated its major victories. While French Gallicanism found a way of remaining within the Roman fold, most other national revolts against papal control, especially in non-Latin countries, led to complete separation from Rome. The new, increasingly competitive Western economy, which, in the political sphere, led to the rise of both economic individualism and "mercantilistic" nationalism, marked in the religious domain the breakdown of Catholic solidarity and the ideological supremacy of the "just price." The interrelations between Protestantism and capitalism have been the subject of extensive discussions during the past half century. The complementary relationships between Protestantism

117

and modern nationalism, though subjected to but incidental scholarly examination, are equally undeniable.

Vernacular Bible translations and liturgies, used by entire congregations rather than specifically ordained mediators, became both a reflection of and a stimulus for cultural nationalism. Similarly, the new organizational forms mirrored national preferences in the area of political organization. Before long, the new ecclesiastical bodies derived much strength from the support of princes, if they were not altogether converted into autonomous agencies of government. The very absence of a hierarchy dependent on extraterritorial authority and the removal of the sacramental distinction between laity and clergy opened the road to the influx of lay, i.e., predominantly nationalist, ideologies and the control by lay, i.e., predominantly state, organs.

1. LUTHER AND CALVIN

Long before the Reformation, secular authorities started impinging upon ecclesiastical jurisdiction. "In England the later state church is discernible in the early fifteenth century. Henry V has virtually anticipated Henry VIII as head of the national church." A duke of Cleve is reported to have said during the Basel schism that he was "pope in his own lands." Luther himself may have considered collaboration with friendly princes as an emergency measure (*Notrecht*), become necessary by the political repression of his religious preachment. He was, nevertheless, driven thereby to increasing recognition of the scholastic doctrine of the state as a necessary remedy to sin. Sharing early Christian pessimism concerning human nature and calling the world a "Satan's inn," he admitted that its redemption may well require the suppression of evil by a state directed by grace divine. He even went beyond Wyclif's paradox of God who "must in this matter obey the devil." By explaining the origin of secular authority (as a "divine instrument") along family lines, Luther included it under the sanctions of the Fourth Commandment. "From the household," he declared, "emerges the city which is nothing but an agglomeration of houses and families. From cities arises the principality, from principalities the kingdom which encompasses them all." [2]

Luther's was not a tolerant brand of religion. Fervently convinced of the truth of his doctrine, he protested against the repressive measures of Catholic princes. His famous declaration of April 18, 1521, "Here I stand, I cannot otherwise, God help me, Amen," has been relegated by modern critics to the realm of legend. But his authentic statement, "I neither may nor will revoke anything, for to act against one's conscience is hard, unwholesome and dangerous," could have served as an equally resounding clarion call to liberty of conscience. He also opposed the long-propagated war against the Turks for, in his opinion, conversion of infidels was none of the emperor's business. With the typical inconsistency of zealots, however, he considered it a primary duty of Protestant princes to outlaw the Catholic mass. Before long he and his followers began calling on the secular arm to eliminate the more radical sectarian movements. By 1532 he formally agreed with his Wittenberg theological confreres that execution of Anabaptists was perfectly legal. Nor did he object to the emperor's abuse of imperial power in the defense of religious convictions, but rather to these convictions as such. "We know," he contended, "that he [the emperor] is not sure thereof and cannot be sure, for we know that he errs and militates against the Gospels. . . . But he is in duty bound to recognize the word of the Lord and to promote it with all his might, as we do." In fact, having repudiated the authority of the church or, to quote his medieval terminology, "It is from the pope that I tear the sword, not from the emperor," Luther had to delegate to the state supreme powers in the suppression of evil.[3]

Luther's assault on the papacy forced him to an alliance with German princes at the price of far-reaching concessions to their political ambitions and their greed in appropriating ecclesiastical domains. Riding on the crest of the rising nationalist revolt against the papacy's universal control, he also became one of the chief molders of early German nationalism. Of course, he shunned the idea of breaking Christendom asunder along national lines even more than that of replacing it by a multitude of competing sects. He never relinquished the hope that, through a new universal council, the long-sought-for "reformation" of Christian doctrine and ecclesiastical organization would re-establish the pristine purity of the church universal. But early in his career he realized that his recognized predecessors, Wyclif and Huss, had owed much of their success to their appeal to their compatriots' national loyalties and that he, too, would have to marshal Germany's resources behind his ideals.

That is why he addressed in 1520 his *Open Letter to the Christian Nobility of the German Nation concerning the Reform of the Christian Estate.* With obvious reference to the Reich's oft reiterated, essentially nationalistic *gravamina* (grievances) against Rome, he explained that

> the distress and oppression which weigh down all the Estates of Christendom, especially of Germany, and which move not me alone, but everyone to cry out time and again, and to pray for help, have forced me even now to cry aloud that God may inspire some one with His Spirit to lend this suffering nation a helping hand.

Apart from fiscal exploitation, he deeply resented the papal claim of supremacy over the empire, the humiliation of the emperor kissing the pontiff's feet and, generally, the purely nominal control exercised by the empire over the body of Christendom. He knew that his people was held in low esteem by its neighbors. "Italy calls us beasts," he declared in one of his "Table Talks" of 1532, "France and England ridicule us, as do all other countries." The "superior" attitude of the papal negotiators, therefore, and their treatment of

Germany as just a recalcitrant province of the church added fuel to his growing resentment. "These ungodly windbags," he exclaimed, "the Prierias, Caietans and their associates, call us Germans fools, simpletons, beasts, barbarians, and laugh over the incredible patience with which we allow ourselves to be cheated and robbed." In answer thereto he constantly extolled the virtues of the German people and finally came to believe that "un-German" and "barbarian" were synonyms.[4]

Less consciously nationalistic in its conception, though in the long run of far greater national influence than these irate exclamations, was Luther's German translation of Scripture. Vernacular Bible translations had long been considered major instruments of reform. Erasmus of Rotterdam, especially, had insistently demanded the translation and extensive popularization of Gospels and Pauline Epistles. All those who wished to appeal from the Catholic tradition to the revealed word of God found that, by directly translating the original Hebrew or Greek texts, they undermined many canonical interpretations of the Vulgate and cut through the maze of exegetical material which had overgrown it in the course of centuries. Indirectly, however, the German public's immediate acceptance of the Saxon chancery language in Luther's translation made possible the subsequent evolution of a uniform German literature which, more than any other single factor, paved the way for ultimate German unity. In the quarter century of 1522 to 1546 the sales of Luther's Bible or sections thereof approximated one million copies. Noteworthy by itself in view of the then widespread illiteracy, this figure is doubly remarkable when one considers that a copy of the New Testament alone sold for one and a half guilders, the "price of a horse." In this sense Luther unwittingly became the real "prophet of the Germans," which high-sounding title he assumed at times to spite his enemies.[5]

Though fully appreciating the richness of regional customs and folklore and, on the other hand, consistently viewing the Holy Roman Empire as a supranational, universal entity, Luther constantly laid stress on the authority of emperor and Diet in all German ecclesiastical affairs. That is why he demanded that his case be adjudicated in Germany rather than Rome and spoke with great pride of the defense of his cause "in Worms before the emperor and the whole empire." He insisted that in certain cases, which clearly belonged to the ecclesiastical jurisdiction, "it might be possible for the primate of Germany to maintain a general consistory, with auditors and chancellors . . . which should be the final court of appeal for German cases." He and his associates of the Nuremberg Diet of 1524 and the League of Schmalkalden also believed that some German city would be the most suitable place for the universal church council whose convocation they insistently demanded.[6]

Under the stress of circumstances, however, Luther's political struggles greatly contributed to the weakening of Pan-German unity. Having failed to secure imperial support, he had to fall back on the individual princes who began to matter most in German political life. Ultimately his preachment helped embroil Germany in an endless series of internecine religious wars, from which she emerged in 1648 as a loose federation of sovereign states, each claiming a specific national character and proving to be a major obstacle to final unification. Ecclesiastically, too, Luther's increasing reliance on the state moved him to sanction the Saxon decree of 1527 which established a regular state organization in control of the new church.[7]

By thus recognizing the state as supreme in its own domain, Luther was led to preach the doctrine of extreme civil obedience. Abandoning the Reformation's revolutionary mainsprings he declared that "the secular empire cannot exist without inequality in persons, that some be free and some in bondage, some masters and some subjects." He demanded, in the name of religion, acquiescence in the existing state of affairs, for "God's Kingdom is a kingdom of grace and mercy, not of wrath and punishment. . . . But the kingdom of the world is a kingdom of wrath and severity. In it there is only punishment, repression, judgment and condemnation, for the suppressing of the wicked and the protection of the good." Despite occasional remarks on the insufficiency of princely power and its dependence on the Lord's inscrutable will, he considered all authority as "God's genuine instrument" and state service on a par with "divine service." With evident reference to contemporary "monarchomach" trends among both Catholic theorists and Protestant sectarians, he condemned tyrannicide as a heathen practice reflecting the pagan quest for human happiness by means of a worldly regime. Before long he, the peasant's son, sided with the princes and nobles against the rebellious German peasantry and, in 1525, published his vehement pamphlet, *Against the Robbing and Murdering Hordes of Peasants*.[8]

In this fashion, driven by circumstances, Luther paved the way for that quietistic, "patriarchal" doctrine of monarchical power which secured, and theologically justified, overwhelming state control over ecclesiastical affairs. It ultimately enabled Prussia to issue in 1817—ironically on the very three hundredth anniversary of Luther's defiant nailing of the *Ninety-Five Theses* on the church doors of Wittenberg—a decree forcing Lutherans and Calvinists to unite. "Everyone could 'adhere to his own faith,' but he was bound to form a single church with men who, according to his faith, were nothing but heretics." Had not Luther's early disciples repudiated Calvinism as a heresy worse than those of Nestorius and Mohammed? It also made possible, more recently, Hitler's all too effective threat to both churches of withdrawing the state's financial support if they disobeyed his dictates.[9]

Calvinism, on the contrary, began with the founder's radical use of state power and ended with the formation of the least politically controlled churches in the history of Christendom since 313. From the outset John Calvin and his followers were far more internationally minded than Luther and his disciples. To be sure, as a born Frenchman, Calvin resented the empire's overbearing claims to universal leadership and generally repudiated the idea of universal monarchy as "most absurd." His own experience also taught him that larger states were less manageable than smaller republics and more inclined to increase their wealth by conquest and extortion. His genuinely international aims were, nevertheless, reflected in his program envisaging the creation of churches all over the world, united not by a hierarchy but by a single Protestant doctrine. His correspondence embraced most Western countries and his influence was, even in his lifetime, Continental in scope.[10]

At the same time Calvin betrayed little of Luther's leaning toward cultural nationalism, although, far beyond Luther, he recognized national differences as a part of the divine scheme of existence. He thus justified the need of peculiar local laws and rituals, for "one nation is more prone than others to some particular vice, unless it be most rigidly restrained." After having taken "the Jewish nation into his special charge, patronage and protection," he also explained, God had enacted the Mosaic law only for the benefit of Jews, with "special regard to their peculiar circumstances." Hence the Christian world was no longer bound by it. But Calvin himself was not a nationalist. A native of France who had become ruler of Geneva, he wrote his famous *Institutes of the Christian Religion* in answer to the repressive policies of Francis I. They were intended, he declared, as an apologia for his French brethren, "whose death was precious in the sight of the Lord," and in order to excite some sympathy for them "in foreign nations." Despite deep-rooted local Swiss patriotism, on the other hand, glorified in the preceding wars of independence and the legends of Tell and Winkelried, no one spoke yet of a separate Swiss nationality, resembling in any way that of other German- or French-speaking areas.[11]

Calvin's political loyalty to Geneva, therefore, had none of the earmarks of political nationalism. Like most other centers of the Reformation, his Geneva was, in some respects, but a link in the perennial struggle of city against bishop, but it was not, as was Luther's state, a political entity outside the church. Under his leadership it became a regular theocracy. Geneva's notorious intolerance, and especially the provisions that citizens refusing to participate in local worship be subject to banishment, evidently inspired Rousseau's extreme demands for a national religion. But while in Rousseau's scheme it would have been the state, in Calvin's it was the church that had supreme authority. For he believed that "no government can be happily constituted, unless its first object be the promotion of piety and that all laws are preposterous which neglect the claims of God, and merely provide for the interests of men." [12]

At the same time Calvin preached loyalty and submission to civil authority, which was "equally as necessary to mankind as bread and water, light and air, and far more excellent." Obedience should spring not only from fear of civil punishment, but also from the fear of the Lord. "We ought to regard them [the princes] as vicars and lieutenants of God whom one cannot resist without resisting God himself," declared the Confession of Faith of 1536, ". . . all Christians are in duty bound to pray to God for the welfare of their superiors and the princes of the lands in which they live." This principle applied also to tyrannical princes, for every people had the rulers it deserved.

> For, though the Lord testifies that the magistrate is an eminent gift of his liberality to preserve the safety of men, and prescribes to magistrates themselves the extent of their duty, yet he at the same time declares that, whatever be their characters, they have their government only from him; that those who govern for the public good are true specimens and mirrors of this beneficence; and that those who rule in an unjust and tyrannical manner are raised up by him to punish the iniquity of the people; that all equally possess that sacred majesty with which he has invested legitimate authority.[13]

These injunctions sound very much like Luther's, but with a significant difference. Calvin never quite abandoned the medieval doctrine of the social compact. In his very formulation of tyrannical rulers we detect an echo, however faint, of the medieval distinction, evidently shoved aside by Luther, Melanchthon and Zwingli, between a good monarch and one who was either a *tyrannus quoad exercitium* (he who abused his rights) or a *tyrannus quoad titulum* (he who usurped authority). In his homilies on the Book of Samuel, especially, Calvin caught some of the latter's antimonarchical spirit and raised the question of constitutional resistance. "Inasmuch as kings and princes," he declared, "pledge their faith to the peoples by an oath that they would administer the law with perfect justice, sincerity and integrity, it is fair to ask, whether, if they break the faith, usurp tyrannical power and permit themselves everything, the people may not themselves consult together and apply a fit remedy to that evil." In his *Institutes*, written under the impact of French persecutions, he had to defend the conscientious resisters. He was thus led to his famous formulation of both the right and obligation of duly elected magistrates, municipal or provincial, to take up the cudgels in behalf of oppressed constituents. Since these magistrates, too, represented authority by the will of God, he taught, they might, by divine ordinance, be called upon to serve as "public avengers," punish unrighteous rulers and deliver a people unjustly oppressed. That this was not sheer theory was evidenced in the contrasting attitudes of the Wittenberg and Geneva theologians to the rebellious inhabitants of Magdeburg. Although professing Lutherans, the latter were severely criticized by Melanchthon for resorting to active resistance, but they found considerable sympathy in Geneva.[14]

Of course, in Calvin's formulation this doctrine still had an aristocratic sound, for most municipal authorities in his day stemmed from patrician classes. But by giving considerable leeway to duly elected magistrates of any kind it unwittingly opened the gate to democratic and revolutionary ideologies. Widely and avidly read, Calvin's works (fully 74 editions in nine languages of the *Institutes* and 435 various editions of one or another of his works are known to have been published before the founding of New England) thus served as a constant source of inspiration to a multitude of liberation movements, both domestic and international.[15]

Unbeknown to the chief protagonists, the main cause of separation between Lutheranism and Calvinism was the difference in their ethical and social, rather than in their strictly theological doctrines. Connected with the former was the divergence, even less conscious, between Luther's intrinsic nationalism and the internationalism propagated from Geneva. In its triumphant march through Western Europe, Calvinism also had to overcome so many political obstacles that rebellion as a sacred duty became one of its dominant religious principles, far outstripping the parallel Catholic teachings of Suarez and Vittoria. Ultimately West European Protestantism, though at first resulting in the establishment of the Church of England and other state-controlled churches, was instrumental in spreading the doctrines of religious toleration, then of complete liberty of conscience and, finally, of separation of state and church.[16]

2. RELIGIOUS AND CIVIL WARS

The Reformation and, in its wake, the Counterreformation contributed greatly to the rise of both modern nationalism and internationalism. Unlike cosmopolitanism or even Catholic universalism, internationalism is, of course, but a function of nationalism, presupposing the existence of fully conscious nationalities. The great Wars of Religion at first sharpened the old international conflicts, for they superimposed on them the ruthlessness of religious fanaticism and the fratricidal venom of civil wars. But though frequently ending in mutual exhaustion, they released so many new energies and helped shape so many new ideologies that, together with the other social forces emerging from the age of geographic and technological discoveries, they wove the main patterns in the fabric of the modern era.

Lutheranism's acquiescence in princely control and Calvinism's aristocratic theocracy failed to stem the powerful revolutionary trends which had come to the fore in the numerous minor sectarian movements. While the two leading reformers undoubtedly played down the "social gospel," others (e.g., Luther's colleague, Andreas Bodenstein von Carlstadt and Thomas Münzer) ardently preached social as much as religious reconstruction.[17] Among the numerous sources of popular disaffection, national oppression loomed ever larger. By adopting or adhering to a different creed many a nationality could now redouble its resistance to the forces of amalgamation by the dominant group.

The Dutch War of Liberation clearly pursued both national and religious aims. Reformatory hatred of Spanish Catholicism and the Inquisition reinforced the struggle for independence which proved successful only in the seven northern provinces where Protestantism had made the greatest inroads. In the southern provinces Catholicism, aided by the Habsburg regime, continued deeply to influence the people's political thinking. A fully conscious Belgian nationalism was awakened much later, as a reaction to Joseph II's Germanizing efforts and the French revolutionary regime. It flowered forth in 1830 to break apart the newly reconstituted unity of the Netherlands and to erect the sovereign kingdom of Belgium. But long before that time incessant religious strife, international as well as domestic, convinced Hugo Grotius, a Dutch student of both law and theology, of the necessity of developing a new rational and secularized legal system, applicable to both national law and the law of nations.

In the Scandinavian countries, too, Sweden's separation from Denmark, with which she had been united by the Union of Kalmar of 1397, was greatly facilitated by the Reformation. While both countries became predominantly Lutheran, the ambitious Christian II began using the Reformation as a means of strengthening the royal power. Even after his downfall in 1523 and another decade of great inner disturbances, the Diet of Copenhagen of 1536 declared Lutheranism the state's official religion and invested the king with the dignity of supreme bishop. This evolution greatly strengthened Danish national unity, but naturally antagonized the Swedes. In 1523, three years after the fateful "Stockholm massacre," Gustavus Vasa was elected king of Sweden. The Lutheran Swedish crown, too, soon assumed full control over ecclesiastical affairs and gradually "nationalized" all ecclesiastical property. The national separation of the two Scandinavian lands thus became an irretrievable historical fact.[18] Within a short century Sweden became the Reformation's most effective champion on the European Continent, the meteoric career of Gustavus Adolphus demonstrating the extent to which such championship could also be utilized for purposes of national aggrandizement.

In Bohemia-Moravia the old Hussite traditions prevented the Czechs from wholeheartedly embracing Lutheranism. They felt that, in all essentials, Luther's critique of Catholicism had been anticipated by John Huss and his disciples who had already repudiated the abuses of papal government, the compulsory celibacy of priests, the veneration of saints, images and relics, the church dogmas of transubstantiation and the purgatory, the sacraments of confirmation and extreme unction, and the use of Latin and liturgical vestments in worship. These heterodox currents, driven underground by the imperial victories over the Taborites and crushingly defeated in 1620, nevertheless nurtured the Czech national spirit among the peasants and made possible its great revival in the nineteenth century. The leading Czech historian, František Palacky, himself a descendant of secretive Bohemian Brethren, glorified the Reformation as the climactic achievement of Czech national culture. Thomas G.

Masaryk, too, the father of the new Czechoslovakia, spoke the mind of many of his fellow nationalists when he declared, almost as a matter of course, that the Bohemian ecclesiastical revolution had initiated the modern period in Europe.[19]

Curiously, the closely related Slovaks, living under Hungarian domination, saw in stanch adherence to Catholicism an effective barrier against denationalization. Similarly the Rumanian shepherds in Transylvania clung firmly to their Greek Orthodox creed as well as to their national language and mores. Even George Rakoczy I's instructions to the bishop of Bihai in 1641 to preach to them in Rumanian so that they "be led from the darkness of superstition to enlightenment," [20] failed to induce them to abandon their ancestral faith. At the same time the Germans living in Hungary adopted for the most part the Lutheran version of the Reformation, while the Magyars themselves were more apt to follow its Calvinist forms. Debreczen, focus of Hungarian Calvinism, long was the center of the Hungarian national movement as well. Despite the successes of the Counterreformation, backed by Habsburg power, strong vestiges of both Calvinism and Lutheranism have remained in the substantial Protestant minority of modern Hungary.

Catholic resistance as an eminent means of national preservation was also demonstrated by papal leadership of the Counterreformation which, though in many ways complicating, in the long run promoted Italian unification. Certainly Spain's new world role of chief defender of the faith helped satisfy many national aspirations abroad and went a long way in forging an all-Spanish national consciousness at the expense of the traditional Castilian, Aragonese and other regional loyalties. It also gave the crown an overpowering control over the church, approximating in practice, if not in theory, that of the French monarchy.[21] Perhaps only Spain's ultimate defeats, combined with its internal economic backwardness and lack of communications, helped salvage enough of Catalan and Basque distinctiveness to flower forth in separatist movements in the new era of nationalist extremes.

French national unity, on the other hand, just achieved at the beginning of the modern period, was now tottering under the blows of internal religious strife and an essentially anti-Catholic foreign policy. At first Calvinism, itself in many respects an offshoot of French Gallicanism, made tremendous gains. The Venetian ambassador to France, as most of his colleagues, a keen observer, wrote home in 1561 about the unbelievable "influence and the great power which the principal minister of Geneva, by name Calvin, a Frenchman and a native of Picardy, possesses in this kingdom." He predicted that "religious affairs will soon be in an evil case in France because there is not one single province uncontaminated." In 1562, two years before Calvin's demise, Coligny enumerated more than two thousand Reformed Church congregations in his country.[22] Internationally, too, the rulers of France entered strange alliances with "infidel" Turks and "heretical" German princes against the Spanish and Austrian Habsburgs. Only utter ruthlessness culminating in the revocation of the Edict of Nantes, abetted by an otherwise enlightened absolutism, a long efficient bureaucracy, progressive "mercantilist" policies and frequent military successes, restored religious and, with it, also national unity.

While in their struggle against the Habsburgs the French often made use of the Protestant loyalties of their German, Swedish or Dutch allies, in their perennial controversies with England they appealed with greater consistency to the anti-British animus, both national and denominational, of the Irish and French Canadians. Catholicism has always been a mainspring of Irish nationalism. Under the Stuarts Anglo-Catholics themselves, acting in the interest of their own church, stirred up Irish resentment. Later again many Englishmen helped awaken Irish national consciousness by invoking British religious and civil liberties. "The question is not," fulminated Henry Grattan, "whether we shall shew mercy to the Roman Catholics, but whether we shall mould the inhabitants of Ireland into a *people*: for as long as we exclude Catholics from natural liberty and the common rights of man, we are not a *people*: we may triumph over them, but other nations will triumph over us." Similarly French-Canadian resistance to amalgamation with their Anglo-Saxon neighbors always had a religious coloring. In his *Declaration Addressed in the Name of the King of France to all the Ancient French in North America*, published in Boston in 1779, Count d'Estaing urged the French Canadians to join the American Revolution by emphasizing their immemorial ties with the French in their common blood, language, customs, and especially religion.[23] The British forestalled that alliance only by granting the French Canadians, in the Quebec Act of 1764, not only full religious liberties but what was tantamount to the establishment of the Catholic Church as the colony's official religion.

Curiously, religious liberty as such could also become a driving force in modern nationalism. In England, Luther's writings began to be read widely as early as 1518. Erasmus himself had sent the *Ninety-Five Theses* to Colet and, in all, eight works of the reformer were translated into English under the reign of Henry VIII. Soon thereafter Calvin's *Institutes* and Bible commentaries became best sellers.[24] Although in its religious teachings and rituals deviating less radically from Catholic patterns, the Church of England likewise handed over the chief episcopacy to the king and nationalized all ecclesiastical property and administration. In all these respects the English Reformation differed but little from the similar interplay of religious and nationalist developments in Germany or Scandinavia.

However, England's traditions of parliamentary and civil liberties strongly operated against her becoming a regular autocracy, despite the unusual succession of monarchs, both gifted and ambitious. Her new economic needs and opportunities also drove her unto the road of a Commercial and Industrial

Revolution, which heralded the coming of the individualistic and freedom-loving "economic man." In subtle intermingling with these political and economic factors, growing religious diversity and individualistic "dissent" undermined all long-range possibilities of authoritarian ecclesiastical control. The union with predominantly Presbyterian Scotland and the evident inefficacy of oppressive measures in Catholic Ireland clearly revealed also the external limitations of the Anglican state church as a nationally unifying force. Only immemorial respect for individual rights prevented this religious disparity from becoming in that religiously enthusiastic age a permanently divisive national force. This mutual respect was now extended to the liberty of religious conscience, especially after the dissenters' temporary victory in the Puritan Revolution.

This type of nationalism differed essentially from all Continental forms. Cromwell's national feeling, rightly comments a recent biographer, was toward a "community decided not by blood, but by faith . . . by adoption and grace after the manner of the Old Testament. . . . It is therefore a nationalism which runs easily and naturally into internationalism." We recall how, a century later, Edmund Burke elevated the British constitutional liberties, including checks and balances between the state church and dissenting groups, to a cornerstone of his nationalist credo. Had not Montesquieu's discerning eye already detected that the English knew "better than any other people upon earth how to value at the same time these three great advantages, religion, commerce and liberty"? This extraordinary combination of religious, economic and political liberties has ever since characterized the English brand of nationalism and its various offshoots in the English-speaking world.[25]

Its climactic form was, naturally enough, achieved in the United States, where dissent was the rule rather than the exception. As early as the 1650's the Dutch West India Company, though restricting public worship to members of the Dutch Reformed Church, had admitted Lutherans, Mennonites, Quakers, Catholics and Jews to its colony of New Amsterdam. In 1663, shortly before surrendering it to the British, the company reprimanded its intolerant governor, Peter Stuyvesant, for banishing a Quaker. It pointed out the benefits of Amsterdam's moderate religious policies which had brought a "considerable influx of people." William Penn's widely advertised proposals to attract new settlers included the promise of religious liberty. Although religious intolerance was still rampant in New England and the southern colonies, the latter living in dread of their Spanish neighbors, liberty of conscience made noteworthy progress in Rhode Island, New York, New Jersey and Pennsylvania. William Gordon, later pastor in Roxbury, Massachusetts, observed on his arrival in Philadelphia in 1770, "how Papists, Episcopalians, Moravians, Lutherans, Calvinists, Methodists and Quakers could pass each other peaceably and in good temper on the Sabbath, after having broke up their respective assemblies."

During the Revolution mutual toleration became the theme song of American nationalism. In his famous Election Sermon before the Connecticut Assembly of 1783, Ezra Stiles, revolutionary preacher and president of Yale College, considered one of the chief reasons for the "future glory of the United States" the fact that

> the Church has never been of any political detriment here, for it never has been vested with any civil or secular power in New England, although it is certain that civil dominion was but the second motive, religion the primary one, with our ancestors in coming hither and settling this land.[26]

Truly, this was the most famous historic instance of religious dissent leading to the establishment of more or less self-governing colonies, from which ultimately emerged the most powerful nation on earth.

From its inception American nationalism, even more pronouncedly than that of Cromwell, bordered on internationalism. Long before Jefferson, Jonathan Edwards eloquently discoursed on Providence's having intended America to be the "glorious renovator of the world." The English dissenter, Richard Price, going far beyond Burke, published in 1784 his penetrating *Observations on the Importance of the American Revolution and the Means of Making It a Benefit to the World*. Believing that God had chosen the Americans to teach the world a lesson in simple, just and egalitarian living, he exclaimed, "O distinguished people! May you continue long thus happy; and may the happiness you enjoy spread over the face of the whole earth!" [27]

Apart from thus furnishing it a semireligious feeling of chosenness Protestant denominationalism made significant practical contributions to the rise of American nationalism. The great cultural heterogeneity of settlers in the thirteen colonies and their diverse, often competitive economic interests threatened to disrupt their unity as soon as the war was over. Andrew Burnaby, an earlier English traveler in North America, had hopefully observed that "fire and water are not more heterogeneous than the different colonies in North America." There were, indeed, strong forces at work trying to vest all sovereignty in the states, loosely tied together in a nominal federation. Here the experiences of various churches, which had long attempted to co-ordinate their work through central or regional bodies, served as both stimulus and model for the creation of federal institutions. Clergymen of various denominations, chief molders of public opinion at that time, eloquently expounded the necessity of preserving national unity through vigorous central organs. John Witherspoon, president of the College of New Jersey (Princeton), asked in and out of Congress:

> For what would it signify to risk our possessions and shed our blood to set ourselves free from the encroachments and oppression of Great Britain, with a certainty, as soon as peace was settled with them, of a more lasting war, a

more unnatural, a more bloody, and much more hopeless war, among ourselves?

He demanded that Congress be given the authority of regulating commerce and levying duties from imported articles. Lay leaders, too, had often gathered their first experience in Continental co-operation while working for their churches. "Alexander Hamilton," writes Edward Frank Humphrey, "was able to produce American financial unity only after he had assisted at the unification of first his church and then his political government." [28]

Thoughtful revolutionary leaders realized that their nation owed its very being to religious disparity and the ensuing need of religious freedom. Witherspoon asserted that fear of a Catholicism established along the lines of the Quebec Act had helped cement the different religious groups into a united belligerent people. Even more biased was, in the presence of numerous loyalist dissenters, the report of the Rev. Charles Inglis of Trinity Church in New York (1776):

> Although civil liberty was the ostensible object, the bait that was flung out to catch the population at large and engage them in the rebellion, yet it is now past all doubt that an abolition of the Church of England was one of the principal springs of the dissenting leaders' conduct; and hence the unanimity of dissenters in this business.

Nevertheless, liberation from the religious control by king and Parliament often served as an added incentive. Time and again Presbyterian leaders contended that "there is no example in history in which civil liberty was destroyed and the rights of conscience preserved entire." Writing under the pseudonym "The Landholder" during the heated controversies over the ratification of the Federal Constitution (1787) Oliver Ellsworth of Connecticut, later chief justice of the United States, commented on the injudiciousness of any religious test for public office. "If it were in favor of either Congregationalists, Presbyterians, Episcopalians, Baptists or Quakers, it would incapacitate more than three-fourths of the American citizens for any public office; and thus degrade them from the rank of freemen." [29]

3. Language and Education

Curiously, what in America and England was achieved by religious freedom and democracy came about in Germany through a combination of military force, cultural nationalism and religious Erastianism. Rousseau's statement to a Catholic friend about the differences between their respective creeds, "Yours is founded upon submission, and you submit. Mine is founded on discussion, and I reason," [30] essentially reflected only Western Calvinistic realities. Luther's successors had largely abandoned the freedom of discussion demanded by their master and fully submitted to authority. In a sort of neo-scholastic doctrine, they justified the existence of three permanent social classes, the princely, clerical and lay, the former exercising by grace divine full control over both state and church. The Lutheran ministry became a pillar of strength for both absolutism and particularism. The bloody Wars of Religion had taught the German people to get along without empire and emperor, and to see its destinies governed by the interests, ambitions, even whims of its regional rulers. *Kleinstaaterei* and *Landeskirche* now became the main features of German public life. Even such Catholic monarchs as Joseph II held undisputed sway over all, except the strictly spiritual, phases of church government.

This atomization of the country into several hundred sovereign principalities, often in alliance with foreign powers against their German neighbors, seemed to run counter to any feeling of an empire-wide German nationalism. Goethe was not the only German who, himself neither Austrian nor Prussian, rejoiced in Frederick the Great's victories over the "imperial" army. Utter failure of all such attempts at religious reconciliation as suggested by Leibniz increased the ordinary subject's readiness to turn from the divisiveness of a religiously heterogeneous Reich to the relative unity and domestic peace of each particular regime. Only in his dreams could even a nationalist like Herder hope that Germany, which had "unhappily divided itself in the century of the Reformation," would someday "have for its mind and heart a national religion, the religion of Christ." It made little difference whether Prussian recruiting officers interrupted the sermon of Gottfried Arnold, the famous Pietist, and carried off all young men for military service, or whether Frederick William I respected the pacifist conscientious objections of some Eastern Prussian Mennonites, whose industrial contributions he valued more highly. It was always the absolutist prince who made the final decision. The Protestant clergy accepted this situation, Pastor Hahnzog's *Patriotic Sermons* (1785) being fairly typical of its regional loyalties. The German people was, indeed, on the road to falling apart into a number of diverse nationalities. Many a state patriot rationalized his opposition to German unity, as did the jurist Johann Stephan Pütter in 1786, by saying that "from earliest times Germany was inhabited by various peoples which may have had a common ancestry . . . but which ordered their own affairs in complete freedom and independence." [31]

Nevertheless, there were powerful forces at work, including religious Pietism, which fostered an all-German nationalism. By teaching religious enthusiasm and the individual's mystic union with his Creator, Pietism not only salvaged German religious feeling from its threatening petrification under overweening state control, but also set the pattern for the national enthusiasm and irrationalism that was to color so deeply all German nationalist thinking in the nineteenth century. Its doctrine of *Wiedergeburt*, of complete rebirth through inner conversion, set the pace also for national regeneration during the Wars of Liberation. The Pietist poet, Klopstock, lent memorable expression to the new German messianic feeling. From the school of Pietism emerged also such early German nationalist thinkers as Herder and the Mosers (father and son). The elder Moser's religious rationale for his German patriotism is typical of the whole group. His concern with Germany arose, he declared, because

> (1) the history of our German Empire had a particular influence on the history of all other Christian states; (2) because Germany is the home of the Reformation and in later times of the Zinzendorf movement [Pietism]; and, finally, (3) because it appears that Germany and its evangelical church have in many respects a particular distinction in the history of the reign of Jesus on earth.[32]

Pietism also laid great stress on the national language and popular education. The same Johann Jakob Moser wrote also a special treatise, *On the Right of the German Language*, showing its close relationship to the old German liberties. Herder rhapsodized on its being an "original language. No one can rob it of that dignity." Johann Georg Hamann, enlightened rationalist turned Pietist, spoke exaltingly of the "sacrament of language." Believing in its truly divine origin ("it was second to none among the works of creation"), Hamann developed a comprehensive psychological theory explaining linguistic peculiarities by the differences in national mentality.

> If our ideas [he wrote] emanate from the attitude of the soul, and the latter, according to many, is determined by the physical constitution, the same may be applied to the body of a whole people. The forms of its speech will correspond to its mode of thought. Every people reveals the latter through the nature, form, rules and mores of its speech, just as much as through its external culture and the exhibition of its public activity. The dialect of the Ionians has been compared to their dress, and the legalism of the Jewish people, which rendered it so blind at the time of the divine visitation, is fully revealed in its language.

Protestantism in general, by abandoning the Vulgate and Latin liturgy, had long met more than halfway these new linguistic aspirations. But after the Wars of Religion man became more fully conscious of the deep interrelations between language, religion and patriotism. Once again it was a Hamann paradox that most clearly expressed this nexus. "The love of one's fatherland," he declared, "is naturally related to its *parties honteuses*: I mean, the mother tongue and the mother church." [33]

National language and literature became, indeed, the main unifying forces in German history. Because Pan-German unity necessarily defied the established particularist regimes, a sharp cleavage arose in the minds of intellectual leaders between political and cultural nationalism. Some became outspokenly unpatriotic. To mention only the three greatest poets: Lessing tolerated patriotism at best as a "heroic weakness I gladly dispense with." Schiller, as late as 1789, cavalierly dismissed interest in one's fatherland as important only for immature nationalities. Young Goethe, reviewing in 1772 a book on patriotism by Joseph von Sonnenfeld, wrote: "Roman patriotism! God save us from it as from a giant's stature! We could not find a chair to sit on, a bed to lie in." A native of Frankfort and minister of the Duke of Weimar, he rejoiced in the spectacular achievements of Frederick the Great. "We were *Fritzisch*," he explained, "for what interest did we have in Prussia?" Even in his old age he persisted in admiring Napoleon in the face of the great anti-Napoleonic frenzy which had seized most of his compatriots. In his letter to Jacobi of 1788, Wilhelm von Humboldt, later a leading Prussian statesman, lightly dismissed all political questions and considered currents of opinion, character building, mores, etc., as the "only genuinely national" problems.[34] No sooner, however, did this combination of rationalist cosmopolitanism and cultural nationalism, aided by the petty states' revolutionary defeats, prove victorious, than it lost most of its cosmopolitan rationalism and, in the romantic movement, inherited much of Pietist irrationalism and mysticism.

Across the ocean, too, American nationalism expressed itself more and more in the linguistic "Americanization" of new arrivals. Gentle pressure of public opinion, rather than governmental enforcement, persuaded, for instance, the Dutch Reformed churches to adopt English versions of their liturgy. Their synod of 1788 graphically explained that "the English language is our national tongue and is making progress, and has already been adopted wholly or in part in worship in most of our congregations, and the rising generation seem to be little acquainted with the Dutch tongue." The English-speaking divines extolled the growing diffusion of their language as a great national as well as humanitarian achievement. "The rough sonorous diction of the English language," prophesied Ezra Stiles in his Election Sermon, "may here take its Athenian polish, and receive its Attic urbanity, as it will probably become the vernacular tongue of more numerous millions than ever yet spake one language on earth." [35]

There was an essential difference, however, between such voluntary "Americanization" of uprooted individuals or groups and the forcible denationalization of long-established minorities through the public school which, though often more annoying than efficacious, became a common practice in the mixed areas of Central and Eastern Europe. In his influential *Ideas on National Education*, published in 1804, Friedrich Zöllner advocated German instruction in order both to develop a national spirit among the German pupils and gradually to replace the Polish and Lithuanian languages in Prussia's eastern districts. For the most part annexed during the preceding eleven years, these districts were nearly one-third of the whole kingdom! Continental nationalists of all denominations also felt that secularization of education necessarily implied its transfer to state control. The nation, they believed, was entitled to indoctrinate its youth with national ideals, just as the church had long indoctrinated it with religious ideals. In his *Essai d'éducation nationale*, published in 1763, Louis René de Caradeuc de La Chalotais insisted that every nation had "an inalienable and imprescriptible right to educate its members." We recall how great a role educational reform had played also in Rousseau's and Fichte's nationalist programs.[36]

Official church leadership, understandably enough, bitterly resented the intrusion of secular education, though it evinced little positive interest in popular education and, on the whole, preferred to develop an intellectual elite holding sway over uneducated masses. Frederick the Great had many ecclesiastical sympathizers when he declared that "le vulgaire ne mérite pas d'être éclairé." In his Cabinet Order of 1769, however, he insisted that "the necessary provisions be made . . . for the children of farmers and villagers to receive more rational and effective instruction in religion, so that their intellect become more enlightened and they be taught better notions concerning their duties." Notwithstanding its obvious authoritarian implications this program found much support among the Pietists who, truer to the spirit of Luther and the early reformers, wished to see the word of God taught to all men and women from early childhood. J. J. Hecker's famous *Generallandschulreglement* of 1763, which laid the foundations for the memorable evolution of Prussia's public school system, was partly inspired by the author's Pietist views.[37]

English and American nationalism, based upon democratic freedoms, naturally presupposed extensive popular education. We recall Jefferson's proud assertion of the American farmer's familiarity with Homer. "Liberty and learning," stated Simeon Howard in a typical Election Sermon (1780), "are so friendly to each other and so naturally thrive and flourish together, that we may justly expect that the guardians of the former will not neglect the latter." Long before Jefferson established the State University of Virginia, a feat he considered on a par with his authorship of the Declaration of Independence, Howard also insisted that, "as it is of great importance to the community that learning and knowledge be diffused among the people in general, it is proper that the government should take all proper measures for this purpose—making provision for the establishment and support of literary schools and colleges." Other religious and lay leaders, however, distrusted state control of education, Joseph Priestley declaring that "education is a branch of civil liberty, which ought by no means to be surrendered into the hands of the magistrate; and that the best interests of society require, that the right of conducting it should be inviolably preserved to individuals." They preferred a rather unilateral arrangement by virtue of which the government would assume all obligations to promote religion and culture, but have no rights whatsoever in directing or controlling the minds and consciences of its citizens. It would be amply rewarded, they believed, by the general benefit of having a religious and cultured citizenry. This point of view essentially prevailed in the Anglo-Saxon countries throughout the nineteenth century and found its classical expression in the Supreme Court's decision against the state of Oregon.[38]

The religious and democratic mainsprings of modern mass education derived great incidental gains from the peoples' growing familiarity with ancient Hebrew and Greek prototypes of ethnic-cultural and religious nationalism. From the Old Testament armory were taken most of the missiles hurled against the divine right of kings. Cromwell led his armies into battle reciting verses from the Old Testament. President Samuel Langdon of Harvard, after citing the classical antimonarchical passages in the Book of Samuel, exclaimed, "The Jewish government, according to the original constitution which was divinely established, if considered merely in a civil view, was a perfect republic." New England Puritans saw in *Moses, his Judicials* by John Cotton an illustration of the ancient Hebrew constitution serving as a model for America. In fact, Cotton's treatise was published in London in 1641 under the characteristic title *An Abstract of the Lawes of New England, As They are Now Established.* "American Israel" became a common phrase, Ezra Stiles stating that all Americans "came hither certainly from the northeast of Asia; probably also from the Mediterranean; and if so, that they are Canaanites, though arriving hither by different routes." Langdon interpreted even America's world responsibility in terms of the divine warning to Israel, "You only have I known of all the families of the earth: therefore I will punish you for all your iniquities." We have here a repetition of that extraordinary Hebrew combination of a "chosen people" bearing a universal responsibility. For such a people political sovereignty appeared but secondary to the truly paramount religious and cultural values.[39]

The Old Testament significantly influenced also cultural, if not political, nationalism in Germany. Luther himself had tried to minimize its importance and to point out the transitory nature of its law. But the German Calvinist, Johannes Althusius, cited it abundantly, laid great stress on the Decalogue and generally admired the Hebrew law and form of government. Among the masses, too, familiarity with the Bible exceeded that with German letters. The founders of the Pietist movement, particularly Philipp Jakob Spener and August Hermann Francke, were diligent students of Hebrew. Despite manifold persecutions, Francke's Collegium Philobiblicum in Leipzig became an important center of independent nationalist thinking. The distribution, within sixteen years, of some 435,000 copies of Scripture by the Canstein Bible Institute, founded in 1712 by one of Spener's disciples, helped greatly to popularize also contemporary Pietist teachings. Many readers undoubtedly learned therefrom the great liberal and nationalist lesson, as proclaimed by Herder:

> For it is what all men have desired, what all wise leaders have tried to accomplish, and what Moses alone and at so early a period had the heart to

realize, namely—that law and not the lawgiver should rule, that a free nation should freely accept and willingly obey the invisible, rational and benevolent power which governs us but does not fetter and chain us.[40]

These nationalist developments came to a climax in the period of the great revolutions. The English Revolution from Cromwell to William and Mary brought about the first full self-realization of English nationalism. The American Revolution paved the way for the new, unique American form of national feeling. The French Revolution, finally, released all the long-accumulating nationalist energies not only in France but throughout the Continent. René Gillouin's apt observation that "the Renaissance was tantamount to the declaration of the rights of man; the Reformation to that of the rights of God" [41] may be extended to the revolutionary era which, with unprecedented vigor, reasserted the rights of nationality.

4. Schleiermacher

Among the chief exponents of the German philosophic answer to the challenge of French nationalism was the great Protestant theologian, Friedrich Daniel Ernst Schleiermacher. His childhood and youth were spent in Frederick the Great's declining years and during the first revolutionary stirrings in Germany. In his middle years he actively participated in the enthusiastic Stein-Hardenberg reform era, whose chief protagonist, Karl vom Stein, was his close friend and admirer. He also partook of the great exaltation of the Wars of Liberation. The last two decades of his life, finally, he spent in the overheated atmosphere of the romantic Teutonomania which gripped Germany under the counterrevolutionary aegis of the Holy Alliance. He was thus able to absorb, and, in his resourceful mind, creatively to reshape the rich and variegated experiences of this eventful historical period. Brought up by a stern father of unflinching orthodoxy [42] and a loving mother of deeply touching piety, he forgot neither the heritage of generations of traditionalist Reformed pastors nor the deep Pietistic imprint of the years spent at the Brethren's school in Herrnhut. At the same time he was a keen student of Spinoza and the German idealistic philosophy. Before long he became not only Germany's most popular preacher but also its leading theologian; one who combined deep religious fervor with philosophic reasoning and keen awareness of national realities. Since his influence was felt far beyond the boundaries of his fatherland, his attitude to political and cultural nationalism is representative of a significant section of Protestant opinion.

Unlike the thinkers of the Enlightenment era and even of German idealism, he used as a starting point not humanity, but God. He believed that God reveals himself in different ways to different peoples. In one of his patriotic sermons, he declared:

Every human institution, in so far as it essentially and genuinely mirrors the spirit of a people, is just as much law divine and revelation of divine power and majesty as were that law and those orders to which the people of the Old Covenant had given that name. For it is God alone and immediately who assigns to each people its peculiar calling on earth and imbues it with its peculiar spirit so that He may glorify himself by each in its peculiar way.

Through this formula Schleiermacher reconciled many contradictions—sympathetic observers may call them polarities—in his conception of life. Originally he had been, like Fichte, an admirer of the French Revolution. Even later he combined advocacy of a true, a "monarchical," monarch and glorification of the Hohenzollern dynasty with a sufficient dose of democratic convictions to be counted among the dangerous "demagogues" by the omniscient police of the Holy Alliance. But he could conscientiously repudiate any imitation of French revolutionary methods in Germany, or what he called "the unfortunate fraud of emulation," by referring to the peculiarities of the German national character. As early as 1793 he confessed to his father that, although disapproving "of all the human passions and exaggerated ideas that have been mixed up with it" (he particularly deplored Louis XVI's execution), he "heartily sympathized" with the French Revolution. But, he added, he was not "seized by the unhappy folly of wishing to imitate it and of desiring the whole world to be remodeled according to *that* standard." In later years he repudiated the medieval doctrine of the state as "a necessary evil," and considered it an essential part of "Christian morality" to refrain from any act of disobedience toward established authority, be it only in the form of passive resistance. If unable to compromise, he stated, the conscientious Christian ought to "withdraw" from the state (Schleiermacher failed to elaborate this equivocal advice) and to suffer quiet martyrdom—or else to emigrate. A convinced believer in religious toleration and a preacher "of liberty of the spirit and the right of conscience," championship of which he considered the greatest humanitarian service ever rendered by Germany, he nevertheless admired King Frederick as one of those "celestial personalities" sent by God to guide the destinies of men. Nor did he see any conflict between his recognition of overwhelming state power and his demand that religion, as well as science, family and social intercourse, should be removed from governmental control.[43]

Of course, Schleiermacher did not preach separation of state and church. He merely realized, as did Luther but not the later German ecclesiastical leaders, that too close an interlocking of the religious and political organizations would in the long run accrue to the benefit of neither. "Such constitutional regulation of political existence," he declared in his famous *Discourses on Religion* of 1799, "affects religious society like the horrible head of a Medusa; everything petrifies as soon as it appears." In practice, however, he often conceded the omnipotent Prussian bureaucracy great ecclesiastical authority. Just as his postulate of independent science did not prevent him from actively collaborating in the establishment of the State University of Berlin, so he never opposed Prussia's strong governmental regulation of Protestant affairs. He was coresponsible for the Union Law of 1817 which imposed upon two historically grown, often antagonistic, Protestant sects a joint ecclesiastical administration. He himself had advanced such a proposal in 1808 and elaborated it in considerable detail, four years later, in a memorandum entitled *A Project of a New Constitution for the Protestant Church in the Prussian State.*

> The clergy must establish vital contacts with one another [he had written] and be forced by the very constitution to engage in more intensive religious and scholarly activities. The state shall retain detailed supervision over orderly procedure and direct surveillance over church property, which must always be considered as derived from, and dependent on, the state. But it must hold completely aloof from the inner administration of the church and rather endow the latter with such a degree of independence that it appear as a fully self-governing organic whole.

In spite of his demand for complete autonomy, he had clearly conceded the primacy of the state and merely advocated that it voluntarily impose upon itself certain limitations in ecclesiastical matters.[44]

Acceptance of state authority did not prevent Schleiermacher from often criticizing the powers that were, however. He voiced, for instance, his keen disappointment with the reforms of the Stein-Hardenberg era, which had not gone far enough. Nor did his admiration of Frederick blind him to the fact that much of what the "great king" had lovingly built would have to be torn down. In the dark years after Jena he prophesied that "only that government, but that one unfailingly, will overthrow Bonaparte on the Continent, which will spontaneously undertake its own regeneration and become intimately united with its people." But he was essentially an optimistic believer in historic progression. In a letter to Henrietta Herz of February 2, 1807, he wrote, "Throughout history we see the genius of man working in the same way. The invisible hand of Providence, and the action of man, is one and the same." That is why he also believed that the peculiar spirit of the nation, emanating from its soil and reflected in both its mores and its scientific achievements, would ultimately right whatever the ruling state powers might wrong.[45]

Curiously, these religious and nationalist convictions led Schleiermacher back to Luther's theoretical demand for separation between the political and religious spheres and placed him in opposition to the dominant patriarchal and quietistic theory of later Lutheranism. In this sense Fichte and Hegel, secular nationalists preaching the state's omnipotence, were more direct continuators of prerevolutionary Protestant political theory. Although he, too, considered the truly national state an "organic planetary work of art," Schleier-macher could not possibly subscribe to Hegel's extreme teachings of the state as "the. rational thing per se," the "reality of the moral idea," or the "reality of concrete liberty." As a compassionate observer of anti-Protestant discrimination in Catholic countries and as a student of Christian martyrology, he clearly perceived that "Christianity can have no more powerful enemy than the egotism of states." [46]

For this reason Schleiermacher consistently demanded that the state leave enough room for independent religious and scientific training of pupils. In general he was a most ardent advocate of national education which alone could instill in youth a communal spirit. He also opposed the type of French education which, customary in German aristocratic circles during the preceding generations, was likely to imbue the pupil with alien ideals. Already in his youth he had reluctantly studied French, on account of its "frivolousness and effeminacy." Later he joined the legions of Hamann and Herder's enthusiastic disciples who viewed the national language as a supreme criterion of each divinely instituted national spirit. "Only one language is firmly rooted in man; he belongs entirely to only one, no matter how many more he may learn." But this very insistence upon an all-German national education made him doubly apprehensive of divisive state control. "In Germany," he once sweepingly declared, "the task is not to let the particular political structure of the individual state influence the type of education." He also argued that, while the state was essentially a relationship between adult individuals, education represented the underlying relationship of successive generations. Hence "education can very well be conceived of without the state and prior to it." The vast compass and multiplicity of aims of a truly national education also militated, in his opinion, against the state's usurping exclusive control. Religious education, in particular, belonged to those internal aspects of religious life in which the state ought to restrict itself to some general regulation and supervision. [47]

Similar nationalist and religious considerations induced Schleiermacher to demand complete religious toleration. Religious and scientific dissent, he admitted, "always involves the assumption that the judgment of the community as a whole is wrong. To make such an assumption with good conscience presupposes, therefore, an almost infinite strength of faith." Since faith is not altogether subject to will, however, the state must not use its legal powers to influence the dissenting minority. National interest, too, demanded legal equality not only of all Christian denominations with their varying ratios in different states, but also of Jews. For many years intimately associated with the Jewish intelligentsia in Berlin and Vienna, Schleiermacher considered it a most serious national loss "to exclude a substantial mass of well-educated members from legal participation in state affairs." [48]

In the long run, however, Schleiermacher was both too ardent a nationalist not to hope for Germany's religious unification and too confirmed a believer not to anticipate the ultimate victory of Protestantism. While advocating Jewish emancipation, he added expressly, "I am also convinced that Judaism will vanish no less speedily after emancipation than before it." Although less outspoken than either Rousseau or Herder, both of whom he greatly admired, he believed in the desirability of national religions or, at least, of national forms of universal Christianity. He merely echoed therein old Pietist opinions, succinctly formulated in Herder's famous query, "Do not nations differ in everything, in poetry, in physiognomy and tastes, in usages, customs and languages? Must not religion, which partakes of all these, also differ among nations?" He sincerely believed that, before very long, Protestantism, the off-shoot of the German national spirit, would prevail over Oriental Judaism and Latin Catholicism. He meant, of course, Protestantism in general, not any of its subdivisions. For, as he wrote in defense of the Union of 1817 against the objections of an orthodox Lutheran, "We ought not . . . to call ourselves Lutheran nor Reformed, but we ought to call ourselves *Evangelical* Christians, after His name and His holy evangel." At the same time he was prepared to see other nations permanently retain their own peculiar national-religious forms. He once asserted that a civilized nation subjecting itself to alien influences, however good in themselves, not only loses its honor, but acts against the divine will. "Only that people relies on the Lord which wishes at all cost to preserve the peculiar purpose and spirit with which He has endowed it. It alone strives to uphold a deed willed by God." [49]

Schleiermacher was doubly skeptical, therefore, of Napoleon's alleged program of reuniting the Catholic and Protestant churches. He believed that the emperor hated "Protestantism as much as he hates speculative philosophy," precisely the two factors on which depended the future regeneration of mankind. In 1806, the dark year of Prussia's downfall, he anticipated an imperial onslaught on the Protestant faith and held himself in readiness to suffer martyrdom, "both religious and scientific." But he felt absolutely confident that the emperor's game—everything was a game to Napoleon—would ultimately fail, "for Germany is still here." [50]

Napoleon's attempt at world domination, indeed anybody's endeavor to build a universal empire, would likewise fail utterly, Schleiermacher thought, because of its underlying denial of the disparate national wills. "The state is not a cosmopolitan entity," he declared, "and its government cannot assume the duty of promoting the welfare of all humanity. It must rather seek to utilize all available resources for the benefit of the people entrusted to it." Every state had, therefore, the unlimited right of waging war, and even a European federation along Kantian lines was utterly utopian. Nevertheless, he condemned extreme state egotism on a par with individual egotism. He believed in the possibility of permanent peace through the nations' rigid adherence to self-imposed compacts and treaties. International public law thus developed would foster peace not by forcible means, for states, as supreme entities, could not recognize any superior outside will, but through moral suasion. Under the operation of such a divinely inspired law, nations would be related to one another, "not like individuals in the state, but as they are . . . in church." In other words, war would vanish not as a result of legal sanctions but because men would voluntarily abandon recourse to arms. The obvious objection, that this expectation failed to take cognizance of the nations' bottomless appetites, was countered by Schleiermacher with both nationalist and religious arguments. Echoing Herder's famous dictum that true "father-lands" never wage war on one another but "live peacefully together and assist one another like families," he insisted that nationalist education must instill in pupils the conviction that "loyalty to one's nationality shall not imply hostility to all outside that group." From the religious angle, too, all history was but an evolution toward the ultimate aims of the Prince of Peace. As a young man he had already written in his *Diary* that "all history is religious, and religion by its very nature must be historical." [51]

Here we perceive the very core of Schleiermacher's nationalist aspiration. He sincerely believed that in the divinely ordained historic evolution the German nation was destined to play a decisive role. Profoundly stirred by Prussia's downfall of 1806 he, too, fell back on the old prophetic rationalization that "divine power often reveals itself in the weak more than in the mighty." In a truly Deutero-Isaianic vein he preached soon after Halle's occupation by the French:

> It is possible that our people, too, will sustain still greater humiliations, that it will be further deprived of its prestige and its position among the powers of the civilized world; if only in lieu of this external power inner strength shall come forth; if only harmony, affection and loyalty shall gain the upper hand . . . then we shall surely stand out as a great example among the nations; then in our very sufferings, through the contrast thus revealed, will most clearly shine forth the majesty of the Divine; then we shall surely become, some day in the future, the focal point around which all the good and the beautiful will be united.

These were Fichtean sounds. Above all personal dislikes (about that time Schleiermacher found Fichte "abominable") they both fell back on the same old messianic hope to weather the great historic crisis. Like most of their contemporaries hard pressed in adjusting their thinking to swiftly moving events, they were confused, even shockingly inconsistent. They may have tried, as Nietzsche punned on Schleiermacher's name, to throw a veil over the eyes of their generation. But by making a virtue of an unprecedented catastrophe, they saw in it but a confirmation of Germany's "chosenness" and a supreme call to the fulfillment of its national-religious mission. "To the imperative, 'Thou shalt' spoken by Fichte," says a recent writer, "Schleiermacher's sermons added the deeply felt 'God wills it.'" [52]

5. IMPERIAL BLANDISHMENTS

History has not borne out Schleiermacher's expectations. German Protestantism became ever more subsidiary to nationalism. The state, through its control of the purse strings and its ramified regulations of ecclesiastical life, made certain that no antinationalist would ever achieve church leadership. But the nationalist sentiments of the bulk of the Protestant population and its lay or clerical spokesmen required little prodding. In the Hegelian philosophy, which supplanted all other offshoots of Kant's idealistic teachings, the Prussian brand of nationalism, with its strong Lutheran moorings, celebrated unprecedented victories. That Hegel himself was a Swabian mattered but little. Just as the Saxon Lessing had been an early admirer of the nascent Prussian regime and vom Stein, a native of Nassau, had become the chief instrument of its regeneration, and just as, a century later, the Austrian Hitler was to personify its climactic achievement, so did Hegel all but canonize the compound of Prussianism and Protestantism which he found in his adopted fatherland.[53] Carried by a band of enthusiastic theological and lay disciples, his message had profound repercussions far beyond Germany's boundaries, for by that time the German theological idiom had become the lingua franca of Continental theology.

The decision, nonetheless, still hung in the balance. German nationalism long sought, in the so-called *grossdeutsch* movement, the inclusion of Catholic Austria, Prussia's old imperial rival. At the same time it pursued generally liberal and humanitarian aims. The revolutionary leaders of the Frankfort National Assembly of 1848 rhapsodized on humanitarian nationalism with almost as much fervor as their French predecessors. But their liberalism frightened the upholders of the sacred alliance between throne and altar. By a concatenation of external and internal developments national unification, that acme of German nationalism, was accomplished not by the liberals of 1848, most of whom were forced to leave their country and preach their doctrines elsewhere, but by Prussia's armies and her "chancellor of blood and iron."

Otto von Bismarck was not altogether a monolithic Prussian aristocrat and royal servant. Unlike his chief military collaborator, Count Albrecht von Roon, who believed in Prussian monarchy's divine mission of maintaining law and order through an inspired and superbly equipped army, the chancellor was a dual personality. Even his wife distinguished sharply between the man and the minister of state. Paradoxically applying Luther's separation between the religious and political spheres, he combined great personal piety with complete absence of moral considerations in politics. The same man who styled himself a "soldier of the Lord" and professed to perform his daily chores "with genuine penitence" did not hesitate to proclaim in his celebrated speech of December 3, 1850, that "the only sound foundation for a great state, which therewith is essentially differentiated from a small state, is its state egotism and not romanticism. It is unworthy of a great state to battle for a cause which is not within the sphere of its own interest." At the same time he constantly reiterated that Germany was a "Christian" state and, as such, in duty bound to alleviate misery and suffering. He was genuinely proud of the extensive social legislation, which had accompanied his outlawry of anti-imperialist and antireligious socialism in 1861 and which made Germany socially the most progressive country of the period. Unconsciously he thus went back of Luther's sharp opposition to mendicancy and reverted to the medieval church's emphasis on charity.[54]

Otherwise Bismarck sharply opposed the Catholic Church, on nationalist even more than on Protestant grounds. As far back as 1853, reporting from Frankfort on the archbishop of Freiburg's victory in an ecclesiastical controversy with Baden, he called it "a defeat of Protestantism, of princely power and of Prussia as the champion of German Protestantism." Later, in the *Kulturkampf*, he hoped to crush Catholicism, the perennial obstacle to Germany's religious unification, and thus resume the work of the Reformation at the point where it had been interrupted by the inconclusive Wars of Religion. He confidently expected support from Protestant England. When in 1873 the Catholic bishop of Nancy instructed his flock, including the inhabitants of a newly ceded district in Lorraine, to pray for the return of the lost provinces to France, Bismarck tried to enlist Queen Victoria's aid in forcing the French government to discipline the bishop. Emperor William I complained to the queen that France abused his country's anti-Catholic struggle for "letting loose and encouraging all those feelings of hatred against Germany . . . and of combating Protestantism." But British diplomacy realized, in the words of Lord Odo Russell, British ambassador in Berlin, that Bismarck's "anti-Roman policy will serve him to pick a quarrel with any power he pleases by declaring that he has discovered an anti-German conspiracy among the clergy of the country he wishes to fight." [55]

In Germany, however, Protestant public opinion meekly surrendered to this imperialist abuse of its faith. There was no vocal opposition to state intervention in matters of conscience so long as it supposedly combated only the organizational excesses of "political Catholicism." But a few shared Hermann Baumgartner's forebodings that the great man might inflict great misery upon the nation. The opposition consisted chiefly of Socialists and Catholics who, though acting in self-defense, long refused to collaborate with each other. Only the catastrophe of the lost First World War brought them together on a platform which was immediately denounced as antinational. Eccentric individuals, like Nietzsche, could decline for themselves the "nationalist mania and patriotic stupidity," but they could not prevent their nihilistic doctrines from whetting nationalist appetites. Beginning with William II's rambunctious address of 1896 at the Second Reich's twenty-fifth anniversary, ever less restrained appeals were addressed to the millions of Germans settled in foreign lands to aid in the fatherland's expansion. The cacophony of Pan-German, racialist, antisemitic propaganda included the voices of religious leaders. Friedrich Naumann, especially, together with the Jew-baiting court preacher, Adolf Stöcker, a most influential spokesman of Christian socialism, achieved notoriety through his elastic *Mitteleuropa* which was to embrace all countries from Berlin to Bagdad. During the First World War, particularly, even calm and composed theologians lost their self-control. Ernst Tröltsch, who had inaugurated his lectures at the University of Berlin with the proud assertion, "I have come here to put an end to the relativity of values," now wrote that he wished that all his words were guns to kill enemies. Only that war's catastrophic finale demolished, for a time, the Bismarckian myth. This psychological transition was graphically described by a contemporary:

> The beginnings of the war and especially the celebration of his hundredth birthday revealed the extent to which he [Bismarck] had appeared to millions of Germans in a transfiguration comparable only to that of deities of primordial days or heroes of primitive sagas, gigantic, eternal and without a peer. Our political and military breakdown at the end of the war opened the gate to voices from the depths which saw in him not a god but a demon, not a faithful Eckhart but the cause of Germany's doom.[56]

These changes in mass psychology were but weakly reflected in the thinking of Protestant leaders. Their "Christian patriotism," or rather their attachment to the old order, survived the downfall of the Hohenzollern dynasty and the separation of state and church. Their bewilderment at the loss of their royal "supreme bishops" was deeply aggravated by the political coloring of the new magistrates. For years the Weimar Republic and most of its member states were controlled by an alliance of Socialists and Centrists, who had been singled out by Bismarckian Germany for ruthless suppression. Taking orders from officials, often personally petty and undistinguished or known for their antireligious or anti-Protestant animus, seemed far more humiliating than acceptance of an evangelical leadership appointed by a Catholic monarch like the emperor of Austria.

Internationally, too, Germany's defeat, combined with the new European hegemony of France, the re-emergence of the Catholic power of Poland and the downfall of Czarist Russia was widely interpreted as a decisive victory of the Roman Church. Devotees of the bon mot had a ready formula for it.

"From the military point of view," they said, "France won the war; from the political, England; from the economic, America; from the cultural, the Jew; from the racial, the Slav; from the religious, the Roman Catholic Church." In Germany, particularly, the sudden separation of state and church affected more severely the politically pampered Protestant leadership than that of the Catholic Church, which, buttressed by its world-wide hierarchy, had long learned to get along without governmental support. The general breakdown in religious allegiance also affected more seriously the industrial centers in the Protestant North than the less urbanized Catholic South. Although conversions of Catholics to Protestantism still exceeded in number the defections from the Protestant to the Catholic camp (the ratio was 11,017 to 8,565 in 1920; and 10,176 to 7,084 in 1922) and intermarriage likewise favored on the whole the Protestant side, the latter was the main loser when hundreds of thousands now formally renounced all church membership.[57]

These withdrawals began tapering off quickly in the following years, however, while many thousands repentantly returned to the fold. There also was a noticeable increase in church attendance. Otto Dibelius claimed that, by finally loosening the ancient bonds between Protestantism and government, separation would usher in a new "century of the church." An outsider, the Rev. R. H. Murray, likewise wrote very hopefully, "Labor has ceased to be hostile to her [the church]. She maintains her hold on the countryside and some of the bourgeoisie." All this proved to be but wishful thinking. The majority of Protestant leaders and theologians belonged to the "national opposition," nonnationalists having lost all standing in the Protestant community. The situation became so serious that Karl Barth wrote in 1931 that "the association and the hyphen between Christianity and nationalism, Protestantism and Germanism has become a permanent fixture in the oral and printed speech of our Church. This is true to such an extent that, one must state, this hyphen has now become the real criterion of Church orthodoxy."[58]

At the same time Barth's own "theology of crisis" helped undermine whatever community of action might have developed between the antinationalist minority and other progressive forces. Ably seconded by such Lutheran theologians as Friedrich Gogarten, Barth preached an extreme form of transcendentalism which condemned as sheer "humanism" all efforts at hastening the establishment of God's kingdom on earth. Only the sudden irruption of supernatural forces, he taught, guided by God's inscrutable will, would someday change the course of history and also bring about the necessary social adjustments. This was an extremely pessimistic reinterpretation of the old Calvinistic doctrine of predestination. Unlike its earlier formulations, therefore, which had often served as spearheads of radical social action, the new theology reinforced the quietistic acceptance of existing realities. If all theology was called by

Shailer Matthews "transcendentalized politics," the theology of crisis certainly became, far beyond the intentions of its founders, a conservative, if not altogether reactionary, political force.[59]

It is small wonder that at the hour of decision the German Protestant Church was found wanting. True, the pressure was enormous. On the one hand, there were the Nazis' lip service to "positive Christianity," their glorification of Luther as the greatest German of all times, and their promise to salvage the world from the "godless" ravages of bolshevism. Even more than its Catholic compatriots, the Lutheran majority, with its deep-rooted Erastianism, sought comfort in Hitler's declaration at the first nazi-controlled Reichstag that "the national government sees in the two Christian denominations most vital factors in the survival of our nationality. Their rights will not be touched." On the other hand, the growingly intensive boring from within by the "German Christians" threatened to weaken the churches' hold upon the masses. German youth, especially, even if not yet dominated by Rosenberg's "blood and soil" ideology, listened with rapt attention to the profession of faith formulated by the Congress of German Christians in April, 1933:

> God has created me a German; Germanism is a gift of God. God wills it that I fight for Germany. War service in no way injures the Christian conscience, but is obedience to God. Faced with a state, which supports the powers of darkness, the believer has the right to revolt. He has the same right when confronted with a church government which does not accept the national resurgence without reservation. For a German the church is a community of believers, which is under the obligation to fight for a Christian Germany. The object of the Faith Movement of German Christians is one Evangelical German Church for the whole Reich. Adolf Hitler's state calls to the church. The church has heard the call.

Puzzled and bewildered, Protestant leadership submitted. Karl Barth bitterly reminisced five years later how, in 1933, "the church had almost unanimously welcomed the Hitler regime with real confidence, indeed, with the highest hopes." Otto Dibelius hailed the new chancellor in an enthusiastic sermon at the inauguration services held at Potsdam. Martin Niemöller, who after serving as U-boat captain during the war became an influential preacher in Berlin, voted for the nazi ticket in 1924 and preached a laudatory sermon on its victory in 1933.[60]

Before very long, however, nazism revealed its true nature. Its essential irreconcilability with any form of Christianity became apparent to all but the most gullible listeners to official outpourings. Though devoid of the guidance of an extraterritorial organ like the papacy, the Protestant leaders began to resist. Other social organizations, including the press, the universities and the once all-powerful labor unions, had gone down in defeat almost without a struggle. But the churches of all denominations put up a relatively valiant fight. To quote Karl Barth again, though "greater proof would in fact have

been possible . . . a *small* proof of the reality of the faith has been given."
In consonance with Schleiermacher's glorification of those Christians who
"rather than become slaves of fear have chosen the wanderer's staff and
abandoned property, native land and forefathers' house, all that is most precious
to man," many Protestant ministers and teachers (Barth among them) voluntarily preferred exile to slavery. Many, including Dibelius, were dismissed
from their posts, which often meant both economic ruin and social ostracism.
To add insult to injury, Dibelius first learned of his dismissal from the newspapers. Others, including Niemöller, suffered imprisonment and torture. Fully
1,300 of the officiating 18,000 Protestant pastors were arrested in the first five
years of the nazi regime.[61]

Nevertheless, Protestant leadership became essentially co-ordinated (*gleich-
geschaltet*) with the regime's other totalitarian phases. A new office of reichs-
bishop was created. The very appointment for life of the first incumbent
without consultation of the congregations and their inability to remove him
ran counter to the old Lutheran doctrine of the priesthood of every believer
and, more sharply, the old congregational emphases of Calvinism. He and
the various church committees appointed by him unstintingly co-operated
with the party's representative, the reichsminister for church affairs. They had
to subscribe to the latter's pious declaration of February 13, 1937:

> National socialism has no other wish than to do the will of our Father in
> heaven. The will of our Father in heaven has been passed into our blood; it
> works through the nation. Everything which national socialism is now doing
> for the community, for the preservation of the nation, is the doing of the will
> of God. Our "neighbor" is he who is indicated to us by blood.

The effects were quickly noticeable. While in 1834 military force had to be
used to persuade Lutheran worshipers in a small Silesian church to adopt
the slightly modified Union ritual, the Protestant congregations now meekly
surrendered to the elimination from prayer book and hymnal of such venerable
Hebrew words as "hallelujah" and "amen" and the suppression of traditional
names like Zion Church or of all references to Jesus on the cross as a "king of
Jews." Even those Protestant writers who in the regime's early years still dared
to reply to Rosenberg's anti-Christian tirades (e.g., Albert Oepke) reiterated
their acceptance, on principle, of the doctrine of race. They merely protested
against its application so as to discourage Jewish conversions to Christianity,
to disqualify non-Aryans from office (there were several hundred non-Aryan
pastors in 1933) and especially to suppress the "Jewish" ingredients of Christianity, including the entire Old Testament. In his famous "Open Letter" to
Reichsminister Kerrl of February, 1937, Dibelius merely argued that the church
could not abandon its belief that Jesus, as a man, was of the House of David
and hence a Jew, or reject the Epistles of Paul (whom German Christians
often chose to call "Rabbi Paul") without ceasing to be the Church of Christ.

Hardly a word was heard about religious liberty as such, an allegedly outworn principle of the discarded liberal era, or about the tortures inflicted upon non-baptized Jews. Few there were indeed who realized, with Barth, that Germany was no longer the type of state, to which obedience had been enjoined in Romans 13, but that it was an outright tyranny which to combat was a religious duty. Far too many were ready to subscribe, despite his general unpopularity, to Pastor Hossenfelder's pious exclamation, "And God said, let there be a people and there was a people. . . . It is from the people that the faith of our time receives its specific meaning." [62] The Second World War finally clinched this surrender of the Protestant majority.

6. Religious Fellowship

In other countries, especially in England and America, but also in Holland and the Scandinavian countries, the picture is far brighter. This is owing in part to their different Protestant traditions and in part to their different types of nationalism. During the past two centuries even the Church of England became less rather than more nationalistic. From the beginning its characteristic spirit of compromise had sprung in part from the desire of combining the nationalist features of a state church with the supranational traditions of Catholicism. This combination accounted for less logical consistency but also for a higher degree of practicality in meeting issues as they arose.[63]

In the nineteenth century the Anglican Church constantly oscillated between reconciliation with the Free Churches on a national basis and reunion with the Roman Church. The sensational conversions of Cardinals Newman and Manning may have been representative of only a small minority. They nevertheless dramatized the possibilities of reunion which would mend the breach of the sixteenth century. Curiously, the re-establishment of the British hierarchy in 1850, intended to accelerate reunion, proved in the long run a serious obstacle. The Anglo-Catholics knew well, say two recent authors, that "the Roman Catholic Cathedral of Westminster would fade into insignificance beside the Cathedral of St. Paul's in the event of Anglicanism attaining the position of a Uniate church. Roman prelates in England will not soon help vote themselves out of office." More important than these petty rivalries, however, was the theological intransigence of the Vatican Council and Popes Pius IX, X and XI, which, after the First World War, rendered completely futile the Anglican leaders' semiprivate "conversations" with Cardinal Mercier and other Catholics in Malines, Belgium.[64]

The simultaneous negotiations with the English dissenters, in the meantime united in a Federal Council of the Evangelical Free Churches, proved equally futile. The bishops of the whole Anglican Communion assembled at the Lambeth Conference of 1920 issued a remarkable *Appeal to all Christian People*, calling for permanent association "in penitence and prayer of all those who deplore the divisions of Christian people, and are inspired by the vision and hope of a visible unity of the whole Church." They also assured the Nonconformists that they would retain in the new union "much that has long been distinctive in their methods of worship and service." Undismayed by Catholic nonco-operation and the breakdown of negotiations with the Free Churches in 1921-25, largely on the issue of episcopal ordination, the Lambeth Conference of 1930 reiterated, in a series of outspoken resolutions, its determination to pursue the quest for "the Unity of the Church." [65]

The Anglican Church had thus traveled very far on the road of religious toleration and international amity. It still remained England's state church, receiving substantial state subsidies and controlled by Parliament even in such spiritual affairs as the revision of its prayer book, but its claim to exclusive religious leadership became progressively weaker. The Catholic emancipation of 1829 and the Reform Bill of 1832 helped shift the political power to classes in which dissent was very strong. Apart from the various freethinking and agnostic movements, the three main Methodist churches (the Wesleyan, Primitive and United) and the numerically insignificant but highly influential Quakers made serious inroads in the Anglican camp. Large-scale immigration of Irish Catholics, Scotch Presbyterians, German Lutherans, Jews, etc., and the lower birth rate of the upper-class membership of the Anglican Church hastened the decline in its proportionate strength.

Even in England, therefore, the equation of Anglicanism with English nationalism became less and less meaningful. It was altogether nebulous among the Anglican minorities of Scotland and Ireland, while the newer nationalist trends in Wales and growing use of Welsh in divine services paradoxically converted the Church of England into a national church of two distinct nationalities. At the same time the growing independence of colonies and dominions resulted in its progressive disestablishment there. As early as 1863 the Privy Council laid down the general rule that "the Church of England, in places where there is no church established by law, is in the same position with any other religious body—in no better, but in no worse position." The colonial and dominion churches of the Episcopal persuasion have generally continued to support the British connection even in the political sphere, but this unity was now of a purely voluntary nature. Australia alone among the dominions expressly stipulated to accept without modification whatever changes in prayer book and church formularies the Church of England might see fit to adopt.[66]

The fact, however, that the Anglican Communion cultivated principally people of British stock and gained few adherents among other immigrant groups gave rise to some antialien trends in the dominions. The impressions gathered by the lord bishop of London, Arthur S. Winington Ingram, during his visit to Canada in the 1920's were fairly typical. On the one hand, he heard frequent complaints about ecclesiastical neglect in the sparsely populated areas of western Canada, a Miss Hazell, for instance, having found on her caravan tour fully one hundred unbaptized babies. He also noted the great need of immigration, especially of agricultural workers. A Vancouver professor told him, "Oh, yes, you can send us as many *serfs* as you like to cultivate our land, our young people don't mean to do it." At the same time, he reported, "every thinking man in Canada sees the danger of outnumbering and swamping the old British stock with every nation under Heaven. The bishop of Edmonton tells me that there are thirty-five languages spoken in Edmonton." [67]

All these undoubtedly were marks of growing nationalism, which incidentally was much more common in lay than in ecclesiastical circles, but they did not infringe on the imperial and international outlook of the Anglican Communion as a whole. The decennial Lambeth Conferences, from their first meeting of 1867 to that of 1930 (the conference of 1940, like its predecessor of 1918, had to be postponed on account of the war), grew into an ever more effective imperial and, in some respects, supraimperial organ. From the outset the American Episcopal Church was an active participant. When the 1897 conference elected a consultative body of eighteen bishops, which subsequently served as a steering committee during the sessions and a continuation committee between them, the American representation of four bishops equaled that of England and Wales together. The colonial churches also were given a larger measure of autonomy or at an earlier date than seemed warranted by the political conditions. Just as the nation-wide church organizations in the American colonies had in many respects adumbrated the later Federal Constitution, so did the growth of these autonomous churches often foreshadow their countries' evolution toward dominion status and ultimately the Statute of Westminster of 1931. Some twenty years before the first British Imperial Conferences, the Lambeth Conferences had thus demonstrated the possibility of voluntary co-operation on the imperial level. Nor does it seem too venturesome to expect that, as those Imperial Conferences were rightly called small leagues of nations, the Lambeth Conferences will have served as a most effective preparatory organ for a genuine World Union of Churches. [68]

In America, too, Protestantism's nationalist function largely consisted in promoting voluntary Americanization, both religious and political. Of course, some Protestant ministers still remembered John Cotton's dictum (in his controversy with Roger Williams) that "it was toleration that made the world anti-Christian." Others were willing to agree with the Rev. Nathaniel Ward of Ipswich that "he that is willing to tolerate any Religion, or discrepant way of Religion beside his owne, unlesse it be in matters meerly indifferent, either doubts of his owne, or is not sincere in it." These words were, after all, but a variation of St . Augustine's *nullum malum pejus libertate errandi* which, long the keynote of medieval intolerance, was quoted with approval by Ward himself. Majority opinion, however, followed William Penn, who had taught with

zest and eloquence that "Imposition, Restraint and Persecution for matters relating to conscience directly invade the Divine prerogative, and divest the
Almighty of a due, proper to none beside himself." [69]

The result was that, while by the end of the Revolution seven states still restricted officeholding to Protestants, "Vermont dropped the clause in its constitution inflicting liabilities on Catholics in 1786, South Carolina followed in
1790 and New Hampshire attempted a similar change in 1792, although public
opinion was still too strong to allow it to be carried out." Delaware, Georgia,
Connecticut, New York and Massachusetts followed with the gradual removal
of all barriers to religious equality. Curiously, public opinion swung to such
anticlerical extremes that many constitutions disqualified the clergy from public office. For the churches, as a whole, were long allied with conservative law-
makers, or, as one of Jefferson's Connecticut followers phrased it, the state was
"under the management of the old firm of Moses and Aaron." Although Jefferson himself soon changed his mind and decided that "after 17 years more of
experience and reflection" he was opposed to such discrimination against the
clergy, these constitutional provisions persisted until 1821 in New York and
much longer in several southern states.[70]

Much of this anticlerical bias was due to the influence of antireligious Enlightenment which for a while dominated large sections of informed opinion
also in England and America. In Bolingbroke and Paine, in Ethan Allen and
Elihu Palmer, to mention only a few, both countries possessed vigorous and
eloquent exponents of deism and freethought, whose spread in the early
United States seemed to presage the formation of a new "republican religion."
Even in the undeveloped Ohio and Mississippi valleys a missionary, J. M. Peck,
complained of "French infidelity that threatened for a time to sweep away
every vestige of Christianity." These movements never struck deep roots, however. While they appealed to a few urban sophisticates, they were much too
abstract for the mass of frontiersmen. Churchmen, moreover, rather than placing obstacles in the way of all progressive movements, kept their fingers on the
pulse of the nation and often led it on the path of its desired evolution. Such
keen European observers as de Tocqueville and James Bryce were struck by the
role which religion continued to play in the daily life of the American people
and how deeply it colored the conduct of all public affairs. Another visitor, Miss
Harriet Martineau, wrote admiringly in 1837, "that the event has fully justified
the confidence of those who have faith enough in Christianity to see that it
needs no protection from the state, but will commend itself to human hearts
better without." Before the end of the century a judge, J. D. Brewer, argued,
though on juridically inconclusive grounds, for considering "the United States
a Christian nation," a doctrine reminiscent of Friedrich Karl Moser's advocacy
of an all-German "Christian patriotism." [71]

Such a combination of nationalist and religious biases was often directed against immigrants of differing faiths. The colony of Massachusetts forbade the importation of Irish persons lest they affect the people with their Catholic views. After the Revolution Jefferson and Madison favored the right of asylum from political and religious persecution, but the Federalist group opposed both immigration and easy naturalization. It was under the Federalist regime that the probationary period for naturalization was first extended to five years and then, in the "Alien Act" of 1798, to fourteen years. The Federalist party bitterly resented the regular pro-Jeffersonian majorities among naturalized voters. A growing fear of foreign "entanglements" also made the American public wary of aliens who, because of their own nationalist biases, tried to embroil it in the controversies of their native lands. The Irish, especially, had early formed a United Irish Society to support the Irish insurrections. Their activities appeared of sufficient importance for the British government to help influence Congress to buttress the "Alien Act" by a "Sedition Law." Both laws were repealed within three years and Irish agitation became the more violent as Anglo-Irish relations deteriorated and Irish immigration increased at a rapid pace. During the Oregon boundary dispute of 1846, especially, and the Young Irish uprising two years later the Irish patriots tried to secure American intervention against England, holding out the old bait of the annexation of Canada. Similarly, tireless propaganda of German and Hungarian refugees after 1848 threatened to drag the United States into unpleasant controversies with the Central European powers.[72]

These suspicions also had serious religious connotations. Making use of their growing voting strength especially on the eastern seaboard, Irish immigrants enhanced the position of their church to an extent resented by conservative Protestants. The Germans, on the other hand, contributed a disproportionate share to the agnostic groups. Within a few years after 1848, a number of revolutionary societies advocated both complete change in government and the abolition of Bible reading, the Puritan Sabbath and formal Christianity as a whole. The Communist Club of New York adopted in 1857 a constitution requiring members to "reject every religious belief, no matter in what guise it may appear, as well as all views not based upon the direct testimony of the senses." Of course, professed agnostics had long espoused their antireligious doctrines before an attentive minority, but the sudden mass influx of fervent preachers of a social and religious upheaval added fuel to the antialien agitation. Since thousands of paupers and criminals also had, with the active support of their governments, found their way across the ocean and become public charges, the antialien furor seized ever-larger sections of the Protestant population in the 1830's and 1840's. The seeds thus sown finally sprouted into that most poisonous plant of the American soil, the powerful Know-Nothing movement.[73]

Samuel Morse, inventor of the telegraph, achieved particular notoriety. In a widely read book on *Foreign Conspiracy* he argued that Catholicism had always been allied with monarchy and that Austria, especially, dreading a revolution stimulated by the American example, was trying to suppress republican institutions everywhere. Morse urged, therefore, the American Protestants to unite against the local Catholic schools and to enact stringent immigration laws, for "we must first stop this leak in the ship through which the muddy waters from without threaten to sink us." He also advocated an amendment providing that "no foreigner who may come into the country, after the passage of the new law, shall ever be allowed to exercise the elective franchise." [74]

Such individual voices soon swelled into a powerful chorus. Various nativist, antialien and anti-Catholic societies sprang up throughout the country. A so-called National Council of the United States of North America, led by James W. Barker of New York, stated that

> the object of this organization shall be to protect every American citizen in the legal and proper exercise of all his civil and religious rights and privileges; to resist the insidious policy of the Church of Rome, and all other foreign influence against our republican institutions in all lawful ways; to place in all offices of honor, trust, or profit, in the gift of the people, or by appointment, none but native-born Protestant citizens and to protect, preserve and uphold the union of these states and the constitution of the same.

The American Society (better known as the Know-Nothing party), allegedly founded in order "to promote the principles of the Protestant Reformation," finally emerged as the political spearhead of these "nativist" forces. In an unprecedented floodtide the party swept state elections and sent seventy-five congressmen to Washington in 1854. In Massachusetts the governor, all state officers and senators were elected on the Know-Nothing platform. A year later Rhode Island, New Hampshire and Connecticut, Maryland and Kentucky became Know-Nothing states. For a while it looked as though the party was to win also the presidential election of 1856, but it polled only 25 per cent of the popular vote.[75]

This nationalist aberration did not last long, however. Its very nationalism antagonized the defenders of state rights. In the South Know-Nothingism, standing for strong national union, soon became identified with abolitionism. Curiously, the antislavery agitation, long successfully led by William Wilberforce's Evangelical movement in England, assumed in America a nationalist hue, for emancipation could be attained only by a strong federal government overruling the southern states. Here, too, economic factors, and especially the old compound of Protestant-capitalist individualism, greatly contributed to the people's growing abhorrence of the unrestricted mastery of man over man. One need note only the strong evangelical as well as nationalist overtones in Lincoln's antislavery speeches. In Know-Nothingism, however, opposition to slavery was suffused with a strong dose of anti-Catholicism. One Know-Nothing convention held at Norfolk, Massachusetts, actually resolved "that there can exist no real hostility to Roman Catholicism which does not embrace slavery, its natural co-worker in opposition to freedom and republican institutions." [76] Nevertheless, emancipation soon became such a paramount issue threatening to disrupt national unity that the ensuing Civil War and need of northern solidarity shoved aside all antialien and anti-Catholic sentiments and put an end to nativism as a major political force.

Since that time American nationalism, at least as represented by its influential spokesmen, has returned to its original principles of religious freedom and international obligation. The anti-Catholic movements stimulated by the American branch of the Evangelical Alliance (founded in 1867) and the Church Union Association never assumed mass character. In periods of great tension certain nationalist groups (e.g., the Ku Klux Klan or the America First propagandists of the Second World War) reverted to radical isolationism, suffused with racial and religious intolerance. Under the stimulus of nazi propaganda, racialism and Jew-baiting found almost as strong an echo among the Protestant masses as among the Catholic followers of "Social Justice." Before 1939 a poll taken by the American Institute of Public Opinion showed that 8,000,000 persons in the United States approved of Hitler's antisemitic policies and barbaric methods. Ironically, the highest percentage of such Hitler sympathizers appeared to live in New England, which had originally been the main haven of refuge from religious persecution and which in 1940 became the stronghold of an interventionist and pro-British agitation directed against the Nazis. [77]

The Protestant churches, as such, however, have kept aloof from these ultranationalist movements which curiously preached internal discord rather than national unity. In fact, some Protestant leaders have become the outstanding champions of a true brotherhood of man transcending racial and national boundaries. The resolutions and committee reports adopted at the Lambeth Conference of 1930 on "Race among the Causes of the Present Unrest" reflect official Protestant opinion far beyond the confines of the Anglican Communion.

> Too frequently [one report reads] our keen appreciation of our own virtues and abilities leads us to feel that any who differ from us in race, color or language are thereby inferior. We are prepared to patronize civilizations far older than our own, and to ignore cultures which we do not understand.

If the status of Negro clergy still leaves much room for improvement, the fault is not principally with America's Protestant leadership, which may be accused of weakness in not forcing the egalitarian issue, rather than of consciously approving the existing inequalities. Neither in the British Commonwealth of Nations, moreover, nor in America have there been mass movements or influential individuals championing a national religion along nazi or "German Christian" lines. George A. Gordon, for example, who in 1913 timidly described what he called "reasonable hope of American religion," hardly caused a ripple in the sea of American sectarianism. Nonetheless, some of the fundamental factors which made possible the rapprochement between German Protestantism and extreme nationalism have also been in evidence in other countries. They may yet someday operate to the grave injury of both religion and those nations themselves.[78]

7. ECUMENICAL MOVEMENT

Protestant leadership is perfectly aware of these dangers. It realizes that so long as states are not "cosmopolitic entities" (to quote Schleiermacher again) but are bent upon safeguarding their particular interests, man's religious brotherhood, too, will remain merely an ideal. As Bishop Brent correctly observed, "The first Christian axiom for international relations is that each nation should view the concerns of its neighbor with solicitude equal to that with which it views its own. This has never been done." While organized religion alone could not enforce such a radical curtailment of sovereignty, it could help create the necessary mental climate for the international treaties designed to achieve it. Combined with the old quest for universal religion, or at least for some universality transcending denominational and territorial bounds, this new attitude created the powerful "ecumenical movement" between the two wars.[79]

Foundations had long been laid by Christian missions which naturally ran counter to both racialist exclusivity and nationalist self-sufficiency. That is why national socialism not only sharply opposed Jewish conversions, but a typical editorial of the *Schwarze Korps*, official organ of the Elite Guard, bitterly denounced also Christian missions in Africa:

> The Negro [it wrote] must remain what he is and not be spoiled by European missions. . . . Christian missions mean a survival of the inferior and the degenerate. . . . Moreover, Christianity with its theory of equality and redemption is a hindrance to the sovereignty of the white man. The greatest danger of the dethroning of white men and their political power comes from the teaching of missions.

Confronted with the loss of German colonies and the need of husbanding its foreign exchange for direct nazi propaganda, the new German regime was even prepared to give up whatever political and economic gains might incidentally accrue to its nation from German missions. In other countries, to be sure, imperialism and the quest for markets often lent a less altruistic coloring to missionary efforts. However, their main objective, certainly in the consciousness of missionaries and their chief backers, was the idealistic wish of spreading the word of God. A very large proportion of funds and personnel of the American Protestant missions came not from the eastern seaboard but from the Middle West, the area of traditional American isolationism and lesser interest in world trade.[80]

Home missions served more directly nationalist purposes inasmuch as whole-sale conversions to the majority creed obviously promoted national homo-geneity. Religious propaganda among Indians and Negroes played a great role in the rise and consolidation of the American national sentiment. In Czarist Russia the more or less forcible Christianization of the Jewish masses became part of the same policy of denationalizing minorities which led to the enforced return of millions of Uniate Ukrainians to the Orthodox fold. In Germany Christian missions among Jews began to flourish in post-Napoleonic Prussia under strong governmental auspices. While the general tenor of these mis-sionary efforts was unfriendly to Jews as well as to Judaism, British and Amer-ican missions often served as spearheads in combating antisemitism. The renowned London Society for Promoting of Christianity amongst the Jews, founded in 1809, contributed greatly to the amelioration of Jewish status all over the world, one of its early leaders, Lewis Way, demanding from Czar Alexander I, and through him from the Congress of Aix-la-Chapelle in 1818, complete emancipation of all European Jewry. Another leader, Anthony Ashley Cooper, the seventh Earl of Shaftesbury, became in the 1840's the chief pro-tagonist of Jewish restoration to Palestine.[81]

On the Continent Methodist, Baptist and other missions were frequently resented on nationalist as well as denominational grounds. The Eastern Churches, particularly after the upset caused by the Communist Revolution, viewed all outside propaganda as a disintegrating force and their delegates at the Stockholm Conference appealed to the Americans to desist from disrupting their ecclesiastical unity. The denominationally heterogeneous English-speak-ing world, on the other hand, nurtured from the springs of religious freedom, viewed with perfect complacency the fact proudly asserted by a student of American denominations that "no form of living Christianity anywhere but has its representative here." The world-famous British and Foreign Bible So-ciety was founded, in 1804, on the initiative of Thomas Charles who, as pastor of a Calvinistic Methodist congregation in Bala, felt the need of supplying Welsh Bibles to his parishioners. None of his colleagues saw in this incidental promotion of the Welsh national tongue the slightest betrayal of English nationalism. Within little more than a century (to 1906) the society dis-tributed nearly 200,000,000 Bibles, of which only some 78,000,000 were in English. The other copies appeared in some 530 different languages and dia-lects, four hundred of which had never had any translation of Scripture. As in the Middle Ages, such versions often became the fountainheads of a new national consciousness.[82]

Anglo-American leadership also brought together the Protestant missions in a world-wide organization. One need not be seriously concerned over the occa-sional verbal lapses, strongly reminiscent of the contemporary imperialist jargon, of some great leaders of the World Missionary Conferences which, first convened in New York in 1854, culminated in the growingly ecumenical gatherings in the same city (1900), Edinburgh (1910), Jerusalem (1928) and Madras (1938). Even the well-known pacifist John R. Mott published in 1897 a book extolling the universities' role in the progress of Christianity by calling them "strategic points in the world's conquest." The distinguished theologian Hendrick Kraemer believed as late as 1938 that he could not praise the Edinburgh Conference more eloquently than by saying that it had focused its attention "on a strategical review of the whole mission field," that "it was the first act of united and coordinated reconnoitring of the non-Christian world," and that it seemed as if the latter "were spread out before the eye as a world to be conquered." But the Continuation Conferences held in various Asiatic lands in 1912-13 and the sessions of the International Missionary Council after the First World War revealed, even verbally, a new understanding of Eastern cultures and national self-determination. By the time the Jerusalem Conference met in 1928, with a much larger participation of the "younger churches" from mission lands, the assumption of Western superiority was wholly abandoned. "A new interest," writes a recent commentator, "in an indigenous Christianity and an indigenous church was manifested, involving new respect for native cultures and a new critique of essential Christianity in differentiation from Western civilization." The conference went so far as to suggest "sharing" with other faiths in the common struggle against the forces of secularism. This line was further pursued by the Laymen's Foreign Missions Inquiry conducted in 1930-32. One of its characteristic conclusions, with special reference to the rise of nationalism in the Orient, reads:

> The connection of Christianity with Western life, formerly a matter of prestige, now has its disadvantages. For the sake of securing for Christianity a fair hearing it is necessary to separate it, as far as possible, from *our* history and our promoting agencies and to present it in its universal capacity.

In fact, the Western leaders now often leaned so far backward in favor of the "younger churches" as to encourage the latter's excessive nationalist proclivities. In Madras, particularly, the rising tide of Eastern nationalism began looming as a new menace to the true brotherhood of man.[83]

Out of this spirit of mutual understanding grew also the new ecumenical movement. The ecumenic idea was as old as Protestantism, indeed as all Christianity. Luther and the other reformers really wanted only to reform the existing church universal. Ulrich Zwingli tried hard to form a federation of all Evangelical churches, while Calvin, too, looked forward to some sort of international organization. A Latin volume published in Geneva in 1581 demanded the "harmony of the various professions of faith . . . in the European kingdoms, nations and provinces." In 1628 John Dury took a vow to devote his life to the reunion of all Christendom. The growth of nationalism, however, and Protestantism's progressive atomization prevented these ideas from assuming tangible form. Even the British effort of 1878 to establish a world church in co-operation with the leaders of Russian Orthodoxy proved an utter failure.[84]

The growing tension in national and international relations at the turn of the century, however, called also for increasing co-operation between the churches. Such co-operation could be secured either by the federation of all Protestant churches in a particular country, world-wide collaboration of single denominations or, most comprehensively, by some truly ecumenical bodies. Despite failure of the Disciples who, instead of uniting all denominations by return to primitive Christianity, had become but another denomination, efforts at unity in country-wide superstructures met with increasing success. The Federal Council of Churches of Christ in the United States, the United Church of Canada, the *Confédération des Eglises* in France, the *Evangelischer Kirchenbund* in both Germany and Switzerland and similar bodies in other countries lent organizational unity to previously disparate efforts. Without infringing on the autonomy of denominations or individual churches these central bodies gave direction to many co-operative efforts. At the same time some denominations began developing world-wide agencies. The Presbyterian Alliance, for example, brought together the Presbyterian churches in a joint representation. Similar functions were performed by new Lutheran and Methodist bodies. The oldest and most effective of these denominational associations were the Lambeth Conferences serving the whole Anglican Communion.[85]

These were milestones on the road toward international organization. Many religious-minded individuals and groups (of women, students, etc.) had long labored in the service of this ideal. As far back as 1893 a Parliament of Religions met in Chicago with the participation not only of representatives of the various Protestant groups but also of Cardinal Gibbons and other Catholics, Rabbis Isaac M. Wise and Gustav Gottheil, several Hindus, Muslims and Chinese.[86] It reconvened sporadically in subsequent years. Along similar lines were the annual meetings of the so-called World Congress of Faiths in 1936-38, the proceedings of which (on "Faith and Fellowship"; "The World's Need of Religion"; and "The Renascence of Religion") indicate the vast range of its debates. Leadership of both organizations clearly rested in the hands of members of Anglo-Saxon Protestant churches, reflecting the deep yearning of English-speaking Protestants for closer contacts with other faiths. But they never were intended to be activist bodies. Their sponsors believed in the intrinsic value of the meeting of minds and personal contacts. Opponents could readily deride them, with far more justice than the League of Nations, as sheer "debating societies." But to religions to whom the "Word" had supreme importance—Protestant leadership ever since Luther and Calvin had paid special homage to the "Word"—even "debates" could not be altogether meaningless.

Principally of theoretical value was also the World Alliance for International

Friendship through the Churches, which was organized by the Church Peace Union with the financial assistance of Andrew Carnegie. Its aims were:

> To organize the religious forces of the world so that the weight of all Churches and Christians can be brought to bear upon the relations of governments and peoples to the end that the spirit of peace and good-will may prevail, and that there may be substituted arbitration for war in the settlement of international disputes; friendship in place of suspicion and hate; co-operation instead of ruinous competition; and a spirit of service and sacrifice rather than that of greed and gain in all transactions between the nations.

It started inauspiciously, by holding its first meeting in Constance, Germany, during the momentous early days of August, 1914. Undaunted the leaders met again in Berne (1915), Holland (1919), Denmark, etc. Although on occasions these gatherings unavoidably reflected outside nationalist controversies, they bore witness to the churches' growing recognition of their share of responsibility in the war tragedies and the nationalist unsettlement of the postwar era.[87]

Together with such related endeavors as the Interchurch World Movement or the circular appeal to the *koinonia ton ekklesion* (union of churches) issued in 1920 by the Greek Orthodox ecumenical patriarch of Constantinople, these activities laid the foundations for the significant ecumenical attempts of the 1920's and 1930's. Here the forces of organized Christianity were to be marshaled not only for the preservation of peace, but also in order to formulate common principles, organize permanent federative agencies, and lay the ground for ultimate organic reunion. From 1916 on Charles S. Macfarland, secretary general of the Federal Council of Churches, labored for the convocation of a world-wide Christian conference. In 1917 Nathan Söderblom, archbishop of Upsala, and the Swiss Federation of Churches issued similar calls. At the session of the World Alliance in 1919 a committee of representatives from the United States, Sweden and Switzerland was entrusted with final preparations.[88]

The outcome was the famous Universal Conference on Life and Work held at Stockholm in 1925. It was attended by delegates from forty-four countries and dominions representing one hundred five independent churches and denominations. Among them were ten branches of the Eastern Orthodox Churches, though no delegates were allowed to come from the Soviet Union. Only the absence of Catholic delegates kept it from being a universal Christian council. The other, even more significant, limitation was that the conference adopted resolutions calling for voluntary acceptance of certain principles, but could not enact binding legal or doctrinal canons.[89]

Stockholm was followed by Lausanne (with a still larger attendance) two years later and by the even more important conferences at Oxford and Edinburgh in 1937. Going beyond sporadic discussions, a permanent World Council of Churches was established with headquarters in Geneva. The enthusiasm revealed in these meetings, the delegates' ability to find areas of agreement, rather than disagreement, and the brilliant leadership of the late Dr. Temple, archbishop of Canterbury and chairman of the World Council, held out great promise for the future. True to the old saying that "doctrine divides but service unites," the American sponsors had originally wished to see the conferences concentrate on such "noncontroversial" fields as education and social work. The Stockholm Conference was, therefore, entirely devoted to the churches' position in "life and work." But it was speedily supplemented by that of Lausanne on the doctrinal and ecclesiastical aspects of "faith and order." Realizing that they were handling dynamite, the leaders abstained from passing formal resolutions. Reports prepared by the committees were read and, without vote, referred to the members for future pondering. A similar division persisted also in Oxford's deliberations on "life and work" and Edinburgh's dedication to the problems of "faith and order." When finally the constitution of the World Council was drafted at Utrecht in 1938, a European member remarked, with general approval, that "no federation for 'social service' alone would come close enough to the fundamental issue to claim the deep allegiance of European Christianity." This realization had already accounted for the far greater concentration on problems of "the church and its function in society" in Oxford than at Stockholm. Even in Edinburgh "definite theological agreements were reached on virtually every important issue save the authority of the ministry and the nature of sacraments." [90]

Unfortunately, the conferences at Oxford and Edinburgh and the World Council worked under the shadow of an approaching war. Though evidently stimulated by the new sense of urgency, they suffered from a growing feeling of futility. However reluctant to intervene in "internal" affairs, they could not remain silent in the face of the nazi threat to all Christianity. As early as January, 1934, Dr. George Bell, archbishop of Chichester, serving as chairman of the World Council of Life and Work, had to lodge a formal protest against the Reich government's obstruction of relations between the German and foreign churches. Undeterred by nazi press attacks on the ecumenical movement, which Alfred Rosenberg soon denounced as an "Ecumenical League of Nations" and a new kind of Freemasonry, the Oxford Conference sent an official message deploring "the absence of their brethren in the German Evangelical Church, with whom they have been closely bound both in the preparations for this conference and in the great tasks which are set before the universal church." The Edinburgh Conference was even more outspoken when it greeted the German Confessional Church, "We are in one heart with all suffering Christians in your land. We reverence the constancy and courage of your witness." Unable to prevent the tragedy of the Second World War which, in its indescribable horrors, exceeded even the darkest moments of its predecessor, the World Council quietly carried on. Its American section even marshaled enough energy to hold a North American Ecumenical Conference in Toronto in 1941. But it is only now after the inauguration of the United Nations organization and its affiliate bodies that the ecumenical movement faces new opportunities, but also new, unprecedented responsibilities.[91]

8. ERASTIANISM VERSUS INDIVIDUALISM

Surveying briefly, as we did, the whole history of Protestant-nationalist interrelations, one is struck by the amazing differences between German and Anglo-Saxon Protestantism which, in their nuclear form, go back all the way to the differences between Luther and Calvin. As is usual with two lines of evolution which, starting at the same point, run at an angle to each other, the distance between them has become ever wider. Luther's intrinsically Germanic and nationalist outlook was still strongly overlaid with a medieval crust of Catholic universality. Calvin's intrinsic internationalism, on the other hand, was temporarily obscured by the façade of a theocratically controlled church-state. Strewn on different national soils and growing in progressively different social and intellectual climates, the seeds sown by the great reformers developed into plants of a fantastically different coloring and texture.

There were, of course, frequent interrelations between these churches. Although lacking central organs, the Protestant communions of various lands always maintained friendly contacts. Anglo-Saxon culture exerted a powerful influence on all walks of German life in the eighteenth and, again, in the twentieth century. In the nineteenth century Germany reciprocated by the world-wide impact of her science and philosophy, including her new "scientific" theology.[92] The break in her historic continuity, which may result from her recent unprecedentedly speedy rise and decline, may reverse the earlier trends. By slow and painful re-education a new and more genuine rapprochement between the German and the rest of the Protestant world may yet be possible.

In the past, however, the Erastianism of the early Lutheran churches led to an ever more intimate alliance of throne and altar, as the German state became increasingly absolutist and bureaucratic. National unification having been achieved by the military prowess of "Protestant" Prussia, the nexus or, as Barth called it, the "hyphen" between Protestantism and nationalism became ever stronger. In its denominational strife with the powerful Catholic minority, climaxed in the *Kulturkampf*, organized Protestantism was allied with radical nationalism in combating the supranational Roman Church. If under Hitler the nationalist Frankenstein finally threatened to destroy all forms of Christianity, as it largely succeeded in destroying German Judaism, it was too late for the Evangelical Church to undergo more than a partial, pathetically inadequate reorientation.

In England, on the contrary, the "national" Anglican Church was the permanent bridge to supranational Catholicism, while the Free Churches moved ever more away from Roman connections. Under these circumstances neither group became wholly ensconced in the destinies of English nationalism, which soon oscillated between loyalty to England, the British Isles and the British Empire, making any form of "integral" nationalism perfectly unrealistic. Nationalist extremism could not possibly be harmonized with either a supra-imperial communion, like the Anglican, represented by almost world-wide Lambeth Conferences, nor with the Free Churches, which deeply cherished their interterritorial connections and missionary efforts. Like the United States, moreover, most British dominions soon had no national churches of their own, often not even a church commanding majority allegiance.[93]

Equally significant was the intimate connection between the Anglo-American liberties and English or American nationalism. Despite all reverses and setbacks, despite Know-Nothingism and the Ku Klux Klan, white supremacy and antisemitism, the basic principles of religious freedom have, at least thus far, prevailed over all forces of intolerance. Woodrow Wilson was perhaps overoptimistic when he predicted:

> Our liberties are safe until the memories and experiences of the past are blotted out and the Mayflower with its band of pilgrims forgotten; until our public school system has fallen into decay and the nation into ignorance; until legislators have resigned their functions to ecclesiastical powers and their prerogatives to priests.

But for the time being even these "ecclesiastical powers" are genuine defenders of religious liberty. From religious groups have come most "conscientious objectors" who, in the midst of their nation's struggle for survival, considered their religious conscience as their ultimate guide. Governments and popular majorities, particularly among the religious-minded, may have doubted the soundness of their judgment, but not their right of following it. Professor Douglas Macintosh, a Canadian member of the Yale Divinity School, was denied American naturalization by the Supreme Court (after a close vote of 5 to 4), because he refused to pledge himself in advance to bear arms in a war which his Christian conscience might consider unjustified. But his stand was applauded by the bulk of informed Protestant opinion.[94] Nothing of that kind could have happened in Germany or almost anywhere else on the Continent.

For this reason the Anglo-Saxon countries have become also the main guardians of religious individualism. The Reformation had preached everywhere the supremacy of individual conscience. German Anabaptists and other sectarians took that principle seriously, as did many Pietists, especially of the Zinzendorf school. But it slowly withered away in the unfavorable clime of state supremacy and nationalist loyalty. Even in the more freedom-loving Scandinavian countries Kierkegaard's appeal to extreme religious individualism was a voice crying in the wilderness. Religious faith, he had taught, precludes all company. "A man, in so far as he is a believer, owes nothing to another man, but everything to God." From this angle any church seemed to him a sort of cowardice.[95] Only England and America could become the physical and spiritual homes of millions of Methodists and Congregationalists, of Baptists, Disciples and Unitarians, who recognized none but the voluntary allegiance of each individual. Most consistently the Baptists refused to recognize the very membership of children baptized by their parents before they reached the age of free individual decision.

Some Germans, even superior theological intellects, looked down condescendingly upon such voluntaristic, and hence artificial, "societies." They much preferred their own ecclesiastical "communities," organically grown from soil and nation. They realized that, far more than even the British churches, those in America were the outgrowth of constant migrations and the intermingling of races and nationalities. In this respect, they admitted, America best typified the modern industrial era, her great missionary successes having been buttressed by the world-wide expansion of her industrial civilization. But hence came also, they believed, her worship of success even in spiritual matters, her concentration upon the "social gospel" and her treatment of the church as merely a function of the kingdom of God.[96]

These criticisms, undoubtedly containing more than a grain of truth, overlooked, however, the simple fact that an industrial civilization may have organic growths of its own kind and that denominations or nationalities built upon personal liberties may grow into organic "communities" of a superior order. Enlightened Anglo-American churchmen realize, of course, the dangers of purely external success and societal anarchy and now pay much closer attention to the church and its function in modern society. They also look forward to an organic, rather than purely federative, development of their ecumenical organs. Certainly the originally consultative Lambeth Conferences have by now become as typical an organic entity as is the largely unwritten, and often admittedly inconsistent, Constitution of Britain or the British Commonwealth of Nations.[97]

Out of this remarkable combination of individualism and liberty-loving nationalism has also grown a new pragmatic approach to the old religious ideal of the brotherhood of man. It is no accident that pious American and British Protestants like Woodrow Wilson, Lord Robert Cecil and Jan Smuts became the protagonists in the first dramatic unfolding of a League of Nations. One of their spiritual disciples, Franklin Delano Roosevelt, became the chief architect of the United Nations. All of them realized that the new world order could be built only upon the foundation of individual liberty and national self-determination, i.e., Wilson's Fourteen Points, Roosevelt's Four Freedoms, and the Atlantic Charter. Similarly the builders of ecumenical Christianity have clearly wished to moor the new structure in the free individual conscience and the full autonomy of all denominational and national groups.

Their internationalism, too, is based on the recognition of certain admirable qualities in both political and cultural nationalism. The idea of self-sacrifice for the nation, in particular, is, even within its nationalist limitations, a truly religious idea. As the Unitarian minister William L. Sullivan once preached:

> Wherever there is a great ideal or something that holds a fair promise of becoming one, it must be kept and not destroyed. You impoverish the world if you destroy it. If you fling away the idea of nationhood and country you wreck one of the highest ideals that ever flowered forth from the spirit of man.[98]

But the ecumenical movement is also mindful of St. Paul's beautiful words: "And though I bestow all my goods to feed the poor, and though I give my body to be burned, and have not charity, it profiteth me nothing."

Chapter VI

ORTHODOX CAESARO-PAPISM

INTERRELATIONS between the Eastern European religions and modern nationalism had many peculiar facets. Because of its unbroken descent from the Eastern Roman Empire, the Orthodox Church's early relations to the Byzantine emperor permanently influenced its destinies in all Eastern realms. It embraced both old nationalities like Greeks and Syrians, and many new ethnic groups which it helped fashion from their tribal amorphousness. Christianity's constant uphill struggle with Islam, finally, the permanent subjugation of Syrians, Copts and other Christians by Arabs, the half millennium of Turkish domination over Balkan Slavs and the two and a half centuries of Tartar rule over Russians likewise left their indelible imprint on the East European evolution.

The Slavonic world itself soon reflected the sharp cleavage between Orient and Occident. Poles, Czechoslovaks and Croats adopted Roman Catholicism and the Latin script and became an integral part of Western civilization. Other Slavonic peoples joined the Eastern Church, adopted its peculiar adaptation of the Greek script and became immersed in the thought patterns, folkways and ritualistic emphases of the Byzantine world. Only Russia's phenomenal expansion during the past three centuries gave the Orthodox Slavs great numerical preponderance over the combined Slavonic Catholics and Uniates.

The overshadowing distinction between the Western, Latin, and Eastern, Greek, civilizations long stimulated supranational, regional loyalties and impeded the growth of national consciousness. However, long before Protestantism's victorious appeal to national and linguistic preferences in worship, the Eastern Churches, confronted by the ancient Syriac and Coptic cultures, which they dared not uproot, tolerated liturgical separatism. That is why they readily yielded also to the liturgical use of the more primitive Slavonic languages. These local liturgies, once adopted, soon became invested with the sanctity of tradition and tended to become crystallized at the early stages of their linguistic evolution. Ultimately, Slavonic liturgy became almost as unintelligible to the ordinary worshipers, lay and clerical, as was liturgical Greek or Latin. Devoid of the latter's universal character it nevertheless seriously impeded the evolution of native languages. Only Peter the Great's act of daring, followed by ruthless suppression of opponents, simplified alphabet and ritual so as to re-establish a measure of conformity between the religious and the secular language.[1]

If ecclesiastical autonomy thus fostered national preservation, caesaro-papism, spreading from the Byzantine Empire to all its dependencies, paved the way for a unity of state and church reminiscent of the ancient empires. True, the Seventh (and last) Ecumenical Council of the Eastern Church, meeting at Nicaea in 787, promulgated the "symphony," i.e., co-operation of emperor and patriarch on the basis of equality. This doctrine was reaffirmed a century later by Emperor Basil the Macedonian in his *Epanagogé*. But neither it nor the occasional sharp controversies between the two powers long deterred the emperors from appointing and deposing patriarchs at will. During the first six years of his reign (1185-91) Isaac II appointed five different dignitaries and often used at his table precious chalices removed from churches.[2] Para-doxically the patriarch often enjoyed greater ecclesiastical authority in Muslim lands. The Ottoman Empire, in particular, long conceded extensive autonomy to its Christian subjects and vested its exercise in the hands of the ecumenical patriarch of Constantinople and the hierarchy under his control.

1. Russia's National Religion

The Russian Church was in many ways instrumental in developing the unity of the various tribes which, in their aggregate, later constituted the Russian nation. It also instilled in them a sense of distinctiveness from their kindred but religiously differentiated neighbors. By adopting Eastern Chris-tianity, Olga, Vladimir and their successors made a vital decision for the entire future of Western civilization. They could have chosen Islam, Judaism or Roman Catholicism, but they decided in favor of Orthodoxy and thus definitely separated their people from Catholic Europe.[3]

At first, this alignment led to complete cultural and religious vassalage. The Russian Church depended not only on the Byzantine hierarchy but also on the emperor. Of the first twenty-three metropolitans of Kiev only three were Russians, another three southern Slavs, whereas seventeen had been native Greeks. All Russian metropolitans were appointed by the patriarch of Constantinople. More astonishingly, the Byzantine emperor was long in-cluded in Russian prayers. As late as 1389 Patriarch Antonius of Constantinople complained to Grand Prince Vasili:

> With sorrow . . . have I heard that thou dost not permit the metropolitan to mention in the liturgy the godly name of the emperor, saying, forsooth, "We have the church, but the emperor we do not have and do not wish to know." This is not well. The holy emperor holds a high place in the church. He is not like other rulers—the local princes and potentates. The emperor in the beginning established and confirmed the true faith for all the world. The

emperors called the ecumenical councils. . . . It is not possible for a Christian to have the church and not the emperor. For the church and the empire are in close union . . . and it is not possible to separate the one from the other.[4]

This dependence diminished with the relative decline of Byzantine versus Russian power. The two and a half centuries of Tartar domination (1228-1462), though generally a bleak period, forced the Russians to rely principally upon their own spiritual and cultural resources. They were aided by the Mongolian invaders themselves who, following the Muslim rulers' example, granted extensive self-government to their Christian subjects and entrusted its exercise largely to the Orthodox hierarchy. Many conquerors, since the Achaemenide Empire, had found that in this way they could maintain large subject populations in a state of relative acquiescence. During that crucial period the Russian metropolitans, since 1300 residing in Vladimir and later in Moscow but often visiting the Mongolian capital of Serai, became the mainstay of Russian national feeling.

At the same time the relinquishing of the metropolitan see of Kiev symbolized the Russian people's growing severance of relations with the West. No longer was any princely throne occupied by a Westernizer of the caliber of Yaroslav of Kiev (eleventh century) who had a Swedish wife, married off three daughters to the kings of England, France and Hungary and a sister to the king of Poland, and trained a son (subsequently the father of another famous prince, Vladimir II Monomachus) to converse fluently in five languages.[5] Tartar domination erected a thick wall of separation even from the Orthodox Lithuanians, who increasingly drifted into the orbit of Catholic Poland.

Forceful Catholic mission which, after the conquest of Constantinople by the Latin crusaders in 1204 had led to the establishment of a Catholic archbishopric in Halich (Galicia), provoked a further Orthodox as well as nationalist reaction. It was deepened by the West's failure to supply effective military aid against the Tartars, just as the papacy's subsequent inability to stave off the Turkish threat to Constantinople completely nullified its diplomatic successes at the Council of Ferrara in 1438-39. When Metropolitan Isidor of Moscow, next to Bessarion chief Orthodox protagonist of the union idea at the council, returned to Moscow in 1441 he was arrested and had to flee for his life. The Union, ultimately consummated in Brest-Litovsk in 1596 between papal and Polish representatives and some "Little Russian" (Ukrainian) spokesmen, was so clearly associated with Poland's imperial aspirations that it became anathema to the Russians.[6] With the continued shift of Russia's center of gravity from the more ancient and populous southwest to the vast open spaces in the northeast, from Kiev and its famous *Lavra* to Moscow and the monasteries of Radonesh, Solovetsk (a White Sea island) or the cities on the Volga, Russia's cultural isolation from the Latin world became well-nigh complete.

"The spiritual contrast between Russia and Europe has been displayed in its fullest significance in the Russian monastery," from which the leading hierarchs were recruited and whose growth in number and affluence far exceeded the general increase in population. According to an admittedly incomplete computation 150 monasteries are known to have been established between A.D. 1000 and 1400: 80 of these were founded in the fourteenth century alone; 70 more were added between 1400 and 1450. Somewhat slowed down in the sixteenth century with its 100 new foundations, progress was resumed in the 1600's when 220 new monasteries were founded. Even more than in the medieval West, these institutions had become focal centers of trade and industry. Many of them exploited vast tracts of land, fisheries and other natural as well as human resources (Radonesh alone was to own in 1764 more than 100,000 villeins), thus furnishing both economic and intellectual leadership to their respective districts. Being integrated under Moscow's hierarchical control, however, they did not promote regional loyalties but became effective instruments of national unity.[7]

Unity was fostered also by the close intermingling of secular and ecclesiastical powers. Otherwise the internecine wars between the princes (there were some 90 such wars in addition to 160 foreign invasions during the Tartar domination) might have broken up the sparse settlements from the White to the Black Sea, possessing woefully inadequate means of communications, into a number of independent tribes. But the ecclesiastical preponderance of the Moscow metropolitanate, whose authority at times extended even over Lithuanian provinces, prepared the ground for the unified monarchy of Ivan the Terrible. Moscow "became the ecclesiastical capital of Rus long before it became the political capital." [8]

Growing political power reciprocally strengthened ecclesiastical control. With the fall of Constantinople and the subjection of all other Greek Orthodox peoples to the rule of Muslim Turkey or Catholic Poland, the Russian Church stood out as the sole independent champion of Orthodoxy. It was quite natural, therefore, for Ivan's successors to establish in 1589 a patriarchate in Moscow to rival and, before long, to exceed in glory the Near Eastern patriarchates. This act of daring was accomplished with the concurrence of the patriarch of Constantinople, who happened to be visiting in Moscow at that time, and was ratified two years later by a council held at Constantinople in the presence of the other Oriental patriarchs. Though not ready to concede to the Moscow hierarch the desired third rank and granting him only fifth place in the patriarchal order, the patriarchs of Constantinople or Antioch, of Jerusalem or Alexandria soon depended on the financial support and political interventions of their Russian coreligionists.[9]

The simultaneous rise of the Muscovite grand prince to the position of czar lent even greater luster to the Russian Church. Having in 1472 married Sophia, niece of the last Byzantine emperor, Ivan III, Russia's liberator from the Tartars, claimed to be the direct successor of the Eastern Roman emperors. The title "czar" often appeared in his formal correspondence with foreign powers. Perhaps at his wife's instigation, he also appropriated the double-headed eagle of Byzantium as Russia's new emblem. Though as late as 1547 Ivan IV asked the patriarch of Constantinople to convoke a council formally to confirm his title of czar, this implied no renunciation of the supremacy of the civil power, long established in the Eastern Church. Ivan's successors, indeed, never again sought at the Bosporus formal confirmation of their ascension to the imperial throne. The impression made by the vivid contrast between Russia's liberation and the fall of Byzantium was best expressed by a contemporary writer who spoke glowingly of Moscow as the "third Rome" destined to supplant the previous Romes at the Tiber and the Bosporus. "For two Romes fell," said Monk Filofei, "and the third stands, and a fourth there will not be." [10]

2. CZARIST AUTOCRACY

The foundations were thus laid for a Russian caesaro-papism which overshadowed even that of medieval Byzantium. Individual patriarchs of great vigor and prestige, like Filaret, the father of Mikhail, founder of the Romanov dynasty (1619-33), or Nikon, in the early days of Czar Alexei (1652-66), evoked the semblance of equality between patriarchate and imperial throne. Filaret actually served as coregent, while during Alexei's absence Nikon issued secular decrees and behaved as if he were Russia's civil ruler as well. The "symphony," long vainly postulated in Byzantium, now seemed close to realization in the Muscovite empire. Some extremists even wished to emulate the papacy's claim to supremacy over the state. Nikon, as strong-willed a hierarch as Gregory VII or Innocent III, accepted the patriarchal office only after the czar promised him complete independence in spiritual affairs. Before long he declared:

> The czar has committed to him the things of this earth but I have committed to me the things of heaven. The czar has committed to him the bodies, but the priest the souls of men. . . . The one acts by compulsion, but the other by counsel. The one uses material weapons, but the other spiritual. The one has his war with men his enemies, but the other with principalities and with the rulers of this world, of the *darkness* of this world. And for this reason the priesthood is a vastly greater thing than the empire. As the moon receives the light from the sun . . . so also the czar derives his consecration, unction and coronation from the bishop. . . . For the episcopal power is in the day, i.e., over souls, but the imperial or royal is in the things of this world, and this power, which is the czar's sword, must be ready to act against the enemies of the Orthodox faith.[11]

This declaration must have sounded like a Russian paraphrase of Boniface VIII's *Unam sanctam!* Not unjustly, therefore, such modern historians as Samarin spoke of Nikon's attempt at establishing a "national papacy."

Unlike the pope, however, the Moscow patriarch lacked the necessary power to validate his extreme demands. He neither had a sovereign state of his own nor could he engage in power politics with the emperor's royal rivals and obstreperous vassals. The days of independent Russian princes and boyars were gone forever, and the national church offered the only domestic counterweight to imperial autocracy. Loyalty to the czar had become so deeply ingrained that a nobleman, impaled by Ivan the Terrible for some minor offense, constantly repeated amidst his excruciating pains, "Great God, protect the czar!" The Russian clergy itself soon voted for Nikon's deposition. The four Oriental patriarchs, too, issued in 1664 a joint declaration condemning Nikon's personal meddling in state affairs and his insistence that the clergy take a vow of obedience to himself, for, in their opinion, in Russia only the imperial authority was unlimited, while that of the patriarch was limited.[12]

Ever since, czar after czar felt free to depose the ecclesiastical leaders and to replace them by others. Peter the Great, going about his self-imposed task of "debarbarizing his native land" (Leibniz), was not satisfied even with Patriarch Adrian's extreme pliability. He first allowed the patriarchal office to remain unoccupied for many years, and in 1721 formally abolished it. Undoubtedly inspired by Lutheran prototypes in Sweden and Prussia, he entrusted the chief ecclesiastical authority to a collegiate body, the Holy Synod. To ensure its permanent acquiescence, he made its members dependent on short-term appointments and obliged them to take an oath "that the supreme judge of this Holy Synod is the emperor of all the Russias." This oath remained obligatory until 1901. The main jurisdiction in ecclesiastical affairs was now vested in the overprocurator of the Synod, a civil official, picked from the army or bureaucracy and subject to dismissal by the emperor at any time.[13]

From that time on the unity of church and state under imperial leadership remained uncontested. The great eighteenth century scholar Lomonosov recklessly extolled Peter: "He is thy God, thy God, O Russia!" Peter himself was more modest. "Here is your patriarch," he exclaimed, thumping on his breast, when a deputation of spiritual leaders asked him to fill the patriarchal chair. His chief ecclesiastical adviser, Theophan, spoke of him as "the anointed," clearly emphasizing his messianic character. Until 1869 all Russian churchgoers listened to the annual recitation of a curse hurled at rebels like Ian Mazeppa and all "who do not know that the Orthodox monarchs have been raised to the throne by virtue of a special grace of God—and that, at the moment the sacred oil is laid on them, the gifts of the Holy Ghost are infused with them anent the accomplishment of their exalted mission." It mattered little that neither Peter nor any of his successors ever repudiated the doctrine that the czar had no authority over matters of faith and dogma, since the Russian Church was but a segment of the Eastern church universal. Peter himself made use of it, whenever it suited his purpose as when he thus excused in 1717 to the doctors of the Sorbonne his inability to promote reunion with Rome. But he readily brushed it aside when he wished to listen to similar proposals from Anglican quarters. He also introduced, on his own, a modicum of liberty of conscience, especially for the numerous foreigners whom he attracted to Russia in connection with his Westernizing reforms.[14]

Catherine II, Peter's stanch admirer, acted with still less restraint as the "head of the church." Personally a typical child of Enlightenment and a religious skeptic, she observed all fasts, took communion once a year, went to church regularly, listened attentively to sermons and treated churchmen with reverence and liberality. In her Coronation Manifesto of 1762 she asserted that "of all the dangers to which Peter III brought Russia none was so great as that of the complete ruin of the Greek religion, whose doctrines were being rooted out in such a way that one had to ask whether the old faith of Russia was not being replaced by one that is new." At the same time she did not hesitate to offer shelter to Jesuits expelled from other European lands and to allow the Polish ruling classes to continue their Romanizing policies among the Uniate and Orthodox peasants of her newly annexed Western provinces. Going far beyond Peter's registration of the vast possessions of Russian monasteries, she confiscated outright most of the monastic wealth accumulated over many generations (1762-64) and added to the state domain some 2,000,000 villeins, or about one-seventh of Russia's entire peasant population. With this one stroke she undermined the monastic clergy's financial independence and control over the secular clergy and converted both into effective agencies of her autocratic government. A few decades later (1839) Marquis Astolphe de Custine observed that "the Graeco-Russian clergy have never been, and never will be anything more than a militia dressed in a uniform rather different from that of the secular troops of the empire." [15]

It was, therefore, with perfect justification that Russia's fundamental law, as promulgated by Nicholas I in 1832 and re-edited in 1906, included the following rhetoric:

> The Russian czar, as a Christian sovereign, is supreme protector and defender of the dogmas of the Graeco-Russian faith and supervisor of Orthodoxy and of good order in general throughout the holy church. In this sense he is spoken of as the head of the church. . . . God himself commands us to obey the czar's supreme authority not from fear alone, but as a point of conscience.

A leading nineteenth century Russian theologian, Filaret Drozdov, though writing in the more liberal era of Alexander II, stated succinctly, "God has given us the autocratic czar after the image of his own universal dominion." [16]

Not that there was lacking opposition to such extremist demands, but under the circumstances it, too, often assumed a religious character. Before the rise of modern revolutionary trends, and later concurrently with them, the existing political and social antagonisms found expression in innumerable sectarian movements. The early sect of "Judaizers," for instance, first appearing in 1370, in many ways reflected the intrachurch struggle against monastic control. The "Old Believers" (*staroobriadtsi*, term and substance would better be rendered by "Old Ritualists"), the largest and most persistent sect in Russian history, doubtless were seriously disturbed by the two rather than three fingers used in making the sign of a cross, the singing of two rather than three hallelujahs at mass, the alleged mispronunciation of the name "Jesus," or the improper shape of the cross. But they would never have formed a regular sect had it not been for the widespread revolt of the lower against the upper clergy. Nor would their sectarian career have been of such strength and duration had not their doctrine exercised a tremendous appeal to national sentiments and religious xenophobia. With the growing interlocking of state and church and the violent, if intermittent, suppression of "heresy," every sectarian movement, however esoteric, of necessity became a political factor, whose significance grew in ratio to the number, concentration and missionary effectiveness of its adherents. Despite the obvious inadequacy of religious statistics, it appears that in nineteenth century Russia 10 to 15 per cent of the population belonged to one or another sectarian group.[17]

Curiously, the sectarians themselves became spearheads of Russia's triumphant progression toward the Pacific Ocean, begun under Peter the Great. Like the religious colonizers of North America, many of them escaped into distant, undeveloped areas out of reach of their persecutors. Others, in this respect resembling the victims of the Spanish Inquisition who helped settle Latin America, furnished ever new contingents of deportees to Siberia. The distinction between ordinary and political crimes being rather tenuous, they often lent moral and intellectual leadership to all pioneering groups there. Persecution and ensuing dispersion reached a climax under Nicholas I. In a decree of 1826, aimed specifically at the pacifist sects of *Molokani* and *Dukhobors*, the czar placed this large and industrious group before the alternative of either enlisting in the army or going to Siberia. Those who chose the army readily performed all pacific tasks, but consistently refused to carry arms. When subjected to cruel tortures, they offered such heroic resistance that their comrades became deeply impressed. Before long the officers protested against their further recruitment as likely to ruin the discipline of the whole army. Similarly, when in 1839-41 Nicholas ordered their dispersal over the Caucasus he "found that to scatter burning coals among combustible material is not the best way to extinguish a fire."[18]

Unlike the British sectarians, however, the Russian schismatics were not raised on traditions of liberty and self-government. From the beginning of the Great Schism (*raskol*) in the seventeenth century, many of them viewed both patriarch and czar as harbingers of Antichrist. Peter's enforced reforms and especially his transfer of the Russian New Year from September 1 to January 1, made him appear to many Old Believers as the very personification of the Evil Principle. Opposition to all authority became ever more vehement, particularly among sects (like the Pilgrims, *Bieguny*) which a governmental classification of 1842 called the "most pernicious." Unlike those current among the North American colonists, however, theirs were anarchist rather than revolutionary ideologies, designed to abolish all governmental constraint. Some schismatics (e.g., the *Filipovtsi* or followers of a monk, Philip) actually preached "baptism by fire" as testimony to the strength of their faith. At the approach of governmental troops they set fire to their settlements and perished in the flames (particularly in 1743 and 1747). The majority, on the other hand, especially among those classified "pernicious" or "less pernicious," opposed the established church but not the imperial government. Even many so-called *Bezpopovtsi*, who repudiated all priesthood and worshiped without the mediation of clergy, bowed to the "white father" of all Russians. In short, rather than becoming a source of imperial disintegration, the Russian sects helped spread Russian nationalism to the far corners of the empire.[19]

So truly Russian were most of these sectarian movements, at least to the end of the nineteenth century, that they stoutly resisted the incursion of Western ideas, Catholic or Protestant. They did it with little inner struggle, often unconsciously, thereby revealing the more clearly the vitality of their national sentiment. The resurgence among *Khlysti* and *Skoptsi* of some old theologumena, cherished by the Montanists of the second century Phrygian Church or by the Bulgarian Bogomils of the ninth century, may have been as much the result of independent religious thinking as of underground historic continuity. Certainly the Judaizers, though blamed by contemporaries on the proselytizing activities of a Jewish merchant-missionary, Zechariah (S'charias), must have sprung from widespread dissatisfaction among the clergy itself. All its founders and early adherents were clerics of the Russian Church.[20]

Catholic propaganda, perhaps because it was supported by the "foreign" powers of the papacy and Poland, made less headway among the sectarians than even among the Orthodox. Somewhat more effective during the romantic reaction after the Napoleonic Wars and Joseph de Maistre's prolonged stay in St. Petersburg, its appeal was still limited to the upper classes. Chaadaev's great, but short-lived, vogue among the intellectual elite came from his outspoken critique of Russia's "backwardness" and his glorification of the Western ways of life rather than from his enthusiasm for the Roman Church. Interest in Catholicism was sufficiently intense, however, for Alexander I, both liberal and mystic though he was, to expel the Jesuit order from all his dominions in

1819. In answer to Chaadaev, Nicholas I intensified in 1841 the repression of all non-Orthodox creeds. Catholic support of the Napoleonic invasion of 1812 and the Polish uprisings of 1831 and 1863, greatly exaggerated in popular imagination, helped antagonize the masses, both Orthodox and sectarian.[21]

Protestant missionary efforts, too, long suffered from the popular association of Protestantism with the hostile powers of Sweden and Germany. In their first onrush, Lutheranism, Calvinism and even anti-Trinitarian Socinianism found many adherents, especially among the nobility. Only sixteen of the five hundred noble families living in the province of Novgorod totally escaped their impact. The Moravian Brethren, on the other hand, appealed more strongly to the peasants. But in his disputation of 1570 with Jan Rokyta, Protestant member of a Polish mission, Ivan the Terrible heatedly repudiated these foreign importations. Nine years later he ordered the burning of two Lutheran churches in Moscow. The protracted wars with Sweden soon placed all Protestant sympathizers under a cloud of suspicion. The inclusion of a large Lutheran population in the Baltic provinces, finally, combined with the vulnerability of the Western frontiers after the partitions of Poland and the disproportionately large representation of Baltic Germans in high military and civilian offices, injected the national issue into the domestic religious controversies as well. In 1845 Nicholas I attempted, with his customary ruthlessness, to convert 1,000,000 Estonian and Latvian peasants to Orthodoxy. Allegedly, nine-tenths were willing, though only 100,000 actually embraced the Orthodox faith.[22]

Not until the end of the nineteenth century, therefore, did Protestantism gain a firm toehold in the Russian people. Carried on by Anglo-Saxon, rather than Continental, missionaries and hence suspected of few outright imperialist motives, Protestant propaganda now made considerable headway. In the 1870's Lord Radstock, associated with V. A. Pashkov, gained numerous adherents among the upper bourgeoisie and bureaucracy of the two capitals, calling forth the Holy Synod's sharp condemnation. If many of these conversions bore the earmarks of intellectual toying, the Baptist missions appealing to the related native groups of *Stundists* and *Dukhobors* made genuine progress. By 1914 some 97,000 Baptists were counted. Their number is said to have reached 4,000,000 in 1925. We may doubt the authenticity of these figures, which included a majority of *Stundists*, but it is evident that, if freed from their antinational stigma, Protestant doctrines and ecclesiastical forms could meet many Russians' spiritual and organizational needs. Their ultimate inefficacy, therefore, doubly underscored the profound interlocking of Russian Orthodoxy and nationalism.[23]

As elsewhere, Russia's national sentiment became clearly crystallized under the impact of the French Revolution. Like Schleiermacher, Alexander I long viewed the Revolution with considerable sympathy. He was prepared to gloss over its terroristic aspects and to admire even Robespierre. But when his conflict with Napoleon sharpened, he fell back upon the nationalist and religious resources of the Russian people. He was convinced by his foreign minister, Prince Adam Czartoryski, that the national enthusiasm of all oppressed nationalities could well be harnessed for the struggle against Napoleon, its great Continental awakener. At the same time it was easy to arouse religious fears of the French emperor's personal agnosticism and political Catholicism. The Holy Synod also played up Napoleon's former appeals to the Muslim world and his convocation of the Paris Jewish Sanhedrin.

> In Egypt [it wrote in one of its proclamations] he associated with the persecutors of the Christian Church, preached the Alkoran of Mahomet, proclaimed himself defender of the creed of the followers of that false prophet, and solemnly demonstrated his contempt for the shepherds of the Holy Church of Christ. . . . Finally to the greater shame of France he assembled there Jewish synagogues, ordered to pay honor to the Rabbins, and established a new great Jewish Synedrion, that same Godless congregation which once dared condemn to crucifixion our Lord and Savior Jesus Christ, and now he attempts to unite the Jews scattered by Divine wrath over the whole earth, and to direct them for the overthrow of Christ's Church and for (O horrible impudence overstepping all his wickedness!) the proclamation of a false messiah in the person of Napoleon.

The height of nationalist and religious frenzy was reached in the War of 1812, when the Russians burned their holy city of Moscow to destroy the invaders.[24]

This combination of concentrated state power, supreme ecclesiastical control, and chauvinist national leadership came to a climax under Nicholas I. Already in his Coronation Manifesto of 1826 the czar adumbrated his policy of suppression of all "impertinent destructive dreams." The new ideology was best expressed by Count Uvarov who in his famous report on the University of Moscow (1831) attacked the pernicious influences of Western ideas. He advocated instead "a regulated, fundamental education with a deep conviction and warm belief in the true Russian conservative principles of Orthodoxy, Autocracy and Nationality, which present the last anchor of our salvation and the surest pledge of the strength and majesty of our country." Later, as minister of education, Uvarov believed that, by stemming the influx of foreign ideas, he would prolong Russia's "youthfulness." If he were only able, he asserted, to keep back the country's development by half a century he would "die in peace." On the tenth anniversary of his ministerial management (1843) he dismissed all opposition to Orthodoxy, autocracy and nationality as objections of irresponsible liberals or mystics,

> of the Liberals, because the Ministry, proclaiming Autocracy, declared its firm desire to return to the Russian Monarchical Principle; of the Mystics—because the word Orthodoxy clearly indicated the intention of the Ministry to

hold fast to the teachings of Christianity and to do away with all the Mystical ghosts that had often obscured the clarity of the Holy traditions of the Church. Finally the word Nationality has provoked our enemies' animosity for the daring assertion that the Ministry considered Russia mature and worthy of marching not behind, but at least alongside with the other European nationalities.

Nationality, he made clear in other connections, meant stressing of Russian against the minority languages. "The very geographic extension of the far-flung empire," he asserted, "and its great heterogeneity make unity of speech and administration absolutely indispensable." Custine was indeed right when, summarizing his impressions of Russia under Nicholas, he said, "Tyranny, rendered calm by the influence of Terror, is the only kind of happiness which this government is able to afford its people." [25]

The Russian people, however, could not forever endure such happiness or retain its calm. After the severe jolt of the Crimean War in which, despite all handicaps of geography, "degenerate" Europe proved victorious, came the reform era of Alexander II. Significant concessions were also wrung from the czarist autocracy by the Revolution of 1905 which followed another humiliating defeat in the Russo-Japanese War. The constant growth of empire likewise created ever-new problems which could not be solved by the simple application of Uvarov's triple formula. At times Russian nationalism was actually at variance with Russian imperialism. The inclusion of millions of Muslims and Asiatics from the Crimea to the Pacific, for example, accentuated not only the former's Mongolian ingredients, but also its intrinsic ambivalence. Whenever Russia's expansionist drive was checked in the west, Asiatic, indeed Pan-Asiatic, tendencies gained the upper hand. In the writings of Prince Ukhtomski, who accompanied the young Crown Prince Nicholas (later Nicholas II) on his journey to the Far East, Pan-Asianism seemed seriously to rival Pan-Slavism as the imperial extension of Russia's nationalist drive. These and other intrinsic contradictions and polarities culminated in the extremist ideology and practice of the era of Pobedonostsev.

3. RUSSIA'S "INTEGRAL ORTHODOXY"

Constantin Petrovich Pobedonostsev left an indelible imprint upon a quarter century of Russian history (1881-1905). A man of fine native intelligence, sound juridical training, good familiarity with both Russian and Western cultures and strong nationalist and religious convictions, he became the master mind of the great reaction which lasted to the Revolution of 1905. The new monarch, Alexander III, was generally indecisive, but distrustful of his father's reforms. He was always glad to refer decisions to his admired mentor, whose official position was only that of overprocurator of the Holy Synod but whom he regularly consulted in the appointment and removal of cabinet ministers and other major affairs of state. Theoretically the Synod was independent of this "eye of the czar," who could not veto any decision, but merely submit it to the sovereign's approval or disapproval. The Synod's clerical members could at any time request an audience with the czar and even discontinue the overprocurator's salary by simply failing to vote for it. In practice, however, Protasov, after quarreling in 1842 with two noted metropolitans, Filaret of Moscow and Filaret of Kiev, refused to summon them for many years to Synod sessions. Going further, Pobedonostsev made it a rule to invite the bishops only for short terms of three, six or twelve months. He also liked to transfer them from one diocese to another and, on the slightest pretext, to send them into retirement. Under his administration most of them served only four years or less in one diocese.[26]

Such transfers could be used also for nationalist purposes. Two former Bessarabian bishops, for instance, were sent to occupy the influential posts of exarch of Georgia and catholicos of Armenia in perfect disregard of the national feelings of Georgians and Armenians. Arbitrary proceedings of this kind, doubly grievous to those who recalled Alexander I's original pledge to respect Georgia's fiscal and ecclesiastical independence, added fuel to nationalist propaganda. Even the Orthodox Seminary in Tiflis became a hotbed of nationalist as well as socialist agitation. In 1886 a seminarist by the name Laguev, a youth of nineteen, assassinated its rector. In his curious report to Pobedonostsev, Exarch Paul of Georgia stressed his personal insecurity and stated that, were it not for his sense of duty, he would prefer a small parish in the least Russian diocese to his exalted post. He recommended a new energetic administrator to purify the contaminated atmosphere of that "seminary of bandits." At the same time he also felt obliged to complain of the excessively generous reception given in Tiflis, on October 11, 1885, to Catholicos Makarii of Armenia. Though fully appreciating that the catholicos, whom he had know in Kishinev, "speaks and acts as a loyal subject of the Russian czar and seeks to inculcate in his coreligionists sentiments of fidelity and loyalty toward Russia," he resented the reception which had caused the Armenians to lift their heads and swagger with nationalist pride. Had Makarii personally been as popular among the Armenian separatists as his "revolutionary" rival, Melchisedek, the homage paid him might have done irreparable damage. The exarch's complaints found receptive ears in St. Petersburg. Before long the entire property of the Armenian Church in the Caucasus, valued at about $75,000,000, was confiscated.[27]

On Pobedonostsev's advocacy the state, beginning in 1893, allotted ever-increasing sums for salaries of the Orthodox clergy. By 1900 more than 43 per cent of all state subsidies to the church amounting to 23,559,685 rubles (approximately $12,000,000), were used for salaries. Five years later they rose further to 12,000,000 rubles. Under the excuse that their parishes could supply them with sufficient livelihood, clerics in the Russian interior received at best 100 to 180 rubles a year. In outlying provinces, however, the salaries ranged from 300 to 600 rubles, while in such exposed dioceses as Riga and Warsaw they increased to between 800 and 1,500 rubles. Through these fiscal measures Pobedonostsev extended his direct control over the lower clergy as well. His was no mean domain. In 1900 it consisted of over 49,082 churches and 18,946 shrines, served by 104,446 secular clergy, and of over 503 monasteries and 325 convents which accommodated 16,668 monks and 41,615 nuns. Although not excessive in ratio to some 90,000,000 Orthodox laymen (including sectarians), such a well-knit organization of 160,000 ecclesiastics proved of tremendous assistance to the czarist regime. Pobedonostsev never hesitated to enlist clerical support, even spying on parishioners, in counteracting the spread of revolutionary ideas.[28]

The clergy could prove most helpful by giving proper religious instruction in schools or, preferably, by concentrating all primary and secondary education in its own hands. Not that Pobedonostsev favored popular education as such. He preserved among his papers a lengthy memorandum by Paul de Derviz (of August 6/18, 1880) which seems to have made on him a lasting impression. Pleading that society's greatest enemy was idleness, the writer demanded that a peasant child be trained chiefly for work in the fields. "Teach him," Derviz added, "the rudiments of reading, writing and arithmetic, if he or his parents demand it, but he should not indulge in these studies except at a time when he has no other, more urgent occupation." Pobedonostsev himself extolled the faith of illiterate masses who, though unfamiliar with Scripture and the meaning of prayers, succeeded in erecting an altar to the "unknown Deity." But since, defying all obstacles, more and more Russians sent their children to school, the overprocurator encouraged state-supported parochial schools in preference even to government schools. Under his prompting the state subsidy to church schools was raised from the paltry sum of 17,000 rubles in 1881, to 7,000,000 rubles in 1900. In 1898 the 40,028 Orthodox Church schools exceeded in number the 37,046 ministerial schools, although the latter still attracted some 63 per cent of all school children. Approximately 60 per cent of all children received no formal education at all, but were occasionally exposed to some sort of religious instruction. A typical catechism, prepared in 1895 by the Synod's School Committee, enjoined the children to believe that the czar was "the father of the whole people and the anointed of God," that all "should be prepared to lay down their lives for him . . . and be obedient to the authorities appointed by him," and that those who shirked their duties toward him were "guilty not only before the sovereign, but also before God." [29]

Pobedonostsev argued against separation of state and church and even against the state's alleged impartiality toward religious minorities on the ground that

> the confidence of the people in its rulers is founded on faith—that is, not only on identity of religious profession but on the simple conviction that its rulers have faith themselves and rule according to it. Even the heathen and Mahometan peoples have more confidence and respect for a government which stands on the firm principles of faith—whatever that faith may be— than for a government which acknowledges no faith, and is indifferent to all.

Russia, in his opinion, was particularly fortunate in having a religion which, though stemming from the Orient and Byzantium, had become so deeply permeated with the Russian national spirit, language and appreciation of beauty as to become, for all intents and purposes, Russia's national religion. In his peroration at the nonacentennial celebration of Russia's conversion to Christianity he not only extolled his country's political independence but also the complete suffusion of its Orthodox creed with "our Russian soul." [30]

This may, indeed, be called "integral Orthodoxy," fully reminiscent of "integral nationalism." It demanded that all ecclesiastical organs bolster the old combination of autocracy, Orthodoxy and nationality. Rather than admitting the obsolescence of these slogans, Pobedonostsev took pride in wanting no innovations whatsoever. Among his first acts as counselor of the new czar was the preparation of an imperial manifesto. In his covering letter to the czar he wrote:

> Please note from the text first the firm determination to retain the autocratic power which is expressed here with full deliberation. This is most essential, for after such an emphatic statement all rumors of the forthcoming enactment of a Constitution today or tomorrow will quickly vanish. Secondly, that announcement is made of the decision not to establish any new institutions, but merely to bring law and order into those which already exist. Finally, that it is clearly stated that the liberation of peasants is irrevocable. Thereby an end will be made to malicious rumors that the peasants are to lose their freedom again. Such a Manifesto must make a most favorable impression both in Russia and in foreign countries. I know, namely, for a fact, that its publication has been awaited impatiently and that there is considerable amazement about its failure to appear.

Whether or not this final hint referred to some intimations by Bismarck, Pobedonostsev was generally most contemptuous of public opinion. While on a visit to Marienbad in 1888 he had nothing but words of utter disdain for the liberal Austro-Hungarian press. Though admitting that the newspaper had become a mighty institution which no government could afford to ignore and that occasionally it might exert a beneficent influence, he believed that it had largely fallen into the hands of ill-informed and self-seeking journalists. "It is hard to imagine," he exclaimed, "a despotism more irresponsible and violent than the despotism of printed words." In 1883 he reintroduced a rigid press censorship.[31]

The overprocurator also roundly condemned trial by jury and parliamentary government. "Among the falsest of political principles," he declared, "is the principle of the sovereignty of the people." He considered even the *zemstvo*, the regional gathering of nobles, at best a necessary evil and condemned believers in this survival of "Novgorod liberties" on a par with liberals and revolutionaries. Curiously, he echoed the revolutionary critique of parliamentarism by Herzen or Bakunin, when he asserted that it made sense in Anglo-Saxon countries where, like the jury, it was the outgrowth of an age-old individualistic tradition, but that it would utterly fail among the communally minded Slavs. Least of all could it expect to cope with an ethnically heterogeneous empire, like Russia, where a central legislature would speedily degenerate, even more than in Austria-Hungary, into a babel of tongues and interests. "It is terrible to think of our condition," he declared, "if destiny had sent us the fatal gift— an All-Russian Parliament! But that will never be." [32]

Russian autocracy obviously went hand in hand only with Orthodoxy. Pobedonostsev always discouraged sectarian movements, although he must have realized that whatever prospects of reconciliation between Orthodoxy and Old Believers had existed in *edinoverie* (one belief) had withered away under Nicholas I's oppressive regime and begun to blossom again only under the milder reign of Alexander II. Under his direction a new law was enacted in 1883 which, outwardly liberalizing outworn provisions of existing statutes, was far more intolerant than the actual practice. In his interesting correspondence of 1901 with the governor of Samara he forbade a local peasant to convert a house into a chapel for Old Believers. He had been told that most of the latter had not prayed in an Orthodox church since infancy and that the younger members had been christened as Old Believers, but he insisted that they all belonged to the Orthodox Church and must not indulge in heretical practices. In 1886 he prevented the establishment of houses of worship by the *Raskolnik* community of Moscow. He even urged Alexander III to reply to the latter's profession of loyalty that their indubitable devotion to the throne "was neither conditioned by the social class or institution to which they belonged nor by the rights and privileges which may have been granted them. It derived from the unshakable love of one's fatherland and from the submission to the czar holding his authority from God, i.e., from sentiments inherent in every Russian and inseparable from Russian nature." He ruthlessly withdrew children of sectarians from parental control and handed them over to Orthodox convents for "proper" education. Irked by Pashkov's extraordinary success in preaching (since 1876 with governmental approval) deeper spirituality at the expense of ceremonial law and submission to the church, he secured complete suppression of that "spiritual pestilence" and sent the founder into exile. But the ultimate outcome of this antiheretical crusade merely was greater underground vitality of the outlaw movements. Most sectarians simply refrained from registering their marriages and births with the official church or else bribed Orthodox clerics to register marriages at which they had not officiated. A new vested interest developed: some priests viewed with alarm any diminution in the number of schismatics which might entail the loss of this revenue.[33]

The *Inorodtsi* (people of foreign stock) felt, even more than the sectarians, the brunt of Pobedonostsev's tyranny. He argued for the dismissal of Count Loris-Melikov as chief minister of state because of the latter's Armenian origin. "Of an altogether Oriental mentality and morality," such a man, he wrote, "does not understand Russia and the Russian people, whose aspirations evoke no echo in his heart." Non-Orthodox Orientals were, of course, even less welcome. A Russian general complained to the exarch of Georgia that, in contrast to the honors paid in Tiflis to the catholicos of 700,000 Armenians, the reception given to the sheikh ul-Islam of 2,000,000 Shiyite Tartars had been entirely informal. The exarch agreed as to the relative injustice, but added, "If you want to know my opinion one should rather suppress all sheikhs ul-Islam and all the muftis. . . . Orthodox Russia may indeed tolerate Islam, Lamaism, etc., but it is not her business to safeguard the prosperity of these creeds." The overprocurator voiced no dissent while calling the czar's attention to the exarch's report.[34]

Pobedonostsev was most concerned about the crucial western provinces. Here the uneducated and, despite government subsidies, underpaid Orthodox clergy had to compete with a highly articulate Catholic priesthood and Lutheran pastorate. Reneging on old privileges, the overprocurator consistently tried to impose Orthodoxy on the Baltic peasants, playing up their hatred of the Lutheran barons. Since aristocracy and clergy resisted furiously and invoked both their ancient rights and their outstanding services in Russia's military and civil administration, he endeavored to fasten on them the stigma of illegality. Many Lutheran pastors, he wrote to the czar on December 21, 1887, "perform baptisms, marriage ceremonies, etc., among the Orthodox and blaspheme in their sermons against both the Russian Church and the authorities." These charges, he admitted, had not been upheld by the courts, which, on the contrary, allowed pending lawsuits against fifty-three pastors to rest for over three years. They were also sharply contradicted by his old friend, Pastor Hermann Dalton, in an *Open Letter* which allegedly impressed even Alexander III. Undeterred, Pobedonostsev repeated them in his formal reply to Edward Naville, chairman of the International Committee of the Evangelical Alliance (March, 1888). "Lutheranism," he declared, "like Catholicism before it, uses in these provinces the mantle of faith to cover up its attempt at domination." In his rage against the internal resisters and foreign interveners, he overlooked the ultimate effects of his policy of encouraging the Estonian and Latvian peasants. Whatever temporary successes he secured for Orthodoxy were more than compensated by his weakening of the traditional pillars of autocracy and by the stimuli he gave to the rise of Baltic irredentas.[35]

At the same time the overprocurator entertained sympathetic relations with individual Protestants and Protestant churches abroad. In 1881 he surprised his coworkers by recommending a Lutheran, Baron Nikolai, for the crucial post of minister of education. At the nine hundredth anniversary of Russia's conversion he contrasted the archbishop of Canterbury's willingness to attend the celebration at Kiev (only the simultaneous Lambeth Conference had prevented the sending of a distinguished Anglican representation) with the absence of the Rumanian clergy for purely political reasons. He was very skeptical, however, of the recurrent talk about reunion. As a nationalist he considered Anglicanism as the typical outgrowth of English individualism and rationalism, in contrast to the Slav communal spirit and mystic attachment to such "superstitions" as relics and ikons. "A Russian feels chilled in a Protestant church," he exclaimed. Deeply egalitarian, the true Slav welcomed the poorest and least educated as a brother in Christ, whereas the Anglican churches clung to existing class distinctions. "The more we consider the distinctive ethnical features of religion the more firmly we are convinced how unattainable is an union of creeds—by a factitious accord in dogma—on the principle of reciprocal concessions in immaterial things.. . . . The essential elements are so involved with the psychical nature of the race, with the principles of their moral philosophy, that it is futile to separate one from the other." [36]

Pobedonostsev consistently regarded the Roman Church as Russia's most dangerous enemy. Paradoxically, he held it responsible for the very doctrine of separation of state and church which everywhere threatened the autocracy's hold on the masses. Unheard of in antiquity, he contended, separation became the obvious corollary of the papacy's claim to supremacy over temporal princes. Even today Catholicism made tremendous strides in the United States, where "restricted by no relation to the state, submitting to no control, the pope freely distributes dioceses, appoints bishops, founds spiritual orders and convents in vast numbers and weaves over the whole territory a close network of ecclesiastical agents and institutions." Despite Leo XIII's conciliatory moves (e.g., his cordial reply of January 28, 1888, to Alexander III's perfunctory congratulations on his sacerdotal jubilee), Pobedonostsev long opposed the admission of a papal nuncio to Russia, which had found considerable support in the Ministry of Foreign Affairs. In his letter to Nicholas II of September 21, 1899, he argued that "the policy of the Roman Curia has been the same for centuries: a policy of ruse and mental reservation. Each rapprochement with Rome, as soon as it is formulated in writing, becomes a menace, for each word uttered is turned by Roman statesmanship into a weapon and a claim, which Rome interprets according to its own desires." He also considered Rome as a permanent ally of those Catholic nations, Austrians and Poles, which belonged to Russia's main domestic and foreign enemies. On account of their "old and still continuing feud" over Russia's southwestern borderlands, the Poles were, in his opinion, the chief protagonists in the struggle against the empire's national homogeneity and the mainstay of all revolutionary forces. Curiously misinterpreting the Russian revolutionaries' pledges of justice and equality for all national minorities, he suspected behind them the machinations of a secret Polish government. His self-imposed blindness to the real causes of disaffection made him exaggerate the indubitable alliance between the Polish and Russian socialist parties into one of the entire Polish nation (led by its Catholic clergy and aristocracy) with Russia's liberal forces.[37]

The Jews, because of their defenseless position, became the most abject victims of Pobedonostsev's oppressive policies. His antisemitism was of a religious and nationalist rather than racial kind, although in exceptional cases he spoke derogatorily of an official's Jewish descent. Possibly having a private ax to grind, he twice denounced the newly appointed governor of Kishinev, Koniard, because of "the inconvenience of appointing a descendant of a family of Jewish bankers to serve as governor of a Jewish district." At the same time he made good diplomatic use of such Jewish converts as J. F. Cyon, a former professor of physiology at St. Petersburg. Working hand in hand with Katkov, Cyon, then living in Paris, became the main Western exponent of Pobedonostsev's governmental ideology and also more helpful than any professional diplomat in preparing the Franco-Russian Alliance. On occasion the overprocurator recommended to the czar artists of Jewish descent. On February 6, 1886, he urged the monarch personally to attend Anton Rubinstein's concert, for the great musician "is a Russian by birth, education, social and family relations, habits and mode of living, and remains in Russia despite wonderful offers from abroad." Three years later, however, he saw in that composer's new opera an almost conscious attempt to "drag into the mud all of Russia's ideals, the czar, the church and the people." Whenever it suited his purposes, he maintained excellent relations even with professing Jews. Samuel Poliakov, one of Russia's foremost bankers and railroad builders, belonged to his principal guides through the maze of diplomatic and financial intrigues which accompanied the growth of the Russian, Balkan and Persian railways.[38]

At the same time, Pobedonostsev and his associates were indubitably guilty of instigation to the widespread massacres of Jews in 1881, 1903 and 1905. In contrast with even medieval Jew-baiting, these pogroms were actually promoted by governmental organs. Censorship allowed the letting loose of such a floodtide of antisemitic writings upon the public that during the decade of 1905-16, for which we have more precise data, 2,837 anti-Jewish publications were distributed in 14,327,000 copies. Nicholas II himself privately subsidized this scurrilous literature to the tune of 12,239,000 rubles. The original version of the notorious *Protocols of the Elders of Zion* was concocted by Sergii Nilus from a variety of spurious sources, one edition appearing in 1903 under the official auspices of the staff of the Military Region of St. Petersburg. This alleged documentation of the Jewish quest for world domination at first failed to impress the masses (its great historic influence was to come after the First World War), but the governmental circles took the myth seriously. In a remarkable memorandum, submitted shortly after Pobedonostsev's resignation, Foreign Minister Count Lamsdorf explained to the czar that the Russian revotionary movement was "actively supported and partly directed by the forces of universal Jewry," centered in the *Alliance israélite* of Paris. He suggested a confidential exchange of views with Berlin and the Vatican for joint defense against the common foe of Christianity and the monarchical order. Though Pobedonostsev himself would hardly have entertained such bizarre notions, Lamsdorf's memorandum was clearly an offshoot of his antisemitic measures. His general aims were well epitomized in his much-quoted, though never fully authenticated, dictum that he wished to see a third of Russian Jewry converted, a third forced to emigrate, and a third allowed to perish.[39]

All of Pobedonostsev's extremist policies ultimately recoiled upon the regime. His church schools made little headway. The theological seminaries, largely recruiting their pupils from priestly families, found them permeated with revolutionary and atheistic doctrines. A group of seminarists in far-off Tobolsk declared, "We do not know of one graduate of our seminary who has entered the priesthood out of sincere conviction." Muzzled by a statute of 1884, higher theological learning declined sharply notwithstanding all efforts of enlightened hierarchs as Metropolitan Antonii of St. Petersburg. Even conservative scholars like Bolotov refused to obtain the much-debased degree of Doctor of Theology. Pobedonostsev lived to see the Moscow clergy publicly protesting against the metropolitan's order to preach sermons favoring reaction, while four of the six priests elected as deputies to the First Duma revealed a decidedly radical frame of mind. His mass conversions likewise proved short-lived. During four years (1905-9) fully 301,450 converts availed themselves of the opportunity, given them by the Revolution, of formally rejoining their former faiths. Countless thousands "relapsed" without formal registration. An ever-increasing chorus (e.g., of participants at the Religious and Philosophical Conferences of St. Petersburg in 1903) demanded far-reaching ecclesiastical reforms. The growing demand for a *sobor* (an all-Russian Council) to restore the patriarchate, much as opinions differed on the latter's functions and attributes, was aimed at abolishing the supremacy of the lay overprocurator. Long before his resignation in 1905 Pobedonostsev himself realized his unpopularity. On March 21, 1901, he wrote to Nicholas II a regular apologia for his life's work, denying both his reputed omnipotence and his opposition to progress. The Russian people knew better. In an early semiprophetic letter (1881) an anonymous Socialist fore-told that the insoluble conflicts inherent in Russia's despotic regime would result in political assassinations and a final socialist revolution which "is the logical and necessary consequence of the Christian idea." Another correspond-ent, Prudnikov, warned the overprocurator by punning on his name that, un-less he changed his course, he would be for Russia not a "harbinger of victory" (*pobedonostsev*) but a "harbinger of misfortune" (*bedonostsev*).[40] Personally a reactionary doctrinaire rather than a farsighted statesman, he contributed, perhaps more than any other individual, to the ultimate downfall of Russian autocracy and Orthodoxy and, for a while also, to the eclipse of Russia's na-tional strength.

4. BALKAN CONFLICTS

The interplay of religion and nationalism was nowhere more vivid than on the Balkan Peninsula. In the Turkish Empire a subject was principally a Mus-lim, Christian or Jew, and only secondarily a Turk, Armenian, Greek or Serb. The far-reaching self-government of "protected" subjects, despite its indubita-ble ethnic and cultural implications, was largely administered by ecclesiastical leaders. Only within the large religious denominations was there room for national disparity. The very ferocity of the endless fratricidal struggles testified to the strong inner ties linking the whole peninsula from time immemorial. Even in the twentieth century, after several generations of militant national-ism, it was still possible for three brothers to claim allegiance to three different nationalities. Many a Bulgarian renegade became overnight a Serbian national-ist or vice versa by slightly changing the ending of his name. By a simple act of conversion the same Bulgarian or Serb could become a Turk. The community of interests and outlook, of institutions and ways of life transcended even the obvious differences in language or religion. In his letter of August 16, 1827, to Kollař, a fellow Slavist, Jan Schaffarik observed that a Serb was individually closer to a Turk than he was to a Czech, Pole or Slovene. A century later Nicholas Iorga, the Rumanian historian, plausibly described the common type of Balkan personality.[41]

Apart from the permanent separation between Orthodox and Catholics and even between Greek Slavs and Roman Slavs, the Orthodox ecclesiastical ad-ministration as such often proved a major obstacle to national self-realization. Ever since Mehmet II, captor of Constantinople, had bribed fugitive Greeks to return to the city and crowned their patriarch with his own hands, the Greek Phanariot clergy served as official representatives of all Balkan Chris-tians. It was in their interest to suppress the national peculiarities of the Slavs entrusted to their care. "During the long rule of the Greek prelates in the Serb provinces," wrote in 1808 Rodofinikin, a Greek-born Russian agent in Serbia, "their servility with respect to the Turkish authorities and their love of money had led their flocks to regard the name *Greek* as almost synonymous to *Turk*, that is to say, *enemy*." To combat the awakening national consciousness among Bulgars and Serbs, the Greek ecclesiastics induced the Porte to abolish in 1766-67 both the Serbian patriarchate of Ipek and the Bulgarian archbishopric of Ochrida. With utter ruthlessness they also destroyed old ecclesiastical and literary records which might stimulate national pride. Modern scholarship has often deplored the ensuing loss of thousands of liturgical and historical manuscripts written in medieval Bulgarian. Even a radical revolutionary like Rhigas dreamed only of the establishment of a unitarian panhellenic state. Article I of his Constitution, published shortly before his execution in 1797, read: "The Hellenic Republic is one, though it embraces different races and religions. It is one and indivisible, though rivers and mountains divide it." For a long time the national distinctions were so blurred that General Ypsilanti began in 1821 the epoch-making Greek revolt against Turkey in Rumania rather than Greece and proclaimed, "Hellenes, the hour has struck! It is time to avenge our religion and our country!" [42]

National differentiation could not be long delayed, however. Ypsilanti himself received an unequivocal answer from the Rumanian peasants. Instead of joining his banners, they followed their own leader, Tudor Vladimirescu, who bluntly reminded the Greek general that "Greece belongs to the Greeks and Rumania to the Rumanians." The successful Greek war of liberation resulted, therefore, in the emergence of the small national state of Greece, rather than a Neo-Byzantine Empire. The new kingdom was endowed with great, for the Balkans quite extraordinary, ethnic and religious homogeneity (in 1928 fully 96.08 per cent of the population professed Orthodoxy) and it could state succinctly in the first article of its Constitution that the Greek Orthodox Church was the country's established religion. Archbishop Damaskinos's recent regency has demonstrated anew the church's relatively firm hold on that highly individualistic people. Though often exploited by reactionary regimes (e.g., by Dictator Metaxas), organized religion had not entirely lost its appeal to the radicals, whose very extremism has its deep roots in the long national and religious struggle for survival led by the much-sung *klephts*, the outlaw assassins of Turkish oppressors.[43]

The Danubian Principalities always enjoyed ecclesiastical and political autonomy, and hence philhellenism could more readily be reconciled with their national aspirations than with that of other Balkan peoples. Neither Rhigas' and Ypsilanti's dreams of a Greek Empire, however, nor the successive occupations by Russia (four times from 1806 to 1856 alone) prevented their gradual severance from the Greek patriarchate, abetted by the growing Latinization of their national culture. Considering themselves descendants of the old Daco-Romans, Rumanian nationalists purged their language of Slavonic and Turkish ingredients and replaced their accustomed Cyrillic script by the Latin alphabet. Self-glorification as the eastern outpost of Latin culture flattered their nationalist ego, but it did not in any way impinge on the Orthodoxy of the masses. Whatever Catholic populations lived in Greater Rumania after 1918 had been Catholic long before their inclusion in the expanded kingdom. In the earlier periods Orthodoxy had substantially helped cement national unity. When, in 1858, the Moldavian and Walachian provincial assemblies, independently meeting in Jassy and Bucharest, elected the same person as their prince, the Moldavian leader, Kogalniceanu, declared:

> We have the same origin as our brothers [of Walachia], the same name and language, the same faith and history, the same institutions, laws and customs; we share the same hopes and fears; the same frontiers are placed under our care. In the past we have suffered the same griefs and we now have to assure for ourselves the same future.

When, on the eve of the Graeco-Turkish war of 1897, the sultan suggested a secret military convention, Rumania demanded in return a Rumanian Orthodox metropolitanate in Macedonia, thus hoping to check the disappearance of the small Vlach minority amidst the hopeless tangle of races in that picturesque province. The sultan is said to have retorted, "Is it wise, at the very moment when I have succeeded in extinguishing one fire, to kindle another?" Though generally more tolerant of religious than national disparity, the Rumanian government always favored the majority's ecclesiastical establishment and disbursed annually substantial sums for salaries of the Orthodox clergy. Religion's continued hold on the masses came clearly to the fore in Corneliu Zelea Codreanu's effective fascist and antisemitic propaganda under the guise of his "League of the Archangel Michael" (doubtless borrowed from a similar league led by the Russian Jew-baiter Purishkevich) and his use of such revivalist tricks as riding from village to village on a white horse with a crucifix in hand. On the other hand, when the government's weak-kneed policies reached an impasse in 1938, King Carol had to call upon the patriarch to form a new cabinet.[44]

Yugoslavia's situation was far more complex. Unlike Greece and Rumania, she embraced ethnically and linguistically related, but religiously much-differentiated groups. Croats and Slovenes were Catholics and used the Latin script even in their secular writings, whereas Serbs and Montenegrins stanchly adhered to their Orthodox faith and Cyrillic script ever since 1217 when St. Sava, Serbia's celebrated national and religious hero, overcame King Stephen, the "papal legate." Only the historic dynamism of Turkey's steady withdrawal toward its ethnographic frontiers, the corresponding expansion of Austria in the eighteenth and Russia in the nineteenth century, the impact of French revolutionary ideologies and Napoleon's short-lived Illyrian Republic helped forge a feeling of unity among these Southern Slav (Yugoslav) tribes. The first popular Serb writer, Dositej Obradovič (eighteenth century), having lived for thirty years in foreign lands, insisted upon the superiority of linguistic over religious ties. He echoed the Enlightenment's religious broad-mindedness, and the Herderian emphasis upon linguistic unity superseding denominational divisions. "Byzantium and Rome succeeded in separating the Serbs and the Croats," later exclaimed Kukulievich, a Croat nationalist leader of 1848, "but the fraternal tie which unites them is so strong that henceforth nothing in the world will be able to sever it." After their political unification in 1919, however, the long-slighted religious and cultural disparity made itself disastrously felt. It converted the traditional Croat feeling of cultural superiority over the "infidel" Serb and the "Oriental" capital of Belgrade into active animosity which, increased by King Alexander's semifascist repression, ultimately played into the hands of the nazi conquerors. It is still hampering full national reconstruction under Marshal Tito (Broz), himself a Croat, notwithstanding the country's division into six autonomous republics along Russian lines.[45]

In some respects the Serbs felt closer to the Orthodox and formerly Turkish Bulgarians. Their dialectal differences were indubitably greater, but their ways of life, liturgy and historic traditions had so much in common as to make them truly "Yugoslav." In 1914 Stamboliiski declared in an open session of the Bulgarian *sobranie* (Diet) that he hoped for a victory of "our brothers, the Serbs" over Austria. Shouted down as traitor and Serb, he exclaimed, "I am neither a Serb nor a Bulgarian; I am a Yugoslav!" Bulgarian majority sentiment, however, was opposed to a comprehensive Southern Slav federation and preferred outright domination over ethnically mixed Macedonia and Dobrudja. Some Bulgarian nationalists, hoping to revive the glories of the medieval Bulgar empires under Boris and Simeon (tenth century) or under the Asenide dynasty (thirteenth century), even toyed with the idea of rapprochement with Rome. After Russia's defeat in the Crimean War, Cankov persuaded Pope Pius IX to consecrate the ex-brigand Sokolski as the first Uniate archbishop of Bulgaria. Almost equally divisive in its effects was the protracted Bulgarian struggle against the Greek patriarchate. Though unable to persuade the Porte to reorganize the empire into a dual Turkish-Bulgarian monarchy along the lines of the Austro-Hungarian agreement of 1867, Bulgarian leaders ultimately secured ecclesiastical autocephaly. On March 11, 1870, an exarchate was established in Sofia which persisted in the face of severe patriarchal condemnation. The Turkish firman, enabling it to establish new dioceses at the request of two-thirds of the population, was turned against both Greeks and Serbs in Macedonia. It is small wonder that all efforts at establishing a Balkan league, with Bulgaria's participation, proved as futile as those to secure peace between "exarchists" and "patriarchists." [46]

Even the blood jointly shed by Greeks, Rumanians, Serbs and Bulgars in the Balkan War against Turkey in 1912 ended in the internecine struggle among the victors, when the three other kingdoms ganged up on Bulgaria, which had carried the main burden. The chasm became so deep that, to spite her more immediate neighbors, Bulgaria forgot her immemorial religious and political links with Russia and joined Germany during the two World Wars. Only the pressure of Russian garrisons, combined with the similarity of aims among the two dominant movements of Communists and agrarians in both Yugoslavia and Bulgaria, may help reduce the latter's resistance to some sort of federal union.

5. PAN-SLAVISM VERSUS AUSTROPHILISM

Austro-Russian imperial conflicts greatly affected the entire modern history of Eastern Europe. After 1806 Austria, though for a time (1816-66) still loosely connected with the Germanic Confederation, became a foremost Slavonic empire. One may doubt the accuracy of the Czech nationalists' statistical computations (according to Schaffarik's *Slavonic Ethnography* there were in 1842 16,791,000 Austrian Slavs in a world Slavonic population of 78,791,000), but there is no question that the Slavs were a majority in both Austria and Hungary. Since most of them were Catholic, the Austrian Empire unwittingly became heir to the age-old struggle between the Catholic Poles and the Orthodox Russians. In the seventeenth and eighteenth centuries Austria seemed in the ascendancy. Prince Eugene appeared as the great Balkan liberator from Turkish oppression and it seemed as if the Habsburgs were to become the permanent protectors of even the Orthodox Serbs and Rumanians. On Austrian invitation the Serbian Patriarch Arsenius left Ipek in 1690 and settled in Hungary together with several thousand Serb families. In the 1699 treaty of Karlowitz (this Austrian city soon was to become a major center of Slavonic culture) the Porte recognized Austria's right to intervene in matters affecting all Turkish Christians.[47]

Austria's counterreformatory heritage, however, proved to be a major obstacle. Inspired by Jesuit advisers the Austrian administration tried to convert the southern populations to the Roman faith and thus missed its greatest historic opportunity. Slowly but surely the religious issue favored Russia's advance into the Balkans. Already in 1657 Patriarch Parthenius of Constantinople was hanged for plotting with the czar. Nineteen years later a Dutch traveler in Turkey, Jacob Spon, observed that "of all the Christian princes none was feared as greatly as the grand czar of Muscovy . . . that which gives him the greatest advantage is that he is the only monarch of the Greek religion." In 1710 during one of the recurrent Russo-Turkish wars a Herzegovinian Serb in Russian service proposed to set in motion an anti-Turkish uprising in his native land and in Montenegro. In a proclamation dispatched to Danilo of Montenegro, Peter the Great expressed his warm concern for the "Slav nation" and his determination "to liberate the oppressed Orthodox Christians from the yoke of the infidel." He also ordered in Amsterdam portraits of himself, bearing the characteristic inscription *Petrus Primus Russo-Graecorum Monarcha*, and distributed them all over the Balkans. In 1768 an impostor posing as the murdered Czar

Peter III found immediate acceptance in Montenegro. During another war with Turkey, Catherine II issued a manifesto "To all Christian Communities of the Greek and Slav Orthodox Nation, our Coreligionists of the Holy Eastern Church," whom she invited to "shake off the oppressive yoke of the infidel." In the treaty of Kuchuk Kainarji of 1774 Turkey was forced to recognize Russia as protector of the Danubian Principalities and to promise good treatment to all her Christian subjects.[48]

Even some Croat Catholics looked up to Russia as the chief protagonist of the Slav world. An early exponent of Pan-Slavism (the term itself was to appear in a pamphlet published by Herke in 1826) was Yurii Krizhanich, a seventeenth century Jesuit and missionary to the Ruthenians who postulated Russian hegemony as a steppingstone toward the final reconciliation of Orthodoxy and Catholicism. In his comprehensive work on *Russia's Politics* he contended that of the six branches of the Slavonic world (Russians, Poles, Czechs, Bulgars, Serbs and Croats) only the first two had retained their national independence and that only by overcoming the schismatic separation between them through union with Rome could the czar bring about the real unification of all Slavs.

> Oh Emperor [he exclaimed] thou holdest in thy hands Moses' miraculous rod and art able therewith to perform miracles. Thou art undisputed master and findest therefore perfect obedience among thy subjects. With God's help thou canst enlighten and glorify not only thine own empire but also the whole Slavic kind, and thereby earn their permanent blessings. To thee alone, Oh glorious Emperor, are turned the eyes of the whole Slavonic nation. Like a father take care of its dispersed children and gather them together.[49]

This pious exhortation proved unrealistic, however. Russia grew to be the foremost Slavonic power, but also the main protagonist of Orthodoxy. Her imperialist-religious dreams were well expressed in the purported Testament of Peter the Great, evidently written during the Napoleonic Wars, in which Peter allegedly enjoined his successors to reach out for both Constantinople and India and, for this purpose, to engage in constant wars with Turkey or Persia. The Russo-Turkish War of 1807, like those which followed, was designed to re-establish the Orthodox dominion over Constantinople as well as to open the Dardanelles to the Russian navy and merchant marine. At this juncture Alexander I concluded a formal alliance with Serb and Montenegrin rebels. Before long three Greeks living in Odessa organized the *Philhellinike Hetairia* which was of greater assistance in the struggle for Greek independence than similar societies elsewhere. Most fittingly Ypsilanti and other Greeks in czarist service were the outstanding leaders of the revolt, one of them, Capodistrias, becoming the first president of liberated Greece.[50]

Religious influences were equally pronounced in so-called Austro-Slavism. Perturbed over the growing nationalist strife in the Habsburg Empire, some Austrian patriots began preaching the unity of the Western, Catholic Slavs

(Poles, Czechs, Slovaks and Croats). Chief exponents of this ideology were the Poles, because of both their numerical strength and their old historic feud with Muscovy. To be sure, the policy inaugurated by Alexander I and Czartoryski soon led to the establishment of the new kingdom of Poland and in 1818 Alexander confidently assured the Poles that their regeneration was "inextricably linked with Russia's destiny." This chance was frittered away, however, by the czar's reactionary advisers. It came to a dramatic end in the Polish uprising of 1830-31, provoked by Nicholas I's highhandedness. After its bloody suppression Slavonic unity could be preached only by Polish messianic dreamers like Towianski and Mickiewicz, or by extreme realists like Count Adam Gurowski. The last-named harped on the theme that historic progress depended on great, rather than small nations and that, since Providence had obviously entrusted Slav leadership to Russia, the Poles should accept this verdict of history. The Austrian Poles, on the other hand, particularly after the Constitution of 1867 had secured their control over Galicia, became the protagonists of a radically anti-Russian orientation. In their petition of December 10, 1866, the leaders of the Galician Diet assured the Austrian emperor that "from our own profound conviction we derive the firm belief that, as a result of its Constitution, Austria will serve as the supreme example for the safeguards of liberty. To the outside world, on the other hand, it will appear as the bastion of Western civilization, of the rights of nationalities, of humanity and justice." Julian Klaczko, a Polish writer of Jewish descent, became the most effective literary exponent of a Western and Catholic orientation. Arguing sharply against both Pan-Slavism and Pan-Germanism, he advocated Austria's voluntary withdrawal from Germany and Italy and her concentration upon liberating Poland and the unification of all Catholic Slavs.[51]

The growing acrimony between the two largest Slavonic peoples strongly emphasized their religious disparity. Katkov expressed the prevailing anti-Polish sentiment after the uprising of 1863, when he declared that it would be suicidal for Russia to consent to the restoration of a decayed Poland. Only a handful of noble and priestly exploiters, he claimed, were the standard-bearers of Polish nationalism. But his and Pobedonostsev's attempt to drive the same class wedge here as between the Baltic barons and peasants must have sounded absurd to the Polish Catholic masses. More progressive views on Polish independence, as expressed by Alexander Herzen abroad and Chernishevski at home, reached only a small Russian intellectual elite. In the border provinces, particularly, which had no Polish majority, the government pursued a rigid policy of both denationalization and de-Catholicization. The incorporation, in 1909, of the Polish province of Chelm in Russia proper (the so-called fourth partition of Poland) was overtly intended to serve both these purposes. The sudden rise of Bismarckian Germany, however, opened the eyes of many Russians, less blinded by the unreasoning hatred of Poles and Catholics, to the real dangers in Russia's international position. After her war with Japan, especially, which had cut off her Far Eastern tentacles and revealed her military and economic unpreparedness, such moderate publicists as Prince Eugene Trubetskoi began preaching reconciliation with the Poles. In his organ *Moskovskii Eshenedelnik* (Moscow Sunday paper) he harped upon the theme:

> We must persuade the Slavonic peoples that it is far from our intention to impinge upon their national peculiarities. . . . In the Balkans Russia has assumed the task of liberator of its brotherly tribes. At home, however, she was the oppressor, indeed the terror of those Slavonic peoples whom she had liberated. All feared to share the fate of Poland and, hence, became alienated from us. . . . We must fill that chasm at whatever cost. This is absolutely necessary for the security of our Western frontiers.[52]

These friendly sentiments were in part reciprocated by those Poles who were more deeply alarmed over Prussia's efficient ruthlessness than over Russia's hit-and-miss tactics. While Pilsudski and the Austro-Polish patriots viewed the forthcoming Russo-German war as an opportunity to resurrect Poland with the aid of the Central Powers, Roman Dmowski and his Russo-Polish associates preferred co-operation with Russia and her Entente allies. Long before 1914, therefore, they preached Russo-Polish rapprochement. History proved them right, though more recently in ways they would not have relished.

The Ukrainians or Ruthenians had even more divided loyalties. Instead of serving as a possible bridge between Orthodoxy and Catholicism, their Uniates were equally as oppressed by the Orthodox Russians in the Ukraine as by the Catholic Poles in Galicia, Germans in the Bukovina or Magyars in Carpatho-Ruthenia. If anything, Russian persecution was more severe, for it aimed at both denationalization and large-scale reconversion. Even a Russian overprocurator admitted (in his report for 1905-7) that "the haste of the civil authorities in the matter of reuniting the Uniates and their use of administrative measures . . . formed the contingent of the so-called determined resisters." Across the border, however, these Russian attempts at forcible assimilation were more readily overlooked. Many Galician Ruthenians were prepared to compromise with the Poles and many more sided with Austria against Russia, but there also was a substantial minority of so-called Moscalophils. Some of them were outright careerists on the Russian payroll (Pobedonostsev, for instance, paid regular subsidies to a Galician priest, Naumovich), in part justifying Polish cynicism concerning "the difference between the pro-Russian and pro-German Ruthenians in Galicia being the same as the difference between the ruble and the mark." But there also were genuine idealists who strove for the realization of an all-Ukrainian national unity and, against all outward evidence, persisted in hoping that the Russians would ultimately grant them complete national and religious autonomy.[53] This hope was suddenly realized in the Soviet Ukraine which at times (1918-19, 1939-41, and since 1944) also extended to the so-called Western Ukraine or Eastern Galicia. But, although the new tolerant policy toward national minorities sharply contrasted with the intransigence of the resurrected Polish Republic, governmentally encouraged agnosticism for a time replaced conversionism as the most serious obstacle to a complete meeting of minds between the two peoples.

The Czechs had no such restraints. Readily overlooking the speedy Russification of a few thousand fellow nationals settled in Volhynia, they saw Russia merely in her role of Slavonic liberator. They belonged to the earliest propagators of a single all-Slav nation or at least of a free federation of all Slavonic tribes. "Whom God hath joined together," rhapsodized Anton Marek in 1814, "let no man put asunder." His friend, Jungmann, rejoiced over the suppression of the Polish uprising in 1831, for therewith was removed Slavism's "worst internal enemy." Two generations later Kramař and other Czech leaders made pilgrimages to Moscow's overtly propagandist Slavonic congresses. With utter abandon they publicly defied the Austrian authorities and preached the unification of all Slavs under Russian leadership. During the First World War Kramař and others were imprisoned; lesser "traitors" were executed. But this did not prevent entire Czech regiments from deserting to the Russians or two Austrian Czechs, Masaryk and Beneš, from engaging in anti-Austrian propaganda in England and America. There is no question that the Slavonic ideal, even in Masaryk's realistically tempered formulations, greatly contributed to the dissolution of the Austro-Hungarian Empire.[54]

Austrophilism had a better chance among the Southern Slavs. In the early nineteenth century the Habsburgs had their most devoted subjects in the so-called Military Frontier. But their growing reliance on the Magyars and the latter's increasing nationalist fervor gradually weakened this attachment. Beginning with the convocation of the Hungarian Diet in 1825 forcible Magyarization was given free rein from Vienna. By 1840-43 Hungarian replaced Latin as the official language. The latter could still be used in Croatia for domestic purposes, but Latin speeches of Croatian deputies at the joint Diet were officially disregarded. Even Lajos Kossuth, himself of Slovak origin, once flippantly asserted that he could not find Croatia on the map. He also consistently rejected the idea of federation either with the Rumanians against the Slavs, as suggested to him by Ion Ghica in February, 1850, or with both Rumanians and Slavs against their royal oppressors, as advocated by Mazzini's Central European Democratic Committee several months later. His main concern was the preservation of Hungary's territorial integrity and he realized that all federative schemes would lead to her ultimate reduction to the Magyar ethnographic area. His follower, Baron Wesselenyi, spoke for the entire revolutionary group when he declared:

The state has the right to force its citizens to learn another language. It may restrict national idioms and, under circumstances, suppress them entirely. Every endeavor to facilitate the use of a non-Magyar tongue outside the family is but the product of a diseased brain and sinful lust.

Of course, during that uprising Vienna was forced into an alliance with the loyalist Croats. But even then sensitive listeners could hear distinct nationalist rumblings in the address of the Croat ban, Jellacič, to the Diet: "Here everything is but one nation. I know of no difference between Croats and Serbs." Neither could Nicholas I's successful intervention, although primarily inspired by the czar's abhorrence of rebellion against established authority, fail to produce the mental association between Russia and Croat national liberation. In 1867, moreover, a vital decision was made. Instead of converting Austria, after her elimination from the Germanic Confederation, into a Western Slavonic power, her ruling classes continued the policy of German-Magyar domination. Since even Croatia's formal autonomy no longer sufficed to forestall Magyar encroachments, she was driven, however reluctantly, into the arms of the anti-Austrian Serbs across the Danube.[55]

The main weakness of Austro-Slavism, however, and probably the most important single cause of its ultimate impotence was its ideological inadequacy. However strongly it appealed at times to Austrian Slavs on opportunistic or narrowly nationalistic grounds, and however justly it invoked Austria-Hungary's long dynastic coëxistence and economic interdependence, it offered nothing comparable to the religious appeal of the Slavophil *mystique*. There certainly was no religious sanction to the conglomeration of nationalities and fragments thereof which had been brought together by the Habsburg dynasty's artificial, often purely connubial policies. Among the Austrian Germans themselves there arose preachers of reunification in a resuscitated *grossdeutsch* Reich which further frightened Germany's Slavonic neighbors into an espousal of the Pan-Slavist cause. Kramař, in particular, tried to convince France and England that the Czechs were the only effective bulwark against Germany's otherwise irresistible expansion to the Persian Gulf. Neither could Catholicism offer a sufficient rallying ground. The Czechs, mindful of their Hussite traditions, had their own national scores with the papacy, which were highlighted by Czech students burning Pope Pius IX in effigy in reprisal for his sharp attack on the heretical power of Russia (1877). Some Czechs were prepared to adopt even the Russian Slavophil theory that Hussitism itself had been but another expression of the old Slavonic opposition to Rome. At the same time the Poles, almost equally threatened by Pan-Slavism and Pan-Germanism, wavered back and forth. While trying to find in ardent Catholicism an antidote to Russia's overpowering absorptive capacity, they viewed Austro-Slavism as at best a temporary expedient. Their ultimate goal remained full national independence, which implied a struggle against all three partitioning powers. Catholicism itself, moreover, had become so supranational in scope and had so many of its historic roots among the Latin and Germanic nations that even the most chauvinistic Slav could not claim for it Slavonic or a particularly Polish, Czech or Croat parentage.[56]

The age-long interdependence of the Russian Church and nationality, on the contrary, and its numerical, political and cultural pre-eminence in the whole Orthodox world lent the identification of Slavism with Russian Orthodoxy a high degree of verisimilitude. In the writings of such Slavophils as Kireevski, Khomiakov, Samarin, the brothers Constantine and Ivan Aksakov and Danilevski, or of such sympathizers as Dostoevski, Russia's old imperial drive received an unmatched religious and humanitarian rationale. These writers utilized Herder and Schlözer's early glorification of Slavonic pacifism and pursued further Schelling's mystical quest for the reunification of Petrine (Catholic) and Pauline (Protestant) Christianity on the theological foundations laid by St. John. They thus ascribed to their nation a messianic role which invested Russia's imperial expansion with qualities redemptive of mankind at large.

It so happened that Russia always had a fairly "good press" abroad. Appealing characteristics of individual Russians and the evident genuineness and depths of their convictions secured a sympathetic hearing to their most fanciful outpourings. The tired and frustrated of Western civilization, especially, often listened with rapt attention to their tirades against Western history filled with war and conquest, as contrasted with the Slavs' perennial desire to be left in peace; Western feudal rule of man over man, as contrasted with the old Russian collectivist farm, the *mir*; Western legal systems forcibly imposed by Roman conquerors, as contrasted with the naturally grown Russian law; Western materialism of workers and entrepreneurs, as contrasted with the spirituality of Russian farmers, the *muzhiks*; even against the materialism of Western Christianity, be it in the form of Catholic "talismanism" (as Khomiakov styled it) or of Protestant rationalism, as contrasted with the spiritual profundities of Russian Orthodoxy. Many were enchanted by Danilevski's *Russia and Europe* (1871), which expatiated on the Russian people's destiny to lead Europe out of its social and spiritual anarchy by effecting a genuinely organic union between religion, culture, politics and social organization, the four main elements of civilization. Overlooking Russia's record in power politics, many eagerly believed General Chernaev when, upon assuming in 1876 the command over the Bosnian and Herzegovinian rebels, he issued a proclamation asserting, "We fight for the sacred idea of Slavdom which is based not upon the quest for power but on the idea of equality of all humanity. We fight for freedom, the Orthodox cross and civilization. Behind us is Russia!" Dostoevski postulated the conquest of Constantinople, "the mother of Orthodoxy," as an indispensable prerequisite for the fulfillment of Russia's mission.

Marching in the vanguard of a united Slavdom [he added] Russia will utter its new, sane, hitherto unheard-of word to all European humanity and its civilization. This greatest of words consists in the commandment of the unity of all mankind, not in the spirit of personal egotism, but in that of genuine and deep love. It will accord with the magnanimous example set for Europe by the Russian people at the head of the free all-Slavonic federation through its care in the preservation of the individuality and freedom of all nationalities for the realization of peace eternal.[57]

Russia's official attitude to Pan-Slavism was rather equivocal. A movement generated by intellectuals, without the benefit of official blessing, was naturally suspect. However reactionary in their social practice (many of them harshly treated their serfs at a time when peasant liberation was the crucial public issue), these writers could not be trusted by the czarist administration since they ventured to think their own thoughts. Pan-Slavism's romantic glorification of the old Slavonic egalitarian structure and the grandeurs of pre-Petrine Russia, unspoiled by contact with the "degenerate" West, implied a critique of the contemporary state. Certainly those Slavophils who inspired the Moscow municipal Duma's address to Alexander II in 1870 must have sounded like out-and-out radicals. "From you alone," these city fathers wrote, "the nation expects the fulfillment of your beneficent promises and first of all—*freedom of opinion and the printed word,* without which the national spirit withers and there is no room for sincerity and truth in relations to the government; *freedom of the church,* without which the preached sermon is impotent; finally *freedom of religious conscience*—the most precious treasure for man's soul." Internationally, too, Nicholas I hesitated to appeal to the uncontrollable forces of Slav nationalism, which had elsewhere proved so subversive of the system established by the Holy Alliance. He even helped his main rival, Austria, in her hour of need in 1849. Four years later he forced Serbia to discharge her leading statesman, Garasanin, because he had become the chief protagonist of a Balkan federation directed against Turkey.[58]

Nicholas's successors were less punctilious. Alexander III the more readily reached an understanding with the Slavophils as they became far "tamer" in domestic affairs and as Russia's imperial position deteriorated after 1871. Count Nicholas Pavlovich Ignatiev, who, as Russian ambassador in Constantinople (1864-77), had long promoted Pan-Slavist aspirations, declared, "The Austrian and Balkan Slavs must be our allies, the weapons of our policy against the Germans." Pobedonostsev lost his temper when he learned in January, 1887, of the election of a Russophobe patriarch at Constantinople. "We Slavs," he bitterly remarked to the czar, "do not know how to conduct our affairs. We are incapable of unity and concerted action in the pursuit of a common purpose. Everywhere intrigues, corruption and mutual suspicion." He and the czar also deeply mourned the death of Ivan Aksakov. Dostoevski's passing likewise appeared to the overprocurator as a personal loss, for "among the Russian writers he was—almost the only one—an enthusiastic preacher of the principles of faith, nationality and patriotism." In the historic days of August, 1914, Czar Nicholas II, finally, proclaimed solemnly, "We fight also for our Slavonic brethren, our coreligionists and blood relations." [59]

6. UNDER THE SOVIETS

This intimate nexus between Russian nationalism and the church was suddenly broken by the Communist Revolution, the impact of which was immediate and world-wide. Going far beyond their earlier demands for a "free church in a free state," the revolutionary leaders turned sharply against all organized religion. Lenin and his associates, implementing the Marxist condemnation of religion as an "opiate" for the people, first disestablished it and, subsequently, undermined its whole structure.[60] At the same time their interpretation of nationalism sharply revised the previous nationalist ideologies. By combining a semimessianic form of internationalism with extensive national minority rights for the numerous ethnic groups inhabiting the Soviet Union, they opened a new chapter in the history of nationalism as well.

Antireligion had older, if not necessarily deeper, historical roots in Russian society than did the new treatment of ethnic minorities. Only in the borderlands, moreover, did the individual Russian feel the brunt of his changed ethnic status. His sensitivities were the less frequently hurt as the previously most militantly nationalistic, non-Orthodox and anti-Russian Poles, Finns and Balts had now seceded from Russia. Most of the minorities remaining within the Soviet Union had never, or at least not from time immemorial, enjoyed full national sovereignty. The largest and most advanced among them, Ukrainians, White Russians and Armenians, faced the alternative of political domination by other, less tolerant neighbors. Czarist officials had long tried to denationalize the minorities by driving wedges between their illiterate peasants and their more outspokenly nationalistic landowners, ecclesiastics and bourgeois intellectuals. Now the Revolution held out to the former the promise of economic and social advancement without the loss of national identity. From the beginning, therefore, they, as well as the Russians living among them, proved exceedingly tractable on the national issue.

The situation was different in the religious sphere which affected the daily life and personal relations of all Soviet peoples. Back in the days of Catherine II a few aristocrats and littérateurs ineffectually toyed with French atheistic Enlightenment and materialism. Not even the revolutionary Decabrists dared raise the religious issue. Only Belinski's identification of religion with superstition along Feuerbachian lines found some eager listeners among his numerous ardent admirers. He was seconded by such famous exiles as Herzen and Bakunin.[61]

With Mikhail Bakunin agnosticism entered a permanent alliance with the

Russian proletarian revolution. Bakunin, more anarchist than socialist and frequently controverted by Marx, became an enemy of both the state and the church. "Church and state," he declared in 1875 in his definitive work on the subject, "are my two black sheep" (*bêtes noires*). "If God exists," he argued like a typical medieval ontologist, "man is a slave; but man can and must be free, therefore God does not exist." In order to secure freedom man must therefore overthrow both civil and ecclesiastical authority. Without its antistatist ingredients this doctrine was shared by Friedrich Engels, who had asserted a year earlier that "atheism is accepted as a fairly self-evident proposition by the European labor parties." Three decades later Lenin restated these views in several essays.

> The impotence of the exploited classes [he wrote] in the struggle against the exploiters engenders faith in a better life beyond the grave just as inevitably as the impotence of the savage in his struggle against nature engenders faith in gods, devils, miracles, and so forth. To him who toils and suffers want all his life religion teaches humility and patience on earth, consoling him with the hope of reward in heaven. And to those who live on the labor of others religion teaches charity on earth, offering them a very cheap justification for their whole existence as exploiters and selling them a suitable price ticket for admission to heavenly bliss. Religion is the opium of the people. . . . Our programme is entirely based on the scientific, that is the materialist world outlook. . . . Our propaganda necessarily includes the propaganda of atheism.

While advocating antireligious propaganda, however, he reminded his readers that Engels had already warned the Socialists not to repeat Bismarck's disastrous *Kulturkampf*. Not the political struggle against clericalism, but the slow and patient organization and enlightenment of the toiling masses was to furnish an effective antidote. As a true Marxist he also believed that a change in the socioeconomic system would automatically alter the ideological "superstructure" of religion. All the party had to do was to popularize the antireligious polemics of French Enlightenment and to undermine the church's control by removing its financial and educational underpinnings.[62]

When Lenin and his associates assumed supreme power in Russia, therefore, they never formally outlawed religion; they merely separated sharply the state from the church. They went therein far beyond the earlier revolutionary regimes of Lvov and Kerensky, which had introduced equal treatment of all faiths but still recognized Orthodoxy as Russia's mother church. In their unprecedented decree of January 23, 1918, they also surpassed the laws of separation in other countries by stating, "Instruction in religious doctrine is not permitted in any governmental or common school nor in private teaching institutions where general subjects are taught. Citizens may give or receive instruction in a private manner." The latter, somewhat equivocal term was interpreted by the courts to refer to the teaching of no more than three children. A later provision, decreed in 1929 and included in the Constitution of 1936 (Art. 124), replaced the original equality of religious and antireligious propaganda by the significant formula: "Freedom for the conduct of religious worship and freedom for antireligious propaganda is recognized for all citizens." Curiously, this legislation affected more severely the dissident groups than the Orthodox Church, Pobedonostsev having rightly emphasized the nonintellectual appeal of Orthodox priests who "teach little and seldom." By seriously hampering the dissemination of sectarian doctrines, it unwittingly strengthened the grip of the Orthodox Church upon its believers.[63]

The church was touched to the quick, however, by the new treatment meted out to its clergy. Unlike Western Europe, where the clergy was often found in the front ranks of fighters for social justice, the number of progressive priests in the Orthodox Church was always small; of those supporting the revolutionary movements practically nil. Nor was the absence of an organized Christian Socialist movement due solely to governmental repression. The first flush of the Revolution of 1905 produced a few progressive clerical deputies to the First and Second Dumas. But the forty-four and forty-three priests serving in the Third and Fourth Dumas, respectively, belonged for the most part to the stanchest supporters of reaction. Many were known to be leaders of the notorious "Black Hundreds." Only direct intervention of the government, dismayed by the prospect of a "priests' duma," forestalled the possible election of some one hundred fifty reactionary clerics. Even the *sobor* (Council), convoked under the Kerensky regime in 1917, clearly mirrored this reactionary state of mind. Bishop Arsenius's assertion that the church was interested in the preservation of the landowners' rights and his reckless exclamation that "the landlord and his church stand together" were quoted with telling effect by the subsequent "godless" agitators.[64]

The church's instantaneous reaction to the communist antireligious moves helped burn the bridges. Even before these were definitely crossed, i.e., four days before the promulgation of the decree of January 23, 1918, but doubtless forewarned, the newly elected Patriarch Tikhon took it upon himself to threaten the new rulers with eternal damnation.

> Recall yourselves [he exclaimed] ye senseless, and cease your bloody deeds. For what you are doing is not only a cruel deed: it is in truth a satanic deed, for which you shall suffer the fire of Gehenna in the life to come, beyond the grave, and the terrible curses of posterity in the present earthly life. By the authority given us by God, we forbid you to present yourselves for the sacraments of Christ, and anathematize you, if you still bear the name of Christians, even if merely on account of your baptism you still belong to the Orthodox Church.

This message was enthusiastically received by the members of the *sobor*. One of them was convinced "that the first collision with the servants of Satan will serve as the beginning of saving the nation and the church from the enemy." [65]

The Soviet government retaliated by relegating all priests to the status of "declassed" persons. It is difficult for a Western reader to imagine the sufferings of a *declassé* under the general stringency of life in the early revolutionary years. Russia was ruined and devastated. The famine of 1921 cost millions of lives. As late as 1932, owing to difficulties in transportation, several millions perished from starvation in some parts of the country, while others suffered but little. A declassed person, legally and socially an outcast, often was excluded from bread rationing and had to forage for himself. As a rule refused shelter in the municipally controlled housing, he had to live in some dilapidated shack on the town's periphery. His children were discriminated against in jobs and schools. If he dared resist he was imprisoned, sent off to hard labor or even executed. To controvert Foreign Commissar Chicherin's assertion at Genoa that Russia enjoyed full freedom of conscience, the Council of the Russian Church produced figures showing that no less than 28 bishops and 1,215 priests had been executed in the five years since the Revolution. To be sure, even accepting the accuracy of these figures, one must bear in mind that such executions affected other classes as well. Had not Alexander Ulianov, Lenin's older brother whose revolutionary martyrdom had left an indelible imprint upon Lenin's mind, issued a manifesto in December, 1886, stating that "the sole method for the [revolutionary] struggle is systematic terrorism"? But in the absence of accurate and detailed statistics it may be assumed that the ecclesiastical profession suffered casualties in excess of its ratio in the population. Legal discrimination was reinforced by administrative measures. Theological schools were closed except for a few small institutions allowed to serve the fairly innocuous Living, or Renovated, Church. Practically all religious publications were gradually suspended. For a while a few small church papers were permitted to appear, but their circulation, always small, was restricted to ecclesiastical circles alone. They practically vanished after 1935, and were not resumed until 1943. Even more serious, because striking at the very roots of religion, was the regime's totalitarian control over the private life and thinking of every citizen. Communism itself was soon felt, by opponents even more than adherents, to be a full-fledged religion aiming at superseding all the traditional creeds. Nicholas Berdyaev found among non-Communists few objectors to his assertion that "communism, both as a theory and as a practice, is not only a social phenomenon, but also a spiritual and religious phenomenon. And it is formidable precisely as a religion." [66]

Despite all this and despite the vigor of the "godless" propaganda abetted by both government and party, the old religions maintained their hold upon large sections of the population. After a decade of antireligious efforts Lunacharski, commissar for public enlightenment, conceded that "religion is like a nail. The harder you hit it the deeper it goes into the wood." This was not merely a reflection of Lunacharski's private bias, although he and many of his more searching colleagues had long indulged in that radical form of "god-seeking" which was condemned by Zinoviev, president of the Third International. Lenin, too, had warned Maxim Gorki that "God-seeking differs from God-creating or God-making and other things of that kind much as a yellow devil differs from a blue devil." [67]

Here is not the place to repeat the thrice-told tale of the trials and tribulations of all churches under the Soviet regime. One might have expected that they would at least tone down their old animosities, but the peculiar venom of fratricidal hatreds and the extreme tenacity of mutual centuries-old sectarian suspicions was demonstrated here again and again. An early telegram of some Muslim leaders appealing for the pope's intervention was an exception confirming the general intransigence of the Muslim rank and file. When, in 1932, 10,000 Uzbek women dropped their veils, many were publicly beaten, while fourteen lost their lives.[68]

The Catholic Church, in particular, was often suspected by Orthodox leaders of trying to utilize the great crisis in the Eastern Church to secure reunion on its own terms. That is why Archbishop Cieplak's impressive defense in his trial for life in 1923 and the martyrology of his associate, Msgr. Budkiewicz, aroused only lukewarm sympathy among the Orthodox clergy. The papacy's efforts at Genoa in 1922 to obtain international safeguards for religious freedom in Russia and its initially promising negotiations with Chicherin and Litvinov raised before the Orthodox world the specter of an alliance between the Vatican and the Soviets. The exiled bishops and lay leaders assembled at Karlovtsi, Yugoslavia, in December, 1921, for a so-called Russian Orthodox synod reciprocated by calling for a Western crusade against their native land. Nor were the Orthodox in Russia particularly elated over the re-establishment in 1934 of a Catholic church in Moscow under an American priest, the Rev. Leopold Braun, as a result of President Roosevelt's formal recognition of the Soviet regime. The subsequent international developments, especially the conflicts in Spain and Mexico, deepened the mutual hatreds. On February 10, 1945, the dignitaries of the Orthodox Church issued a proclamation in which they raised "their voices against those—the Vatican especially—who try to protect Hitlerite Germany from responsibility for crimes committed by her and ask forgiveness for Fascists who spilled the blood of innocent victims all over Europe." [69]

The conflict over Soviet policies, social and ecclesiastical, cut across national lines, both in Russia and in other lands. As early as 1913 Joseph Stalin wrote that "a nation has the right to arrange its life on autonomous lines. It even has the right to secede." Although he added that secession may not be most beneficial to a particular nationality, i.e., its toiling masses, the right to it was upheld by Lenin's government at the Peace Conference of Brest-Litovsk which proclaimed the independence of Finland, Poland and the Baltic States. It nullified in short shrift Russia's western expansion laboriously achieved over a period of two centuries. Later, in order to put an end to the war with resusci- tated Poland, the Soviet leaders consented in the Treaty of Riga to the subjec- tion of millions of Ukrainians and White Russians to Polish domination, readily relinquishing what Ivan III had called his "patrimony" half a millenni- um before. Within the Union, too, they went out of their way to detect new nationalities among the backward tribes of their far-flung empire. Often they had to invent new alphabets and lay the first foundations for new national literatures.[70]

Not that Soviet leadership was nationalistic for nationalism's sake. On the contrary, it so stanchly adhered to Marxist internationalism that Lunacharski stated in 1923, "The teaching of history which would stimulate the children's national pride, their nationalistic feeling and the like must be banned, as well as such teaching of the subject which would point at stimulating examples in the past for imitation in the present. For I do not know what kind of thing is a healthy love for one's fatherland." To reconcile this obvious contradiction Lenin and Stalin used Marxian dialectics. Just as in Marxian theory, they con- tended, the state was ultimately to "wither away" completely, so would all national distinctions melt away in communism's final stages. Interveningly, however, concentrated state power under the dictatorship of the proletariat alone could break the resistance of vested interests, lay down effective plans for years ahead, and usher in the successive stages of socialism and communism. Similarly, by allowing the untrammeled development of each nationality and thereby eliminating national strife, communism would prepare the ground for the ultimate merger of all into an all-embracing human civilization. In his report to the Sixteenth Congress of the Communist Party in 1930 Stalin clearly stated:

> We must let the national cultures develop and expand, revealing all their potential qualities, in order to create the necessary conditions for fusing them into one common culture with one common tongue. The flourishing of cul- tures, national in form and socialist in content, in the conditions of a prole- tarian dictatorship in one country, for the *purpose* of their fusion into one common socialist culture, common both in form and in content, with one common tongue, when the proletariat is victorious throughout the world and socialism becomes an everyday matter—in this lies the dialectical quality of the Leninist way of treating the question of national cultures.

From this obvious rationale of existing nationalist rivalries stemmed the policy of granting minority rights to some hundred eighty nationalities (like the American sects some of these number only a few-score members), although the Soviet Union was never committed to it by international treaties. Apart from its propagandistic value abroad, it proved to be the most eminent means of securing domestic peace and enabling the population to concentrate on the complex tasks of socialist reconstruction.[71]

The advent of nazism marked a turning point for the Soviet Union, too. Hitler's hysterical calls for an antibolshevist crusade and the early successes of his "blood and soil" ideology revealed the inherent weaknesses of all previous efforts at international co-operation. As in all other crises the Russian nation rallied behind its leaders, who read the new signs on the wall and began stressing the virtues of Russian nationalism. Reversing Lunacharski's stand, they now extolled loyalty to one's fatherland and in 1934 gave the capital offense of "treason against the nation" a national, rather than exclusively counter-revolutionary connotation. The history of Russia's earlier wars, her successful defense against the Tartars and Napoleon and her national heroes were now glorified through literature and school, press and film and all the other media of popular enlightenment. When the shadows of the Second World War lengthened after Munich, *Pravda* approvingly reported the thundering applause with which the youth of Moscow had greeted the motion picture *Alexander Nevski*. "They did it," wrote this official party organ, "because the Russian nation is imbued with flaming patriotism and had been imbued with it throughout its history." A month after Hitler's entry into Prague the government paper, *Izvestia*, commented, "The readiness of the present generation to give everything to protect the Russian country against invaders, the struggle for its independence has deep historic roots. . . . Soviet patriotism is national and historical. National and historical has also been the Russian Revolution which has continued the tradition of the Russian nation." On December 20, 1943, finally, the "International" was formally replaced by Russia's new national anthem.[72]

Internationalism as such was not abandoned, however. To be sure, the steady growth of the Russian ethnic element within the Union from less than 53 per cent in 1926 to 58.4 per cent in 1939 was not due to natural causes alone. But neither was it the result of the majority's conscious assimilatory efforts. It rather was the unintentional by-product of the rapid growth of great industrial centers which, for the most part located in the Russian "heartland," attracted labor from all over the Union. The new settlers came under the spell of the Russian language and culture and the more readily lost their ethnic consciousness the shallower were its historic roots. Officially, however, the various nationalities were still encouraged to cultivate their historic traditions.[73]

Before long it began to dawn upon many minds that perhaps religion, too, a most vital link in national tradition, should be allowed to play a role during the intermediary socialist stage, if not in the ultimate communist society. Certainly the old alliance between the autocratic state and the Orthodox Church had already been broken. No longer did church leaders hurl anathemas on the new regime, nor did anyone dare to call on all believers as had Patriarch Tikhon on January 19, 1918, to defend "our insulted and oppressed Holy Mother." In the meantime, Tikhon himself had retracted. In a much-debated confession, undoubtedly prompted by the co-operative spirit of the Second All-Russian Sobor in May, 1923, he had admitted that

> having been nurtured in a monarchist society, and until my arrest having been influenced by anti-Soviet individuals, I was filled with hostility against the Soviet authorities, and at times my hostility passed from passivity to active measures, as in the instance of the proclamation on the occasion of the Brest-Litovsk peace in 1918, the anathematizing of the authorities in that same year, and finally, the appeal against the decree regarding the removal of church treasures in 1922.

Subsequently, the danger of counterrevolution became so remote that the state slowly withdrew its tacit support of the more amenable Living Church, although the latter had in the meantime secured official recognition from the patriarchs of Constantinople, Alexandria and Antioch. The supremacy of the Patriarchal Church, in 1927 readmitted to official registration, became ever less contested. Since the new generation was largely growing up without religious instruction, even the "godless" agitation began losing ground. In 1937 Yaroslavski, chief of the Godless Society, admitted complete failure. The party's changed attitude came most clearly to the fore during the preparations for the new Russian Constitution of 1936, when Stalin himself significantly declared that "not all former kulaks, white guards or priests are hostile to the Soviet power." [74] Like other declassed persons, the priests were now admitted to full Soviet citizenship and franchise. Party members were still expected to subscribe to the materialistic conception of life, but some of them began practicing religious rites and attending church services without suffering expulsion.

Reconciliation was clinched after the outbreak of the war. Russia, then still at peace with Germany, occupied the Baltic States and eastern Poland, where she could the more readily appeal to the workers and peasants to turn against their Polish masters, as they mostly were Ukrainians or White Russians and professed Orthodoxy. The Polish administration had often been accused before (e.g., by the exiled leader, Glubokhovski, at the Ecumenical Conference in Stockholm) of destroying Orthodox churches and undermining the authority of the Orthodox priesthood. In 1939 Metropolitan Sergius simply welcomed back these Orthodox populations as long-lost children of the Russian Church. Following czarist precedents, the Ukrainian and Estonian churches were granted a considerable measure of autonomy, but those of Latvia and Lithuania were incorporated without much ado into the Russian ecclesiastical structure. Soviet publications circulated a picture of Sergius surrounded by three Baltic bishops, which symbolized the re-established church unity complementing political unification. More significantly, anticipating the unavoidable clash with Germany, the press now sang the praises of the old religious heroes who had served Russia well in earlier emergencies. Many an oldtime Communist must have rubbed his eyes while reading in the *Krasnaya Zvezda* (of September

8, 1940) about the exploits of St. Dmitri Donskoi against the Tartars: "The victory of the Kulikovo Pole," declared the Red Army paper, "opened the way for the growth of the national Russian state. The Russian people realized that only unity gives strength and secures a glorious future to the fatherland." [75]

This call to unity did not remain unheeded. In June, 1941, the church rallied to the nation in its hour of need. Metropolitan Sergius immediately issued an appeal to all the Soviet nationalities stating that the Russian Church, as a church of the people and not of the state, shared all the dangers confronting the people. In his sermon at the Bogoiavlenski Cathedral in Moscow four days after the German invasion, Sergius called "all hands on deck."

> Deeply in error are they [he exclaimed] who think that the present enemy will not affect our holy things or touch our faith. Observation of German life tells us quite a different story. . . . Can we stand by satisfied with folded arms? Can we exchange Christ for some sort of imagined god, created by the unhealthy imaginings of men descended into beasts?

This appeal to religious loyalties proved extremely effective. Even in the Ukraine, where nationalist as well as Uniate aspirations had long militated against complete solidarity with Greater Russia, intensive German propaganda made little headway. The Ukrainian nationalist Polycarp, appointed by the Nazis to replace the Kiev Metropolitan Nicholas who had escaped to Moscow, had almost as small a following as the "phony" Russian Metropolitan Seraphim of Berlin. Majority and minority peoples alike believed Stalin when, in his urgent radio appeal of July 3, 1941, he asked them all (mentioning a dozen by name) to realize that "the issue is whether the peoples of the Soviet Union shall remain free or fall into slavery." Even during the First World War the minorities had dutifully defended the oppressive czarist regime, but now they fought with greater valor and consciousness in the defense of their homesteads however collectivized, their new social status, and their new national opportunities. [76]

Whatever religious resentments they still nurtured were mitigated by the new spirit of toleration displayed by government and High Command. The resurgence of religion within the Red Army is the more remarkable as that segment of the new Soviet aristocracy of labor had long been the object of special attention by the Godless Society, and as its early battles had been fought against the priest-ridden, ikon-displaying legions of Kolchak and Denikin. Now many soldiers carried crosses and insisted upon religious services in army camps and at burials. The government, though not going the whole length of appointing army chaplains and (through Kalinin) still proclaiming adherence to the materialist doctrine, tolerated these religious manifestations with a newly discovered friendliness. In *Truth about Religion in Russia*, published in 1942, various contributors contended that religion had not suffered from the forcible separation of state and church because it more than made up in spiritual appeal for what it lost in outward prestige. Churches and priests were now allowed to grow in number. The *Soviet War News* of August 22, 1941, reported the existence of 5,665 priests (contrasted with 50,960 in 1917) serving 4,225 licensed Orthodox churches. By June, 1945, the number of all churches in the Union's enlarged area was estimated at more than 16,000.[77]

From October, 1943, on, an official State Council on Greek Orthodox Church Affairs has formally protected its constitutional rights. The council's communist leader, Georgi Karpov, though personally professing no faith, stated to a *New York Times* correspondent in 1945 that "during the last ten years nothing negative [toward the regime] could be observed about the clergy. The state never has opposed the people for believing in God, but only for antipopular activities." In 1943 the government also consented to Sergius's elevation to the patriarchate and, early in 1945, to his successor Alexei's ceremonial installation in the presence of many Orthodox churchmen from foreign lands. As patriarch, Sergius, who ever since Tikhon's death had been chief administrator of the Russian Church, still was only *primus inter pares* among the Russian bishops. But the prestige of his office enabled him to make better use of his earlier training as Marxist, member of the "god-seeking" Religious and Philosophical Circle of 1903, and of the Living Church in the 1920's (for which he had to do humiliating penance) in finding some common ground between the church and communism.[78]

Internationally, to be sure, the relations with the Vatican have not become friendly. Even in satellite Poland, with its formerly strong Catholic attachments, the new regime has evinced great antipathy to papal leadership. The age-old suspicions, which had induced Patriarch Tikhon pointedly to ignore the Catholic Church in his appeals for famine-stricken compatriots, were now reinforced by the papacy's frequent attacks on communism and the Soviet Union. But there has been an ever-growing understanding with the Protestant churches abroad. In the 1930's visiting Protestant ecclesiastics received a fine welcome from both Russian colleagues and government officials. The qualified recognition of the Anglican ordination by the Eastern patriarchs and Metropolitan Sergius's still more qualified concurrence removed an old stumbling block to reunion. Sergius wrote in 1935 that, by retaining the apostolic succession, the Anglicans were "of the church" (*ek tes ekklesias*), if not yet in complete communion with it. Russian collaboration was eagerly sought, on the other hand, by leaders of the ecumenical movement, despite the difficulty of balancing the émigré anti-Soviet churches against the hierarchy in Russia. Mutual understanding reached a new height after the German invasion. Evidently shaken by the sweeping advances of the nazi armies in the first ten days, Stalin himself comforted his people with the forthcoming aid of its "trusty allies," referring particularly to Churchill's "historic declaration" and the readiness of the United States government to give immediate help (July

3, 1941). These sentiments were echoed in church circles, especially during the archbishop of York's visit to Moscow in the fall of 1943. After recounting the long story of attempts at rapprochement, Metropolitan Nicholas of Kiev added:

> The present war against the evil force of Hitlerism has shown the two churches' complete community of attitude to the brutal common foe. This community of feeling unites our churches in sacred wrath. We have a common belief in the ultimate triumph of light and truth over the darkness and abomination of nazi banditry.[79]

7. MESSIANIC NATIONALISM

The outlook for the future is still uncertain, however. The war's devastation of western Russia and the enforced removal of industries and populations into the European interior, the Urals or Siberia has shifted the center of gravity from the old civilized areas to new regions and seriously weakened the historic roots of religion and church. Even before 1941 the successive Five-Year Plans had thus undermined many religious institutions. Magnitogorsk, the new iron metropolis of the Urals, had no place of worship for years. Its hundreds of thousands of younger workers, stemming from all over Russia, had never undergone any intensive religious training. Their few believing members were divided into many sects, and unable to organize effective communities. During the war Magnitogorsk and other new industrial centers assumed ever-greater importance and offered an increasingly realistic background to the party's materialistic program. The mere toning down of atheistic propaganda need not, therefore, in itself augur well for organized religion, for atheistic sermonizing became meaningless to youngsters in whose life and thinking religion had never played a significant role. Unaided by government and public opinion, but also less hampered by them, the religious leaders merely have a chance now of proving their mettle.

Nor are the nationalist trends devoid of confusing crosscurrents. The Soviet annexation of vast areas east of the Curzon line, including territories which had never belonged to Russia (Eastern Galicia, Carpatho-Ukraine, parts of Bukovina, Moldavia, and East Prussia), has increased the ratio of nationally conscious and self-assertive minorities. On the other hand, the war transferred untold multitudes into the Russian heartland. Some of these may return to their old homes. Others may cultivate their cultural and linguistic heritage in their new environment. The majority, however, will undoubtedly be absorbed, sooner rather than later, by the main stream of Russian culture. The numerous Russians, on the other hand, who will doubtless permanently reside in the reoccupied or newly annexed areas, unless speedily assimilated by the local majorities, may become spearheads of Russification. Aided and abetted by a superior culture, perhaps also supported by a rejuvenated Orthodox Church, both expanding through the persuasiveness of genuine economic and social needs rather than through government fiat, these Russian nuclei may yet help develop a far more effective "melting pot" than the spasmodic efforts of Nicholas I or Pobedonostsev. The German Volga Autonomous Republic, oldest self-governing national unit, unavoidably vanished when its settlers were forcibly dispersed, because they could not be trusted against the approaching Nazis. The Crimean Tartars, the Kalmuks on the Caspian Sea, and two other autonomous areas lost their privileged status after their reconquest by the Russians. Even Tartar and Kalmuk town names have already been replaced, in part, by Russian names. Such repression may be explained by local causes, e.g., excessive collaboration with the Germans. It nevertheless seems to illustrate the resumption of the old historic process of Russification, which is likely to gather momentum in the next few decades.[80]

Another resumption of an old historic process led Russia back into the Balkans, resuscitating the memories of Orthodox as well as Slavonic solidarity which lay buried under the altar erected to the goddess of World Revolution. Consciously the Russian Communists were anything but Slavophils. Without subscribing to Marx and Engels's condemnation of all Slavs ("the racial dregs of a thousand years' confused development") for their role in the suppression of the Magyar revolt of 1848, the Russian Socialists equated the Slavophil movement with czarist reaction and imperialism. Mikhail Bakunin's eloquent *Appeal to the Slavs* of 1848 was well-nigh forgotten. After the debacle of the First World War, the Slavonic members of the Little Entente appeared alongside of Poland, Rumania and the Baltic States as parts of the *cordon sanitaire* designed to check the growth of the Union. Prague and Belgrade extended generous hospitality to "White" Russian aristocrats and churchmen and gave them ample opportunities to preach a world crusade against bolshevism. There were only two definitive remedies: the overthrow of the hostile regimes and moderation of nationalist fervor. That is why the Balkan Communist parties were encouraged to stress national pacification as an integral part of the social revolution. They thus harked back to the Serbian Socialist Markovich, who in 1875 had proposed Serbia's federation first with the kindred Bulgarians and then with all the other Balkan peoples as a demonstration of the "socialist negation of nationality." At its conference in Sofia in January, 1920, the Balkan Socialist Federation, soon renamed Balkan Communist Federation and affiliated with the Third International, adopted a resolution stating that "nothing but the proletarian revolution and the dictatorship of the proletariat . . . will liberate the Balkan nations from all oppression and will afford them the possibility of self-determination in uniting them all into one Balkan Soviet Socialist Republic." [81]

Little did these early enthusiasts foresee that a quarter century later Russian armies would enter their countries as liberators from German oppression (this was true even in regard to Germany's satellites), but would nevertheless hesitate to force the pace of social revolution and Balkan federation. As in the old days of czarist Pan-Slavism, the destinies of the Balkan peoples seemed to be considered primarily from the angle of Russia's security and interests. Just as czarist diplomacy had often propagated liberal constitutions in the Balkans, so have the Soviet occupation forces thus far helped bridle their local allies' enthusiasm for speedy nationalization of all means of production. In resuming her old historic drive toward Constantinople and the Straits, Russia has also spared the religious sensitivities of the Balkan peasants. Under her official auspices the religious schism in Bulgaria was quickly settled and the leading Balkan churchmen, most of whom had stanchly resisted Hitler's blandishments, foregathered in Moscow for the installation of the new Russian patriarch. The only important absentee was the metropolitan of Athens, thus symbolically underscoring the emancipation of the Slavonic churches from the tutelage of the Greek mother church.[82]

This is, of course, Pan-Slavism under a new guise. By a curious twist of history, the old ideal of an all-Slav federation under Russia's leadership, with the Rumanians and Magyars added for geographic reasons, has come closer to realization now under the aegis of the most outspoken Westernizers than it had ever been under that of their Slavophil foes. The preachers of a "scientific" and "materialistic" world outlook thus unwittingly became heirs to the Orthodox-Slavonic ideal of unity. This ideal could the more readily become associated with the idea of world revolution, as Slavophilism itself, on its highest levels, was a profound synthesis of universalism and nationalism. In the works of its masters, Kireevski, Khomiakov or Dostoevski, the Russian nation was conceived as a far more genuine *Menschheitsnation*, than Germany or Italy in those of Fichte or Mazzini, for they organically combined Russian nationalism with the old ecumenic ideals of the Orthodox faith. Dostoevski's celebrated Pushkin address of 1880 sounded the keynote to Slavophil idealism.

> Yes, the vocation of the Russian man [the great novelist declared] is doubtless universal-European and even ecumenical. To become a true Russian, entirely Russian, means perhaps only (in the last issue, please emphasize this) to be brother of every man, to become an "All-man," if you wish. All our Slavophil and Western movement is but a great misunderstanding, even if historically necessary. . . . To become then truly Russian means to provide the solution of European contradictions . . . to receive with brotherly love all brothers into his Russian soul, and perhaps even finally to be able to utter the word of universal great harmony, of final brotherly concord between nations, according to Christ's commandments.[83]

In essentially the same vein wrote also the other great masters of Russian thought: Leo Tolstoi, whose independent preachment of Christian ethics as exemplified by the Russian *muzhik* made him anathema to the official church; or Vladimir Soloviev, whose depths of theosophic universalism as reflected in the Orthodox doctrine of salvation were entirely beyond the ken of such official reactionaries as Pobedonostsev.[84] Essentially the same conviction inspired, on the other hand, social revolutionaries like Plekhanov to insist that Russia, though industrially backward, was destined to lead the other nations on the path of socialization. In view of the old Russian traditions of *mir* (communally held land)—Stolypin's agrarian reform of 1911 was to prove but a brief interlude between the *mir* and the collective Soviet farm —Plekhanov believed that Russia could skip the otherwise unavoidable intermediate stage of capitalism and build directly a communist society not only for itself but for the world at large. Mikhail Bakunin was, indeed, right when he said that theoretical materialism may turn out to be more idealistic than many a school of idealistic philosophy.

For lack of a better term, therefore, we may perhaps designate Russia's peculiar national loyalties as *messianic* nationalism. Deep down in the heart of almost every great Russian lay dormant the feeling, even when paradoxically expressed in Chaadaev's glorification of the Catholic West, that humanity would ultimately be redeemed by Russia's spirit and Russia's might. Instinctively the masses, too, were permeated with that sentiment of "manifest destiny" for which they were ready to offer supreme sacrifices. In their quest for mankind's ultimate happiness they forswore pursuit of personal happiness the more readily as centuries of Orthodox asceticism, made realistic by the penury of an overwhelming majority, had instilled in them a sense of guilt for every this-worldly enjoyment. Christian humility and suffering was nowhere taught with greater zest of conviction and nowhere found more fervent listeners. For this reason, too, the ordinary Russian never developed that craving for personal and civil liberties which is so deeply embedded in the Anglo-Saxon tradition. Unless he went to the other extreme of nihilism or anarchism, he generally condemned such liberties, with their checks and balances, as leading to society's atomization and ultimate dissolution. So long, moreover, as he had to fight his centuries-long battles for survival against Tartars or Turks, Poles, Swedes or French, or, more recently, the growing threat of a united Germany, and as, finally under the Soviets, he believed himself constantly menaced by a world conspiracy of capitalist powers, he gladly renounced his individual freedoms in favor of an autocracy which would see him through the recurrent emergencies.

At the same time the Russians decidedly felt that they belonged to an essentially egalitarian society. An autocracy, as Aristotle recognized, differed from a democracy largely by making all, except the supreme power, equally rightless. This feeling of equality was the more deeply ingrained as Russia had never really gone through the transition from feudalism, with its powerful nobility, to capitalism, with its class divisiveness. It was mightily reinforced by the Communist Revolution's proclamation of a basic economic "democracy" which, because of the (professedly temporary) autocratic controls, appears so strange to Western "democrats" thinking primarily in terms of individual and political freedoms. Even in the religious sphere the Russian had long learned to accentuate not individual conscience but the church's authoritarian teachings and to yearn for universal rather than personal salvation.

> In the innermost of his soul [wrote Kireevski] he is not alone and does not act for himself alone, but he participates in the common work of the whole church of all mankind, for whom the redemption has taken place and a small part of which he himself is. He can be redeemed only together with the whole church and in living community with it.[85]

Under these circumstances separation of state and church meant in Russia something diametrically different from what it meant in the United States. It had been a serious new venture even for France, inured for it by age-old traditions of militant anti-Catholicism. In Russia the sudden transition from caesaro-papism to a "free church in a free state" would have been an historic upheaval of prime magnitude even if it had not been accomplished under the aegis of historic materialism and accompanied by a fervent atheist propaganda. The old caesaro-papism, however, had doomed itself by its very excesses and its degradation of the church into a political instrument. Even the extremely conservative *Novoe Vremia* wrote after the elections to the Fourth Duma that "no heresy or schism ever brought so much harm to the church and so damaged the authority of the clergy in the eyes of the population as the degrading role which was imposed upon the priests in the last elections." [86] Such a regime could not possibly survive its great defeats during the First World War. In the fantastic reign of Rasputin it wrote its own macabre finale.

The breaking of the caesaro-papist link, an evident historic necessity, may therefore yet prove to be of great benefit to a revitalized Orthodox Church. In retrospect we may perhaps assert that the Russian Church had outgrown its czarist attachments. Russia's unique "messianic" nationalism was largely based on her faith which, because of her own growing numerical and political pre-eminence, was sufficiently Russian to be a close substitute for a national religion, and because of its Near Eastern roots and the millions of its non-Russian adherents, was sufficiently ecumenical to be also a universal religion. So long as the Russian people was weak, czarism performed the necessary function of emphasizing the particularist, national element. Hence the old legend that Jesus' brother, Adrian, had directly transplanted Christianity to Russia. Hence also Ivan the Terrible's irate denial that the Russian Church had been an offshoot of the Greek Church. By the nineteenth century, however, czarism's preponderant power began to menace the church's ecumenical foundations. So deeply engrossed had the church become in these czarist entanglements that few of its official spokesmen sensed this danger and still fewer dared to mention it publicly. It was left to the intelligentsia of Slavo-phils or Westernizers, of Tolstoian cosmopolitans or Solovievian and Gorkian "god-seekers," of liberal internationalists or socialist champions of a world proletariat constantly to remind their people of its universal mission. The crescendo of these voices grew in proportion to the ever more abysmal depths of czarism's power politics and domestic oppression.

Now that the church has been ousted from its nationally dominant posi-tion, it has been forced to stress again its perennial, universalist aspects. At the same time the internationalist Communist Revolution has progressed in the opposite direction. The toning down of World Revolution was accom-panied, particularly during the Second World War, by a strong resurgence of Russian nationalism. These recent developments, essentially marking the resumption of long-term historic processes, may yet open untold opportunities to that remarkable compound of universalism and particularism which is his-torically represented by the Russian Orthodox Church.

Chapter VII

JEWISH ETHNICISM

Like all other Christian combinations of universalism and particularism that of the Russian Church goes back to the early teachings of the Israelitic prophets. Jewish nationalism has indeed been an integral phase of the entire history of interrelations between religion and nationalism, irrespective of the number of Jews accepting or repudiating it. For some three thousand years the Jewish people has represented a synthesis of internationalism and nationalism, shedding a remarkable light on the history of both and on their interplay in the various historical periods.

The impact of modern nationalism and secularism and the new "political" zionism have given a new turn to the ancient relationship. The upbuilding of a Jewish national home in Palestine has had strong repercussions all over the world. Conversely, modern antisemitism which used the Jewish question as an instrument of nationalist as well as international power politics has, in its very spread and virulence, highlighted a negative aspect of interdependent religious and national animosities. At the same time unprecedented migratory movements brought the Jewish people into intimate contact with all varieties of national and religious thinking. Reflecting in many ways the ideologies shaped under the peculiar conditions of their varying environments, often helping to formulate the new nationalist theories, various segments of Jewry searched for a comprehensive rationale of their own to maintain their world-wide ethnic and religious unity.

1. Ancient Roots

Some peculiarities of Jewish nationalism reach back into the people's origins. The greatest achievement of Israelitic prophecy was universal ethical monotheism based on religion's supremacy over state and territory. Under the stress of an extraordinary world situation and peculiar domestic tensions, the prophets severed the fate of their people, which they extolled as the chosen bearer of God's universal message, from the destinies of its country. They constantly reminded the Israelites that they had originally come from Chaldea and spent a long time in Egyptian bondage; that their miraculous Exodus from

213

Egypt, desert migrations and Sinaitic revelation had fashioned both their nationality and their religion outside the confines of Palestine; that their acquisition of the Holy Land was the effect of a divinely granted privilege and not of conquest by their own might or merit. No other people on earth had to listen to such prophetic exhortations as were ascribed to Joshua, the great conqueror himself, "And I [the Lord] have given you a land for which ye did not labor, and cities which ye built not, and ye dwell in them; of the vineyards and oliveyards which ye planted not do ye eat." [1] With an enthusiasm often called disloyal but tested by subsequent history as the main safeguard for Jewish survival, these immortal leaders viewed the victorious enemy as but a "rod of God's anger" and the downfall of their country as part of the divine guidance of history. At the same time they proclaimed that the Jewish people must and will be preserved to the end of days.

In this way Israel's prophets, lawgivers and priests came to preach also "historical monotheism," i.e., the doctrine that God revealing himself and operating through the history of mankind and their own people teaches them to overcome the forces of nature. They reinterpreted, in particular, their religious festivals so as to "purify" them of their natural backgrounds and to lend them some new historical significance. The traditional spring festival, for example, became for them the Passover celebration of the freedom gained through the Exodus. The harvest festival received new meaning as a commemoration of the desert migration. Even their weekly day of rest received a new sanction because of its association with both Creation and Exodus. Similarly, these teachers taught, the nation's ethnic and religious loyalties ought to surpass its "natural" attachments to state and territory. Of course, they did not object to their people's political self-determination. But they found harsh words to castigate the abuses of power politics and the monarchy, the social inequalities and the degradation of the poorer members of an essentially egalitarian community—all of which had appeared to advocates of the established order as but natural consequences of state rule and landownership. Evidently rationalizing their people's political weakness, when contrasted with mighty Assyria, Babylonia and Egypt, they preached:

> The Lord did not set His love upon you nor choose you, because ye were more in number than any people—for ye were the fewest of all peoples—but because the Lord loved you and because He would keep the oath which He swore unto your fathers, hath the Lord brought you out with a mighty hand, and redeemed you out of the house of bondage, from the hand of Pharaoh king of Egypt.[2]

The Israelitic prophets and priests may thus be designated the first exponents of a religious and cultural nationalism, in which culture was equated with religion but in which all political aspirations were considered secondary.

Through another concatenation of historic circumstances the fall of Jerusalem was followed within a few decades by partial restoration.[3] Most exiles remained in the Dispersion, but those who returned founded a national home permanently enjoying ethnic and religious self-government. The new "theocratic" regime (a designation apparently coined by Josephus), with spiritual control over a far-flung Diaspora, had few earmarks of political nationalism. Under its priests and scribes the Second Jewish Commonwealth was a church-controlled state rather than the usual state-controlled church of antiquity, and as such a prototype of Calvin's Geneva, only far more successful and enduring. Despite the eighty years' interlude of the Maccabean sovereign state, it thus underscored the people's detachment from the accepted idea of an all-pervasive state. It also helped the Jewish masses in the Dispersion to resist complete absorption and to strengthen their life as a permanent ethnic-religious minority. So prepared, they survived the second fall of Jerusalem without undergoing any fundamental change in ideology or organizational structure.

Under the stress of exile they developed a new form of organization, the Diaspora community, which helped them overcome the enormous centrifugal forces characteristic of their minority existence. Centered around the synagogue, which for the first time detached divine worship from the territorial moorings of a temple, the postexilic community developed an extensive educational system which, even before the end of the Second Commonwealth, led to the establishment of regular public schools for boys of six or seven. The ancient and medieval rabbis long anticipated Rousseau and Herder in their emphasis on the national as well as religious significance of popular education. Already in the first century the philosopher Philo and the historian Josephus boasted before their Greek readers of the great familiarity of Jewish children with the vast range of Jewish law.[4]

The increasingly powerful communal organization provided the Jews with that minimum of political coëxistence without which even their ethnic-religious life could not long endure. It served as a fairly effective substitute for their state, just as their segregated living quarters, sporadically recorded in antiquity but become permanent features in the Muslim and Christian Middle Ages, gave them an approximation of self-contained territories. These makeshifts merely accentuated the fundamental will to survive of the people which defied the "natural" will of the national majorities in various lands to assimilate it through religious conversion. Time and again it readily gave up a centuries-old residence and wandered into other lands, carrying with it its spiritual and ethnic heritage which it had refined in the course of its perennial migrations.

This peculiar ethnic-religious nationalism was complemented by a genuine political internationalism which, again the effect of both circumstances and conscious adaptation, helped strengthen Jewish religious universalism. Generally admitting that the abnormality of Diaspora life was the result of their forefathers' sins, Jewish thinkers did not condemn the state as the result of sin, but considered it merely as a divinely ordained temporary expedient. Ever since Jeremiah the Jews had learned to pray for the welfare of the countries of their residence, often confusing the welfare of men and classes in control of countries with that of the countries themselves. That is why their prayers for and frequent financial support of the royal power often embroiled them in considerable difficulties in revolutionary periods and made them special targets for attack by insurrectionary forces. At the same time their living among many nations and creeds all over the then known world conditioned their welfare on the well-being of all humanity.

> All the peoples of the world should know [wrote Azariah de' Rossi, a six-teenth century Jewish historian] that as long as we, the remnant of Israel, live as strangers and sojourners in a land which is not ours, we are obliged, in accordance with the words of the prophets and the custom of our fathers which is law, to pray for the peace of the kingdom which rules over us. Especially at a time like this, when our sins have caused our dispersion to the four quarters of the world, we also have to invoke Heaven to grant peace to the whole universe, that no people should raise arms against another.

Even in the Middle Ages, when war was considered a normal activity and spring was styled the season in which kings go to war, the Jews on both ideological and selfish grounds were induced to pray fervently for the preservation of peace.[5]

Jewish messianism itself had all the earmarks of a synthesis of ethnic-religious nationalism with political internationalism. The hope of an ultimate miraculous restoration to Palestine was a necessary counterpart to the political resignation of ancient and medieval Jewry. Without such a hope the Jewish people, despite its nonpolitical orientation and existing nonpolitical substitutes, would hardly have weathered the recurrent storms of persecution and intolerance. In periods of crisis the messianic yearnings often assumed exaggerated, even grotesque forms. Time and again certain religious enthusiasts or fakers, psychopaths or genuine mystics believed that they were the divinely chosen instruments of redemption and were prepared to face the consequences. According to Maimonides, one of these would-be saviors was asked by a Yemenite ruler to prove his supernatural mission. He unostentatiously offered his head to be cut off, so certain was he of his miraculous survival. Entire communities often yielded to the messianic frenzy.

> Nearly a millennium ago sophisticated Baghdad Jewry, with its merchants and diplomats, physicians and men of science, unflinchingly exposed itself to the ridicule of its neighbors when it spent a night on the rooftops in the expectation that the coming of the Redeemer foretold for that night would suddenly endow it with wings to fly to the Holy Land. When the first rumors of the appearance of the false Messiah Shabbetai Zevi reached Hamburg, the

hard-headed bankers and businessmen of this capitalistically most advanced community immediately called a meeting and decided to dispatch envoys to pay homage to the new king of Israel.[6]

Restoration to Palestine was, of course, more than a mere political aspiration. Even those rabbis who tried to tone down the exorbitant hopes and expected the messianic era to bring about only the Jewish people's release from foreign domination admitted that, in its ultimate effects, it would pave the way for a truly universal religion and a universal reign of justice and peace among men. In its more moderate, authoritative formulation by Maimonides the messianic hope meant that

> The sages and prophets have not yearned for the days of the Messiah in order that the Jews shall rule the world, exercise dominion over heathens or receive homage from the nations, nor that they shall eat and drink and enjoy life. Only in order that they may be free to dedicate themselves to learning and wisdom, without the interference of an oppressor and disturber, so that they may secure life in the world-to-come. . . . And at that time there shall be no hunger, nor war, nor envy and rivalry, for there will be an abundance of all good things and all the priceless commodities will be as readily available as dust, so that the world's only preoccupation will be with the quest for the knowledge of God. In this fashion the Jews will become great sages, understanding the mysteries of existence, and will achieve the knowledge of God to the limit of human capacity.

Popular imagination, on the other hand, ran riot in depicting the advent of the new miraculous era which would put an end to the struggle for subsistence. The universal significance of a Jewish restoration to Palestine was widely acknowledged also in the Christian world, which often regarded it as an indispensable preliminary to the second and final coming of Christ.[7]

2. EMANCIPATION AND ASSIMILATION

This rather precarious, but effective, balance between ethnic-cultural nationalism, religious universalism and political internationalism was suddenly upset by the American and French revolutions. The new increasingly monolithic and egalitarian state gradually superseded the corporate divisions of medieval society. The old-type Jewish community, too, began to be resented as an anachronistic survival of the corporate age. Curiously, the same political, economic and cultural factors which accounted for the rise of European nationalism long contributed to the complete denial of Jewish nationalism. The French revolutionary leaders in lengthy debates made it perfectly clear that they expected the Jewish citizens to be full-fledged members of the French nationality, both politically and culturally. The Girondist Count Clermont-Tonnère, speaking for the progressive majority in the National Assembly, advocated full equality of rights for Jews as individuals, but no rights whatsoever for them as a national group. The Jews were advised to give up their

peculiar "state within the state," of which the antisemitic and clerical opponents of Jewish equality so bitterly complained, to discard their separate laws
and self-governing institutions and, except for their purely religious disparity,
unequivocally to accept French national culture. Otherwise, added Clermont-
Tonnère, as befitted one of Rousseau's faithful disciples, "let them say so
[that they refuse] and then let them be banished!" [8]

When, in the following years, the Revolution was finally driven to the suppression of all established religions and their substitution by the Religion of
Reason, the Jews faced the alternative of either suffering religious persecution or completely losing their identity. Within a few years they saw their
government, whose progressive and humanitarian ideas many of them had
exultantly shared, refuse to recognize them as either a national or a religious
group. Before long they heard a government official in Strasbourg express,
rather crudely, the views of many zealotic adherents of the new faith.

> There exists among these people [he declared] the inhuman law of perform-
> ing a bloody operation on every male child after birth, as if nature would not
> be perfect. They wear long beards out of ostentation and in order to ape the
> patriarchs, whose virtues they have not inherited. They make use of a lan-
> guage which they do not know and which has been dead for a long time. I ask,
> therefore, the Provisional Commission to forbid them these practices and to
> order that an auto-da-fé be made to Truth of all Hebrew books and particularly
> of the Talmud, whose author had the effrontery of permitting them to lend,
> on usury, to men professing a different creed.

Some Jews, especially in the more orthodox communities of Alsace-Lorraine,
were prepared to bear the new religious intolerance as just another episode
in their age-old persecutions. Others, like Jean Mendès in Paris, shared the
fate of some Catholic compatriots in suffering religious martyrdom. But there
were also many who gleefully dedicated their synagogues to serve as temples
of Reason or delivered their religious books to be burned in public bonfires.[9]
In the humanitarian embrace of all races, creeds and nationalities it looked,
indeed, as if the death knell had been sounded for all organized forms of
Jewish life.

Under the Directorate and Napoleon the established religions were again
given full legal recognition. But apart from becoming, along with the other
denominations, a state-controlled rather than a truly self-governing religious
group, the Jewish community had to agree, on principle, to give up all those
"national" peculiarities which had segregated it from other Frenchmen. The
dramatically convoked Paris Sanhedrin, intended by its name and external
pomp to resurrect the memory of the ancient legislature of world Jewry, was
to help denationalize the Jewish creed. In the midst of his strenuous campaigns
Napoleon took time off to dictate the questions which the minister of cults
was to submit to the Jewish leaders together with the replies which he was to

secure. If the emperor's wishes had been fully met, the Sanhedrin would have decreed that every third marriage contracted by Jews should be with members of the Christian faith. To be sure, this dictatorial stroke miscarried. The Jewish Assembly merely conceded the legal validity of mixed marriages, but refused permission to rabbis to officiate at them. In all other respects, however, it clearly accepted the governmental ideology that the new age, though tolerant of religious disparity, demanded unqualified Jewish surrender to French political and cultural nationalism.[10]

Thus was ushered in, under the great fanfare of equality, liberty and fraternity, the era of Jewish emancipation combined with Jewish ethnic assimilation. Country after country in Europe extended to the Jews equality of rights so as to facilitate their incorporation into the national majority. Other countries temporarily withheld equality, until the Jews, through complete re-education and the adoption of the language and mores of their environment, would demonstrate their preparedness for assimilation. Of course, these views were never expressed in the crude terms of a legal condition. There is no historic evidence to support the "contract myth" which, invented by Jew-baiters late in the nineteenth century, contended that the Jews had entered a contractual agreement with the emancipatory governments that they would accept assimilation as a price for equality.[11] But there existed more or less everywhere in the minds of progressive Christians and Jews alike the ideological nexus between emancipation and assimilation. It is still much alive among liberals of both faiths in many Western countries.

The religious adjustments resulting from this nexus were slow and painful. The Reform movement, though stemming principally from inner Jewish developments, was considered by many of its adherents as the most effective instrument for the adjustment of Judaism to the new national situation. Though by no means denying the religious unity of all Israel and the unbroken continuity of the Jewish heritage,[12] it eliminated most ritualistic laws which had helped segregate the Jews from their non-Jewish neighbors, reduced the Hebrew prayers to a minimum and reinterpreted the messianic hope so as to divest it of the idea of a physical restoration to Palestine. In this fashion the Reformed Jew of the mid-nineteenth century felt fully prepared to become part and parcel of the national majority. Even conservative Jews of various shades persuaded themselves and their neighbors that their traditional creed and ritual belonged exclusively to that realm of religion in which the liberty of individual conscience had long been recognized by public law. In their rush to absorb the national cultures of their environment many young Jews neglected their religious education, and often viewed the outstanding contributions of individual Jews to Western arts and sciences as an incontrovertible testimony to their own complete cultural assimilation.

These professions were undoubtedly sincere and as such accepted by the liberal wings of non-Jewish opinion. However, they failed to prevent the re-crudescence of old anti-Jewish prejudices and even the rise of a new type of postemancipatory antisemitism. The Jew-baiters, who had formerly complained of Jewish separatism, now bitterly resented the large Jewish student bodies at universities and the numerous Jewish writers, artists, scientists and journalists. Jewish "domination" of national culture now became a major antisemitic slogan. Increasing Jewish participation in the so-called liberal professions also provoked economic jealousies, further exacerbating antagonisms long nurtured from the historic springs of the Jews' disproportionate share in commerce and banking. Forgetting the peculiar historical and sociological causes and over-looking the millions of poverty-stricken Jews, the Western masses watched with amazement the rise of the Jewish house of Rothschild to all-European leadership. Theodor Mommsen was undoubtedly right in stating that "the history of the house of Rothschild is more important for world history than the inner evolution of the state of Saxony." [13] Although, on the whole, the Rothschilds were a political liability rather than an asset to the Jewish people, the European masses listened indiscriminately to self-seeking agitators who denounced "international Jewish banking" as the chief vehicle in the alleged Jewish drive for world domination. The upshot was that so long as there was any religious disparity at all, in some cases even after an individual's conver-sion to Christianity, Jews were suspected of maintaining a particular brand of group solidarity and of revealing in their behavior certain characteristics which set them aside from the rest of the population. Loud professions to the contrary, a large body of non-Jewish opinion simply refused to acknowledge Jewish assimilation as an accomplished fact or to believe in its effective realiza-tion in any foreseeable future.

If the elimination of Jewish religious nationalism had thus proved to be futile, the compromises imposed upon Jewish religious universalism, though less obvious, were equally profound and equally unavailing. The most ardent Reformers sincerely believed that, by giving up the nationalist ingredients of their faith, they merely emphasized its universalist content. Even Abraham Geiger, fine scholar and thinker that he was, failed to perceive the fallacy of this position in an age of rampant nationalism. Commenting in 1870 on the important Jewish assemblies of Leipzig and Philadelphia, Geiger believed that "cultural evolution is now becoming conscious of its general humanitarian character. Judaism, too, must give up its national limitations and, assured of its eternal content, unhesitatingly penetrate the wide halls of humanity." In his and his confreres' opinion, the main justification for the Jews' perse-verance in their religious dissidence was their "mission" to uphold the purity of ethical monotheism among the nations. A secular writer, like Jakob Wasser-mann, somewhat more realistically but no less stanchly rhapsodized, "For me the Jew of the Dispersion is the Jew of destiny. This is my unshakable conviction, despite all evils and all sufferings or rather because of the evils and suffering. There exist many nations; alas! But the Jews must not be a nation. And they can be a people only among the peoples, or above them." [14]

Few of these men realized the anachronistic nature of such a mission in a nationalistically overheated historical epoch. Still conceivable in the Middle Ages, religious and cultural rapprochement could not be attained by the Jews of the nineteenth or twentieth century with humanity or even Western civilization at large, but only with one or another particular brand of nationalism. All humanitarian professions notwithstanding, therefore, however genuinely meant, Jewish assimilation proceeded apace in the direction not of an abstract humanity but of its empirical nationalist segments.

If completed, this process would evidently have robbed Judaism of both its universalist and nationalist ingredients and undermined its very *raison d'être*. Moreover, by making of Jews exclusively members of various Western nationalities, it would have broken asunder the unity of Israel and converted the Jewish people into separate groups of Frenchmen, Germans, Englishmen, Americans and so forth, whom nothing would bind together but an ever-decreasing conformity in belief and observance and some pale, vanishing memory of a common past. Logically this might have been a feasible solution, but in the realm of historic fact it proved to be utterly unrealistic.

Not only were Jews of various lands held together by a powerful tradition and emotional attachments incomprehensible to Western thinkers living out of touch with their Eastern masses, but their solidarity was constantly reinforced by the unceasing flow of migrations; the struggle for equality of rights in which the emancipated Western Jews aided their less fortunate Eastern coreligionists; interterritorial Jewish charities and last, but not least, the more or less universal anti-Jewish prejudice. "Scattered on the surface of the whole globe," wrote Abraham Benisch in a memorandum submitted to the British government in 1842, "the Jews still form in their religious sentiments an irrefragable unity, and a benefit conferred on any of them fills the hearts of even their ocean-separated brethren with purely grateful feelings." [15] Experience had, indeed, taught them that their fate in any country was deeply affected by developments in another land, however distant. Only the blind or the indifferent could still believe that the total solution of the Jewish problem could be achieved within the boundaries of any single nation.

3. Varieties of Nationalist Affirmation

Out of this international as well as inner Jewish situation was born the new Jewish nationalism. Its rise has frequently been ascribed, especially by opponents, to a Jewish reaction to modern antisemitism. Unquestionably the new pseudo-scientific Jew-baiting of the 1870's in Germany, the agitation of Drumont and the integral nationalists in France, and the governmentally instigated Russian pogroms of 1881-1905 all helped shatter the belief of Jewish liberals in the efficacy of assimilation. In the relatively quiet prenazi period one could even hear various paraphrases of the overcharitable characterization of antisemitism as an "international benevolent society for the preservation of Judaism." [16]

Such influence of external forces, often heatedly disclaimed by Jewish nationalists, need not astonish anyone familiar with their enormous impact on the destinies of any people. Without necessarily sharing Ranke's doctrine of the general primacy of foreign over domestic affairs, historians have long realized that many domestic situations and ideologies were influenced, directly or indirectly, through parallel or opposing trends abroad. Even America, separated by thousands of miles from any powerful neighbor, has often deeply reacted to "foreign" developments. What would its recent history have been without the world-wide forces of communism and fascism, international arts and sciences, a world-wide economic depression, indeed all those factors which had inescapably drawn it into the whirlpool of two world wars? Certainly a sensitive minority living a dispersed life among varying national majorities would respond even more directly to such external influences and particularly to the great menace of antisemitism.

At the same time numerous internal, though often contradictory, factors likewise favored the rise of a strong Jewish national movement. The tremendous increase in Jewish population, especially in Central and Eastern Europe, had forced its leaders to seek ever new outlets of emigration. Almost every third Jew living in Europe during the generation preceding the First World War left it for overseas. With millions on the march the people's old hopes of restoration to Palestine also assumed a more tangible shape. The progressive secularization of Western life likewise increasingly affected the Jews. Having given up their traditional beliefs without sharing those of another faith, many lost souls roamed the whole area of Jewish existence in search of new roots. These men were particularly impatient with the doctrine of the "chosen people," which to some appeared as sheer arrogance. Others agreed with Heymann Steinthal, the famous ethnopsychologist, when he thus explained its meaning:

> We call ourselves the chosen people, not in order to indicate the height on which we stand or ever stood, not in order to appear superior to our fellow men, but in order constantly to visualize the chasm separating our reality from the ideal tasks of our morality, the chasm between our shortcomings and the model life sketched for us by the prophets. The ugliness of each act of vulgarity and coarseness shall seem to us more repulsive when we have to admit to its being found in a "kingdom of priests"; and even the virtues which we might feel entitled to claim shall fall short of the demands of a "holy nation."

But even they balked against carrying the burden without believing in its supernatural sanctions or looking forward to its supernatural rewards. They yearned to become "normal" people, with normal, not priestly, tasks and a legitimate indulgence in all human frailties.[17]

Secular nationalism, akin to the healthy cultural loyalties of other peoples, seemed to offer the best solution for those who considered their life without roots a menace to themselves and their environment. They watched the disastrous psychological effects on many Jewish individuals of what we have, perhaps uncharitably, called "inverted Marranism," or the necessity of nominally belonging to the Jewish group merely because the outside world refused to open acceptable avenues of escape. Keen disappointment with the indifferent effects of assimilation, the realization that even a century after the American and French revolutions they were still denounced as "aliens" by many European and American compatriots likewise led many to look for some more effective solutions.

To clinch it all came the intensification of nationalist movements in Austria-Hungary and Russia, which at that time embraced the bulk of world Jewry. Apart from their direct impact on Jewish thinking, the ever-sharpening nationalist controversies placed the Jews in an extremely uncomfortable position. If in Bohemia, for instance, Jews sided with the Germans, as many of them did for cultural and historic reasons, all of Bohemian Jewry became a target for Czech chauvinists. In 1897 anti-Jewish riots in several Bohemian cities widely publicized such nationalist resentment. If, on the other hand, a few Jews subscribed to the Czech program, they were denounced as betrayers of the higher German *Kultur* and as traitors to the unity of the Austrian Empire. Under such circumstances it often seemed more convenient to declare one's neutrality by claiming to belong to a third, the Jewish national group.

Cultural assimilation, too, which had attracted the best minds of Jewry when it called for absorption of a world culture like the English, French or German, sounded far less alluring in some of the backward areas of the Balkans or Russia. While some Russified Jews condemned Jewish mass emigration as a betrayal of "Mother Russia," there was little intellectual recompense in a Russian Jew becoming a Latvian, Lithuanian or Estonian nationalist. These nationalities had just begun to develop modern literatures which did not measure up even to the achievements of the relatively young, modern Yiddish letters. How could one expect Jews to forfeit for their sake their millennial Hebraic heritage? Purely political assimilation might still have been feasible were it not for the coincidental shift of emphasis from political to cultural nationalism in both Austro-Hungarian and Russian empires, stimulated by teachings of the Austrian Socialists Renner and Bauer. Whether or not they hoped to become someday a political nationality, in the stricter sense, by erecting a state of their own, most East European Jews now began asserting that their national culture was distinct from that of all other cultural and linguistic groups.

The complexities of the Jewish situation, however, arising from the extraordinary heritage of a universalist-ethnic religion, the ubiquity of Jewish dispersion and the vast differences in environmental pressures led to a great variety of nationalist and antinationalist formulations. Practically all shades of nationalist and cosmopolitan thinking are reflected in Jewish ideologies developed during the fourscore years since Moses Hess's *Rome and Jerusalem* (1862) had sounded the clarion call for the solution of this "ultimate problem of nationalism." An early fundamental cleavage developed particularly between the so-called Diaspora nationalists and the Zionists or other territorialists.

The Diaspora nationalists found influential spokesmen among middle-class publicists like Simon Dubnow, but their main strength rested with proletarian groups, especially the *Bund*. Dubnow and his confreres believed in the essential sameness of Jewish destiny in various lands and periods. Slowly developing their doctrine of nationality along the Austrian socialist lines and claiming that, despite local diversities, the Jewish people had maintained its essential "community of destiny and culture," they insisted upon its right to untrammeled cultural evolution. Most of them also adopted Ahad Haam's doctrine that every nation possesses a native will to survive which assumes different forms in different periods. Long expressed in religious forms, this national will was now seeking to preserve Jewish cultural values through secular self-governing institutions. Communal autonomy, Dubnow contended, had always characterized the history of Diaspora Jewry. In lieu of the old religious community, however, a new national community must be built which, likewise endowed with the authority of public law, would be in exclusive charge of Jewish education and culture. "You are children of your people to the extent that you help build it [a play on the words "banim" and "bonim"], that you combine faith with deeds and strive with utmost devotion for its survival and its inner autonomy in all the lands of its dispersion." [18]

Some extremists, like Noah Prilucki's Populist party, demanded that such multinational states as Russia and Austria-Hungary become federations of major national groups, divided not along territorial, but along cultural lines. Their federal parliaments were to be elected through national *curiae* embracing the voting members of each nationality, irrespective of their place of residence. Others, more moderate, wished to entrust foreign, military and fiscal affairs to legislative and executive organs elected jointly by all federated peoples, but demanded for each nationality complete autonomy in the use of its language and full control of its cultural and educational institutions supported by strictly proportionate allotments from the government's school budget. "The Jews," Dubnow exclaimed, "equal in civil law, should also attain national equality within the limits consistent with the integrity of a given state." Minority rights of this kind, he believed, could be established not only in the ethnically heterogeneous countries of Central and Eastern Europe, but throughout the world wherever Jews lived in significant numbers. Using Hegelian terminology, Dubnow often reiterated his conviction that the medieval "thesis" of Jewish autonomy without equality had been followed by the antithetical evolution of equality without autonomy in the Emancipation era. Now, however, the time had come for a "synthesis" of both equality and autonomy. Emancipation, he answered its critics during the turbulent 1930's, "brought with it assimilation, but it also brought freedom and human dignity; it revived in the Jew the feeling of being a free man. The task of our great national movement during the last half a century has consisted in our struggle for emancipation *without* assimilation, for combined civil and national rights." [19]

Jewish Socialists went further. They wished to superimpose upon the democratic system of political and civil equality the economic equality of all men, including Jews. Peace among national groups, too, they believed, would be assured by the cessation of class struggle. While some considered national aspirations as a hindrance to the realization of their supranational socialist program, others admitted at least the necessity of nationally and linguistically differentiated approaches to the masses of workers. Aron Liberman, a pioneer of Jewish socialism, asked in 1878 by a Vienna court to state his religion, replied tersely, "I am a socialist. . . . By nationality I am a Jew, but I belong to no denomination." He nevertheless found it advisable to publish in 1877 a Hebrew periodical, *Ha-Emet* (The Truth) for the propagation of his socialist ideas among the Jewish workers.

> Not love of our people [he expostulated] has prompted us to publish this periodical, but the love of men generally and the love of our co-nationals, because they are men—this alone induced us to address them in a language which they understand and to tell them the value of truth.[20]

One could doubt the efficacy of Hebrew propaganda among the Jewish workers of Vienna or London, where Liberman lived. But one could not deny that the majority of Jewish workers in Russia and Poland understood little Russian or Polish and that Yiddish alone could help spread among them the socialist gospel. In 1897 the *Bund* was founded principally for this utilitarian purpose. Its leaders nevertheless had to struggle long and hard to justify their "separatist" organization to the Russian Socialist party which not only resented the loss of influential Jewish members, but also suspected the *Bund* of camouflaging deep-seated nationalist aspirations behind that linguistic mask. Most Jewish Socialists themselves at first felt, as did at that time Vladimir Jochelson, who later reminisced:

> We maintained a negative attitude toward the Jewish religion as to all religions. The [Yiddish] jargon we considered to be an artificial language, and

Hebrew a dead language, of interest only to scholars. National beliefs, traditions and language in general did not seem valuable to us from the common standpoint of humanity. But we were sincere assimilationists, and it was to the Russian enlightenment that we looked for salvation for Jews. . . . One must also confess that Russian literature, which implanted in us love of culture and of the Russian people, also in some degree implanted in us a conception that Jews were not a people but a parasitic class.

Before long, however, these practical revolutionaries learned that their estrangement from Jewish ways of life had opened a chasm between them and the Jewish workers of Russia and Galicia. They also realized that, besides sharing the general class struggle, the Jewish working class had to carry on a specific battle against anti-Jewish discrimination and that, despite the egalitarian convictions of enlightened leaders, the rank and file of non-Jewish laborers at times betrayed outright antisemitic feelings. Close observation also revealed that, to quote Juli Martov (Zederbaum), "a working class, which is content with the lot of an inferior nation, will not rise up against the lot of an inferior class. . . . The growth of national and class consciousness must go hand in hand." [21]

Martov himself may have changed his mind later and gone over to the *Iskra* faction within the Russian Socialist party, which became the major opponent of Jewish "separatism." But his fellow Socialist Chaim Zhitlovsky consistently tried to harmonize Jewish nationalism with Marxian internationalism. His ideas, first formulated in an essay, *A Jew to Jews* (1892), gained ever-wider currency in *Bund* circles, confronted by the rising tide of nationalist and zionist sentiments among Russian Jews. Vladimir Medem soon became the outstanding Russian exponent of social democracy's role in the solution of national questions. To be sure, as late as 1911 he vigorously attacked Dubnow's middle-class Diaspora nationalism, as well as every shade of zionism, and particularly combated the notion of a Jewish world-wide *Kulturgemeinschaft*. He pointed out that there was little community of culture between the French and Bulgarian Jews and that "a type of American Jewry is being formed which diverges more and more from Russian Jewry and which might well form a new national type." But he stanchly defended the right of Russian Jews to national existence and self-determination. The *Bund* itself in its Fourth Conference at Bialystok of 1901 adopted a resolution demanding that Russia "be reconstructed as a federation of nationalities with complete national autonomy for each nationality, independent of the territory in which it is located." Although still denying here the timeliness of a struggle for recognition of Jewish national rights, the *Bund* continued thenceforth to defend the Jewish claims to minority safeguards. In 1903 it seceded on this score from the Russian Socialist party. It maintained its position stanchly also after its return in 1907 to the fold of the larger movement, which now evinced greater understanding at least for the rights of other national minorities.[22]

4. Zionist Renascence

There were, on the other hand, many Jewish nationalists, both proletarian and middle class, who felt that, even if national minority rights could be universally secured, which they seriously doubted, the status of the Jewish people would remain highly abnormal. Other nationalities, living in compact masses, constituted the majority of at least their particular regions. Apart from such minor ethnic residua of historic ravages as the Gypsies, the Jews alone were the permanent and universal minority. Even in areas of their mass settlement they constituted only from 5 to 13 per cent of the population.

Permanent minority status implied more than mere numerical inferiority. The evolution of modern nationalism had amply demonstrated the instability of political frontiers. The rise of many small nationalities to sovereign status inspired the territorially segregated ethnic groups with the hope that someday, as a result of as yet unforeseeable historical processes, they, too, would achieve political sovereignty or become semisovereign members of larger federations. The Jews alone could never dream of political independence in the countries of their settlement. Close territorial settlement had also long proved the most eminent means of safeguarding national identity. Great as was the success of Germanization or Russification among the upper classes and in the cities of Bohemia, the Baltic lands and the Ukraine, the national sentiment survived among the peasant masses to blossom forth into full-fledged national cultures in the era of conscious nationalism. The Jews, on the other hand, a permanent urbanized minority, were everywhere exposed to overwhelming forces of amalgamation which threatened to break apart the unity of their world community. The great pressure of population and imperative need of economic restratification, impossible amidst the growingly overcrowded and land-hungry peoples of East-Central Europe, added a note of realistic immediacy and urgency to these ideological considerations.

Philanthropists as well as nationalists, therefore, longingly turned to the vast, unexploited areas in the Old and New Worlds, where closely knit Jewish agricultural colonies seemed to promise speedy relief. Nationalists, however, saw beyond the immediate benefits of reconstruction prospects for a permanent territorial solution of the Jewish question. All through the nineteenth century visionaries and hardheaded businessmen, idealists and self-seeking promoters, even outright antisemites, devised schemes of transplanting millions of Jews to some undeveloped regions. A German nationalist like Karl Freiherr vom Stein, a Russian revolutionary like Pavel Ivanovich Pestel, and a French Socialist like Charles Fourier, all agreed, largely on antisemitic or anticapitalist grounds, on the desirability of removing most European Jews to a country of their own. Among the Jews, Judge Manuel M. Noah's Ararat project of 1825, though more of a publicity stunt than a realistic effort, attracted widespread attention. Jacques Altaras's project of transplanting Russian Jews to Algiers led in 1846 to his abortive negotiations with the Russian government. Only the *Am Olam* movement of the 1880's and 1890's established a number of Jewish agricultural colonies in the United States. Although it, too, bogged down in the face of natural difficulties and the lack of properly trained personnel, it helped pave the way for the fairly extensive participation of American Jewry in agricultural pursuits.[23]

The most ambitious and well-endowed project of this kind was that initiated in 1891 by Baron Maurice de Hirsch's Jewish Colonization Association (ICA). Its grandiose plan of transferring some 3,000,000 Russian Jews to Argentina within a quarter of a century ended in failure, but it succeeded in acquiring land and helping colonize or otherwise readjust Jews economically in various lands, including Palestine. In 1903, finally, the British government officially offered the Zionist Organization, then only a few years old, a portion of British East Africa (Uganda) for colonization as a Jewish homeland. Theodor Herzl and other Western leaders were tempted to accept that offer, at least as a preliminary step toward the ultimate Jewish restoration to Palestine. But they had to yield to the wave of protests from Russian Jewry, which saw in this scheme a betrayal of the zionist ideal. A minority led by Israel Zangwill, however, seceded from the Zionist Organization and formed an independent Jewish Territorial Organization (ITO) to continue the quest for a Jewish state anywhere on the surface of the globe. While some extreme territorialists ruled Palestine out because of its inadequate natural resources and its large Arab population, Zangwill himself merely believed that the Jews would greatly benefit from an intervening preparation in another self-governing community. Ultimately, he wrote grandiloquently in reply to a questionnaire, "If the vast majority of the Jews will return to Palestine, then the nations they quit will sustain an immense loss, politically, economically and spiritually, while the Jews themselves will lay the foundation of a state that will within a century or two recall 'the glory that was Greece and the grandeur that was Rome.' "[24]

The Palestine ideal alone reflected the age-old yearnings of the Jewish people. From ancient times generation after generation of pious Jews made pilgrimages to the Holy Land. Some settled there permanently in order to be buried in the holy soil and thus be spared that mystic subterranean migration which would otherwise precede their bodily resurrection in Palestine upon the advent of the redeemer. James Finn, British consul in Jerusalem in the 1850's often embroiled in local religious controversies, impatiently observed that "the numbers [of Russian Jews] repairing to Jerusalem for the inestimable privilege of being buried there became alarming." Diaspora Jewry lavished of its money and learning upon this ever self-rejuvenating remnant in Zion which, largely consisting of scholars and devotees, could not possibly be self-supporting. The *Halukkah* (distribution of Palestine relief) was subject to much abuse and maladministration, but it helped maintain a permanent vital link not only between the Holy Land and the communities of the Dispersion, but also among the latter in relation to one another.[25]

These deep-rooted loyalties explain the immediate response of Jewish masses to Hess and Pinsker's calls to national action. As a medical man Leo Pinsker was stirred to the depths by the manifestations of mass psychopathology in Russia's anti-Jewish riots of 1881. In his *Auto-Emancipation* he brilliantly analyzed the permanent psychological effects of antisemitism in the Emancipation era. He came to the reluctant conclusion that only complete abandonment of assimilation, which he had espoused for many years, and formation of a self-governing Jewish nation on its own soil would furnish the necessary antitoxin.[26] He joined the "Lovers of Zion" organization which a few years before had begun slowly to settle Jews in Palestine aided therein by parallel, more purely philanthropic efforts of Baron Edmond de Rothschild. These and other brooks and rivulets were united into a broad stream of political zionism under the colorful leadership of Theodor Herzl.

Out of Herzl's broodings over the Dreyfus Affair was born the pamphlet *A Jewish State* (1896) which, despite its occasional eccentricities, became a classic of political zionism. His starting point was antisemitism. The Jewish question, he contended, that remnant of the Middle Ages, still "exists wherever Jews live in perceptible numbers. Where it does not exist, it is carried by Jews in the course of their migrations." Everyone trying to understand the complex phenomenon of antisemitism from the Jewish standpoint but without fear or hatred must come, he believed, to the inescapable conclusion that the Jewish question was essentially a national, rather than a social or religious question. It could, therefore, be solved only "by making it a political world-question to be discussed and controlled by the civilized nations of the world in council." Assimilation had proved totally ineffective. It could succeed only if there was continuous large-scale intermarriage, contingent not only on the legal capacity to marry outside the fold (denied, for instance, to Austrian Jewry) but also on the widespread desire of the majority peoples to enter mixed marriages with Jews. There was no evidence of any such widespread desire. A recent Hungarian decree legalizing marriages between Jews and Christians had ironically led to the union of a baptized Jew with a professing Jewess. The only answer, therefore, Herzl declared, would be the creation of a Jewish state.

> We are one people—our enemies have made us one in our despite, as repeatedly happens in history. Distress binds us together, and, thus united, we suddenly discover our strength. Yes, we are strong enough to form a state and a model state. We possess all human and material resources necessary for the purpose.

To allay apprehensions of various nations that a sudden exodus of Jewish financiers and businessmen might leave behind an economic vacuum and cause far-reaching dislocations, Herzl advocated a gradual and well-planned evacuation under the management of a Society of Jews acting as *gestor Judaeorum*. Supported by world opinion and sympathetic governments, this society would carry out ambitious colonization schemes through the instrumentality of a "Jewish Company" which, in building the new Jewish state, would try to steer clear of the numerous ills of modern society. Therefore, Herzl triumphantly concluded, "prayers will be offered up for the success of our work in temples and in churches also; for it will bring ease from a burden which has long weighed on all men. . . . The world will be freed by our liberty, enriched by our wealth, magnified by our greatness." [27]

This line of reasoning was, of course, territorialist rather than Palestinocentric. In fact, Herzl long wavered between accepting any suitable country and insisting upon the ancient homeland. But when he phenomenally succeeded, within two years, in convoking the first Zionist Congress to Basel (1897), the pro-Palestinian sentiment of the two hundred delegates admitted no debate on this issue. The deliberations in committees and public sessions were confined essentially to details of organization and phrasing. The Basel Program, adopted by the Congress and since stanchly adhered to, read that the aim of the new organization was "to establish for the Jewish people a publicly and legally assured home in Palestine."

Uppermost in the delegates' minds was the postulate of a Jewish state. But since this goal could be reached only through the circuitous road of diplomatic negotiation, especially with the sultan, the equivocal term "home" was preferred. Its ambiguity made it a ready target for such critics as Ahad Haam who ridiculed it as a "monument of diplomacy." [28] It also was to cause endless complications in more recent years. In 1897, however, it not only helped reconcile differences of opinion among delegates, but it also served to enlist the support of statesmen and publicists who would have shied away from advocating a Jewish state *before* mass colonization demonstrated the Jews' ability to build a self-sustaining economy and autonomous society in that long-neglected land. The argument was clinched by the British offer of Uganda. The outburst of protests by old Zionists, particularly in Russia, was so strong that Herzl's very leadership seemed endangered. To his amazement even the two delegates from Kishinev, just ravaged by a bloody pogrom, voted in the negative. Herzl saved his authority, and with it the unity of the movement, only by outright rejection of the British proposal, which he had previously considered a magnificent political achievement.

Despite its immediate failure, the proposal was indeed a great diplomatic success. Herzl's dramatic negotiations with the sultan, the Kaiser and other rulers really led nowhere. At the Porte he vainly pitted his great personal charm and deep idealistic conviction against the wiles of Oriental diplomacy. The Turkish government was bent upon securing a large loan to buttress the tottering empire while giving as little as possible in return. William II heartily enjoyed the histrionic performance of meeting a great Jewish leader and discussing with him the historic redressing of an ancient wrong. But, like other monarchs and statesmen, he had a ready subterfuge against taking the initiative by pretending that it might be misinterpreted as an attempt to enforce the emigration of his own Jewish subjects. The British government alone, prompted by Colonial Minister Joseph Chamberlain, ventured to make a public offer. Perhaps it felt assured of its long record in combating world-wide antisemitism. In these days of bitter anti-British feeling among Zionists, it may well be remembered that, as Joseph Klausner recently noted, "no European country has had statesmen with such understanding for the Jewish messianic idea as did Great Britain, and no European literature has brought forth poets dreaming of the song of our restoration as did the English literature." [29] The British East African proposal, officially recognizing the Zionist Organization, placed it, as it were, on the world's diplomatic map. It also initiated that long chain of negotiations which during the upheaval of the First World War led to the Balfour Declaration and, subsequently, the British mandate over Palestine.

This is not the place to narrate the long vicissitudes of political zionism. When, especially after Herzl's death, diplomatic negotiations offered few prospects, the Zionist Organization returned to the "practical" work of Palestine reconstruction, initiated by the "lovers of Zion." When, on the other hand, the First World War and the forthcoming dissolution of the Ottoman Empire opened unexpected new opportunities, diplomatic action took precedence over all other efforts. Of course, its pace often failed to satisfy ardent expectations. Vladimir Jabotinsky, especially, became the stormy petrel of movements designed to obtain a quick decision. From the beginning of the First World War he combated the official "neutrality," necessarily assumed by the Zionist Organization with a membership recruited equally from the Central and Allied Powers. He and his associates cast their lot with the Allies, organized a Jewish legion which fought with the British in Gallipoli and Palestine, and hoped to reap a speedy reward by the formal establishment of a Jewish state. Thus was born the Revisionist party, which believed in direct action and, if necessary, in military suppression of any Arab opposition. Only as an afterthought did it also advocate certain internal measures designed to eliminate class struggle (it was provoked thereto by labor's stanch opposition to its "undemocratic" methods) and to promote totalitarian control for more effective action. It was often branded "fascist," although it evidently cherished none of the fascist ideals of corporative society, imperial expansion, and race inequality. Its agitation frequently caused much embarrassment to the parent body which, in 1935, finally placed severe curbs on its activities. The revisionists retaliated by forming a New Zionist Organization of their own, some also going under the name of a Jewish State party. Not until 1946 was the breach completely healed.[30]

The "cultural" Zionists raised different objections to the methods, if not necessarily the ultimate aims of political zionism. Unable to forgo entirely the idea of Jewish mission, they viewed the building of a Jewish homeland as a major humanitarian effort. Already Moses Hess, "the socialist rabbi," had written, "We are on the eve of the Sabbath of history and should prepare for our last mission." He believed that the prophetic "end of days" was not to be the eschatological end of the world, but the period of highest human achievement. Such a period had already been ushered in by the teachings of Spinoza and the egalitarian successes of the French Revolution, but it was up to the Jewish people to bring about its final fruition. "When I labor for the regeneration of my own nation," Hess exclaimed, "I do not thereby renounce my humanistic aspiration," for modern nationalism was essentially but a reaction "against the leveling tendencies of modern industry and civilization which threaten to deaden every original organic life force by introducing a uniform inorganic mechanism." In reply to Gustave d'Eichthal's demand of a new synthesis of Judea, Hellas and Rome, Hess expressed his credo:

> We, too, believe in the revival of the genius of our race, which lacks but a center of activity where a nucleus of persons devoted to the religious mission of Israel could gather, so that they may develop anew from thence the eternal principles which unite humanity with the Universe and the Universe with its Creator. These persons will rediscover one another some day in the ancient state of Israel. For this purpose their number is irrelevant. Judaism has never been represented by a numerous people; the golden calf always attracted the majority, and only a handful of Levites kept the holy flame of our religion burning on its ancient hearth.[31]

The idea of Palestine as a cultural center for world Jewry was more fully developed by Ahad Haam (Asher Ginzberg). Even Herzl realized, as he told the first Zionist Congress, that "zionism is a return to Judaism, even before the return to the Jewish land." But, without being a mere political opportunist as alleged by Ahad Haam, he chiefly meant the return of the stray, assimilated sons to the fold of the Jewish nation. Ahad Haam went further in demanding the solution of problems affecting "Judaism first, and those of the Jews will ultimately take care of themselves." For him Jewish culture embodied the biological drive for self-preservation characteristic of every living national group, for which all forms of national existence are means rather than ends. Territorial moorings were important, but so were language and religion. Self-preservation might even assume such paradoxical forms as when, in order to survive emancipation, Western Judaism accepted ethnic assimilation in return for the untrammeled pursuit of its mission in behalf of ethical monotheism. The effects of this impossible compromise upon the Jewish psyche, however, only generated "spiritual slavery in the midst of political freedom" compared with which the political oppression of East European Jewry was decidedly the lesser evil. To redress the balance a spiritual center in Palestine was indispensable. Like Hess, Ahad Haam was not interested in numbers and often stressed the physical impossibility for Palestine to absorb more than a fraction of world Jewry.

> After two thousand years of untold misery and suffering [he also declared] the Jewish people cannot possibly be content with attaining at last to the position of a small and insignificant nation, with a state tossed about like a ball between its powerful neighbors, and maintaining its existence only by diplomatic shifts and continual truckling to the favored of fortune.

But even one per cent of the Jewish population, he believed, if properly selected and guided by a wise leadership in Palestine, might regenerate the whole people. Such a renaissance would re-emphasize Israel's adherence to the principles of justice and bring it close to the realization of its prophetic dream of living as a "kingdom of priests" for the benefit of themselves and the world at large.[32]

Cultural zionism had many strong affinities with Diaspora nationalism for it was also interested in the preservation of Diaspora culture as an end in itself. Herzl, too, after a while began counseling his followers to "conquer the communities," but for him this was only a political stratagem to overthrow their entrenched antizionist leadership and to use their large financial and educational resources for the realization of his zionist program. To Ahad Haam the reconstruction of Jewish communal life and thorough reform of Jewish education were major postulates, the more vital as they alone promised the rejuvenation of Hebrew culture on a world-wide scale. Many of his sympathizers, working within the Zionist Organization and led by Martin Buber and Berthold Feiwel, successfully stressed, from 1902 on, the cultural *Gegenwartsarbeit* in the Dispersion.[33]

The prolonged failure of diplomatic negotiations, highlighted by the controversy over the Uganda project, clinched the argument in their favor. Like the *Bund*, the Russian Zionists at first failed to wax enthusiastic over the struggle for national minority rights, seeing in it a dangerous diversion from their main Palestinian objective. But in 1903-5 they, too, changed their minds. The Helsingfors Conference of Russian Zionists, meeting in 1906, adopted a resolution demanding that

> the organs of national self-government possess the right to found, conduct and support all kinds of institutions which serve the ends of 1) national education, 2) national health, 3) mutual and labor aid, 4) emigration and 5) matters of faith . . . as also to issue in accordance with the laws of the state and the province . . . ordinances and regulations for their institutions.

During the First World War the ever-expanding drive for national self-determination found such an enthusiastic response in the East European communities that the Zionist World Organization, though concentrating on the realization of the Balfour Declaration, was forced to assume leadership in the struggle for Jewish minority rights as well. Its "Copenhagen Manifesto" of October, 1918, finally, ratified in 1921 by the Zionist Congress in Carlsbad, offered a most authoritative exposition of the demanded safeguards.[34]

Labor Zionists, representing various combinations of zionism and socialism, on the whole, co-operated with the cultural Zionists in both the struggle for Jewish rights in the Dispersion and the practical colonization of Palestine. The Jewish colonies in Palestine, wrote Ber Borochov in 1917, however small and full of shortcomings, "did more toward enlightening the Jewish nation than a thousand beautifully worded programs and diplomatic negotiations." At the same time, as true Marxists, Borochov and his associates believed in the inevitability of a world revolution which alone would pave the way for the ultimate solution of the Jewish question. But they agreed with Martov that "one who has no national dignity can have no class dignity." They viewed with particular alarm the incipient signs of anti-Jewish discrimination among non-Jewish workers. When, after prolonged negotiations Gentile weavers in Bialystok admitted a few Jewish comrades out of "socialist pity," some *Bund* leaders hailed this agreement as a socialist victory. Borochov, however, vigorously denounced it as a "*numerus clausus* in the factories." Like middle-class Zionists, therefore, he and his associates came to this doleful conclusion:

> The *galut* [Diaspora] condition of the Jewish nation is not only tragic, but also hopeless. Our *galut* tragedy is not temporary, but permanent. We do not fight for a Jewish cause; we suffer for foreign interest. We do not possess our own land, and are neglected by this colossal world which has its own troubles. . . . Our fate is always determined by the fate of other nations. . . . We Socialists-Zionists are convinced that our freedom depends primarily upon the national self-help of the Jewish masses.[35]

Another brand of labor zionism was represented by Aaron David Gordon. Its frequent designation as "national socialism" should not place it on a level with German nazism, for it had none of the latter's characteristic racial, fascist or militaristic features. But its socialism was also distinctly anti-Marxian. As a disciple of both the prophets and Tolstoi, Gordon rejected the idea of class struggle, denounced both capitalism and Marxism as two facets of the same mechanistic civilization. "Socialism," he declared, "is just the opposite of nationalism. It is based entirely on technique and industry, while nationalism is entirely based on life and creation." Supranational Christianity, on the other hand, had failed because it started with the doctrine of love, that is, at the summit of human achievement, instead of placing it as an ultimate goal toward which humanity should strive throughout its historic career.

In nationalism there is a cosmic moment, as if to say the natural spirit of the fatherland has combined with the spirit of the nation. And that is essential. That is the very foundation of the national soul; and in this lies the difference between the nation which is an organic and creative body and society which is a mechanical and unstable entity.

But just as an individual, in order to live justly, must be a human man, so must nations become humanized and avoid bloodshed and mutual degradation. "We were the first to say that the individual was created in God's image; we must amplify this by saying that the nation must likewise be formed in God's image." Such a full development of the Jewish human personality as well as humanized nation was possible only in Palestine, where alone the Jew could achieve the "unfathomable depths" of experience to build a living spiritual center far superior to Ahad Haam's purely rational and "visible" center.[36]

Gordon lived as he preached. At the age of forty-eight he tore up his roots in Russia and, without outside compulsion, settled in Palestine. His way of living added a fascinating hue to his *Hapoel Hasair* (Young Worker) organization. Long at loggerheads with the Marxist *Ahdut ha-abodah* (Unity of Labor), the Young Workers realized, over Gordon's protests, the need for unity in action which would transcend ideological differences. In January, 1938, the two factions, finally, got together in the General Federation of Jewish Labor (*Histadrut*) which, because of its overshadowing importance in the upbuilding of Palestine, has not unjustifiably been called "a labor commonwealth in the making." Uniting in its practical program the various combinations of zionism and socialism formulated by the disciples of both Borochov and Gordon, the federation helped build the collectivistic Jewish colonies which, often outspokenly anticommunist, gave a new communal coloring to the entire zionist enterprise. It also fostered many other co-operative efforts which, though leaving ample room for private enterprise and a profit economy, have laid the foundations for a social-democratic society, which may yet serve as a model for the entire Near East and beyond it. Its philosophy was well summarized by Solomon Schiller, one of Palestine labor's pioneer leaders:

> Now the synthesis of the two elements, the nationalist and the socialist, in Labor Zionism, will certainly be able to mend the defects on both sides. The socialist idea, which stands for justice . . . will not allow our national movement to degenerate into narrow-minded chauvinism. On the other hand, the national consciousness of the workers, the knowledge that a whole people knocks at the gates of the country with no one to open them, the feeling that, as things stand at present, each day allowed to pass without practical achievement spells irretrievable loss for the nation and its future—all this will not allow them to become submerged in the "world as it is." [37]

Despite these serious divergences of opinion, often expounded with considerable heat and mutual animosity, zionism has become the most representative type of Jewish nationalism. Gradually subduing almost all nationalist opposition outside the Soviet Union, it has also become the most influential and profound intellectual movement in modern Jewish history. It has reached out far beyond Western Jewry into the long-isolated settlements in Yemen, Kurdistan and Bokhara. After securing international recognition it has built a Jewish national home by methods so novel and in the face of difficulties so staggering as to overtax the physical and spiritual resources of many another people. It has embarked upon establishing a state without the backing of state power, of colonizing without a motherland, and of recruiting manpower and marshaling funds without any possibility of enforcement. It has succeeded in reversing a world-wide trend from country to city, from agriculture to industry and professions and converted thousands of skilled professionals into farmers and road builders. It has also long dreamed of setting still another historic precedent by colonizing a country *with* the consent of the natives. It has, finally, undertaken to build the new commonwealth on unparalleled foundations of social justice, thus eliminating class struggle, that greatest source of dissension in the modern world.

All these are ideals. Like all ideals, they may be cheapened by contact with reality. As ideals, they also evidently transcend the Jewish nationality and are intended to serve the cause of all humanity.[38]

5. Religious and Socialist Controversies

These ideals are clearly a revival of the old combination of nationalism and universalism, given in a modern, secular garb. There is little distinction in this respect between political and cultural zionism, since even the former is in so far essentially nonpolitical as it has little understanding "for the essence of power and the struggle for power." [39] Most political Zionists really espouse an ethical cause and appeal to the world's conscience in behalf of suffering multitudes and Jewish cultural values. The cultural Zionists, on the other hand, have come to recognize the need of political methods for the building of a "cultural center" as well. And it was their leader, Chaim Weizmann, who, under propitious circumstances, realized the political program much more fully than any of the political dogmatists of the pre-Balfourian era. The official position of the Zionist Organization, reflecting the perfect blending of political and cultural programs, is well summarized in its memorandum to the League of Nations' Council, submitted in July, 1922, on the eve of the League's confirmation of the Palestine mandate.

> It would be a profound mistake [it wrote] to regard the Zionist Movement as an artificial attempt to reverse the course of history and to restore the political conditions which existed when the Jewish State came to an end. If the Jews now ask for an opportunity of rebuilding their national home, they base their claim not only on the existence of a Jewish State in remote antiquity, but on the unwavering concentration on Palestine of the Jewish hopes and prayers

from the moment of the dispersion up to the present day. The connection be-tween the Jews and Palestine has never been broken. . . . They are per-suaded that in Palestine alone is it possible for Jews as such to live their corporate life and attain their full stature as a people in perfect harmony with their environment. They are not less firmly persuaded that it is in the interests of the new world order that the discord in the Jewish soul should be resolved, and that the Hebrew genius, restored to Hebrew soil, should have an assured opportunity of once more making its characteristic contribution to the com-mon stock.[40]

Of course, stress on the humanitarian aspects of their movement was charac-teristic of most nationalists in the early, "heroic" stages of their movement. In fact, Fichte's ideology, his emphasis upon the German *Menschheitsnation* as a nation without state and political history, which out of its ideal "Thou shalt" was to create both a state and a new history, struck a responsive chord among Jewish nationalists, too. In the Jewish case, however, the ancient traditions of Israelitic prophecy and the old messianic ideals lent a peculiar coloring to such humanitarian professions.

Despite its outward secularization, therefore, its professed attempt at "nor-malizing" Jewish existence on the level of other nations, and its endeavor to unite the whole people from the extreme orthodox to the extreme agnostics, the zionist movement was but an offshoot of the traditional Jewish messianic idea. Little wonder that it has often been criticized as such by religionists of all camps. The Basel program of 1897 immediately evoked a sharp protest from the Executive Committee of the German Rabbinical Assembly.

1. The efforts of so-called Zionists [wrote its five rabbinical spokesmen] to erect in Palestine a Jewish national state, run counter to Judaism's messianic hopes, as expressed in Scripture and later religious sources.
2. Judaism imposes upon its adherents the obligation to serve with devotion the country to which they belong and to promote its national interests whole-heartedly and with all their strength.
3. There is no conflict, however, between this obligation and the noble endeavors aiming at Jewish agricultural colonization in Palestine, for these have no connection whatsoever with the establishment of a national state.

Reform Jews, in particular, long saw in zionism the abandonment of Judaism's religious mission and a denial of its true religious universalism. "He who, as a matter of principle, reserves the basic teachings of Judaism for the Jewish people alone," said the distinguished philosopher, Hermann Cohen, "denies therewith the one and only God of messianic humanity." Frankfort neo-orthodoxy, on the other hand, violently objected to zionist toleration of wide-spread nonconformity among Palestinian settlers. Certainly the Biblical postu-lates of a sabbatical year, tithe, etc., were felt as a serious hindrance in a modern agricultural economy and were brushed aside by most pioneers, with the tacit concurrence of officials in charge of colonization. To Isaac Breuer the professed religious indifference of the zionist movement appeared as an outright denial of the true essence of Jewish nationality which, as a unique *Religionsnation*, had always been centered around its religious law.[41]

Eastern orthodoxy always was more Palestinocentric. It remembered the exultant praises showered on the country by its hasidic and rabbinic teachers alike. It recalled, for instance, the inspired words of Rabbi Ber, the great Preacher of Meserich, "Zion is the very essence of the world, it is the lifeblood of the universe; that is why it contains a portion of all countries, and every country draws her lifeblood and nourishment from that portion which is hers in Zion." [42] But at least in the early stages of the zionist movement the Orthodox violently objected to the secularization of messianism and the expectation that the people's restoration to Palestine could be achieved without the supernatural intervention of a personal redeemer.

Curiously, pious Christians rarely objected to zionism once their apprehensions concerning the Holy Places had been allayed. Old prophecies concerning the second coming of Christ, combined with a feeling of guilt for anti-Jewish persecutions and a humanitarian concern for a suffering people, often created a positively prozionist attitude. The 320 Christian signatories of the memorial submitted to Lord Palmerston on March 2, 1841, expressed beliefs shared by many Protestants and Catholics alike.

> Your Memorialists [they wrote] beg leave further to remind Your Lordship that the Land of Palestine was bestowed by the Sovereign of the Universe upon the descendants of Abraham as a permanent and inalienable possession nearly 4000 years ago, and that neither conquests nor treaties among men can possibly affect their Title to it. He has also decreed that they shall again return to their country and that the Gentiles shall be employed as the means of their restoration.

The famous declaration later issued by another British foreign secretary, Lord Arthur James Balfour, was greeted with general acclaim by distinguished churchmen in many lands. The Anglican bishop of Chelmsford declared that "from a religious point of view I think the decision of the English government relating to the future of the Holy Land is not only the most interesting but the most important incident of the war which has yet been recorded." [43] Today, too, zionism has some of its stanchest supporters among the American clergy, many of whom have joined such organizations as the American Christian Palestine Committee.

The constant growth of the movement and the fact that it increasingly met the people's real needs, material as well as spiritual, has largely silenced Jewish religious opposition, too. In 1902 Orthodox Jewry organized a special zionist faction, the so-called *Mizrahi*, which, under the leadership of Rabbi Isaac Reines of Lida, propagated a religious form of zionism adumbrated by the zionist pioneers Alkalai, Kalischer and Mohilewer.[44] Even many of those who held aloof from the Zionist Organization began to collaborate with it in the practical realization of its program.

Reform Judaism, too, long a major objector, has largely given up its opposition. The Central Conference of American Rabbis, which from the first Zionist Congress to the Treaty of Versailles had often gone on record as opposing political zionism, has during recent years included the zionist anthem in its hymnal and adopted a resolution endorsing the zionist program. While this militant pronouncement induced the opposing minority to form the new anti-zionist American Council for Judaism, there is little doubt that the vast majority of Jews favor keeping Palestine open to unrestricted Jewish immigration and even an ultimate Jewish majority and commonwealth. A poll taken in November, 1945, by Elmo Roper showed that 80.1 per cent of the Jews of America favored a Jewish state, while only 10.5 per cent opposed it.[45]

The main Jewish opposition to zionism has come all along from those secularist groups which have looked forward to the reconstruction of Jewish life under a new social order. Through the years some Socialists and Communists condemned zionism, including its laborite wings, as bourgeois and reactionary. Some invoked Marxian internationalism and contended that the Jewish people has always been but a religious community. Under the new social order, they asserted, which would eliminate all religious "opiates," anti-Jewish prejudice would die out of itself. The Jews should therefore refrain from injecting another source of disturbance into a world already convulsed by bitter nationalist strife. Others, interpreting literally the irate remarks of Karl Marx in his early essays "on the Jewish question," asserted that Judaism had merely been the ideological superstructure of a peculiar Jewish economic function and that with the elimination of the latter under the new order the superstructure, too, would crumble. An Austrian Jewish Communist, Otto Heller, published in 1931 a volume predicting on this score the forthcoming "decline of Judaism." [46]

Russian Jewish Communists, on the contrary, early recognized the overwhelmingly nationalist sentiment of the Russian Jewish masses. Fully 90 per cent of all Jewish votes cast at the last "free" election of 1917 had gone to nationalist, principally zionist candidates. Though vigorously opposing zionism, the Jewish Communists, as well as the government, were forced to recognize the Jews as a national minority entitled to the political safeguards pledged by the new regime to all national minorities. For Lenin this meant a dialectical *salto mortale*. Before his rise to power he had long denied the existence of a Jewish nationality and in numerous articles from 1903 to 1914 urged the Russian Jewish workers to give up the *Bund* and join the Russian Socialist party. With his customary vigor he had arraigned them:

The Jews in the civilized world are not a nation, they have become most of all assimilated, affirm Karl Kautsky and Otto Bauer. The Jews in Galicia and Russia are not a nation, they unfortunately (and not through their fault, but owing to the Purishkeviches) are still a *caste*. This is the unquestioned conclusion of people who are unquestionably well informed on the history of the Jews.

What do these facts indicate? They indicate that "assimilation" can be denounced only by the Jewish reactionary petty bourgeois, who wish to turn back the wheel of history, and to force it to move, not from the conditions of Russia and Galicia to the conditions of Paris and New York, but in the opposite direction.

After 1917, however, he and Stalin, in consonance with their general policy of pacifying the national minorities, promoted an extensive Jewish national school system from elementary schools to "sectors" in universities and academies of science, special Jewish peoples' courts and Jewish soviets in areas of Jewish mass settlement. They also encouraged agricultural colonization in close Yiddish-speaking settlements and the formation of autonomous regions. Finally, as a counterpart to the British mandate in Palestine, the Soviet regime invited its Jewry to develop Far Eastern Biro-Bidjan into a Jewish state ultimately functioning as still another federated Soviet republic. At the same time the Jewish religion, Hebraic culture and zionism were thoroughly discouraged.[47]

Even outside the Soviet Union the various socialist movements became zionism's greatest rivals, particularly because of their powerful appeal to youth. Whether in its internationalist or its assimilationist aspects, socialism with its religious fervor and messianic hopes became a factor in Jewish, as in non-Jewish life far beyond its numerical strength. In Russia before 1939 communism held undisputed sway over some 3,000,000 Jews or one-fifth of world Jewry. Today the Soviet Union and its satellites embrace perhaps 30 per cent of the entire Jewish population. Speaking in religious terms, one may consider the communist movement as a new Jewish schism of major proportions and envisage the ultimate breakup of Jewish unity as a result of sectarian clashes outstripping in violence the Pharisaic-Sadducean or Rabbanite-Karaite controversies. Since the Jewish people had never before lived without religion, many observers predict the Jews' speedy assimilation in the Soviet Union and with it the weakening of the communist factor in Jewish life. More recently hopes have been expressed that the change in Russia's international policies, its wartime rapprochement with the Western democracies, and the toning down of its antireligious crusade would lead to the reorientation of its policy toward both the Jewish religion and Palestine reconstruction. The survival of a strong zionist sentiment within the Soviet Union, despite a quarter of a century of outlawry, is asserted by many observers. According to a newspaper report, the Germans once tricked the Jewish population of an occupied Crimean community into appearing en masse in order allegedly to be sent to Palestine. All Jews, without exception, are said to have gathered at the stated hour and become easy victims of the nazi extermination squads.[48]

A major inconsistency, on the other hand, in the behavior of Zionists sheds a characteristic light on their alleged unregenerate secularism. The first Czechoslovak census of 1921, revealing that eleven residents of Prague and hundreds more throughout the country registered as belonging to the Jewish "nationality" and the Roman Catholic "religion," came as a shock to the zionist leaders. Six other Prague Jewish "nationals" stated that they professed Protestantism or Greek Orthodoxy.[49] The Zionists had long received with open arms Jews having no religious affiliation, but they drew the line in the case of converts to another faith. Long before "racialism" became the great menace to world Jewry, zionist opinion resented religious apostasy as a betrayal of the Jewish national cause as well. This would have been illogical if ethnic descent, and not religion, were the exclusive criterion. But it was an inescapable reflection of the Jewish people's semiconscious realization that, however secularized, it still was a "religious nationality," glorying in its religious past and essentially held together by a common religion. It knew that, however weakened their faith may have become by sectarian disharmonies and widespread indifference, the overwhelming majority of its members continued entering after birth the covenant of Abraham and finding after death a permanent resting place in a Jewish religious cemetery. They thus unwittingly testified to the strength of the immemorial religious ties in the most critical moments of life and death.

For these reasons the much-debated conflict between the Jewish religion and Jewish nationalism has become almost meaningless today. So long as the Jewish faith will largely be restricted to descendants of Jews (paradoxically of religious, and not "racial" Jews); so long as Judaism refrains from being again an active missionary religion trying to convert vast Gentile masses; and so long as the Jews, with individual exceptions, fail to adopt other religions and formally adhere to their forefathers' creed or profess religious indifference—Judaism of every shade will appear to Jews and, still more, to their neighbors as an ethnic religion, however peculiar and unique. These widespread practical appraisals received a severe jolt, but were never completely abandoned, even after the revolutionary transformations brought about by the long nightmare of nazism and the Second World War.

6. IMPACT OF WARS

The First World War had suddenly brought the Jewish national program closer to realization than anyone could reasonably have expected before 1914. The upsurge of nationalist sentiment throughout Central and Eastern Europe; the destruction of the Austro-Hungarian and Ottoman empires and the separation of the western provinces from Czarist Russia; and the vigorous espousal of national self-determination by progressive leaders from Wilson to Lenin opened new opportunities for the safeguarding of national minority rights by both domestic constitutions and international treaties. Nor was the example set by the Soviet Union in 1917 completely lost on its neighbors.

The representatives of East European Jewry appearing before the Peace Conference of Paris were fairly unanimous in demanding national minority rights for Poland, Czechoslovakia, Rumania, the Baltic lands, etc. They were vigorously supported therein by American and, to a lesser extent, by British Jewry. Some American leaders like Louis Marshall were personally anti-nationalist, but they refrained from injecting their personal biases into peace settlements affecting only their Eastern coreligionists. Under the peculiar historic circumstances Jewish leadership was in a position effectively to champion the cause of all national minorities. The Allied and Associated Powers, including newly arisen Poland and Czechoslovakia, annexed as many territories as they could possibly claim under the national principle. Few of their own nationals now remained under the sovereignty of other states. The chief minorities were recruited from the defeated Central Powers (Germans, Austrians, Hungarians, Bulgarians and Turks) whose representatives had little influence at the Peace Conference and mainly bargained for more favorable territorial adjustments. They were much more interested in forestalling the transfer of conationals to other sovereignties than in protecting their rights thereafter. The Jews alone were certain of retaining their minority status regardless of the new boundaries. Having influential coreligionists in the United States, Great Britain, France and Italy, they unwittingly became the spearheads in the movement for securing domestic national rights through international agreements. Thus were created those famous minority clauses in the Peace Treaties of 1919 which constituted a significant innovation in international public law. The Jews were mentioned specifically only in the Polish and Turkish treaties. The special safeguards for the Jewish educational structure and Sabbath observance in Poland were deemed necessary "in view of the historical development of the Jewish question and the great animosity aroused by it" there. But it was agreed that Jewish rights would be equally protected by the more general clauses in the other treaties.[50]

The zionist program made even greater headway. The great sufferings of the Jewish masses, whose East European heartland had been converted into a bloody battlefield, made Jewish emigration doubly imperative. While the Western Hemisphere was becoming less and less hospitable to large-scale immigration, the dissolution of the Ottoman Empire opened untold vistas for Jewish settlement in Palestine. The British government, in particular, soon realized the benefits it might derive from espousing the zionist cause. There had existed a century-old tradition of British humanitarian and religious, as well as imperial interests in Palestine Jewry. Now in her life-and-death struggle against the Central Powers Britain needed badly the support of world Jewry which she hoped to secure by issuing the Balfour Declaration. The British government was, of course, fully aware of the so-called MacMahon Correspondence of 1915-16 and its promises to the Arabs, whom it had urged to revolt against the Turks. But it soon recognized that, as the wartime prime minister David Lloyd George later publicly testified in Parliament (June 19, 1936), "it was vital we should have the sympathies of the Jewish community." As late as June 3, 1940, the Laborite leader, Noel Baker, while moving in Parliament for censure of the government's land regulation in Palestine, quoted a statement made by Winston Churchill, another member of the War Cabinet, seven years previously. The Balfour Declaration had been issued, Churchill had said, in "the dire need of the war with the object of promoting the general victory of the Allies, for which they expected and received valuable and important assistance." Lloyd George underscored this quotation by exclaiming, "Hear! Hear!" At the same time, there was a strong idealistic streak in Arthur James Balfour, who considered Jewish restoration to Palestine a turning point in human history. According to his niece, Mrs. Edgar Dugdale, he asserted during his last illness that "nothing he had done or tried to do would prove of more permanent value to the world than this support of the Jewish national cause." [51]

To be sure, the British government did not accede to all zionist demands. It soon became known—Ahad Haam himself made much ado about it [52]— that the British had refused to accept the zionist formula postulating "Palestine as the national home of the Jewish people." Instead they promised only to try to secure a Jewish national home in Palestine. This formula was equivocal not only in the term "home," a heritage of the studied ambiguity of the Basel program, but also in failing to delimit frontiers. Very soon, indeed, the Peace Treaty of San Remo and subsequent mandate by the League of Nations opened wide new possibilities for whittling it down. By separating, in 1922, Transjordan from Western Palestine for the first time in recorded history, the mandatory power removed a vast undeveloped area from the potential Jewish national home. In the so-called Churchill White Paper it also informed the Jews that, although they were coming to Palestine "as of right and not on sufferance," they were not to expect Palestine to be "as Jewish as England was English." Moreover, the Balfour Declaration itself had already provided that the building of a Jewish national home was not to "prejudice the civil and religious rights of existing non-Jewish communities in Palestine." Like every other mandate, that of Palestine imposed upon the mandatory power the obligation to develop its self-governing institutions. If fully developed, before the Jews attained a majority of the population, the predominantly Arab legislature could readily prohibit Jewish immigration and defeat all other measures taken to establish a Jewish national home. In view of these numerous contradictions and ambiguities the local administration had much leeway in interpreting the mandate less favorably to Jewish aspirations than had originally been intended.

This is not the place to describe in detail the vicissitudes of either the up-building of Jewish Palestine or of the Jewish minority rights in Europe. As often before, the high-strung expectations generated by a great war had to be toned down in contact with reality. In Europe the national majorities as a rule refused to live up to the minority safeguards in the treaties even if they had willingly signed them. Two major culprits, Poland and Rumania, often contended that their signatures had been placed under duress. The peacemakers had also failed to provide detailed sanctions. The League of Nations, a cumbersome infant trying to get on its feet, wasted several years discussing the procedure in handling petitions submitted by aggrieved minorities. The accused governments could accompany each petition with whatever answers they saw fit. Nor could they easily be prevented from taking punitive action against the petitioners who, not being the League's official members, never had equality of representation.

The League itself, weakened by the nonco-operation of the United States and the prolonged exclusion of Russia and Germany, could never quite justify the discriminatory treatment of a few member states subjected to the minority provisions of the Peace Treaties, while the bulk of its membership had retained complete sovereignty in domestic affairs. The much-debated "universalization of minority rights," like the promised general disarmament, was frustrated by a vocal opposition which refused to surrender any particle of its sovereignty. Such influential non-European statesmen as Mello-Franco of Brazil often found vigorous words of condemnation for every attempt at extending the peace provisions to other lands. In retrospect his fears have not proved altogether unfounded. By granting minority rights to her three largest minorities, the Germans, Italians and Japanese, often living in close territorial settlement, Brazil might have strengthened the pro-Axis forces during the Second World War.[53] The upshot was that, among all the signatories, Czechoslovakia and Estonia alone tried to fulfill their treaty obligations. By 1934 Colonel Joseph Beck of Poland startled his colleagues in the League by declaring, with obvious reference to the Jewish minority, that his country would no longer co-operate with League organs in problems affecting national minorities.

This general disregard of minority rights significantly contributed to the progressive decline of European Jewry. Palestine Jewish colonization, on the other hand, made steady progress, in spite of all obstacles placed in its way by an increasingly unsympathetic mandatory administration. Its constant growth was made possible only by the almost superhuman effort of thousands of pioneers and endless sacrifices of the Jewish people as a whole.[54] Nevertheless, the international status of the national home was gradually deteriorating. The historic, cultural and economic differences between the Arab-speaking countries from Iraq to Morocco did not prevent enthusiastic Arab nationalists from now asserting the unity of a Pan-Arab nation and from insisting upon its unrestricted control over all of Palestine. Future historians may well prove that zionism was the most important single factor in the rise of the Pan-Arab movement, since peoples have often attained their unity more easily on a negative than on a positive platform.

At the same time the British auspices embroiled zionism in the historic controversies of the British Empire. The Soviet Union, for instance, a major enemy of British imperial power, long condemned zionism as an ally of British imperialism. The empire's general retreat was accelerated by fascist Italy's Near Eastern aspirations and, still more, by nazi Germany's resumption of the historic *Drang nach Osten*. In the late 1930's British power in the Near East was seriously undermined by effective nazi and fascist appeals to Arab nationalism, now intermingled with fervent Judeo- and Anglophobia. In both Europe and the Near East the Chamberlain administration long pursued the futile line of "appeasement," the White Paper of 1939 being but another inglorious monument to that policy shortly before the outbreak of the Second World War. Even the Permanent Mandates Commission of the League had to condemn it as contrary to the provisions of the mandate.[55]

The war did not immediately change this Near Eastern policy, while it catastrophically affected the Jews of Europe. Since it was fought between an outspokenly anti-Jewish power and the democratic alliance, no effort was needed to secure Jewish goodwill for the Allied cause. Even Jewish citizens of neutral countries had no alternative but to fight Hitler. In fact, insidious nazi propaganda had so well succeeded in presenting the war as the effect of "Jewish warmongering" that Roosevelt and Churchill were often apprehensive of strengthening the hands of their enemies by taking sides with Jews. In the realistic game of power politics, moreover, the Jews had no additional *quid* to offer for the *quod* of active Allied support.[56]

The manifest political weakness of the Jewish people gave no occasion for the issuance of another Balfour Declaration or for the reiteration of its ultimate objectives. On the contrary, the policy of reducing its pledges now continued unabated. Many British statesmen believed that the British imperial interest now lay in exploiting to the full the Near Eastern oil resources, eliminating France from the Levant and staving off the threat of Russian expansion. The attainment of all these objectives was, in their opinion, contingent on their reaching full agreement with the Arab states. They helped, therefore, organize the Arab League, which covered up the transfer of the "independent" states of Syria and Lebanon from French to British control and erect a barrier, built on religious and class apprehensions, against Soviet penetration. These realistic long-distance considerations have undoubtedly carried far greater weight with the successive British administrations than the professed fear of an immediate Arab armed uprising.[57]

On closer examination, however, it appears that, by allying themselves with the present Arab states, the British rely on classes now in power, especially the so-called *effendis*. But by that very fact they play into the hands of Russian propagandists among the peasant masses and the nascent industrial proletariat. The multicolored religious and ethnic patterns of the Near East likewise promote Russian interests in view of the tremendous appeal exercised on all Asiatic minority groups by the Soviet treatment of national minorities.

Perhaps the entry of the United States into Near Eastern and especially Palestine politics, as exemplified by the recent Anglo-American Commission of Inquiry, may help alter the hopeless course of British imperial policy. The United States had long had a genuine interest in Near Eastern affairs. In August, 1921, Secretary of State Charles Evans Hughes demanded for his country an equal voice in all decisions over formerly Ottoman territories, because of America's contribution to the victory over Germany.[58] Although the United States soon withdrew from active participation in international affairs, it signed a treaty with Britain safeguarding its and its nationals' rights under the Palestine mandate. Its experiences during the Second World War and its present assumption of a leading role in world affairs, combined with such specific interests as the exploitation of Near Eastern oil fields and the satisfaction of demands voiced by its large Jewish population, have created some counterweight to British policy which may make itself increasingly felt in the years to come.

Whatever may be the outcome of international deliberations, the Jews of both Palestine and Europe are determined to go ahead with the building of their national home. They have the active support of world Jewry which, in its overwhelming majority, favors at least unrestricted Jewish immigration. The extermination of more than five million coreligionists and the reduction of their total number by more than a quarter has convinced the Jews everywhere that, biologically at least, they had lost the war despite the political and military victory of the democratic alliance, of which, in a sense, they had been the earliest members. Certainly, the "defeated" Axis nations have not lost anything like a quarter of their number. There are some 4,000,000 more Japanese in the world today than in 1937 during the so-called "China incident." Before long there will probably be more Germans in Central Europe than there were in 1939. The Jewish people, however, has little chance of biologically recuperating in the near future. This stark tragedy has led most thoughtful Jews to despair of any future for the age-old centers of Jewish culture in Germany and Poland, while extremists envisage the ultimate Jewish exodus from all countries of the Dispersion.

Under these circumstances Jewish minority rights in Eastern Europe would have lost much of their meaning even if the general outlook for such rights were far more promising today. The prevailing trend all over Europe, west of the Curzon line, is to secure national homogeneity, if need be by the wholesale deportation of minorities. Czechoslovakia, formerly a faithful adherent of minority provisions, now sets the pace in the evacuation of Germans and Hungarians. Its venerable president, Eduard Beneš, for forty years an eloquent champion of minority rights, has clearly indicated his change of mind. In an interview with the correspondent of the Jewish Telegraphic Agency of August 10, 1945, for instance, he stated bluntly:

> The establishment of a Jewish Home in Palestine is a necessity for all nations, because antisemitism is a regrettable but practically inevitable social phenomenon. It will not vanish till the creation of a Jewish country granting citizenship to all Jewry. It would be difficult to repatriate all Jews there, but it could be done soon at least for the European Jews. Those who would not leave for Palestine ought to be assimilated completely to the people of the country they want to live in, or live there as citizens of a foreign state.

This trend may not be permanent, but it certainly ought to be reckoned with as a major factor in shaping the status of East European Jewry in the next generation.[59]

7. JEWISH MISSION

Whatever the future may hold for the realization of the zionist ideal or of Jewish minority rights, there is no question that during the past half century Jewish nationalism and, especially, zionism have profoundly transformed the spiritual and material physiognomy of the Jewish people. They have also contributed a noteworthy new chapter to the development of both nationalism and religion. Being in its early stages of aspiration rather than realization, zionism still has the grandeur of the other "heroic" national movements and bears the earmarks of the revolutionary, Fichtean and Mazzinian ideology. Will it, too, deteriorate in the course of time? Will it also degenerate into an integral nationalism of a Maurras or a Rosenberg?

It is, of course, too early to judge. Anti-Zionists point to the growth of the revisionist movement and the "terroristic" acts of Palestinian hotheads as adumbrating such future degeneration. Many Zionists, however, hopefully contend that their case is different; different not only because of the millennial tradition of Jewish ethics and the extraordinary historic experiences of the Jewish people, but also because of differing contemporary and prospective realities. Even after the establishment of a Jewish commonwealth, they contend, Palestinian Jewry would be confronted by a strong Arab minority and be surrounded by large Arab states. For generations to come, the majority of the Jewish people would still live outside of Palestine as a minority dependent on the goodwill of majorities. Such goodwill would certainly be affected, positively or negatively, by what Palestinian Jewry might do in regard to its own Arab minority. These Zionists trust, therefore, in the creative élan of their people to find some unprecedented answers. They believe that, just as their prophetic ancestors, acting from necessity, discovered memorable new approaches vital to all of Western civilization, so will the Jews of a new Palestine, acting under the stress of new stupendous difficulties, help devise some new ways out of the present world crisis.

Of course, this is the old religious idea of "Jewish mission" brought back to life. Vocal protests to the contrary, this modern translation of the ancient messianic hope is but another illustration of the fundamental fact that religion and nationalism are for Jews, not contrasting, conflicting categories, as they often appear in the modern world at large, but an extraordinary organic wholeness. In fact, one may legitimately doubt whether these terms genuinely correspond to Jewish reality. After all, the Bible, that most religious of all books, has no word for "religion." Nor has the Talmud, that other authoritative expression of traditional Judaism. When modern Hebrews began looking for a designation of what their neighbors came to call religion, they had to borrow the word "dat" which originally meant something more akin to law and mores. Judaism has indeed always been more a way of life than a system of beliefs and doctrines. Since Mendelssohn, Jewish theologians and philosophers of religion have carried on a debate, still unfinished, as to whether their faith recognizes any dogmas. Such a well-defined way of life could naturally be particularistic, i.e., based on a particular ethnic group of adherents, while its doctrinal superstructure was fully universalistic.

> To Judaism the existence of the Jewish people is essential and indispensable, not only for its realization in life, but for its very idea; not only for its actuality, but for its potentiality. The Jewish religion without the "chosen people" is unthinkable. Neither could it, like the other religions be transplanted from the Jewish to another people.[60]

There are, on the other hand, untold numbers of Jews who neither profess nor practice their religion, and yet consider themselves and are considered by their neighbors as Jews. At the same time, as a nationality, the Jewish people, or at least its non-Palestinian majority, lacks some of the usual criteria of language, territory and statehood. It must lean heavily on its religious heritage as the main positive basis for its unity. This heritage is reinforced by a certain community of physical descent which, far from being "racial" in the technical sense—even ancient Israel already was a racial mixture of ethnic groups speaking a variety of Semitic and non-Semitic dialects—has nevertheless helped maintain the historic links with a hundred earlier generations. This extraordinary combination of substantial physical and cultural continuity amidst great territorial diversity, of religious particularism and universalism, of obvious national insufficiency and high messianic aspiration has often defied classification under the usual categories of thinking and been a source of irritation to the social theorists and practitioners alike. But it is in this very uniqueness of Jewish religious ethnicism, often a source of great suffering to themselves and some annoyance to their neighbors, that many Jews see their greatest challenge and an opportunity for realizing some of those ancient dreams which always seemed to justify their people's mission on earth.

How long will they be able or be allowed to carry on in this increasingly unitarian, though nationalistically strife-torn world? Or will they ultimately give up and, except for the remnant saved in Zion, surrender their identity and their messianic mission to the overwhelmingly assimilatory forces of their respective environments? Even the most extreme Jewish secularist will reply with some profession of faith, rather than with pure logic.

Chapter VIII

POSTWAR CHALLENGES

THE intimate relationships between nationalism and religion have now entered a new phase. We have seen that even modern, secularized nationalism could not quite dispense with religious attachments. Not only in those Asiatic, African and Balkan lands where religious allegiance has remained the prime criterion of cultural and national identity, but also in Western countries religious denominationalism or, in some cases, religious liberty has time and again served as a major force of national cohesion. Curiously, this influence has made itself felt quite irrespective of the depth of religious conviction or ritualistic observance of individual members. People who never went to church, synagogue or mosque have frequently, in periods of crisis, recalled their denominational solidarity with members of their own faith also in matters of national concern. The same Argentinian who drove his wife and children to church but himself refused to enter has nevertheless often fought for religious instruction in school and defended Catholic interests in his country or those of Franco Spain and the Vatican in international affairs. In decisive moments most Western men have asserted their religious allegiance, unless they were militantly atheistic; that is, unless they professed the counterreligion of atheism. It is a matter of common knowledge that the vast majority of citizens in the most secularized Western countries still go through baptism or circumcision and find their permanent resting place in one or another denominational cemetery. Certainly those who in the eighteenth century predicted the speedy disappearance of both religion and nationality in the new rational and cosmopolitan civilization of Enlightenment have come to grief on both national and religious issues.[1]

Has the catastrophe of the Second World War had any bearing on these ancient interrelations? There is a widespread feeling, shared even by those who expect a third world war in the not too distant future, that that catastrophe has ushered in a new historic era which will deeply affect the national and religious evolutions. Of course, almost every generation has considered itself living on the threshold of a new era. Generations emerging from some major cataclysm have particularly been inclined to draw a sharp line of demarcation between the past and the future. One can readily understand that the same people who today feel that, for example, the generation living between 1420 and 1450 was but a link between those which preceded and followed it are somehow convinced that their generation, living between 1920 and 1950, marks a unique departure from the past and opens a new chapter for the future. Such psychological egocentrism of each generation, which has justified the satirical observation that Adam and Eve had already lived in a period of transition, is closely akin to the individual egocentrism underlying the basic Fichtean division between "I" and "Thou" with which everybody confronts the entire universe outside himself. Even discounting this natural proneness to exaggeration, we may admit the legitimacy of taking the present postwar period as a starting point for some really new, as yet but dimly foreseeable, developments.

1. RELIGIOUS REVIVAL

There is much talk about a religious revival all over the world. Soldiers and sailors serving in the armed forces of various countries, including the Soviet Union, doubtless evinced a new feeling for religion, which most of them never had shown in civilian life. To be sure, an investigation conducted during the First World War revealed that, while most young men in the American armed forces had become more consciously religious, they rarely inquired about the fundamentals of their faith and were hardly disturbed by the differences between one religion and another. A member of the Committee of Six in charge of this survey has thus defined their attitude in 1917-18:

> God was a power controlling destiny, to whom one prayed but His character was ill-defined, and He could almost as easily be identified with the fatalistic God of Mohammed as with the God and Father of our Lord and Savior, Jesus Christ. Prayer was instinctive and chiefly for personal and private matters. . . . The sense of personal sin was conspicuous by its absence. . . . The Bible . . . was carried even when it was not read, but there is little evidence of intelligent and sympathetic acquaintance with its contents.[2]

Even this modicum of religious feeling, moreover, was not, as a rule, carried over into the postwar era. Expectations voiced during the war that men, having found their God while facing eternity, would continue cherishing him in all the years thereafter, failed to materialize. On the contrary, as a result of a widespread pacifist revulsion against the bellicose patriotism of the war years, many churches suffered severe decline in prestige and popular appeal because of their war record. The accusation that they had abandoned their pacific mission, blessed the arms of all belligerents and exhorted their respective uniformed flocks to exterminate one another as a sacred, religious duty carried the more conviction as indeed far too many churchmen of all denominations had surrendered to the war psychosis. Even where the conduct of individual ministers was beyond reproach, the principal religions were affected by the general disillusionment of a generation suffering from the aftermath of an abysmal breakdown of accepted values. Widespread revolutionary movements, long confronted by the old alliance between throne and altar, attacked altars along with thrones. The upsurge of Marxian socialism, in particular, strengthened the antireligious forces on the European Continent and exerted a powerful influence also on the minds of many young non-Europeans.[3]

Today the situation seems rather different. The religious awakening during the Second World War was more intensive and reached wider circles than that of three decades ago. Its depth, to be sure, has been variously assessed. A Presbyterian army chaplain, Russell C. Stroup, found that "in the thinking of the average G.I. the Church of Jesus Christ shares a place with the Society for the Prevention of Cruelty to Clay Pigeons. . . . The typical soldier, if such there is, has no quarrel with the Church. He is no more interested in closing the church doors than he is in entering them . . . a Church which has the world's indifference is a Church moribund." [4] Other observers, though less pessimistic in their immediate appraisals, predicted that little of the new religious enthusiasm would remain after the cessation of hostilities.

On the other hand, this time the churches, on the whole, held aloof from the nationalist frenzy. Although the provocation was much greater and everybody realized that the very foundations of Western civilization were under attack, religious leaders largely succeeded in holding fast to the fundamentals of their faiths in the midst of the war hysteria. Perhaps it was easier this time. They did not have to resort to any name calling or to "drag politics into the pulpit." They merely had emphatically to restate their time-honored religious truths to make them effective patriotic exhortations. To quote Karl Barth:

> When they preach about the sole sovereignty of Jesus Christ, His human origin among the people of Israel, His triumph over powers and dominations . . . about the impossibility of serving two masters, about freedom, and the service of the children of God conceived in the Holy Spirit, they are inevitably preaching, through a simple, strict interpretation of the biblical texts . . . against Hitler, Mussolini and Japan, against antisemitism, idolization of the state, oppressive and intimidating methods, militarism, against all the lies and the injustice of national socialism and fascism.[5]

More, these nationalist excesses of the 1930's and 1940's themselves led many men, in uniform and civilian garb alike, to detect a new appreciation of religion as one of the few genuinely international forces. They have seen it survive under the severe blows of a hostile communist regime, and come out of the crucible of persecution with greatly diminished worldly resources but with renewed spiritual vigor. They have seen that, while almost all other great social organizations, including universities, newspapers and labor unions, had gone down in defeat before the nazi onslaught, the churches had at least put up a fight. The fight may have been neither active nor persistent enough. The number of both Protestant and Catholic resisters to the last ditch may have been pitifully small and their following too weak in both body and spirit. The official church leadership may belatedly and halfheartedly have expressed its abhorrence of nazi crimes. Even today one rarely hears leading German ecclesiastics voice candidly and unreservedly their own and their people's sense of guilt, as does, for instance, the Heidelberg philosopher Karl Jaspers or as did, on a special occasion, the Brandenburg Synod of the Evangelical Church. The latter called for a day of penance because "we Germans have removed the Ten Commandments from our public life, and have acted contrary to the law of God. . . . All the innocent bloodshed cries to God against us, all the inhumanities which took place in our midst." [6] The official circles of both major denominations, however, prefer to indulge in apologetical exaggeration as to the number of their martyrs or in finding mitigating circumstances, even for some former Nazis. And yet, the fact that the churches resisted as much and as effectively as they did in the face of a most ruthless and efficient tyranny has given fresh hope to many despairing souls.

Equally significant has been religion's growing self-assertion. The era of religious relativism seems to have come to an end. Even liberal Protestantism or Reform Judaism have tended in recent years to search for more absolute values and demand more rigid observance. The Catholic Church, long on the defensive, has made considerable gains, particularly in countries where it is in minority and hence less intimately linked to their national struggles and aspirations. Although it has lost much ground in Poland, Czechoslovakia and Hungary, because of its implacable enmity toward communism, it has gained many new adherents elsewhere, largely because of its insistence on the superiority of its "perennial philosophy" over the transitory philosophies of the modern relativistic era. From Pius XII to Archbishop Temple, Patriarch Sergius and Chief Rabbi Kuk, from Jacques Maritain to Karl Barth, Nicholas Berdyaev and Leo Baeck, there has been a universal quest for religious absolutes to satisfy the cravings for spiritual security of a generation which had come to cherish security almost above anything else. Ceremonialism, too, long in disrepute among the more advanced religious and social thinkers, has since gained in both popular favor and intellectual acceptance. Reinforced by the constant toning down of Biblical criticism, itself the effect of both greater knowledge of ancient history and the decline of historic relativism, and the growing realization of a certain independence (despite obvious interdependence) of faith and history, the new self-assertion of religious leadership has begun to exert a powerful attraction on the minds of this generation.[7]

Will these new opportunities be utilized to the full or will they be allowed to wither away under constant interdenominational bickering or catering to vested interests? The answer, which will gradually unfold in the course of several decades, will largely depend on the new relationships between organized religion and the national and international forces taking shape under the impact of the new era.

2. REGIONALISM OR WORLD GOVERNMENT

Modern nationalism has evidently overreached itself in the two world wars. Even before 1939 there were powerful forces at work undermining the predominance of national allegiance. The struggle between communism, fascism and democracy cut across national boundaries and the internal divisions on these issues often overshadowed the national controversies. Though some of the fifth columns were nurtured from nationalist, particularly separatist, resentments, many others consisted of classes and men bent upon the defense (or the negation) of certain socioeconomic and political interests. In France, many rightist elements preferred a victory of Hitlerite Germany to one of French communism. At the same time French Communists before Germany's attack on Russia sharply agitated against the "imperialist" war indirectly helping their rightist foes to bring about France's surrender in 1940. "Hitler's successes are basically rooted," wrote a keen observer at the height of the dictator's military glory, "not in his extreme nationalism, but on the contrary in his shrewd judgment of the decay of nationalism among his neighbors." [8]

This decline of the national state has been accentuated by the war. Long before 1914 such imperialists as Bismarck or Pobedonostsev stressed the unique rights as well as the obligations of the great powers, which alone possessed sufficient strength to carry out their sovereign decisions. "Political thinkers in England began to believe, not so long after Maitland, that the sovereign state as well as being discredited in theory, was also decaying in fact." The First World War, fought by the Allies to a victorious conclusion under the Wilsonian doctrine of national self-determination (reinforced by the Leninist recognition of the disaffected nationalities' right of secession from the Russian Empire), temporarily reversed that process. But the period between the two wars demonstrated ever more clearly the anarchical nature of a system based upon the sanctity of the national state. Europe's "Balkanization" at a time when technologically and culturally the world had become more and more interdependent involved organized humanity in endless contradictions, which were ultimately resolved only by the power of the sword. The Second World War confirmed beyond peradventure the fact that the smaller states had become but play balls of their mighty neighbors. Old and established nations like Holland, Belgium and Norway were occupied within a few days. Poland, a ranking second-rate power, went down in defeat within little more than a fortnight. Denmark and Czechoslovakia surrendered without firing a shot. Switzerland and Sweden, on the other hand, escaped a similar fate for reasons equally beyond their control. This must have persuaded all but the most stubborn champions of political nationalism that the days of limitless sovereignty of the small national state had passed and that the political future of mankind will be determined only by the great powers.[9]

In the next generation or two the fate of humanity will be decisively influenced by what the Big Three are going to do or fail to do. Their veto power in the Social Security Council of the United Nations is, therefore, not merely a whim of power-drunk statesmen, but inherent in the international situation. For, whether we morally agree to it or not, "it would be folly to neglect the overwhelming evidence that modern national governments cannot and will not observe international treaties or rules of international law when these become burdensome or dangerous to the welfare and security of their own nation." Under the existing conditions of power it matters relatively little whether one of the smaller nations wishes to violate international agreements, for it can be held in check by the big powers acting in unison. The record of the League of Nations in this respect is truly illuminating. As long as the League had to maintain peace among the lesser powers, to tackle the difficult tasks of exchanging the Graeco-Turkish populations or internationally to administer (before Germany's rearmament) such recalcitrant areas as the Saar, Memel and Danzig, Upper Silesia and Thrace, it proved eminently successful. But already its supervision of mandated territories, where it had to deal with the great mandatory powers, left much to be desired. It broke down completely in the face of Japanese, Italian and German aggression, since only a display of overwhelming military force could have checked those recklessly expansive regimes. Even today there is little more than its own will and agreement to prevent the lawbreaking by a great power.[10]

This is, unfortunately, a far cry from that system of international justice which many idealists, including leaders of organized religion, would like to see established. While restricting the sphere of war to the greatest powers and probably reducing its frequency, the present methods of settling international disputes make the armed clashes the more destructive and sanguinary the more power is marshaled on either side. They have merely reduced the areas of friction and the ability of any number of petty nationalist leaders to set the world aflame. Perhaps someday a real world government will become possible—a government whose federal powers will transcend, in practical application as well as in theory, the powers of any constituent members. Such a possibility undoubtedly exists, despite the absence so far of a world-wide organic community and the enforced reliance, therefore, of any world government upon the essentially contradictory principle of the full sovereignty of member nations. However, many constitutional experiments throughout the ages have shown that such artificial structures, after taking root in society, have often grown into new organic entities. The story of the American Constitution is not wholly comparable with what might happen at the United Nations. It has nevertheless demonstrated that thirteen independent states, sharply separated from one another by mores, economic interests, religious establishments and political factions, could band together into an effective union with a functioning federal government, which ultimately helped unify the American nation and thereby reciprocally strengthened its own organic basis. At the time of the American Revolution the differences between the individual colonies seemed almost as insuperable as those between members of the United Nations today. Prompted by necessity, however, as well as great vision, the founding fathers overcame all these obstacles to genuine organic growth.

In the following century, other parts of the British Empire achieved independence in different ways. The rise of dominions which, without severing their imperial ties, achieved sovereign status evolved into another historic experiment in collective federalism organically blended with individual sovereignty. Perhaps the Statute of Westminster, in operation only for a decade and a half, does not yet warrant generalization. Certainly the Irish Free State's near-secession during the war has cast long shadows upon the whole structure. But the fact that, with this exception, wholly understandable because of age-old animosities, and that of the Arab Near East, a recent and unwilling partner, the Commonwealth has weathered the storm of ages augurs well for the future. Viscount John Halifax was not excessively optimistic when he extolled the potentialities inherent in the Anglo-Saxon constitutional evolution, which had grafted upon the ancient Greek idea of democracy ever more advanced forms of the free coëxistence of peoples. Beginning with the English representative government and parliamentary system, he declared, this evolution proceeded to American federalism and the British Commonwealth of Nations. The latter, he concluded, presents a novel "method of combining complete freedom with the requisite unity in action and is the beginning of yet another grafting on the democratic plant." [11]

The Soviet Union, on the other hand, with its hierarchical structure of sixteen Soviet republics and thirty-odd autonomous republics, autonomous regions and national districts, has pointed the way toward a reconciliation of its over-all national sovereignty with the legitimate interests of its ninescore national minorities. Its program, early formulated by Stalin, overcame the centrifugal drives inherent in the first three propositions by the strong cohesive forces emanating from the fourth proposition. The Communist party here proposed to put an end to nationalist strife by "(a) the recognition of the right of peoples to secession; (b) regional autonomy for peoples which remain within the given state; (c) specific laws guaranteeing freedom of development for national minorities; (d) a single indivisible, proletarian collective body, a single party for the proletarians of all the nationalities in the given state." [12] The latter could, of course, be accomplished only by a dictatorship of the proletariat, and even by the dictatorship of a number of party leaders over the proletariat. But since both the proletariat and its leadership were recruited from all nationalities on a consciously nondiscriminatory basis and since Stalin himself, as well as his greatest rival, Trotsky, had come from minority groups, this equilibrium between cultural self-determination and the imperial unity of economic and political action has proved itself in the great hour of trial.

All these may prove to be, from some future historical perspective, preliminary steps in the direction of a constitutional world government. Those may be right who speak of our "living during the last phase of an apparently inevitable historical process, which is likely to end in the emergence of a single all-powerful world-state, similar on a far grander scale to the Roman Empire." [13] But even if a world government were to be proclaimed right away, which is inconceivable under the existing division of power, it could not generate the underlying organic world community in less than several generations. With the United Nations constitution as now adopted, such organic growth must be postponed for several more generations. The coming century of human history is likely, therefore, to be dominated not by a single will of all humanity but by the diverse, often conflicting, wills of the major powers, which roughly correspond to the earth's major regions. For the time being the United States, the British Empire and the Soviet Union are such major regional groupings whose lead the smaller national states will have to follow. Later China and, possibly, India may also become leading regional powers. Nor is it impossible for Europe outside Britain and the Soviet Union to find someday a way of overcoming its age-old antagonisms and organizing a United States of Europe equal in rank to the other regional groupings. However, there is little talk today about Winston Churchill's wartime proposals concerning the formation of a Council of Europe, Council of Asia, etc., while his more recent advocacy of a European federation is too pointedly anti-Soviet to be truly constructive. Be that as it may, the present Big Three, including the British Empire whose decline has so often been foretold in vain, are going to focus all of organized humanity's conscious desires.[14]

These regional powers are anything but national states. Certainly the British Empire, consisting of sovereign dominions, colonies, mandates and trusteeship areas and inhabited by the greatest conglomeration of races, creeds and cultures known in history, is the very antithesis of a national state. It would be such, even if its heartland, the United Kingdom, had been more nationally homogeneous. But apart from the obvious Welsh, Scotch, Ulster-Irish national trends, the English themselves "have most completely solved the problem of nationality because they have most completely divorced it from politics." For this reason, rightly states Sir Alfred Zimmern, the designation "British" had "become nationally colorless in order to become politically significant." [15] In the Soviet Union the large Russian Republic is confronted by fifteen other Soviet Socialist republics, largely organized along national lines. The Union includes further national subdivisions, organized into sixteen autonomous republics, six autonomous regions and ten national districts, which embrace both local majorities and minorities. Despite the undeniable process of assimilation and the steady percentage growth of the Greater Russian majority, there is little doubt that in any foreseeable future the Union will remain a heterogeneous multinational structure, not quite inappropriately styled "the Soviet League of Nations." It was more than a mere wartime exhortation to supreme effort when Stalin in November, 1944, asserted that "Soviet patriotism does not disunite, but on the contrary consolidates all nations and nationalities in our country into one single fraternal family." [16]

Only the United States among the Big Three has some characteristic features of at least a national state in the making. But its very size and regional diversities, its combination of state rights, societal autonomy and cultural liberties impedes its becoming a typical national state like Germany, France or Italy. Moreover, it has legitimately been called a "nation of nations," inasmuch as it has grown out of a stupendous agglomeration of racial, national and religious strains which, despite its melting-pot ideology, have left their indelible imprint on its national physiognomy. Religious sectarianism, too, the existence of more than two hundred different denominations, may well prove a permanent obstacle to its unification into a national state in its usual totalitarian meaning. That is why the progressive forces of America have long learned to appreciate the merits of cultural pluralism as opposed to "hundred per cent" nationalism and isolationism. What is more, its very geographic position and economic necessities have placed the United States in a position of leadership for the whole Western Hemisphere. Disregarding such jingoistic declarations as Secretary of State Richard Olney's pronunciamento of 1895 (with reference to the British-Venezuelan controversy), "To-day the United States is practically sovereign on this Continent, and its fiat is law upon the subjects to which it confines its interposition," [17] these hemispheric responsibilities have existed since the enactment of the Monroe Doctrine and the conference of several Latin-American states convened in Panama in 1826. The growing economic dependence, particularly of the Caribbean and Central American countries upon the United States markets and common defense needs have always far overshadowed the occasional inter-

American controversies or the frequent denunciations of Yankee imperialism and dollar diplomacy south of the Rio Grande. However many cracks in the structure of Pan-American solidarity may yet become visible in normal times, one need not doubt that in all major crises the United States will function as the chief agent of hemispheric thinking and action. For these reasons it, too, has been representative of a multinational state far more than of the growingly defunct national state.

3. Religion and Regionalism

This new world situation has created new opportunities for organized religion. If a genuine world government were possible now, one would have to insist, indeed, on the formation of full-fledged ecumenical bodies or parliaments of religion, endowed with executive power and promoting that organic understanding in life and work between the denominations which would correspond to and help foster humanity's growth into an organic world community. Even in the more moderate setup of the present United Nations one may envisage an organization like United Religions, advocated by D. Luther Evans, to supplement its political work. Such "a global religious organization," says Evans, "could benefit contemporary religion in areas of belief, worship and action. . . . [It] might legitimately interpret a particular religion to show the significance of its basic doctrines for a universal religious perspective, but it could not have the experience or authority to originate creeds of its own." Of course, just as the UN must create a machinery to accommodate and help develop new national sovereignties, without initiating them, so would the UR have to find ways of admitting new religious groups, if and when such should emerge. Otherwise, both organizations might degenerate into bodies designed to preserve the status quo. As illustrated by the failure of the League of Nations, such a conservatory attitude would convert them sooner or later into instruments of reaction—many progressive trends today undoubtedly will become reactionary at some future time— and ultimately make them fall prey to inevitable historical changes. But if able to preserve its adaptability to ever-changing needs, to quote Mr. Evans again:

> A UR could include religions with contradictory metaphysical assumptions as legitimately as the UN includes nations with opposite philosophical postulates. It would be utterly foolish for a UR to exclude the common beliefs of humanists and theists regarding human dignity because these two groups accept divergent philosophical theories of ultimate reality. In fact, it is very doubtful if philosophies will ever come to fundamental agreement in theory until they cooperatively test the worth of their respective philosophies in the realm of joint social action. Only when the religions of the world replace religious argumentation with religious affirmations will human beings find in religion resources of heroic idealism.

We need not agree with this low estimate of religious argumentation for heroic idealism, but rather consider religious controversies to be as legitimate as national disputes, and yet believe that, just as the UN will try to adjust the latter amicably, so will the UR, even at the risk of becoming a sounding board for major disagreements, endeavor to find the basic areas of agreement. It will the more readily accomplish this task as religions, unlike nations, have long learned to recognize existing and potential differences of belief and opinion without resorting to violent methods of resolving them.[18]

For this reason the Protestant ecumenical movement and the World Council of Churches, although a step in the right direction, are, because of their obvious denominational limitations, not far-reaching enough. It was perfectly legitimate for the Oxford Conference of 1937 to declare that "no international order which can be devised by human effort may be equated with the Kingdom of God" and to explain the widespread disillusionment about international affairs by man's forgetfulness "that to all human institutions clings the taint of sin." But this statement of belief and the ensuing conclusion that "a true conception of international order requires a recognition of the fact that the state, whether it admits it or not, is not autonomous, but is under the ultimate governance of God" will carry no weight with atheists or humanists. If it were made a sole basis for co-operation with other international organs, it would sound too much like the Vatican's readiness to co-operate —on its own terms.[19]

Such spiritual intransigence, of course, leads nowhere; certainly no further than, for instance, a declaration of the Comintern that true international amity could be achieved only by the recognition of the materialistic world outlook and the universal elimination of the profit system. Apart from such tactical considerations, it may perhaps be useful for all great religious organizations to be simultaneously "extrovert" enough to become effective agencies in the outside world and sufficiently "introvert" to examine their own shortcomings. They may well remember that, at least in so far as they are human institutions, they, too, are tainted with sin and apply to themselves Vladimir Soloviev's beautiful exhortation to Russian patriots, that "the most essential, even the only essential question is not the question of Russia's might or mission, but that of the sins of Russia." [20]

Mankind's leading religious bodies have shown greater awareness of the danger of unwittingly mirroring the class structure of their home churches. Especially in Anglo-Saxon lands the transfer of power to new social classes has not yet been fully reflected in their lay or professional leadership. Perhaps the dependence of all American and the British Free Churches on voluntary financial contributions makes them cater to larger donors and thus helps warp their representative character. Certainly the ecumenical movement ought to take heed of Kenneth Leslie's recent warning, and beware of being something artificially induced "by men accustomed to the rationalizations of business, men who having succeeded in monopolizing and stabilizing a portion of the business world wish to do something of the same sort with the churches, one of their motives being their fear of religion itself as a possible source of instability." [21]

Today, the control over the Church of England is gradually shifting, via Parliament, to the British Labor party. The next Lambeth Conference may, therefore, better reflect England's mass mind, long left to the almost exclusive tutelage of dissenting organs. Perhaps it is not too venturesome to hope that the present ecumenical movement, if so broadened as to become an interdenominational movement transcending the Christian faith, will, by steadily perfecting its own outlook and structure, help shape the new institutions of the United Nations. It would thus repeat on the world scene what the American ecclesiastical organizations of the colonial age had done in foreshadowing the Federal Constitution and what the Lambeth Conferences achieved in paving the way for the British Commonwealth's Statute of Westminster. Such a genuine world-wide interdenominational movement, spearheaded though not dominated by Anglo-Saxon religious leaders, could the better assist the organic growth of the United Nations, as the latter, too, is likely to follow, on a higher plane, the basic patterns of American federalism and of British and Pan-American regionalism.

Will not the new trend toward regionalism, however, become a fresh, insurmountable obstacle to the world-wide collaboration of all creeds? In the present writer's opinion, regionalism, though creating some new temporary difficulties, will, in fact, help remove the greatest obstacle of all, namely, the churches' nationalist limitations. In nationalism, even in political and economic nationalism, because of its subtle interlocking with cultural nationalism, religion found something akin to itself in spirit and institution. Much too frequently, therefore, Erastianism and other forms of religious nationalism have taken hold of the spiritual leaders of world religions. Too many churchmen have become too deeply involved in nationalist controversies to serve as genuine spokesmen of the brotherhood of man. "It is certain," says Sir Frederick Pollock, "that the church could not have prevented Christian rulers from making war upon each other . . . the Holy Father himself, as a temporal prince, was often a belligerent, and his adversaries felt no diffidence about invoking their patron saints against him." [22]

Now, however, national loyalties may soon be subordinated to regional feelings of solidarity, just as clan and tribal loyalties were once synthesized in national patriotism. In its extreme form such supranational patriotism might become regional imperialism and isolationism, and ultimately a source of new wars. Unlike political nationalism, however, regionalism would not be abetted by the deeper springs of cultural and religious unity, barring the wholly exceptional case when cultural and religious boundary lines would coincide with a new regional grouping. Such was, in the past, the medieval experience, when the Catholic Occident, Greek Orthodox Byzantium and the Muslim Caliphate were vast regional units based on religion. Today, however, two of the largest regional units, the British Empire and the Americas, embrace a variety of Christian denominations, the former also the majority of the world's Muslims and Hindus. The Soviet Union, even if it were formally to revert to Greek Orthodoxy, would embrace powerful dissident minorities of sectarians, Muslims, Jews, etc. Even during the heyday of "godless" agitation Stalin essentially adhered to his and Lenin's early pledge to the Soviet Union's 30,000,000 Muslims "that henceforth your beliefs and customs, your national and cultural institutions are free and inviolable." [23] Certainly culturally and religiously the United States will have more in common with England, Canada and Australia than with its Latin-American collaborators, or than England will with her Hindu or Arab fellow imperials. By continuing to foster, as they always did, the various positive forms of cultural nationalism, the great world religions thus might significantly contribute toward counteracting the expansive forces of regionalism and preventing their conversion into new chauvinist and bellicose civilizations.

Religion's constructive contribution may make itself most deeply felt in its strengthening the positive forces of human co-operation to outweigh the hitherto prevailing negative factors. Without going the whole length of Ranke's primacy of foreign over domestic relations, we shall admit that heretofore the unity of human groups was forged largely in the heat of external tensions and dangers. States and nations usually achieved and maintained their unity under the impact of outside enmities, often so permanent as to become "hereditary." Human nature being as it is, hatred of nonnationals has often brought men together more forcefully and permanently than their love of one another. This has largely held true also of the present regional groupings. The Pan-American idea, although partially sustained by growing economic interdependence, has derived its main strength from the negative Monroe Doctrine and common defense needs. What would the British Commonwealth have been without British sea power, which had so greatly reduced the defense responsibilities of the dominions (also of all American republics) and enabled them to concentrate on their pacific tasks? True, this reliance on the British fleet has also retarded their growth and helped keep them in that state of underpopulation and underdevelopment over which Australia, for instance, almost came to grief during the war. It has also held in abeyance the starkly anachronistic racial and economic situation in the Union of South Africa. But perhaps just because it made possible these isolationist excesses and delusions of sovereignty—another essentially negativistic factor—it smoothed the path for the daring architects of the British Commonwealth. It is equally clear that fear of encirclement and constant dread of foreign invasion have helped cement the unity of the peoples of the Soviet Union and made them willingly sustain the untold hardships of rapid industrialization. Today again the new Five-Year Plan, based upon further years of deprivation, appears tolerable to the Soviet masses only because they are impressed with the danger of another foreign intervention. Fear and mutual suspicion is also at the root of that other major obstacle to the world's pacification, namely, "the disposition of Soviet diplomacy to pursue democratic ends by undemocratic means in the border zones, and the propensity of Anglo-American leaders to employ democratic slogans to promote undemocratic purposes in the same areas." [24]

If the United Nations is to have a chance, therefore, man must learn more and more to co-operate positively rather than negatively, for the sake of his own self-enlightened long-range interests rather than against somebody else's interests, out of love rather than hatred or fear. In this respect the United Nations is something fundamentally, and not merely quantitatively, different from even the greatest regional combines. To achieve its aims, it may well require a thoroughgoing and universal re-education, if not a basic change in what is usually called human nature. Here religion's task is clearly set. Perhaps because it had succeeded, after long inner struggles, in overcoming its initial motivation of the fear of the Unknown (if, indeed, *timor fecit deos*) and in reaching out for a positive affirmation of the divine guidance of the universe, it may also be in a position to help replace fear of fellow man by a genuine brotherhood of man as the propelling force in international relations. In further long and arduous struggles it may thus help convert charters like that of the UN into a forceful reality.[25]

4. HUMAN RIGHTS

Of course, we have not yet arrived at the millennium. To expect that after the cataclysm of the past decade humanity will emerge purified of all its sins and permanently live up to the religious ideals of brotherhood is starkly utopian. But we ought not to take it lightly if we have moved only a small step forward on the road toward this goal.

It would be a significant step, indeed, if the peace treaties of the 1940's were to duplicate, on another plane, the achievements of similar treaties signed three centuries ago. The devastating sixteenth and seventeenth century Wars of Religion, culminating in the Thirty Years' War, laid Central Europe waste beyond recognition. There is good reason for believing that, for instance, the Holy Roman Empire had entered that war, in 1618, with a population of some 25,000,000 and emerged from it thirty years later with but 13,000,000 inhabitants. The economic and cultural ravages were equally profound, and it took more than a century for Germany to regain her former strength. However, out of this catastrophe emerged the Treaty of Westphalia based on the realization that no peace could prevail in Europe without the recognition of the right of religious minorities to worship God in their own way. The peacemakers of 1648 concluded, therefore, that they must give up the requirement of absolute religious conformity within the boundaries of each country. They recognized that the rule of *cuius regio eius religio*, i.e., that the state could insist on religious homogeneity and banish, or forcibly convert, all dissidents, had been a festering wound in the European body politic and that it had to be replaced by what might be called international guarantees for religious minority rights. Different, but equally obnoxious, experiences with religious intolerance in Britain and the British colonies finally led to the proclamation of liberty of conscience as the cornerstone of any structure of domestic and international peace.

Wars of Religion have been replaced in the past two centuries by equally ruthless and fanatical wars of nationalism. The pernicious doctrine of *cuius regio eius religio* reappeared now under the guise of the national state demanding unequivocal national uniformity of its subjects. *Cuius regio eius natio* increasingly became the disruptive slogan of the new age. The minorities were again unwilling and unable to accept the violation of their conscience and Europe, in fact the whole world, became increasingly embroiled in war. These clashes of conflicting national claims, finally, culminated in the new Thirty Years' War of 1914-45.

Once again nations and leaders must realize that there can be no permanent peace unless a new type of toleration and a new type of liberty of conscience are universally proclaimed and respected. The treaties of 1919 already undertook to safeguard national as well as religious minority rights. But they did it halfheartedly, restricting the safeguards to certain areas and failing to provide for their effective application. The United Nations need not go back to the particular formulas of a quarter century ago, outworn and impracticable as some of them have proved to be. But, if undismayed by the stupendous complexity of their task, they will strive with all their might to lend expression to these deep yearnings of humanity they will find new formulas to eliminate, or at least greatly to reduce, the main nationalist causes of friction.

Here religion and its leadership have their greatest chance. Having lived through the desolating experiences of religious intolerance, having learned through enormous sufferings both the short-lived hypocrisy of enforced conformity and the impossibility of safeguarding peace without respect for conscientious scruples, the religious bodies are most qualified to lead the way in this process of agonizing self-purification. They might bear in mind that, according to ancient Jewish sages, peace is given especially to repentant sinners.

Fortunately the religious bodies, and particularly the Protestant ecumenical and other world-wide organs, need not concern themselves too much about formal safeguards for the free exercise of religion, public or private. Even twenty-eight years ago the world had traveled far enough for the statesmen assembled at Paris to offer little resistance to the incorporation of such safeguards in the respective peace treaties. Whatever impediments a pious worshiper may still encounter in a "godless" environment, such as existed in the Soviet Union, and whatever hardships he may undergo in running counter to some governmentally encouraged patterns of behavior have long been of a largely extralegal nature and could hardly be mitigated by express provisions in international charters. The religious leaders must, therefore, use the more indirect approach of securing peace by insisting upon mutual toleration of opposing dogmas and by securing justice to all racial, ethnic and other social groups. They must try to implement the joint Catholic, Jewish and Protestant Declaration on World Peace of October, 1943, which demanded, among other measures:

> The rights of all peoples, large and small, subject to the good of the organized world community, must be safeguarded within the framework of collective security. The progress of undeveloped, colonial or oppressed peoples toward political responsibility must be the object of international concern. . . .
> National governments and international organization must respect and guarantee the rights of ethnic, religious and cultural minorities to economic livelihood, to equal opportunity for educational and cultural development, and to political equality.[26]

The present trend toward regionalism, by overcoming the limitations of political nationalism, essentially encourages such minority and other subnational loyalties. Man's attachment to his soil, to his village, town or district, as well as his allegiance to a particular social group, has long been impeded by nationalist centralization. The basic ingredients of folk creativity, like folklore, dialects and local customs, extolled by such early cultural nationalists as Herder and the Grimms as the very lifeblood of nations, have been stifled in those vast, standardized and metropolitanized civilizations developed by the large modern nationalities. Those romantics who, like Barrès, denounced the "uprootedness" of modern nationalism vainly tried to turn back the wheels of history. They ultimately fell into the other extreme of "integral nationalism" to which mother earth itself became as much of an abstraction as the myths of blood and race. Regionalism in this sense, i.e., man's loyalty to some definite small geographic region, was doomed by the all-devouring moloch of political and economic nationalism. Only now with the apparently irresistible growth of regionalism in the supranational sense, regionalism of this subnational variety may become possible once again. These two mutually complementary types of regionalism may also lead to the unshackling and new flowering of individualism, which, once a major source of inspiration to national movements, has in recent generations fallen prey to the ever more exacting demands of political nationalism. It may create the conditions necessary for the realization of Bakunin's old dream that there should "arise free unions organized from below by the free federation of communes into provinces, of provinces into the nation, and of nations into the United States of Europe." Without its anarchistic rationale and with the addition of the pivotal supraregional structure of United Nations, such a hierarchical pyramid may indeed become a reality before very long. In some respects, this would seem to be but a recrudescence of the medieval system, which as Gierke said, "started from the idea of the whole and of unity, but to every lesser unit, down to and including the individual, it ascribed an inherent life, a purpose of its own and an intrinsic value within the harmoniously articulated organism of the world-whole filled with the Divine Spirit." But being inextricably interwoven with the permanent modern fabric of equality and liberty, it would be devoid of those gross inequalities associated with the medieval corporate hierarchy of rights and duties.[27]

Because of its inherently democratic checks and balances the new system, whether world-wide or regional, would give to nationalism, too, both political and cultural, its rightful place. While restraining the excessive appetites of national majorities and preventing them from violently swallowing their minorities, it would also stave off the danger of minority rights as such becoming a fetish and a cause of both progressive social pulverization and permanent unrest. The revival of individual self-assertion and, with it, of the ultimate responsibility of individual conscience also in regard to national allegiance may secure a far better equilibrium between conflicting national claims. Father John LaFarge is quite right in emphasizing the peculiar American approach to national problems.

> Does the individual [he asks] exist *for the minority,* so that the paramount interest of anyone who belongs to a minority group is to be found precisely in the interests of that minority? Or does the individual exist for a life of his own; so that his belonging to this or that minority is but an accident insofar as his civic life is concerned; an important and even desirable accident, but not to be placed before the spiritual good of his own soul or the existence of those social and national institutions through which his spirit functions. The latter view is our American philosophy of minorities.

As a matter of fact, the main difficulty facing American minority groups is the unwillingness of many of their own members to identify themselves with them and the latter's preference, if not prevented by racial or religious biases from doing so, to be counted among the majority. Even the Soviet Union, which has pushed recognition of national minority rights to all practicable limits, has never prevented individuals from transferring their allegiance to another national group, notably to the Greater Russians. Champions of minority rights, who always stress the absence of objective criteria for nationality and assert that ultimately individual decision must be allowed to prevail, cannot deny that such decision may work both ways. On the other hand, it is also perfectly clear that a line must be drawn somewhere. If we wish to prevent the atomization of society into ever smaller national units, each demanding complete national self-determination, we must basically accept the decision of the Permanent Court of International Justice of 1928 (with reference to the interpretation of the Polish minorities' treaty) that "the question whether a person does or does not belong to a racial, linguistic or religious minority . . . is a question of fact and not solely one of intention." [28] In short, if national self-determination ceases to be the overpowering obsession of many national groups and if both supra- and subnational regional loyalties partially supersede it, there may indeed be far more room for individual self-determination in the choice and intensity of one's national allegiance.

This is ultimately also the meaning of the new drive for "human rights" in which various religious bodies have so actively participated. The accent rests entirely upon the individual and his rights, which must, of course, be complemented by a system of his duties toward society. Essentially, however, human rights are group rights, for the rights of any individual would be safeguarded only in so far as he belongs to a particular group. No one intends, for example, to extend international protection to an individual deprived of his employment because his employer dislikes him, unless such dislike be derived from prejudice against the employee's race, religion or nationality. Similarly freedom of speech or worship, while protecting the rights of any "crackpot" to voice his ideas and to worship God in his own way, is of practical significance primarily because it safeguards the right to self-expression of members of political and religious minorities.

Organized religion is interested in human rights, in the first place, because of the old struggle for the freedom of individual conscience, but indirectly it is also much concerned with all the other freedoms. With a bit of overstatement one could even assert that "it is arguable in logic and demonstrable in history that freedom of worship implies the other three: to achieve it is to achieve freedom of speech and freedom from want and fear." Certainly sermons freely delivered depend on freedom of speech. Similarly nondiscrimination, social justice and the other ingredients of freedom from want and fear are not only germane to free religious preachment but would largely be effected by the voluntary adherence of the masses of believers to their religious precepts.

What is more, human rights, if properly administered, may help establish the supremacy of moral law in international relations. In most ancient and medieval periods a sovereign king was *under* the authority of his religious law. The extremes to which Biblical law and practice went in restraining the arbitrary proclivities of Israelitic kings may have no parallel in other ancient or medieval constitutions. But almost everywhere even the ancient king-gods or sons of gods usually hesitated to run counter to the established religious laws and morals. In the Middle Ages the Holy Roman emperors by grace divine often ran up against the insurmountable barrier of local custom as well as of the "natural law" stanchly upheld by the international church.[29] Only in modern times has the secularized sovereign state, with its exclusive concentration on the *raison d'état,* divested itself completely of any such outside restraints. We have all learned to our chagrin the dismal effect of national sovereignty run amuck.

This extreme doctrine of sovereignty also led to another pernicious principle of international law, the noninterference in internal affairs of other states. Farsighted liberal thinkers have long realized the dangers of this principle to the survival of liberalism in a world dominated in part by despotic regimes. In his essay "A Few Words on Non-Intervention" written in 1859 John Stuart Mill warned that England would be forced to take the initiative in fighting off the threat of Continental despotism to her free institutions.

> There are few questions [he wrote] which more require to be taken in hand by ethical and political philosophers, with a view to establish some rule or criterion whereby the justifiableness of intervening in the affairs of other countries, and . . . the justifiableness of refraining from intervention, may be brought to a definite and rational test. . . . The time may not be distant when England, if she does not take this heroic part because of its heroism, will be compelled to take it from consideration for her own safety.

This terrifying contingency was staved off for three-quarters of a century by the might of the British navy. In the Second World War, however, it became manifest that no geographic barriers can prevent injustice in one land from ultimately jeopardizing the interests of any other country. In our growingly interdependent world, justice as well as peace has become indivisible.[30]

Human rights, and particularly the prospective International Bill of Rights, to be administered by a special Commission on Human Rights under the Social and Economic Council of the United Nations, will make possible the necessary equilibrium between organized humanity's social responsibility and the right of each state to regulate its internal affairs. Unfortunately the United Nations Charter, though paying great verbal homage to the principle of human rights, has not endowed their administration with any powers of enforcement. Edward Stettinius, at that time United States secretary of state and chairman of the San Francisco Conference, prompted by American church and lay liberal groups, was largely instrumental in inserting the human rights provisions into the Charter. But he subsequently reported to President Truman that the Charter had pledged the various members to co-operate with the United Nations in the achievement of its economic and social objectives "without infringing upon their right to order their national affairs according to their own best ability, in their own way, and in accordance with their own political and economic institutions and processes." After numerous delays the commission was finally organized in 1947 under the chairmanship of Mrs. Eleanor Roosevelt, a devoted champion of human rights. But even now the discussions are still in their initial stages. Here the impact of religious bodies can make itself felt most strongly and effectively.[31]

5. NATIONALISM IN RELIGION

To achieve this aim religion must try to purge itself of some of its nationalist biases. Statements like those of Dean William Ralph Inge, "It is impossible to converse long with a Catholic without being conscious of an insurmountable barrier; and if we consider what this barrier is, we find that we cannot confidently appeal to those instincts and moral traditions which are the common heritage of all English people," reveal not only religious bias, but one which takes recourse to alleged national loyalties. Toleration of race distinctions, as in the treatment of Negro preachers by their own denominational bodies in the southern United States, however enforced by lay prejudice, is a serious obstacle to the achievement of human rights within the churches and must weaken their position in the struggle for human rights outside. Similarly antisemitism, though largely discredited in official church circles, still counts many more adherents in the rank and file and the lay or professional leadership than is ascertainable by public opinion polls or other statistical devices. Acceptance, however passive, of Jew-baiting within the church not only plays into the hands of such godless movements as national socialism, but even the so-called "Christian Americanism" is forgetful of the fundamental reason why Hitler considered the Jew as a major obstacle to his new order. To quote Karl Barth:

> The existence of the Jew probably is the symbol of the objective metaphysical fact, independent of all intellectual countermovements, that the Christian root of Western culture is still alive. Without credit to him, and even against his will, the Jew is witness to the continuing vitality of the Old and New Testament revelation, by virtue of which Western culture, despite the degree of its present and possible future apostasy, is separated as by an abyss from the inherent godlessness of national socialism.[32]

Theologically this is but a restatement, in modern terms, of the old Christian doctrine of Jewish testimony to the truth of Christian tradition which, for nearly two millennia, has been at the root of all Judeo-Christian relations. Stripped of its theological verbiage, however, it simply means that the entire Judeo-Christian heritage has been endangered by the rise of the neopagan forms of extreme nationalism and the idolization of race and state and that only a profound reaffirmation of its traditional values, based on the dignity of man and his inalienable rights, will be able to save and advance our civilization.

It is really the progress, however slow, in the realization of these traditional values which has hitherto marked the major advances in the patterns of our existence and which inspires at least the Western peoples with some hope for the future. After analyzing in 1937 the ravages of national sovereignty, the Marquess of Lothian could only quote the words of an Oriental scholar, "that all the real achievements of Western civilization, the respect for human personality, the humanitarian movement, the abolition of slavery, individual freedom, the emancipation of women, the ideal of moral purity, the concept of social reform, the rise of democracy, the assault on war, the idea of the League of Nations, have all derived their greatest support and their greatest driving power from those who have drawn their courage and inspiration and devotion to God and man from the eternal springs of the Bible." [33] Their courage was not weakened by their realization, likewise reinforced by Scripture, of the sinfulness of human nature, the imperfections of human institutions, and the slow historic progression, interrupted by frequent relapses, from barbarism to civilized life.

The polarity of human existence being what it is, pessimists, both religious and secular, will find in the present state of world affairs plenty of reasons for a feeling of hopelessness, if not of utter despair. With states, large and small, unwilling to renounce any essential particle of their sovereignty, the law of the jungle still reigns supreme in international relations. Perhaps the cynics are right in claiming that hatred is stronger than love and that men will not permanently co-operate unless they fight somebody else. Hence the United Nations, they derisively say, will not become sovereign in its own right until such time as man will have to marshal all his resources for some interplanetary struggle— a remote contingency, indeed.

Pessimistic forecasters of this kind, however, though never devoid of supporting evidence, have always proved to be evil counselors. At least one basic obstacle to human understanding has progressively been weakened by modern evolution. What has been called the "small-scale nature" of man, his real attachment only to his small group or locality, the only true expanse of his intellectual horizon, has been inescapably broadened by modern technology, economics and science. Modern nationalism has already superseded these small-scale loyalties by broader national allegiance. Supranational regionalism has somewhat weakened these nationally centripetal forces and helped reestablish the subnational attachments, but it has also begun to broaden further the intellectual horizons of the man in the street as well as of the intellectual elite. The last step, therefore, toward a large-scale, all-embracing mentality may not be so far distant as is assumed by persons of a natively pessimistic or highly impatient disposition.

Organized religion can do much in accelerating this broadening process. The world religions have long represented large-scale approaches to the riddles of existence. While stressing individual beliefs and observances and, at times, overemphasizing parochial duties and attitudes, they also have taught man to think in terms of a universal godhead, the cosmic relevance of even minutiae of ethical behavior and the essential nature of an all-human brotherhood. Now that the world evolution has given them a real chance to divest themselves of some of their own nationalist biases, without in any way interfering with their positive contributions to "good" and healthy forms of nationalism, particularly in the cultural sphere, they may indeed help create that large-scale climate of opinion requisite for the creation of a constructive world order. By turning inwardly and detecting ever new ways of human co-operation in the spiritual sphere they will also help devise means for a new human co-operation in the worldly sphere. By reforming themselves, they will help reform the world.

NOTES

Chapter I

Varieties of Nationalist Experience

1. New York, 1924, p. xi.
2. Martin Buber, *Kampf um Israel, Reden und Schriften* (1921-1932), Berlin, 1933, p. 232. Cf. also Guido Zernatto, "Nation: The History of a Word," *Review of Politics*, VI (1944), 351-66.
3. Johann Gottlieb Fichte, *Sämmtliche Werke*, ed. by J. H. Fichte, Berlin, 1845-46, VII, 569.
4. Colbert, whose name became a symbol of extreme economic nationalism, declared in 1669 that France had achieved prosperity not only in itself, but also "in the condition of want it has created in the neighboring states. Extreme poverty appears everywhere." Cited by Shepard B. Clough, *France: A History of National Economics*, New York, 1939, p. 21.
5. Ernest Renan, *Qu'est-ce qu'une nation?* Paris, 1882, p. 27.
6. T. Walek-Czernecki, "Le rôle de la nationalité dans l'histoire de l'antiquité," *Bulletin of the International Committee of Historical Sciences*, II, Pt. 2 (1929-30), 307. These views are colored by the author's profound faith in the constructive force of nationalism, which was undoubtedly inspired by his own Polish patriotism and his belief that, in contrast to the supranational Roman Empire, the contemporary Western civilization would be saved from its much-prophesied decline by its nationalist vitality (*ibid.*, p. 320). Hence the difference between him and Eduard Meyer, who, using other criteria, found in antiquity only three real nationalities, the Jews, Iranians and Greeks, is largely terminological.
7. Cf. Martin Noth, *Das System der zwölf Stämme Israels*, Stuttgart, 1930.
8. Salo W. Baron, *A Social and Religious History of the Jews*, 3 vols., New York, 1937, I, 77.

9. Herodotus, VIII, 144 (Loeb Classics, IV, 153).
10. Euripides, *Andromache*, 1237; *Orestes*, 1584 (Loeb Classics, II, 265, 509); Gen. 34:7, etc. Cf. Ernest L. Hettich, *A Study in Ancient Nationalism: The Testimony of Euripides*, Williamsport, Pa., 1933, p. 56, and, more generally, Julius Jüthner, *Hellenen und Barbaren*, Leipzig, 1923; Hans Kohn, *The Idea of Nationalism: A Study in Its Origins and Background*, New York, 1944.
11. E. L. Woodward, *Christianity and Nationalism in the Later Roman Empire*, London, 1916, pp. 43 f., 48. In "The Patriarchate of Alexandria: A Study in National Christianity," *Church History*, XV (1946), '81-100, E. R. Hardy, Jr., concludes that "the ancient Church of Alexandria has an important place both in the general history of Christianity and in the national history of Egypt. Its rise and decline is on the whole a glorious story of resistance to either pagan or officially Christian imperialism, and a valuable exhibition of the strength and limitations of a predominantly national form of Christianity."
12. Cf. Hans von Schubert, *Das älteste germanische Christentum oder der sogenannte "Arianismus" der Germanen*, Tübingen, 1909, p. 14.
13. F. J. C. Hearnshaw in *The Social and Political Ideas of some Great Mediaeval Thinkers*, London, 1923, pp. 216 f. Cf. also Herbert Brook Workman's detailed study of *John Wyclif*, Oxford, 1926.
14. Martin von Nathusius, *Die christlich-socialen Ideen der Reformationszeit und ihre Herkunft*, Gütersloh, 1897, pp. 76 f. In his suggestive essay on "The Beginnings of National Self-Determination in Europe," *Review of Politics*, VII (1945), 29-42, Roman Jakobson traces the earliest formula-

tion of the national idea to St. Cyril's eulogy of national letters in the 800's and believes that the "sacramental character" vested in the national language by the Slavonic liturgy left a permanent imprint upon the other European nations. Cf. also Kamil Krofta, "L'aspect national et social du mouvement hussite," *Le Monde Slave*, V, Pt. I (1928), 321-51; and Chap. IV. For Luther see below Chap. V.

15. This point is stressed particularly by Albert Brackmann in "Der mittelalterliche Ursprung der Nationalstaaten," *Sitzungsberichte der Preuss. Akademie der Wissenschaften*, Phil.-hist. Klasse, Berlin, 1936, pp. 128-42.

16. Leopold von Ranke, *Weltgeschichte*, 9 vols., Leipzig, 1881-88, IX, Pt. 2, p. 68; Dietrich Schäfer, *Deutsches Nationalbewusstsein im Licht der Geschichte*, Jena, 1884, p. 17.

17. *Monumenta Germaniae historica, Constitutiones*, IV, 139 ff.; John of Salisbury, *Epistolae*, LIX, in Migne's *Patrologia latina*, CIC, 39; H[einrich] Finke, *Weltimperialismus und nationale Regungen im späteren Mittelalter*, Freiburg i.B., 1916, pp. 14 ff.; Albert Brackmann, "Die Ursachen der geistigen und politischen Wandlung Europas im 11. und 12. Jahrhundert," *Historische Zeitschrift*, CIL (1934), 234 f. Petrus de Flotte, France's royal emissary, conceded the pope's possession of both the spiritual and the temporal powers, but added laconically, "However, sire, your power is verbal while ours is real." *Acta inter Bonifacium VIII . . . et Philippum Pulchrum*, 1614, fol. 164v, cited by W. Ullmann in "A Medieval Document on Papal Theories of Government," *English Historical Review*, LXI (1941), 181. This essay analyzes fully the *Rex Pacificus* which, apparently written by theologians of the University of Paris under Boniface VIII, became a fountainhead for the antipapal, nationalist theories of John of Paris and Marsiglio of Padua.

18. Karl Lamprecht, *Deutsche Geschichte*, 6th ed., Berlin, 1920, I, 16 f., 29; St. Stephen's *Monita* in Migne's *Patrologia latina*, CLI, 1240; Carl Conrad Eckhardt, *The Papacy and World Affairs*, Chicago, 1937, p. 7.

19. St. Gregory Nazianzien, *Theological Orations*, 43, 14 ff. in J. P. Migne's *Patrologia graeca*, XXXVI, 513 ff.; G. G. Coulton, "Nationalism in the Middle Ages," *Cambridge Historical Journal*, V (1935), 18

f., 20, 24, 27. The "seven nations" of the University of Orléans were allowed to have "certain superstitious celebrations, vulgarly known as the feasts of the nations" which often gave rise to nationalist quarrels interfering with orderly academic pursuits. Cf. the Statute of the German Nation of Oct. 4, 1382, excerpted by Lynn Thorndike in his *University Records and Life in the Middle Ages*, New York, 1944, pp. 255 f. Cf. also *ibid.*, pp. 169 ff.; and Louis Rigaud, "La nation germanique de l'ancienne Université d'Orléans," *Revue d'histoire de l'Eglise de France*, XXVII (1941), 46-71.

20. Carlton J. H. Hayes has turned special attention to this factor and suggested fuller scholarly treatment. Cf. "The Church and Nationalism: A Plea for Further Study of a Major Issue," *Catholic Historical Review*, XXVIII (1942), 3 f.

21. Marcel Handelsman, "Le rôle de la nationalité dans l'histoire du moyen-âge," *Bulletin of the International Committee of Historical Sciences*, II, Pt. 2 (1929-30), 238 ff.

22. Ernest Lavisse, *Histoire de France*, 9 vols., Paris, 1903-11, IV, Pt. 2, p. 364; Coulton, *op. cit.*, pp. 31 f.

23. George C. Powers, *Nationalism at the Council of Constance (1414-1418)*, Washington, D. C., 1927, pp. 59 ff., 104, 108 f., 119; Louise R. Loomis, "Nationality at the Council of Constance," *American Historical Review*, XLIV (1938-39), 508-27; Eckhardt, *op. cit.*, p. 26; William Boulting, *Aeneas Silvius*, London, 1908, p. 207.

24. *The Commentaries of Pius II*, English transl. by Florence Alden Gragg, in *Smith College Studies in History*, XXII (1936-37), 99.

25. The interplay between the Occidental and national consciousness in various medieval periods is succinctly analyzed by Richard Wallach in *Das abendländische Gemeinschaftsbewusstsein im Mittelalter*, Leipzig, 1928.

26. Cecil Roth, "Marranos and Racial Antisemitism," *Jewish Social Studies*, II (1940), 239-48. Guido Kisch goes too far in denying these sentiments merely because the original sources fail to call them by their modern names. Cf. his "Nationalism and Race in Medieval Law," *Seminar*, I (1943), 48-73.

27. Stephen P. Ladas, *The Exchange of Minorities: Bulgaria, Greece and Turkey*,

New York, 1932, pp. 437 ff. Another 1,100,-000 Greek Orthodox had emigrated from the area of the new Turkish Republic during the preceding decade.

28. League of Nations, *Official Journal*, V (1924), 1354. Cf. Ladas, *op. cit.*, pp. 386 f.; C. A. Macartney, *National States and National Minorities*, Oxford, 1934, p. 9.

29. Romulus Candea, *Der Katholizismus in den Donaufürstentümern*, Leipzig, 1916, pp. 62 f., 90, 110. In Russia, too, Turks and Tartars retained their ethnic identity only when they persevered in their ancestral, Muslim faith.

30. John Fordun, *Scotichronicon*, with a continuation by Walter Bower, 2 vols., Edinburgh, 1759, II, 262, 264; Coulton, *op. cit.*, p. 31. Finke (*Weltimperialismus*, pp. 61 f. n. 90) correctly stresses the frequency of such deprecatory utterances throughout medieval Europe. On the whole the closer one's neighbor the less well he was thought of.

31. Cf. Louis Franck, "La nationalité belge et le mouvement flamand," *Séances et Travaux* of the Académie des Sciences Morales et Politiques, XC, Pt. 2 (1930), 490-516; Shepard B. Clough, *A History of the Flemish Movement in Belgium*, New York, 1930, pp. 5, 44 ff. Thomas Harrison Reed has rightly stressed the remarkable phenomenon that "French villages have confronted Flemish villages, the Flemish side of the street the French side, time out of mind, without one tongue gaining on the other, and without any tendency toward the formation of a common speech." Cf. his *Government and Politics of Belgium*, Yonkers, N. Y., 1924, p. 4. Cf. also Vicomte Ch. Terlinden, "Les Jésuites et la nationalité belge," *Etudes classiques*, XIII (1945), 153-66.

32. Cf. Kenneth Scott Latourette, *A History of the Expansion of Christianity*, 7 vols., New York, 1937-45, IV, 123 ff.; Alfred Fischel, *Der Panslawismus bis zum Weltkrieg*, Stuttgart, 1919, p. 379; Macartney, *op. cit.*, pp. 132, 147 n. 1, 457 ff. For a graphic description of the drastic methods employed by Nicholas I's administration in converting the Uniates, cf. Hugh Y. Reyburn, *The Story of the Russian Church*, London, 1924, pp. 232 f.

33. Paul Joachimsen, *Vom deutschen Volk zum deutschen Staat*, Leipzig, 1920, p. 104.

34. Cf. Otto Vossler, *Mazzinis politisches Denken und Wollen in den geistigen Strömungen seiner Zeit*, Munich, 1927, pp. 56 f. See also below Chap. II.

35. Coulton, *op. cit.*, p. 28 n. 36.

36. Cf. Salo W. Baron, "Nationalism and Intolerance," *Menorah Journal*, XVI (1929), 405-15; XVII (1929), 148-58; *idem*, A *Social and Religious History of the Jews*, II, 38 ff.; III, 107 f.

37. Ranke, *Abhandlungen und Versuche*, Leipzig, 1872, pp. 38 f.

38. A. Dove, "Der Wiedereintritt des nationalen Prinzips in die Weltgeschichte," in *Ausgewählte historische Schriftchen*, Leipzig, 1898, p. 5.

39. Even today, e.g., the Catholic hierarchy in Latin-American countries effectively opposes the intrusion of Protestant missionaries by stressing the dangers of religious disparity to national unity. As a result, there are no more than 2,000,000 Protestants south of the Rio Grande, despite the influence exerted by 52 Protestant theological colleges and 155 church publications. Cf. George P. Howard, *Religious Liberty in Latin America?* Philadelphia, 1944.

Chapter II

Nationalist Fathers

1. Lenin, "Socialism and Religion" (1905) in English transl. in V. I. Lenin, *Selected Works*, 12 vols., New York, n.d., XI, 659. Cf. also *idem*, "The Attitude of the Workers' Party Towards Religion" (1909), *ibid.*, pp. 663 ff.

2. Mme. de Staël, *Considérations sur les principaux événemens de la Révolution française*, IV, in *Œuvres complètes*, Paris, 1820-21, XIII, 369.

3. J. N. Bauman, *Eloge de J.-J. Rousseau*, Paris, 1803, pp. 22 ff., cited by Pierre Maurice Masson in *La Religion de J.-J. Rousseau*, 3 vols., Paris, 1916, III, 263 f. Cf. also *ibid.*, pp. 226, 267.

4. Giorgio del Vecchio, *Sui caracteri fondamentali della filosofia politica del Rousseau*, Genoa, 1912, p. 4 (reprinted from *Rivista Ligure di Scienze, Lettere ed Arti*, XXXIX). Cf. also Ernst Cassirer, "Das Problem Jean Jacques Rousseau," *Archiv für Geschichte der Philosophie*, XLI (1932), 177-213, 479-513; and E. H. Wright, *Meaning of Rousseau*, London, 1929.

5. Rousseau's letter, written but not sent to Mirabeau, about March 25, 1767, in his *Correspondance générale*, ed. by Théophile Dufour, 20 vols., Paris 1924-34, XVII, 2 f. Cf. Jacques Maritain in his *Three Reformers: Luther — Descartes — Rousseau*, English transl., New York, 1937, p. 223.

6. *Discours sur l'origine et les fondements de l'inégalité parmi les hommes* in Rousseau's *Political Writings*, ed. by C. E. Vaughan, 2 vols., Cambridge, 1915, I, 146; Masson, *op. cit.*, III, 44 f.

7. A reckless exclamation like that in Lettre à Madame [la Comtesse de Wartensleben] of Sept. 27, 1866, in Rousseau's *Correspondance générale*, XVII, 77: "In my opinion the blood of a single man is of higher value than the liberty of the whole human race," clearly controverted his general conviction that liberty alone distinguishes human beings from animals. Cf. *Discours sur l'inégalité, l.c.*, I, 149. Cf. also Charles Borgeaud, *Jean-Jacques Rousseau's Religionsphilosophie*, Leipzig, 1883, pp. 37 f., 73 ff.

8. The fullest analysis of these passages and their historical background is given in the three volumes of Masson's *op. cit.*

9. *Mémoires et correspondance de Mme. d'Epinay*, Paris, 1818, II, 63; Rousseau, *La "Profession du foi du Vicaire Savoyard,"* critically ed. by P. M. Masson, Paris, 1914, p. 404; Lettre à M. de Beaumont in Rousseau's *Œuvres complètes*, 4 vols., Paris, 1835-39, II, 772. Voltaire's caustic remark is cited by Masson (*loc. cit.*) from the marginal notes in Voltaire's copy of *Emile*.

10. To be sure, like most of his contemporaries, Rousseau addressed himself to the educated upper strata and not directly to the masses whose cause he championed (his mass popularity was to come much later). Even his arguments against the atheistic and materialistic doctrines were written principally for an audience familiar with some outstanding agnostic manuscripts of limited circulation. Cf. Masson, *Religion*, III, 19 ff. Nonetheless, his critique of the existing conditions was so far "national" in scope as to any intellectual of the pre-Revolutionary period the French nation was, as Aulard has shown, identical with *la France lettré ou riche*.

11. Rousseau, Preface to *Narcisse* in *Œuvres*, III, 193; *Contrat social*, IV, 8 (Chap. on Civil Religion), in *Political Writings*, II, 130. Cf. Masson, *op. cit.*, II, 183; Machiavelli, *Political Discourses upon the First Decad of Livy*, II, 2 in *Works*, transl. by Ellis Farneworth, 2d ed., 4 vols., London, 1775, III, 218 f.

12. *Contrat social, l.c.,* p. 128; *Lettre de la Montagne,* I, 1 in *Œuvres,* III, 14; *Considérations sur le gouvernement de Pologne,* III; *Que l'état de guerre naît de l'état social* in *Political Writings,* I, 293 ff.; II, 432. Cf. also Henri Rodet, *Le Contrat social et les idées politiques de J.-J. Rousseau,* Paris, 1909, pp. 334 f.; and Karl Dietrich Erdmann, *Das Verhältnis von Staat und Religion nach der Sozialphilosophie Rousseaus (Der Begriff der "religion civile"),* Berlin, 1935. Erdmann emphasizes the chronological sequence in the Rousseauan dichotomy between "man" and "citizen" from the initial statement in the first two *Discours,* through the attempts at harmonization in the *Contrat* and *Emile,* to the breakdown of his solution in the *Considérations.*

13. *Contrat social,* IV, 8; *Considérations,* II, in *Political Writings,* II, 128, 428; *Lettre à M. de Beaumont,* in *Œuvres,* II, 786. Cf. also the fuller passage on the longevity of the Jews cited from a manuscript draft, probably dating from the last fifteen years of Rousseau's life, by Masson, *op. cit.,* II, 240. Rousseau's fearless and somewhat irreverent attitude toward the Old Testament contrasted with his far more reserved approach to the New Testament. Cf. Masson, *op. cit.,* II, 63 f., 106. But this contrast was not unusual then even among such outstanding Biblical critics as Baruch Spinoza and Jean Astruc.

14. Letter to Mme. [de Créqui] of July 21, 1764 in *Correspondance,* XI, 198. Cf. also his *Nouvelle Héloïse,* VI, 8, in *Œuvres,* II, 353; Jean Baptiste Tollot's letter about Rousseau of 1754 published by Eugène Ritter in the *Annales de la Société J.-J. Rousseau,* III (1907), 203; Gaspard Vallette, *Jean-Jacques Rousseau: genevois,* Paris, 1911.

15. *Contrat social,* IV, 8, *l.c.,* II, 132; *Profession,* ed. Masson, p. 309.

16. *Projet de constitution pour la Corse,* II, in *Political Writings,* II, 350; *Contrat social,* I, 6, *ibid.,* pp. 32 ff.; Montesquieu, cited by Rodet, *op. cit.,* p. 268. Cf. also Montesquieu's *Pensées et fragments inédits,* ed. by Gaston de Montesquieu, 2 vols., Bordeaux, 1899-1901, II, 262 f. (is more sorry for Louis XIV and the Catholic Church than for the Huguenots), 344; Rousseau's letter to Voltaire of Aug. 18, 1756, in *Correspondance,* II, 322 ff.; and *Profession,* ed. Masson, pp. 393 f., 423, 453 ff. Rousseau speaks there, on the one hand, of the "cruel

dogma of intolerance" which would vitiate any acceptable hypothesis of the divine government and, on the other hand, glorifies fanaticism as the "great and strong passion which elevates man's heart . . . and which only requires little direction to produce the most sublime virtues." For a brief analysis of the crucial term "general will" cf. Rudolf Stammler, "Notion et portée de la 'volonté générale' chez Jean-Jacques Rousseau," *Revue de Metaphysique et de Morale,* XX (1912), 383-89. This anniversary issue of the *Revue* contains also a number of other pertinent essays.

17. Cited by Henry H. Walsh in *The Concordat of 1801,* New York, 1933, p. 27. Cf. also Erdmann, *op. cit.,* pp. 68 ff.

18. Burke had avoided the "insane Socrates" during the latter's brief stay in England as David Hume's temperamental guest. This much-debated unpleasant visit is treated with full documentation by Margaret H. Peoples in "La querelle Rousseau-Hume," *Annales de la Société J. J. Rousseau,* XVIII (1927-28), 1-331. Cf. also J. Y. T. Greig's edition of *The Letters of David Hume,* 2 vols., Oxford, 1932, II, 54 ff., 384 ff.; and Henri Roddier's "La querelle Rousseau-Hume," *Revue de littérature comparée,* XVIII (1938), 452-77.

19. *Reflections on the Revolution in France* in Burke's *Writings and Speeches,* 12 vols., Boston, 1901, III, 459; James Prior, *Memoir of the Life and Character of the Right Hon. Edmund Burke,* 2 vols., Boston, 1854, II, 45. Cf. also the comparative study of *Rousseau and Burke* by Annie Marion Osborn, London, 1940; and of several of Burke's English contemporaries by Alfred Cobban in his *Edmund Burke and the Revolt against the Eighteenth Century,* London, 1929.

20. *Observations on a Late Publication Intituled "The Present State of the Nation"* (1769) in *Writings,* I, 398; *Speech on Moving Resolutions for Conciliation with America* (1775), *ibid.,* II, 179.

21. *Speech on American Taxation* (1774), *ibid.,* II, 25; *Reflections, ibid.,* III, 274, 312, 344 f.; *Letters on Regicide Peace,* IV, *ibid.,* VI, 60; Voltaire, *Lettres philosophiques,* VIII (1726) in *Œuvres complètes,* 52 vols., Paris, 1877-85, XXII, 104. Cf. Lord John Acton's pointed critique of Burke's appraisal of the statesmen of 1688 in his *History of Freedom and Other Essays,* London, 1907, p. 53.

22. *Reflections, l.c.,* III, 359; John Mac-Cunn, *The Political Philosophy of Burke,* London, 1913, p. 60.

23. *Reflections, l.c.,* III, 307, 310, 345, 355, 559; *Regicide Peace,* I, in *Writings,* V, 284. Cf. Louis Bernstein Namier, *The Structure of Politics at the Accession of George III,* 2 vols., London, 1929, I, 79, 182.

24. *Conciliation, l.c.,* II, 141, 145, 180; *Speech on American Taxation, l.c.,* II, 75 ff.; *The Epistolary Correspondence of . . . Burke and Dr. French Laurence,* London, 1827, p. 54. This letter, written on July 28, 1796, had all the earmarks of a testamentary injunction.

25. *Regicide Peace,* Letter I, *l.c.,* V, 307, 317 f., 324 ff.; Letter II, *ibid.,* pp. 345 f.

26. Joseph Priestley voiced the prevailing view when he wrote to Burke, "that an avowed friend of the American Revolution should be an enemy of that of the French, which arose from the same general principles and in a great measure sprung from it, is to me unaccountable." Cf. his *Letters to the Right Honourable Edmund Burke occasioned by his Reflections on the Revolution in France,* Birmingham, 1791, p. iv. For the same reason Robert M. Hutchins concludes his analysis of "The Theory of the State: Edmund Burke," *Review of Politics,* V (1943), 139-55, on the note of censure: "He fashioned his theories to serve the purpose he had in view. Contrary to the advice he offered the world, he made his reason subordinate to his will."

27. Sir Philip Magnus, *Edmund Burke; A Life,* London, 1939, pp. 55, 69 f., 77 ff.; Oliver Goldsmith, *Retaliation* in *Works,* ed. by Peter Cunningham, 8 vols., Boston, 1900, I, 94; Lord John Morley, *Burke* in the series of *English Men of Letters,* ed. by him, New York, 1930, p. 167.

28. *Reflections, l.c.,* III, 368; *Regicide Peace,* I, *l.c.,* V, 309 f., 316.

29. *Reflections, l.c.,* III, 350 f., 354, 361; *Speech on the Petition of the Unitarians* (1792), *ibid.,* VII, 43.

30. *Reflections, l.c.,* III, 351, 429 f.; Letter to his son, Richard, of 1793 in *Writings,* VI, 399; Speech of Dec. 4, 1781, in T. C. Hansard's *Parliamentary History of England,* XXII, 775. Cf. also *Tract on the Popery Laws,* III (after 1765) in *Writings,* VI, 336, where Burke climaxed his harangue against these laws by exclaiming, "In proportion as mankind has become enlightened, the idea of religious persecution, under any circumstances, has been almost universally exploded by all good and thinking men."

31. *Conciliation with America, l.c.,* II, 123; *Speech on Relief of Protestant Dissenters* (1773) in *Writings,* VII, 23 ff.; *Speech on the Acts of Uniformity* (1772), *ibid.,* p. 13; Speech of March 2, 1789, in Hansard's *Parliamentary History,* XXVIII, 432 ff., 441.

32. *Relief of Protestant Dissenters, l.c.,* VII, 36.

33. Magnus, *op. cit.,* pp. 5 f., 11, 111.

34. Burke emphasized this point in his literary debut, *The Vindication of Natural Society* (1756), written against Bolingbroke's "natural religion," in *Writings,* I, 45 f.

35. Burke, *Regicide Peace,* I, *l.c.,* V, 326; *Conciliation with America, l.c.,* p. 181; Rousseau, *Considérations,* III in *Political Writings,* II, 432.

36. *Conciliation with America, l.c.,* II, 120, 124. Cf. Gilbert Chinard's *Thomas Jefferson: The Apostle of Americanism,* Boston, 1929, pp. vii, 80 ff.; and his introduction to the edition of *The Common Place Book of Thomas Jefferson,* Baltimore, 1926.

37. There was a widespread feeling among the colonists, as voiced by the *Pennsylvania Packet* in its support of the French alliance, that severance from the British would help eliminate the unfortunate influences of the "pomp" of the Anglican Church, English class distinctions, and the English Constitution, "so perfect in theory, but so corrupt in practice." Cited by Evarts Boutell Greene in his "Imponderables in Early Americanism," *Thought,* XVIII (1943), 221. Cf. also *idem, The Revolutionary Generation 1763-1790,* New York, 1943.

38. William Stevens Perry, *The Faith of the Signers of the Declaration of Independence* (reprinted in the *Magazine of History,* XXIX, 1926, 215-37), pp. 26 f. (218). Cf. also *idem, Influence of the Clergy on the War of the Revolution,* New York, 1891, p. 6.

39. John Adams to Jedediah Morse, Dec. 2, 1815, in Adams's *Works,* ed. by Charles Francis Adams, 10 vols., Boston, 1850-56, X, 185; Burke, *Conciliation with America, l.c.,* II, 120; Jefferson, *Notes on Virginia* in *Writings,* 9 vols., ed. by H. A. Washington, New York, 1853-54, VIII, 398 (unless otherwise stated, all following references are to this edition). Cf. Edward Frank Humphrey,

Nationalism and Religion in America, 1774-1789, Boston, 1924, pp. 24 f.; Charles F. James, *Documentary History of the Struggle for Religious Liberty in Virginia*, Lynchburg, Va., 1900, p. 197. "I fully concur with your grand maxim," wrote Isaac Backus, chief Baptist champion of separation of state and church, to John Adams on Jan. 19, 1774, "that it is essential to liberty that representation and taxation go together. Well, then, since people do not vote for representatives in our legislature from ecclesiastical qualifications but only by virtue of those which are of a civil and worldly nature, how can representatives thus chosen have any right to impose ecclesiastical taxes?" Cf. Humphrey, *op. cit.*, pp. 362 f.

40. Letters to Paine of March 17, 1789; the Baptist Associations of Danbury and Baltimore of Jan. 1, 1802 and Oct. 17, 1808, respectively; George Flower of Sept. 12, 1817; and John Adams of Nov. 25, 1816, in *Writings*, III, 8; VII, 45 f., 84; VIII, 113, 138; *Notes on Virginia, ibid.*, VIII, 330 f. In regard to the British fleet he wrote apprehensively to Robert R. Livingston, then American minister in Paris (April 18, 1802) that, should France take possession of New Orleans, "from that moment we must marry ourselves to the British fleet and nation." A year later (June 30, 1803), viewing with great concern the jeopardy in which England was placed by Napoleon's expansionist designs, he stated to Sir John Sinclair that America "should be sincerely afflicted were any disaster to deprive mankind of the benefit of such a bulwark against the torrent which has for some time been bearing down all before it." *Ibid.*, IV, 432, 491.

41. Letters to Earle of Sept. 24, 1823; Adams of Aug. 1, 1816; Priestley of Jan. 27, 1800; and Kerchival of July 12, 1816, in *Writings*, IV, 318; VII, 14 f., 27, 310 f. Cf. also his letters to Madison of Sept. 6, 1789, and Governor Plumer of July 21, 1816, *ibid.*, III, 103; VII, 19. It may be noted that, with one exception, all these statements were written after Jefferson's stay in Paris, which did not mark quite that radical break with his previous thinking as is presented by Otto Vossler in *Die amerikanischen Revolutionsideale in ihrem Verhältnis zu den europäischen untersucht an Thomas Jefferson*, Munich, 1929, pp. 105 ff.

42. Letters to George Washington of

May 2, 1788; Monroe of June 17, 1785; William Lee of Jan. 16, 1817, in *Writings*, I, 352; II, 375; VII, 56 f.; John T. Morse, Jr., *Thomas Jefferson*, Boston, 1895, p. 49. In an opinion written on Nov. 29, 1790, however, Jefferson criticized the "disgusting monotony" of Philadelphia's buildings. Cf. his *Writings*, Memorial Edition, ed. by Albert Ellery Bergh, 20 vols., Washington, 1907, III, 84.

43. Letters to William Lee of Jan. 16, 1817; John Manners of June 12, 1817 (referring to an act drawn by him in 1776 for the Virginia Code); Walter Jones of March 5, 1810; Lafayette of April 2, 1790, and Inaugural Address of 1801, in *Writings*, III, 132; V, 509 ff.; VII, 56 f., 73; VIII, 4. He anticipated his letter to Jones by almost nine years when in his first Annual Message to Congress of Dec. 8, 1801, he advocated revision of the naturalization laws, for "shall oppressed humanity find no asylum on this globe?" *Ibid.*, VIII, 14. This idea had been voiced by Madison and others before him. Cf. also below Chap. V n. 72.

44. Letters to James Madison of Nov. 24, 1801; Alexander von Humboldt of June 13, 1817; James Monroe of June 11, 1823; de Marbois of June 14, 1817; Adams of Aug. 1, 1816, in *Writings*, IV, 420; VII, 27, 75, 77, 288; to Dr. Mitchell of June 13, 1800, cited from ms. by Chinard, *op. cit.*, p. 398; Inaugural Address of 1801 in *Writings*, VIII, 3 f. Cf. also *ibid.*, V, 164 f., 444 f.; VII, 67 f.

45. Letters to Benjamin Rush of April 21, 1803; Peter Carr of Aug. 10, 1787; Ezra Stiles of June 25, 1819; Jared Sparks of Nov. 4, 1820, in *Writings*, II, 238 ff.; IV, 479; VII, 127 f., 185 f.; Morse, *op. cit.*, pp. 45 ff.

46. Letters to Short of Oct. 31, 1819 and April 13, 1820; Adams of Aug. 15, 1820, and April 11, 1823; Augustus Woodward of March 24, 1824, in *Writings*, VII, 138 ff., 155 ff., 176 f., 281, 339. Cf. also the lengthy letter to Benjamin Waterhouse of June 26, 1822, *ibid.*, pp. 252 f., where Jefferson spoke of the "demoralizing dogmas of Calvin" and of the true Christians who followed the simple doctrines of Jesus rather than those of "the impious dogmatists, as Athanasius and Calvin." For Bolingbroke's influence on young Jefferson, cf. Chinard's edition of Jefferson's *Literary Bible*, Balti-

more, 1926. Jefferson often thought of translating Epictetus into English side by side with an abstract of the finest teachings of Jesus. Cf. Adrienne Koch, *The Philosophy of Thomas Jefferson* (New York, 1943, pp. 9 ff.), who points out, however, that Jefferson's Epicureanism was greatly diluted by a strong dose of Stoicism and modern ethical philosophy. Cf. also the essays published in *Ethics*, LIII (1942-43), 237-310, particularly Gilbert Chinard's "Jefferson among the Philosophers" (especially pp. 263 ff.) and Herbert W. Schneider's "The Enlightenment in Thomas Jefferson."

47. Letters to John Adams of Jan. 11 and May 5, 1817, and Gideon Granger of May 3, 1801, in *Writings*, IV, 395; VII, 55, 62; *Common Place Book*, ed. by Chinard, p. 362. One such New England "hierocrat," Judah Champion, Congregational minister in Litchfield, Conn., publicly prayed for Jefferson, then vice-president: "Oh Lord, wilt Thou bestow on the Vice-President a double portion of Thy grace, for Thou knowest he needs it." Cf. Alain C. White, *The History of the Town of Litchfield, 1720-1920*, Litchfield, 1920, p. 163. It is doubly remarkable that Jefferson firmly opposed the exclusion of clergy from public office which many state legislatures considered their most effective safeguard for the separation of state and church. Cf. Evarts B. Greene, *Religion and the State*, New York, 1941, pp. 82, 95 f.

48. Humphrey, *op. cit.*, pp. 25 ff., 368; Morse, *Jefferson*, pp. 339 f.; Jefferson's letters to Benjamin Waterhouse of June 26, 1822, and Lafayette of May 14, 1817, in *Writings*, VII, 66, 252 f.

49. Letters to Mann Page of Aug. 30, 1795; John Adams of Sept. 24, 1821, and Cornelius Camden Blatchly of Oct. 21, 1822, in *Writings*, IV, 119; VII, 219, 263.

50. Letters to de Crèvecœur of Jan. 15, 1787, and John Jay of April 7, 1809, in *Writings*, II, 98; V, 440.

51. Letters to Mrs. Bolling cited by Francis W. Hirst in *Life and Letters of Thomas Jefferson*, New York, 1926, p. 206; John Adams of Aug. 1, 1816, in *Writings*, VII, 27; Chinard, *Jefferson*, pp. 9, 99, 511 f.

52. This is really the import of Fichte's critique of Rousseau's emotionalism, "Action, action, that is what we are for." *Einige Vorlesungen über die Bestimmung des Gelehrten* (1794), V, in his *Sämmtliche*

Werke, VI, 345. Rousseau, thus censured, had said almost exactly the same thing some forty-two years earlier, however. Cf. Franz Haymann, *Weltbürgertum und Vaterlandsliebe in der Staatslehre Rousseaus und Fichtes*, Berlin, 1924, p. 47 n. 2. In general Fichte so penetratingly understood Rousseau that without knowing of the preliminary draft of the *Social Contract* then unpublished, in which the author had declared, "I am searching for right and reason, I am not disputing the facts," Fichte used almost verbatim the same formula in describing Rousseau's aim. Cf. Georg Gurwitsch, "Kant und Fichte als Rousseau-Interpreten," *Kant-Studien*, XXVII (1922), 158. Before long he believed that he understood Rousseau better than the latter understood himself. Cf. *Einige Vorlesungen*, etc., V. in *Sämmtl. Werke*, VI, 337. Ironically Fichte's teachings, too, became the subject of most divergent interpretations by his successors. Cf. the brief survey in H. C. Engelbrecht's *Johann Gottlieb Fichte. A Study of his Political Writings with Special Reference to his Nationalism*, New York, 1933, pp. 160-90.

53. *Beitrag zur Berichtigung der Urtheile des Publicums über die französische Revolution* in *Sämmtliche Werke*, VI, 71; *Rückerinnerungen, Antworten, Fragen* (1799), *ibid.*, V, 343. Cf. also *Grundzüge des gegenwärtigen Zeitalters*, *ibid.*, VII, 30, 96 f.

54. *Beitrag*, *l.c.*, p. 95. Only the first part of this work defending the legitimacy of the Revolution was published in 1793 and republished in 1795. The whole work appeared much later *ibid.*, III, 37-288.

55. *Reden an die deutsche Nation*, III, in *Sämmtl. Werke*, VII, 313 f., 460.

56. *Der Patriotismus und sein Gegentheil* (1807) in *Nachgelassene Werke*, III, 228 f.

57. *Der geschlossene Handelsstaat* in *Sämmtl. Werke*, III, 387-513. In his *Reden an die deutsche Nation*, delivered a decade later, Fichte reminded his listeners of the "passionate hatred" with which these proposals had been greeted. *Ibid.*, VII, 466 f.

58. *Ibid.*, pp. 423, 431; *Grundzüge, ibid.*, pp. 203 f., 207 f. (here Fichte lightly dismissed the Malthusian fears of overpopulation).

59. *Staatslehre* (1813), III, *ibid.*, IV, 431 ff.; *Politische Fragmente, ibid.*, VII, 565. A curious juxtaposition of freedom and com-

pulsion is found *ibid.*, p. 571, where Fichte contended in a single breath that Germany's geographic position would enable it "to force the other nations to maintain peace and thus become the first permanent seat of freedom." Cf. also *ibid.*, p. 578, etc. As early as 1799 Anselm Feuerbach noted that Fichte "would be capable of playing the role of Mohammed, were the time still ripe for a Mohammed, and of enforcing his Theory of Science by sword and imprisonment, were his professorial chair a royal throne." Cf. Ludwig Feuerbach, *Anselm Ritter von Feuerbachs Leben und Wirken*, Leipzig, 1852, I, 51 f. Cf. also Kuno Fischer, *J. G. Fichte und seine Vorgänger* in his *Geschichte der neueren Philosophie*, V, 2d ed., Munich, 1884, pp. 243 ff.

60. *Grundzüge, l.c.*, VII, 98 ff., 104. Cf. fragment, *Ueber Ehe u.s.w, ibid.*, pp. 599 f., where summing up his views on the contrast between the "god of nature" of the ancient heathens and the "moral lawgiver of liberty" in early Christianity Fichte added, "Here is demonstrated once again, what the Germans are: the *national* counterpart of the principles contained in Christianity. Only through them can the Christian state be attained and it is their historic task to bring about its realization." Cf. also Haymann, *op. cit.*, p. 36; Karl Haack, *Der religiöse und ethische Charakter der Vaterlandsliebe Fichtes* (Diss. Erlangen), Wohlau, 1927, pp. 55 f.

61. Cf. Nietzsche, *Jenseits von Gut und Böse*, no. 244 in his *Werke*, 20 vols., Leipzig, 1895-1926, VII, 209 (= *Beyond Good and Evil*, authorized transl. by Helen Zimmern, New York, 1907, pp. 197 f.): "Jean Paul knew what he was doing, when he declared himself incensed at Fichte's lying, but patriotic, flatteries and exaggerations—but it is probable that Goethe thought differently about Germans from Jean Paul, even though he acknowledged him to be right with regard to Fichte." Cf. also *ibid.*, XIII, 14.

62. *Politische Fragmente, l.c.*, VII, 565.

63. *Ueber Ehe, ibid.*, VII, 601; *Grundl. des Naturrechts* (1796), *ibid.*, III, 377 ff.

64. It was published some four decades later by his son in *Sämmtl. Werke*, VII, 530-45.

65. "Eleusinen des 19. Jahrhunderts," *l.c.*, II, 22. Cf. also Haymann, *Weltbürgertum*, pp. 59 ff.

66. *Reden, l.c.*, VII, 379, 384; *Politische Fragmente, ibid.*, pp. 556 f., 609.

67. "Foi et avenir" (1835) in Mazzini's *Scritti editi ed inediti Edizione nazionale* (subsequently quoted as *Ed. naz.*), 89 vols., and appendix vols. II-IV, Imola, 1906-40, VI, 263 f. For a somewhat different English translation cf. *Life and Writings of Joseph Mazzini*, 6 vols., London, 1890-91, III, 117 f. Herder's influence on Mazzini was far more direct than that of Fichte. Cf. Vossler, *Mazzinis politisches Denken*, pp. 32 ff., 78 ff.

68. From *Italia del Popolo* of June 18, 1848, reprinted in *Ed. naz.*, XXXVIII, 82; Review of Renan's *La reforme intellectuelle et morale* in *Scritti editi e inediti*, 18 vols., Milan, 1861-91 (subsequently quoted as *Scritti*), XVI, 126; "Nationalité. Quelques idées sur une Constitution nationale" (1835), in *Ed. naz.*, VI, 125, 127. Another definition ("I collaboratori della *Giovine Italia* ai loro concittadini" [1832], *ibid.*, III, 64) stressed even more the spirituality of national feeling. Nationality appears here as "the totality of citizens speaking the same language, associated, under equality of civil and political rights, in the common purpose of progressively developing and perfecting the social forces and the activity of these forces." As late as 1871 he still insisted (in his "Nazionalismo e nazionalità" in *Scritti*, XVII, 164 f.) that language, territory and race are at best symptoms of national feeling, but that they are completely ineffective unless they are reinforced by a unity of purpose, a historic tradition and a long evolution of collective life. Cf. also other passages analyzed by Giovanni Gentile in *I profeti del Risorgimento italiano*, Florence, 1923, pp. 36 ff.

69. J. A. R. Marriot in *The Makers of Modern Italy*, Oxford, 1937, p. 16; Heinrich Finke, "Die Nation in den spätmittelalterlichen allgemeinen Konzilien," *Historisches Jahrbuch*, LVII (1937), 337 f.; Arndt, *Germanien und Europa*, Altona, 1803, p. 385. The French, on their part, always claimed the Rhine as their natural though not their linguistic frontier. For the medieval period, cf. Wallach, *op. cit.*, pp. 38 f. Cf. also Friedrich Meinecke, *Weltbürgertum und Nationalstaat*, 7th ed., Munich, 1928, p. 63.

70. Cf., e.g., "Condizioni e avvenire dell'-Europa" (1852), *Ed. naz.*, XLVI, 262 ff. The "thirteen or fourteen nuclei" of Euro-

pean reconstruction, based on a radical adjustment of existing boundaries, are scattered in Mazzini's writings. For a systematic survey cf. Giuseppe Calabrò, *La dottrina religioso-sociale di Giuseppe Mazzini: La religione dell' avvenire*, Palermo, 1912, pp. 150 ff.; and Gaetano Salvemini, *Mazzini*, Rome, 1920, pp. 73 ff.

71. "Sull' enciclica di Papa Pio IX" (1849), *Ed. naz.*, XXXIX, 357 f.; "De l'initiative révolutionnaire en Europe" (1834), *ibid.*, IV, 140 f.; "Istruzione generale per gli affratellati nella Giovine Italia," *ibid.*, II, 54 f. (a somewhat different English transl. in *Life and Writings*, I, 110 ff.).

72. "Del ordinamento del Partito" (1858), *Ed. naz.*, LXII, 59; "Foi et avenir," *ibid.*, VI, 248 (English transl. in *Life and Writings*, III, 101). Cf. also his sharp antipapal harangues in "Roma e il governo di Francia" (1849), *ibid.*, XXXIX, 238; "Le prigioni del Papa" (1865), *ibid.*, LXXXIII, 145 ff.; and Vossler, *Mazzinis politisches Denken*, pp. 55 ff.

73. "Dei doveri dell' uomo" (1860), *Ed. naz.*, LXIX, 1 ff. (English transl. in *Life and Writings*, IV, 209 ff.); letter to Francesco Bertioli of January, 1833, *ibid.*, V, 216. For a summary of Mazzini's acknowledged divergences from official Catholicism cf. his open letter of 1865, "A Pio IX, Papa," *ibid.*, LXXXIII, 45 ff. In his "Moto antipapale germanico" of 1871 (in *Scritti*, XVIII, 209 ff.) he even condemned the Old Catholic movement against papal infallibility as well as the Christian-socialist movements among English Protestants. All these progressive movements proved, in his opinion, only that "Christianity feels that it had been overtaken by the moral and intellectual conquests of civilization." In themselves, however, they had "not the slightest promise of a future" (*ibid.*, pp. 211, 218). Cf. also his "Sulla Rivoluzione Francese del 1789. Pensieri" (1871), *ibid.*, XVI, 54-93; "Questione morale" (1866), *Ed. naz.*, LXXXIII, 199 ff.; letter to Luigi Amedeo Melegari, *ibid.*, V, 257 ff.; and "Ai Signori Tocqueville e Falloux" (1849), *ibid.*, XXXIX, 161 ff. (English transl. in *Life and Writings*, V, 222 ff.).

74. "Foi et avenir," *Ed. naz.*, VI, 260 ff. (English transl. in *Life and Writings*, III, 113 ff).

75. Correspondence with Sismondi of 1832 in *Ed. naz.*, III, 14, 19 f.; Letter to Me-

legari of July 22, 1838, *ibid.*, XV, 91; "Foi et avenir," *ibid.*, VI, 260 (English transl. in *Life and Writings*, III, 113); *Duecento lettere inedite di Giuseppe Mazzini*, ed. by Domenico Giurati, Turin, 1887, pp. 62, 319. By a curious irony the International Congress of Freethinkers meeting in Rome in 1905 celebrated the hundredth anniversary of Mazzini's birth. Cf. Salvemini, *op. cit.*, p. 13 n. 1.

76. "Ai Giovani d'Italia" (1859), *Ed. naz.*, LXIV, 180 f.; "Lettere d'un esule, II" (to Ernest Hang of April, 1863), *ibid.*, LXXV, 118 ff.; letter to Melegari of 1838, *ibid.*, XV, 90 f.; "La santa alleanza dei popoli" (1849), *ibid.*, XXXIX, 203 ff. (English excerpts of this work are given in *Life and Writings*, V, 265 ff.). Cf. Salvemini, *op. cit.*, pp. 102 f. Curiously, Mazzini's free association was not too far removed from the ideology of the Holy Alliance. It, too, was to be founded on faith and its avowed aim was to protect the faith rather than any particular national or imperial interests. Nor was it to be any less intolerant of opposing viewpoints. Gentile (*op. cit.*, p. 46) goes too far, however, in contrasting the Mazzinian ideas of international collaboration with Wilson's League of Nations.

77. "Questione morale" (1866), *Ed. naz.*, LXXXIII, 205 f.; reprint from *Italia del Popolo* of July 26, 1848, *ibid.*, XXXVIII, 175; "A un inglese" (1850), *ibid.*, XLVI, 30. Cf. also *ibid.*, XXXIX, 191, 218; Salvemini, *op. cit.*, p. 59 n. 1.

78. These ideas were most fully developed in his essay, "Thoughts upon Democracy in Europe" republished in *Ed. naz.*, XXXIV, 91 ff. Cf. also his various essays in *La Roma del Popolo* of 1871, "Le classi artigiane," "Questione sociale," "Il moto delle classi artigiane e il congresso" (especially the beginning), "Alle società operaie" in *Scritti*, XVI, 165 ff., 182 ff., 206 ff., 214 ff.; Salvemini, *op. cit.*, p. 137.

79. Letter to his mother of Dec. 10, 1851, in *Ed. naz.*, XLVII, 127; "Doveri dell' uomo" *ibid.*, LXIX, 127 (English transl. in *Life and Letters*, IV, 354); "Letter to Daniel Stern" (pseud. of Marie C. S. D'Agoult) of Sept. 16, 1864, *ibid.*, LXXIX, 61; reprint from *Italia del Popolo* of July 15, 1848, *ibid.*, XXXVIII, 165 ff. In his "Sull' enciclica di Papa Pio IX" (1849), *ibid.*, XXXIX, 350, however, he objected to the pope's confounding socialism with communism, while

"the former philosophically contradicts the latter." Cf. also Jessie W. Mario, *Della vita di Giuseppe Mazzini*, Milan, 1885, pp. 349 f.; and Mormina Perma, *L'idea sociale di Giuseppe Mazzini e i sistemi socialisti*, Bologna, 1907.

80. *Lettres intimes*, ed. by D. Melegari, Paris, 1895, p. 146.

81. Vincenzo Gioberti, *Del Rinnovamento civile d'Italia*, ed. by Fausto Nicolini, 3 vols., Bari, 1911, I, 349; Salvemini, *op. cit.*, pp. 101 n. 1, 173; Gentile, *op. cit.*, pp. 83, 88 ff.

82. Letter to Giorgio Pallavicino of Oct. 6, 1860, in *Ed. naz.*, LXVI, 255. For a brief analysis of Mazzini's influence in England cf. Maria Schubiger's *Giusseppe Mazzini im englischen Geistesleben* (Diss. Zurich), Uznach, 1930.

83. In his letter of April, 1867, to Ludmila Assing, the German translator of his works, Mazzini modestly expostulated for his philosophic insufficiency for a German reading public. Cited from his *Schriften*, 1868, p. iii, by Vossler, *Mazzinis politisches Denken*, p. 1. Such insufficiency was often criticized also by thoughtful Italians, among them Gentile. But for what they lacked in precision and logical cogency Mazzini's writings made up by their eloquence, sincerity, and most of all, their deep religious fervor.

84. Louis de Bonald, intellectual father of the Counterrevolution, was right in stating that "from the Gospel to the *Social Contract* books have created revolutions." Cited from his *Recherches philosophiques* by Alexandre Koyré in "Louis de Bonald," *Journal of the History of Ideas*, VIII (1946), 70 f. Despite de Bonald's advice of strict censorship, Rousseau's writings in post-Revolutionary France enjoyed great popularity and a governmental inquiry showed that in seven years (1817-24) their sales exceeded half a million volumes. Cf. Albert Schinz, *Etat présent des travaux sur J.-J. Rousseau*, New York, 1941, p. 14. Schinz's survey, incidentally, is in itself an eloquent testimony to the sustained interest in Rousseau's work in recent generations.

85. Herder, who fully realized the difficulty of describing in words the "profundity" of each people's national feeling, also observed that "every nationality bears in itself the focus of its own happiness." Cf. his "Philosophie der Geschichte zur Bildung

der Menschheit" in *Sämmtliche Werke*, ed. by Bernhard Suphan, 33 vols., Berlin, 1877-1913, V, 502, 509; "Ideen zur Philosophie der Geschichte der Menschheit," *ibid.*, XIV, 227 f. Cf. also Robert Reinhold Ergang, *Herder and the Foundations of German Nationalism*, New York, 1931.

86. *Considérations*, XII in Rousseau's *Political Writings*, II, 491.

87. Cf. Henri Hauser, *Le principe de nationalités: Ses origines historiques*, Paris, 1916, p. 24. As a Frenchman Fustel de Coulanges was perfectly right in reprimanding Theodor Mommsen for not being aware that "it is neither race nor language that makes nationality." Cited by Michael Tierney in his "Nationalism: A Survey," *Studies*, XXXIV (1945), 475. It was, indeed, a sign of the complete Teutonization of French "integral nationalism," when Charles Maurras declared, "We have not willed our nationality . . . the *patrie* is a natural or, what is the same, an historic society. We no more choose our fatherland than we select our father or mother." Cf. *Mes idées politiques*, Paris, 1937, p. 252, and below Chap. III. Cf. also the naïve illustration of subconscious French feelings in Bismarck's letter of Sept. 15, 1855, in *Briefe an den General Leopold von Gerlach*, ed. by Horst Kohl, Berlin, 1896, pp. 246 f.

88. Hauser, *op. cit.*, pp. 20 ff.; Rühs, *Das Verhältniss Holsteins und Schleswigs zu Deutschland und Dänemark*, Berlin, 1817; Treitschke, *Politik*, 2 vols., Leipzig, 1897-98, I, 24; Joachimsen, *op. cit.*, p. 97. Meinecke's description of Ranke's "nationalist sentiment" and of its cultural and "pantheistic" mainsprings applies to many other German nationalists as well. "Here it is not stated," says Meinecke, "that a nation is [the group] that wants to be a nation—but on the contrary: a nation is regardless of whether the individuals composing it wish to belong to it or not. It rests not upon free self-determination, but upon predetermination." Cf. *Weltbürgertum*, p. 290.

89. Cf. especially the discussion between Karl Kautsky and Otto Bauer in the socialist weekly, *Die Neue Zeit*, XXVI, Pt. 1, (1908). Kautsky in his essay "Nationalität und Internationalität" published there in Ergänzungsheft no. 1 criticized Bauer's *Die Nationalitätenfrage und die Sozialdemokratie* for repudiating language as the main

criterion of nationality. In his "Bemerkungen zur Nationalitätenfrage" (pp. 792-802), Bauer vigorously defended his position. The debate was concluded by Kautsky's final note which stressed that, despite this sharp theoretical divergence, he largely agreed with Bauer in the practical solution of national problems.

90. Giuseppe Prezzolini, *Fascism*, English transl., New York [n.d.], p. vii.

91. Paul Janet, *Histoire de la science politique dans ses rapports avec la morale*, 2 vols., 3d ed., Paris, 1887, II, 546 f.; Novalis, *Blüthenstaub* (1798) in *Schriften*, critically ed. by Ernst Heilborn, Berlin,

1901, II, Pt. 1, p. 31: Burke "has written a revolutionary book against the Revolution." Cf. also Vossler, *Amerikanische Revolutionsideale*, pp. 18 f.

92. Jefferson, letters to Edward Carrington of Jan. 16, 1787, and John Hollins of May 5, 1811, in *Writings*, II, 100; V, 597. The dichotomy between Jefferson's general insistence on freedom of the press and his frequent objections to its contemporary abuses is analyzed in Frank L. Mott's *Jefferson and the Press*, Baton Rouge, 1943.

93. Jefferson, "Inaugural Address" 1801 in *Writings*, VIII, 3 f.

94. Maritain, *Three Reformers*, p. 155.

Chapter III

Nationalist Epigoni

1. Cf. William Curt Buthman, *The Rise of Integral Nationalism in France*, New York, 1939, pp. 14 f.

2. Lord Hugh Cecil, *Nationalism and Catholicism*, London, 1919, p. 30. Maurras himself must have been surprised to find his incoherent ideas described as a system of "hierarchies and certainties" by the academician, Joseph de Pesquidoux, who as an adolescent had already been indoctrinated in Maurras's teachings by his royalist father. Cf. his Preface to Maurice Clavière's *Charles Maurras ou la restauration des valeurs humains*, Paris, 1939, pp. 7, 11.

3. *Romantisme et révolution*, Paris, 1925, pp. 5 f.; "Sur les idées de Rousseau," *Revue critique des idées et des livres*, XVII (1912), 648-52. In that issue of June 25, 1912, largely dedicated to the debunking of Rousseau, Maurras's friends, Paul Bourget, Pierre Gilbert, etc., made a concerted attack "contre la glorification de Rousseau." They also republished a series of older appraisals of the Genevan's works by such opponents as de Bonald, Proudhon and Lemaître and reproduced Barrès's anti-Rousseauan harangue at the Chamber of Deputies. Cf. also Maurras's *Dictionnaire politique et critique* (articles selected by Pierre Chardon), 5 vols., Paris, 1932-34, V, 130 ff. (especially p. 131 citing excerpts from Maurras's article in *Action française* of June 28, 1912); and Schinz, *op. cit.*, pp. 76 f.

4. *Quand les Français ne s'aimaient pas: chronique d'une renaissance, 1895-1905*, Paris, 1916, pp. 27 ff.

5. *La démocratie religieuse*, Paris, 1921, pp. 26, 190, 195, 223 ff., 235; *Romantisme et révolution*, pp. 4 f.; *Enquête sur la monarchie*, Paris, 1925, p. 506. Cf. also various other passages excerpted in *Dictionnaire politique*, IV, 197 ff.; and Buthman, *op. cit.*,

pp. 151 f., 156, 283. Maurras was deeply skeptical about the possibility of harmonious coëxistence of Protestants and Catholics in any country. He therefore discounted the progress of Catholicism in the United States, the "American-Catholic façade," and predicted that the descendants of Puritans would soon resume their traditional antipapism. "Blood will flow perhaps." *La démocratie rel.*, pp. 321 f.

6. *Ibid.*, pp. 182, 194; *Enquête*, pp. 481, 505; J. Vialatoux, *La doctrine catholique et l'école de Maurras*, Lyons, 1927, p. 25.

7. Georges Bernanos, *La grande peur des bien-pensants: Edouard Drumont*, Paris, 1931, p. 128.

8. *La démocratie religieuse*, pp. 185, 199, 226, 334. In the midst of the acrimonious debate on separation of state and church Maurras quoted Waldeck-Rousseau's earlier statement concerning the inner affinities between Protestantism and liberalism since both are based on the principle of free inquiry. *Ibid.*, p. 247 n. 1. Cf. also Carlton J. H. Hayes, *The Historical Evolution of Modern Nationalism*, New York, 1931, p. 204 f. Despite Dreyfus's retrial and complete rehabilitation, the *Action française* never conceded his innocence, preferring to pick minor flaws in the presentation of the affair's chief recorder, Joseph Reinach. Cf. e.g. Henri Dutrait-Crozon, *Joseph Reinach historien*, Paris, 1905, which Maurras provided with an extensive foreword. Cf. also *La démocratie rel.*, p. 334. Without Maurras, asserts Albert Thibaudet, "the Dreyfus case might have been but a three-act play . . . he kept it going for five acts, indeed, never let it die." Cf. *Les idées de Charles Maurras*, 6th ed., Paris, 1920 (in his *Trente ans de vie française*, I), p. 86; Denis W. Brogan, "The Nationalist Doctrine of M. Charles Maur-

ras," *Politica*, I (London, 1934-35), 290.

9. Max Nordau, "Etudes littéraires," *La Grande Revue*, VI, Pt. 3 (1902), 490.

10. Brogan, *op. cit.*, p. 295; Urbain Gohier, *Les gens de roi: Sidi Maurras ben Ma'aras, ou le maure pion*, Paris, 1926.

11. Paul Bourget, *Outre-mer* (*Notes sur l'Amérique*), 2 vols., Paris, 1895, II, 319 ff. (modified in the English transl.). Maurras, going beyond Bourget, believed that there was an essential difference between the French and American national spirits: "It suffices to read some of the more beautiful discourses held by American bishops." *La démocratie rel.*, p. 356; *Quand les Français ne s'aimaient pas*, pp. 359 ff.

12. Buthman, *op. cit.*, pp. 231 f., summarizing two articles on the Jewish question published in *La Gazette de France* of Jan. 4 and 7, 1899; *La démocratie rel.*, p. 351.

13. *Ibid.*, pp. 214, 247 ff., 342. Here, too, Maurras vigorously denied that his views had anything in common with the "simpleton deductions" of racial antisemitism which had "poisoned Germany for the last fifty or sixty years." Cf. *Action française* of Oct. 27, 1930; *Dictionnaire politique*, II, 368 n. 1.

14. *La démocratie rel.*, pp. 316, 320, 342; *Dictionnaire politique*, V, 185 ff. (especially pp. 189 f.). Cf. also Charles A. Micaud, *The French Right and Nazi Germany 1933-1939*, Durham, N. C., 1943, p. 17. Maurras and his associates often invoked the shades of Proudhon whom Louis Dimier included among *Les Maîtres de la Contre-Révolution au dix-neuvième siècle*, Paris, 1917. There certainly was much in both Proudhon's socialism and his opposition to Napoleon III's policy of liberation of European nationalities to recommend him to the French Right of the twentieth century. Cf. J. Salwyn Schapiro, "Pierre Joseph Proudhon, Harbinger of Fascism," *American Historical Review*, L (1944-45), 714-37. Sorel's syndicalism likewise often appealed to them. Cf. Waldemar Gurian, *Der integrale Nationalismus in Frankreich. Charles Maurras und die Action française*, Frankfort, 1931, pp. 113 ff. We see here the usual conglomeration of muddled, undigested, and often contradictory socialist doctrines found useful in combating both entrenched capitalism and its Marxist assailants.

15. *La démocratie rel.*, pp. 295, 405 ff., 523.

16. *Lettre du 12. octobre addressée par*

Charles Maurras à Sa Sainteté de Pape Pie XI, Versailles, 1927 (includes Gasparri's reply). Vaugeois's definition was cited with approval by Maurras himself in his *Au signe de flore: la fondation de l'Action française, 1898-1900*, Paris, 1931, p. 122. For the "goddess of France" cf. the same article in which the term "integral nationalism" was coined, *Le Soleil* of March 2, 1900; Buthman, *op. cit.*, p. 111. As early as 1913 Count Bernard de Vesius published a fairly extensive list of *Action* converts to Catholicism in his "La foi catholique et l'Action française," *L'Action française*, of May 23. Maurras considered this article sufficiently significant to reprint it in the appendix to his *La démocratie rel.*, pp. 548 f. Cf. also Clavière's testimony, *op. cit.*, p. 203. The dichotomy in the mutual relations between Maurras and the Church is discussed on the basis of a vast controversial literature by Gurian in *Der integrale Nationalismus*, pp. 53 n. 2, 54, 101 ff. Cf. also E. Renauld, *L'Action française contre l'église catholique et contre la monarchie*, Paris, 1936.

17. *La démocratie rel.*, p. 244; *L'Europe Nouvelle* of July 29, 1939, cited by Micaud, *op. cit.*, p. 225.

18. *De la colère et la justice. Reflexions sur un disastre*, Geneva, 1942, p. 43. With his customary opportunism Maurras, in his prefatory "Letter to a Genevan Magistrate," admitted that Swiss democracy had been quite successful. But he expostulated that this success had been possible only because the Swiss had retained their military spirit, their religious and social morality, and a deep reverence for their past. All of these had been ruined in France by the progressive parties. *De la colère*, p. 12. Maurras now stands formally convicted of responsibility for the arrest and torture of Frenchmen and of having publicly denounced Georges Bidault and other resistance leaders as "De Gaullist conspirators." Cf. *New York Times* of Sept. 21, 1944.

19. Martire, "I culti acattolici e l'articolo I° del Concordato," *Corriere della Sera* of May 7, 1929, cited by Mario Missiroli in his *Date a Cesare. La politica religiosa di Mussolini*, Rome, 1929, pp. 159 ff.; Mussolini's speech on "The Tasks of Fascismo" delivered at Trieste on Sept. 20, 1920, and reprinted in *Mussolini As Revealed in His Political Speeches*, ed. by Baron Bernardo Quaranta di San Severino, London, 1923, p.

109; Prezzolini, *op. cit.*, pp. 118 f. (translator's note). Mussolini's figures were justified in so far as Italian emigration from 1901 to 1914 alone had averaged more than 600,000 a year, although there was also a substantial reimmigration. Cf. Robert F. Foerster, *The Italian Emigration of Our Time*, Cambridge, 1919, pp. 7 ff. Even nationalists like Scipio Sighele proudly stressed the difference between their nationalist doctrine and that of the reactionary clerical, legitimist and antisemitic *Action française*. Cf. his *Pagine Nazionaliste*, Milan, 1910, p. 218. Cf. also Arcangelo William Salomone, *Italian Democracy in the Making . . . 1900-1914*, Philadelphia, 1945, pp. 81 ff., 93 n. 41, 96, discussing also Italian freemasonry and Mussolini's early opposition to it.

20. Mussolini, *The Doctrine of Fascism*, Florence, 1936, pp. 7 f., 23, 50; Carlini, *Filosofia e religione nel pensiero di Mussolini*, Rome, 1934, p. 31.

21. Georges Sorel is reputed to have called him a "new condottiere" as early as 1912. Cf. Herbert W. Schneider, *Making the Fascist State*, New York, 1928, p. 10; and the editor's remark in Mussolini's *Speeches*, p. 143.

22. Mussolini, *Scritti e discorsi*, definitive ed., vols. I-XI, Milan, 1934-38, VII, 230; cited briefly in the notes to his *Doctrine*, p. 51. Mussolini used with predilection his own revolutionary, and in some respects anti-Christian calendar. When he published, for one example, his speeches on *Gli Accordi del Laterano*, 2d ed., Rome, 1929 (with a documentary appendix), the Preface reproduced in facsimile not only his signature, but also the date, "Roma 14 giugno dell' anno VII."

23. *Speeches*, pp. 201 ff.; Prezzolini, *op. cit.*, p. 135. There were many straws in the wind indicating the Vatican's readiness to compromise the issue. See below Chap. IV.

24. Gentile, *Che cosa è il fascismo*, English excerpts in Schneider, *op. cit.*, p. 352. Cf. also *ibid.*, pp. 106, 221. In time Mussolini's portrait or portraits far overshadowed both the royal picture and the crucifix.

25. Cf. Mussolini's speech before the Chamber on May 13, 1929, in *Gli Accordi del Laterano*, pp. 64 ff., 82 ff. In view of the lira's depreciation the total amounted to only some 400,000,000 gold lire or less than $80,000,000. Though doubtless temporarily helpful to the Holy See, this comparative pittance was not a weighty inducement to its renunciation of major permanent claims. The events connected with the Franciscan celebration of that year, though undoubtedly a source of great annoyance to the Church, served to publicize widely its rapprochement with fascism. On the day following the celebration at Assisi the Fascists staged a big Mussolini festival in near-by Perugia (Oct. 4-5, 1926). "The net effect of the whole performance, for the thousands who had gathered in that region from all over Italy, was to make it a two-day celebration . . . the first devoted to the great Italian saint of the Roman Church and the second to the *Duce* of Imperial Rome re-arisen." Schneider, *op. cit.*, p. 226. At that time a Catholic priest, Paolo Ardali, wrote an essay on *San Francesco e Mussolini* in which he compared the self-abnegation and other virtues of the Duce to those of the saint. This essay was soon reprinted, together with the same author's similar mental acrobatics, *Pio XI e Mussolini*, in one of the monthly pamphlets, *Mussoliniana*, no. 28.

26. These and other contemporary comments are summarized by Missiroli, *op. cit.*, pp. 20 ff.

27. *Gli Accordi*, pp. 88 f., 113 ff.; *L'Osservatore Romano* of June 6, 1929, cited by Missiroli, *op. cit.*, pp. 363 ff. The pope pointed out, by way of illustration, that Louis Duchesne's *Early History of the Christian Church*, Mussolini's chief authority, had ever since 1912 been on the papal Index. Curiously, in defending Italian theological learning against Mussolini's slurs, the pope reversed the tables on the nationalist exponent of Italy's cultural supremacy in all fields.

28. G. Monti, *La libertà della scuola (Principi, storia, legislazione comparata)*, Rome, 1928, pp. 22 ff.; Missiroli, *op. cit.*, pp. 256 f., 359 f.

29. *Gli Accordi*, p. 117; *Doctrine*, pp. 8 f., 10 f., 12 f., 60; Carlini, *op. cit.*, p. 50. In another speech at the Chamber Mussolini admitted that it was "curious" that in the three months between the conclusion of the Lateran Treaties and the discussion of their ratification he had suppressed more Catholic journals than in all the preceding seven years. "This was perhaps the only way of bringing them back to the correct intonation." *Gli Accordi*, p. 105. Before long fascist rowdies, unhindered by the

police, attacked the "Catholic Action's" schools and clubs. Guido Zernatto points out that the weakening of the religious antidotes to the fear of death lent deep meaning to the perspectives opened by Mussolini's peroration: "We are an immortal country of greatness and fame. Your death signifies nothing since you continue to live in this honorable society, of the past, the present and the future." The semireligious fascist roll call of the dead, when at the reading of the name of a dead man someone shouted, "present," left a lasting impression on the audience. Cf. Zernatto's "Religion and Nationality," *Thought*, XIX (1944), 474.

30. *Doctrine*, pp. 26 f., 32; *Speeches*, pp. 55 f.; *Gli Accordi*, pp. 117 ff. Mussolini personally never countenanced the anti-intellectualism of such other influential leaders as Farinacci and Finzi. Forgetting his quotation from Renan which he used to bolster his attack on the League of Nations, he assured the foreigner, Emil Ludwig, "For me the honor of the nations consists in the contribution they have severally made to human civilization." Cf. *Ludwig's Talks with Mussolini*, English transl., Boston, 1933, p. 203. Addressing the Seventh Italian Congress of Philosophy in May, 1929, he vigorously denied that fascism had lowered intellectual standards. He blamed the existing shortcomings on "the period of transition" and promised a speedy new flowering of Italian arts and philosophy. Cf. Missiroli, *op. cit.*, pp. 335 f. At the same time he insisted that Italy, an empire in the making, could not afford to indulge in universalist cultural pursuits, as could other Western nations which had already "arrived."

31. Gentile, *Che cosa* in Schneider's transl., *op. cit.*, p. 350; Mussolini's *Doctrine*, pp. 14 f.

32. Cf. Joshua Starr, "Italy's Antisemites," *Jewish Social Studies*, I (1939), 105-24.

33. Nathaniel Micklem, *National Socialism and the Roman Catholic Church*, London, 1939, p. 104, citing the *Figaro* and *Germania*; Galeazzo Ciano's *Diaries, 1939-1943*, ed. by Hugh Gibson, New York, 1946, p. 423.

34. Nietzsche, *Thus Spake Zarathustra*, X, XVIII, English transl. by Thomas Common in *The Philosophy of Nietzsche*, New York, 1937 (Modern Library), pp. 62, 80; *Beyond Good and Evil*, transl. by Helen Zimmern, *ibid.*, p. 4 (the passages here cited are somewhat modified better to convey the meaning of the original). Some of these passages are rightly brought into connection with Rosenberg by Friedrich Grünagel in his Heidelberg dissertation entitled *Rosenberg und Luther*, Bonn, 1934, pp. 4 ff. Nietzsche lent himself particularly well to propagandistic abuse because his scintillating, none-too-precise epigrams furnished sharp criticisms of the existing political and intellectual systems without necessarily harmonizing among themselves. Mrs. Foerster, Nietzsche's sister and executrix, was certainly right when, though appreciating Hitler and Mussolini's unfailing remembrance of her brother's recurrent anniversaries, she confided to a friend that neither dictator "had the ghost of an idea of what Nietzsche really meant." Cf. Cornelius Kruse's review in the *Journal of Religion*, XXI (1941), 485. For a spirited negative answer to the question, "Was Nietzsche an Anti-Christian?" cf. Roger Hazelton's essay, *ibid.*, XXII (1942), 63-88.

35. Paul de Lagarde, "Diagnose" in *Deutsche Schriften*, 4th ed., Göttingen, 1903, pp. 97, etc. Some of these Lagardian pronunciamentos are quoted with great veneration and emphasis by Alfred Rosenberg in *Der Mythus des 20. Jahrhunderts*, 177-181st ed., Munich, 1941, pp. 457 f.; and in his essay on Lagarde reprinted in *Blut und Ehre. . . . Reden und Aufsätze von 1919-1933*, Munich, 1937, pp. 228-30. Cf. also his comments on Lagarde's controversy with Abraham Berliner in *An die Dunkelmänner unserer Zeit*, 28th ed., Munich, 1935, pp. 22 ff.

36. Cited by Ismar Freund in *Der Judenhass*, Berlin, 1922, pp. 36 ff. This is a clear illustration of ruthless chauvinism bridging the chasm between nationalism and imperialism which of necessity transcended national boundaries. Cf. Hannah Arendt, "Imperialism, Nationalism, Chauvinism," *Review of Politics*, VII (1945), 441-63.

37. A. S. Duncan-Jones (Dean of Chichester), *The Struggle for Religious Freedom in Germany*, London, 1938, p. 25; Hitler, *Mein Kampf*, 706-710th ed., Munich, 1942, pp. 506 ff.

38. Waldemar Gurian, *Der Kampf um*

die Kirche im Dritten Reich, Lucerne, 1936, pp. 48 ff.

39. *Blut und Ehre*, pp. 56 f., 176 f., 334 f., 381; *Mythus*, pp. 215, 520; *Gestaltung der Idee. . . . Reden und Aufsätze von 1933-1935*, 2d ed., Munich, 1936, p. 215.

40. *Ibid.*, pp. 20 f., 37, 81, 108, 115; *Mythus*, pp. 51, 169, 186; *Blut und Glaube*, p. 245.

41. *Mythus*, pp. 13, 74 ff., 219, 604, 616 f. In contrast to this "bastardization, Orientalization and Judaization of Christianity" Rosenberg invoked (in a way reminiscent of Fichte) the testimony of the Gospel of John which "is still permeated with the aristocratic spirit." The gnostic Marcion's revolt against the God of the Old Testament is likewise gratefully recorded as that of the Nordic idea of organic stages in the world order against the Semitic conception of an arbitrary divine power. *Ibid.*, pp. 75 f. Of course, Fichte, and still more Rosenberg, vastly exaggerated "the antisemitism of the Fourth Gospel." Cf. the judicious analysis of this problem by Walter W. Sikes in the *Journal of Religion*, XXI (1941), 23-30.

42. *Mythus*, pp. 12, 70 f., 74 ff., 480, 605 f.

43. *Ibid.*, pp. 12, 87 ff., 128, 145 ff., 169 f., 215, 236 f., 243, 395 f., 597 f., 607, 624; *Blut und Ehre*, pp. 255, 338 f.; *Dunkelmänner*, pp. 56 ff. Through Karl Marx bolshevism, too, has become affected by the materialism of the Old Testament and the Talmud. *Mythus*, p. 128. Cf. also Albrecht Oepke, *Der Mythus, Rosenbergbetrachtungen*, Leipzig, 1935.

44. *Mythus*, pp. 2, 23, 33, 114, 614 f.; *Blut und Ehre*, p. 339. In invoking the testimony of the "great Isocrates" in favor of racial purity, Rosenberg conveniently overlooked the sophist's numerous anti-racialist utterances. Cf. e.g., *Panegyricus*, 50 (Loeb Classics, I, 149): "the name 'Hellenes' suggests no longer a race but an intelligence, and that title 'Hellenes' is applied rather to those who share our culture than to those who share a common blood." Cf. also Jüthner, *Hellenen und Barbaren*, pp. 34 ff.

45. *Mythus*, pp. 114, 225, 238, 258 f., 441, 445, 514, 565 ff., 598, 601, 616 f. Rosenberg, of course, never mentioned that Eckhart, whose mystic writings had long been extant only in scarce medieval manu-scripts, had borrowed certain significant doctrines from medieval Jewish philosophers, especially Ibn Gabirol and Maimonides. Cf. Joseph Koch, *Meister Eckhart und die jüdische Religionsphilosophie des Mittelalters*, Breslau, 1928. For a cautious critique of Rosenberg's tenuous interpretation of Eckhart, cf. Grünagel, *op. cit.*, pp. 47 ff. Cf. also in general E. C. Salzer, "Il maestro Eckhart nella critica tedesca contemporanea," *Rivista di filosofia neoscolastica*, XXXI (1939), 136-44.

46. *Mythus*, pp. 5 ff., 10, 107, 133, 175 f., 485 ff., 526, 531, 565, 571, 574, 607 f., 612, 620 f., 628, 635; *Blut und Ehre*, pp. 55, 58 f., 62 f., 181, 222 f., 252; *Gestaltung der Idee*, pp. 23 f., 45 f., 177; *Dunkelmänner, passim*; Oepke, *op. cit.*, p. 46.

47. Duncan-Jones, *op. cit.*, p. 300. At the Nuremberg Party Congress of 1937 Rosenberg likewise declared that "the Churches had the grand opportunity of putting their work at the disposal of Adolf Hitler, as the new state was being built up, and of marching with him. They have let the opportunity slip, and when one does not, or will not, recognize such chances of world history, one has spoken the verdict of destiny." Cited by Micklem, *op. cit.*, p. 82.

48. *Ibid.*, pp. 223 f. and *passim*; Harry C. Koenig, ed., *Principles for Peace (Selections from Papal Documents, Leo XIII to Pius XII)*, Washington, D. C., 1943, p. 539. This, as well as other passages from Koenig's compilation, has been quoted in this volume with the kind permission of the publisher, the National Catholic Welfare Conference in Washington, D.C., which is hereby gratefully acknowledged. Cf. also Duncan-Jones, *op. cit., passim*.

In the early years of the nazi regime a few mild replies by Protestant and Catholic theologians were allowed to be published, but their enforced overcautiousness made them totally inadequate. Cf. the analysis by Albert R. Chandler in his *Rosenberg's Nazi Myth*, Ithaca, 1945. The *New York Times*, of Jan. 7, 1944, reported, on behalf of the Office of War Information, about an "apparent about-face" of the nazi fanatics and their declaration that "religion has again become modern." But the excerpts from Rosenberg's Russian-language propaganda paper, *Novoe Slovo*, make no reference to Christianity, except for stating that "even those who did not believe in Christ must admit that His coming was the birth of a new era." This is a far cry from a repentant sinner's renunciation of his "religion of blood."

49. Maritain, *Three Reformers*, pp. 106, 225; Gordon H. McNeil, "The Cult of Rousseau and the French Revolution," *Journal of the History of Ideas*, VI (1945), 197-212; Karl Alexander von Reichlin-Meldegg, "Der hundertste Geburtstag Johann Gottlieb Fichtes. Eine übersichtliche Darstellung der Fichtefestschriften," *Zeitschrift für Philosophie und philos. Kritik*, n. s. XLII (1863), 247-77. "In days to come," wrote Alfred Baeumler in an admiring biography, "one will adore in Rosenberg one of the greatest German educators against halfness." Cf. his *Alfred Rosenberg und der Mythus des 20. Jahrhunderts*, Munich, 1943, p. 107, cited by Max Weinreich in his *Hitler's Professors: The Part of Scholarship in Germany's Crimes Against the Jewish People*, New York, 1946, p. 23.

50. Belloc, *The Crisis of Our Civilization*, London, 1937, p. 6. "Our own nation," writes Ernest Barker, "has suffered from its moments of aberration, in which it has dreamed sad dreams of an English God and God's Englishmen; but in its more sober and permanent disposition it has been inspired by a not ignoble notion of national duty to aid the oppressed—the persecuted Vaudois, the suffering slave, the oppressed nationality—and it has been most charac-teristically national when it has most felt such inspiration." Cf. his *Christianity and Nationality*, Oxford, 1927, p. 28.

51. Cited from Moser's *Von dem deutschen Nationalgeist* by Kohn in his *Idea of Nationalism*, p. 350.

52. H. Finke has collected a number of interesting illustrations showing the longevity of certain peculiar characteristics of European nations as reflected in the observations of their neighbors. Cf. his *Weltimperialismus*, pp. 37 f. In his "Europe: Its Traditions and Its Future," *Christendom*, XII (1942), 144-56, Christopher Dawson stresses the importance of the glorification of the soil by such writers as Maurice Barrès and D. H. Lawrence. But he adds: "It is characteristic that while the Continental European writers looked for inspiration to the subterranean forces in their own national cultures, Lawrence and the other English and American writers turned to the exotic traditions of American Indians or Negroes; a fact which suggests that the relation between the national English and American cultures is more closely related to modern cosmopolitan civilization, than are those of the Continental nationalities, so that it is not easy for the Englishman or the American to escape from modern civilization without at the same time renouncing his own past." *Ibid.*, pp. 149 f.

53. *Der Fels*, XXIX (1934-35), no. 1, quoted by Rosenberg in his *Dunkelmänner*, pp. 102 f.

Chapter IV

Catholic Interterritorialism

1. Francis Mannhardt, "The Roman Catholic Church since the Reformation," in A. S. Peake and R. G. Parsons, eds., *An Outline of Christianity: The Story of Our Civilization*, 5 vols., London, n. d., III, 119. In 1921-22 the number of episcopal sees increased from 839 to 874 and of the apostolic vicarates from 197 to 206. In 1923 three new archdioceses were established, as were 14 dioceses, one apostolic delegation, 7 vicarates and 7 prefectures. Cf. Adolf Keller and George Stewart, *Protestant Europe: Its Crisis and Outlook*, New York, 1927, p. 169. Even monastic orders and religious congregations, defying the general trend toward secularization, have been constantly expanding in modern times. "In the hundred years after 1815," says Prof. Kenneth Scott Latourette, "more new orders and congregations came into existence through which men and women devoted themselves to the Church than in any previous period of equal length." Cf. his *History of the Expansion of Christianity*, IV, 26.

2. Cf. Pius XI's encyclical, *Divini Redemptoris*, on atheistic communism of March 19, 1937, in Koenig, *op. cit.*, p. 527.

3. Pius XII's Christmas Allocution of Dec. 24, 1945, in the *New York Times* of Dec. 25, p. 14; Laurence Frederick Schmeckebier, *History of the Know Nothing Party in Maryland*, Baltimore, 1899, p. 121; Bishop Doane cited by John Ireland in his essay on "Catholicism and Americanism" (1913), reprinted in John A. Ryan and Francis J. Boland's *Catholic Principles of Politics*, New York, 1940, p. 350. This was, of course, an old argument. Cf. for instance, the interesting reasoning of Philipp Jakob Spener, the early eighteenth century German Pietist, in his *Theologische Bedenken* (4 vols., Halle, 1712-15, IV, 470) in regard

to the legal discrimination against Catholics in Protestant states. Such discrimination was justified, Spener contended, because Catholics formed everywhere a state within the state and owed allegiance to a foreign prince, the pope. Protestants, on the other hand, were unquestionably loyal even to their Catholic rulers and were, therefore, entitled to claim perfect equality. Cf. Koppel S. Pinson, *Pietism as a Factor in the Rise of German Nationalism*, New York, 1934, p. 86.

4. The petition of 1783 with the accompanying letter by John Carroll (subsequently Archbishop of Baltimore) and the negotiations leading to the papal bull of Nov. 6, 1789, are analyzed by John Gilmary Shea in his *History of the Catholic Church in the United States*, 4 vols., New York, 1886-92, II, 208 ff., 249 ff., 336 ff. Cf. also Humphrey, *Nationalism and Religion*, pp. 239 ff., 430 ff. By that time the London vicar apostolic, Msgr. Challoner, himself felt that his jurisdiction over the American colonies had outlived its usefulness and repeatedly asked to be relieved. Cf. Laval Laurent, *Quebec et l'Eglise aux Etats Unis sous Mgr. Briand et Mgr. Plessis*. Washington, D. C., 1945, pp. 14 ff. Curiously, Benjamin Franklin was ready in 1783 to accept the appointment of a Frenchman as the ecclesiastical superior of American Catholics, while the more farsighted French statesman, Vergennes, intimated his preference for a resident of the United States. Of course, the American episcopacy did not silence all criticisms and Bishop England of Charleston, chief Catholic apologist of the early nineteenth century, was forced to make impassioned professions of loyalty to the Constitution. "Let the pope and the cardinals," he declared, "and all the powers of the Catholic world united make the least

encroachment on that Constitution, we will protect it with our lives. Summon a General Council—let that Council interfere in the mode of our electing but an assistant to a turnkey of a prison—we deny the right, we reject the usurpation." Quoted by Conrad Henry Moehlman in *The Catholic-Protestant Mind*, New York, 1929, pp. 128 f. Later in the century the patriotic American teachings of Isaac Thomas Hecker (died 1888) and of such distinguished churchmen as Cardinal Gibbons, Archbishop Ireland and Bishop Keane, first rector of the Catholic University, were seized upon by European Catholic modernists and advocates of separation as a cloak for their own biases. The ensuing "Americanist controversy" lasting from 1895 to 1900 was not completely settled by Leo XIII's moderate condemnation of the new heresy in 1899. Cf. the recent analyses by Thomas T. McAvoy, "Americanism and Frontier Catholicism," *Review of Politics*, V (1943), 275-301; and "Americanism: Fact and Fiction," *Catholic Historical Review*, XXXI (1945), 133-53.

5. Ant. Huonder, *Der einheimische Klerus in den Heidenländern*, Freiburg i.B., 1909, pp. 4 ff.; Latourette, *op. cit.*, IV, 61 ff., 125 f.

6. Cited by Louis Le Fur in his *Le Saint-Siège et le Droit de Gens*, Paris, 1930, pp. 202 f. Essentially the same idea was expressed also by Bismarck when on Nov. 30, 1881, he declared at the Reichstag that he considered "the Catholic Church in Germany, together with the papal superstructure belonging to it, as a native institution of the German Confederate States or of the German Reich." It was confirmed more recently by Pius XI when, on Aug. 17, 1925, in addressing 8,000 pilgrims from Milan, he emphasized the universality of the Church rather than his personal Milanese or Italian loyalties, and by Pius XII when he assured the Noble Guards on Dec. 31, 1944, "that the love and the solicitude of the Vicar of Christ, although being himself necessarily a son of one people, does not exclude but belongs equally to the love of all in the charity of Christ." In his Christmas Allocution of 1945 Pius XII likewise asserted that, precisely because the *Sancta Mater Ecclesia* is a mother of all, "she does not and cannot belong exclusively to this or that people, nor even more to one than to others but equally to all." Cf. Hubert Bastgen, *Die*

römische Frage, Dokumente und Stimmen, 3 vols., Freiburg i.B., 1919, III, 19; Friedrich Ritter von Lama, *Papst und Kurie in ihrer Politik nach dem Weltkrieg,* Illertissen, Bavaria, 1925, pp. 662, 669; *New York Times* of Jan. 3, and Dec. 25, 1945.

7. *Ep. ad Diognetum,* V; Origen, *Contra Celsum,* VIII, 75, in Migne's *Patrologia graeca,* II, 1173; XI, 1625 ff.; Tertullian, *Apologeticum,* 32, 39, etc., in Migne's *Patrologia latina,* I; Finke, *Weltimperialismus,* p. 22. Cf. above Chap. I n. 17.

8. In Peake and Parsons, *op. cit.,* III, 125.

9. Carl Mirbt, *Quellen zur Geschichte des Papsttums und des römischen Katholizismus,* 2d ed., Tübingen, 1901, pp. 386 ff.; Eckhardt, *op. cit.,* pp. 4 f. H. Pfeiffer (in his "Katholizismus-Marxismus-Protestantismus," *Allgemeine Rundschau,* Sept. 25, 1924) has shown that the popular vote in twenty-six predominantly Protestant districts had given the Marxist parties (Socialists, Independent Socialists and Communists), an absolute majority. But in the ten overwhelmingly Catholic districts they marshaled only 31 per cent of the total vote. The ensuing deficiency of some 3,000,-000 votes reduced to 44.2 per cent their representation at the National Assembly and forced them to make substantial concessions to their Liberal and Centrist allies. Cf. Lama, *op. cit.,* pp. 87 f.

10. Ryan and Boland, *op. cit.,* p. 315. When on Nov. 1, 1939, Pius XII in his encyclical *Sertum laetitiae* extolled the American hierarchy's continued growth in numbers, affluence and effective service, he reminded it nevertheless of Leo XIII's "warnings and directions which were evidence alike of his goodwill and of his great prudence." Cf. Charles Rankin, *The Pope Speaks . . . The Words of Pius XII,* New York, 1940, pp. 199 ff. American Catholics, on the other hand, often insisted on the superiority of the American system. It was with obvious reference to Leo XIII's encyclical that Cardinal Gibbons, upon taking possession of his titular church in Rome, voiced the "deep sense of pride and gratitude that I belong to a country where the civil government holds over us the aegis of its protection without interfering with us in the legitimate exercise of our sublime mission as ministers of the Gospel of Christ." Cited by Moehlman in *The Catholic-Protestant Mind,* p. 130.

11. Walsh, *op. cit.*, pp. 37, 95 f.; J. L. de Lanessan, *L'état et les églises en France depuis les origines jusqu'à la séparation*, Paris, 1906, pp. 125 n. 1, 137. Cf. the careful analysis by André Latreille of *Le catéchisme impérial de 1806* (Paris, 1935, pp. 19 ff., 80 ff., 128 ff., 177 ff.) showing the unprecedented character of Leçon VII on the duties toward the government, its extensive application in 1806-8 and its gradual decline from 1809 on.

12. Charles Stanley Phillips, *The Church in France, 1848-70*, London, 1929, pp. 20 f.; Lanessan, *op. cit.*, pp. 154 f. Sporadic voices in favor of papal infallibility rose to a powerful chorus at the Vatican Council of 1870 which formally embodied that principle in the Catholic system of beliefs and, by the unprecedented absence of secular princes, demonstrated the exclusion of the secular arm. Cf. Johann Friedrich, *Geschichte des Vatikanischen Konzils*, 3 vols., Bonn, 1877-87.

13. Koenig, *op. cit.*, p. 119. "There were hardly any Republican priests in 1871," says Father Edouard Lecanuet in his fully documented *L'Eglise de France sous la Troisième République*, 2 vols., Paris 1907-10, I, 180. When, in 1890, Cardinal Lavigerie of Algiers sounded the keynote for the *ralliement*, he was denounced by the Catholic press "as a freemason, a 'sans-culotte' and ranked with apostates and the defrocked clergy." Cf. J. V. Ducatillon, "The Church in the Third Republic," *Review of Politics*, VI (1944), 75, 81. Cf. also Evelyn M. Acomb, *The French Laic Laws, 1879-1889*, New York, 1941.

14. (Anatole P. A.) de Monzie, *Rome sans Canossa, ou la diplomatie de la présence*, Paris, 1918; Lama, *op. cit.*, pp. 172 ff., 183 ff. De Monzie and his associates had been dissatisfied with the handling of all Allied interests by the British envoy who, on French initiative, had been sent to the Vatican at the beginning of the war. In 1918 the individual Allied powers had started to jockey for positions at the prospective peace settlements and French and British diplomacy no longer agreed on all major issues. Soon afterward, moreover, the reorganization of Catholic dioceses in reconquered Alsace-Lorraine called for direct negotiations with the Holy See. Cf. in general Jules Delahaye, *La reprise des relations diplomatiques avec le Vatican*, Paris, 1921. The attitude of the Catholic aristocracy is perhaps best illustrated by the experience of an army chaplain serving with the American Expeditionary Forces in France who one evening accompanied a group of doughboys entertained by a French marquise. The Americans, stimulated by excellent French wines, became hilarious, sang lustily some popular songs and failed to live up to a French château's customary decorum. The next morning the chaplain apologized to the marquise. To his amazement, however, he learned that she had been seriously shocked only by the singing of the "Marseillaise" which had never before been sung in her château.

15. Cf. especially Bismarck's letter to General von Gerlach of Jan. 20, 1854, in his *Briefe an . . . Gerlach*, p. 122.

16. Candea, *op. cit.*, p. 110; Koenig, *op. cit.*, p. 137; Rankin, *op. cit.*, p. 274.

17. Marriott, *op. cit.*, p. 159; Lanessan, *op. cit.*, pp. 169 f., 262 ff.; Charles L. Souvay, "The Church in Contemporary France," in Peter Guilday, ed., *The Catholic Church in Contemporary Europe, 1919-31*, New York, 1932, pp. 73 f. Italian illiteracy also had considerable bearing on the franchise. In 1871 only 1.98 per cent of the Italian people were allowed to vote, largely because the incidence of illiteracy reached 72.96 per cent. Cf. Gaetano Salvemini's Introductory Essay to Salomone, *op. cit.*, p. viii. In Belgium during the 1870's the hierarchy openly defied the government's attempts at secularization of education and forbade the Catholic pupils to attend the public schools. Nineteen hundred and thirty-six (out of a total of 2,515) municipalities established "free," i.e., parochial schools. Leo XIII's reluctant support of this ecclesiastical obstructionism led, in 1880, to the rupture of diplomatic relations between Belgium and the Vatican. There was, of course, full reconciliation after the Catholic party's electoral victory in 1884. Cf. E. Jarry, *L'église contemporaine*, Paris, 1936, pp. 101 f.; E. de Moreau, "Le parti catholique belge, des ses origines à 1884," *Nouvelle Revue théologique* (1946).

18. 268 U. S. Reports, 510-36; Greene, *Religion and the State*, pp. 126 f. Cf. also Conrad Henry Moehlman, *School and Church: The American Way*, New York, 1944, especially, pp. 123 f., 139 f.; *idem*, *The Catholic-Protestant Mind*, pp. 144 ff.

In England, the higher standards and increased costs of schoolhouses since the Balfour Act of 1902 helped accelerate the decline of registration in religious schools. Between 1896 and 1923 the number of pupils in Anglican schools diminished by 600,000; in nonconformist schools by 400,-000. The Catholic schools, however, increased their enrollment by 36,000 to a total of 425,000, a significant number in a population of 2,000,000 only. Cf. Daniel Sargent, "The Catholic Church in Contemporary England," in Guilday, op. cit., pp. 60 f.; and, more generally, Henry O. Evennett, The Catholic Schools of England and Wales, Cambridge, 1944. However, in America and elsewhere some Catholics join in deploring the nationally divisive force of the parochial school. An anonymous Catholic priest once marshaled many weighty arguments against "The Heresy of the Parochial School" in the Atlantic Monthly, CXLI (1928), 158-66 (one of three essays attempting to reappraise the relations between "The Catholic Church and the Modern World"). On the other hand, the parochial school could be made to serve nationalist purposes, inasmuch as it helped preserve German, Italian and other minority languages and cultures. When the Bennett Law, adopted by the legislature of Wisconsin in 1889, demanded that certain classes be conducted in English, the German bishops of Milwaukee became "chief defenders of the parochial schools and implicitly of the German language schools." They found little sympathy, however, among such exponents of Americanization as Archbishop Ireland. Cf. Daniel F. Reilly, The School Controversy (1891-1893), Washington, 1943, pp. 55 ff.; McAvoy in Catholic Historical Review, XXXI, 138; and John J. Meng, "Cahenslyism," ibid., pp. 389-413; XXXII (1946-47), 302-40. Other confusing crosscurrents came to the fore, e.g., during the protracted hearings before the Senate Committee on Education in 1945 on the two opposing bills S. 181 (Thomas-Hill Bill concerning federal aid to public schools) and S. 717 (Mead-Aiken Bill for aiding also nonpublic schools). Cf. the summary of the voluminous Official Record in Thomas Bledsoe's sharp attack on "The Hierarchy's School Fund Holdup," Protestant, VII, no. 4 (Oct.-Nov., 1946), 38-49.

19. Koenig, op. cit., p. 389; Ludwig Bergsträsser, Der politische Katholizismus. Dokumente seiner Entwicklung, 2 vols., Munich, 1921-23, II, 382; Duncan-Jones, op. cit., pp. 174 f.

20. Thomas Aquinas, Summa theologica, II, 2, 42, 2, 3 (in the English transl. by the Dominican Fathers, II, Pt. 2, no. 1, London, 1917, p. 518); Bastgen, op. cit., III, Pt. 1, p. 65; Leo XIII's letter Reputantibus of Aug. 20, 1901, in Koenig, op. cit., p. 106. Cf., however, the more detailed exposition of Thomas Aquinas' views in his De regimine principum, 6, culminating in the statement that "to proceed against the cruelty of tyrants is an action to be undertaken, not through the private presumption of a few, but by public authority"—a theory reminiscent of the later doctrine of limited resistance by John Calvin. Cf. Gerald B. Phelan's English transl., On the Governance of Rulers, London, 1938, p. 58.

21. Clough, Flemish Movement, pp. 94 ff., 130 ff., 222 f.

22. Benedict XV's letters, Commisso divinitus nobis, of Sept. 8, 1916, and Litteris apostolicis, of June 7, 1918; Leo XIII's letter, Saepe nos, of June 24, 1888; and encyclical, Caritatis, of March 19, 1894; Pius X's letter Poloniae populum, of Dec. 3, 1905, in Koenig, op. cit., pp. 46, 87, 117, 212, 254.

23. L'Osservatore Romano of May 13 and July 7, 1918, cited by Lama, op. cit., pp. 217 ff.; Benedict XV's letter, Nel grave periodo, of Oct. 15, 1918, in Koenig, op. cit., pp. 255 f. Of course, "the essential price of the triumph of Irish nationalism was partition." This was the first time the British government consented to partition in lieu of maintaining a binational dominion as it did in Canada or South Africa. Cf. Alfred Cobban, National Self-Determination, London, 1945, p. 85. This deviation was in part enforced by the sharp religious cleavage between Ulster and Southern Ireland.

24. Lama, op. cit., pp. 240 ff., 265 ff.

25. Keller and Stewart, op. cit., pp. 298 ff.; Lama, op. cit., pp. 281 ff., 303, 310, 313; Zernatto in Thought, XIX (1944), 477. As late as 1930, the Czech National Church still counted some 800,000 members. Cf. in general Alfred Fischel's historical sketch in Das tschechische Volk, 2 vols., Breslau, 1928, II, 27 ff.; and Hubert Beuve-Méry,

"L'Etat tchecoslovaque et les églises," *Le Monde slave*, n.s., XV, Pt. 1 (1938), 177-204.

26. Rankin, *op. cit.*, pp. 165 f.; Koenig, *op. cit.*, pp. 598 (a diluted official transl.), 757. The famous papal "Five Point Peace Plan" of 1939 demanded in Point IV special consideration of "the real needs and the just demands of nations and populations, and of racial minorities." Koenig, *op. cit.*, p. 637; Rankin, *op. cit.*, p. 232. Cf. also Pius XI's address to the Rumanian prelates of Feb. 18, 1940, *ibid.*, p. 243. The pope's Christmas Allocution of 1941 greatly displeased Mussolini, since he considered four of its five points as directed against the dictatorships. Cf. Ciano's *Diaries*, p. 424.

27. Rousseau in a note to his *Contrat social* in *Political Writings*, II, 127 n. 1; Jarry, *op. cit.*, p. 82. One must also bear in mind the clergy's numerical strength, e.g., the ratio of 1:55 to the rest of the population, found in the Papal States in 1862. Henry Charles Lea, "The Religious Reform Movement in Italy" (1868) in *Minor Historical Writings and Other Essays*, Philadelphia, 1942, p. 278.

28. Carlton J. H. Hayes, *France, A Nation of Patriots*, New York, 1930, pp. 105 f. (citing also Poincaré's reminder to the French Parliament of 1923 concerning the French missionaries' "radiating French civilization"); Latourette, *op. cit.*, pp. 60 ff.; Lama, *op. cit.*, pp. 56 ff.

29. Shea, *op. cit.*, II, 148 ff., 352 f.; Victor Coffin, "The Province of Quebec and the Early American Revolution," *Bulletin of the University of Wisconsin*, I, Pt. 3 (1896), 275-562; Humphrey, *op. cit.*, pp. 125 ff., 425 f.; Greene, *Religion and the State*, pp. 74 f. The French-Canadian clergy, however, always felt more reassured in facing the Protestant majority under British imperial overlordship than in a wholly sovereign Canadian republic. Cf. Georges Vattier, *Essai sur la mentalité canadienne-française*, Paris, 1927, pp. 315 f. Reminiscing on his years of activity at the Prussian Diet, August Reichensperger admitted that "anything referring to Poles attracted my special attention. I do not wish to conceal the fact that I was influenced by religious sympathies. . . . In the Grand Duchy of Posen denationalization had often proceeded hand in hand with decatholicization." Cf. the

excerpts from his "Survey" written in 1864 in Bergsträsser, *op. cit.*, I, 251. A similar pro-Polish stand was taken at the Frankfort National Assembly by such Catholic spokesmen as Döllinger and Clemens, cf. Roy Pascal, "The Frankfort Parliament, 1848, and the *Drang nach Osten*," *Journal of Modern History*, XVIII (1946), 113.

30. Bergsträsser, II, 74 ff., 140 f., 146 ff.; Gurian, *Kampf*, pp. 18 f. Less successful were Bismarck's earlier attempts to induce the papacy to influence Centrist policies and to declare publicly that the "highest authority of the Church did not approve of the aggressions against the state in which respectable members of the Church had become involved by malcontent laymen." Cf. Bismarck's letter to Tauffkirchen, the Bavarian minister in Rome of Jan. 12, 1872, in his *Gesammelte Werke*, Berlin, 1924-25, VIc, no. 18, pp. 15 f.; and, more generally, E. L. Woodward, "The Diplomacy of the Vatican under Popes Pius IX and Leo XIII," *Journal of the British [Royal] Institute of International Affairs*, III-IV (1924-25), 127 f., 130 ff.; (this essay was brought more up to date by Algernon Cecil in his "Vatican Policy in the Twentieth Century," *ibid.*, IV, 1924-25, 1-29); Francis A. Arlinghaus, "The Kulturkampf and European Diplomacy, 1871-75," *Catholic Historical Review*, XXVIII (1942), 340 ff.

31. Encyclical *Etsi nos* of Feb. 15, 1882, in Koenig, *op. cit.*, pp. 15 f. Cf. also Pius XII's more recent remark in his encyclical *Summi pontificatus* of Oct. 20, 1939: "Italy, always a fruitful seed-ground for the Catholic faith which the Prince of the Apostles planted there, has, since the Providential signing of the Lateran Treaty, held a place of honor among the states which have regularized relations with the Roman Bishop." Rankin, *op. cit.*, p. 155.

32. Auguste Leman, *Urbain VIII et la rivalité de la France et de la Maison d'Autriche de 1631 à 1635*, Lille, 1920; Eckhardt, *op. cit.*, pp. 63, 75, 77, 147, 212 f.; Lanessan, *op. cit.*, pp. 121 f. Napoleon's success in deluding the Catholic world was truly amazing. Even in the far-off Danubian principalities Catholic priests and missionaries hailed him as liberator of the Church and conducted *Te Deum* services on his ascension to the imperial throne. Cf. Candea, *op. cit.*, p. 131.

33. Consalvi to Cardinal Pacca, Vienna, Sept. 26, 1814. Cf. Erwin Ruck, *Die römische Kurie und die deutsche Kirchenfrage auf dem Wiener Kongress*, Basel, 1917.

34. Jarry, *op. cit.*, pp. 6, 11; Lanessan, *op. cit.*, p. 196. Lanessan points out that not only could the Franco-German War have been averted, if France had accepted the offered Triple Alliance with Austria and Italy in return for Rome, but that on July 22, 1871, after her disastrous defeat, 350 members of the French National Assembly still voted to forward to the Ministry of Foreign Affairs a petition demanding the restoration of the pope's temporal powers. Bismarck, on the other hand, explained to the British ambassador, Lord Augustus Loftus, on Nov. 2, 1867, that his representative at the suggested European Conference on the Roman question would have to be but "a passive listener," for "Prussia could not fight against the pope, on account of her Catholic subjects, neither could she fight for the support of the papacy, as she would thereby risk offending her Protestant subjects." Cf. Loftus, *Diplomatic Reminiscences, 1862-1879*, 2d series, London, 1894, I, Pt. 2, p. 197.

35. Francesco Salata, *Per la storia diplomatica della questione romana*, Milan, 1929, I, 134 ff.; Koenig, *op. cit.*, p. 290; Salomone, *Italian Democracy*, pp. 35 ff. In the late nineteenth century even the visit of a Protestant monarch (e.g., that of William II in 1888) was viewed by Catholics with considerable misgivings. The German Center party would have preferred if the emperor had called on the Italian king in Florence or Milan. Cf. Windthorst's cautious instructions to the Centrist press of September, 1888, in Bergsträsser, *op. cit.*, II, 156 f. The idea of a papal asylum outside Italy had first been suggested during the critical year of 1870 when Archbishop Ledochowski, allegedly acting on Pius IX's orders, broached the subject of German hospitality. According to Grand Duke Frederick I of Baden, Bismarck, with his usual cynicism, weighed the advantages of a temporary papal residence on German soil, as "direct observation of Rome's priestly regime would help cure the Germans." Cf. Bastgen, *op. cit.*, III, Pt. 1, pp. 112 ff.; and, in general, Salata, *op. cit.*, pp. 261 ff.; Arlinghaus, *op. cit.* There is no evidence, however, to support Benedetto Croce's theory (advanced in his *Storia d'Italia dal*

1871 al 1915, 2d ed., Bari, 1928, p. 34) that the papacy refused to accept the Law of Guarantees because it feared to underscore thereby its Italian character in the eyes of foreign Catholics. It evidently was not prepared to relinquish those claims to temporal power which Pius IX had restated with so much vigor only a few years before. Cf. Samuel William Halperin, *Italy and the Vatican at War: A Study of the Relations from the Outbreak of the Franco-Prussian War to the Death of Pius IX*, Chicago, 1939; *idem*, *The Separation of State and Church in Italian Thought from Cavour to Mussolini*, Chicago, 1937; Daniel A. Binchy, *The Church and State in Fascist Italy*, New York, 1942.

36. Art. 15 of the Treaty of London of April 26, 1915; Eckhardt, *op. cit.*, pp. 237 ff., 243 f.; Koenig, *op. cit.*, p. 550; Art. 24 of the Lateran Treaty. The papacy's changed attitude to the League in the mid-1930's is reflected in William Teeling's testimony of having "heard it openly commented on at the Vatican that it is impossible for Rome to look with any favor on a League of Nations run by Russians, by the Protestant Great Powers, and by an anti-clerical Power." Cf. his *The Pope in Politics, The Life and Work of Pope Pius XI*, London, 1937, p. 253.

37. Portalis' speech is cited from *Rétablissement de la religion en France*, Leyden, 1802, pp. 8 f. by Masson, *op. cit.*, III, 262. As far back as 1311, however, the Council of Vienne heard the complaint from the bishops of the archdiocese of Sens that men and women of all classes attached so little importance to anathemas that one seldom met a person hesitating to live under a ban for many years. Cf. Ewald Müller, *Das Konzil von Vienne 1311-1312*, Münster, 1934, p. 458 (also *ibid.*, pp. 443, 471); Lanessan, *op. cit.*, p. 17.

38. Bruno Bauer, *Einfluss des englischen Quäkertums auf die deutsche Kultur und auf das englisch-russische Project einer Weltkirche*, Berlin, 1878, pp. 200 ff.; Allen Sinclair Will, *Life of Cardinal Gibbons, Archbishop of Baltimore*, 2 vols., New York, 1922, I, 569 ff. Gibbons himself felt the need of explaining his broad-mindedness to the Vatican. On Oct. 26, 1893, he recorded in his Journal: "Sent Cardinal Rampolla a long statement regarding the work of the Parliament of Religions in Chicago, and the hopes entertained of its results." *Ibid.*, p.

573. The pope was under considerable pressure for Gibbons' and Ireland's reconciliation with America's republicanism and "natural virtues" was often invoked by Continental advocates of separation of state and church. Cf. McAvoy in *Catholic Historical Review*, XXXI, 139; Vincent F. Holden, "A Myth in 'L'Américanisme,' " *ibid.*, pp. 154-70.

39. *The Great Encyclical Letters of Pope Leo XIII*, translated from approved sources with Preface by Rev. John J. Wynne, New York, 1930, pp. 350 ff.; Lama, *op. cit.*, pp. 657 ff.; *Sixteen Encyclicals of His Holiness Pope Pius XI*, Washington, D. C., 1926-37, no. 2 (transl. by Rev. R. A. McGowan), p. 14; Rankin, *op. cit.*, pp. 50 f. Cf. also *ibid.*, pp. 65 f.; W. H. McLellan, *The Catholic Attitude towards Conferences on Christian Unity*, New York, 1927; Nils Karlström, "Rom und die Stockholmer Bewegung. Ein chronologischer Beitrag," *Kyrkohystorisk Årsskrift*, XXXI (1931), 100-12 (with documents of 1918). Some Catholic leaders, to be sure, evinced considerable sympathy toward the ecumenical movement. A German Jesuit, Max Pribilla, wrote about it with much understanding in his book, *Um kirchliche Einheit — Stockholm-Lausanne-Rom. Geschichtlich-theologische Darstellung der neueren Einigungsbestrebungen*, Freiburg i.B., 1929. Another, more outspoken, *Catholic Plea for Reunion*, however, published by a Jesuit (Father Jerome or Albert Gille) in London, 1934, led to the author's forcible retirement from the Society of Jesus, just as the earlier appeal of a priest, J. D∪ggan (*Steps towards Reunion*, London, 1897), had been placed on the papal Index. The foreboding of an eminent English Jesuit proved right, when upon reading Gille's chapters he exclaimed, "Thank Heaven for the book, but God help the writer." Cf. Gille's Prefatory Note and Henry R. T. Brandreth, *Unity and Reunion: A Bibliography*, London, 1945, nos. 539, 845. Cf. also below Chap. V. What the official Church understood by collaboration had already come to the fore during the convocation of the Vatican Council. In June, 1868, both the Eastern and the Protestant bishops were asked to attend—on Catholic terms. Of course, they refused. Similarly when Leo XIII, in his encyclicals, *Provida matris*, of May 5, 1895, and *Divinum illud munus*, of May 9, 1897, set aside the days before Pentecost for annual prayers to "hasten the work of reconciliation with our separated brethren," he had in mind reconciliation on the basis of Catholic doctrine alone. More recently, the incipient understanding with the Greek Orthodox Church illustrated by the Constantinople patriarch's unprecedented willingness to be represented at Pius XII's coronation (Rankin, p. 48) has been exposed to severe shocks by the renewed attacks of the reconstituted Russian Orthodox Church on the Vatican, the Soviet Union's most implacable enemy. Cf. also M. J. Congar, *Divided Christendom: A Catholic Study of the Problem of Reunion* (English transl., London, 1919), culminating in the assertions, "with the East we firmly believe that some day we shall have complete reunion. Where Protestants are concerned the outlook is very different. . . . Reunion will only become possible when Protestantism has got rid of those fundamental oppositions, which, with the intention of doing Him honor, belittle and defame the creative operations of God. . . . Of reunion, as of the second Coming of the Lord, we can only say that God alone knows the time, and it is in vain for us to try to determine the day or the means" (pp. 273 ff.).

40. Pius XI's address to the diplomatic corps of March 9, 1929, cited by Missiroli, *op. cit.*, pp. 18 ff.; Acton, *op. cit.*, p. 206; Koenig, *op. cit.*, p. 340; Ryan and Boland, *op. cit.*, p. 124.

41. Benedict XV's encyclical, *Ad beatissimi*, of Nov. 1, 1914, in Koenig, *op. cit.*, p. 136; Rankin, *op. cit.*, pp. 272 f. (although invoking the shades of Leo XIII, this encyclical repeated with less restraint the hackneyed arguments of liberal economists against the "sophistries of demagogues"); Pius XI's remark quoted, after an interview with the pope, by Abbé Cardijn, founder of the French association of Catholic Working Youth. Cf. Jacques Maritain, *Christianity and Democracy*, English transl., New York, 1944, p. 28.

42. Edmund A. Walsh, "The Catholic Church in Contemporary Russia" in Guilday, *op. cit.*, p. 265; Rankin, *op. cit.*, p. 84. Cf. below Chap. VI.

43. Benedict XV's motu proprio, *Bonum sane* on Devotion to St. Joseph, of July 25, 1920; Pius XI's address at the International Catholic Press Exposition of May 12, 1936; his encyclical, *Divini Redemptoris*, of March 19, 1937; and his address in Spanish, *Con*

inmenso gozo, in Koenig, *op. cit.,* pp. 263, 294, 510 ff.; Rankin, *op. cit.,* pp. 134 ff.; *Patriotism, Nationalism and the Brotherhood of Man,* Report of the Committee on National Attitudes (Carlton J. H. Hayes, chairman) of the Catholic Association for International Peace, Washington, 1937, pp. 36 ff. Popular propaganda was likewise very effective. A pamphlet, entitled *The Soviet Campaign against God* and published by the British Catholic Truth Society, became a best seller. With 50,000 copies distributed in 1930, it ranked only behind the prayer book in the sale of Catholic publications. Cf. Sargent in Guilday, *op. cit.,* pp. 63 f. The Vatican must have realized that in the Spanish question it did not command the undivided allegiance of Catholic masses. George Seldes pointed out, on the basis of contemporary polls, that the Spanish issue had created a deep cleavage between the American hierarchy, which was almost unanimously pro-Franco, and the Catholic laity, of which a third could not make up its mind, while among the rest 42 per cent voiced pro-Loyalist sentiments. Cf. *The Catholic Crisis,* New York, 1939, pp. 4, 11 f. The papacy's protracted silence in the face of Mussolini's unprovoked aggression in Ethiopia, underscored by widespread rumors that it had influenced some Latin-American republics to vote against League "sanctions," not only hampered Catholic missionary efforts among the colored peoples, but also antagonized numerous antifascist Catholics. Cf. Teeling, *op. cit.,* pp. 130, 253.

44. Gurian, *Kampf,* pp. 90 ff.; Micklem, *op. cit.,* p. 104.

45. Koenig, *op. cit.,* p. 501; Duncan-Jones, *op. cit.,* pp. 225 ff.; Ryan and Boland, *op. cit.,* p. 125. Britain's Cardinal Hinsley, too, declared in a letter to the London *Times* that "in the name of reason and of faith, in the cause of humanity and religion, the creed of nazism must be denounced as the archenemy of mankind." Incidentally this was not the first time that Pius XI and his secretary of state, Pacelli, employed drastic means in evading totalitarian repression. In countering Mussolini's order dissolving the Catholic Action groups in Italy, they convoked an international congress of Catholic Action by an encyclical flown to Paris by two young monsignori (one of them, Francis Spellman, the present Archbishop of New York) and released to newspapermen before Mussolini's

henchmen were able to interfere. Cf. Rankin, *op. cit.,* pp. 11 f., 115 f.

46. Camille M. Cianfarra, *The Vatican and the War,* New York, 1944, pp. 269 f. Although written in the vein of an apologia, this volume reproduces a number of interesting observations from close range. Only churchmen living in close proximity with the Nazis, like the Bishop of Linz (Austria), realized at an early date that nazism was more dangerous than communism. Cf. Karl Rosenfelder's chronicle in *Nationalsozialistische Monatshefte,* VIII (1937), 836 (citing other Austrian and Swiss "criminal" utterances in the same vein). Spain's closest neighbor, Portugal, likewise saw more clearly the dangerous implications of the Franco rebellion. Cf. the discourse of Cardinal Cerejeira delivered in Lisbon on Nov. 18, 1938, and cited by Jacques Maritain in *The Twilight of Civilization,* English transl., New York, 1943, p. 49. Taught by bitter experience, Catholic members of the French Resistance movement likewise argued, at least on opportunist grounds, that one must oppose first the nazi stranglehold as "the more immediately threatening . . . while Bolshevism (which must be opposed afterwards) is at the other end of Europe." Cited from the underground paper, *Courrier français du témoignage chrétien,* by Georgette Vignaud in "The Catholics in France from the Autumn of 1942 to the Invasion," *Review of Politics,* VI (1944), 523.

47. Duncan-Jones, *op. cit.,* pp. 158 f. During the war it was the papacy rather than the German Church that kept on protesting against the nazi closing of churches under the pretext that they were too distant from air-raid shelters and the elimination of all but five Catholic magazines because of the paper shortage. Cf. Cianfarra, *op. cit.,* pp. 190, 219 f. Cf., however, the data on "Catholic Resistance in Nazi Germany," assembled by F. Baerwald in *Thought,* XX (1945), 217-34.

48. Vignaud in *Review of Politics,* VI, 517; George Doherty, "The Cross and the Sword: A Catholic View of Argentina," *Harper's Magazine* of January, 1945, pp. 109 ff. The somewhat analogous distortions of the venerable idea of penitence and other words of the same kind in Pétain's "pharisaical ideology," were characterized by Maritain as "synonyms of sickly self-accusation which is demanded of enslaved people in

order to furnish the really guilty ones with an alibi." Cf. his *Christianity and Democracy*, p. 20. Cf. also his *Twilight of Civilization*, pp. 45 f.; Vignaud (*or* Vignaux), "The Catholics in France since the Armistice," *Review of Politics*, V (1943), 194-215; Peter Masten Dunne, "Church and State in Argentina," *ibid.*, VII (1945), 395-417. Extremists, like Roberto Farinacci, denounced the papal organ, *L'Osservatore Romano*, of being "the evident mouthpiece of the Jews." Cianfarra, *op. cit.*, pp. 220 f.

49. Pius XI's encyclicals, *Ubi arcano Dei*, of Dec. 23, 1922, and *Studiorum ducem*, of June 29, 1923, in Koenig, *op. cit.*, pp. 343, 347, 364; *Civiltà cattolica* of 1929, cited by Missiroli, *op. cit.*, pp. 352 f. In his Allocution to Student Priests of July 12, 1939, Pius XII advocated "freedom of research," provided it led to a better understanding of Aquinas. For "it is characteristic of Thomas Aquinas to shed light on the truths that are accessible to human reason and to gather them into compact unity; to make them adaptable to the illustration and defense of dogma; and to dispose efficiently of fundamental errors that are of all times." Rankin, *op. cit.*, pp. 140 f. Cf. also the pope's injunctions of the same year to the American hierarchy, *ibid.*, pp. 208 f. Curiously, in 1887 when the "dark ages" were still held in fairly general disrepute, Leo XIII in his epistle to Cardinal Rampolla felt prompted to repudiate the identification of the Church's political theories with the medieval spirit. Cf. Bastgen, *op. cit.*, III, Pt. 1, p. 56. He felt that his profound admiration for Aquinas, which had found expression in his founding the St. Thomas Academy in Rome and his encouragement of a critical edition of the Angelic Doctor's works, had nothing to do with restoration of the medieval system. No such apologies seemed necessary in the 1920's or 1930's, when the return to medieval unity and discipline, in contrast to modern disharmony and anarchy, had a welcome ring not only among profascist romanticists but also among many disillusioned progressive intellectuals.

50. Eckhardt, *op. cit.*, p. 177. This doctrine had long and venerable antecedents. To mention only two authoritative utterances:

Innocent III declared that "according to the canons, faith is not to be kept with him who keeps not faith with God." The Council of Constance likewise decreed that "no faith or promise is, by natural, divine or human law, to be observed which shall be to the prejudice of the Catholic faith." Charles Henry Lea, *History of the Inquisition*, New York, 1887, I, 228; Mansi, *Concilia*, XXVII, 791; James MacKinnon, *The Origins of the Reformation*, New York, 1939, pp. 187 f.

51. Lanessan, *op. cit.*, pp. 68 f.; Missiroli, *op. cit.*, pp. 368 f.; Belloc, *op. cit.*, pp. 195 f. Dr. Eduard Seitz, a Catholic spokesman at the Hessian Diet, combated the legal validity of marriages between Christians and Jews in the name of liberty. "True liberty of conscience," so ran the curious argument in his address to the Diet of 1847, "consists in the respect paid by state law to the religious convictions of all its members and in its avoiding any semblance of approving a transgression, however slight, of the ecclesiastical laws." Bergsträsser, *op. cit.*, I, 103.

52. William Barry, "Leo XIII, a Retrospect," *Dublin Review*, CXXXIII (1903), 248, cited by Eckhardt, *op. cit.*, p. 247: Joannes Gerson, *De potestate ecclesiastica*, Consideratio XIII in Melchior Goldast von Heimingsfeld's *Monarchia S. Romani Imperii*, 3 vols., Frankfort, 1611-14, II, 1403 f.; Pius XII's Christmas Allocution of Dec. 24, 1944 (official English translation), *Catholic News*, LIX, no. 18 (Dec. 30, 1944), 4 f.; Acton, *op. cit.*, pp. 191 f.; Maritain, *Twilight*, p. 54.

53. G. A. Borgese, "The Pope and the Peace," *Nation*, CLIX (1944), 430. Cf. also Joseph Bernhart, *The Vatican as a World Power*, English transl., London, 1939 (a historical survey); Luigi Sturzo, "The Vatican's Position in Europe," *Foreign Affairs*, XXIII (1944-45), 211-21; and D. A. Binchy, "The Vatican and International Diplomacy," *International Affairs*, XXII (1946), 47-56.

54. Leo XIII's Allocution, *Molti e segnalati*, of Dec. 23, 1893; and Pius XI's encyclical, *Ubi arcano Dei* of 1922, in Koenig, *op. cit.*, pp. 86, 343, 347. Cf. also Bastgen, *op. cit.*, III, Pt. 1, pp. 148 f.; [Hayes], *Patriotism*, pp. 13 f.

Chapter V

Protestant Individualism

1. William Adams Brown, *The Church in America*, New York, 1922, p. 8 n. 1. A Frenchman, contrasting the American conditions with those in his native land, exclaimed, "Mon Dieu! A country with two hundred religions and only one sauce!" Cf. Winfred Ernest Garrison, *The March of Faith. The Story of Religion in America Since 1865*, New York, 1933, pp. 100 f.

2. MacKinnon, *Origins of the Reformation*, pp. 409 f.; Luther, *Enarratio Psalmi CXXVII* in his *Opera latina*, ed. by Christoph St. Th. Elsperger, Joannes Conrad Irmischer, *et al.*, 67 vols., Erlangen and Frankfort, 1826-57, XX, 65 f., 108 f. MacKinnon (p. 84) points out the dependence of Wyclif's doctrine of state and private ownership on Richard Fitzralph's *De pauperie salvatoris*. Cf. also Reginald Lane Poole's Preface to his ed. of Wyclif's *De dominio divino*, pp. xlvii f. and to his critical edition of *De pauperie* in the Appendix thereto, pp. 257 ff., in Wyclif's *Latin Works*, London, 1885 ff.

3. Luther, *On War against the Turk* (1529) in *Works*, English transl., 6 vols., Philadelphia, 1915-32, V, 104; *Bedenken über die Abschaffung der Messe und des Klosterlebens* in *Werke Kritische Gesammtausgabe*, ed. Weimar (subsequently cited as *Werke*), *Briefwechsel*, V, 615; Walther Köhler, *Luther und das Luthertum in ihrer weltgeschichtlichen Auswirkung*, Leipzig, 1933, pp. 34, 96 f.; Heinrich Boehmer, *Luther and the Reformation in the Light of Modern Research*, English transl., New York, 1930, pp. 292 ff. Cf. also Nik. Paulus, *Luther und die Gewissensfreiheit*, Munich, 1905; Paul Wappler, *Inquisition und Ketzerprozesse in Zwickau zur Reformationszeit*, Leipzig, 1908; Heinrich Hoffmann, *Reformation und Gewissensfreiheit*, Giessen, 1932.

4. Luther, *Works*, II, 63, 108, 155 f.;

Tischreden, ed. Weimar, II, 98, no. 1428. Cf. Theodor Pauls, *Luthers Auffassung von Staat und Volk*, Bonn, 1925, pp. 106, 123 f., 136; R. H. Murray, "Lutheranism" in Peake and Parsons, *Outline of Christianity*, III, 18. In his treatise on "Trading and Usury" Luther complained, "God has cast us Germans off. We have to throw our gold and silver into foreign lands and make the whole world rich, while we ourselves remain beggars." *Works*, IV, 13. For this reason he felt, as early as 1525, that his reform had ushered in a "magnificent transformation in German lands." *Ermahnung zum Frieden* in *Werke*, XVIII, 293. Whenever it suited his purpose, however, he was prepared to attack the German people with equal vehemence. "We Germans are Germans and remain Germans, that is swine and stupid beasts," or "We horrible Germans are for the most part such vile pigs that we possess neither discipline nor reason"—such are some shafts from his inexhaustible armory of vituperation. Cf. his *Ob Kriegsleute auch in seligem Stande sein können* (1526) in *Werke*, XIX, 631; *Dass diese Worte Christi "Das ist mein Leib" noch fest stehen* (1527), *ibid.*, XXIII, 149; and in general Hartmann Grisar's sharply critical biography of *Luther*, English transl., 6 vols., 2d ed., London, 1914-19, III, 93 ff.; Hermann Meltzer's admiring description of *Luther als deutscher Mann*, Tübingen, 1905; J. Declareuil's anti-German evaluation of "Luther, l'homme allemand," *Revue des questions historiques*, CXVI (1932), 317-54; CXVII (1932), 45-64; and Imbart de la Tour's suggestive reasoning, "Pourquoi Luther n'a t-il créé qu'un christianisme allemand?" *Revue de Métaphysique et de Morale*, XXV (1918), 575-612.

5. Köhler, *op. cit.*, pp. 37 f.; Luther, *Warnung an seine lieben Deutschen* (1531) in

302

Werke, XXX, Pt. 3, p. 290. Cf., however, his denial of being a prophet in his letter to the Archbishop of Mayence of July 6, 1530 (*ibid.*, Pt. 2, pp. 411 f.), and the editor's note thereon. Curiously, the ultranationalist Paul de Lagarde accused Luther of using the ugly Saxon chancery language in preference to the beautiful German prose of the fourteenth and fifteenth centuries and of having thus permanently despoiled the beauty of the national language. Cf. "Die revidierte Lutherbibel des Halleschen Waisenhauses," *Göttingische Gelehrte Anzeigen* of Jan. 15, 1885, pp. 57-96, reprinted in his *Ausgewählte Schriften*, ed. by Paul Fischer, Munich, 1934, pp. 252 ff. But even Lagarde did not gainsay Luther's great linguistic contribution to German unity. No Protestant has ever paid a more eloquent tribute to that contribution than did the Catholic Ignatius von Döllinger when he wrote in 1872: "He [Luther] alone impressed upon the German language and the German spirit alike his own imperishable seal, so that even those amongst us who abhor him from the bottom of our hearts as the mighty heresiarch who seduced the German nation cannot help speaking with his words and thinking with his thoughts." Cited by Grisar, *op. cit.*, III, 102.

6. Luther, *Brief an die Fürsten zu Sachsen über den aufrührerischen Geist* (1524), in *Werke*, XV, 214; *Donatio Constantini* (1537), *ibid.*, L, 79 ff.; *Open Letter to the Christian Nobility* (1520), in *Works*, II, 104; *On the Councils and the Churches* (1539) and Charles M. Jacobs's Introd. thereto, *ibid.*, V, 127 ff. Köhler (*op. cit.*, p. 15) has pointed out that already at Charles V's election the new capitulations submitted by the electors of Germany included for the first time the provision that no German should be summoned before any non-German court. It was suggested by Frederick the Wise of Saxony, evidently with an eye to the pending case of the Wittenberg professor.

7. The gradual transition in Luther's advocacy of a national all-German Church to that of territorial churches is analyzed by Alfred Adam in "Die Nationalkirche bei Luther," *Archiv für Reformationsgeschichte*, XXXV (1938), 39-62. Cf. also the same author's *Nationalkirche und Volkskirche im deutschen Protestantismus*, Göttingen, 1938. Related thereto is also Luther's contention that all law is essentially the law of peoples

(Iures consulti igitur proprie non habent ius naturale, sed tantum ius gentium, quod profluit ex ratione humana). Cf. his *Tischreden*, I, no. 581 (1533); and Otto Scheel, *Evangelium, Kirche und Volk bei Luther*, Leipzig, 1934, p. 54. This is doubly remarkable as he otherwise was a strong believer in "natural law." Cf. John T. McNeill, "Natural Law in the Thought of Luther," *Church History*, X (1941), 211-27; *idem*, "Natural Law in the Teaching of the Reformers," *Journal of Religion*, XXVI (1946), 168 ff.

8. *Works*, IV, 248 ff.; *An Open Letter concerning the Hard Book against the Peasants* (1525), *ibid.*, p. 265; *Tischreden*, II, 209, no. 1762; 222, no. 1810; *Von weltlicher Oberkeit* (1523) in *Werke*, XI, 257 f.; *Ob Kriegsleute auch in seligem Stande sein können* (1526), *ibid.*, XIX, 633. Of course, Luther insisted also on the complementary obligations of the prince, who should "realize that he is in charge not of his private but of divinely entrusted affairs." *Annotationes in Deuteronomion Mosi* (1525), *ibid.*, XIV, 554. Cf. Köhler, *op. cit.*, p. 48; Pauls, *op. cit.*, pp. 8 f. For Luther's generally pessimistic view of worldly existence, cf. Johannes Kunze's address, *Das Christentum Luthers in seiner Stellung zum natürlichen Leben*, Leipzig, 1918.

9. Böhmer, *op. cit.*, pp. 287 ff.; Gurian, *Kampf*, p. 12; Ernst Troeltsch, *Die Soziallehren der christlichen Kirchen und Gruppen* in *Gesammelte Schriften*, 4 vols., Tübingen, 1912, I, 680 (somewhat weakened in the English transl., entitled *The Social Teaching of the Christian Churches*, 2 vols., New York, 1931, II, 624). Cf. also, for instance, Polycarp Leyser's pamphlet, *Eine wichtige . . . Frag: ob, wie und warumb man lieber mit den Papisten gemeinschafft haben und . . . mehr Vertrawen zu ihnen tragen solle, denn mit und zu den Calvinisten*, Leipzig, 1620. Although unduly minimizing the importance of the "patriarchal" theory of government in Luther's political teachings, Günther Holstein has carefully analyzed their great influence on the preachers and writers of the seventeenth and eighteenth centuries in *Die Staatsphilosophie Schleiermachers*, Bonn, 1923, pp. 10 ff.; *Luther und die deutsche Staatsidee*, Tübingen, 1926. Cf. also the critique of earlier views, *ibid.*, pp. 26 f.; Friedrich Meinecke, "Luther über christliches Gemeinwesen und christlichen Staat," *Historische Zeitschrift*, CXXI (1920), 1-22;

and Gerhard Ritter, "Die Ausprägung deutscher und westeuropäischer Geistesart im konfessionellen Zeitalter," ibid., CXLIX (1934), 247 f. The difficulties of reaching general agreement in regard to Luther's views on any subject have long been recognized. R. N. Carew Hunt once suggested that in view "of the incoherence of his thought with its opponencies and contradictions exaggerated by the habitual intemperance of his language" we should abandon the normal method of critical examination and "appeal from the comparison of isolated and seemingly inconsistent utterances to the personality which his life and writings reveal"—a desperate expedient, indeed. Cf. his review article on "Luther's Theory of Church and State," Church Quarterly Review, CVII (1928-29), 27. Since Herder and the romantics many German nationalists have invoked the shades of the great reformer as an abettor of their own nationalist credo. Houston Stewart Chamberlain exclaimed with his usual abandon: "Luther is above all a political hero. . . . His patriotism was absolute, his learning limited. . . . Luther was more of a politician than a theologian." Cf. his Foundations of the Nineteenth Century, English transl., 2 vols., London, 1911, II, 367, 373, 375. This is, of course, a gross exaggeration, though one must not overlook the profound affinities, despite equally profound divergences, between the preachment of Luther and that of national socialism. "The Lutheran Reformation is therefore," writes Reinhold Niebuhr, "that particular locus in the history of Christendom where the problem of justice is most clearly disavowed. It is therefore no accident of history that nazi pessimism, with its glorification of force as the principle of order, its unqualified affirmation of the state, its disavowal of all concepts of justice and its rejection of all universal standards of morality, should grow upon this soil." Cf. his Christianity and Power Politics, New York, 1940, p. 51. Cf. also William Montgomery McGovern's From Luther to Hitler, the History of Fascist-Nazi Political Philosophy, Boston, 1941.

10. Calvin, Commentary on Isaiah (47: 10) in his Opera quae supersunt omnia, 59 vols., Brunswick, 1863-1900, XXXVII, 167 f. Cf. also his Praelectiones on Daniel (2:36 ff.), ibid., XL, 596 ff. (on the four universal monarchies, including an interesting polemic against Abravanel's Jewish interpretation);

and Hans Baron, Calvins Staatsanschauung und das konfessionelle Zeitalter, Munich, 1924, p. 60. Calvin's sharp condemnation of the ancient Roman Empire as "the great piratical center" and a nation of "proud barbarians" likewise had a contemporary sound. Cf. the numerous passages quoted by Josef Bohatec in his minute analysis of Calvins Lehre von Staat und Kirche, mit besonderer Berücksichtigung des Organismusgedankens, Breslau, 1937, pp. 608 ff. Nevertheless, "during the later years of his life in Geneva Calvin ruled by his influence an ecclesiastical organization scarcely less united and scarcely less extensive than that which acknowledged the Pope." W. R. Matthews, "John Calvin" in The Social and Political Ideas of Some Great Thinkers of the Renaissance and the Reformation, ed. by F. J. C. Hearnshaw, London, 1925, p. 196.

11. Calvin, Institutes, IV, 20, 16; in the English transl. by John Allen, 6th American ed., 2 vols., Philadelphia, 1928, II, 650; Preface to his Commentary on the Psalms in Opera, XXXI, 23. In one of his typical sermons he fulminated against his native land, "for one now sees the country of France infested with every kind of impiety. For the most part they are but dogs and swine who have no religion." Sermon XXIX (on Galatians 4:21-25), ibid., L, 640. Cf. Herbert D. Foster, "Calvin's Programme for a Puritan State," in Collected Papers, 1929, p. 32. But he was no less outspoken in his condemnation of his fellow Genevans whom he often accused of manifestly despising God, living a dissolute life and being outright heretics, indeed worse than papists, Turks or pagans. Cf. his Sermons XX, XXII, LXXV-LXXVI (on Deut. 4, 11 and 13) in Opera, XXVI, 123, 138; XXVII, 89 f., 237 f.; Sermon XXVI (on I Tim. 3), ibid., LIII, 315 f., etc. It should be noted, however, that the successful struggle of the Swiss farmers against the Austrian knights in the fourteenth century had left a permanent imprint on all subsequent liberation movements in Central Europe. The term "Schweiz" actually became a German synonym for revolutionary disaffection. Cf. Nathusius, op. cit., p. 81.

12. Calvin, Institutes, IV, 20, 9, p. 641. After electing princes or other magistrates, Calvin insisted, the people ought to pray to God that "He should direct them by His inspiration and supply them with gifts which are known to be necessary for the faithful

execution of the charge to which they had been called. For it is certain that without such special divine grace they could not carry out anything that is right but rather commit all sorts of injustice. . . ." Sermon XXXIII (on I Sam. 10) in *Opera*, XXIX, 604. In the note of 1762 to his *Contrat social*, II, 7 (Vaughan's ed., II, 52 n. 5) Rousseau wrote: "Those who consider Calvin only as a theologian little realize the breadth of his genius. The promulgation of our wise laws in which he had a large share, does him as much honor as his *Institutes*." Cf. Foster, *op. cit.*, p. 66; Rodet, *op. cit.*, p. 32. The stringent theocratic regime in Geneva is described in Eugène Choisy's *La théocratie à Genève au temps de Calvin*, Geneva, 1897; and his *L'état chrétien calviniste à Genève au temps de Théodore de Bèze*, Geneva, 1902. Cf. also the interesting illustrations, cited in part from the experiences of Rousseau's own family by Masson, *Religion de Rousseau*, I, 16 f.; and more generally Henri Naef, *Les origines de la Réforme à Genève*, Geneva, 1936.

13. *Institutes*, IV, 20, 3 and 25, pp. 635, 656 f.; "Confessions de la Foy" (1536) in *Opera*, IX, 700; "Commentary on Romans 13," *ibid.*, XLIX, 248 ff. Cf. also Marc-Edouard Chenevière, *La pensée politique de Calvin* (Diss. Geneva), Paris, 1937, pp. 297 ff.

14. Sermon XXIX (on I Sam. 8) in *Opera*, XXIX, 552; *Institutes*, IV, 30-31, pp. 661 f.; Letter to an unnamed church of May 28, 1559, in *Lettres*, ed. by Jules Bonnet, Paris, 1854, II, 270 ff.; Foster, "Political Theories of Calvinists before the Puritan Exodus to America," *op. cit.*, p. 102. Cf. also the extensive discourse on the duty of obedience and the obligation to revolt in his Sermon IX (on Dan. 6:22-24) in *Opera*, XLI, 414 ff., and, more generally, Bohatec, *op. cit.*, pp. 75 ff., 247 ff., 619 ff.; McNeill in *Journal of Religion*, XXVI, 179 ff.; Georges de Lagarde, *Recherches sur l'esprit politique de la Réforme*, Paris, 1926, pp. 233 ff. The latter, however, understates the distinction between Calvin and Luther. Cf., for instance, E. G. Schwiebert, "Medieval Pattern in Luther's View of the State," *Church History*, XII (1943), 98-117.

15. Foster, *op. cit.*, pp. 78 f. The parallel effects of the teachings of Wyclif which, though likewise "aristocratic" and nonrevolutionary in aim, had "aroused and kept alive the spirit of revolt against a corrupt and tyrannic ecclesiastical domination" have been analyzed by James MacKinnon in *A History of Modern Liberty*, Vols. I-IV, London, 1906-41, I, 322 ff.

16. Troeltsch, *Social Teaching*, II, 624 ff. In this sense Merle d'Aubigné was perfectly justified in calling Calvin "one of the founders of modern liberties." Cf. also E. Doumergue, "Calvin le fondateur des libertés modernes," *Revue de théologie et des questions religieuses*, VII (1898), 685-713; and Hans Baron, "Calvinist Republicanism and Its Historical Roots," *Church History*, VIII (1939), 30-42.

17. For a brief survey of these radical movements cf. Roland H. Bainton, "The Left Wing of the Reformation," *Journal of Religion*, XXI (1941), 124-34.

18. Cf. Köhler, *op. cit.*, pp. 79 f. Although emphasizing that "the northern countries may be regarded as a stronghold of the Lutheran Confession," Bishop Valdemar Ammundsen pointed out numerous differences between Scandinavian and German Lutheranism and the former's affinities with the Anglican Communion. Cf. his paper on "The Anglican Church and the Lutheran Churches of Scandinavia" read at the Church Congress at Cheltenham in 1928 and published in the *Anglican Communion, Past, Present and Future*, ed. by H. A. Wilson, London, 1929, pp. 367-83. Evidently the national homogeneity of the Scandinavian countries (except Finland) accounted for part of that evolution. Cf. also John Wordsworth, *The National Church of Sweden*, Milwaukee, 1911.

19. Böhmer, *op. cit.*, pp. 255 f.; Thomas Garrigue Masaryk, *The Spirit of Russia*, English transl., 2 vols., London, 1919, I.

20. Cited by Hans Kohn in his *Idea of Nationalism*, p. 528.

21. Commenting on the situation in Spain's American colonies, Joaquin Garcia Icazbalceta writes: "The kings of Spain came to acquire such a hand in the ecclesiastical government of America that with the exception of the purely spiritual, they exercised an authority which appeared to be pontifical. . . . Always the civil power interposes itself between our Church and the Supreme Pastor." Cited by J. Lloyd Mecham in his *Church and State in Latin America*, Chapel Hill, N. C., 1934, p. 43.

22. Cited by Archibald Main in his essay on "Calvin and the Reformed Churches" in Peake and Parsons, *op. cit.*, p. 27.

23. Henry Grattan, *Speeches in the Irish and in the Imperial Parliament*, ed. by his son, 4 vols., London, 1822, I, 103; Humphrey, *Nationalism and Religion in America*, p. 128. Cf. also above Chap. IV n. 29.

24. Köhler, *op. cit.*, pp. 81 ff.; Foster, *op. cit.*, pp. 78 ff.

25. Ernest Barker, *Oliver Cromwell and the English People*, Cambridge, 1937, pp. 82 f.; Montesquieu, *The Spirit of Laws*, XX, 6 [7], English transl., 2 vols., Worcester, 1802, II, 14. Cf. also Max Weber, *The Protestant Ethic and the Spirit of Capitalism*, English transl., London, 1930, p. 45; Franklin Le Van Baumer, "The Church of England and the Common Corps of Christendom," *Journal of Modern History*, XVI (1944), 1-21; Arthur Barker, *Milton and the Puritan Dilemma, 1641-1660*, Toronto, 1942; and the extensive documentation in Wilbur Kitchener Jordan's *Development of Religious Toleration in England*, 4 vols., Cambridge, Mass., 1932-40. The transfer of power from the monarchy to Parliament in 1688 opened the gate for the incursion of party politics into church management. The subsequent gradual extension of political rights to nonconformists, Catholics, Jews and atheists produced "the crude fact that not a Christian but a non-Christian Parliament controls the Church of England." Cf. Bishop Herbert Hensley Henson, *The Church of England*, Cambridge, 1939, pp. 20 ff. The rejection by Parliament, in 1927-28, of the revisions in the Book of Common Prayer suggested by the bishops evoked many protests from the Church and led to some such reappraisals of "The Establishment of the Church of England: Its Constitutional and Legal Significance" as that of F. W. Buckler in *Church History*, X (1941), 299-346. But Parliamentary control helped the Church to listen to the ever-changing voice of the people and to forestall petrification at a particular stage of its sociopolitical evolution.

26. William Gordon's sermon of 1774 and Ezra Stiles' sermon of 1783, reprinted in John Wingate Thornton's *Pulpit of the American Revolution*, Boston, 1860, pp. 216 note, 491. Cf. also Thornton's Introd., *ibid.*, pp. xix, xxix f.; Greene, *Religion and State in America*, pp. 28 ff., 53 f., 59. Even Virginia, long known for her intolerant policies, was warned by the English Board of Trade that religious freedom was "so valuable a branch of true liberty and so essential to the enriching and improving of a trading nation." Herbert L. Osgood, *The American Colonies in the Eighteenth Century*, 4 vols., New York, 1924, III, 475.

27. Preserved Smith, *History of Modern Culture*, 2 vols., New York, 1930-34, II, pp. 202 f.; Richard Price, *Observations on the Importance of the American Revolution and the Means of Making It a Benefit to the World*, London, 1785, pp. 57 f. Cf. Vossler, *Die amerikanischen Revolutionsideale*, pp. 45 ff. In his aforementioned sermon of 1783 Ezra Stiles contended that, on the basis of the existing population trends, "it is probable that within a century from our independence the sun will shine on fifty millions of inhabitants of the United States" and that before the end of the millennium the latter may exceed in number the population of China. "Should this prove a future fact," he exclaimed, "how applicable would be the text, when the Lord shall have made his American Israel high above all nations which he has made, in numbers, and in praise, and in name, and in honor!" Thornton, *op. cit.*, pp. 439 f. In his sermon on the "Divine Goodness Displayed in the American Revolution," delivered in 1780, John Rodgers of the Wall Street Presbyterian Church in New York likewise declared the United States taking its "station among the nations and the empires of the earth" to be "an event of such magnitude, that it forms a new era in the history of mankind." Cf. *The Patriot Preachers of the American Revolution*, New York, 1860, pp. 312 ff. These exalted expectations were well in line with the older rationalizations of the New England Puritans that with their settlement in the New World "God was actually taking a hand in establishing his kingdom on earth." Cf. Herbert Wallace Schneider, *The Puritan Mind*, New York, 1930, pp. 8 ff., 31.

28. Andrew Burnaby, *Travels through the Middle Settlements in North America in the Years 1759 and 1760*, 3d ed., London, 1798, pp. 121 f. (Burnaby actually believed that were the colonies to secure independence, "there would soon be a civil war from one end of the continent to the other." Among the reasons for discord he observed that "religious zeal, too, like a smothered fire, is secretly burning in the hearts of the different sectaries that inhabit them and

were it not restrained by laws and superior authority, would soon burst out into a flame of universal persecution"); John Witherspoon, *Works*, 4 vols., Philadelphia, 1800-1, IV, 348; Humphrey, *Nationalism*, p. 15. Cf. also *ibid*., pp. 1 ff., 439 ff.; Claude H. Van Tyne, *The Causes of the War of Independence*, Boston, 1922, pp. 74 ff., 82. One may readily admit that intercolonial church organization was still very loose (this point is stressed by Greene in his *Revolutionary Generation*, pp. 110 f.) and yet concede both its superiority over the existing political institutions and the great educational value of the manifold attempts at strengthening it.

29. Witherspoon's sermon of May 17, 1776, cited by Martin I. J. Griffin in "The Anti-Catholic Spirit of the Revolution," *American Catholic Historical Researches*, VI (1889), 147; Inglis's Report in *Ecclesiastical Records of the State of New York*, published under the supervision of Hugh Hastings, state historian, 7 vols., Albany, 1901-16, VI, 4292; Pastoral Letter of the New York and Philadelphia Presbyterian synods of 1775 (almost verbatim repeated a year later by Witherspoon in one of his sermons, cf. his *Works*, V, 176 ff.); "The Landholder" (Ellsworth) in the *Connecticut Courant* of Dec. 17, 1787; Ray Allen Billington, *The Protestant Crusade, 1800-1860: A Study of the Origins of American Nativism*, New York, 1938, pp. 17 f.; Humphrey, *op. cit*., pp. 28 ff., 75 ff., 91, 462 ff. During the fierce debate on ratification at the Virginia State Convention of 1778 James Madison exclaimed, "This freedom [of religion] arises from that multiplicity of sects which pervades America, and which is the best and only security for religious liberty in any society." Jonathan Elliott, *The Debates in the Several State Conventions on the Adoption of the Federal Constitution*, 2d ed., 5 vols., Philadelphia, 1836-59, III, 330. Because it simply could not get along without religious and civil liberties the American people adopted the doctrines of John Locke with greater zeal than Locke's own compatriots. Locke's teachings, moreover, largely stemmed from the same Calvinist sources which independently inspired many revolutionary leaders. That is why his *Two Treatises of Government*, essentially a rationalization of the principles proclaimed by the English

Revolution of 1688, were, according to Pierre Bayle, the "gospel of the day among Protestants." With even greater emphasis Josiah Tucker, Dean of Gloucester, remarked during the American Revolution that "the Americans have made the maxims of Locke the ground of the present war." Cf. Foster, "International Calvinism through Locke and the Revolution of 1688," *op. cit*., pp. 147 ff. Foster points out that, although Locke sparingly cited his authorities, he referred in his *Two Treatises* to seven Calvinists (Hooker, Bilson, James I, Milton, Hunton, Ainsworth and Selden), one ex-Calvinist, Grotius, and but one non-Calvinist, the Scottish Catholic, Barclay.

30. Rousseau's letter to Chevalier [Charles] d'Eon of March 31, 1766 in *Correspondence*, XV, 139.

31. Jean Baruzi, *Leibniz et l'organisation religieuse de la terre, d'après des documents inédits*, Paris, 1907; Franz Xaver Kiefl, *Leibniz und die religiöse Wiedervereinigung Deutschlands; seine Verhandlungen mit Bousset und den europäischen Kirchenfürsten über die Versöhnung der christlichen Konfessionen*, 2d ed., Regensburg, 1925; J. Minton Batten, "Political Factors in Movements toward Christian Unity in Seventeenth-Century Europe," *Church History*, XII (1943), 163-76; Herder, "Ueber National-Religionen" (*Adrastea*, VII, 1802), in *Sämmtliche Werke*, XXIV, 49; Pinson, *Pietism*, pp. 12, 183 f.; Weber, *Protestant Ethic*, p. 44; Chr. Ludwig Hahnzog, *Patriotische Predigten oder Predigten zur Beförderung der Vaterlandsliebe für die Landsleute in den Preussischen Staaten*, Halle, 1785; Johann Stephan Pütter, *Historische Entwickelung der heutigen Staatsverfassung des Teutschen Reichs*, 2d ed., 3 vols., Göttingen, 1788, I, 2. Cf. also *ibid*., III, 276 f., 299. In a similar vein Johannes Müller wrote to Friedrich Heinrich Jacobi on May 23, 1782, that "subjection of the whole of Europe under one monarch, I regard as death; subjection of the German Empire in the heart of Europe under one monarch, I regard as the harbinger of death." Cf. his *Briefe an Freunde* in *Sämmtliche Werke*, ed. by Johann Georg Müller, 40 vols., Stuttgart, 1831-35, XXXVII, 273. Cf. also Kohn, *op. cit*., pp. 372, 691 n. 100.

32. Johann Jakob Moser, *Der dreyfache Entwurf einer Historie des Reichs Gottes auf Erden*, 1745, pp. 345 ff., cited by Marianne

Fröhlich in *Johann Jakob Moser in seinem Verhältnis zum Rationalismus und Pietismus*, Vienna, 1925, p. 124; Pinson, *op. cit.*, passim.

33. Moser, *Vermischte Schriften über mancherley das Teutsche Staatsrecht betreffende Materien*, 2 vols., Frankfort, 1733-36, I, 398-471; Fröhlich, *op. cit.*, pp. 57 f.; Herder, "Ueber die neuere deutsche Literatur, III," in *Sämmtliche Werke*, II, 248; Johann Georg Hamann, "Biblische Betrachtungen" (1758); "Kreuzzüge des Philologen" (1762); "Zwey Scherflein zur neuesten deutschen Litteratur" (1780) in *Schriften*, ed. by Friedrich Roth and Gustav Adolf Wiener, 8 vols., Berlin, 1821-43, I, 107 f.; II, 122 f.; VI, 25. In his "Selbstgespräch eines Autors" (1773) Hamann addressed "the men of Europe" in behalf of the "sacred language of my fathers" and sarcastically stated, "The zeal for the honor of my fatherland is too magnificent a sin, for you to excuse it." *Ibid.*, IV, 89 f. Cf. also K. H. Gildemeister, *Johann Georg Hamanns des Magus in Norden Leben und Schriften*, 6 vols., Gotha, 1857-73 (Vols. I-III in 2d ed., 1875), IV, 154 ff.; Rudolf Unger, *Hamanns Sprachtheorie im Zusammenhange seines Denkens*, Munich, 1905, pp. 126 ff.; Erwin Metzke, "J. G. Hamanns Stellung in der Philosophie des 18. Jahrhunderts," *Schriften der Königsberger Gelehrten Gesellschaft*, X (1934), 246 ff.

34. Gotthold Ephraim Lessing, Letter to Johann W. L. Gleim of Feb. 14, 1759, in his *Sämmtliche Schriften*, ed. by Karl Lachmann, 3d ed. revised by Franz Muncker, 23 vols., Leipzig, 1886-1924, XVII, 158 (cf. also Lessing's preceding letter to Gleim, *ibid.*, p. 156); Goethe's review in *Frankfurter Gelehrte Anzeigen* of May 22, 1772 in his *Sämmtliche Werke*, Jubiläum-Ausgabe, 40 vols., Stuttgart, 1902-7, XXXVI, 68 (and the editor's comments thereon, *ibid.*, p. 323); Humboldt's letter to Jacobi of Oct. 26, 1798 in his *Briefe an Friedrich Heinrich Jacobi*, ed. by Albert Leitzmann, Halle, 1892, p. 61. Cf. also Paul Kluckhohn's anthology, *Die Idee des Volkes im Schrifttum der deutschen Bewegung*, Berlin, 1934, pp. 5 ff.; Ergang, *Herder*, pp. 31 ff.; Joachimsen, *op. cit.*, pp. 40, 44 f.

35. Humphrey, *op. cit.*, pp. 283 ff., 292 ff., 295; Thornton, *op. cit.*, pp. 461 f. Cf. also Witherspoon's remarks on the American use of English which, though less refined than

among the corresponding educated classes in England, was superior among the common men, in his *Druid*, V (1781), reprinted in his *Works*, IV, 181; Greene, *The Revolutionary Generation*, p. 184.

36. Johann Friedrich Zöllner, *Ideen über National-Erziehung*, Vol. I, Berlin, 1804; Louis-René de Caradeuc de La Chalotais, *Essai d'éducation nationale ou Plan d'études pour la jeunesse*, new ed., Paris, 1825. It should be noted, however, that clerics of all denominations often objected to such extremes. Following Herder, who had opposed Joseph II's forcible Germanization of his non-German subjects, Latvian pastors, meeting in Mitau in 1819, went on record against the foisting of German upon the Latvian peasants. Persistence in addressing the masses in German, they felt, would destroy the efficacy of their religious preaching. One pastor, Watson, stated unequivocally that "each people can be educated only in its native language given to it by God as a guardian of its nationality." Cf. Hans Rothfels, "Reich, Staat und Nation im deutsch-baltischen Denken" in his *Ostraum, Preussentum und Reichsgedanke*, Leipzig, 1935, p. 115 (also pointing out that a German pastor, Heinrich Adolphi, had been the first to publish a Latvian grammar in 1685). Nor can the contribution of the Catholic monks, Voigt, Dobner and Pelzel to the rebirth of Czech nationalism be easily overestimated. Though themselves Germans and but superficially acquainted with the Czech language, these Piarists, because of their contacts with the Bohemian peasantry, became foremost students of the Czech language, folklore and history.

37. Cf. Elisabeth Gloria, *Der Pietismus als Förderer der Volksbildung und sein Einfluss auf die preussische Volksschule*, Osterwieck, 1933, pp. 27 ff., 52.

38. Howard, Election Sermon of 1780 in Thornton, *op. cit.*, pp. 367, 392; Joseph Priestley, *An Essay on the First Principles of Government*, 2d ed., London, 1771, p. 109. Cf. in general, F. A. Cavanagh, "State Intervention in English Education," *History*, XXV (1940-41), 143-56. The liberal attitude was naturally more pronounced among dissenters than in the Established Church which leaned heavily upon both the state and the upper classes. The Bishop of London's remark in 1803 (cited *ibid.*, p. 144): "Men of considerable ability say that

it is safest for both the government and the religion of the country to let the lower classes remain in that state of ignorance in which nature has originally placed them," well echoed prevailing Continental biases. For the dissenting groups, on the other hand, cf. e.g., Olive M. Griffiths, *Religion and Learning. A Study in English Presbyterian Thought from . . . 1662 to the Foundation of the Unitarian Movement*, Cambridge, 1935, pp. 31 ff.

39. John Cotton, *Moses, his Judicials*, reprinted in Peter Force's *Tracts and Other Papers Relating Principally to the Origin, Settlement and Progress of the Colonies in North America from the Discovery to the Year 1776*, Vol. III, Pt. 9, Washington, 1844; Samuel Langdon, Election Sermon of 1775 in Thornton, *op. cit.*, pp. 239, 248 f. (with reference to Amos 3:2); Stiles, Election Sermon, *ibid.*, pp. 409 f.

40. Cf. especially Althusius's *Politica methodice digesta*, Herborn, 1603, *passim*; and the analysis by Otto Gierke of *Johannes Althusius und die Entwicklung der naturrechtlichen Staatstheorien*, 4th ed., Breslau, 1929, pp. 20 ff., 56 ff.; Weber, *Protestant Ethic*, p. 164; Horst Stephan, *Der Pietismus als Träger des Fortschritts in Kirche, Theologie und allgemeiner Geistesbildung*, Tübingen, 1908, pp. 14 f.; Herder, *Vom Geist der ebräischen Poesie*, II (1783) in *Sämmtliche Werke*, XII, 117. Growing admiration for the ancient Greeks likewise helped to displace the Roman imperial tradition in the minds of influential German thinkers and writers.

41. Cited by Chenevière, *op. cit.*, p. 356.

42. The relationships between father and son are well illustrated by various letters. Cf. *The Life of Schleiermacher as Unfolded in his Autobiography and Letters*, English transl. by Frederica Rowan, 2 vols., London, 1860, I, 46 ff., 50 ff.

43. Schleiermacher, *Predigten*, 4 vols., Berlin, 1843 (= *Sämmtliche Werke*, 33 vols., Berlin, 1835-64, Vols. XIV-XVII), I, 353 ff., 364 (1808); IV, 34 (1809); Rowan, *op. cit.*, I, 109; "Zur Theologie" ("Die christliche Sittenlehre"), *Sämmtliche Werke*, XII, 455, 472. Cf. Ernst Müsebeck, *Schleiermacher in der Geschichte der Staatsidee und des Nationalbewusstseins*, Berlin, 1927, pp. 56 ff. Schleiermacher developed further his view of the hero's role in history in another commemorative address, "Ueber den Begriff des grossen Mannes," delivered on Jan. 24, 1826. Its extant, incomplete text is included in Schleiermacher's *Werke. Auswahl in vier Bänden*, ed. by Otto Braun and Johannes Bauer, Leipzig, 1910-13, I, 520-31. For his dynastic attachments cf., for instance, his sermons of Oct. 22, 1815, and Nov. 17, 1822, in *Predigten*, IV, 90, 176 ff.; and his genuinely felt letter of thanks of Jan. 1831, when he finally received the much-delayed royal recognition in the shape of an Order of the Red Eagle Third Class. Cf. Rowan, *op. cit.*, II, 317 f.

44. *Ueber die Religion. Reden an die Gebildeten unter ihren Verächtern*, 5th ed. by Rudolph Otto, Göttingen, 1926, p. 131 (211); "Der Kirchenverfassungs-Entwurf von Schleiermacher," published by A. L. Richter in the *Zeitschrift für Kirchenrecht*, I (1861), 326-41 (Richter has conclusively proved Schleiermacher's authorship). To make the new constitution truly effective, Schleiermacher wrote here, "it is absolutely necessary to abolish completely the ecclesiastical differentiation between Lutherans and Reformed, so that the Protestant Church in this state be but One." The earlier memorandum, evidently written in a similar vein, is no longer extant. Though submitted in 1808 to Stein at the latter's request, it no longer appealed to the Prussian bureaucracy after Stein's resignation and was simply set aside. Cf. *ibid.*, p. 326. In his sermon of March 31, 1822 (*Predigten*, IV, 162 ff.), Schleiermacher still sang the praises of both a local and an all-Prussian union of the two denominations. A year later, while fearing dismissal for his allegedly liberal leanings, he wrote to Arndt about the possibility of his moving elsewhere, e.g., to England. But he declared, "I would be of no earthly use beyond the limits of Germany, and within these, I should prefer above all others a constitutional country in which the two confessions are united." Rowan, *op. cit.*, II, 209. But he became increasingly critical of overpowering state control which left no room for the expression of popular will. Cf. Adam, *Nationalkirche*, pp. 104 ff. Adam sees in Schleiermacher's stronger emphasis upon the "people's church" (*Volkskirche*) on this occasion a major theological contribution. Cf. also Arthur von Ungern-Sternberg, *Schleiermachers völkische Botschaft aus der Zeit der deutschen Erneuerung*, Gotha, 1933, pp. 31 ff., 156 f.; and E. L. F. Henke's address,

Schleiermacher und die Union, Marburg, 1868.

45. Address delivered on Jan. 24, 1833, in Sämmtliche Werke, XXVI, 164 f.; Rowan, op. cit., II, 77; Schleiermacher als Mensch . . . Familien- und Freundschaftsbriefe, ed. by Heinrich Meisner, 2 vols., Gotha, 1922-23, II, 89, 119. Cf. Ungern-Sternberg, op. cit., pp. 20, 149.

46. Schleiermacher, "Brouillon zur Ethik" (1805-6) in Ausgewählte Werke, II, 149; "Die christliche Sittenlehre" in Sämmtliche Werke, XII, 491; "Die Lehre vom Staat," ibid., XXXII, passim; Hegel, Grundlinien der Philosophie des Rechts, 257, 258, 260 in Sämmtliche Werke, ed. by Georg Lasson, VI, 3d ed., Leipzig, 1930, pp. 195, 202. In "Die christliche Sittenlehre" (Sämmtliche Werke, XII, 491) Schleiermacher even went so far as to declare that "a people can act in good conscience only if it pursues its civilized career as an organ of the whole human kind." For a brief comparison between his and Hegel's theory cf. Holstein, Staatsphilosophie Schleiermachers, pp. 202 ff.

47. Rowan, op. cit., I, 69; Schleiermacher, "Erziehungslehre," Sämmtliche Werke, XXXIII, 101, 534 f., 538 f., 702 f.; Andrew R. Osborn, Schleiermacher and Religious Education, London, 1934, passim. Cf. also Anton Strobel's dissertation Die Pädagogik und Philosophie Schleiermachers in ihren Beziehungen zu J. J. Rousseau, 1928, pp. 142 ff., 174 ff., 331 ff. In his essay of 1814, "Ueber den Beruf des Staats zur Erziehung" (Sämmtliche Werke, XXVI, 237, 244 f.), Schleiermacher argued for the priority of tribal customs and mores, but concluded that "sooner or later a time will come when it [the government] will note the necessity of submerging multiplicity in genuine unity so that love of tribe and country shall not run counter to the love of fatherland and people." Cf. Hans Reuter, "Schleiermachers Stellung zur Idee der Nation und des nationalen Staats," Theologische Studien und Kritiken, XCI (1918), 473 ff. Even in his postulate of a new theological school Schleiermacher pursued national as well as religious aims. In writing to his friend G. von Brinckmann about his hopes for the new school (Dec. 17, 1809), he described it as an institution which would "develop and revitalize Protestantism, as it must be now, and at the same time leave open, or perhaps pave the way for the ultimate overcoming

of the contrast between the two Churches." Cf. Aus Schleiermachers Leben. In Briefen, ed. by Ludwig Jonas and Wilhelm Dilthey, 4 vols., Berlin, 1858-63, IV, 172 f. This letter, incidentally, confirms Schleiermacher's authorship of the aforementioned memorandum of 1808.

48. "Die christliche Sittenlehre," Sämmtliche Werke, XII, 489; "Die Lehre vom Staat," ibid., XXXII, 66 ff.

49. Ibid.; Ueber die Religion (Otto's ed.), pp. 175 ff. (286 ff.); Herder, "Ueber NationalReligionen" in Sämmtliche Werke, XXIV, 38 ff.; Rowan, op. cit., II, 206 f.; Predigten, IV, 75. Schleiermacher was so convinced of the nexus between religion and the national spirit that, on his visit to Prague in 1818, he explained the population's indifference to its beautiful monuments by the Catholic Counterreformation. "Protestantism has been wrenched from the people with unheard-of cruelty, but Catholicism they cannot prevent from rotting among them." Rowan, II, 269 f.

50. Letters to Henrietta Herz of Nov. 21, 1806, to E. von Willrich of Dec. 1, 1806, and to Georg Reimer of Dec. 20, 1806, ibid., pp. 70, 73; Schleiermacher als Mensch, ed. by Meisner, II, 83 f.; "Zusatz" to the 2d ed. of his Ueber die Religion (written in Aug. 1806), Berlin, 1806, p. 371.

51. "Ueber die Auswanderungsverbote" (1817) in Sämmtliche Werke, XXV, 339; "Die Lehre vom Staat," ibid., XXXII, 31 ff.; "Die christliche Sittenlehre," ibid., XII, 48 ff., 454; "Erziehungslehre," ibid., XXXIII, 31; Predigten, IV, 673 f.; Herder, "Briefe zur Beförderung der Humanität," V, no. 57 end in Sämmtliche Werke, XVII, 319. In the same sermon, "Der rechte Dank für die Errettung des Vaterlandes," Schleiermacher also noted that the contemporary revolutionary trends had created inner dissensions often exceeding in bitterness the conflicts between states. "Two parties seem to oppose each other with undisguised hostility in all states, two historical eras oppose each other among all nations." Predigten, IV, 675. His skepticism concerning a world state is put into bolder relief by Friedrich von Schlegel's profession of faith in the practical possibility of a world republic. Cf. Schlegel's "Versuch über den Begriff des Republikanismus" (written in 1796, long before he embraced the Catholic faith) in Friedrich Schlegel, 1794-1802: Seine Prosaischen Jugendschrif-

ten, ed. by J[akob] Minor, 2 vols., 2d ed., Vienna, 1906, II, 57-71.

52. Schleiermacher's letter to Friedrich von Raumer of Jan. 12, 1807, in *Schleiermacher als Mensch*, II, 87 f.; *Predigten*, I, 258 ff.; Nietzsche, *Ecce homo* in the Modern Library ed., p. 128. Cf. Ungern-Sternberg, *op. cit.*, pp. 15 ff., 18 f. Schleiermacher's dislike of Fichte was of old standing. Cf. his unsympathetic comments on "Fichte's little humiliation" in his letter to Henrietta Herz of May 2, 1799, Rowan, *op. cit.*, I, 211.

53. Joachimsen, *Vom deutschen Volk*, p. 83. There was, of course, also some opposition. Even the great historian, Leopold von Ranke, himself a pious Protestant and confirmed nationalist, viewed the extremes of modern nationalism with considerable alarm. Approaching the subject as a keen investigator of world realities, rather than from the angle of philosophic speculation, he knew that further untrammeled growth of nationalism would ultimately endanger the survival of both civilization and Christianity. Ranke's views on nationalism, however, because largely empirical were not always consistent. Cf. A. Gasparian, *Begriff der Nation in der deutschen Geschichtsschreibung*, Leipzig, 1916, pp. 10 ff.; Meinecke, *Weltbürgertum*, pp. 283 ff.

54. Köhler, *op. cit.*, p. 128; *Die Reden des Abgeordneten von Bismarck-Schönhausen in den Parlamenten, 1847 bis 1851*, ed. by Th. Riedel, Berlin, 1881, p. 110 (cf. Hans Blum's biography, *Fürst Bismarck und seine Zeit*, 7 vols., Munich, 1894-99, I, 247); Meinecke, *Weltbürgertum*, p. 320 (referring to an interesting Ranke parallel); William Harbutt Dawson, *Bismarck and State Socialism*, London, 1891. Cf. especially *ibid.*, pp. 23 f., for several interesting excerpts from Bismarck's speeches ranging from 1847 to 1882 and harping on the theme of Prussia and Germany's mission as a Christian state. Cf. also Carl Schweitzer's analysis of *Bismarcks Stellung zum christlichen Staate*, Berlin, 1923.

55. Bismarck's *Briefe an General Leopold von Gerlach*, 1896, pp. 107 f.; William I's letter of Feb. 26, 1874, in *Letters to Queen Victoria*, Second Series: 1862-1878, 2 vols., New York, 1926, II, 327; Russell's letter to Lyons of Feb. 20, 1874, in Lord Thomas W. L. Newton, *Lord Lyons: A Record of British Diplomacy*, 2 vols., London, 1913, II, 53; Arlinghaus in *Catholic Historical Review*, XXVIII, 355 f., 363 ff. At the same time the British government was anything but sympathetic to "political Catholicism." Widespread anti-Catholic feeling, nurtured by the aggressive policies of Cardinals Wiseman, Newman and Manning, had created a substantial following for the anti-Catholic Evangelical Alliance (founded in 1846). Gladstone's fulminations against the "antisocial power" of the Church rose to a high pitch after the uncompromising Vatican Council. Though out of office at that time, he corresponded with Bismarck at length on the great menace threatening the entire Protestant world. Cf. John Morley, *The Life of William Ewart Gladstone*, 3 vols., New York, 1903, II, 512 ff., 520 f. Cf. also Gladstone's own polemical work, *Vaticanism. An Answer to Replies and Reproofs*, London, 1875; and Kurt O. Rabe, *Christentum und Volkstum bei W. E. Gladstone*, Munich, 1936 (with special reference to Gladstone's attacks on Disraeli's Eastern policy at the Congress of Berlin).

56. Joachimsen, *op. cit.*, pp. 85, 103, 108; Nietzsche, *Werke*, 1895-1926, XIII, 351 no. 871; Keller and Stewart, *Protestant Europe*, p. 126; Friedrich Naumann, *Central Europe*, English transl., New York, 1917. Cf. also *idem, Freiheitskämpfe* (collection of essays, 1904-11), Berlin, 1913; and Alfred Neumann, *Friedrich Naumanns christlicher Sozialismus*, Leipzig, 1927. Arthur Bonus pointedly characterized Naumann's early activity as the beginning of the "Teutonization of Christianity." Cited by Adam, *Nationalkirche*, p. 164. Cf. also Paul Sweet, "Recent German Literature on Mitteleuropa," *Journal of Central European Affairs*, III (1943-44), 1-24.

57. Before 1914 rarely more than 12,000 Germans withdrew from church membership in the course of a year. In 1919 their number suddenly increased to almost 230,000 and in 1920 to over 305,000. Only about one-ninth of the latter, however, had left the Catholic fold, which contrasted with the general Catholic ratio of one-third of the population. Cf. Keller and Stewart, *op. cit.*, pp. 80 f., 157, 160 f., 217 f.

58. *Ibid.*, p. 218 (on pp. 104 f. the lower figure of 246,075 is given for 1921); R. H. Murray in Peake and Parsons, *op. cit.*, III, 18; Dibelius and Barth, cited by Gurian, *Kampf*, pp. 22 f., 30 f. Officially the relations between the churches and the republic were

perfectly correct, of course. As late as July, 1929, the Prussian Evangelical Oberkirchenrat urged its member churches to hold religious services at the annual celebration of the Weimar Constitution, emphasizing how much it had done in establishing a firm legal foundation for the free evolution of religion. Cf. the circular letter published in *Evangelischer Pressedienst* of July 31, 1929.

59. To justify their "aloofness" from the great social drama that was played before their eyes, some of these leaders cited Luther's aforementioned passage stating that the Gospels were not concerned with worldly things. Hans Michael Müller argued that "taking sides on any cultural or political issue from the standpoint of the Gospels lends absolute value to a particular human onesidedness and an historically conditioned order." Cf. his *Macht und Glaube*, Munich, 1933, p. 196. Karl Barth himself, for a while, tried to evade the political challenge of nazism. Several months after Hitler's rise to power he still wrote: "I am withstanding a *theology* which today seeks refuge in national socialism, not the national socialist ordering of state and society." (Cf. *The Church and the Political Problem of Our Day*, English transl., New York, 1939, pp. 32 f.; Barth apologized here merely for his lack of foresight in December, 1933). As if these two elements could be separated at all in nazi theory or practice! Within a few months, however, Barth publicly asserted that the Church could not "fail to appreciate that of all tyrannies, religious tyranny, the rule over the consciences of men, in matters of minor or major importance, in the name of God, carried through by external or spiritual means, is its most fearful, yes, its most accursed form." Cf. his address on "The Church" delivered in Paris in April, 1934, and published in his *God in Action*, English transl., New York, 1936, p. 35. Cf. also such works of nazism's theological opponents as Walter Künneth's *Antwort auf den Mythus. Entscheidung zwischen dem nordischen Mythus und dem biblischen Christus*, Berlin, 1935; Grünagel, *Rosenberg und Luther*, pp. 29 f.; Gregory Vlastos, "The Religious Foundations of Democracy, Fraternity and Equality," *Journal of Religion*, XXII (1942), 140.

60. Duncan-Jones, *Struggle for Religious Freedom in Germany*, pp. 30, 34 f., 150 f.; Barth in his Introduction to the English ed.

of Arthur Frey's *Cross and Swastika: The Ordeal of the German Church*, London, 1938, p. 15. Cf. also his *The Church and the War*, English transl., New York, 1944, p. 8. Niemöller later realized nazism's real implications and published a pamphlet, *Die Staatskirche ist da!* (1936), which was speedily suppressed by the Gestapo. But he unrepentingly mentioned his earlier nazi sympathies at his trial of Feb. 7, 1938, which nevertheless resulted in his condemnation. Cf. also his *From U-Boat to Pulpit*, English transl., Chicago, 1937, including an Appendix, "From Pulpit to Prison," by Henry Smith Leiper.

61. Barth, *Trouble and Promise in the Struggle of the Church in Germany*, Oxford, 1938; Schleiermacher, "Ueber das Verhältnis des Christen zu seiner Obrigkeit" (1809), *Predigten*, IV, 34; Duncan-Jones, *op. cit.*, pp. 260 f., 267. In 1938 the army chaplains warned Hitler that the mass arrests of the clergy had affected the morale of the armed forces.

62. Oepke, *Mythus*, p. 52; Dibelius "Open Letter" to Kerrl in Duncan-Jones, *op. cit.*, pp. 303 ff.; Barth and Hossenfelder cited by Curian, *Kampf*, pp. 58 ff., 111 f. The immediate acceptance in 1938 of the Hitler regime by the small Evangelical Church of Austria showed how superficial had been the ecclesiastical opposition to nazism even outside the immediate range of the Gestapo and Goebbels's propaganda machine. Exceeding in obsequiousness even Cardinal Innitzer's sudden reversal of his pro-Dollfuss stand, the Protestant leaders informed the conqueror on April 9, 1938, that "the Evangelical Church in Austria is happy to be allowed to bring you, through her highest leaders, the solemn promise of loyalty." Having ceased to be a long-slighted minority and become part of a favored majority throughout the Reich, it attracted most of the 46,000 Austrians who, within six weeks, deserted their Catholic creed. Cf. Duncan-Jones, *op. cit.*, p. 243; Micklem, *National Socialism*, p. 212. (Incidentally, twenty-six persons embraced Judaism, which appears less paradoxical when one realizes that in the 1930's non-Aryan Christians shared in practically all the disabilities of professing Jews, but were deprived of the few countervailing benefits of membership in the organized Jewish community.) No sharper contrast to the behavior of Austria's Protestant churches need be

adduced than the later *Fight of the Norwegian Church against Nazism* documented by Bjarne Höye and Trygve M. Ager in New York, 1943, Cf. also *Die evangelische Kirche in Deutschland und die Judenfrage. Ausgewählte Dokumente . . . 1933 bis 1943*, Geneva, 1945.

63. "There is at least so much truth in the 'compromise' theory, that the statesmen and ecclesiastics who guided the course of the English Reformation fell back, perhaps to some extent unconsciously, upon the idea of a national Church, as an autonomous portion of the universal or Catholic Church." H. C. Shuttleworth, "The Church of England," in *Religious Systems of the World*, London, 1901, p. 508. Bishop Herbert Hensley Henson aptly observed that the Church of England would long ago have fallen apart into several groups if English religious life were governed by sheer logic. Cf. his autobiography cited by Nathaniel Micklem in his brief analysis of the present "Religious Situation in Great Britain" in the *Journal of Religion*, XXVI (1946), 46. Even the Anglo-Catholics have become more tolerant. "What has happened," explained Herbert Leslie Stewart, "is a vast deepening of our sense of the mystery of things, and a consequent increase in our intellectual indulgence toward honest guessing." Cf. *A Century of Anglo-Catholicism*, New York, 1929, pp. 347 f.

64. Keller and Stewart, *op. cit.*, pp. 151 f.; Pribilla, *Um kirchliche Einheit*, pp. 20 f. Pius XI's encyclical, *Mortalium animos* of Jan. 6, 1928, marked the final condemnation of Anglo-Catholicism and spelled the end for all attempts at reunion. Cf. the text in *Sixteen Encyclicals of His Holiness Pope Pius XI, 1926-37*, no. 2.

65. These resolutions were published semi-officially by the Society for Promoting Christian Knowledge in *The Lambeth Conference*, 1930, pp. 48 ff. Cf. William Redmond Curtis, *The Lambeth Conferences: The Solution for Pan-Anglican Organization*, New York, 1942, pp. 297 ff. Earlier proposals were the subject of an extensive monograph by H. Mason Baum, entitled *Church Reunion, Discussed on the Basis of the Lambeth Proposals of 1888*, New York, 1890. Cf. also H. A. Wilson's survey, *Episcopacy and Unity: A Historical Inquiry into the Relations between the Church of England and the Non-Episcopal Churches at Home and Abroad, from the Reformation to the Repeal of the Occa-*

sional Conformity Act, London, 1912; and Robert Frederick Lau's brief remarks on *The Lambeth Conferences and the Orthodox in America*, New York, 1930. Considerable progress was indeed made in the Church of England's negotiations with the Eastern churches, the Continental Old Catholics, the Church of Sweden, and in the proposal for a United South India Church. Cf. S. C. Carpenter, *Church and People, 1789-1889*, London, 1933, pp. 581 ff. The difficulties of reunion between "Anglicanism and Nonconformity" were discussed with considerable frankness at the Anglican Church Congress of Cheltenham (1928), especially by A. E. Garvie in a paper subsequently published in the *Anglican Communion*, ed. by H. A. Wilson, pp. 413-21. The Free Churches most willingly co-operated, however, in such joint enterprises as the various ecumenical meetings or the Copec Conference (Conference on Christian Politics, Economics and Citizenship) held in Birmingham in 1924. Devoted to a discussion of social problems, this conference was attended by 800 official delegates of various churches and 700 other churchmen. In Scotland the Church of Scotland and the United Free Church of Scotland, after prolonged negotiations, concluded a formal union. It was dramatically clinched in an impressive ceremony at St. Giles Cathedral in Edinburgh on Oct. 2, 1928.

66. W. R. Curtis, *op. cit.*, pp. 58, 110. The Church of England was formally disestablished in Wales in April, 1920, after a protracted struggle in which Welsh nationalists joined forces with English protagonists of religious freedom. Cf., e.g., the Memorandum of Lord Stuart Rendel in his *Personal Papers*, ed. by F. E. Hammer, London, 1931, pp. 303 ff.; William George Addison, *Religious Equality in Modern England, 1714-1914*, London, 1944, p. 170. This dual Anglo-Welsh background was, in some respects, adumbrated already by Queen Elizabeth who, reversing her father's legislation, ordered that Scripture and prayer book be translated into Welsh and that services be held in that language. In this way, she believed, her Welsh subjects might partake of the same "unspeakable joy" with which the English had received the prayer book "in the vulgar English tongue." Cited by Macartney in his *National States*, pp. 42 f. Cf. also John Ballinger and J. I. Jones, *The Bible in Wales*, London, 1906.

67. Arthur F. Winnington Ingram, *Some World Problems*, London, 1927, pp. 7, 9, 11. Cf. also George M. Wrong, "The Growth of Nationalism in the British Empire," *American Historical Review*, XXII (1916-17), 45-57, sketching the earlier stages of Canadian and other dominion nationalism.

68. Curtis, *op. cit.*, pp. 284 ff. Cf. also Sidney Dark, *The Lambeth Conferences, Their History and Their Significance*, London, 1930. The growth of the Lambeth Conferences cannot be fully understood without reference to the operation of such socioeconomic factors as the migrations of Englishmen to empire countries and the general transition in the 1870's from the old colonial system to the new imperialism. It was more than sheer coincidence that the first Lambeth Conference met in 1867, the year of the Canadian Confederation which, though achieving a prime goal of Canadian nationalism, strengthened the cohesive forces in the empire. Cf. Robert Livingston Schuyler, *The Fall of the Old Colonial System . . . 1770-1870*, London, 1945, especially pp. 234 ff., 278 ff. The Second World War, especially Britain's perilous position after the fall of France, hastened the processes of both international thinking and interdenominational collaboration. In a remarkable letter addressed to the London *Times* in December, 1940, the Archbishops of Canterbury and York joined hands with the Free Church Federal Council and Cardinal Hinsley in advocating a peace program which embodied the pope's Five Points together with five principles proposed at the Oxford Conference of 1937. Cf. Paul Hutchinson, *From Victory to Peace*, New York, 1943, Appendix 1; Micklem in *Journal of Religion*, XXVI, 47. For the views of the late Archbishop Temple cf. especially his last work, *The Church Looks Forward*, New York, 1944; and John C. Bennett's brief sketch, "William Temple," *Anglican Theological Review*, XXV (1943), 257-71.

69. William Penn, *The Great Case of Liberty of Conscience* (1670) in *Select Works*, 3d ed., 5 vols., London, 1782, III, 12; Greene, *Religion and State*, pp. 43 f., 48 f., 56 f. Cf. Elizabeth Feist Hirsch, "John Cotton and Roger Williams: Their Controversy concerning Religious Liberty," *Church History*, X (1941), 38-51. In addressing on March 21, 1772, the inhabitants of the West Indies in behalf of the College of New Jersey, John Witherspoon said about himself, "And,

as he hath ever been in that [established] Church an opposer of lordly domination and sacerdotal tyranny, so he is a passionate admirer of the equal and impartial support of every religious denomination which prevails in the northern colonies and is perfect in Pennsylvania and the Jerseys, to the unspeakable advantage of those happy and well constituted governments." *Works*, IV, 356. Nevertheless, missionary activities among Indians and Negroes or, for that matter, among recent immigrants remained an essential part of the churches' Americanizing as well as religious task. The royal charter of 1606 had already emphasized that the new colony of Virginia was to propagate the Christian religion among the natives living in "miserable ignorance of the true knowledge and worship of God." Greene, p. 32.

70. Billington, *The Protestant Crusade*, pp. 22 f.; Abraham Bishop, *Oration in Honor of the Election of Jefferson*, 1804, p. 20, cited by Richard J. Purcell, *Connecticut in Transition, 1775-1818*, Washington, 1918, p. 212; Jefferson, Letter to Jeremiah Moor of Aug. 14, 1800, in *Writings*, ed. by Paul Leicester Ford, 10 vols., New York, 1892-99, VII, 454 f. Cf. also Witherspoon's remarks "On the Georgia Constitution" in his *Works*, IV, 227 ff. Sister Mary Augustina (Ray) has pointed out how frequently these early constitutions combined sweeping professions of religious liberty with discriminatory provisions in detail. Some of the latter, however, went into disuse long before their formal repeal. Cf. her *American Opinion of Roman Catholicism in the Eighteenth Century*, New York, 1936, pp. 350 ff. Cf. also William Clarence Webster, "A Comparative Study of the State Constitutions of the American Revolution," *Annals of the American Academy of Political and Social Science*, IX (1897), 380-420.

71. G. Adolf Koch, *Republican Religion . . . The American Revolution and the Cult of Reason*, New York, 1933; Herbert M. Morais, *Deism in Eighteenth-Century America*, New York, 1934; John M. Mecklin, *The Story of American Dissent*, New York, 1934, pp. 350 ff.; Harriet Martineau, *Society in America*, 3 vols., 2d ed., London, 1839, III, 273; J. D. Brewer, *The United States a Christian Nation*, Philadelphia, 1905. An opposing view is presented, for instance, by Max J. Kohler in "The Doctrine that 'Christianity Is a Part of the Common Law' and Its Recent Judicial Overthrow in England, with Particu-

lar Reference to Jewish Rights," *Publications of the American Jewish Historical Society,* XXXI (1928), 105-34. A few early instances of clerical exponents of social reform in England are cited by Carpenter, *op. cit.,* pp. 17 f.

72. Arthur Cushman McGiffert, Jr., "Protestant Liberalism," in *Liberal Theology. Essays in Honor of Eugene William Lyman,* ed. by David E. Roberts and Henry Pitney Van Dusen, New York, 1942, pp. 107 f., 111 f.; *Records of the Governor and Company of the Massachusetts Bay in New England (1628-1686),* ed. by Nathaniel B. Shurtleff, 5 vols., Boston, 1853-54, III, 291; Claude G. Bowers, *Jefferson and Hamilton: The Struggle for Democracy in America,* Boston, 1925, pp. 264 f., 374 ff. (Jefferson denounced the Alien Bill as "detestable." Madison predicted that it would be "a monster that will disgrace its parents," but the Jeffersonian party was unable to prevent the enactment of political measures principally aimed at its own following); Billington, *op. cit.,* pp. 23, 327 ff.; Edward O'Meagher Condon, "Irish Immigration to the United States since 1790," *Journal of the American-Irish Historical Society,* IV (1904), 89.

73. Billington, *op. cit.,* pp. 35 f., 328 f.; Albert Post, *Popular Freethought in America, 1825-1850,* New York, 1943, p. 186 and *passim.* Cf. also William Frederic Kamman, *Socialism in German American Literature,* Philadelphia, 1917; C. F. Huch, "Die freireligiöse Bewegung unter den Deutschamerikanern," *Mitteilungen des Deutschen Pionier-Vereins von Philadelphia,* XI (1909), 1-33. A typical denunciation by a congressman read: "The foreigner believes that America is the natural rendezvous for all the exiled patriots and disappointed and turbulent persons of the earth, and that here they are to meet to form plans and concoct schemes to revolutionize all creation and the rest of mankind." Cited from *Congressional Globe* by Schmeckebier in his *History of the Know Nothing Party in Maryland,* p. 48. Even before the mass immigration of German freethinkers, however, Ezra Stiles Ely, a Presbyterian pastor in Philadelphia, indulged in intemperate denunciations of all "opponents of Christianity" and preached "the duty of Christian freemen to elect Christian rulers" (1828). The forces behind Elyism and the vigorous opposition thereto are analyzed by Joseph L. Blau in "The Christian Party in Politics," *Review of Religion,* XI (1946-47), 18-35.

74. Samuel F. B. Morse, *Foreign Conspiracy against the Liberties of the United States,* 7th ed., New York, 1852, p. 143. For Morse's travels abroad, his stay in Italy in 1830-31, where he learned of an alleged conspiracy against the United States, and his disappointing struggles with the English and French governments in securing patents for his newly invented telegraph, cf. Samuel Irenaeus Prime, *The Life of Samuel F. B. Morse,* New York, 1875, pp. 186 ff., 347 ff., 728 f. Morse's singling out of Austria for his anti-Catholic barbs was undoubtedly owing to Metternich's reactionary reputation. But he may also have had in mind the considerable support extended by Austrian Catholics to their American coreligionists. Cf. the documentation in Benjamin J. Blied, *Austria's Aid to American Catholics, 1830-1860,* Milwaukee, 1944.

75. M. W. Cluskey, *Political Text-Book,* Philadelphia, 1860, p. 57. Cf. also Schmeckebier, *op. cit.,* pp. 219 ff.; Billington, *op. cit.,* pp. 386 ff., 430, 437 ff.; George H. Haynes, "The Causes of Know-Nothing Success in Massachusetts," *American Historical Review,* III (1897-98), 67-82. Haynes's careful analysis sheds light on the conditions in other states as well. His concluding remarks are particularly worth pondering today in the new era of "widespread political unrest."

76. John [H.] Harris, *A Century of Emancipation,* London, 1933, pp. 1 ff., 52 f.; Billington, *op. cit.,* pp. 424 f. Britain, which in 1807 abolished the slave trade and in 1833 formally suppressed slavery throughout the empire, led also in the struggle for its international outlawry. Her efforts date back to 1662 and in the century following 1807 she "concluded nearly 600 treaties and international instruments designed either to check or abolish the slave trade." Harris, pp. 216 ff.

77. Garrison, *March of Faith,* pp. 9, 103 f.; John Moffatt Mecklin, *The Ku Klux Klan,* New York, 1924, pp. 127 ff., 157 ff.; Seldes, *The Catholic Crisis,* pp. 22 f. Cf. also Donald S. Strong, *Organized Anti-Semitic Movements in America: The Rise of Group Prejudice during the Decade 1930-40,* Washington, 1941.

78. *The Lambeth Conference,* 1930, p. 96; Curtis, *op. cit.,* pp. 329 f.; George A. Gordon, "Reasonable Hope for American Religion," *Atlantic Monthly,* CXI (1913), 824-36. Yves Simon is perfectly right in concluding his stimulating analysis of the "Secret Sources of the Success of the Racist

Ideology" (Review of Politics, VII, 1945, 74-105) by stating: "The cause of racism will not be definitely shaken until the day when our moderate, secret racists, will find, facing them, not smiling analysts and hairsplitting 'logicians' but men with tightened fists, determined to commit themselves thoroughly, determined to run risks, determined to call people and things by the right names; men who refuse to enjoy a life from which justice is absent; men who have for their motto: *justice or death*."

79. Charles E. Brent, "European Nations and Christian Statesmanship," in Peake and Parsons, *op. cit.*, p. 180. The term "ecumenical" was popularized by Count Keyserling, fashionable philosopher of the 1920's, who spoke of the new "ecumenical era" which had dawned upon the growingly interdependent world. Cf. John A. Mackay, "The Biblical and Theological Bases for the Ecumenical Goal" in *Toward World-Wide Christianity*, ed. by O. Frederick Nolde, New York, 1946, p. 41.

80. *Das Schwarze Korps* cited by Vlastos in *Journal of Religion*, XXII, 142 f.; Latourette, *op. cit.*, IV, 5, 75.

81. Johann F. A. de le Roi, *Geschichte der evangelischen Juden-Mission seit Entstehung des neueren Judentums*, 2 vols., Leipzig, 1899; *idem*, "Judentaufen im 19. Jahrhundert. Ein statistischer Versuch," *Nathanael*, XV (1889), 65-118; William Thomas Gidney, *The History of the London Society for Promoting Christianity amongst the Jews, from 1809 to 1908*, London, 1908; Anna M. D. W. Stirling, *The Ways of Yesterday; Being the Chronicles of the Way Family from 1307 to 1885*, London, 1930, pp. 83-290; Edwin Hodder, *The Life and Work of the Seventh Earl of Shaftesbury*, 3 vols., London, 1888; Latourette, *op. cit.*, IV, 112 ff., 155; Nahum Sokolow, *History of Zionism, 1600-1918*, 2 vols., London, 1918, I, 121 ff.; David Max Eichhorn, "Mission to the Jews," *The Universal Jewish Encyclopedia*, 11 vols., New York, 1939-44, VII, 584 f., in part summarizing the author's unpublished study, *A History of Christian Attempts to Convert the Jews of the United States and Canada*. Only in comparison with the new racialist emphases since the foundation of the Second Reich did the *Institutum Judaicum* in Berlin and its leaders, Franz Delitzsch and Hermann Strack, give the impression of defending the rights of individual Jews, if not of the Jewish faith.

82. Brown, *Church in America*, p. 354; John Owen, *The History of the Origin and First Ten Years of the British and Foreign Bible Society*, 3 vols., London, 1816-20, I, 15 ff., 138 f.; William Canton, A *History of the British and Foreign Bible Society*, 2 vols., London, 1904, I, 5 ff.; II, 469 ff. (giving a list of versions and their distribution to the end of 1853).

83. John R. Mott, *Strategic Points in the World's Conquest. The Universities and Colleges as Related to the Progress of Christianity*, New York, 1897; Hendrik Kraemer, *The Christian Message in a Non-Christian World*, London, 1938, p. 36 (this volume, described by the Archbishop of York in his Foreword as "the classical treatment of its theme," was prepared at the request of the International Missionary Council in advance of the World Conference of 1938); Lyman Van Law Cady, "The Liberal Attitude Toward other Religions," *Liberal Theology*, ed. by Roberts and Van Dusen, pp. 139 ff.; Latourette, *op. cit.*, IV, 106; Laymen's Foreign Missions Inquiry, *Re-Thinking Missions: A Laymen's Inquiry after One Hundred Years*, New York, 1932. The numerous contributors to the volume *The Missionary Outlook in the Light of the War*, published in New York, 1920, were for the most part members of missionary societies and citizens of different countries. Yet they all agreed on the need of adjusting the traditional missionary methods to the new cultural awakening of the Eastern peoples. Cf. also the detailed report of the *Ecumenical Missionary Conference, New York, 1900* (2 vols., New York, 1900), which includes a brief sketch of earlier gatherings, I, 19 ff.; and the literature, both bibliographical and descriptive, listed below n. 86.

84. *Harmonia confessionum fidei Orthodoxarum et Reformatarum Ecclesiarum . . . Europae Regnis, Nationibus et Provinciis*, Geneva, 1581, revised and enlarged by Peter Hall, London, 1842; J. Minton Batten, *John Dury, Advocate of Christian Reunion*, Chicago, 1944, p. 19; F. Böhl, "Was lehrt uns die ökumenische Bewegung?" *Aus Theologie und Geschichte der Reformierten Kirche. Festgabe für E. F. Karl Müller-Erlangen*, Neukirchen, 1933, pp. 321-45. Cf. also Baumer in *Journal of Modern History*, XVI, 21.

85. Cf. Garrison, *March of Faith*, pp. 217 f. Cf. also, e.g., John A. Hutchison, *We are not Divided: a Critical and Historical Study*

of the *Federal Council of the Churches of Christ in America*, New York, 1941; Henry R. T. Brandreth, *An American Plan for Unity: A Study of the Anglican-Presbyterian Negotiations in America*, London, 1945 (a brief survey of the negotiations since 1937); R. J. Pierce, "The Church of England in Canada and Reunion," *Theology*, XLI (1946), 354-59 (describing the present state of negotiations). In 1922 Paul Hutchinson argued that a world-wide Methodist organization was preferable to interdenominational country-wide bodies which could only aggravate the existing national divisions. William Adams Brown replied that denominationalism might be as divisive as nationalism and that Christian unity would be poorly served by overemphasizing the rivalries of either kind. Brown, *Church in America*, p. 273 n. 1. Neither author would deny, however, that, if animated by genuine yearning for human brotherhood, both organizational forms could well serve as intermediary links between individual congregations or regional groups and the really ecumenical, i.e., supranational as well as supradenominational organs. Such sociological factors as progressive urbanization and growing mobility of the population enhanced the intermingling of Protestant groups and the weakening of interdenominational barriers. As a result millions of Christians, particularly in the United States, have fluctuated from one denomination to another. In 1920 the Congregational churches admitted 92 ministers ordained by other denominations in addition to 96 men ordained by themselves. In the following five years 38 per cent of all new Presbyterian ministers had "infiltrated" from other churches. Cf. H. Paul Douglass, "Ecumenicity in America" in Nolde, *op. cit.*, pp. 179 f.

86. This Parliament was sharply attacked by integral nationalists. Maurras quoted with relish Bourget's derision of the "sacred parade" whose *bizarrerie* had often bordered on the grotesque, and Frederick Harrison's description of the "Jewish conference presided over by a Catholic cardinal." Cf. his *Quand les Français ne s'aimaient pas*, p. 371. For interesting memoirs of the English Methodist, Sir Henry S. Lunn, publisher of the *Review of the Churches* and initiator of the Reunion Conference at Grindelwald, Switzerland, in 1892, cf. his *Chapters from My Life. With Special Reference to Reunion*, London, 1918. The early history of

"ecumenical movements" in the wider sense is described by Gaius Jackson Slosser in his *Christian Unity: Its History and Challenge in all Communions, in all Lands*, New York, 1929; and William Adams Brown, *Toward a United Church: Three Decades of Ecumenical Christianity*, New York, 1946 (including "An Ecumenical Bibliography," compiled by Paul Griswold Macy). Cf. also René Heinrich Wallau, *Die Einigung der Kirche vom evangelischen Glauben aus*, Berlin, 1925; Nolde, *op. cit.*; and Henry R. T. Brandreth's Introduction to his *Unity and Reunion*. This critical survey of existing literature well supplements Auguste Senaud's *Christian Unity: a Bibliography*, Geneva, 1937. "The literature on this question," Adolf Keller noted already a decade ago, ". . . has become measureless in extent; and no one can claim to possess even a general grasp of the thought and labors of Christendom through the centuries" in this endeavor. Cf. his prefatory essay to Senaud's bibliography on "The Meaning and Task of the Oecumenical Movement." The last decade has, of course, been even more articulate.

87. Keller and Stewart, *op. cit.*, pp. 192 f.

88. *Ibid.*, pp. 190 ff. As an influential official at the various conferences and continuation committees, Dr. Keller had much inside information. Cf. also Charles S. Macfarland, *International Christian Movement*, New York, 1924; *idem, Christian Unity in Practice and Prophecy*, New York, 1933; Tor Andrae's biography of *Nathan Söderblom*, German transl., Berlin, 1938; and Adolf Deissmann's address, *Die ökumenische Erweckung. Ein Jahrzent zeitgenössischer Kirchengeschichte*, Berlin, 1929.

89. A full analysis of the Conference work, its antecedents and results was given by Nathan Söderblom, its prime mover, in his well-documented *Kristenhetens Möte i Stockholm*, Stockholm, 1926. This volume well supplements the official report, ed. by G. K. A. Bell, Oxford, 1926. Cf. also Söderblom's detailed comments on Pribilla's aforementioned work in his "Pater Max Pribilla und die ökumenische Erweckung; Einige Randbemerkungen," *Kyrkohistorisk Arsskrift*, XXXI (1931), 1-99; and Pribilla's restatement, in reply thereto, of the "Drei Grundfragen der ökumenischen Bewegung," *ibid.*, pp. 113-27.

90. William Adams Brown,"The Church," in Roberts and Van Dusen, *op. cit.*, pp. 265 f.; *idem, Toward a United Church, passim;*

Henry Smith Leiper and Abdel R. Wentz, "The Rise of Ecumenical Organization" in Nolde, *op. cit.*, p. 97. The vast range of these ecumenical discussions, for which only a few brief hints could be given here, is reflected in the voluminous official publications covering the proceedings of the conferences, reports of various committees and the World Council, etc. Apart from church organs the world press also paid more than casual attention to these meetings and official announcements.

91. Samuel McCrea Cavert, "Outlook for Church Unity," *Journal of Religion*, XXII (1942), 419; Duncan-Jones, *op. cit.*, pp. 73, 248 ff., 309, 311; Micklem, *op. cit.*, pp. 179 f. "There is no question," writes Sherman Elbridge Johnson, "that the singling out of the nazis and the silence on the Russian situation has discredited Oxford in the minds of many." Cf. "The Churches Feel Their Way" (a review of the Oxford Conference Report), *Anglican Theological Review*, XX (1938), 211. Anticipating these criticisms A. S. Oldham wrote in his Introd. to that report (*The Oxford Conference*, Chicago, 1937, pp. xiv f.), "There [in fascist countries] the menace to the Church is not that it may be wiped out but that it may be prostituted to the purposes of a state which itself would become supreme even over Christ." Nevertheless, Karl Barth's critique of the ecumenical bodies' protracted silence at decisive moments, though perhaps unbecoming in view of Barth's own previous record, merits full consideration: "Not in 1933 (the start of the German church struggle), nor in the summer and fall of 1938, when the political storm was gathering, nor in 1939, when it broke loose, neither at the time of the catastrophe of 1940 nor since then, was there directed to Christendom and to mankind a witnessing, clarifying and comforting word from the ecumenical centers." Barth was probably also right in asserting that the World Council should have assumed some real ecclesiastical power, even at the risk of being blamed for having overstepped its authority. Cf. his *Church and the War*, pp. 46, 48. We must bear in mind, however, the difficulty of squaring an effective world-wide ecclesiastical power with the sectarian traditions of most Protestant churches. Reinhold Niebuhr has rightly pointed out that the debates at the Ecumenical Conferences have often appeared remote, even irrelevant, to

American Protestants, because their religious organizations are still under the influence of "the 'sect' protest against the order, the liturgy and the theology of the Church." Cf. his discussion of "The Ecumenical Issue in the United States," *Theology Today*, II (1945-46), 525-36.

92. Adolf Deissmann was not overcourteous when he informed the Cheltenham Church Congress of 1928 that, despite, for example, Zinzendorf's influence on John Wesley, "the effects of England on Germany and other Protestant regions in the field of spiritual life seem to me to have been greater than our effects on England." Cf. his "Anglicanism and Lutheranism" in *The Anglican Communion*, ed. by Wilson, pp. 395 f.

93. There also was a widespread feeling that its theological position of "bridge Church" between Catholicism and the Free Churches predestined the Anglican Church to serve as the major instrument of reunion. Cf. Henry L. Goudge, *The Church of England and Reunion*, London, 1938, and the essays answering in the negative the question *Is Christ Divided?* ed. by William Temple, Harmondsworth, 1943.

94. Albert W. Beaven, "The Meaning for Religion of the Trend toward Nationalism," *Annals of the American Academy of Political and Social Science*, CLXXIV (1934), 71 ff.

95. Søren Aabye Kierkegaard, *Philosophische Brocken*, German transl., in *Gesammelte Werke*, 12 vols., Jena, 1909-22, VI, 92 f.

96. Cf. the illuminating critique of "Die gestaltenden Kräfte des westlichen Protestantismus und die protestantische Einheit" by Heinrich Frick in *Protestantismus als Kritik und Gestaltung*, ed. by Paul Tillich, Darmstadt, 1929, pp. 103-44.

97. This is essentially also the underlying distinction between W. A. Visser t'Hooft and H. Paul Douglass's appraisals of the ecumenical movement. The former denies its being in any way a manifestation of the *Una Sancta* and believes that it constitutes "a movement *about* Church unity rather than a demonstration *of* that unity." Douglass, on the other hand, is convinced that "these things, as manifestations of the *koinonia*, are the very stuff of unity." Cf. Nolde, *op. cit.*, p. 171.

98. William L. Sullivan, *Righteous Nationalism: A Sermon*, New York, 1919, p. 13.

Chapter VI

Orthodox Caesaro-Papism

1. Greek, long the sacred tongue of all Christians, rapidly lost ground in the West and even such distinguished theologians as Gregory the Great no longer knew it. Before long Latins began viewing all Greeks with suspicion and condemning their church as outright heterodoxy or even infidelity on a par with Islam. Enea Silvio, the later Pope Pius II, believed that Emperor Heraclius had inspired Mohammed to found the new sect. A sincere friend of reunion argued for the elimination of Greek from the list of "sacred tongues," because of its association with the Eastern Church's "evil attitude" in religious matters. In Venetian possessions religious prejudice became so rampant during the fourteenth century that Orthodox converts to Catholicism were sharply discriminated against in all ecclesiastical appointments. Byzantine writers reciprocated by harping especially on the moral inferiority of Latins and proclaiming Constantinople as the only home of divine truth and orthodox observance. Cf. Harold Steinacker, "Die römische Kirche und die griechischen Sprachkenntnisse des Frühmittelalters," *Festschrift Theodor Gomperz*, Vienna, 1902, pp. 324-41; Wallach, *Das abendländische Gemeinschaftsbewusstsein*, pp. 4, 8, 13 f., 16, 30, 48 ff. There is no question, however, about the intrinsic merits of the Slavonic liturgical language. "It is not only the Church language of all the Russias," writes one of its apologists, "but of Moldavia, Wallachia, Serbia, Bosnia, Montenegro, Slavonia proper, Dalmatia and Bulgaria. . . . Unlike its rivals in this respect, Greek and Latin, it had no previous literature; it was adapted to ecclesiastical purposes in its full freshness and vigor, not in its decay; and it has not, like the Latin, served as the medium of works purely literary. The Church gave it its letters and its letters,

obsolete in other respects, now serve only for the use of the Church." John Mason Neale, *A History of the Holy Eastern Church*, 5 vols., London, 1847-73, II, 821 f. Cf. Hugh Y. Reyburn, *The Story of the Russian Church*, London, 1924, pp. 8 f. Similar apologias for the "unhistoric" Slavonic languages were heard already in the tenth and eleventh centuries, the Russian Metropolitan Illarion claiming that, just as new wines require new skins, a new faith requires new words and letters. Cf. Jakobson in *Review of Politics*, VII, 39.

2. Canon 3 of the Council of Nicaea (later included in *Corpus iuris canonici*, XLIII, 7) cited in Greek by Charles Joseph Hefele in his *Histoire des conciles*, French ed. by H. Leclercq, Vols. I-X, Paris, 1907-38, III, 778; John Shelton Curtiss, *Church and State in Russia. The Last Years of the Empire 1900-1917*, New York, 1940, pp. 5 f.; Lysimaque Oeconomos, *La vie religieuse dans l'empire byzantin au temps des Commènes et des Anges*, Paris, 1918, pp. 118 ff., 123 f. (quoting the contemporary chronicler, Nicetas).

3. Though oversimplified in the chronicler's recital of Vladimir's conversion, the reasons for his decision were not derived from high theologica! or moral considerations. The prince's objections to Islam, for example, were primarily based on its prohibition of liquor. "Drinking is the delight of Russians, and we cannot live without it." The Latin Church was dismissed curtly with the remark that "our ancestors have not admitted any of these things." Vladimir repudiated Judaism, recommended to him by emissaries from neighboring Khazaria, because of its political impotence. "Where is your country?" he asked. The argument was finally clinched by a visit of Vladimir's emissaries to Constanti-

319

nople where they were deeply impressed by the grandeur of the imperial court and the splendor of the Orthodox ritual. Cf. Nestor's twelfth century chronicle in the English transl. by Samuel H. Cross entitled, *The Russian Primary Chronicle*, Cambridge, Mass., 1930, pp. 183 ff., 204; Alexander Haggerty Krappe, "La chutte du paganisme à Kiev," *Revue des études slaves*, XVII (1937), 206-18 (with special reference to the Perun cult).

4. Masaryk, *Spirit of Russia*, I, 36 f.; Curtiss, *op. cit.*, pp. 7 f. Cf. also, in general, M. V. Dovnar-Zapolskii, *Tserkov i dukhovenstvo v do-mongolskoi Rusi* (Church and Clergy in Pre-Mongolian Russia), Moscow, 1906. "While after the fall of Kherson [in 989]," says George Vernadsky, "the emperor had to recognize a *de facto* autocephalous Russian Church under the authority of the archbishop of Tmutorskan, the patriarch was obviously reluctant to grant it *de jure* recognition." Vladimir's independence also antagonized the authorities in Constantinople to such a degree that they resisted his canonization until after 1263. Cf. "The Status of the Russian Church during the First Half-Century following Vladimir's Conversion," *Slavonic Year-Book (Review)*, XX (1941), 294 f., 309. Somewhat different views are expressed by Ernest Honigmann in "The Foundations of the Russian Metropolitan Church according to Greek Sources," *Byzantion*, XVII (1944-45), 128-62. In any case, Vladimir's successors proved far more pliable. Cf. also S. H. Cross, "The Results of the Conversion of the Slavs from Byzantium," *Annuaire de l'Institut de Philologie et d'Histoire Orientales et Slaves* of the Université libre in Brussels, VII (1939-44), 71-82; Am. Gasquet, *De l'autorité impériale en matière religieuse à Byzance*, Paris, 1879. Gasquet believes that some vestiges of the ancient imperial worship, now somewhat purified of its overtly pagan ingredients, persisted to the fall of Constantinople. *Ibid.*, pp. 67 ff., 82.

5. D. N. Bonwetsch, *Kirchengeschichte Russlands im Abriss*, Leipzig, 1923, pp. 5 f.; Reyburn, *op. cit.*, p. 22.

6. Joseph B. Koncevičius, *Russia's Attitude towards Union with Rome (9th to 16th Centuries)*, Washington, 1927, pp. 111 ff., 120 ff. Cf. also Adolf Ziegler, *Die Union des Konzils von Florenz in der russischen Kirche*, Würzburg, 1938; and, for the later period, E. F. Schmurlo, *Le Saint-Siège et l'Orient*

orthodoxe russe, 1609-1654 (Russian, with French summaries and Latin documents), Prague, 1928. Polish nationalism colored the entire history of the Orthodox Church in Poland, as told in Kazimierz Chodynicki's careful monograph, *Kościół prawosławny i Rzeczpospolita Polska* (The Orthodox Church and the Republic of Poland, 1370-1632), Warsaw, 1934.

7. Masaryk, *op. cit.*, I, 2 f.; Bonwetsch, *op. cit.*, pp. 36 f. Cf. also Igor Smolitsch, *Das altrussische Mönchtum (11-16 Jahrhundert)*, Würzburg, 1940 (brief sketch, discussing in particular the work of St. Sergii of Radonesh, Iosif of Volotsk and Nil of Sorsk).

8. V. O. Kluchevsky, *A History of Russia*, English transl., 5 vols., London, 1911-31, I, 289 f. The rule enunciated by the eleventh century metropolitan, John II, "Cleave ever unto the law of God—not unto the custom of the land," however imperfectly applied, also served as a major unifying factor. So were undoubtedly the constant migrations and large-scale transfers of population by both foreign invaders and local princes, resulting from the widespread medieval practice of *polon*, or capture. Cf. *ibid.*, pp. 176 f., 188 ff. These factors may also help explain the relative absence of pronounced regional and dialectal differences in modern Russia.

9. Reyburn, *op. cit.*, pp. 114 f. Russia's influence now began to be felt even in the field of Orthodox theology. A Russian catechism, first adopted by the Kiev Synod of 1640, was accepted, with but minor modifications, by the four Oriental patriarchs three years later, as valid for the whole Anatolian Church. The opposition, which objected, among other matters, to "Russia teaching us our faith," merely succeeded in postponing its publication in print till 1662. Cf. Bonwetsch, *op. cit.*, pp. 48 f.

10. Curtiss, *op. cit.*, p. 13. The European importance of the title "czar" and its gradual recognition by the other powers is analyzed in the somewhat colored description of *Russlands Eindringen in Europa in der Epoche Peters des Grossen* by Heinrich Dörries, Königsberg, 1939, pp. 145 ff. While Moscow became the "third Rome," the ancient capital of Kiev soon claimed to be the "second Jerusalem." This designation, originally appropriated by Constantinople is analyzed by Robert Stupperich in "Kiev—das zweite Jerusalem," *Zeitschrift für slavische*

Philologie, XII (1935), 332-54. For a lucid analysis of the early stages of "Nationalization of Faith and Church" in Russia, cf. Paul Miliukov, *Outlines of Russian Culture*, English transl., 3 vols., Philadelphia, 1942, I, 9-26.

11. William Palmer, *The Patriarch and the Tsar*, 6 vols., London, 1871-76, IV, 328 f. An Oriental clergyman attending services in Moscow in 1655 wrote with amazement: "Nikon blessed the czar. . . . All listened in silence and more than all the czar. . . . What a spectacle: The ruler with his head uncovered, the patriarch in his mitre—like servant and lord. My heart was burning for the czar." Cited by Richard Salomon in his brief summary, "Patriarch Nikon and the Russian Church," *Anglican Theological Review*, XXVI (1944), 201.

12. Palmer, *op. cit.*, III, 317 ff.; Albert F. Heard, *The Russian Church and Russian Dissent*, London, 1887, pp. 51 f. In 1666 the patriarchs of Antioch and Alexandria personally attended the Council at Moscow which, after listening to Alexei's accusation and Nikon's stubborn defense, approved the latter's deposition and exile to a monastery, as in accordance with Greek Canon Law (*can. apost.* 81). Cf. also the fully documented biography of *Patriarkh Nikon* (Russian) by Mikhail V. Zyzykin, 3 vols., Warsaw, 1931-38; and Matthew Spinka's remarks on "Patriarch Nikon and the Subjection of the Russian Church to the State," *Church History*, X (1941), 347-66.

13. Anatole Leroy-Beaulieu, *The Empire of the Tsars and the Russians*, English transl., 3 vols., New York, 1893-1902, I, 286 ff.; Curtiss, *op. cit.*, pp. 23 f., 26; Masaryk, *op. cit.*, I, 61 f.

14. *Ibid.*, pp. 62, 65; Curtiss, *op. cit.*, pp. 27, 39 ff.; Reyburn, *op. cit.*, pp. 182 f., 184 f.; William Stanley (or Standley), *Treuhertzige Warnung an die Muscovitische Kirche, für die Nachstellungen der Römischen Kirche sich zu hüten*, German transl., Berlin, 1708. The attempts at rapprochement between "the Church of England and the Eastern Churches" are discussed by Arthur C. Headlam in his *History, Authority and Theology*, Milwaukee, 1910, pp. 146 ff.; and, more generally, by John A. Douglas in *The Relations of the Anglican Churches with the Eastern Orthodox*, London, 1921. The approach of the Sorbonne theologians in 1717 and the opposition of Buddeus thereto in 1719 are analyzed by Ernst Benz in "Ein Unionsversuch unter Peter dem Grossen," *Evangelium und Osten*, VIII (1935), 114-24 (not available here). Bruno Bauer goes decidedly too far, however, when he compares Peter's hesitant moves toward religious toleration with its outspoken and effective championship by William Penn. Cf. "Peter der Grosse und William Penn" in his *Einfluss des englischen Quäkertums*, pp. 9-15; and, more generally, Robert Stupperich, *Staatsgedanke und Religionspolitik Peters des Grossen*, Königsberg, 1936; Dörries, *op. cit.*

15. Reyburn, *op. cit.*, pp. 189, 195, 201, 267; Igor Smolitsch, "Katherinas II religiöse Anschauungen und die russische Kirche," *Jahrbücher für Geschichte Osteuropas*, III (1938), 568-79; Alexander Kornilov, *Modern Russian History*, English transl., new ed., 2 vols., New York, 1943, I, 18 f., 21, 32. Custine's observation (in his *Russia*, English transl., 2d ed., 3 vols., London, 1844, III, 341) is borne out by the government's insistence that the priests immediately report to the police subversive acts made known to them under the seal of confession. With typical casuistry the legislator argued that "the sanctity of the confessional is not infringed by this disclosure, for the admission of an intended lawlessness which the confessing person is not ready to renounce and does not include in his sins is not a confession or a part of a confession, but a cunning trick to seduce the conscience." Curtiss, *op. cit.*, p. 25. Cf. also *ibid.*, pp. 27, 73 f., 249; Julius Hecker, *Religion under the Soviets*, London, 1933, pp. 26, 52 f.; and below n. 28. The immediate effects of Catherine's confiscations upon peasant liberation were largely neutralized by her numerous transfers of state lands to the nobles. Cf. Geroid Tanquary Robinson, *Rural Russia under the Old Regime*, London, 1932, pp. 27, 30. But, in the long run, they increased the economic, political and sectarian unrest among the masses which colored so much of Russia's modern history. Particularly her freeing the landowners from military service removed the props from under the whole system of villeinage, long justified only by the country's defense needs. Many peasants actually believed that, simultaneously with the privilege for the landowners, the empress had enacted the complementary restoration of their former freedom and landholdings to the villeins, and that only the landowners had fraudulently

suppressed that information. Cf. Karl Nötzel, *Die Grundlagen des geistigen Russlands,* Jena, 1917, p. 11.

16. Masaryk, *op. cit.,* I, 109 f. At the accession of Alexander II to the throne Constantine Aksakov, famous Slavophil leader, implored the czar not to allow any restrictions on the imperial autocracy which alone, in his opinion, fully conformed with the spirit of the Gospels. This petition was published in 1881 for the edification of the new czar, Alexander III. Cf. Leroy-Beaulieu, *op. cit.,* III, 49.

17. Bonwetsch, *op. cit.,* pp. 29 f., 57 ff.; Masaryk, *op. cit.,* I, 49 n. 1; Kornilov, *op. cit.,* I, 295 ff. During the five years 1847-1852 no less than 26,456 persons were tried for belonging to the schism. *Ibid.,* p. 297. Unfortunately the checkered history of Russian sectarianism has not yet been sufficiently elucidated. It may never become fully known because of the secretiveness, both voluntary and enforced, of most sectarian groups. Many kept no records, others destroyed them in periods of persecution. Some, like the *Khlysti* (men of God), exacted from every new member the pledge of absolute silence. Except for chance discoveries, our information is largely derived from evidence gathered at successive court trials (e.g., the Khlysti trials of 1732, 1745, etc.). Of course, neither prosecution nor defense was interested in producing more than fragmentary data to bear out some specific contentions. Also few original works of sectarian leaders (many had never confided their teachings to writing) were published. One of the most significant books, however, the account of Avvakum, leading seventeenth century heresiarch and spiritual father of the "Old Believers," is available also in the English transl. by Jane Harrison and Hope Mirrlees entitled, *The Life of the Archpriest Avvakum by Himself,* London, 1924. Cf. also Pierre Pascal, *Avvakum et les débuts du raskol,* Paris, 1938. Much material, both documentary and analytical, has been assembled also in such works as Vasilii I. Kelsiev, *Sbornik pravitelstvennikh svedenii o raskolnikakh* (Collection of Government Testimonies on the Schismatics), 3 vols., London, 1860-62 (including many documents smuggled out of Russia); Karl Konrad Grass, *Die russischen Sekten,* 2 vols., Leipzig, 1905-14, and voluminous documentary collections in Russian by Vladimir Bonch-Bruevich, 7 vols., St. Petersburg,

1908-16; and I. Aivazov, 5 vols., Petrograd, 1915-16. Cf. also Leroy-Beaulieu, *op. cit.,* III, 280 ff.; Frederick C. Conybeare, *Russian Dissenters,* Cambridge, Mass., 1921; and V. V. Andreev, *Raskol i ego znachenie v narodnoi russkoi istorii* (The Schism and Its Meaning in Russia's National History), St. Petersburg, 1870. Other literature in Russian is included in the bibliography appended to Curtiss, *op. cit.*

18. Reyburn, *op. cit.,* pp. 238 f.; Kornilov, *op. cit.,* I, 294 ff.

19. Bonwetsch, *op. cit.,* pp. 59 f., 62; Reyburn, *op. cit.,* pp. 236 f., 264. This ambivalent attitude comes clearly to the fore in Avvakum's aforementioned autobiography. Though suffering severe persecutions, the heresiarch could not conceal his sympathy for the czar, the misguided disciple of the "wolf and apostate," Nikon. Cf. especially, *op. cit.,* pp. 52 f., 100 ff., 108, and Avvakum's epistles to the czar written from his exile in Pustozhersk and published in *Pamiatniki istorii staroobriadtchestva XVII v.* (Memoirs for the History of Old Belief in the Seventeenth Century), Leningrad, 1927 (Arkheograficheskaya komissiya, *Russkaya istoricheskaya biblioteka,* vol. 39), pp. 723 ff.

20. Domet Oljančyn, "Was ist die Häresie der 'Judaisierenden'?" *Kyrios,* I (1936), 176-89 (also quoting the extensive previous literature).

21. Reyburn, *op. cit.,* pp. 211 f., 224, 236 f. Chaadaev's writings (available in a good Russian edition by M. Gershenzon, 2 vols., Moscow, 1913-14), which had caused an intellectual upheaval in the 1830's and 1840's became widely known in the West, too, through the publication in Paris, 1862, of his *Œuvres choisies* by Prince I. S. Gagarin of the Society of Jesus. For an analysis of Chaadaev's views and their affinity to the early Slavophil doctrines, cf. Masaryk, *op. cit.,* I, 222 ff.; Charles Quénet, *Tchaadaev et les Lettres Philosophiques; contribution à l'étude du mouvement des idées en Russie,* Paris, 1931; Eugene A. Moskoff, *The Russian Philosopher Chaadayev, His Ideas and His Epoch,* New York, 1937. Heterodox missionary activities were often outlawed. In a decree included in the official Code (*Svod zakonov*) the governors were enjoined to protect the various faiths practiced freely within the empire, but to make sure "that no one shall be led astray into these faiths from Orthodoxy." Curtiss, *op. cit.,* p. 38.

22. Masaryk, *op. cit.*, I, 45, 68; Bonwetsch, *op. cit.*, pp. 46, 73 f., 76, 83 f.; Avrahm Yarmolinsky, "Ivan the Terrible contra Martin Luther, A Sixteenth Century Russian Manuscript," *Bulletin of the New York Public Library*, XLIV (1940), 455-60. Polish imperialism, however, at that time allied with the Catholic Counterreformation was combated in Poland-Lithuania itself by such a Protestant-Orthodox Alliance as is discussed in Domet Oljančyn's "Zur Frage der General-Konföderation zwischen Protestanten und Orthodoxen in Wilna, 1599," *Kyrios*, I (1936), 29-46, 198-205. Foreign Protestants, like Gustavus Adolphus of Sweden and Betlen Gabor of Transylvania, frequently conspired with the Polish Orthodox against the territorial integrity of Poland. Cf. Chodynicki, *op. cit.*, pp. 305 ff., 348 ff., 376 f., 512 ff. Cf. also Dm. V. Tsvetaev, *Protestanstvo i protestanti v Rossii do epokhi preobrazovanii* (Protestantism and Protestants in Russia to the Period of Reformation), Moscow, 1890; and Oreste Tafrali, "Chiesa ortodossa e riforma," *Religio*, XI (1935), 126-45, 505-22 (on the sixteenth and seventeenth centuries).

23. Constantin Pobedonostsev, *L'autocratie russe. Mémoires politiques, correspondance officielle et documents inédits . . . (1881-1894)*, Paris, 1927, pp. 304 f.; Latourette, *Expansion*, IV, 142 f.; Keller and Stewart, *Protestant Europe*, pp. 97, 335 ff.; J. H. Rushbrooke, *Baptists in the U.S.S.R.*, Nashville, 1943, pp. 3 ff. The rapprochement between the Orthodox and Anglican churches through the work of the Russian Bible Society, stimulated by its London prototype, is yet to be examined in full detail. Through its distribution of some 600,000 copies in 45 languages in the fourteen years of its untrammeled activity (1812-26) the society greatly influenced popular religious thinking. It withered away under Nicholas I, but from 1839 on the vacuum was partly filled by a branch of the British and Foreign Bible Society which at the turn of the century circulated several hundred thousand copies annually. Cf. Reyburn, *op. cit.*, pp. 221 ff. The idea of reunion, always present under the surface, came up for more serious consideration during the liberal reign of Alexander II (1867-70). After J. J. Overbeck submitted a petition signed by 120 Anglicans to the Holy Synod, the metropolitan of St. Petersburg appointed a Committee of Seven, including Overbeck and Archpriest Popoff of the Russian embassy in London, to consider the proposal. But nothing tangible came out of these deliberations. Cf. Bauer, *op. cit.*, pp. 200 ff. For an equally futile previous attempt by William Palmer of Magdalen College, Oxford, cf. the latter's *Notes of a Visit to the Russian Church in the Years 1840, 1841*, Selected and Arranged by Cardinal Newman, London, 1892; Stanislas Tyszkiewicz, "Un épisode du mouvement d'Oxford, la mission du William Palmer," *Etudes*, CXXXVI (1913), 43-63, 190-210, 329-48; and William J. Birkbeck, *Russia and the English Church during the Last Fifty Years*, Vol. I, London, 1895 containing Palmer's extensive correspondence with Khomiakov from 1844 to 1854.

24. Kornilov, *op. cit.*, I, 118 ff. Czartoryski later reminisced: "I spoke only of the progressive emancipation of the nations which had been unjustly deprived of their political existence, and I named the Greeks and Slavs as those whose restoration to independence would be most in conformity with the wishes and the opinions of the Russians." Polish independence, on the other hand, was but tacitly conceded by the emperor, for "no Russian was ever on his own initiative or of his own will favorable to Poland." *Memoirs*, ed. by Adam Gielgud, 2 vols., 2d ed., London, 1888, II, 11 f. Cf. also Marceli Handelsman, *Czartoryski, Nicolas Ier et la Question du Proche Orient*, Paris, 1934; and, more generally, A. N. Pypin, *Die geistigen Bewegungen in Russland in der ersten Hälfte des XIX Jahrhunderts*, German transl., Berlin, 1894, I, 394 ff., 399 ff.; Alexandre Koyré, *La Philosophie et le problème national en Russie au début du XIX siècle*, Paris, 1929, pp. 153 ff., 194 ff.

25. Kornilov, *op. cit.*, pp. 236, 280, 288 f.; Fischel, *Panslawismus*, p. 179; Custine, *Russia*, III, 329. Two other passages from Uvarov's pronunciamentos in 1833, largely harping on the same themes, are cited by Masaryk, *op. cit.*, I, 109. Cf. L. Strakhovsky, *L'empereur Nicolas Ier et l'esprit national russe*, Louvain, 1928. No less than a thousand detailed provisions pertaining to "the protection of the church by the state" were included in Vol. XIV of the Russian code (*Svod*) alone. Even a conservative like Ivan Aksakov commented that "in perusing that volume one is amazed by the extent to which every minutia of religious guidance is here

defined, provided for, formulated in a police regulation and subdivided into articles, sections and paragraphs." Cf. his editorials in *Moskva* of April 16 and 19, 1868, cited in "Russische Kirchenpolitik," *Russisch-Baltische Blätter*, III, Pt. 4 (1889), 70.

26. Curtiss, *op. cit.*, pp. 26, 41 ff., 49, 51. Interesting data on the early relationships between "Pobedonostsev and Alexander III" are supplied, particularly on the basis of Pobedonostsev's letters to the daughters of the poet Tiuchev, by an anonymous writer in the *Slavonic Review*, VII (1928-29), 30-54. His influence began to wane under Nicholas II whose personal weaknesses were exploited by a determined czarina and a succession of charlatans, rightly nicknamed the czar's "bedchamber councilors."

27. Pobedonostsev, *L'autocratie russe*, pp. 336 ff., 391 ff.; Reyburn, *op. cit.*, p. 281. The students of the Tiflis Seminary later included Joseph Djugashvili (Stalin).

28. Curtiss, *op. cit.*, pp. 71 f., 92 f., 123 f. In 1867, writes O. V. Kluchevsky, there were "six times as many ecclesiastics in the Orthodox *gubernii* [or *guberniias*, provinces] of Russia proper as in the Catholic *gubernii* of the Vistula region, and nearly six times as many, as in the Protestant *gubernii* of Esthonia." *Op. cit.*, IV, 349. Despite Pobedonostsev's heated denial, Witte's accusation that priests had been forced to break the seal of confession was borne out by the testimony of unwilling and remorseful confessors themselves. Curtiss, *op. cit.*, p. 73 f., 249; Hecker, *op. cit.*, pp. 26, 52 f. M. N. Katkov, Pobedonostsev's close journalistic collaborator, rationalized czarism's claim to religious distinction: "All power has its derivation from God; the Russian czar, however, was granted a special significance distinguishing him from the rest of the world's rulers. . . . He is a successor to the Caesars of the Eastern Empire, the builders of the Church and its conclaves, the founders of the very creed of the Faith of Christ. . . . Herein lies the mystery of the deep distinction between Russia and all the nations of the world." Cited from *Moskovskiia Vedomosti* of Nov. 8, 1882, by Moissaye J. Olgin in *The Soul of the Russian Revolution*, New York, 1917, p. 58. This was but a nineteenth century Russian version of an old claim of Byzantine emperors.

29. Pobedonostsev, *L'autocratie russe*, pp. 31 ff., 36; Curtiss, *op. cit.*, pp. 182, 186. Cf.

also the brief essays on "Public Instruction" and "Faith" included in Pobedonostsev's famous *Collection of Muscovite Studies*. This collection is available also in an English transl., entitled *Reflections of a Russian Statesman*, London, 1898, and in a somewhat different German transl. (from the 4th Russian ed.) by C. E. Wohlbrück under the title, *Sammlung Moskowitischer Studien über das politische und geistige Leben der Gegenwart, mit Bezug auf Russland*, Dresden, 1904. A typical passage reads (*Reflections*, p. 79): "Few reflect that, by tearing the child from the domestic hearth for such a lofty destiny, they deprive his parents of a productive force which is essential to the maintenance of the home, while by raising before his eyes the mirage of illusory learning they corrupt his mind, and subject it to the temptations of vanity and conceit." Cf. also *ibid.*, pp. 138, 148 f. The ultimate result of these obscurantist views is well illustrated by the school statistics accusingly marshaled by Pastor Hermann Dalton in his *Offenes Sendschreiben an den Oberprokureur des russischen Synods . . . Pobedonoszeff*, Leipzig, 1889, pp. 20, 60 f. Esthonia had a public school for every 546 inhabitants, Latvia for 711 (comparing favorably with Germany's average of 734) and even the Muslim Tartars averaged one for every 780 members . . . but the rest of Russia (apart from the Baltic States, Finland and the Caucasus) possessed only one school for 3,216 inhabitants. The Russian people gradually overcame all these obstacles, however, even before the educational reforms of 1908 had taken effect. As late as 1914 only one-half the children of school age were enrolled, but the percentage of literates among military recruits rose from 49 in 1900 to 73 in 1913. Cf. Robinson, *Rural Russia*, pp. 256 f.

30. "Church and State" in *Reflections*, pp. 1, 15 f.; *L'autocratie russe*, p. 536.

31. Pobedonostsev's letters translated into German by Elias Hurwicz in his selection from Pobedonostsev's papers appended to Friedrich Steinmann's biography, *Konstantin Petrowitsch Pobjedonoszew . . . der Staatsmann der Reaktion unter Alexander III*, Königsberg, 1933, pp. 54, 149 ff., 210; "The Press" in *Reflections*, pp. 68 f.; *L'autocratie russe*, pp. 263, 267. Alexander III and his chief adviser nevertheless attentively listened to the brilliant Moscow journalist, M. N. Katkov. A former resident of the ancient

capital, Pobedonostsev himself glorified it as the real center of Russian thought and read the *Moskovskiia Vedomosti* as a genuine mouthpiece of the autochthonous interior, in contrast to much-Westernized St. Petersburg. Cf. Steinmann-Hurwicz, *op. cit.*, p. 62.

32. Cf. especially his sharp attacks in 1881-82 on the constitutional proposals of Loris-Melikov and the *zemskii sobor* (regional council) suggested by his own henchman, Ignatiev, *ibid.*, pp. 141, 159; and his essays on "The New Democracy," "The Great Falsehood of Our Time," and "Trial by Jury" in *Reflections*, pp. 28 f., 32 ff., 47 f., 49 ff., 60 f. Cf. also the antiparliamentary outburst of one of Pobedonostsev's spiritual disciples, Prince Nikolai D. Zhevakhov, who served as associate overprocurator of the synod during the crucial years before the revolution, in his *Vospominaniia* (Reminiscences), 2 vols., Munich-Novi Sad, 1923-28, I, 83, also cited by Matthew Spinka in *The Church and the Russian Revolution*, New York, 1927, p. 8. It mattered little that Pobedonostsev's critique of democracy was "based upon—or more correctly copied from —the theories and ideas of the Frenchman, Le Play, the Englishman, Maine, and the Jew, Max Nordau." Cf. A. S. Rappoport, "Pobiedonostzev, the Apostle of Absolutism and Orthodoxy," *Fortnightly Review*, LXXXVII, 1907, 869. The more mediocre and unoriginal his views, the more representative were they of the ruling oligarchy.

33. Curtiss, *op. cit.*, pp. 132 f., 135, 141 f., 146; *L'autocratie russe*, pp. 370 f.; Steinmann-Hurwicz, *op. cit.*, pp. 214 ff. Pobedonostsev saw in all heterodoxy but the misguided assertion of an ego which believes that it alone had grasped the truth, while everyone else is plunged in error and deceit. "The same phenomena," he declared, "appear in the history of all sects, from the gnostics and the Arians to the nihilists of today, the disciples of Pashkov, of Sutaev, of Tolstoi." Cf. "The Malady of Our Time" in *Reflections*, p. 99. An inquiry instituted by the Ministry of Internal Affairs for ten provinces and districts over the five-year period of 1899-1903 revealed that of 29,431 marriages among the Old Believers and other sectarians, only 1,840 were entered in the record books, notwithstanding the stigma of illegitimacy placed upon offspring of non-registered marriages. There were 131,730 births, but only 1,340 were registered. Of 91,634 deaths only 552 were formally recorded. Cf. Curtiss, *op. cit.*, p. 150 citing a report by the Octobrist, Kamenskii, at the Third Duma in 1909.

34. *L'autocratie russe*, pp. 61 ff., 339.

35. Steinmann-Hurwicz, *op. cit.*, pp. 72 ff., 77 ff., 81, 229 ff.; *L'autocratie russe*, pp. 401 ff. (referring to a report of the poet K. K. Sliuchevskii of May 29, 1886, concerning the alleged misgovernment of the German clergy), 556 ff., 568 ff. (Pobedonostsev received a large number of "fan" letters from various more or less highly placed Russian personages expressing their appreciation of his reply to Naville); Dalton, *Offenes Sendschreiben, passim*; "Russische Kirchenpolitik," *Russisch-Baltische Blätter*, III (1887), 69-99; "Lettisch-estnische Wandlungen," *ibid.*, pp. 115-34; "Dem Herrn Pobedonoszew," *ibid.*, IV (1888), 67-99 (including a retranslation into German of the overprocurator's correspondence with the Schaffhausen pastors). The latter essays, written in a German nationalistic vein, stress the impact of Bismarckian Germany on the overprocurator's anti-Lutheran policies. The Russian press suspected even the Baltic-German fire brigades of being but Prince Bismarck's "militia" prepared to side with Germany against their own country. Cf. also Hans Rothfels, "Bismarck und die Nationalitätenfragen des Ostens" in his *Ostraum*, pp. 65-92. Before 1871 Russian statesmen were more dispassionate. Prince Gorchakov, writing in March, 1865, about the inefficacy of Nicholas I's conversionist efforts in the Baltic provinces, commented that "the peasants turned Orthodox soon learned that they had gained nothing in worldly well-being by their change of faith. At the same time they had exchanged an educated clergy and beautiful houses of worship for an ignorant priesthood and churches which, to say it mildly, are unworthy of any divine service." Cf. his correspondence with d'Oubril, republished in German in *Russisch-Baltische Blätter*, I, Pt. 4 (1886), 79 ff. Cf. also Wilhelm Grass's brief historical sketch of *Die Verfolgung der evangelisch-lutherischen Kirche in den Ostseeprovinzen von seiten der Russen*, Libau, 1934.

36. *L'autocratie russe*, pp. 564 ff. (letters exchanged in 1888 by Edward, archbishop of Canterbury, and Platon, metropolitan of Kiev); Steinmann-Hurwicz, *op. cit.*, pp. 208 f.; Pobedonostsev, "The Church" in *Reflec-*

tions, p. 195. Metropolitan Platon sounded the nationalist keynote of the Russian Church when he wrote: "The Orthodox Christian faith, which our Holy Church professes, has exercised a great and beneficent influence upon the destinies of Russia until today. From it our most pious sovereigns have derived their strength and firmness; it has aided our armies animated by the love of Christ to conquer the enemy legions; it inspires the Orthodox Russian to acts of devotion which enable him to sacrifice everything, his life itself, for the good of the faith, the czar and the fatherland." Cf. also the solemn declaration of the leading ecclesiastics concerning the utter immutability of the divine doctrines preserved by the Orthodox Church, cited by Hecker, *op. cit.*, pp. 26 f.

37. "Church and State" in *Reflections*, pp. 2 f., 21; *L'autocratie russe*, pp. 555 f.; Steinmann-Hurwicz, *op. cit.*, pp. 68 f., 220 f., 237 f. Leo XIII's congratulatory letter to Alexander II, on the latter's twenty-fifth anniversary on the Russian throne (Aug. 12, 1880), sharply contrasted with Pius IX's fervent attacks on the "schismatic" power and its persecutions of Catholics (e.g., in the Jubilee Allocution of April 30, 1870). Resumption of diplomatic relations was to serve also Russia's domestic purposes. The *Journal de Saint-Pétersbourg* of June 6, 1894, anticipated from the recent appointment of a Russian minister to the Holy See "a most salutary influence upon the Catholic populations of Russia. It will help maintain among the clergy and the faithful those sentiments of loyalty which had been recommended to them by the spiritual head of Catholicism as recently as in his encyclical to the Polish bishops." Cf. Placido de Meester, *Leone XIII e la Chiesa Greca*, Rome, 1904, pp. 10 f., 51 ff.; Fischel, *Panslawismus*, pp. 417 f., 476 f. Cf. also Adrien Boudon, *Le Saint-Siège et la Russie; leurs relations diplomatiques au XIX siècle*, 2 vols., Paris, 1922-25 (covering the period 1814-83); and Mieczyslaw Zywczynski's review article on "Some Studies and Literature on the Catholic Church in Russia and the Kingdom of Poland during the Nineteenth Century" (Polish), *Nova Polonia Sacra*, 1936, 100-40 (not available here).

38. Steinmann-Hurwicz, *op. cit.*, pp. 183, 262 ff.; *L'autocratie russe*, pp. 220 f., 359 ff., 364 ff., 427 f., 473 f. For Katkov's interesting defense of Cyon cf. his letter to Pobedo-

nostsev of June, 1887, *ibid.*, pp. 492 f. Russian diplomacy attached great importance to the French alliance, cf. Laurence B. Packard, "Russia and the Dual Alliance," *American Historical Review*, XXV (1919-20), 391-410; Baron Boris Nolde, *L'alliance franco-russe: les origines du système diplomatique d'avant guerre*, Paris, 1936, in part quoting Elie de Cyon's own *Histoire de l'entente franco-russe*, 3d ed., Paris, 1895. The governmentally encouraged antisemitic movement in Russia during Pobedonostsev's regime is described, with considerable bitterness, by Simon M. Dubnow in his *History of the Jews in Russia and Poland*, English transl., 3 vols., Philadelphia, 1918, II, 243 ff.; III, 1 ff. Cf. also the brief essay on "Antisemitism in Tsarist Russia" by Mark Vishniak in *Essays on Antisemitism*, ed. by Koppel S. Pinson, 2d ed., New York, 1946, pp. 121-44; and A. B. Tager, *The Decay of Czarism. The Beilis Trial*, English transl., Philadelphia, 1935.

39. Hermann Bernstein, *The Truth about "The Protocols of Zion,"* New York, 1935; John S. Curtiss, *An Appraisal of the Protocols of Zion*, New York, 1942; Vishniak, *op. cit.*, p. 138 n. 26; Rappoport in *Fortnightly Review*, LXXXVII, 871; S. W. Baron, *Social and Religious History of the Jews*, II, 286 f., 294 f.; Lucien Wolf, *Notes on the Diplomatic History of the Jewish Question*, London, 1919, pp. 57 ff. The reiterated pro-Jewish interventions of foreign churches were consistently repudiated by Pobedonostsev's underlings as an unwarranted interference in Russia's internal affairs. Cf., e.g., Archpriest Ianichev's reply, with the czar's approval, to the Archbishop of Canterbury, referred to in *L'autocratie russe*, p. 601 f.

40. Curtiss, *Church and State*, pp. 182 f., 196, 199, 202 f., 206 f., 212 ff., 228 f., 354; Steinmann-Hurwicz, *op. cit.*, pp. 267 ff.; *L'autocratie russe*, pp. 187 ff., 194 ff.; Masaryk, *op. cit.*, I, 176. Cf. also *ibid.*, II, 356 f., 441, 467 n. 1, 502 f. n. 1. Before long a radical wing in the Church, represented by the so-called "Group of Thirty-Two Priests" and led by a priest, Peter Kremlevskii, began advocating a fairly broad socialist program. Cf. Alexander T. Vvedenskii, *Tserkov i gosudarstvo* (Church and Government, 1918-1922), Moscow, 1923, p. 24; Spinka, *Church*, p. 51.

41. R. W. Seton-Watson, *The Rise of Nationality in the Balkans*, London, 1917,

pp. 129 f.; Fischel, *Panslawismus*, p. 26; N. Iorga, *Le caractère commun des institutions du Sud-est de l'Europe*, Paris, 1929. Certain basic semantic, morphological and phonetic similarities have been detected also between the various Balkan languages. Cf., e.g., A. Seliščev, "Des traits linguistiques communs aux langues balkaniques," *Revue des études slaves*, V (1925), 38-57.

42. L. S. Stavrianos, "Balkan Federation. A History of the Movement toward Balkan Unity in Modern Times," *Smith College Studies in History*, XXVII (1941-42), 13 f., 19, 33, 35; Ap. Dascalakis, *Rhigas Velestinlis: La Révolution française et les préludes de l'indépendance hellénique*, Paris, 1937, *passim* (Rhigas's Constitution is available also in Greek and a French transl. by Dascalakis in the appendix to the latter's bibliographical study of *Les œuvres de Rhigas Velestinlis*, Paris, 1937, pp. 73-125); Seton-Watson, *Rise of Nationality*, pp. 21 ff., 50 f., 78, 80 f. Cf. also Cons. G. Papadopoulos's careful analysis of *Les Privilèges du Patriarcat Oecuménique (Communauté Grecque Orthodoxe) dans l'Empire ottoman*, Paris, 1924. In his *Paternal Instructions* of 1798 (during Napoleon's Near Eastern campaign) Patriarch Anthimos of Jerusalem declared bluntly that he preferred the Turkish government to one of anti-Christian Franks. A Francophile nationalist, Korais, replied anonymously in a pamphlet, *Brotherly Instructions*, in which he attacked the "rapacious" clergy who "fear the destruction of the Ottoman Empire and the attainment of liberty, because it will mark the beginning of their own misfortune." Cf. Stephen George Chaconas, *Adamantios Korais: A Study in Greek Nationalism*, New York, 1942, pp. 86 ff.

43. Seton-Watson, *Rise of Nationality*, p. 51; David Mitrany, *The Land and the Peasant in Rumania*, London, 1930, p. 24; Joseph S. Roucek, *The Politics of the Balkans*, p. 103. Most revolutionaries agreed with Korais in opposing foreign missionary efforts on the ground that by introducing denominational divisions they would tend to break up the Greek national unity. Chaconas, *op. cit.*, p. 121. Cf. also Theodor Haralambides, "Die Kirchenpolitik Griechenlands (1821-1935)," *Zeitschrift für Kirchengeschichte*, LV (1936), 158-92; and for a historical outline D. S. Balanos, "Kirche und Nation in der orthodoxen Kirche Griechenlands," *ibid.*, LVII (1938), 554-65.

44. W. G. East, *The Union of Moldavia and Wallachia, 1859*, Cambridge, 1929, pp. 22 f. and *passim*; Trandafir G. Djuvara, *Mes missions diplomatiques . . . 1887-1925*, Paris, 1930, p. 48; Stavrianos, *op. cit.*, pp. 27 f., 140; Roucek, *op. cit.*, pp. 30 f., 45. Rumania's nationalist and religious biases, as usual interwoven with a variety of economic interests, have led to many domestic and international complications in the Jewish question as illustrated by the treaties of 1856, 1878, 1918-19, 1944, etc., and by endless diplomatic intercessions of the great powers in the intervening years. Cf. Cyrus Adler and Aaron M. Margalith, *With Firmness in the Right: American Diplomatic Action Affecting Jews, 1840-1945*, New York, 1946, pp. 99 ff.; S. W. Baron, *The Jews in Rumania*, New York, 1930; Joshua Starr, "Jewish Citizenship in Rumania (1878-1940)," *Jewish Social Studies*, III (1941), 57-80.

45. Joseph Matl, "Der heilige Sawa als Begründer der serbischen Nationalkirche—Seine Leistung und Bedeutung für den Kulturaufbau Europas," *Kyrios*, III (1938), 23-37; Charles Loiseau, "La question religieuse en Yugoslavie," *Le Monde slave*, n.s. II (1924-25), 349-68 (the author's facile optimism was disproved by events); Dragoslav Stranjaković, "La collaboration des Croates et des Serbes en 1848-1849," *ibid.*, n.s. XII, Pt. 2 (1935), 394-404; Seton-Watson, *Rise of Nationality*, pp. 27 ff.; Dinko Tomašić, "Nationality Problems and Partisan Yugoslavia," *Journal of Central European Affairs*, VI (1946), 111-25 (analyzing present-day difficulties). In his essay on "Jugoslavia and the Croat Problem" (*Slavonic Review*, XVI, 1937-38, 102-12), Seton-Watson called attention to the fact that "the problem which faces Jugoslavia is one of a triple nature—constitutional, national and economic—and it is not the least blunder of the dictatorship that the three have become inextricably mingled and can no longer be solved separately." He might have added that behind them all lurked the perennial religious issue, further complicating the prospects for satisfactory solution. The general historic evolution is described by Emile Haumant in *La formation de la Yugoslavie (XVᵉ-XXᵉ siècles)*, Paris, 1930, while the long-controversial data on the origin of the two main components are reviewed again by Henri Grégoire in

"L'origine et le nom des Croates et des Serbes," *Byzantion*, XVII (1944-45), 88-118.

46. Stavrianos, *op. cit.*, pp. 20, 89, 107 f., 121, 140; Seton-Watson, *Rise of Nationality*, p. 82. Because of Russian influence, Patriarch Cyril of Jerusalem declined to join the Synod of Constantinople in excommunicating the Bulgarians in 1872. The lasting effects of the ensuing controversy between the patriarchate and the Arab Orthodox community were so grave that the British administration felt prompted to appoint in 1925 a special commission. Cf. the report of the commissioners, Sir Anton Bertram and J. W. A. Young, *The Orthodox Patriarchate of Jerusalem*, London, 1926. Any rapprochement between Bulgaria and the Roman Church was, of course, viewed with alarm by Russia. Cf., e.g., Ignatiev's fears expressed to Pobedonostsev in 1881 (*L'autocratie russe*, pp. 94 f.) that, although the establishment of the exarchate had checked the pro-Catholic orientation, the Treaty of Berlin of 1878 had given it a new impetus. Ignatiev, who had served for years as Russian ambassador at Constantinople, where his devious diplomacy earned him the nickname of "pasha of lies," spoke with considerable authority on this subject. Cf. also Cyril E. Black, *The Establishment of Constitutional Government in Bulgaria*, Princeton, 1943 (chiefly on the period of 1878-1885); A. P., "Les aventures du Tsarisme en Bulgarie," *Affaires étrangères*, VI (1936), 379-84 (on Russian diplomacy's contribution to the revolutionary movements following Alexander's overthrow in 1886); L. S. Stavrianos, "L'institution de l'exarcat bulgare. Son influence sur les relations interbalkaniques," *Les Balkans*, XI (1939), 56-69; Hans Roger Madol, *Ferdinand von Bulgarien. Der Traum von Byzanz*, Berlin, 1931.

47. Seton-Watson, *The Southern Slav Question and the Hapsburg Monarchy*, London, 1911; Jan Schaffarik, *Slawische Ethnographie*, 1842, quoted by Fischel, *Panslawismus*, pp. 101 f. Fischel points out that this obviously dry statistical work enjoyed wide popularity and appeared in several editions as well as in Polish and Russian translations, all because, in the words of Kopitar, it had become "another stone in the structure of Panslavism." Kopitar himself had claimed as early as 1808 that Aus-

tria's population consisted of 13,000,000 Slavs as against 7,000,000 Germans, Magyars, Jews, etc. *Ibid.*, pp. 233. "In a hundred years," enthusiastically asserted Jan Kollar, "Slavonic life will spread over the whole world like a deluge." Cf. his *Ueber die literarische Wechselseitigkeit zwischen den verschiedenen Stämmen und Mundarten der slawischen Nation* (2d ed., Leipzig, 1844). The hundredth anniversary of the first publication of this classic of cultural Panslavism was celebrated by the Czech Academy of Sciences in an interesting collection of Czech essays, ed. by Jiři Horak under the title, *Slovanska Vzajemnost, 1836-1936*, Prague, 1938.

48. Seton-Watson, *Rise of Nationality*, pp. 13 f., 16 f., 26 f., 31 f., 34 ff., 45 f.; Jacob Spon and G. Wheler, *Voyage d'Italie, de Dalmatie, de Grèce et du Levant fait ès années 1675 et 1676*, 4 vols., Lyons, 1678-80, I, 355 f.; Stavrianos, *op. cit.*, pp. 6 f., 9, 11, 22. Stavrianos stresses the Russian practice of extensively employing Balkan Christians as dragomans, real or fictitious, and of granting to many Greek merchantmen the right of flying the Russian flag. In his essay, "Ortodossia orientale e unificazione nazionale" (*Religio*, XII, 1936, 200-14), Costantino Andreescu minimizes the imperialistic element in the Russian interventions, and argues for "the existence of an idea of a unitarian Orthodoxy, a Pan-Orthodoxy, an Orthodox nationality." Here the pendulum has swung too far to the other extreme.

49. Fischel, *Panslawismus*, pp. 20 f.; Cyril Bryner, "The Political Philosophy of Yuri Krizhanich," *New Scholasticism*, XIII (1939), 133-68.

50. George Vernadsky, "Alexandre I et le problème slave pendant la première moitié de son règne," *Revue des études slaves*, VII (1927), 95-111; Virginia Penn, "Philhellenism in Europe, 1821-1828," *Slavonic Review*, XVI (1937-38), 638-53. Cf. also Edward M. Earle, "American Interest in the Greek Cause, 1821-1827," *American Historical Review*, XXXIII (1927-28), 44-63. The real initiator of this policy was Czartoryski. In his Memorandum of 1804 he urged Alexander to satisfy a minimum of the demands of the great powers for "rectification" of territories. But "the mass of the Turkish territories in Europe should be divided into separate states, governed locally, and bound

to each other by a federation, upon which Russia would be able to secure to herself a decisive and lawful influence by means of the title of Emperor and Protector of the Slavs of the East, which would be accorded to his Imperial Majesty." Cf. his *Memoirs*, II, 55. Cf. also Handelsman, *Czartoryski, passim*; H. Batowski, "Un précurseur polonais de l'union balkanique—le prince Adam Czartoryski," *Revue internationale des études balkaniques*, II (1936), 149-65.

51. Fischel, *Panslawismus*, pp. 196 f., 201 ff., 292 ff., 335, 338; Julian Klaczko, "Le congrès de Moscou et la propagande panslaviste," *Revue des deux mondes*, LXXI (1867), 132-81. Cf. also Count Valerian Krasiński's *Panslavism and Germanism*, London, 1848; and, more generally, Marceli Handelsman, *Les idées françaises et la mentalité politique en Pologne au XIXe siècle*, Paris, 1927, emphasizing the conflict between the Polish liberals (especially among the émigrés) who were stimulated by the revolution, Benjamin Constant and the socialists, and the conservatives, led by Czartoryski at home and influenced by the ideas of Montalembert and Tocqueville.

52. Fischel, *Panslawismus*, pp. 372 ff., 516 f., 545 f. In his remarkable letter of Feb. 11, 1888, Pobedonostsev advocated even the support of a Russian church in far-off Buenos Aires, as both an outpost of Russian culture and a possible place of refuge for Russian ships in case of war. *L'autocratie russe*, pp. 523 f.

53. *Ibid.*, p. 276; Curtiss, *Church and State*, pp. 178 f.; Fischel, *Panslawismus*, pp. 311, 358 f., 377 ff., 461, 497, 502 f., 521 ff. Austria succeeded, to Pobedonostsev's chagrin, in preventing the Rumanian Bishop Melchizedek from spending his vacation in Kiev attending the celebrations of 1888—the overprocurator irately submitted copies of the correspondence between the Rumanian government and the bishop which he had secured from a "sympathetic" Rumanian—but a number of her own Ruthenian and Slovakian citizens smuggled themselves over the frontiers. Cf. Steinmann-Hurwicz, *op. cit.*, pp. 208 f. Pobedonostsev had rejoiced, however, when ten Galician delegates, including Naumovich, two students and a peasant, participated in the millenary celebrations for Cyril and Methodius in 1885, *L'autocratie russe*, pp. 320 f. Cf. also René Mardel, "La politique

slave de la Russie d'avant guerre: le procès ukrainien de Marmaros-Sziget," *Affaires étrangères*, VI (1936), 623-34; and Enrico Insabato, *L'Ucraina e la chiesa cattolica*, Rome, 1933 (from the fascist standpoint, mainly interesting because it lists the Uniate churches throughout the world, pp. 21 ff.).

54. Fischel, *Panslawismus*, pp. 88 ff., 468 f., 477 ff., 484, 499 f., 541 f. Interveningly, however, farsighted Czech leaders sought to come to terms with Austria. While afraid of Greater Germany, Palacký was equally apprehensive that Russia's further expansion would give birth to "a universal monarchy, that is to say, an infinite and inexpressible evil, a misfortune without measure and bound, such as I, though heart and soul a Slav, would nonetheless profoundly regret from the standpoint of humanity, even though that monarchy were proclaimed a Slavonic one." He propagated, therefore, the idea of a Danubian federation. Cf. Otakar Odložilik, "A Czech Plan for a Danubian Federation—1848," *Journal of Central European Affairs*, I (1941-42), 253-74. For Masaryk's wartime activities, cf. especially R. W. Seton-Watson, *Masaryk in England*, Cambridge, 1943 (including valuable unpublished materials). Cf. also Alfred Fischel, *Das tschechische Volk*, I, chiefly describing the Czechs' role in the dissolution of the Austro-Hungarian Empire and the rise of the Czechoslovakian Republic. Czech nationalism naturally enough evoked a strong reaction among the Sudeten Germans. Cf. the jubilee volume, *Das Sudetendeutschtum, Sein Wesen und Werden im Wandel der Jahrhunderte*, ed. by Gustav Pirchan, *et al.*, Brünn, 1937, and especially Josef Pfitzner's "Nationales Erwachen und Reifen der Sudetendeutschen," *ibid.*, pp. 419-47.

55. Fischel, *Panslawismus*, pp. 67 ff., 119, 152 f., 212, 257; Mazzini, *Scritti, Ed. naz.*, XLIV, 318; R. W. Seton-Watson, *Racial Problems in Hungary*, London, 1908, p. 42; Stavrianos, *op. cit.*, pp. 44, 69 ff.; G. Horn, *Le compromis de 1868 entre la Hongrie et la Croatie et celui de 1867 entre l'Autriche et la Hongrie*, Paris, 1907. Magyar conservative opinion agreed with the radicals. Count Karl Zay, inspector general of the Slovak-Lutheran churches and schools, declared in 1840 in the name of liberty, intelligence and Protestantism, that "magyarization of the Slavs is the most

sacred duty of every true Hungarian patriot, every fighter for liberty and reason and
every faithful subject of the imperial House
of Austria." The expected pro-Serbian and
Russophil reaction in Croatia came clearly
to the fore, e.g., in the "Pan-Slavist Memorandum of Liudovit Gaj in 1838," published
by Philip E. Mosely in the *American Historical Review*, XL (1934-35), 704-16.

56. Karel Kramař, "Europe and the Bohemian Question," *National Review*, XL
(1902-3), 183-205; Fischel, *Panslawismus*,
pp. 417 f., 423, 478 f. Kramař's arguments
were greatly expanded during the First World
War by such writers as Louis Leger in *Le
panslavisme et l'interêt français*, Paris, 1917.
The theory concerning Hussitism's old Slavonic origins is now reinforced by Jakobson's
pertinent remarks in the *Review of Politics*,
VII, 41. The Polish hesitancy, on the other
hand, is well illustrated by Marceli Handelsman's brief survey, "La politique slave de la
Pologne du XVIII° et XIX° siècles," *Le
Monde slave*, XIII (1936), 427-55. Cf. also
Friedrich A. Rager, "National Autonomy in
the Austro-Hungarian Monarchy," *Journal
of Central European Affairs*, I (1941-42),
417-27.

57. Fischel, *Panslawismus*, pp. 412, 416
f.; Nicholas Arseniev, *Holy Moscow*, London, 1940, pp. 108 ff.; Avrahm Yarmolinsky, *Dostoevsky*, New York, 1934, pp. 334
ff. Cf. also Masaryk, *op. cit.*, I (excellent
summary of Panslavist ideologies); Georg
Sacke, *W. S. Solowjews Geschichtsphilos-
ophie*, Diss. Leipzig, 1929, pp. 7 ff.; Clarence Augustus Manning, "Khomyakov and
the Orthodox Church," *Review of Religion*,
VI (1941-42), 169-78; *idem*, "Dostoyevsky
and Western Christianity," *Anglican Theological Review*, XII (1929-30), 399-410. As
early as 1858 A. I. Kochelev had emphasized in his reply to Ivan Aksakov that
"without Orthodoxy our nationality is nothing; with Orthodoxy our nationality has
universal significance." Cited by Paul N.
Miliukov in his lecture on the "Decom-
position of Slavophilism," as illustrated in
the teachings of Danilevski, Leontiev and
Soloviev. Cf. his *Le mouvement intellectuel
russe*, Paris, 1918, p. 419. The religious appeal of Neoslavism on twentieth century intellectuals is best characterized by the lyrical
passages in A. N. Berdyaev's biography of
A. S. *Khomyakov* which appeared in Russian
in 1912. "Slavophilism," wrote this disap-

pointed Marxist turned religious philosopher,
"brought to conscious ideological expression
the eternal truth of the Orthodox East and
the historical order of the Russian land,
uniting these organically. The Russian land
was for the Slavophils the bearer of Christian truth, and the Christian truth was in
the Orthodox Church." Cited by Hecker,
op. cit., p. 131. How Russian mysticism
and messianism, however, could be turned
against Panslavism and extreme nationalism
was demonstrated by Vladimir Soloviev, especially in his polemical essays of 1883-91,
assembled in his *Natsionalnii vopros v Rossii* (The National Problem in Russia), in his
collected works (*Sobranie sotshinenii*), ed.
by S. M. Soloviev and E. L. Radlov, 10 vols.,
St. Petersburg, n.d., Vol. V. Cf. Michael
Karpovich's brief analysis of "Vladimir
Soloviev on Nationalism," *Review of Politics*, VIII (1946), 183-91.

58. Kornilov, *op. cit.*, II, 194 f. (the ad-
dress of 1870 was edited by the leading
Slavophils, Ivan Aksakov, Yurii Samarin and
Prince Cherkaskii); Seton-Watson, *Rise of
Nationality*, pp. 144 ff.; Stavrianos, *Balkan
Federation*, p. 121.

59. Pobedonostsev's letters to Alexander
III of Jan. 21, 1881; Jan. 27, 1886; Feb. 6,
1887, in Steinmann-Hurwicz, *op. cit.*, p. 203;
L'autocratie russe, pp. 358, 408 f.; Fischel,
Panslawismus, pp. 542 f., 581. For Pobedonostsev and Alexander III's earlier leanings
toward Panslavism, cf. the letters cited in
Slavonic Review, VII, 40 ff. The German
threat soon began looming so large that some
Slavophils considered even Austroslavism as
the lesser evil. In May, 1910, General Volo-
dimirov asserted that with respect to the
forthcoming world conflict, "the Austroslavs,
who are at the same time Neoslavists, are
genuine Russophils." Fischel, pp. 542 f.

60. Marx first used this stock phrase of
militant atheism in his essay, "Zur Kritik
der Hegelschen Rechtsphilosophie" in
Deutsch-Französische Jahrbücher of 1844,
reprinted in his and Engels's *Werke. Gesamt-
ausgabe*, ed. by N. Rjazanov, Frankfort,
1927 ff., I, 607. Cf. the discussion between
Reinhart Seeger in his *Herkunft und Bedeutung des Schlagworts "Die Religion ist
Opium für das Volk*," Halle, 1935 (ascrib-
ing its coining to Bruno Bauer), and Ewald
Schaper in his "Religion als Opium für das
Volk," *Zeitschrift für Kirchengeschichte*,
LIX (1940), 425-30 (citing Feuerbach's

more qualified utterance of 1838). One wonders whether Marx, Bauer and Feuerbach were not directly indebted to Rousseau, since they had all doubtless read the *Nouvelle Héloïse* (VI, 8) where Julie's husband characterizes her love for God, "sa dévotion est un opium pour l'âme."

61. Herzen was not altogether consistent. While condemning the political quietism of Christianity, that "apotheosis of death," he was deeply impressed by Catholicism. Himself czarism's unrelenting critic, he found it possible to defend Russia and the czar against Michelet. He finally declared that Russia would ultimately rejuvenate decrepit old Europe by its socialism, a socialism in many ways analogous to Christianity. Alexander Herzen, *Le peuple russe et le socialisme. Lettre à M. J. Michelet*, 2d ed., Paris, 1852 (reprinted from *L'Avénement du peuple* of Nov. 19, 1851); Masaryk, *op. cit.*, I, 354 ff., 393 ff., 412, 422. Cf. also Raoul Labry, *Herzen et Proudhon*, Paris, 1928; and, more generally, J. P. Voronizhin, *Istoriia ateizma* (History of Atheism) 5 pts., Moscow, 1928-29; and Fritz Mauthner, *Der Atheismus und seine Geschichte im Abendlande*, 4 vols., Stuttgart, 1923.

62. Bakunin, *Dieu et l'Etat*, Paris, 1882; Masaryk, *op. cit.*, I, 433 ff.; Lenin, "Socialism and Religion," in his *Selected Works*, XI, 658, 661. Cf. Edward H. Carr, *Michael Bakunin*, London, 1937, especially pp. 167 ff., 327 ff.; and Gerd Machers, *Bakunin und Lenin: die Integranten der russischen Revolution* (Diss. Heidelberg), Offenbach, 1932. The more recent role of socialist as well as fascist parties in Russia, Germany, Turkey, Mexico, Spain and England in *The War against God* is described briefly by Sidney Dark and R. S. Essex in a volume published in New York, 1938. Cf. also Johanna Gunz, *Sozialismus und Religion in Deutschland der Nachkriegszeit*, Munich, 1933.

63. Spinka, *Church*, pp. 104 ff., 147 ff.; Paul B. Anderson, *People, Church and State in Modern Russia*, New York, 1944, pp. 9 f.; Pobedonostsev, "Faith" in *Reflections*, p. 138. The general disorganization of church life, however, more than counteracted these educational difficulties and the dissident sects made successful inroads into the shrinking total of professing Christians. Among the reasons for their relative success, the Orthodox Church Synod of 1925 mentioned

their "social and political slogans which are akin to the communist ideas, for which they were formerly prosecuted but which now are looked on with tolerance by the new regime." Cited by Hecker, *op. cit.*, p. 71. In the early years some Soviet Baptists were even allowed to participate in the Baptist World Congresses at Stockholm (1923) and Toronto (1928). Cf. Rushbrooke, *op. cit.*, p. 16. Cf. also Sergius Troitsky's analysis of "The Living Church" in William Chauncey Emhardt, *Religion in Soviet Russia: Anarchy*, Milwaukee, 1929; Robert Stupperich, "Das russische Sektenwesen der Gegenwart," *Osteuropa*, X (1934-35), 553-64; and, in general, the materials assembled in Vvedenskii, *op. cit.*; P. V. Gidulianov, *Otdelenie tserkvi od gosudarstva v S.S.S.R.* (Separation of State and Church in the Soviet Union), 3d ed., Moscow, 1926 and B. V. Titlinov, *Tserkov vo vremia revolutsii* (The Church in the Period of Revolution), St. Petersburg, 1924.

64. Spinka, *Church*, pp. 58 f., 79 ff.; Robinson, *Rural Russia*, pp. 183 f., 196 f.; Anderson, *op. cit.*, pp. 49 ff. For the main reactionary organization, the so-called *Soius russkago naroda* (The Union of the Russian People), cf. the volume under this title, ed. by A. Chernovskii, Moscow, 1929. Cf. also Boris P. Kandidov, *Tserkov i fevralskaia revolutsiia* (The Church and the February Revolution: The Class Position of the Orthodox Church in the Period of February, 1917), Moscow, 1934; and, for the general background, Frank A. Golder's *Documents of Russian History, 1914-1917*, New York, 1927; M. V. Rodzianko's memoirs, *The Reign of Rasputin*, London, 1927; and Sir Bernard Pares's *The Fall of the Russian Monarchy: a Study of the Evidence*, New York, 1939.

65. Hecker, *op. cit.*, pp. 200 f.; Spinka, *Church*, pp. 118 ff. Tikhon's rashness may in part be explained by his own sense of insecurity. The momentous decision to restore the patriarchate had been made less than three months before (Oct. 30, 1917) by the *Sobor*, with only 265 (of 564) delegates present and only 141 voting in the affirmative. He himself was elected by lot from a slate of three candidates, among whom Metropolitan Antonii Khrapovitskii of Kharkov, a former leader of the "Black Hundreds," had clearly been the assembly's first choice. *Ibid.*, pp. 87 ff.

.66. Reyburn, *Russian Church*, pp. 259, 295 f.; Anderson, *op. cit.*, pp. 12 f.; Nicholas Berdyaev, *The Russian Revolution*, English transl., London, 1932, pp. 59 f.; Hecker, *op. cit.*, pp. 186 ff. Hecker quotes the following passage from A. Lunacharski: "The new [socialist] religion, the religion of humanity, the religion of toil, has no guarantees, but I suppose that even without God and without guarantees, which are but masks of the same God, it remains a *religion*."

67. Lenin's Letters to Gorki of November and December, 1913, in *Selected Works*, XI, 675 ff. Cf. Walsh in Guilday's *Catholic Church in Contemporary Europe*, pp. 218 f.; Sir Bernard Pares, *Russia and the Peace*, New York, 1944, p. 40.

68. Walsh in Guilday, *op. cit.*, pp. 251 f.; Hecker, *op. cit.*, pp. 226 f. Because Monsignor d'Herbigney, president of the Pontifical Commission for Russia, cited the Muslim telegram without giving its place of origin or the names of its signatories, its authenticity was doubted. Such skepticism seems excessive, however, in the light of the then existing circumstances.

69. Pares, *Russia*, pp. 39 f.; Koenig, *Principles of Peace*, p. 324 (Cardinal Gasparri's memorandum to the Genoa Conference); Lama, *Papst und Kurie*, pp. 379 ff.; Alice Burke's interview with Father Braun in the *Boston Traveler* of Jan. 4, 1946; the declaration of Feb. 10, 1945, cited by Peter Charanis in "The Schism between the Greek and Roman Church and Its Significance," *Journal of Central European Affairs*, V (1945), 260. The Karlovtsi Synod and its overtly counterrevolutionary leadership are briefly described in Spinka's *Church*, pp. 166 ff. The Russian government played up these mutual antagonisms as when at the Cieplak trial it conceded the archbishop the mitigating circumstance that his church had been oppressed under czarism and the bourgeois republic of 1917. Cf. Adolf Ziegler, *Die russische Gottlosenbewegung*, Munich, 1932, p. 166. Catholic reaction to Orthodox intransigence is best illustrated by Max Pribilla's bitter comment, that many Orthodox seem to "prefer to perish in a Bolshevik or Turkish way, rather than be saved in Roman fashion." Cf. his *Um kirchliche Einheit*, p. 130. Cf. also Walsh's sharply worded pamphlet, *Why Pope Pius XI Asked Prayers for Russia on March 19, 1930?* New York, 1930; Joseph McCabe's antipapal essay on

Russia and the Roman Church, London, 1941; and the more dispassionate study of P. Mailleux, "The Catholic Church in Russia and the Exarch Feodorov," in *Religion in Russia*, ed. by Count George Bennigsen, London, 1940, pp. 31-48.

70. Stalin, *Marxism and the National and Colonial Question* (collection of essays), English transl., new ed., New York, 1942, p. 20; Pares, *Russia*, p. 91. Cf. the "Resolution on the Question of Nationalities" adopted by the Comintern with special reference to the situation in the Balkans and published in the English ed. of the *Communist International*, n.s., IV (1924), 86-98; and, in general, Hans Kohn, *Nationalism in the Soviet Union*, New York, 1933; Oscar I. Janowsky, *Nationalities and National Minorities (With Special Reference to East-Central Europe)*, New York, 1945, pp. 69 ff.; Corliss Lamont, *The Peoples of the Soviet Union*, New York, 1946. In the liberal era of Alexander II and under the stimulus of early Panslavist humanitarianism, the czarist administration itself laid stress upon the great national diversities within the empire. They were graphically displayed in the picturesque Dashkov Museum, founded in Moscow on the occasion of the Slavic Congress of 1867. Cf. its description by Leroy-Beaulieu, *op. cit.*, I, 57 ff. Under Alexander III, however, these diversities were acutely felt as a source of weakness. The reversal of policies under the Soviets was particularly evident with respect to Jews. While before 1917 antisemitism had full government sanction, it was now formally outlawed and made a heinous counterrevolutionary crime. On the enactment of this prohibition in July, 1918, Lenin delivered a memorable radio address. Cf. I. Larin, *Evrei i antisemitizm v S.S.S.R.* (Jews and Antisemitism in the Soviet Union), Moscow, 1929; and Avrahm Yarmolinsky, *The Jews and other Minor Nationalities under the Soviets*, New York, 1928.

71. N. S. Timasheff, "Russian Nationalism under the Soviets," *Thought*, XX (1945), 443 f.; Stalin, *Political Report to the Sixteenth Party Congress of the Russian Communist Party*, English transl., New York, 1930, p. 191. The ambiguity in Marx's numerous, but incidental, remarks on nationalism is analyzed by Solomon F. Bloom in *The World of Nations. A Study of the National Implications in the Work of Karl Marx*,

New York, 1941. Cf. also the brief analysis by B. Moore, Jr., of "Some Readjustments in Communist Theory," in the *Journal of the History of Ideas*, VI (1945), 468-82, showing the changes which took place since 1917 in various other phases of the Marx-Leninist theory.

72. *Pravda* of Nov. 7, 1938; *Izvestia* of April 17, 1939, cited by Timasheff, *op. cit.*, pp. 447, 455. Cf. also the same author's "Four Phases of Russian Internationalism," *Thought*, XX (1945), 37-54, and more generally, *The Great Retreat: The Growth and Decline of Communism in Russia*, New York, 1946. Though somewhat colored by th:: author's anticommunist bias (how many studies on the Soviet Union lack bias of one kind or another?), these studies succinctly summarize the evident recent transformations in the Soviet Union's national ideologies, complementing the author's earlier review of *Religion in Soviet Russia 1917-1942*, New York, 1942. Cf. also Max M. Laserson's pertinent remarks on the "rehabilitation of national history" in his *Russia and the Western World: The Place of the Soviet Union in the Comity of Nations*, New York, 1945, pp. 138 ff.

73. Cf. the brief summary by Rose M. Somerville, "Counting Noses in the Soviet Union: 1939 Census," *The American Quarterly on the Soviet Union*, III (1940), 51-73. Although emphasizing that the two censuses are not absolutely comparable, for the definition of "nationality" (*natsionalnost*) in 1939 differed somewhat from that of "ethnic group" (*naradnost*) in 1926, Frank Lorimer points out that "the number of persons reporting themselves as Russians in 1939 was 27 per cent higher than the number classified as 'Russian' in 1926, in contrast to an increase of slightly less than 16 per cent for the total population," and that "the decrease in the number of persons reported as Ukrainian was probably due, in the main, to increasing identification with the Russians, especially in the case of Ukrainians living in the R.S.F.S.R." Cf. *The Population of the Soviet Union: History and Prospects*, Geneva, 1946, pp. 137, 139. It stands to reason that the war strengthened these assimilatory trends. The Red Army, in particular, long an unconscious instrument of Russification, now served as a gigantic melting pot for untold millions recruited from national minorities. Cf. John Maynard, *The Russian Peasant and Other*

Studies, London, 1942, p. 393. Nevertheless, the present writer recalls his amazement when, on his visit to the Soviet Union in 1937, he heard an old Jewish Communist leader and stanch fighter for the use of Yiddish as against the "bourgeois" Hebrew language, extol the virtues of medieval Hebrew literature. The Communists, he was told, had all come to recognize the fact that no great nationality could begin dating its cultural history with the revolution of 1917.

74. Anderson, *op. cit.*, pp. 65 f., 82 ff., 86, 89 f., 140 f. The second Sobor of 1923, controlled by a reformist majority of the "Living Church," adopted a resolution reading in part: "The Sobor affirms that every honorable Christian should take his place among these warriors for humanitarian truth, and use all means to realize in life the grand principles of the October Revolution." Spinka, *Church*, p. 237.

75. Anderson, *op. cit.*, pp. 167 ff.; Timasheff in *Thought*, XX, 447. Lama's reply (*Papst und Kurie*, p. 265 n. 1) to Glubokhovskii that even in Rome the Catholic Church had preserved pagan temples and merely converted them to Catholic uses is, of course, beside the point. The Orthodox resented just as much the conversion of their churches into Catholic places of worship as they did the leveling of their historical monuments. The Russian Church was also perfectly consistent inasmuch as Tikhon had formally repudiated the Treaty of Brest-Litovsk as dangerous to Russia. Spinka, *Church*, pp. 135 f. Cf. also James T. Shotwell and Max M. Laserson, *Poland and Russia, 1919-1945*, New York, 1945, discussing the political rather than the religious or cultural issues between the two countries.

76. Anderson, *op. cit.*, pp. 170 f., 194 ff., 199 f.; Pares, *op. cit.*, p. 47.

77. Ziegler, *op. cit.*, pp. 30 f.; P. E. T. Widdrington, "The Religious Situation in Russia," *Christendom*, XII (Oxford, 1942), 11-18; Pares, *op. cit.*, p. 49; Anderson, *op. cit.*, pp. 159 f., 207 ff.; Cyrus L. Sulzberger's correspondence to the *New York Times* of June 7, 1945. The importance attached in czarist circles to the battle use of ikons is luridly demonstrated by Zhevakhov's reminiscences. The empress shared his conviction, the associate overprocurator asserted, that the World War lasted so long only because no heed had been paid to St. Joasaph's order (given Zhevakhov in a dream) that his ikon

be displayed in various parts of the front. *Op. cit.*, I, 33, 50; Spinka, *Church*, p. 8.

78. Sulzberger, *l.c.* Similar recognition was extended also to other denominational bodies. According to the *Izvestia* of Oct. 27, 1943, a Muslim congress meeting at Tashkent on Oct. 15-19 elected an Uzbek octogenarian as presiding mufti of the Muslim administration in Central Asia and Kazakstan. J. H. Rushbrooke, president of the Baptist World Alliance, quoted recent news as stating that the government is "doing everything possible to help believers," *op. cit.*, p. 3; Anderson, *op. cit.*, pp. 213 f.

79. *Ibid.*, pp. 180 ff., 188 f., 191, 206 ff. The difficulties of recognizing the Anglican ordination in the light of accepted Greek Canon Law are well illustrated by four papers submitted, at the request of the Archbishop of Canterbury, by leading theologians at the University of Athens. These papers published in the *Ekklesia* are summarized by J. Gill in "The Orthodox Church of Greece and Anglican Orders," *Orientalia Christiana Periodica*, V (1939), 239-44.

80. Cf. the analysis of the new election districts in the U.S.S.R. (listed in *Pravda* on Oct. 17, 1945) in the *New York Times*, of Nov. 30, 1945. The annexation of Viborg and Königsberg by the Russian S.S.R., the largest unit in the Union, was clearly dictated by strategic considerations. The inclusion of East Prussia in either of the neighboring republics of Lithuania or White Russia, though geographically more logical, would have added another recalcitrant minority and immeasurably increased the burdens of either government. Ultimately the potentially irredentist German (and Finnish) residents may be marked for evacuation or assimilation.

81. Herman Wendel, "Marxism and the Southern Slav Question," *Slavonic Review*, II (1923-24), 289-307 (citing also Wilhelm Liebknecht, Jean Jaurès and even the Communist International of 1920 among those lacking in sympathy for Southern Slavs); Tomašić in *Journal of Central European Affairs*, VI, 111 f. Bakunin, too, was so in-

censed over the Croat contribution to the defeat of the Magyar revolution that in his "Second Appeal to the Slavs" he exhorted the Austrian Slavs to get rid of their traitors (among whom he included Palacký). Cf. the German text published by Václav Čejchan in his *Bakunin v Čechách* (Bakunin in Bohemia), Prague, 1928, and cited by Odložilik in *Journal of Central European Affairs*, I, 260 n. 7.

82. The relatively amicable attitude of the Russian occupational authorities to the Bulgarian "enemy" effectively controverted the predictions of Bulgarian Nazis who, before the war, had proclaimed the end of Panslavism and endeavored to deny even Russia's Slavonic character. Cf. Janko Janeff, "Der Untergang des Panslawismus," *Nationalsozialistische Monatshefte*, VIII (1937), 881-88. Today it is the turn of the 2,000,000 Germans in the Balkans to pick up their old roots and return to the Fatherland. Cf. Joseph B. Schechtman, "The Elimination of German Minorities in Southeastern Europe," *Journal of Central European Affairs*, VI (1946), 157-66.

83. Dostoevski, "Speech on Pushkin," English transl. in *Pages from the Journal of an Author*, Boston, 1916, pp. 66 f. (the preferred translation as given in the text is taken from Arseniev, *Holy Moscow*, pp. 108 ff.). Cf. also Yarmolinsky, *Dostoevsky*, pp. 366 ff.

84. Cf. Pobedonostsev, *L'autocratie russe*, p. 531.

85. Cited by Arseniev, *op. cit.*, p. 87. This is, indeed the keynote of Kireevski's highly influential essay of 1852 in which he contrasted European with Russian civilization to the latter's obvious advantage. This essay is available in a German translation entitled *Russlands Kritik an Europa*, Stuttgart, 1923. Kireevski's anti-individualistic interpretation, moreover, is shared by such other representative thinkers as Khomiakov, Soloviev, Bulgakov and Berdyaev. Cf. C. Swietlinski, *La conception sociologique de l'oecumenisme dans la pensée religieuse russe contemporaine*, Paris, 1939.

86. Curtiss, *op. cit.*, p. 343.

Chapter VII

Jewish Ethnicism

1. Joshua 24:13. Joshua's authorship of this statement has been disputed by modern Biblical critics, but there is almost general consensus as to its pre-exilic origin. Cf. also Deut. 6:10-11. Even later some descendants of Canaanites disputed the Jews' possession of Palestine. Cf. Hans Lewy, "Ein Rechtsstreit um den Boden Palästinas im Altertum," *Monatsschrift für Geschichte und Wissenschaft des Judentums*, LXXVII (1933), 84-99, 172-80.

2. Deut. 7:7-8. The Sabbath rest commandment is justified in Ex. 20:11 by reference to God's rest after the six days of creation, but Deut. 5:15 speaks only of its social purpose which should, however, remind every Israelite of his liberation from Egyptian bondage. The meaning and implications of Israel's "historical monotheism" are briefly explained in the author's *Social and Religious History of the Jews*, I, 4 ff. The reader will find in this work (especially in its third volume) fuller documentation for the evolution of both Jewish nationalism and religion.

3. There are few scholars today who still doubt the historicity of either the exile or the restoration. Such doubts had been voiced with much learning and ingenuity especially by Charles C. Torrey, in his *Ezra Studies*, Chicago, 1910; *The Second Isaiah*, New York, 1928; *Pseudo-Ezekiel and the Original Prophecy*, New Haven, 1930; and "Certainly Pseudo-Ezekiel," *Journal of Biblical Literature*, LIII (1934), 291-320. While the literary evidence by the very nature of the Biblical sources could not be absolutely conclusive, archaeological excavations of the 1920's clearly demonstrated that Palestine had suffered great losses of population in the sixth century B.C. which could be explained only by large-scale destruction and deportation. Cf. William F. Albright, *The Archaeol-*

ogy *of Palestine and the Bible*, 3d ed., New York, 1935, pp. 169 ff., 218 ff. Nor is there any question as to the existence of a vast and growing Jewish dispersion even before the fall of Jerusalem and its persistence after the restoration. Cf. Antonin Causse, *Les dispersés d'Israël; les origines de la Diaspora et son rôle dans la formation du judaïsme*, Paris, 1929. Unfortunately its life in the postexilic age is almost completely shrouded in darkness, broken only by occasional flashes emanating from the records of Ezra and Nehemiah's work in Palestine or from the Aramaic papyri illustrating the life of a rather atypical Jewish military colony in Elephantine, Egypt.

4. Philo Judaeus, *Opera*, ed. by Th. Mangey, London, 1742, VI, 204; Josephus, *Against Apion*, II, 18, 175, in *Works*, ed. by H. Thackeray and Ralph Marcus, London, 1926 (Loeb Classical Library), I, 362 ff. Cf. Nathan Morris, *The Jewish School: An Introduction to the History of Jewish Education*, London, 1937; and Nathan Drazin, *History of Jewish Education from 515 B.C.E. to 220 C.E.*, Baltimore, 1940. The pre-exilic antecedents of both the exilic community organization and the synagogue (Palestine's geographic regionalism, extensive municipal self-government, imageless cult, and the Deuteronomic centralization of worship), are fully discussed by the present writer in *The Jewish Community: Its History and Structure to the American Revolution*, 3 vols., Philadelphia, 1942, I, 31 ff., 55 ff.; III, 6 ff., 10 ff. Even such critics as Siegmund Mowinckel, who believe that the issue of imageless worship had not been decided until the days of Amos and Hosea (cf. his "À quel moment le culte de Jahvé à Jérusalem est-il officiellement devenu un culte sans images?" *Revue d'histoire et de philosophie religieuses*,

335

IX, 1929, 197-216), would concede several generations for such preparation of the exilic community. In his *Du groupe ethnique à la communauté religieuse*, Paris, 1937, Antonin Causse defends the thesis that the pre-exilic Judean nationality was changed into a purely religious Jewish community after 586. This view overlooks the basic ethnicism of the very Diaspora community and has even less justification than the long-discarded opinion of Theodor Mommsen that the Jews ceased to be a national group after the second fall of Jerusalem in A.D. 70. Cf. Jean Juster, *Les Juifs dans l'empire romain*, 2 vols., Paris, 1914, II, 19 ff.

5. Azariah de' Rossi, *Meor eynaim* (Light of the Eyes, a collection of historical essays), ed. by David Cassel, Vilna, 1864-66, p. 446, quoting many older sources. In a lengthy discourse Solomon Ephraim Lentshits, a seventeenth century preacher, argued in favor of peace among nations because of their common descent from Adam and Eve. He conceded, however, the permissibility of interdenominational wars—a characteristic reflection of that era of religious wars. Cf. his *Olelot Ephraim* (Homilies), Amsterdam, 1710, no. 374. Cf. also Moses Sofer in his *Hatam sofer* (Responsa), VI, 86, fol. 28 b.

6. Maimonides, "Letter on Astrology," ed. by Alexander Marx in "The Correspondence between the Rabbis of Southern France and Maimonides about Astrology," *Hebrew Union College Annual*, III (1926), 356 f.; Salo W. Baron, "Prospects of Peace in Palestine" in *The Near East: Problems and Prospects*, ed. by Philip W. Ireland, Chicago, 1942, pp. 109 f. Cf. also Jacob Mann, "The Messianic Movements during the First Crusades" (Hebrew), *Hatekufah*, XXIII (1925), 243-61; XXIV (1928), 335-58; and more generally Julius H. Greenstone, *The Messiah Idea in Jewish History*, Philadelphia, 1906; Hugo Gressmann, *Der Messias*, Göttingen, 1929; Joseph Klausner, *Ha-Raayon ha-meshihi be-Yisrael* (The Messianic Idea in Israel), 2d ed., Jerusalem, 1927; and Abba Hillel Silver, *A History of Messianic Speculation in Israel, From the First through the Seventeenth Centuries*, New York, 1927.

7. Maimonides, *Mishneh Torah* (Code of Laws), end. Isaiah's prediction of the "remnant" which shall "return" (10:22), reinforced by St. Paul (Romans 9:27), exerted a powerful influence on pious minds, both Catholic and Protestant. Even Duns Scotus,

though affected by the widespread agitation for the expulsion of the Jews from England, could merely suggest that it "might suffice to allow a few of them segregated on some island to observe their law, so that they may fulfill that Isaianic prophecy." *Sententiae*, IV, dist. 4, qu. 9 in *Opera omnia*, Paris, 1891-95, XVI, 489. Cf. Salo W. Baron, "The Jewish Factor in Medieval Civilization," *Proceedings of the American Academy for Jewish Research*, XII (1942), 36 ff. Cf. also Louis Finkelstein, "Some Aspects of Early Rabbinic Nationalism," *The Brandeis Avukah Annual of 1932*, ed. by Joseph Shalom Shubow, Boston, 1932, pp. 78-96; Martin Buber, "The Beginnings of the National Idea," *Review of Religion*, X (1945-46), 254-65 (analyzing the teachings of the sixteenth century rabbi, Loewe ben Bezalel); N. M. Gelber, *Zur Vorgeschichte des Zionismus. Judenstaatsprojekte in den Jahren 1695-1845*, Vienna, 1927; Sokolow, *History of Zionism, passim*; Francesco Ruffini, "Alessandro Manzoni e il Ritorno d'Israele," *Atti della R. Academia delle Scienze di Torino*, Classe di scienze morali, LXV (1929-30), 167-94, 224-30.

8. Clermont-Tonnère's address at the National Assembly of Dec. 23, 1789, reproduced in *Revue des grandes journées parlementaires*, ed. by Gaston Lèbre and G. Labouchère, I (1897), 10. The French Revolution offers a convenient illustration of the main emancipatory trends because of its dramatic reversal of previous conditions and trends, its clearcut discussions on the Jewish question, and its immediate influence on the status of the majority of world Jewry living on the European continent. In addition to the literature listed in Baron's *History* (III, 146 ff.), cf. such recent studies as S. Posener, "The Immediate Economic and Social Effects of the Emancipation of the Jews in France," *Jewish Social Studies*, I (1939), 271-326; Adolf Kober, "The French Revolution and the Jews in Germany," *ibid.*, VII (1945), 291-322; *Di Yidn in Frankreich* (Jews in France), ed. by Elias Tscherikover, 2 vols., New York, 1942. But this evolution had long been adumbrated by new social, economic and political developments in Holland and the Anglo-Saxon countries. Under the impact of the Commercial Revolution, Enlightenment, and the Wars of Religion there were distinctly new approaches to the Jewish question in Hugo Grotius' proposals for the formal ad-

mission of Jews to Amsterdam in 1617, the Naturalization Bill for Britain's North American colonies in 1740, Pelham's "Jew Bill" of 1753, and finally, the Constitution of the United States. Cf. such more recent works as *Geschiedenis der Joden in Nederland*, ed. by Hendrik Brugmans and A. Frank, Vol. I, Amsterdam, 1940; and Cecil Roth, *History of the Jews in England*, Oxford, 1941, pp. 149 ff.

9. Robert Anchel, *Napoléon et les Juifs*, Paris, 1928, pp. 14 ff., 18; Ernest Ginsburger, *Le Comité de surveillance de Jean-Jacques Rousseau, Saint-Esprit-Les-Bayonne*, Paris, 1934; *idem*, "Les Juifs de Peyrehorade," *Revue des études juives*, n. s. IV (1938), 35-69.

10. This keynote, sounded by the obsequious speakers at the Assembly of Jewish Notables and the Grand Sanhedrin, soon permeated the correspondence between the newly created Central Consistory in Paris and its dependencies in France, Italy and Holland and influenced also the Jewries of other lands. Cf. for instance, the memorandum submitted to Napoleon during his visit to Amsterdam in 1811 by a leader of Dutch-Jewish Enlightenment and published in the Appendix to S. W. Baron's "Moses Cohen Belinfante" (Yiddish), *Yivo Bleter*, XIII (1939), 441 ff. (cf. also *idem* in *Historia Judaica*, V, 1943, 1-26). Later rabbinic glorification of the French Revolution is illustrated by B. Mossé's collection, *La Révolution française et le rabbinat français*, Avignon, 1890.

11. Cf. the brief remarks of Harry Sacher in his *Jewish Emancipation—the Contract Myth*, London, 1917. Of course, many Continental governments tried to promote Jewish assimilation, especially in its early stages by a variety of legislative stimulants. Cf. the brief survey by Kurt Stillschweig, "Jewish Assimilation as an Object of Legislation," *Historia Judaica*, VIII (1946), 1-18.

12. A curious illustration of both affirmations was the contention of the first German Rabbinic Conference, which met in Brunswick in 1844, that it was but a continuation of the Paris Sanhedrin. Similarly the preliminary meeting of 1889 in Detroit, which paved the way for the Central Conference of American Rabbis, accepted the work of the Brunswick and other German conferences as the basis for its own program, "in an endeavor to maintain in unbroken historic suc-cession the formulated expression of Jewish thought and life of each era." Cf. the resolution published in the Central Conference's *Yearbook*, I (1890-91), 4.

13. Theodor Mommsen, *Auch ein Wort über unser Judentum*, 3d impression, Berlin, 1880, p. 8.

14. Abraham Geiger, "Die Versammlung zu Leipzig und die zu Philadelphia," *Jüdische Zeitschrift für Wissenschaft und Leben*, VIII (1870), 2; Jakob Wassermann, "Der Jude der Bestimmung" in *Antisemitismus und jüdisches Volkstum* (Sonderheft of *Der Jude*), Berlin, 1925, p. 85. Cf. also the latter's autobiographical credo, *Mein Weg als Deutscher und Jude*, Berlin, 1921.

15. Salo W. Baron, "Abraham Benisch's Project for Jewish Colonization in Palestine (1842)," in *Jewish Studies in Memory of George A. Kohut*, ed. by him and Alexander Marx, New York, 1935, pp. 78 f.

16. There exists as yet no comprehensive scholarly history of modern antisemitism. Apart from some good encyclopedia articles supplying also bibliographical data, one may mention especially W. ten Boom, *Die Entstehung des modernen Rassen-Antisemitismus (besonders in Deutschland)*, Leipzig, 1928; Israel Schapira, *Der Antisemitismus in der französischen Literatur*, Berlin, 1927; Roberto Mazzetti, *L'antiebraismo nella cultura italiana dal 1700 al 1900. Antologia storica*, Modena, 1939; and more generally, Hugo Valentin, *Antisemitism, Historically and Critically Examined*, English transl., New York, 1936; *Jews in a Gentile World*, ed. by Isaque Graeber and Stuart H. Britt, New York, 1942; and *Essays on Antisemitism*, ed. by Pinson. The literature on, for, and against antisemitism makes up in staggering quantity for what it lacks in scholarly qualities. Cf., e.g., the list of more significant items published in the short span of two years in Salo W. Baron's *Bibliography of Jewish Social Studies, 1938-39*, New York, 1941, pp. 112 ff., 236 ff. Antisemitism has been treated here merely as a background for the rise of modern Jewish nationalism, although it exerted, of course, a powerful influence also on other phases of Jewish, as well as non-Jewish, life and thought. In 1848 Gabriel Riesser, stanch champion of Jewish emancipation, declared at the Frankfort National Assembly (of which he was soon to become second vice-president) that "one must not think that exceptional laws can be enacted [against

338   MODERN NATIONALISM AND RELIGION

a particular group] without causing a dangerous rupture in the entire system of liberty."
Cf. his *Gesammelte Schriften*, ed. by M.
Isler, 4 vols., Frankfort, 1868, IV, 410. More
recently M. Müller-Claudius, observing the
adverse effects of the growing antisemitic
propaganda in Germany before Hitler's rise
to power, wrote succinctly: "Antisemitism
works injustice not only on the Jew, but also
has unwholesome biological effects on the
hater himself. It lays the ground for a patho-
logical state of mind." Cf. his "Antisemitismus als Angriff auf die Seele." *Der Morgen*,
VII (1931), 157. It took a world war to impress both these lessons on all Western
peoples.

17. Heymann Steinthal, "Das ausgewählte
Volk" (1890), in *Ueber Juden und Judentum, Vorträge und Aufsätze*, ed. by Gustav
Karpeles, 3d ed., Berlin, 1925, p. 13. Cf. also
various other pertinent excerpts culled from
Jewish and Christian writings in *Die Lehren
des Judentums*, ed. by Simon Bernfeld *et al.*,
5 pts., Berlin and Leipzig, 1923-28, IV, 153
ff. Commenting in 1897 on the role of "the
eternal Jew," Theodor Herzl pointed out
that the modern Jewish migratory movements had numerically dwarfed the famous
barbarian migrations which had marked the
turn from ancient to medieval times. Cf. his
Zionistische Schriften ed. by Leon Kellner,
2 vols., 2d ed., 1920, I, 266.

18. Dubnow, "Foundations of Jewish Nationalism," *Reflex*, I, Pt. 4 (1927), 47; *idem*,
"The Mystery and Law of Survival of the
Jewish People" (Hebrew), *Heatid*, IV (2d
impression, 1923), 117. The latter essay appeared as part of a symposium on the future
of Judaism. Dubnow himself succinctly
stated the affinities, as well as the differences, between his and Ahad Haam's views
in his Hebrew essay on "Negation or Affirmation of the Diaspora in Ahad Haam's Doctrine," *Hashiloah*, XXX (1914), 206-10. He
had previously developed his general views
on Jewish nationalism in his *Pisma o starom i
novom evreistvie* (Letters on Old and Modern Judaism, 1897-1907) which first appeared in his monthly *Voskhod* and were
reissued in book form in St. Petersburg,
1907. They were subsequently translated
into Hebrew by A. Levinson, Tel-Aviv, 1937.
Dubnow's autonomist reinterpretation of
Jewish history underlay also his *Weltgeschichte des jüdischen Volkes* (10 vols.,
Berlin, 1925-29) and his numerous other

writings listed in the bibliography compiled
by Josef Meisl and published in *Festschrift zu
Simon Dubnows siebzigstem Geburtstag*,
Berlin, 1930, pp. 266 ff. Cf. also his autobiography completed a few years before his
death at the hand of nazi assassins in Riga
and first published in Russian (2 vols., Riga,
1934-35). Excerpts in German entitled *Mein
Leben* and. ed. by Elias Hurwicz appeared in
Berlin, 1937, and were followed by a full
Hebrew version.

19. Dubnow, *Pisma*, p. 83; *idem*, "What
Are We to Do in the Days of Haman?" (Yid-
dish), *Oifn Scheidweg*, II (Paris, 1939), 6.
Cf. also his Yiddish review of the writer's
Social and Religious History in *Di Zukunft*,
XLII (1937), 765 ff.

20. N. M. Gelber, "Der erste Sozialist in
der hebräischen Literatur" in *Aus Zwei Jahr-
hunderten, Beiträge zur neueren Geschichte
der Juden*, Vienna, 1924, p. 190; *Ha-Emet*,
Vienna, 1877, Introd. (also new ed., Tel-
Aviv, 1938). Cf. also Dov (Bernard) Wein-
ryb, "The Ideological Evolution of A. S.
Liberman" (Hebrew), *Zion*, IV (1939),
317-48; Borys Sapir, "Liberman et le socialisme russe," *International Review for Social
History*, III (1938), 25-88.

21. Jochelson and Martov cited by Koppel S. Pinson in his "Arkady Kremer, Vladimir Medem and the Ideology of the 'Bund',"
Jewish Social Studies, VII (1945), 235 f. Cf.
also *Arcady: Essays Dedicated to the Memory
of Arcady Kremer* (Yiddish), New York,
1942 (includes excerpts from Kremer's writings); *Vladimir Medem: On the Twentieth
Anniversary of his Death* (Yiddish), New
York, 1943; and such memoirs of less important early members as B. Michalewicz's
Zichroines fun a yidishen sotsialist (Reminiscences of a Jewish Socialist) 3 vols., Warsaw,
1922-25; Hillel Katz Bloom's *Zichroines fun
a bundist* (Reminiscences of a Bundist),
New York, 1940; and, more generally, the
Yiddish Scientific Institute's voluminous collection of *Historishe Shriften* (Yivo Studies
in History), Vol. III: The Socialist Movement among the Jews up to 1897, ed. by F.
Kursky, A. Menes, A. Rosin, E. Tscherikover,
Vilna, 1939 (especially the introductory
article by Menes).

22. Zhitlovsky, *Gezamelte Shriften* (Collected Works), 10 vols., New York, 1912-19
(VI, 13-55: "A Jew to Jews"); Medem,
"The World-Wide Jewish Nation" (1911),
in his *Zichroines un artiklen* (Memoirs and

Essays), Warsaw, 1918, pp. 100 f.; *idem, Sotsialdemokratiia i natsionalnii vopros* (Social Democracy and the National Question), 2d ed., St. Petersburg, 1906; Pinson in *Jewish Social Studies,* VII, 248 n. 38; Oscar I. Janowsky, *The Jews and Minority Rights (1898-1919),* New York, 1933, pp. 79 f.

23. Stein's suggestion to populate the North African coast with Jews in *Wilhelm und Caroline von Humboldt in ihren Briefen,* ed. by Anna von Sydow, 7 vols., Berlin, 1907-16, V, 228; Pavel I. Pestel, *Russkaia Pravda* (Russian Truth), St. Petersburg, 1906, pp. 50 ff.; Charles Fourier, *Le nouveau monde industriel et societaire,* Paris, 1829; Mordecai M. Noah, *Discourse on the Restoration of the Jews,* New York, 1845; Isaac Goldberg, *Major Noah: American Jewish Pioneer,* Philadelphia, 1936, pp. 189 ff.; Saul M. Ginsburg, "Jacques Altaras, the Predecessor of Baron de Hirsch" (Yiddish) in *Historishe Verk* (Historical Works), 3 vols., New York, 1937, II, 203-19; Gabriel Davidson, *Our Jewish Farmers,* New York, 1943, pp. 194 ff. Cf. also Israel M. Lubin, *Zur Charakteristik und zur Quellenanalyse von Pestel's "Russkaja Pravda,"* Hamburg, 1930, p. 26 n. 2; Gelber, *Zur Vorgeschichte,* pp. 56 ff.; Edmund Silberner, "Charles Fourier on the Jewish Question," *Jewish Social Studies,* VIII (1946), 245-66; and, more generally, Jacob Lestchinsky, "Jüdische Wanderungen und Staatsträume im Lichte der Vergangenheit," *Monatsschrift für Gesch. und Wiss. des Judentums,* LXXV (1932), 429-43; Abraham G. Duker, "Jewish Territorialism: An Historical Sketch," *Contemporary Jewish Record,* II, Pt. 2 (1939), 14-30.

24. Zangwill, in Werner Sombart, A. Landsberger, *et al., Judentaufen,* Munich, 1912, p. 144; *idem, Speeches, Articles and Letters,* ed. by Maurice Simon, London, 1937; *idem, The Voice of Jerusalem,* New York, 1921, especially pp. 263 ff. Cf. also Margit Freund, *Israel Zangwills Stellung zum Judentum,* Diss. Berlin, 1927. It may be noted that, while presenting the Uganda project to the Zionist Congress on Aug. 22, 1903, Herzl, too, had made it perfectly clear that British East Africa "is not Zion and can never become Zion. It is merely a provisional measure of colonization, but, be it noted, on a national and self-governing basis. . . . It is and must remain an emergency measure which is to remedy the present chaotic power-

lessness of all philanthropic undertakings, and obviate the loss of scattered sections of the race." Curiously, even in Uganda there already were white "natives" who, according to Zangwill (*Voice,* p. 277), "could not have filled a village church," but who nevertheless objected to the immigration of "alien Jews." Cf. Jacob de Haas, *Theodor Herzl,* 2 vols., Chicago, 1927, II, 162, 198 f.

25. James Finn, *Stirring Times or Records from Jerusalem Consular Chronicles of 1853 to 1856,* ed. by his widow, 2 vols., London, 1878, I, 113. Cf. also Albert M. Hyamson, *The British Consulate in Jerusalem in Relation to the Jews of Palestine, 1838-1914,* 2 vols., London, 1939-41; and the literature listed by S. W. Baron in *Community,* III, 213 ff.; and by him and Jeannette M. Baron in "Palestinian Messengers in America, 1849-79: A Record of Four Journeys," *Jewish Social Studies,* V (1943), 115-62, 225-92.

26. Leo Pinsker, *Auto-Emancipation,* English translation newly edited together with several addresses and letters in *Road to Freedom,* with an Introduction by B. Netanyahu, New York, 1944; Alter Druyanov, "Pinsker and His Period" (Hebrew), *Hatekufah,* XII (1921), 214-50; XIII (1921), 275-320; XVI (1922), 308-25 (incomplete). There is a vast literature dealing with the early projects of Jewish restoration to Palestine and other phases of zionist thought and activity. In this area, too, Napoleon made dramatic history, when during his Near Eastern campaign of 1799 he "issued a proclamation inviting all the Jews of Asia and Africa to assemble under his flag in order to re-establish ancient Jerusalem." Cf. the Constantinople report in the official *Moniteur* of Germinal 28, 1799. For some, rather dubious, sustaining evidence, cf. Franz Kobler, "Napoleon and the Restoration of the Jews to Palestine: Discovery of an Historical Document," *New Judaea,* XVI (1940), 189-90. This manifesto and the emperor's subsequent convocation of a Jewish Sanhedrin made a deep impression even in far-off Virginia as illustrated by a local newspaper debate. Cf. Joseph J. Shulim, "Napoleon I as the Jewish Messiah: Some Contemporary Conceptions in Virginia," *Jewish Social Studies,* VII (1945), 275-80. Cf. also, in general, Sokolow, *History of Zionism; idem, Hibbath Zion (The Love of Zion) . . . 1840-1897,* Jerusalem, 1941; Gelber, *Zur Vorgeschichte;* Adolf Böhm, *Die zionistische Bewegung,* Vols. I-II, Berlin,

1935-37 (up to 1925); the valuable collections of source material by Alter Druyanov in his *Ketabim le-toledot hibbat Zion ve-yishub Eres Yisrael* (Documents for the History of "Love of Zion" and Palestine Colonization), 3 vols., Odessa-Tel-Aviv, 1918-32; and by Ben-Zion Dinaburg in his *Sefer ha-siyonut* (The Book of Zionism, an Anthology), Vol. I, Tel-Aviv, 1938; and other writings listed by Baron in *Social and Religious History*, III, 167 f.; and his *Bibliography of Jewish Social Studies*, pp. 126 ff., 240 f.

27. Herzl, *A Jewish State: an Attempt at a Modern Solution of the Jewish Question*, revised English transl., with notes by Jacob de Haas, New York, 1904, pp. 4 ff., 24 f., 93 ff., 101 f. Herzl readily conceded the impact of the Dreyfus Affair on the sudden reversal of his earlier, assimilationist views. In 1899 he explained: "The Dreyfus case embodies more than a judicial error; it embodies the desire of the vast majority of the French to condemn the Jew and to condemn all Jews in this one Jew. . . . When a people which in every other respect is so progressive and so highly civilized can take such a turn, what are we to expect from other peoples?" Cited by Alex Bein in his *Theodore Herzl: A Biography*, English transl., Philadelphia, 1940, pp. 115 f. Herzl's reiterated definitions of Jewish nationalism likewise emphasized this negative force of cohesion: "A nationality is an historic group of people demonstrably belonging together and held together by a common enemy." Cf. his reply to "Dr. Güdemann's 'National-Judentum' " (1897), reprinted in his *Zionistische Schriften*, I, 175; his "Rede in der Oesterreichisch-israelitischen Union" (1896), *ibid.*, p. 157, etc. Nevertheless, Max Nordau, his closest collaborator, was essentially justified in stating that "in the case of most Zionists antisemitism was only a stimulus causing them to reflect upon their relation to the nations, and their reflection has led them to results that must remain for them a permanent intellectual and spiritual possession, even if antisemitism were to vanish completely from the world." Cf. his *Zionism: Its History and Its Aims*, English transl., London, 1905, pp. 7 f.

28. Ahad Haam (Asher Ginzberg), " 'Statehood' and Palestine Colonization" (Hebrew, 1898), in his *Al parashat derakhim* (On the Crossroads: Collected Essays), 4 vols., 3d ed., Berlin, 1921, II, 36. This was the second of Ahad Haam's three essays published under the impact of the Basel Program. Only the first is available in English translation in *Ten Essays on Zionism and Judaism*. London, 1922, pp. 32-55.

29. Joseph Klausner, "Byronism in Modern Hebrew Poetry" (Hebrew), *Melilah*, I (1944), 152-65. Cf. also Albert M. Hyamson, *British Projects for the Restoration of the Jews*, London, 1917 (also in a more fully documented version in the *Publications of the American Jewish Historical Society*, XXVI, 1918, 127-64).

30. Vladimir Jabotinsky, *Medinah ibrit* (A Jewish State: The Solution of the Jewish Question), Tel-Aviv, 1937; idem, *The Story of the Jewish Legion*, English transl., New York, 1945; idem, *Evidence Submitted to the Palestine Royal Commission, House of Lords, February 11, 1937 on behalf of the New Zionist Organization*, London, 1937; idem, *The Jewish War Front*, London, 1940. Cf. also Shalom Schwartz's biography of *Jabotinsky, lohem ha-ummah* (Jabotinsky, the People's Warrior), Jerusalem, 1943. In her "Zionism Reconsidered," *Menorah Journal*, XXXIII (1945), 162-96, Hannah Arendt rightly suggests that "the revisionist program, so long bitterly repudiated, has proved finally victorious." Evidently the victory, even if temporary, of a radical wing within any movement is the historic rule rather than exception. Certainly the combined impact of the war ravages, the inescapable need of European-Jewish emigration to Palestine and stubborn British resistance thereto has greatly strengthened the belief in extremist programs.

31. Moses Hess, *Rome and Jerusalem: A Study in Jewish Nationalism*, English transl. with notes by Meyer Waxman, New York, 1943, pp. 48, 54 f., 122 f., 138; idem, Review of Gustave d'Eichthal's *Les trois grands peuples méditerranéens et le Christianisme* in *Archives israélites*, XXVI (1865), 485 f. (also in his *Jüdische Schriften*, ed. by Theodor Zlocisti, Berlin, 1905, p. 78). Cf. in general Zlocisti's biography of *Moses Hess, Der Vorkämpfer des Sozialismus und Zionismus 1812-1875*, Berlin, 1921; and Martin Buber, "Moses Hess," *Jewish Social Studies*, VII (1945), 137-48.

32. Ahad Haam, *Al parashat derakhim*, I, 84 f., 120 ff.; II, 29 f.; III, 53; IV, 160. Cf. in general M. Glikson's brief Hebrew biography of *Ahad Haam*, Jerusalem, 1927; and Jecheskel Kaufman, "The Principal Teach-

ings of Ahad Haam" (Hebrew), *Hatekufah*, XXIV (1925), 421-39.

33. Ahad Haam's emphasis upon both Hebrew and the Palestinian center naturally brought him into sharp conflict with the largely Yiddishist Diaspora nationalists. He co-operated with them, however, in such immediate practical tasks as organizing an armed Jewish self-defense during the massacre of 1903. Cf. "Ahad Haam's Secret Circular" published in Hebrew by Simon Dubnow (a cosigner), *ibid.*, pp. 416-20; Böhm, *Die zionistische Bewegung*, I, 297 ff.

34. Janowsky, *Jews and Minority Rights*, pp. 110, 272 f.

35. Ber Borochov, *Nationalism and the Class Struggle. A Marxist Approach to the Jewish Question. Selected Writings*, English transl. with Introduction by Abraham G. Duker, New York, 1937, pp. 83, 85 f., 91 f., 96 f. A fuller collection of essays in the original Yiddish appeared under the title *Poale Zion Shriften*, 2 vols., New York, 1920-28. Cf. also the writings of such other labor zionist leaders as Hayyim Arlosoroff, *Kitbe*, ed. in Hebrew by J. Steinberg, 7 vols., Tel-Aviv, 1934-35; and Nahman Syrkin, *Kitbe*, ed. by Berl Kaznelson and Yehudah Kaufman, Vol. I, Tel-Aviv, 1939.

36. A. D. Gordon, *Kol Kitbe* (Collected Writings), 5 vols., Tel-Aviv, 1925-30, II, 36, 43 f.; IV, 255; V, 14. Cf. also his *Selected Essays*, English transl. with a biographical sketch by Eisig Silberschlag, Boston, 1938; Nathan Rothenstreich, *Ha-Ummah be-torato shel A. D. Gordon* (The Nation in the Doctrine of A. D. G.), Jerusalem, 1942; Reuben Wallenrod, "The Teachings of A. D. Gordon (1856-1922)," *Jewish Social Studies*, VII (1945), 337-56.

37. Solomon Schiller, *Principles of Labor Zionism*, New York, 1928, pp. 9 f. Cf. also the more recent publications of the Poale-Zion-Zeire Zion Organization, *Palestine and Jewish Freedom: A Symposium*, New York, 1942; and *The Jewish Frontier Anthology*, 1934-1944, New York, 1945. Gordon's somewhat doctrinaire opposition to the designation of his own movement as "socialist" and co-operation with other socialist parties aroused the ire of even such a close friend as the novelist I. Ch. Brenner. Admitting the shortcomings of disciples hiding behind high-sounding slogans, Brenner censured his friend's insistence upon calling the passionate hatred of parasitism and intense belief in the

necessity of nationalization of all means of production "nationalism," rather than "socialism." "It is no less strange stubbornness bordering on sin when one adheres, with all his might, to a particular content and repudiates forcefully and angrily the word which describes it." Cf. "On Terminological Disputes" (Hebrew), *Yalkut ahdut ha-abodah*, I (1929), 51. The religious, though perfectly unorthodox, strain in labor zionism, came to the fore also in Palestine's famous collective settlements. After a few months in several such colonies, a recent English visitor was greatly impressed by their truly religious spirit of self-sacrifice. He was particularly "struck by the parallel of the monastic life in the Christian scheme of things." C. Witton Davies, "Impressions of Life in a Jewish Settlement in Palestine," *Christendom*, XIV (Oxford, 1946), 209. Cf. also the brief analysis by Shalom Wurm, *The Kvutza: The Structure, Problems and Achievements of the Collective Settlements in Palestine*, English transl., New York, 1942.

38. Cf. Robert Weltsch, "Zionismus als unendliche Aufgabe," in *Der Jude*, Sonderheft V: Zu Martin Bubers fünfzigstem Geburtstag, Berlin, 1928, p. 37: "What we have understood under zionism never was a single, this-worldly—political or practical—economic enterprise. Buber has indeed expressed the deep conviction of the Jewish national psyche when he emphasized that our ideal could not possibly be the creating of a new petty, national state. From the teachings of Ahad Haam we have definitely learned that political zionism, if measured quantitatively, could solve only a small fraction of the Jewish question, but that from the point of view of quality a Jewish settlement in Palestine can be of immeasurable value to world Jewry."

39. Adolf Grabowsky, "Das Schicksal Palästinas und die Krise des Zionismus," *Zeitschrift für Politik*, XIX (1929-30), 530. Even the Revisionists, whose understanding of the need of power politics Grabowsky admires, were only "the Don Quixotes of Zionism," (*ibid.*, p. 537). Though often exaggerating and in many essential points disproved by subsequent events, Grabowsky's critique is not completely devoid of merit even today.

40. This statement was underscored two years later in *The Establishment in Palestine of a Jewish National Home*, memorandum

submitted by the Zionist Organization to the secretary-general of the League of Nations for the Information of the Permanent Mandates Commission, [Geneva], 1924, p. 5.

41. The rabbinical protest published in the *Berliner Tageblatt* is quoted by Herzl in his reply entitled "Protestrabbiner," *Zionistische Schriften*, I, 211 ff.; Hermann Cohen, "Religion und Zionismus" in his *Jüdische Schriften*, ed. by Bruno Strauss, 3 vols., Berlin, 1924, I, 323; Isaac Breuer, *The Jewish National Home*, English transl., Frankfort, 1926. As far back as 1886 Leo Pinsker had to defend himself against the accusation that he favored freethinkers in Palestine. Cf. especially his letter to the "Lovers of Zion" in Bialystok published by Druyanov in his *Ketabim*, I, 635 ff. Whatever one thinks of the authenticity of this letter (cf. the editor's note thereon), there is no doubt that the attacks of such old Orthodox leaders, as Rabbi Samuel Mohilewer, upon Pinsker's evident "neutrality" in religious matters brought about the latter's resignation from the presidency of the Odessa Committee in 1887. But the debate has continued ever since among the "Lovers of Zion" and their zionist successors.

42. Ber (Baer) of Meserich, *Or Torah* (Hasidic Commentary on the Five Books of Moses), Koretz, 1804, section Va-Erah.

43. Sokolow, *History of Zionism*, II, 408; *Great Britain, Palestine and the Jews: A Survey of Christian Opinion*, London, 1918, p. 5.

44. Cf. Isaac Reines, *Or hadash al Siyyon* (New Light on Zion), Vilna, 1902; Jehudah Leb Fishman, *The Misrachi Movement*, English transl., New York, 1928; *idem*, "The Division between the Mizrahi and the 'Agudah'" (Hebrew), *Sinai*, III (1938), 187-92; Moses Ostrowsky, *Toledot ha-mizrahi be-Eres Yisrael* (A History of the Mizrahi in Palestine), Jerusalem, 1944. Cf. also Abraham Bick's anthology, *Exponents and Philosophy of Religious Zionism*, Brooklyn, 1942.

45. Beryl Harold Levy, *Reform Judaism in America: A Study in Religious Adaptation*, New York, 1933, pp. 131 ff.; Elmer Berger, *The Jewish Dilemma*, New York, 1946 (an exposition of the American Council's antizionist philosophy); Elmo Roper, "U. S. Jews' Stand on Palestine," *New York Herald Tribune* of Nov. 22, 1945. The issue came to a head in 1942, when as a result of the prozionist stand of the majority of the Central Conference ninety reform rabbis published a statement opposing political zionism. In reply a joint declaration of 831 Orthodox, Conservative and Reform rabbis declared that "zionism is not a secularist movement. It has its origins and roots in the authoritative religious texts of Judaism. . . . Antizionism, not zionism, is a departure from the Jewish religion." Both statements are reprinted in *Jewish Post-War Problems. A Study Course*, Unit VI: Palestine in the New World, ed. by Abraham G. Duker *et al.*, New York, 1943, pp. 58 ff. For Germany under Hitler, cf., e.g., Ignaz Maybaum, "Zionismus und Zionsliebe," *Der Morgen*, XIII (1938), 510-16; *idem*, "Der Zionismus als sekulärer Idealismus und als religiöse Bewegung," *ibid.*, XIV (1938), 5-14.

46. Karl Marx, "On the Jewish Question" (1844), English transl. in *Selected Essays*, transl. by H. J. Stenning, London, 1926, pp. 40-97; Otto Heller, *Der Untergang des Judentums. Die Judenfrage, ihre Kritik, ihre Lösung durch den Sozialismus*, Vienna, 1931. Marx's sharply anti-Jewish utterances, doubly remarkable in a born Jew and scion of a long line of rabbis and communal leaders (cf. Bernard Wachstein, "Die Abstammung von Karl Marx," *Festskrift . . . Professor David Simonsen*, Copenhagen, 1923, pp. 277-89), has intrigued many scholars. Cf., e.g., Solomon F. Bloom, "Karl Marx and the Jews," *Jewish Social Studies*, IV (1942), 3-16.

47. V. I. Lenin, "The National Spectre of Assimilation" (1913), excerpted in English transl. in *Lenin on the Jewish Question* (a collection of essays), New York, 1934, p. 15. There exists no comprehensive and authoritative statement of the Jewish Communists' national doctrine. The numerous essays on the subject reveal large divergences and inconsistencies, wholly explainable under the combined impact of the sudden break with the Jewish heritage and the dynamic transformations in the general Soviet attitude to nationalism and patriotism. For an example of curious intraparty dialectics cf. B. Akselrod and I. Gershanbaum, "Against Bourgeois Nationalism" (Yiddish), *Ofn visenshaftlechn front* (III-IV, Minsk, 1933, 80-99), written before the general nationalist revival in the Union. The vicissitudes of Zionists and especially of the zionist Young Pioneers (Hehalus) in the early years of the Soviet regime are told with considerable documentation by Dan Pines in his *He-Halus be-khur*

ha-mahapekhah (Hehalus in the Crucible of Revolution), Vol. I: 1917-24, Tel-Aviv, 1938.

48. We have no absolutely objective study of the Jewish status in the Soviet Union. Perhaps none is possible in the light of the ideological pressures in the country and the limited information available outside of it. The relatively fullest treatments are by Yarmolinsky, *Jews and Other Minor Nationalities*, passim; Otto Heller, *Untergang*, pp. 175 ff.; Abraham Heller, *Die Lage der Juden in Russland von der Märzrevolution 1917 bis zur Gegenwart*, Breslau, 1935; Jacob Lestchinsky, *Dos sovetishe Yidentum* (Soviet Jewry: Past and Present), New York, 1941; and L[ev] Zinger, *Dos banaite folk* (The People Reborn; Figures and Facts concerning the Jews in the U.S.S.R.), Moscow, 1941. Even at the time of their publication, however, most of these works were subjected to numerous strictures, both scholarly and partisan. Today they are the less adequate as the war and postwar developments in the Union and its new attitude to both nationalism and religion have deeply affected Russian Jewry. First greatly increased by the Union's territorial expansion in 1939, which added some 1,500,000 Jewish citizens of the annexed areas in addition to several hundred thousand refugees from western Poland, the Soviet Jewish population suffered severely from nazi ravages. Of the 5,334,824 Jews estimated to have lived in the enlarged area in 1941 (cf. Lamont's "Chart of Soviet Nationalities" in his *Peoples of the Soviet Union*, p. 212) perhaps only one-half or less have survived. The fragmentary information now available allows for neither an objective appraisal of their present status nor a reasonable assessment of the prevailing ideological trends among them.

49. Cf. Karl Baum, "Das jüdische Prag der Gegenwart in Zahlen," *Monatsschrift für Gesch. und Wiss. des Judentums*, LXXIII (1929), 361 f. These manifestations of ethnicist extremism were confirmed by the contemporary censuses in Poland and other Eastern European countries.

50. Clemenceau's letter to Paderewski of June 24, 1919. Cf. Janowsky, *Jews and Minority Rights*, pp. 264 ff.; E. Landauer, *Das geltende jüdische Minderheitenrecht. Mit besonderer Berücksichtigung Osteuropas*, Leipzig, 1924; Kurt Stillschweig, *Die \uden Osteuropas in den Minderheitenver-*

trägen, Berlin, 1936; idem, "Die nationalitätenrechtliche Stellung der Juden in den russischen und österreichischen Nachfolgestaaten während der Weltkriegsepoche," *Monatsschrift für Geschichte und Wissenschaft des Judentums*, LXXXII (1938), 217-48; idem, "Die nationalitätenrechtliche Stellung der Juden in der Tschechoslovakei," *Historia Judaica*, I (1938), 39-49. The enormous literature on minority problems is reviewed by Jakob Robinson in *Das Minoritätenproblem und seine Literatur*, Berlin, 1928. Another volume bringing this bibliographical survey up to date would fill a much-felt lacuna.

51. The Royal Institute for International Affairs, *Great Britain and Palestine, 1935-39*, Revised ed., London, 1939, p. 9; *New Judaea*, XVI (1939-40), 86 ff.; Mrs. Edgar (Blanche E. C.) Dugdale in her Foreword to *The Balfour Declaration: Origins and Background*, London, 1940. The MacMahon Correspondence, though often referred to in previous controversies, was published by the British government only in 1939 (Cmd. 5957) in connection with the London Round Table Conference of Jews and Arabs which, because of Arab refusals, never met for joint deliberations. It nevertheless resulted in the issuance of the antizionist White Paper of 1939. The story of negotiations leading up to the Balfour Declaration is narrated as fully as is possible without access to British and other governmental archives by N. M. Gelber in his *Hazharat Balfour ve-toledoteha* (A History of the Balfour Declaration), Jerusalem, 1939. The Arab case is stated most elaborately against the background of a century-old historical evolution by George Antonius in *The Arab Awakening: The Story of the Arab National Movement*, new impression, New York, 1946. Cf. also Paul L. Hanna, *British Policy in Palestine*, with an Introd. by Josephus Daniels, Washington, 1942.

52. Cf. Ahad Haam's Introd. to the third edition of his *Al parashat derakhim*, pp. xx f., or the English excerpts therefrom, entitled "Build Palestine on Realities," *Commentary*, I, Pt. 6 (April, 1946), 55.

53. It was also on Brazil's motion that the Pan-American Conference at Lima resolved sweepingly in 1938 that "the system of protection of ethnical, language or religious minorities cannot have any application whatsoever in America, where the

conditions which characterize the groups known as minorities do not exist." Cited by John P. Humphrey in *The Inter-American System: A Canadian View*, Toronto, 1942, p. 162.

54. Of the vast literature on the subject of Palestine's Jewish colonization, cf. especially Abraham Revusky, *Jews in Palestine*, 3d ed., New York, 1945; Alex Bein, *Toledot ha-hityashbut ha-siyonit* (A History of Zionist Colonization from the Period of Herzl until Today), Jerusalem, 1943; and Gerhard Muenzner, *Jewish Labour Economy in Palestine*, London, 1945 (in collaboration with Ernst Kahn). Cf. also the publications listed in Baron's *Bibliography of Jewish Social Studies*, pp. 180 ff., 249 f.; and the recent comprehensive study of *Palestine*, sponsored by the Esco Foundation for Palestine and published in 2 vols., New Haven, 1947.

55. Zionists consistently refused to recognize the validity of the White Paper of 1939 (Cmd. 6019). They were supported by such venerable exponents of international amity as Lord Robert Cecil who, together with several others, declared in a letter to the London *Times* of April 12, 1940, that "those who have repeatedly protested against the policy of the White Paper must not be taken as being in any way bound by it."

56. Despite lacking recognition, Palestinian Jews, like the rest of world Jewry, contributed significantly to Allied victory. Apart from frightful Jewish losses in nazi-occupied Europe, the large Jewish communities of the United States and the Soviet Union, it appears, served in the armed forces of their countries in larger numbers, suffered more casualties and received more decorations for valor than was warranted by their numerical strength. Similarly Palestinian Jewry mobilized its economic and manpower resources for the successful prosecution of the war. Almost all its young men and many young women volunteered for military service. As many as were admitted by the British fought valiantly in North Africa and Italy, whether or not they were allowed to serve in the special Jewish brigade. Cf., e.g., the moving *Letters from the Desert* by Moshe Mosenson, English transl., with an Introd. by Shlomo Grodzensky, New York, 1945; and the Jewish Agency's brief survey of *The Economic War Effort of Jewish Palestine*, Jerusalem, 1946.

57. This threat always offered a ready excuse, however. The King-Crane Commission sent by President Wilson in 1919 to investigate the conditions on the spot, arrived in Jaffa on June 10. Two days later it already expressed doubt that "any British or American official here believes it is possible to carry out the zionist program except through the support of a large army." Cf. Harry N. Howard, "An American Experiment in Peace-Making: The King-Crane Commission," *The Moslem World*, XXXII (1942), 132 f. The historic record indicates, however, that a mere display of firmness, as under the regime of Lord Plumer (1923-28), sufficed to maintain order, while a vacillating policy ultimately encouraged the Arab revolt of 1936-38. Despite strong backing by the Axis, this revolt was speedily quelled when Britain showed real determination, backed up by the presence of only 16,000 troops under General Dill.

58. Cf. Quincy Wright, *Mandates under the League of Nations*, Chicago, 1930, p. 54. The general American attitude to the upbuilding of the Jewish homeland in Palestine is presented, with detailed documentation, by Reuben Fink in his *America and Palestine*, New York, 1944.

59. The more optimistic views expressed as late as 1943 by the contributors to the volume, *Were Minorities Treaties a Failure?* ed. by Jacob Robinson, New York, 1943, have largely been controverted by subsequent events.

60. Baron, *Social and Religious History*, I, 3.

Chapter VIII

Postwar Challenges

1. This religious conformity by otherwise religiously indifferent or even professedly agnostic persons has often evoked the ire of freethinkers. In *Le livre de l'Exilé: Lettre à Eugène Sue sur la situation religieuse de l'Europe*, Paris, 1856, p. 458, Edgar Quinet called it a shame for true republicans to invite priests to bless their dead or to baptize their children. "Why do you chain with your own free hands this helpless creature who cannot resist?" All such exhortations were unavailing, however (except in the Soviet Union at the height of its "godless" agitation), against deep-rooted habits, reinforced by such rationally uncontrollable feelings as filial piety, fear of the unknown, and taking no chances with the hereafter.

2. W. A. Brown, *Church in America*, pp. 19 f., summarizing *Religion among American Men: As Revealed by a Study of Conditions in the Army*, New York, 1920, Chap. III. "There is a well-substantiated story," writes Elisha Atkins on the experiences of the Second World War, "that some of the marines getting ready to make landings on the island of Bougainville in the Solomons prepared themselves by hanging both a cross and the tablets of the law about their necks. . . . Viewed in such a manner religion becomes a sort of last-minute everlasting life insurance which can be bought with low premiums and pays big dividends." Cf. "A Soldier's Second Thoughts," in *Religion of Soldier and Sailor*, ed. by Willard L. Sperry, Cambridge, Mass., 1945, pp. 102 f. For the impact of earlier wars cf. Karl Holl, "Die Bedeutung der grossen Kriege für das religiöse und kirchliche Leben des deutschen Protestantismus" (1917), in his *Gesammelte Aufsätze zur Kirchengeschichte*, 2d ed., 3 vols., Tübingen, 1923-28, III, 302-84.

3. The general disillusionment largely explains also the fact, observed by a well-informed British clergyman, that, while many irreligious persons had become believers, the war had shattered the faith of many alleged believers.

4. Russell C. Stroup, "A Soldier Looks at the Church," *Harper's Magazine*, CLXXXIX (1944), 397-402.

5. Barth, *Church and War*, pp. 30 f.

6. Cited by Charles W. Iglehart in his "Ecumenical Fellowship during the War," in Nolde, *Toward World-Wide Christianity*, p. 124. In *The Rebirth of the German Church* (New York, 1946, p. xvi), Stewart W. Herman quotes a much weaker statement of the German church leaders at their first postwar meeting in Treysa (August, 1945). The ample data, however, gathered in that volume reflect, for the most part, an unregenerate attitude of the mass of German laity and clergy. That the author himself, a former minister of the American Church in Berlin, unwittingly betrays a certain forbearance toward that attitude merely heightens the impression of its universality and respectability in ecclesiastical circles. Even Martin Niemöller, who, in his Introduction to Herman's work states, "Guilt for the past rests on us—a guilt that is terrible in the eyes of men, terrible also and enormous in the eyes of God," expatiates there at much greater length on God's forgiveness to sinners. At the Treysa Conference he had opposed the ruthless suppression of former Nazis for there were, he said, worse things than a converted Nazi; at least such men showed that they were capable of having *convictions. Ibid.*, pp. x, 115 n. 4. This expostulation, having a strong personal ring, must have sounded incongruous even to the Germans, the overwhelming majority of whom, immediately upon occupation, had

345

begun vociferously disclaiming any nazi associations.

7. Growing moderation in both Old and New Testament criticism, since its heyday at the beginning of this century, seems to have gone further than similar modifications in the critical evaluation of Graeco-Roman or other ancient sources. Cf., e.g., Joseph Coppens, *The Old Testament and the Critics*, English transl., Paterson, N. J., 1942. Most of the recent histories of the ancient Hebrew and Christian religions also betray a new predilection for theological rather than strictly historical, i.e., relativistic, interpretations. The very question of relationships between faith and history, readily disposed of by fundamentalist Christians and Orthodox Jews but long decided by liberals of both faiths in favor of history, has been answered by a new emphasis on the autonomy of each in its own sphère in such works as Reinhold Seeberg's *Die Geschichte und Gott. Betrachtungen über Wesen und Sinn der Geschichte*, Bonn, 1928; Arthur Weiser's *Glaube und Geschichte im Alten Testament*, Stuttgart, 1931; and Herbert George Wood's *Christianity and the Nature of History*, Cambridge, 1938.

8. Franz Borkenau, *Socialism, National or International*, London, 1942, p. 165.

9. W. Friedman, *The Decline of the National State*, London, 1943; Cobban, *National Self-Determination*, pp. 66 ff., 76. In this fine study Cobban also points out that, despite his advocacy of the right of secession, Lenin was not a real friend of the small state. He realized that in modern times small nations had become parasitical, their very existence often depending on the conflicting imperialisms of great powers. Hence "the advantages of large states both from the point of view of economic progress and from the point of view of the interests of the masses, are beyond doubt." Cf. "The Socialist Revolution and the Right of Nations to Self-Determination" (1916), in his *Selected Works*, V, 270.

10. Edward Hallett Carr, *Nationalism and After* (London, 1945, p. 31), referring, for example, to Britain's repudiation of the American loans, which was as much a blow to her deep-rooted pride of honoring international commitments as it was to the American creditors. J. B. Condliffe may have gone too far in arguing that after the war

"the United States will in fact determine by its own actions what degree of international cooperation will be possible. . . . Any limitations of sovereignty the United States is willing to accept, they [other countries] will be almost bound to accept." Cf. his *Agenda for a Postwar World*, New York, 1943, p. 221. But there is little doubt that the United States and for that matter also Britain and the Soviet Union will, by their decisions reached under fluctuating internal and external pressures, decisively influence the entire political evolution. Most of the lesser powers themselves, vocal protests to the contrary, will resignedly subscribe to the statement of Ezequiel Padilla, Mexico's secretary of state, at the Inter-American Conference at Chapultepec of February, 1945: "The small nations do not pretend to equal participation in a world of unequal responsibilities. What they do desire is that when injustice may strike at the door of small nations, their voices may be heard." Cited by Roberto Herrera in his "Evolution of Equality of States in the Inter-American System," *Political Science Quarterly*, LXI (1946), 111.

11. Halifax, "Roads to Victory," *Proceedings of the Academy of Political Science*, XX (1943-44), 448.

12. Joseph Stalin, *Marxism and the National and Colonial Question*, p. 66. In the discussion which followed that resolution at the Seventh All-Russian Conference of the party in May, 1917, Stalin admitted that "every national movement is a reactionary movement," but stressed the democratic nature of, e.g., the Irish movement "which is striking a blow at imperialism." *Ibid.*, p. 67.

13. Tierney in *Studies*, XXXIV, 482.

14. Much water has spilled over the dam since the late Lord Lothian, writing under the impact of the Munich crisis, predicted (in the *Observer* of Nov. 27, 1938): "Though few yet realize it, the old anarchy of multitudinous national sovereignties . . . is going to disappear, either through federation, which is the democratic way, or through an integration consequent on the rise of the great totalitarian powers. That the world is going to fall into four or five main political and economic groups, each in great measure self-supporting, each under the leadership of a great state, equipped with modern military and air power, at any

rate for a time, seems certain. Nothing that we can do can prevent it." But this forecast is still valid today notwithstanding the defeat of the totalitarian powers and the weakening of autarchic-isolationist trends everywhere else. G. D. H. Cole seems to have gone too far, however, in asserting that the small states will "be kept alive, if at all, only when they are in the position of buffers between the great." Cf. his *Europe, Russia and the Future*, London, 1941, p. 101.

15. Alfred Zimmern, *The Third British Empire*, 2d ed., London, 1934, pp. 150, 156. In these lectures delivered at Columbia University in 1925 Zimmern went so far as to assert that "the more the different nations of the Empire find themselves spiritually, the easier it will be for them to solve their political problems." *Ibid.*, pp. 155 f.

16. Lamont, *The Peoples of the Soviet Union*, pp. 3, 7, 13. The number of Soviet subdivisions is here given according to the status of January, 1946.

17. Gaston Nerval (Raul Diez de Medina), *Autopsy of the Monroe Doctrine: The Strange Story of Inter-American Relations*, New York, 1934, p. 207, citing *Foreign Relations in the United States, 1895*, I, 552 ff.

18. D. Luther Evans, "United Religions for United Nations," *Journal of Liberal Religion*, VII (1945-46), 213. One must bear in mind, however, Alfred Loisy's warning (to him rather a hope) that a system like the League of Nations or the United Nations "requires a religion of humanity. When the league will have become fully conscious of its unity, it will naturally produce and in a sense be such a religion, just as in ancient times the peoples gathered under the imperial rule of Rome received the religious and moral consciousness of their unity in Catholic Christianity." Loisy compared that city of the future with the heavenly city of the Book of Revelation (21:10-27), but believed that it would be "even more celestial, that is to say more truly spiritual and more ideal." Cf. his *Y a-t-il deux sources de la religion et de la morale?* Paris, 1933, pp. 190, 195.

19. Cf. *The Oxford Conference (Official Report)*, ed. by J. H. Oldham, Chicago, 1937, p. 155 (Report of the Section on the Universal Church and the World of Nations). This statement is reminiscent of an earlier dictum by Archbishop Temple, the Oxford Conference's leading spirit. In his Paddock Lectures on *Church and State*, delivered soon after the outbreak of the First World War (London, 1915, p. 57), William Temple had declared that "nothing but such a spiritual society can secure fellowship among nations. . . . What will secure this, except the realization of common membership in the Kingdom of God, and in the Christian Church, its herald and earnest?" Compared with such rather blunt exclusion of non-Christians from the building of a genuine international fellowship, the aforementioned Five-Point Program of Pope Pius XII, the Ten Peace Points of British Anglican, Free Church and Catholic ecclesiastics in their letter to the London *Times* (later concurred in by Jewish leaders), the joint declaration of American Catholics, Protestants and Jews of October, 1943, and the most recent "declaration of human rights" of the National Catholic Welfare Conference seem far less intransigent. Cf. the texts in Koenig, *Principles of Peace*, pp. 636 f.; Nolde, *Toward World-Wide Christianity*, New York, 1946, pp. 158 ff., 166 ff.; *New York Times*, of Feb. 2, 1947.

20. Soloviev cited by Karpovich in *Review of Politics*, VIII, 191; Kenneth Scott Latourette, "The Church and Christian Society Today in the Perspective of History" in *The Gospel, the Church and the World*, ed. by him, New York, 1946, pp. 83-110.

21. Kenneth Leslie's editorial in the *Protestant*, VII, Pt. 4 (October-November, 1946), 2, with reference to the World Council's pamphlet describing the Conference of Church Leaders on International Affairs held in Cambridge, England, in August, 1946.

22. Cited by Bishop Brent in Peake and Parsons, *Outline of Christianity*, V, 142.

23. Lamont, *op. cit.*, p. 5.

24. Frederick L. Schuman, *Soviet Politics At Home and Abroad*, New York, 1946, p. 609.

25. Writing toward the end of the first Thirty Years' War (1643), Johann Amos Comenius declared: "Nothing is more necessary for the stability of the world, if it is not to perish completely, than some universal rededication of minds. Universal harmony and peace must be secured for the whole human race. By peace and harmony, however, I mean not that external peace between

rulers and peoples among themselves, but an internal peace of minds inspired by a system of ideas and feelings." Cited by I. L. Kandel in his *Intellectual Cooperation: National and International*, New York, 1944, p. 78. What Comenius advocated three centuries ago and what Kandel envisaged by man's total re-education under the direction of an International Office of Education is beginning to take shape through the work of UNESCO, however faltering its first steps necessarily are. Cf. also Alexander Meiklejohn, *Education Between Two Worlds*, New York, 1942. Some incipient stages of positive affirmation are distinctly manifest, for instance, in the relations between the United States and Canada or Britain. According to Sir Alfred Zimmern, the popular phrase that war between these countries is "unthinkable" really connotes that, in the very unlikely event of its occurrence, most citizens of these countries would regard the conflict as something akin to "civil war." This means that, "although for purposes of government, or, shall we say, administration, the two areas remain separate, they have become, so far as resort to violence is concerned, a single society." Zimmern also refers to Sir William Harrison Moore's explanation of the particular *quality* of relations between members of the British Commonwealth. They are expected not only to adhere scrupulously to the letter of their mutually agreed covenants, but "charity is conceivable between them—free gifts." Cf. Zimmern, "The Ethical Presuppositions of a World Order" in *The Universal Church and the World of Nations* (The Official Oxford Conference Books, no. 7, Chicago, 1938), pp. 51 ff. To reinforce scrupulous observance of all international covenants and suffuse them with the spirit of charity is, indeed, the formidable task confronting organized religion.

26. Nolde, *op. cit.*, pp. 166 f. To be sure, some spadework for securing international guarantees for freedom of worship was performed during the First World War by the American Committee on the Rights of Religious Minorities. But despite the frequent interlocking of national and religious controversies, particularly in those very lands which in 1919 became the main objects of minority provisions, there is little evidence of any sustained opposition to the incorporation of the guarantees of liberty of conscience into the treaties. Even their restriction *to* creeds, "whose practices are not inconsistent with public order and public morals," was largely academic. Cf. the list of articles concerning minority rights in the Treaties of 1919 in Keller and Stewart, *Protestant Europe*, p. 177. Cf. also *ibid.*, p. 192. Woodrow Wilson and Lord Robert Cecil vainly tried, however, to insert binding clauses against interference with religion or discrimination against adherents of any particular faith in the League Covenant itself. Cf. Luther A. Weigle, "Religious Liberty in the Postwar World," in *Religion and the World Order*, ed. by F. Ernest Johnson, New York, 1944, p. 30.

27. Michael Bakunin's speech at the Geneva Congress of "all friends of free democracy" of 1867 quoted from his later summary by E. H. Carr, *Bakunin*, p. 331; Otto von Gierke, *The Development of Political Theory*, English transl., New York, 1939, p. 257. Cf. Cobban, *op. cit.*, pp. 148, 151, 155.

28. John LaFarge, "Injustice in Peace Fosters Reasons for War," *America*, LXII (1939-40), 371; Georges Kaeckenbeeck, *The International Experiment of Upper Silesia: A Study of the Working of the Upper Silesian Settlement, 1922-1937*, London, 1942, p. 326, summarizing the Permanent Court's judgment no. 12 of April 26, 1928, in Series A, no. 15.

29. Addison, *Religious Equality*, p. 2. The present absence of moral standards by which the conduct of nations might be judged and the conviction of many politicians and lawyers that the actual practice, as expressed in usages and customs among nations, constituted the only valid approach to international law, was censured even by some prominent jurists. The Inter-American Juridical Committee condemned "the exponents of this mistaken theory [who] came to determine the existence of rules of international law by the record of the conduct of nations, instead of judging the conduct of nations by the principles of law." Cited by Clyde Eagleton in his "Reconstruction in International Law," in Johnson's *Religion and the World Order*, p. 140.

30. John Stuart Mill, *Dissertations and Discussions: Political, Philosophical and Historical*, 3 vols., Boston, 1865, III, 251, 263. Commenting on the basic principles of the League of Nations' Covenant, Sir Alfred

Zimmern remarked that it had asked the member states "to insure political order over the whole peace-keeping area by substituting a system of active relations for a system of passive relations, or, in the language of the present day, a system of social responsibility for a system of non-intervention." Cf. his "Ethical Presuppositions," pp. 55 f. This applies with even greater force to the Charter of the United Nations.

31. Stettinius, *Report to the President on the Results of the San Francisco Conference,* Washington, 1945 (Department of State, Publication 2349), pp. 115 f. Stettinius also referred to the unanimous decisions of the Conference Committee stating that "nothing contained in Chapter IX [of the Charter] can be construed as giving authority to the Organization to intervene in the domestic affairs of member states." Cf. Oscar I. Janowsky, "The Human Rights Issue at the San Francisco Conference. Was It a Victory?" *Menorah Journal* (XXXIV, 1946, 29-55), emphasizing the superiority of the League of Nations' safeguards of minority rights to the United Nations Charter's provisions for human rights. In his authoritative analysis of *An International Bill of the Rights of Man* (New York, 1945, p. 221), however, H. Lauterpacht argues that "an effective International Bill of the Rights of Man—which attempts to solve an abiding problem of human freedom in the relation of man to state in a manner transcending the protection of national and linguistic minorities—would be a proper and desirable substitute for the system of protection of minorities by treaties binding upon a limited number of states and safeguarding a limited area of rights of limited members of the population. There is in the Minorities Treaties no substantive right and no procedural safeguard which is not to be found in the Bill of Rights as here proposed." Unfortunately the peacemakers of 1946-47 have neither restated the old minorities safeguards for national groups as such in their treaties with Rumania, Hungary, etc., nor adopted a binding universal Bill of Rights similar in content to Arts. 3-4 of the Rumanian, or Arts. 6-7 of the Finnish, Treaty. This sin of omission, though understandable in the heat of controversy between the powers and the specific uncertainties of the future status of many minorities affected by large-scale deportations, doubtless will plague the United Nations councils for many years to come.

32. William Ralph Inge, *England,* New York, 1926, pp. 68 f. (with reference to Santayana's *Soliloquies in England,* contending that an Englishman can never be really a Catholic); Barth, *Church and War,* p. 5. Cf. also A. Roy Eckardt's forthcoming volume on *Christianity and the Children of Israel,* offering both an analysis of church attitudes to antisemitism and suggestions for a theological solution; and Mark Vishniak's suggestions for *An International Convention against Anti-Semitism,* New York, 1946.

33. Marquess of Lothian, "The Demonic Influence of National Sovereignty," in *The Universal Church and the World of Nations,* p. 23.

INDEX

MERIDIAN BOOKS

12 East 22 Street, New York 10, New York

MERIDIAN BOOKS

12 East 22 Street, New York 10, New York

Titles listed here are not necessarily available in the British Empire

MERIDIAN BOOKS

12 East 22 Street, New York 10, New York

MERIDIAN GIANTS

MERIDIAN LIBRBRY